PUBLICATIONS OF THE
MINNESOTA HISTORICAL SOCIETY

EDITED BY

SOLON J. BUCK
SUPERINTENDENT OF THE SOCIETY

A HISTORY OF MINNESOTA
VOLUME IV

WILLIAM WATTS FOLWELL
[From a photograph taken about 1905, in the museum of the Minnesota Historical Society.]

A HISTORY OF MINNESOTA

BY

WILLIAM WATTS FOLWELL

IN FOUR VOLUMES
VOLUME IV

PUBLISHED BY THE
MINNESOTA HISTORICAL SOCIETY
SAINT PAUL, 1930

History is the judgment of humanity.
Schiller, "Resignation."

EDITOR'S INTRODUCTION

THE history of an American commonwealth in the period since the Civil War has so many facets that it cannot adequately be told in a single continuous narrative. The author of this work chose therefore to present in the third volume a running sketch of the political and administrative history of the state and to devote this fourth volume to a series of essays on special topics mainly in the fields of economic and social history. No attempt was made to cover these fields completely, however, and the author was well aware of the fact that many important topics were neglected. He made tentative beginnings on several additional essays, but dropped them because of limitations of space and the desirability of bringing the work to a close. Despite advancing age and increasing infirmities the author continued his work of writing, supplementing, and revising his history until the summer of 1929, when he pronounced it finished. He was not destined to see the volume in print, however, for his long career came to an end on September 18, 1929, but it was a matter of great satisfaction to him that he had been able to complete his self-appointed task. During the last few years of his life, at intervals in the work on the history, he also wrote and dictated a very interesting volume of reminiscences, which is now being prepared for publication by the University of Minnesota Press.

The six essays that comprise the chapters of this volume are notable contributions to Minnesota history, and some of them might properly be called monographs. Here will be found for the first time on a comprehensive scale the remarkable story of the development of iron-mining in Minnesota and the tragic and often sordid record of the dealings of white men with the Chippewa Indians. In the chapter on the University of Minnesota no attempt is made to give a general history of that institution, but certain aspects of its story not adequately told elsewhere are presented in considerable detail. The account of public education is more general in character but includes fairly full discussions of certain incidents and aspects of special interest. The chapter entitled "The Will of the People" outlines the changes in "the sovereign power" as constituted by "the deposit of the elective franchise" and discusses the development of electoral procedure. The final chapter contains brief discussions and appraisals of the work of twelve Minnesotans, who, because of their fundamental contributions to the economic and cultural development of the state, are considered worthy to be designated as "apostles."

The introduction to the first volume of this work announced that a general bibliography would be included in the final volume. On further consideration, however, in view of the inclusion of complete bibliographical information with the first reference in each volume to each work cited, it seemed that the principal object of such a bibliography would be achieved by listing the works in the consolidated index, printed in this volume, with references to the first citations. Undoubtedly a systematic bibliography of Minnesota history would be very useful, but there is no special reason why it should be included in this work. All manuscripts and newspapers cited, unless otherwise indicated, will be found in the collections of the Minnesota Historical Society. These include, in the Folwell Papers turned over to the society by the author and his family, correspondence and records of interviews with many persons who possessed first-hand information.

Acknowledgment is due to the graduate school of the University of Minnesota for successive annual grants which made possible the employment of a part-time assistant to help the author in assembling and digesting material. Similar services were also rendered from time to time by members of the society's staff. Two expert editorial assistants, Miss Mary E. Wheelhouse and Miss Livia Appel, have had charge at different times, under the direction of the editor, of the detailed work of verification, revision, and proofreading on the final volume. The maps were planned by the editor, with some suggestions from the author, and were drawn by Dr. Warren Upham. The consolidated index is mainly the work of Miss Appel, who made the indexes to the preceding volumes. For the selection of the illustrations the editor is responsible.

SOLON J. BUCK

MINNESOTA HISTORICAL SOCIETY
    September, 1930

CONTENTS

I. THE MINNESOTA IRON MINES

PAGE

EARLY EXPLORATIONS FOR MINERALS 1
THE VERMILION LAKE GOLD RUSH 4
THE VERMILION IRON DISTRICT 8
THE MESABI IRON RANGE 17
THE CUYUNA IRON RANGE 22
MARKETING THE MINNESOTA ORES 23
COMBINATIONS OF MINE OWNERS 28
THE FUTURE OF THE ORE DEPOSITS 41
THE ORIGIN OF THE MINNESOTA ORES 43
THE LOSS OF THE MOUNTAIN IRON MINE PROPERTY 44
THE OWNERSHIP OF LAND UNDER PUBLIC WATERS 48
THE GROWTH AND DEVELOPMENT OF MINING COMMUNITIES . . 50
THE TAXATION OF MINING PROPERTIES 53
THE LEASING OF STATE ORE LANDS 58

II. THE UNIVERSITY OF MINNESOTA

THE MINNESOTA PLAN OF ORGANIZATION 60
THE HIGH SCHOOL BOARD 72
THE AGRICULTURAL COLLEGE OF MINNESOTA 77
THE SCHOOL OF AGRICULTURE 85
THE DOUBLE UNIVERSITY LAND GRANT 97
THE COLISEUM 103
THE MAYO FOUNDATION 108
THE EUSTIS TRUST 122
THE REVOLUTION OF 1928 126

III. PUBLIC EDUCATION

THE ESTABLISHMENT OF THE PUBLIC SCHOOL SYSTEM 135
THE DEVELOPMENT OF HIGH SCHOOLS 141
SCHOOL TAXES 142

PAGE

THE PERMANENT SCHOOL FUND 145
STATE AID FOR SCHOOLS 149
TEXTBOOK LEGISLATION 151
COMPULSORY EDUCATION 162
CONSOLIDATED SCHOOLS 168
RELIGION IN THE SCHOOLS 170
THE FARIBAULT PLAN 174
STATE SUPERVISION OF SCHOOLS 183

IV. CHIPPEWA INDIAN PROBLEMS

EARLY EFFORTS TO CONCENTRATE THE CHIPPEWA 190
THE NORTHWEST INDIAN COMMISSION, 1886 198
THE NELSON ACT OF 1889 219
THE UNITED STATES CHIPPEWA COMMISSION 226
THE APPRAISAL AND SALE OF CEDED PINE LANDS 235
THE LOGGING OF DEAD AND DOWN TIMBER 243
THE MORRIS ACT 249
THE CHIPPEWA NATIONAL FOREST 253
THE TRAGEDY OF WHITE EARTH 261
THE WHITE EARTH LITIGATION 283
THE RED LAKE CHIPPEWA 296
THE BATTLE OF SUGAR POINT 312
THE PRESENT SITUATION 323

V. THE WILL OF THE PEOPLE

THE ELECTIVE FRANCHISE 330
THE DEVELOPMENT OF THE ELECTION CODE 338
ELECTION PROCEDURE 341
THE AUSTRALIAN BALLOT 353
THE REGISTRATION OF ELECTORS 356
ABSENTEE VOTING 360
THE GROWTH OF THE PRIMARY SYSTEM 365
" CORRUPT PRACTICES " LEGISLATION 374

VI. THE ACTS OF THE APOSTLES

CHRISTOPHER C. ANDREWS, APOSTLE OF FORESTRY 386
THEOPHILUS L. HAECKER, APOSTLE OF AGRICULTURAL
    COOPERATION 402

CONTENTS

PAGE

HASTINGS H. HART, APOSTLE OF PUBLIC CHARITIES 407

CHARLES N. HEWITT, APOSTLE OF PUBLIC HEALTH 413

CHARLES M. LORING, APOSTLE OF PARKS AND PLAYGROUNDS . . 425

EDWARD D. NEILL, APOSTLE OF EDUCATION 434

WILLIAM S. PATTEE, APOSTLE OF JURISPRUDENCE 442

LE GRAND POWERS, APOSTLE OF LABOR 448

MARIA SANFORD, APOSTLE OF CULTURE AND PATRIOTISM . . . 459

THOMAS B. WALKER, APOSTLE OF ART 465

HENRY B. WHIPPLE, APOSTLE TO THE INDIANS 472

NEWTON H. WINCHELL, APOSTLE OF SCIENCE 478

CONSOLIDATED INDEX 487

ILLUSTRATIONS

WILLIAM WATTS FOLWELL . . . . *Frontispiece*
THE FIRST PIT OF ORE AT MOUNTAIN IRON, 1890 . . 20
AN OPEN PIT AND AN UNDERGROUND MINE 32
THE OLD MAIN BUILDING AND THE COLISEUM,
     UNIVERSITY OF MINNESOTA 106
AN EARLY SCHOOL AND A CONSOLIDATED SCHOOL . . 168
A CHIPPEWA BIRCH BARK AND GRASS WIGWAM AND
     GRAVES OF CHIPPEWA MEDICINE MEN AND CHIEFS 208
CHIPPEWA INDIANS RECEIVING LAND ALLOTMENTS . . 268
CHRISTOPHER C. ANDREWS AND THEOPHILUS L.
     HAECKER 402
HASTINGS H. HART AND CHARLES N. HEWITT 412
CHARLES M. LORING AND EDWARD D. NEILL 434
WILLIAM S. PATTEE AND LE GRAND POWERS 448
MARIA SANFORD AND THOMAS B. WALKER 464
HENRY B. WHIPPLE AND NEWTON H. WINCHELL . . . 478

MAPS

THE IRON MINING REGION OF MINNESOTA 8
CHIPPEWA LAND CESSIONS IN MINNESOTA, 1837–66 . . 191
RESERVATIONS FOR THE CHIPPEWA OF THE MISSISSIPPI,
     1863–67 194
WHITE EARTH INDIAN RESERVATION 233
THE UPPER MISSISSIPPI RESERVATIONS 257
RED LAKE INDIAN "RESERVATION," 1863–1930 . . . 298

ILLUSTRATIONS

William Watts Folwell . . . . Frontispiece
The First Pit of Ore at Mountain Iron, 1890 20
An Open Pit and an Underground Mine 32
The Ore Mass Building and the College,
    University of Minnesota 106
An Early School and a Consolidated School 108
A Chippewa Birch Bark and Canvas Wigwam and
    Chiefs of Chippewa Mourning Men and Chiefs . . . 208
Chippewa Indians Receiving Land Allotments 268
Christopher C. Andrews and Herman
    Haecker 407
Hastings H. Hart and Charles W. Hart 412
Charles M. Loring and Edward D. Neill 431
William S. Pattee and Le Grand Powers 453
Maria Sanford and Thomas B. Walker 564
Henry B. Whipple and Newell H. Winchell 478

MAPS

The Iron Mining Region of Minnesota 8
Chippewa Land Cession in Minnesota, 1837-66 191
Reservations for the Chippewa of the Mississippi,
    1867-67 194
White River Indian Reservation 235
The Upper Mississippi Reservations 267
Red Lake Indian "Reservations," 1863-1930 278

A HISTORY OF MINNESOTA

VOLUME IV

I. THE MINNESOTA IRON MINES

EARLY EXPLORATIONS FOR MINERALS

IT IS related that Champlain, passing a winter with the Hurons on Lake Simcoe, heard from them reports of a "grand lac" far to the west and was shown nuggets of copper said to have been brought from its shores. Later French explorers held to the belief that metallic deposits would be found there. The tradition must have descended to the English, for in 1770 Alexander Henry obtained permission for himself and two others to work "the mines of Lake Superior." The enterprise was without any notable result.[1]

The tradition was passed on to Americans. It was not until May 24, 1815, that the British actually evacuated the Northwest. Lewis Cass, who was governor of the vast Territory of Michigan at the time, desired to become acquainted with its topography and resources. Early in 1820 he obtained from Calhoun, secretary of war, leave to make an expedition to the Lake Superior region. One purpose suggested by him was to investigate reported mineral deposits of great variety and richness there. In the spring of the same year he conducted his memorable expedition to what he supposed was the head of the Mississippi. His movement was too rapid to permit of a search for minerals, and other objects were more interesting. He did not lose interest in minerals, however. When, in 1826, he traveled to the West again and negotiated a treaty with the Chippewa of Lake Superior on the site of Fond du Lac, Minnesota, he persuaded them to

[1] See *ante*, 1: 4; James H. Baker, "Lake Superior," in *Minnesota Historical Collections*, 3: 340; and Alexander Henry, *Travels and Adventures in Canada and the Indian Territories between the Years 1760 and 1776*, 220 (James Bain, ed.— Boston, 1901).

1

cede the right to search for minerals in their country and carry them away.[2]

Governor Ramsey, coming to Minnesota in 1849, must have been told the story of deposits of minerals to be found on Lake Superior. He had not been in the territory a hundred days when, on September 4, he advised the legislature that a good road ought to be made to Lake Superior to open the mineral regions on the shore of that lake. It is well known that the Chippewa cession of 1854 was obtained in expectation, in part, that minerals — copper certainly, and gold or silver probably — would be found in that region. The construction of the canal about the falls of the Sault de Ste. Marie to be completed the next year may have been an occasion for the negotiation of the treaty. Thereafter the "triangle" was not out of the world.[3]

It is not necessary here to arbitrate the claims made by or for persons to the first discovery of iron ore on the north shore. Hunters and trappers, government surveyors, and timber cruisers had penetrated the region and had brought away samples of the red rock. It is important only to record the serious exploitations promoted by capitalists, carried on by men of science, and encouraged by legislation. Governor Ramsey appears to have held steadily to the belief that there was great mineral wealth in the triangle. In his message to the second state legislature, delivered on January 2, 1860, he reminded that body that the mineral lands of the Lake Superior region were "not only of magnificent extent, but the ores, both of iron and copper" were "known to be of singular purity." The legislature was sufficiently interested to provide for the appointment of two commissioners to make a preliminary report on the geology of the state and present a plan for a geological survey. Their reports, dated January 25, 1861, contained little infor-

[2] See *ante*, 1: 101–106, 306, and *American State Papers: Indian Affairs,* 2: 318–320.

[3] See *ante*, 1: 249, 306, and Minnesota Territory, *House Journal*, 1849, p. 16.

mation, but plenty of good advice about the importance of making geological surveys and of avoiding the mistake made by other states in appointing as state geologists politicians without qualifications.[4]

Governor Swift must have inherited the tradition. In recommending to the legislature of 1864 a rearrangement of groups of counties so that Carlton, St. Louis, and Lake counties might have fairer representation in the legislature, he stated that there were precious metals in those counties, and that mining companies were operating there. The legislature, thus informed, authorized the governor to appoint a competent person to make, under his direction, a geological survey of the lands on the north shore of Lake Superior and elsewhere and appropriated two thousand dollars for services and expenses. The governor's appointee, Dr. Augustus H. Hanchett, accepted the duty, declined compensation, and turned the field work over to Thomas Clark, one of the commissioners of 1860. The reports of Hanchett and Clark, written in November and December, 1864, stated that a portion of the north shore had been visited and that beds of copper, iron, and slate had been observed. The appropriation was too meager to permit of a general examination.[5]

The next legislature, that of 1865, was disposed to continue the quest for minerals, but it diverted half of the two thousand dollars it was willing to spend to a geological exploration of the St. Croix Valley. Governor Miller appointed Henry H. Eames to continue the survey on the north shore. Eames, with his brother Richard, penetrated

[4] House Journal, 1860, p. 180; Senate Journal, 673; Charles L. Anderson and Thomas Clark, Report on Geology and Plan for a Geological Survey of the State of Minnesota (St. Paul, 1861). Clark recorded observations made during six years of travel and railroad surveying. He prophesied that Minnesota would supply the upper Mississippi Valley with iron from mines discovered but held secret.

[5] Henry A. Swift, Message, January 11, 1864, p. 23; Stephen Miller, Message, January 4, 1865, p. 15; General Laws, 1864, p. 111; Hanchett and Clark, Report of the State Geologist, together with the Physical Geography, Meteorology, and Botany of the Northeastern District of Minnesota, 3–10 (St. Paul, 1865).

to Vermilion Lake, where he found iron ore exposed from fifty to sixty feet in thickness, presenting "quite a mural face." But he took but slight interest in this discovery, because he was looking for more precious metals.[6]

THE VERMILION LAKE GOLD RUSH

On September 19, 1865, the secret leaked out that Governor Miller had the day before received from the United States mint at Philadelphia an official statement that a certain specimen of quartz rock had yielded upon assay $25.63 in gold and $4.42 in silver to the short ton. It was understood that the specimen had come from Vermilion Lake. There was, says the *Saint Paul Pioneer*, "a flutter in our financial market second to no excitement ever witnessed in St. Paul." Sioux half-breed scrip jumped from $3.25 an acre to $12.00, and at sunset none was to be had at any price. The *Pioneer* instantly started Ossian E. Dodge as special correspondent to the Vermilion gold field. His letters describing his journey and observations, signed "Oro Fino," were written in a lively mood. He landed from his canoe on an immense bed of iron ore and saw, or was told of, gold veins "from three inches to ten feet in width, and . . . many miles in length."[7]

On October 28 Eames and his brother were back in St. Paul, speaking cautiously about the gold finds but confident of their great extent and richness. Intimations of the report Eames would make to the governor were not widely diffused for a month or more. About the middle of December the craze broke out. Numerous companies were organized, with such titles as " The Mutual Protection Gold Miners Company of Minnesota," of which Thomas M. Newson was president; " The Vermillion Falls Gold Mining Company," which owned

---

[6] *General Laws*, 1865, pp. 84–86; Henry H. Eames, *Report on the Metalliferous Region Bordering on Lake Superior*, 10 (St. Paul, 1866).

[7] *Saint Paul Pioneer*, 1865: September 19, p. 1; 20, p. 1; 21, p. 4; 30, p. 2; October 5, p. 2; 8, p. 2; 15, p. 1; 21, p. 2; 24, p. 2; 25, p. 2.

the falls on the South Vermilion River and the eighty acres
from which Eames took his specimens; and "The Minnesota Gold Mining Company," of which Sibley was president,
Governor Miller, secretary, and John S. Prince, treasurer.
On December 27, 1865, an expedition of about thirty-five
men, including a number of returned soldiers sent out by
the Mutual Protection Company, took the road from St. Paul,
equipped with ox sleds, an ammunition wagon, and a car
for eating and sleeping. Duluth was reached and on January 27 the party proceeded from there, but it took more
than thirty days to cut and clear a road to Vermilion Lake.
In March it was reported that there were about a hundred
men encamped around the lake. Thomas M. Newson, known
to the reader as the author of *Pen Pictures,* on his return
from Vermilion Lake in May, 1866, wrote an account of
the march for the *Pioneer.* By that time there were about
three hundred white people at the lake, and a sawmill and
fourteen houses had been erected.[8]

The legislature of 1866 was impressed, but not stampeded,
by the revelations of Eames in his report for 1865. On
March 2 a bill was passed appointing Eames state geologist
for the year 1866. The act fixed his salary at two thousand
dollars and provided for an additional three thousand dollars
for the expenses of geological surveys.[9]

In his report for 1865, submitted to Governor Miller
early in the following year, Eames states: "I have dis-

[8] *Saint Paul Pioneer,* 1865: October 31, p. 4; December 14, p. 1; 16, p. 2;
21, p. 2; 24, p. 4. For reports of the expedition from St. Paul and Newson's
story of the trip, see the *Pioneer,* 1865: December 14, p. 1; 27, p. 4; 1866:
February 17, p. 4; March 16, p. 4; May 9, p. 1; and May 25, p. 2. Richard
and Samuel H. Chute of St. Anthony were named as two of the seven directors
of the Minnesota Gold Mining Company and Henry T. Welles of Minneapolis
and Daniel S. Norton of Winona were among the stockholders. The Vermillion Falls Gold Mining Company was first in the field after the assays
were made. Ossian E. Dodge located with Sioux half-breed scrip the eighty
acres on the lake where Eames found the gold. Dodge was treasurer of the
company and James Gilfillan, afterwards chief justice of the state supreme
court, was attorney.

[9] *General Laws,* 1866, p. 98. For his services and expenses in 1866 the
state geologist was paid $6,050.87. State Treasurer, *Reports,* 1866, pp. 36, 37.

covered gold and silver in the quartz veins traversing the talcose and siliceous slates of Vermilion Lake, in the county of St. Louis. These veins are from an inch to several feet in width . . . their extent and richness can only be determined by practical working." In an appendix he gives the results of four assays of specimens from Vermilion Lake yielding from $25.63 to $32.35 in gold to the short ton. The formal publication in an official report of these results, already known in a general way, added violence to the existing craze. A trek to the gold mines, not only of individual prospectors but also of parties with tools and machinery for mining and with necessary supplies, set in. In the early season of 1866 a typical mining camp grew up at Vermilion Lake. Shafts were sunk into quartz veins and mining works were constructed. Three stamp mills were erected. The town site of Winston was laid out and shacks were erected on it. Saloons and other places of entertainment were opened. But the craze was short lived. Assayers who had been brought along did not find with their field apparatus any such values of gold and silver as the enterprising Eames had reported in 1865, and by midsummer the newspapers had ceased to print scare heads about the gold mines.[10]

The state geologist's report of his activities in 1866 was submitted to Governor Marshall, as the date on the title-page indicates, before the close of the year.[11] " The result of the practical workings in the quartz veins of Vermillion Lake and its vicinity," Eames wrote, " leads conclusively to the belief that they will be found remunerative in the extraction of gold and silver and will, undoubtedly, be the

[10] Newton H. Winchell, *The Geology of Minnesota*, 1: 95 (Geological and Natural History Survey of Minnesota, *Final Report*—St. Paul, 1884–1901); Walter Van Brunt, *Duluth and St. Louis County, Minnesota*, 1: 343–348 (Chicago and New York, 1921); Geological and Natural History Survey, *Reports*, 1878, p. 23. Five thousand copies of Eames's report, a pamphlet of twenty-three pages, were printed by order of the legislature of 1866.

[11] Eames, *Geological Reconnoissance of the Northern, Middle, and Other Counties of Minnesota* (St. Paul, 1866). On the Eames surveys, see Winchell, *Geology of Minnesota*, 1: 95.

means of developing other metals . . . in that region." His reconnoissance, extended into the counties of St. Louis, Lake, Itasca, Cass, Todd, Otter Tail, Douglas, and Stearns, was cursory and not important here or elsewhere. The further prosecution of the survey about Vermilion Lake he delegated to his assistant and brother, Richard M. Eames, whose report was made part of the report of the state geologist. After preparing sketches for a geological map showing the formations of the region, the assistant geologist examined and recorded his observations of twenty-three veins of quartz of varying width between walls of slate. In sixteen of them shallow shafts had been sunk, in but two of which he mentions having found gold. In the last paragraph of his report, dated September 5, 1866, he cautiously remarks that his examinations have led him " to suppose, that the hidden sources of wealth, lying buried in the strata, would justify the investment of capital." An appendix gives the results of seven assays of specimens from Vermilion Lake. The average yield in one " selected specimen " was $62.81 in gold and $7.05 in silver per two thousand pounds of ore; in another specimen, $32.06 in gold and $12.73 in silver; in a third, $27.34 in gold and $5.35 in silver; and in a fourth, $24.61 in gold and $2.00 in silver. The other assays showed small values, in one case only a trace of gold. The name of the assayer is not given. As the numbers of the assays do not correspond to the numbers of the samples collected by the assistant geologist, the exact source and the time of collection are left in doubt. He made no mention of parties still at work in the mines.

In 1880 a competent expert, employed by private parties, was sent out to make a reëxamination of the Vermilion Lake region. In his report he states that he looked over the so-called gold deposits and collected from many quartz veins specimens, which he had carefully assayed. " Not a trace of gold was discovered," he said. Where Eames obtained the specimens that yielded so promisingly is a question that awaits solution.[12]

THE VERMILION IRON DISTRICT

If Eames had not been so much interested in gold and silver and could have divined the extent and richness of the iron ore bed he saw, iron mining on Vermilion Lake might not have been delayed for nearly twenty years. But the belief in the existence of great metallic wealth on the north shore survived and extended. Alexander Ramsey appears to have cherished his belief that some day rich deposits of iron ore would be developed in the triangle. Early in the congressional session of 1869–70 he introduced into the Senate a bill to make a grant of public lands to Minnesota to aid in the construction of a railroad from Lake Superior to Vermilion Lake. On March 2, 1870, it was reported from the committee on public lands with amendments. On April 25 it was up on general orders. Objection was made to consideration on the ground that the bill would call out discussion. A senator said, " Can we not vote on it without talking?" and Senator Ramsey replied, " Certainly we can." But the bill went over and no vote was reached.[13]

George C. Stone, a native of Massachusetts, settled in Duluth in 1869, the year before that town was incorporated as a city. Perhaps because the various enterprises in which he made ventures did not turn out to his satisfaction, he gave

[12] Albert H. Chester, " The Iron Region of Northern Minnesota," in Geological and Natural History Survey of Minnesota, *Reports*, 1882, pp. 155, 166. Winchell, in Geological and Natural History Survey, *Reports*, 1889, pp. 19, 21, gives his opinion that there is no *a priori* obstacle to the expectation that there may be gold in the quartz of the region and that there is some positive basis of fact to show that it exists there in sufficient quantities in some instances to make a valuable ore if mined by the methods employed in the Black Hills.

[13] *Congressional Globe*, 41 Congress, 2 session, 1623, 2893, 2957, 4310. One senator withdrew his objection upon the request of Ramsey, " who thinks the Senate are unanimous for Senate bill No. 124." Another senator objected and the bill went over. Ignatius Donnelly appears to have been in Washington at the time and interested in the bill. In the Donnelly Papers is a letter from W. L. Banning, dated April 13, 1870, appealing to Donnelly

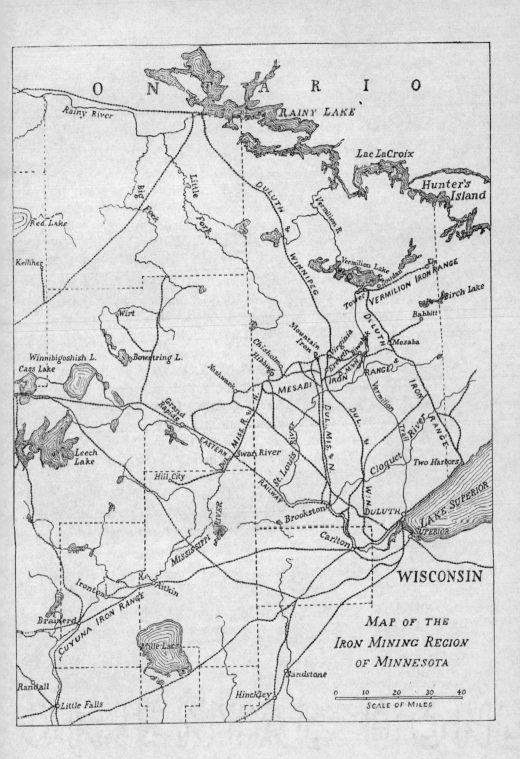

MAP OF THE
IRON MINING REGION
OF MINNESOTA

0   10   20   30   40
SCALE OF MILES

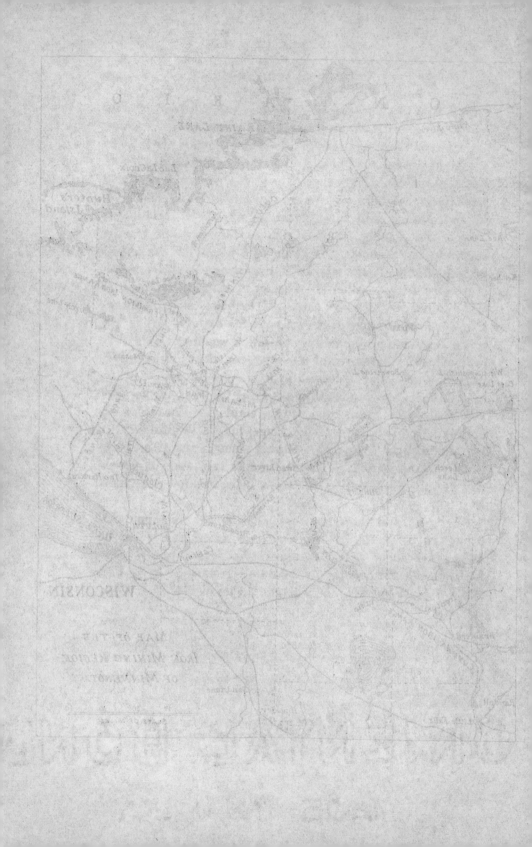

attention to the rumors and reports of the existence of iron
about Vermilion Lake and along the conspicuous elevation
in St. Louis County, already called " the range." There was
abundant capital for opening and working mines if an adequate profit could be expected. Convinced by converging
indications that there was ore in large quantities on the range,
in 1875 Stone laid his information before Charlemagne
Tower of Pottsville, Pennsylvania, an attorney for mining
interests, and Samuel A. Munson of Utica, New York, and
persuaded them to arrange for an exploring expedition to the
region. Professor Albert H. Chester of Hamilton College at
Clinton, near Utica, was employed to head the expedition.
Extensive explorations were made in the eastern part of the
range and some preliminary exploration was made near Vermilion Lake. Exposures of ore were found in township 59,
range 14 west, and in township 60, ranges 12 and 13 west,
on the range, and in township 62, range 15 west, in the Vermilion district. In his report to his employers Chester spoke
unfavorably of the ores of the range, but the Vermilion district he thought " deserved further most careful and exhaustive examination." The report, the substance of which
was not published until some years later, had no immediate
results.[14]

The great and thorough geological survey of Minnesota
conducted by Professor Newton H. Winchell was begun in
1872. For some years its operations were properly confined to the older counties of the state. It was not until 1878
that a visit was made to the triangle. In townships 59 and 60,

to have a certain amendment made. " With the bill thus amended," Banning
wrote, " we can secure the iron formation in direction of Vermillion." In a
letter to Donnelly, dated April 13, 1870, Jay Cooke wrote: " Try & get it
as near as possible to our views and then *pass it* quickly. I wrote Ramsey
yesterday. Confer with him."

[14] *Special Laws*, 1870, pp. 5–43; Van Brunt, *Duluth and St. Louis County*,
1: 350–355. On pages 351–358 Van Brunt gives extracts from a paper by
Chester on his explorations and investigations in Minnesota in 1875 and
1880. The substance of Chester's reports to Munson and Tower on these
explorations is given in his " The Iron Region of Northern Minnesota," in
Geological and Natural History Survey, *Reports*, 1882, pp. 155–167. George

range 14 west of the fourth principal meridian, Winchell found, where Chester had seen it, as it later appeared, an exposure of magnetic oxide of iron of high metallic content. It resembled, said Winchell, ores of Scandinavia and Russia, desirable for steel production. There was plenty of hardwood from which to make charcoal for reduction and a good farming country round about; and he thought that the ores might easily be made accessible by the construction of roads from Thomson, Duluth, or Beaver Bay. In his tenth annual report, that of 1881, Winchell exhorted the board of regents of the University of Minnesota to become " directly instrumental " in the development of the great industry that was to ensue. Private parties from the East, he said, had already made costly examinations and laboratory assays. The geologist predicted that the iron ores would yield a great revenue to the state. Minnesota, he said, had " every requisite and every facility " for the production of iron. The great regions to the west and northwest would be supplied from Minnesota with iron as with lumber. As Winchell did not suggest any particular way in which the regents could become " directly instrumental " in opening mines, his exhortation was without effect upon the board. Neither the regents nor the state authorities could take much interest in the statements of the man of science supported only by field notes and hand specimens.[15]

In the summer of 1880 Chester was sent by Tower and Munson on a second exploration in northern Minnesota — this time in the neighborhood of Vermilion Lake, where " an exhaustive examination of the whole district was made." His discoveries, kept secret for some years, led him to predict " the development there of an iron district of immense value and importance." Tower, however, was in no haste

R. Stuntz, a pioneer resident of Duluth and a government surveyor, was guide and explorer for the expedition of 1875. In regard to Stuntz, see Van Brunt, *Duluth and St. Louis County*, 1: 2, 64–68, 344–347, 352–354, 356, 360, 373.
   [15] Geological and Natural History Survey, *Reports*, 1878, pp. 21–23; 1881, p. 8; 1882, p. 156.

to invest large money until assured that mining property in Minnesota would not be unreasonably taxed. So George C. Stone saw to it that iron ore should not be taxed to such an extent that capital would be scared away from Minnesota. It was due to his efforts that the legislature of 1881 passed an act the obvious intent of which was to exempt iron ore from taxation, except a scintilla for purposes of statistics. It imposed a tax of one cent a long ton on iron ore mined, shipped, or disposed of, one-half to go to the state and one-half to the county or counties in which the mines were located. Every mining company was required to make to the state auditor an annual report, duly verified, of the amount of ore mined, sold, or disposed of.[16]

Late in the following year, on December 1, 1882, the Minnesota Iron Company was incorporated, the charter members being Charlemagne Tower, George C. Stone, Charlemagne Tower, Jr., George R. Stuntz, and two others. It was obvious, of course, that mining property sixty miles or more from transportation facilities would be of little value. A way was found to obtain a railroad charter and, incidentally, a considerable public contribution. It appears that on December 24, 1874, the Duluth and Iron Range Railroad Company had been organized, Stone having been one of the incorporators. The immediate purpose of the organization was soon apparent. With the aid of the influential state senator from the twenty-ninth district, Charles H. Graves, the legislature of 1875 was moved to pass an act calculated to secure a basis of credit for building a railroad. The act authorized the Duluth and Iron Range Railroad Company to build a railroad from Duluth to the northeast corner of township 60, range 12. It seems probable that the proposed railroad was to run in a nearly direct line between the termini, distant about sixty miles. To aid in construction the act granted

16 Van Brunt, *Duluth and St. Louis County*, 1: 355–358; Chester, in Geological and Natural History Survey, *Reports*, 1882, pp. 160–167; *General Laws*, 1881, extra session, 55. The word " ton " as used hereafter refers to the long ton of 2,240 pounds, unless the short ton of 2,000 pounds is specified.

to the corporation an amount of state swamp lands equal to ten sections for each mile of road completed. If there should not be found swamp lands enough within the prescribed limits, the company was authorized to locate other state swamp lands in St. Louis, Lake, or Cook counties to make up the deficiency. But the company, as originally organized, never built a mile of railroad and, of course, never earned any swamp land.[17]

The members of the Minnesota Iron Company knew, of course, that a railroad connection between their iron mines and Lake Superior was an absolute necessity; and it did not require much genius to strike out a plan to capture the dormant Duluth and Iron Range Railroad Company's franchise and its swamp-land grant. They accordingly, in 1883, bought the control on terms not now known and not here important. Uncertain, however, as to whether all its original rights and immunities had survived, they sought and obtained from the legislature of 1883 an act to continue the corporate existence of the Duluth and Iron Range Railroad Company, retaining all its original rights, with power to relocate its line so that its northern terminus should be in township 62, range 15, a point on the southern limb of Vermilion Lake, where the town site of Tower had been laid out and platted in 1882. The change of route of this railroad led to difficulties and misunderstandings, which were not settled for many years, in regard to the location of the swamp lands.[18]

[17] *Special Laws*, 1875, p. 286; Van Brunt, *Duluth and St. Louis County*, 1: 350, 359, 361, 393; *Duluth Minnesotian*, December 26, 1874, p. 2; January 16, 1875, p. 4; Fremont P. Wirth, "The Disposition of the Iron Lands in Minnesota," 119 (transcript of a University of Chicago manuscript thesis, 1925, in the library of the Minnesota Historical Society). In his preface Wirth states that he visited the principal mining towns on the ranges. In Duluth he found important manuscript material in private libraries and interviewed well-informed persons. Adequate references are made to government documents and to the records of the general land office. An alternative title might have been: "The Iron Lands of Minnesota; How They Were Acquired by Private Individuals and Corporations." The author acknowledges his indebtedness to Wirth in preparing the present account.

[18] *Special Laws*, 1883, p. 203; Van Brunt, *Duluth and St. Louis County*, 1: 350, 361.

Charlemagne Tower must have been satisfied by the report of Chester in 1880 that a large amount of rich iron ore lay about the shores of Vermilion Lake in northern Minnesota, since he began in that year to acquire lands thereabout. George C. Stone was his agent also in this part of the enterprise. In the course of three years Tower obtained possession of seventeen thousand acres at a cost of forty thousand dollars. The land, of course, passed to the Minnesota Iron Company.[10]

At this point some reader may inquire how such large purchases were possible in a mining region. In a country abundant in natural resources it has been the American policy virtually to give away to lucky discoverers and prospectors mineral deposits, forests, water powers, and fisheries. The great expansion of mining, especially of gold, silver, and copper mining after the gold finds in California in 1848, led to the conviction that limits ought to be set to mining claims. By an act of Congress of May 10, 1872, the mining laws of the United States were codified. Mineral lands were taken out of the category of public lands in general and mining claims were restricted to rectangles six hundred by fifteen hundred feet in surface. In the next session of Congress, at the instance of the Michigan delegation, an amending act was passed expressly excluding the operation of the code on all mineral lands in the states of Michigan, Wisconsin, and Minnesota. In the brief discussions in the two houses one of the reasons given for the amendment was that the law of 1872 was not intended to apply to the copper, coal, or iron mines of the Lake Superior region. The effect in Minnesota was to leave all its mineral lands open to preemption, homesteading, or purchase by cash or scrip in

[19] Van Brunt, *Duluth and St. Louis County*, 1: 358, 359. On page 359 Van Brunt states that half-breed scrip, picked up at four dollars an acre, was located on some of the best pieces and that " for the rest they paid $500 a quarter-section to entrymen, who took up farms on the barren rocks and commuted them at $1.25 an acre, with a minimum of time and easy swearing." See also Wirth, " Disposition of the Iron Lands," 123–125.

legal subdivisions like arable or timber lands. Citizens, therefore, were within their rights in 1880 in acquiring all the ore lands they wanted.[20]

The ways and means, sanctioned by the ethics of the border, by which valuable timber lands were acquired at low cost, such as locating half-breed and soldiers' additional scrip and bogus preëmptions and homesteads, have been, some or all, sufficiently described in earlier parts of this work; so also have sales at public auction, at which lumbermen were too polite to bid against one another and suffered the land advertised to go unsold, to be left to private entry the next day. All these methods were worked for all they were worth by Tower's agents and parties let in on the ground floor to obtain title to lands thought to contain iron ore. The details of the transactions cannot be gone into here. A few examples will be enough. Ex-Governor William R. Marshall, appointed by the government as special agent of the land office to investigate alleged frauds in the Duluth land district, testified in 1882, in a prosecution brought by the government to cancel alleged fraudulent homestead entries, that in traveling over ten or more townships he did not find an actual settler. "This land," he said, "is situated in a forest region of rocks, swamps and marshes, and is not suitable for farming purposes. . . . I saw no place on this claim where five acres would be plowed, even if cleared of timber and brush thereon. . . . This land is accessible only by travel through the woods on foot, or by canoe on the rivers . . . and at the time I was there there was no settlement nearer than Duluth." He added that there were "90 miles of this land." Marshall investigated a number of preemption claims and reported that he had found forty-seven of them in one township with improvements consisting of shanties four poles high and ten feet square, without roof or

[20] *Statutes at Large*, 17: 91, 451; *Congressional Globe*, 42 Congress, 3 session, 962, 1322.

floor and with a hole in one side for a door. In another township he had found nineteen preëmptions and in a third, twenty, all without habitable houses; in still another he had found ten, with no improvements and no signs of white men.[21]

There was a public sale of timber lands in Duluth in 1882, attended by a number of big buyers. A timber cruiser put in a bid for a thousand acres for a group of buyers. "That for yourself, George?" asked A. J. Whiteman, a Duluth real estate dealer. George said it was. "Then I'll not bid against you," said Whiteman. One of the Pillsburys asked how many pieces were on his list. "Twenty-six," said George. "Looks like a good deal for a cruiser," said the Minneapolis man, "but if all the rest will hold off, I will." The accommodating cruiser got a twenty-dollar bill for his work. That land contained seventy million tons of ore. This is one example of many cases in which buyers of timber in good faith, without knowledge of ore deposits on the lands, acquired large fortunes.[22]

The Duluth and Iron Range Railroad Company, its charter extended and its land grant assured, in the spring of 1883 was a living concern, with Charlemagne Tower, Jr., as its president and George C. Stone as its vice president and treasurer. In the middle of May a contract was let for building the road, not from Duluth, its technical southern terminus, but from Agate Bay in Lake County, some twenty miles down the north shore. This was a temporary disappointment to the hopeful townsmen of the "Zenith City." In that high latitude the winters are long and often severe. It was not until midsummer of the following year that the road was completed. It was a standard-gauge road — four feet eight and one-half inches — and its construction cost $1,996,633.04. The purchase of equipment brought expenditures to $2,454,938.24. Of that amount, $1,750,000 was furnished by Charlemagne

21 See *ante*, 1: 470–478, 482–486; 2: 332; Wirth, "Disposition of the Iron Lands." 74–118, especially 82, 84, 130.
22 Van Brunt, *Duluth and St. Louis County*, 2: 539, quoting John S. Pardee.

Tower, who took the railroad company's mortgage bonds at par.[23]

The Minnesota Iron Company owned ore lands on Vermilion Lake and was having a railroad built to transport ore on the way to market, but there were no miners in that remote wilderness.   To supply the need the company brought from Quinnesec in the Menominee iron region in the northern peninsula of Michigan a colony of Cornishmen and Swedes, headed by Captain Elisha Morcom. Liberal wages, comfortable dwellings, and permanent employment were promised. After traveling by rail to Superior and thence by sleighs, the first group reached Soudan on March 17, 1884 They found ready built for their shelter twenty-eight houses. The company had built a sawmill to manufacture the lumber and a gang of carpenters had been sent up to build the houses. A company store had been provided to furnish food, clothing, and other necessaries and some comforts.

As soon as the people could be settled in their homes the miners began work on two pits, drilling by hand and wheeling out the ore in barrows. When the pits became deeper, derricks were run up and tackles were rigged to hoist the ore by horse power. By the time the first railroad train arrived a considerable stockpile had been accumulated. That was on July 31, 1884. A half holiday was declared and the whole population, including some visiting Chippewa, joined in loading 220 tons of ore into the ten empty cars. This was the first shipment of iron ore from a Minnesota mine. By the close of the season 62,124 tons of ore had been delivered at Two Harbors, the settlement at Agate Bay. The annual shipments for the next three years from Soudan were respectively 225,484 tons, 307,948, and 394,910. These great and increasing outputs aroused wide attention to the Vermilion district; speculators in timber and mineral lands

[23] Van Brunt, *Duluth and St. Louis County,* 1: 362; *Duluth Daily Tribune,* 1883: April 17, p. 4; 25, p. 1; 27, p. 4; May 16, p. 2; Railroad Commissioner, *Reports,* 1883, p. 73; 1884, p. 199; 1885, pp. 205, 207.

appeared in numbers and, in the early part of 1887, a veritable mining boom set in. By the close of the year 1890 no fewer than 284 mining and quarrying companies had been incorporated under the laws of Minnesota.[24]

Prospecting went on in the Vermilion Lake iron region, at first by hand drills and later by the diamond drill driven by steam. No new discovery of importance was made until 1886, when a very promising ore deposit was disclosed at a point twenty miles northeast of Tower. Because the Minnesota Iron Company was not interested there the railroad was not extended to the town of Ely, which had been laid out, until October 1, 1888. Before the close of the season the famous Chandler Mine was opened and 54,612 tons of ore were shipped. The next year, 1889, the output ran up to 316,120 tons of high-grade Bessemer hematite. Four other mines were opened at Ely.[25]

THE MESABI IRON RANGE

The grade of the ore found by the Hamilton College professor in 1875 on township 59, range 14 west, was not considered by his employers to be high enough to warrant an

[24] *Duluth Herald*, December 9, 1911, p. 13; Van Brunt, *Duluth and St. Louis County*, 1: 362, 370; Elisha J. Morcom, "The Discovery and Development of the Iron Ore Industry," 2-4, a paper read at a meeting of the St. Louis County Historical Society in 1926, a copy of which is in the possession of the Minnesota Historical Society; Wirth, "Disposition of the Iron Lands," 16, 39; Newton H. and Horace V. Winchell, *The Iron Ores of Minnesota; Their Geology, Discovery, Development, Qualities, and Origin, and Comparison with those of Other Iron Districts*, 1, 335-349 (Geological and Natural History Survey of Minnesota, *Bulletins*, no. 6 — Minneapolis, 1891). The last work is an octavo of 430 pages with 41 plates and 2 large maps in pockets. On pages 335-349 is a list of the mining and quarrying companies incorporated up to December 1, 1890. The work is of a summary character, describing the ores, their geological and geographical situation, important mines of the Vermilion district, and methods of exploration and mining. It includes a treatise on the origin of iron ores, with an elaborate bibliography. On page 112 it is stated that, "although there is at present no mining" in the ores of the Mesabi Range, a full description of them is given because they "are destined to play a very important part in the future development of the iron industry of the state."

[25] Winchell, *Iron Ores of Minnesota*, 171-175, 196, 208; Van Brunt, *Duluth and St. Louis County*, 1: 365-369, 382.

investment. A decade ran by during which the opinion, if
there was any, prevailed that there was no pay ore in that
township. In 1888 Newton H. Winchell advised John Mallmann, who had been his guide in 1878, to make an exploration of the " red cut " in township 59 on the line of the
railroad to the Vermilion mines. Mallmann persuaded the
Minnesota Iron Company to furnish means for a practical
test and a vertical shaft was sunk into a bed of good ore.
The deposit was not a large one, however, and the mine
established did not become of much importance; but the
find encouraged further explorations in the region.[26]

Leonidas Merritt, who was born in Chautauqua County,
New York, had come in his boyhood to Minnesota, had served
in Brackett's Battalion in the Civil War, and afterwards had
settled in a suburb of Duluth. He and his six brothers,
some or all, became cruisers for pine timber, of which there
were fine stands in St. Louis County. In the course of their
wanderings they struck the red dirt in places and felt confident that iron ore would be found in some of them.[27]

In the session of 1889, at the instance of the state auditor,
William W. Braden, the legislature authorized the auditor,
as state land commissioner, to lease mineral lands belonging to the state. This made prospecting thereon feasible,
since it was not necessary to purchase the land. Any applicant, upon payment of twenty-five dollars, could obtain the
right to prospect for minerals for one year on the leased
land, which was not to exceed a quarter section, or 160 acres.

[26] Newton H. Winchell, in *Minnesota in Three Centuries*, 4: 382 (New
York, 1908); Winchell, " The Discovery and Development of the Iron
Ores of Minnesota," in *Minnesota Historical Collections*, 8: 33; Winchell,
Iron Ores of Minnesota, 202; Geological and Natural History Survey, *Reports*,
1889, p. 7. Evidence that Winchell was deeply impressed with the extent
and value of ore lands on the Mesabi is the fact that several times prior to
1888 he advised the state auditor to hold state lands on the Range, as they
might be rich in ore. *House Journal*, 1897, appendix, 87–94.
[27] Charles K. Leith, *The Mesabi Iron-bearing District of Minnesota*, 27
(United States Geological Survey, *Monographs*, vol. 43 — Washington, 1903;
printed also as 57 Congress, 2 session, *House Documents*, no. 429 — serial
4513); Van Brunt, *Duluth and St. Louis County*, 1: 395–398.

At any time before the expiration of the year he could, upon payment of one hundred dollars, lease the land for fifty years for the purpose of mining ore. For each ton of ore mined and shipped the lessee was obligated to pay to the state a royalty of twenty-five cents.[28]

In the year 1890 Leonidas Merritt took out 141 leases, 117 on school sections. Whether the Merritt brothers formed a partnership or a corporation does not appear in the annals of the time, but they are credited with starting the new movement. On November 16, 1890, one of their exploring parties, headed by Captain J. A. Nichols, struck ore in township 58, range 18, just north of where the Mountain Iron Mine was later to be opened, four miles west of the present village of Virginia. In the following summer a cruiser of the Merritts noticed red earth turned up by the roots of a fallen tree about ten miles east of Virginia. A test pit was sunk, which was the beginning of the Biwabik Mine. The discovery of ore where Eveleth was later built, five miles south of Virginia, and at Hibbing, some twenty miles westward, converted the belief that there was another iron range into full assurance of facts.[29]

As later explored, the Biwabik formation — the iron-bearing formation — of the Mesabi Range extends along the range for its entire length, from a point near Grand Rapids west of the Mississippi to the south shore of Birch

[28] *General Laws*, 1889, pp. 68–73. The constitutionality of the leasing act was not doubted until it had been in operation for about fifteen years. The question was then raised whether the language of article 8, section 2, of the state constitution, providing for the sale of the school lands from time to time and turning the proceeds into a perpetual fund, authorized the leasing of them. The state supreme court, on September 7, 1906, sustained the constitutionality. State *v.* Mabel Evans and others, 99 *Minnesota*, 220–229.

[29] Winchell, *Iron Ores of Minnesota*, 350–355; Winchell, in *Minnesota in Three Centuries*, 4: 383, and in *Minnesota Historical Collections*, 8: 38; Leith, *Mesabi District*, 27; Van Brunt, *Duluth and St. Louis County*, 1: 397, 398, 444, 447. Van Brunt, on page 397, quotes a remark of Pardee's that the tradition that ore was first revealed on the Mesabi on the roots of an upturned tree must be true, since four different locations had been given for the tree. On page 418 Van Brunt quotes Alfred Merritt's claim that he had discovered ore on township 58, range 18, in the summer of 1890.

Lake on the eastern border of St. Louis County, a distance of nearly 110 miles. The general direction is northeast, but there are numerous bends and a great flexure called "the horn" in range 17. The exposure varies in width from a quarter of a mile to three miles, the average being a mile and a quarter. In the eastern part there are elevations of eighteen and nineteen hundred feet above sea level; to the west the range drops down to the general level of the countryside. The adjacent lands are comparatively low and flat.[30] Explorations were rapidly extended over all the areas where surface conditions indicated ore and a boom set in similar to that which followed the opening of the Vermilion district, but even more extravagant and frenzied. Duluth was the center of mining speculations running into millions.[31]

Millions of tons of iron ore on the Mesabi Range could have no commercial value until there was a railroad to carry the ore raised from its beds to market. The Merritt brothers, after having failed to induce the Northern Pacific or the St. Paul and Duluth to extend a track to the range, organized on February 11, 1891, the Duluth, Missabe, and Northern Railway Company, with five of the family on the list of incorporators. As a temporary outlet, the company built forty-five miles of track from the Mountain Iron Mine to Stony Brook, now Brookston, to connect with the Duluth and Winnipeg Railroad, with its eastern terminal in Superior. On October 17, 1892, the first and only trainload for the season, 4,245 tons, was shipped from the Mountain Iron Mine. In the next year, 1893, the Duluth and Iron Range having extended its line westward to Virginia and the Duluth,

[30] Leith, *Mesabi District*, 20–23; Charles R. Van Hise and Charles K. Leith, *The Geology of the Lake Superior Region*, 159, 164 (United States Geological Survey, *Monographs*, vol. 52 — Washington, 1911). The best map of the Mesabi region, corrected to 1911, about nine feet long, is in the pocket at the end of the latter volume, and a map of the Vermilion iron-bearing district may be found facing page 118. For a description of the surface geology of the region, see Winchell, *Geology of Minnesota*, 4: 262–265.

[31] Wirth, "Disposition of the Iron Lands," 21–23; *Duluth Evening Herald*, 1892: February 27, p. 3; March 5, p. 3; 26, p. 1; *Duluth Daily News*, 1892: February 27, p. 4.

The First Pit of Ore at Mountain Iron, 1890

[From a photograph in the museum of the Minnesota Historical Society.]

Missabe, and Northern having built a branch from Iron Junction to Biwabik, 613,620 tons were shipped from eleven mines on the Mesabi. In 1896, the fifth year of mining operations, 2,882,079 tons were carried from twenty mines; in 1901, the tenth year, 9,004,890 tons were carried from thirty mines on the Mesabi. The total for the decade was 40,404,967 long tons. Minnesota had become the largest producer of iron ore in the Union.[32]

The sudden, great, and then continuous production of ore from the Mesabi Range was due not so much to its superior richness as to its physical character and the nature of the ore bodies. The ore deposits of the Vermilion district, together with the inclosing rocks, originally sedimentary and horizontal, had been tilted by geological cataclysms to the vertical, or so nearly so that the ore could be reached only by shafting nearly vertically. Practically all mining was underground. In contrast, the Mesabi ore bodies lie in the horizontal, with but slight dip, in detached masses, shallow and irregular, running lengthwise in the range like islands formed in an old river bed. In depth they are generally less than two hundred feet, but in a few instances reach five hundred feet. An overburden of glacial drift covers the whole district, varying from a few feet to one hundred feet or more, the average thickness being between twenty and forty feet. It was necessary only to strip this overburden to reach great masses of ore.

This location of the deposits near the surface without overlying rock greatly reduced the cost of mining, and that reduction was immensely increased by the physical character of the ore. While the Vermilion ores were hard rock, those

[32] Van Brunt, *Duluth and St. Louis County*, 1: 286–288; Railroad and Warehouse Commission, *Reports*, 1893, pp. 277, 295; Leith, *Mesabi District*, 28, 287–289; United States, Bureau of the Census, *Mines and Quarries, 1902*, 417 (*Special Reports* — Washington, 1905). The shipments from the Mesabi mines in 1928 were 35,398,660 tons. The total shipments from the Mesabi Range from 1891 to 1928, inclusive, were 815,688,058; those from the Vermilion Range were 54,770,276; and those from the Cuyuna, 27,201,381. Minnesota School of Mines Experiment Station, *Mining Directory of Minnesota*, 1929, p. 193 (University of Minnesota, *Bulletins*, vol. 32, no. 21).

of the Mesabi Range, as first developed, were soft ores varying from fine dust to coarse gravel. This characteristic led immediately to the introduction of a new method of mining on the Mesabi Range — if it really be mining — the so-called " open-pit method," with the use of the steam shovel both for stripping the overburden and winning the ore. It was found that " the fines " could be scooped up at once by the shovel and dropped onto ore cars waiting on standard-gauge tracks and conveniently moved from time to time. Compacted beds could be handled in the same way when loosened up by blasting. As successive horizontal slices of ore were taken off, the mine took on the appearance of a ter-raced amphitheater. The whole cost of underground operations — shafting, drifting, timbering, tramming, and hoisting — was saved.[33]

THE CUYUNA IRON RANGE

A third Minnesota iron range, lying westward of and parallel to the old ranges, was traced out and developed in the second decade of the present century. A surveyor named Cuyler Adams as early as 1895 suspected the existence of iron ore in Crow Wing County from the dip of the magnetic needle. Desultory exploration went on but tardily, probably because of the absence of surface indications. A mine

[33] Van Hise and Leith, *Lake Superior Region*, 137–139, 179; Leith, *Mesabi District*, 207, 223, 280–282, plates xxii–xxviii; Geological and Natural History Survey of Minnesota, *Reports*, 1891, p. 129; Van Brunt, *Duluth and St. Louis County*, 1: 419, 446, 449. On early mining methods on the Vermilion Range, see Winchell, *Iron Ores of Minnesota*, 176–186 and plates 21–36. Winchell, in his *Geology of Minnesota*, 4: 595, wrote: " The hard hematite ore of the mines at Soudan comes out of the ground in masses too large to be handled easily in shipping or charging at the furnace. Formerly the large blocks were broken by hand, and a man with a twenty-pound sledge hammer would pound for hours . . . before reducing a particularly hard and tough lump to convenient size." By that time, 1899, power crushers were employed. A photograph of a section of the iron-bearing Biwabik formation of the Mesabi district is given in Van Hise and Leith, *Lake Superior Region*, plate ix, facing p. 180. The tendency is more and more toward open-pit mining in Minnesota. According to F. A. Wildes, state superintendent of mines, 30,035,260 tons of ore were produced by open-pit mining in 1928, and 8,669,889 tons by underground methods.

was opened in 1911, the Kennedy Mine, and a first shipment of ore was made in April of that year. The Cuyuna
Iron Range, so far as identified, extends northeast from the
village of Randall in Morrison County to a point just east of
Aitkin, a distance of about sixty miles. Although the country
is flat, with a mere drainage divide, the term " range " came
easily into use. The ore lenses, nearly vertical, varying in
width from a few inches to 125 feet on the south range and
up to between 400 and 500 feet on the north range, lie in the
axes of the double range. The greatest depth known on the
north range is 850 feet and that on the south range, about
250 feet. As all the beds lie under a heavy mantle of drift,
with a few exceptions, mining is underground. The ores, soft
and hard with many varieties of color and texture, contain
from forty-five to sixty-three per cent of iron. On the average eleven and one-half cubic feet of the soft ores and ten
cubic feet of the hard ores contain one ton of iron. It is hydrated hematite, more or less magnetic. The distinguishing
characteristic of the Cuyuna ores is that, with variations, they
are rich in manganese, running from two to twenty-five per
cent. Manganese, as is well known, plays an important part
in the production of steel, whether by the crucible or " Bessemer," or by the open-hearth process. The manganiferous
Cuyuna ore soon found a market, which was enlarged in the
years of the World War, and the demand has been continuous. In the year 1925 there were shipped from the Cuyuna
district 1,514,053 tons, nearly all from a group of mines
near the village of Ironton in Crow Wing County.[34]

MARKETING THE MINNESOTA ORES

The enormous output of the Minnesota mines will have
aroused the wonder of the thoughtful reader. It is not mere
tonnage, however, that determines the value of a mine or a

[34] Van Hise and Leith, *Lake Superior Region*, 216, 219, 223; *Mining
Directory of Minnesota*, 1926, p. 185; Van Brunt, *Duluth and St. Louis
County*, 1: 329; William R. Appleby and Edmund Newton, *Preliminary Con-*

district. The ores of the eastern, central, and western parts
of the Mesabi Range differ widely in richness and purity.
Variations in quality frequently occur in the same mine.
With ore at the mine worth two dollars and a half a ton, a
variation of one per cent in quality means twenty-five thousand dollars on a shipment of a million tons. Ores are therefore constantly assayed at the mine and the market and are
bought and sold on guaranties of richness. If the hematites
of the Minnesota ranges were absolutely unadulterated every
hundred pounds would contain seventy pounds of iron. Such
ore does not exist. In the first place, the ore is hydrated; that
is, it contains moisture. The ores from the Mesabi and
Cuyuna ranges contain more than eleven per cent, by weight,
of water, and those from the Vermilion district, less than
seven per cent. There are also physical admixtures of
abraded rock, sand, clay, and earthy material, estimated as
high as thirty per cent of the ore from the beds. Less in
amount, but more difficult and costly to eliminate, are chemical admixtures, of which the principal ones are silica, manganese, and phosphorus. Ore containing more than .045
per cent of phosphorus is not adapted to the production of
Bessemer steel, according to present practice. In the earlier
years of Minnesota mining it was found that ore from the bed
must contain from 60 to 65 per cent of metal to be profitably
mined and sent to the distant markets on Lake Erie. That
standard later was lowered to 51.50 per cent. As rich ores
became scarce and vast amounts of lower grade ores were

centration Tests on Cuyuna Ores, 11 (University of Minnesota, School of
Mines Experiment Station, Bulletins, no. 3 — Minneapolis, 1915); Dwight E.
Woodbridge and John S. Pardee, eds., History of Duluth and St. Louis County,
Past and Present, 2: 667 (Chicago, 1910). Pages 648 to 685 of the last work
contain a well-briefed account of the development of the three ranges. For
maps of the Cuyuna district, see Van Hise and Leith, Lake Superior Region,
plate 14, and Mining Directory of Minnesota, 1926, pp. 38–44. Warren Upham,
in Minnesota Geographic Names, 1, 157 (Minnesota Historical Collections, vol.
17 — St. Paul, 1920), states that Cuyler Adams named the range for himself
and his dog, Una. The word is said to have been coined by Adams' wife.
A comprehensive bibliography of Minnesota iron mining may be found in
Winifred Gregory, Bibliography of Minnesota Mining and Geology (Minnesota
School of Mines Experiment Station, Bulletins, no. 4 — Minneapolis, 1915).

discovered, the problem arose how, if possible, to raise the quality of the leaner ores enough to render them marketable. The obvious solution was, if possible, to eliminate the waste nonmineral portions of the raw ore. Various processes — washing, crushing, drying, screening, sintering, and magnetic separation — have been devised and put into operation. In the year 1925 more than one-third of all the Minnesota shipments were of ores thus bettered — in the dialect of the mining people, " beneficiated." [35]

The immense deposits of iron ore on the Minnesota ranges would have been of no use without coal to furnish the great heat necessary to drive out the oxygen and leave the metal; and their value depended upon a market for the ore when mined and for the iron when extracted. Both of these needs were supplied. The city of Pittsburgh, a little more than a hundred miles from the south shore of Lake Erie, had long been the leading seat of blast furnaces and steel plants and of factories for converting iron and steel into numberless useful forms. That city lay on the edge of vast coal fields and in the heart of an immense iron and steel consuming area. The Pittsburgh smelters, after some experiments, adjusted their processes to the rich and fine-grained Minnesota ores and were pleased to pay enough for them to cover the long carriage.

To move the great and increasing output of the Minnesota mines a transport of large proportions was needed. It was not difficult, when capital was found, to multiply railroads and equipment to bring the ore down to Two Harbors, Duluth, or Superior and steamboats to carry it on through the Great Lakes to Cleveland, Conneaut, Ashtabula, Lorain,

---

[35] *Mining Directory of Minnesota*, 1926, pp. 186, 198, 203–205; Van Hise and Leith, *Lake Superior Region*, 489, 493; Winchell, *Iron Ores of Minnesota*, 187, 188. See Tax Commission, *Reports*, 1922, pp. 30–39, for descriptions of the various processes of beneficiation. The report also gives a list of sixteen washing plants on the western Mesabi, a description of the concentration plant of the United States Steel Corporation near Coleraine, and a description of the magnetic concentration plant at Babbitt on the eastern Mesabi. From rock carrying only twenty-four per cent of magnetic iron, the plant at Babbitt

and other lake ports. The number of vessels needed was greater because they had to lie idle during the five months in which the lakes were locked in ice. The transfer of the millions of tons of ore from railroad to ships' holds was a problem that challenged the skill of engineers. It was solved by the design and erection of the great ore docks so conspicuous at the upper lake ports mentioned. They are in fact extensions of railroads, the tracks being supported by trestles reaching out many hundreds of feet to deep water. Whole trains are backed out on them and the hopper bottoms of the cars are dropped, their loads falling into bins, called pockets, on both sides of the dock. An ore-carrying vessel, whose coming has been signaled, runs alongside the designated part of the dock with open hatches. The bottoms of the pockets fall down and ten thousand tons of ore slide into the ship's hold in the course of six hours. During the season an approximate average of twenty boats leave the head of the lake daily. In 1926 the " dumping charge " was ten cents a ton. At the Lake Erie ports the docks are equipped with unloading machines that drop automatic buckets into the holds of the boats, lift out several tons of ore at a grab, and drop it onto waiting cars. In 1925 it cost only three cents more a ton to unload the boats than to load them.[36]

The idea of reversing the practice of sending Minnesota iron ores to Pennsylvania to be smelted by bringing the coal to the head of the lake for furnaces to be built there was

extracts a sinter of sixty-four per cent. The *Mining Directory of Minnesota,* 1926, p. 182, lists forty beneficiation plants on the Minnesota iron ranges, and on page 186 it gives 13,539,431 as the number of tons of beneficiated ore shipped from the state in 1925. See also Edward W. Davis, *The Future of the Lake Superior District as an Iron-Ore Producer,* and his *Magnetic Concentration of Iron Ore* (Minnesota School of Mines Experiment Station, *Bulletins,* nos. 7, 9 — Minneapolis, 1920, 1921).

[36] Van Brunt, *Duluth and St. Louis County,* 1: 288, 290; Charles E. Van Barneveld, *Iron Mining in Minnesota,* 208–214 (Minnesota School of Mines Experiment Station, *Bulletins,* no. 1 — Minneapolis, 1913) ; Leith, *Mesabi District,* 285; *Mining Directory of Minnesota,* 1926, p. 204; Minnesota Tax Commission, *Reports,* 1922, p. 19; Crowell and Murray, *The Iron Ores of Lake Superior,* 79–88 (Cleveland, 1920). The Duluth newspapers note daily the arrivals and departures of ore vessels.

early entertained by enterprising citizens of Duluth. Soon after the opening of the great Mesabi Range a company was formed, a furnace was built, and a beginning was made in smelting. For reasons not known the venture was not a fortunate one and was soon suspended. In 1902 the Zenith Furnace Company was organized and it took over and put into operation the plant of the defunct concern. It is still in existence, with a capacity of some 300,000 tons of pig iron consuming 650,000 tons of ore.

The gigantic United States Steel Corporation, organized on February 23, 1901, owning mines of iron in Minnesota and of coal in Pennsylvania, was best situated economically to undertake smelting at Duluth. Repeated appeals from the business interests of that city to the great corporation did not meet with a ready response. It was not until 1907 that a subsidiary corporation, the Minnesota Steel Company, was ready to buy fifteen hundred acres of land, which was later included in the city. More than eight years passed before the plant was put into operation. On December 15, 1915, the first shipment of steel billets was made. The plant consisted of two blast furnaces, ninety-two coke ovens, ten open-hearth steel furnaces, and numerous auxiliary mills and shops, the whole valued at more than twenty-five million dollars. For two years the plant was occupied with the manufacture of war material.

In 1922 the United States Steel Corporation, following a policy of distributing its various kinds of steel production to different subsidiary corporations in many states, assigned to the Minnesota Steel Company as its principal manufacture the production of wire and wire products and nails. For these products, especially for bale ties and wire fencing with steel posts, there has been and will continue to be a large and increasing demand in Minnesota and the prairie states. When in full operation, the steel plant, according to statistics of 1926, consumes about 700,000 tons of Minnesota iron ore a year, about the same quantity of coal, and about 220,000 tons of limestone.

To house a nucleus of its operatives, the Minnesota Steel Company, while constructing its plant, laid out on its lands a residence quarter called "Morgan Park," using as its agent the Morgan Park Company. That company graded and paved the wide streets with concrete, put in a sewage system, and erected dwellings, a hospital, and a clubhouse, with ample spaces about them. The company maintains the whole quarter as a park. The rentals are moderate.

About the time of the completion of the Minnesota Steel Company's plant, the Universal Portland Cement Company, another subsidiary of the United States Steel Corporation, put into operation a cement mill in Morgan Park. This plant, which makes Portland cement from the slag of blast furnaces with other composits, principally limestone and coal, has a capacity of 6,500 barrels of cement a day. The Morgan Park steel, wire, nails, and cement establishments are the most considerable of all the industries of the ambitious and prosperous city of Duluth; but the million tons of iron ore that the steel company and the Zenith Furnace Company capture out of the forty millions sent down from the ranges is not a large percentage.[37]

Combinations of Mine Owners

In a period in our history when properties and industries were combining into large incorporated holdings at a rate without precedent, it was inevitable that mine owners, or some of them, would also combine for coöperative management or for absorption into heavily capitalized corporations. As already related, the Merritt brothers of Duluth, by leases or otherwise, had obtained equities in numerous mining properties on the Mesabi Range. Mention has been made

[37] Van Brunt, *Duluth and St. Louis County*, 1: 310–315; Minnesota Steel Company, *How Steel Wire and Wire Products Are Made*, 2, 32 (Duluth, n.d.) ; H. L. Hosford to the author, January 18, 1927, Folwell Papers.

of the organization of the Duluth, Missabe, and Northern Railroad Company by the Merritt brothers to carry ores from certain mines to the head of the lake. To finance an extension and the building of ore docks in 1893, a block of $1,600,000 worth of bonds was offered by them in New York. John D. Rockefeller took a quarter of the amount and the remainder was worked off tardily, widely margined. Early in the season of that panic year there was a shortage of money to pay contractors building the road and the docks. In July the Merritts were in danger of losing the collateral securities they had pledged for loans. As Rockefeller had already made an investment, it was hoped that he would be willing to add to it. The result of negotiations between his representative and the Merritts was the organization on August 28, 1893, of the Lake Superior Consolidated Iron Mines Company, into which the Merritts merged their railroad stock and their stock in five mines and Rockefeller, mining stock owned by him. Rockefeller further agreed to finance the railroad to the amount of $500,000 and to buy all the ore that the Mountain Iron Mine should produce that fall. For his share in the deal, Rockefeller took the bonds of "the Consolidated"; the Merritts were content to take stock, hold apparent control, and direct operations. Inexperienced in financial affairs and ill advised, they authorized and issued absurdly excessive amounts of stock.

The railroad was finished, and the Merritts were happy in spite of an ominous cloud of maturing obligations incurred in a variety of private adventures. At the close of the year 1893, however, they were desperate. In January, 1894, they offered Rockefeller ninety thousand shares of their stock at ten dollars a share. He accepted the proposition, paid them in stocks and bonds of two companies in which he was interested, and granted them an option to recover fifty-five thousand shares at any time within a year at the same price, with interest. Instead of redeeming the fifty-five thousand shares of stock, the Merritts, conceiving that Rockefeller had deceived them by paying them in securities of companies that he knew at the time were insolvent, brought suit against him for damages, charging him with fraud and misrepresentation. The result of a tedious litigation was a settlement. But the Merritts lost control of the Consolidated. "Rockefeller men" became directors and officials.[38]

For the eight years during which the company remained in independent existence, its mines on the Mesabi yielded great and increasing amounts of ore and the "Missabe" railroad did a thriving business hauling it to Duluth. Absurdly over-capitalized — nearly thirty million dollars' worth of stock was authorized — the company never paid a dividend; but there came a time when the shares were good property. On February 23, 1901, the United States Steel Corporation was organized and in April it absorbed the Consolidated, paying $79,417,542 in equal amounts of common and preferred "United States Steel" in exchange for its $29,424,594 in shares of stock. The estimated amount of iron ore thus conveyed was between three hundred and four hundred million tons, of which half, or thereabout, lay in the ore beds of the Mesabi Range.[39]

Another pioneer mine operator in Minnesota was Henry W. Oliver of Pittsburgh. Oliver was at the Republican

[38] Henry R. Mussey, *Combination in the Mining Industry: A Study of Concentration in Lake Superior Iron Ore Production*, 115 (Columbia University, *Studies in History, Economics, and Public Law*, vol. 23, no. 3, whole no. 60 — New York, 1905) ; Van Brunt, *Duluth and St. Louis County*, 1: 287, 399–408; testimony of Alfred and Leonidas Merritt, in United States House of Representatives, *Hearings before the Committee on Investigation of the United States Steel Corporation*, 3: 1845–1881, 1897–1933 (Washington, 1912). The *Hearings* are in eight volumes, the first seven of which are paged consecutively. They will be cited hereafter as *Steel Corporation Hearings*. See also Frederick T. Gates, *The Truth about Mr. Rockefeller and the Merritts*, 7, a pamphlet of thirty-two pages published in or after 1911; Dwight E. Woodbridge to the author, January 26, February 2, 1927, in the Folwell Papers; and Rockefeller *v.* Merritt, in *Federal Reporter*, 76: 909–919. The case was settled in 1897.

[39] Van Brunt, *Duluth and St. Louis County*, 1: 405, 412; United States Commissioner of Corporations, *Report on the Steel Industry*, part 1, pp. 12, 29, 66, 106, 114, 147–149. This report is bound in *Steel Corporation Hearings*, vol. 8.

national convention in Minneapolis in June, 1892, which nominated Benjamin Harrison. Out of curiosity Oliver made an excursion to the Mesabi Range and penetrated, over corduroy roads and through woods and swamps, to the site of the Missabe Mountain Mine, near which the village of Franklin afterwards grew up. He was so much impressed with appearances that he leased the mine of the Merritts at sixty-five cents a ton, including the state royalty. On September 30 he, with others, organized the Oliver Iron Mining Company, with an authorized capital of a million dollars, which took over the lease. Oliver's original purpose was to obtain ore for his own furnaces. It is understood that in them were made the improvements that rendered the smelting of the Mesabi ores practicable and economical. He was presently so much impressed with the value of ore property that he planned to enlarge his holdings. Before the year was over he gave to the Carnegie Steel Company one-half of the stock of the Oliver Iron Mining Company in consideration of a loan of half a million dollars, to be spent in developments.

A few years later, in 1896, Oliver arranged a deal with the Rockefeller interests, successors to the Merritts and owners of the Duluth, Missabe, and Northern Railroad. The Oliver company was to lease the Lake Superior Consolidated Iron Mines properties on the Mesabi on a royalty basis of twenty-five cents a ton and to mine and ship over the Rockefeller railroads and lake vessels 1,200,000 tons of ore a year for fifty years. To add to his working capital and to enlarge his credit, Oliver made over one-third of his mining stock to the Carnegie Steel Company and thus control passed to the larger concern. The big transaction "knocked the price of ore from $4.00 down to . . . $2.50 a ton." Owners of Minnesota ore properties were keen to sell and they found the Carnegie-Oliver combination ready to buy. In the course of a few years the combination acquired, with a comparatively small capital, a large number of leaseholds and through them controlled an extensive reserve of tonnage. When the Carnegie Steel Company passed over its great properties to the United States Steel Corporation, its ore lands in Minnesota were included. The exact amount of tonnage thus transferred was not known to the parties themselves and it is still a question for actualities; but it was a great addition to the tonnage acquired from the Lake Superior Consolidated Iron Mines Company.[40]

Another of the constituent members of the United States Steel Corporation was the Federal Steel Company, which was organized as a holding company in 1898. Upon its organization the Federal Steel Company had taken over all the ore lands of the Minnesota Iron Company, the Duluth and Iron Range Railroad, and a fleet of lake vessels and barges. The absorption by the United States Steel Corporation passed all these properties to the giant combination. It then proceeded to merge the Federal Steel Company, the Lake Superior Consolidated Iron Mines Company, and the Carnegie-Oliver company into one subsidiary, which was called the Oliver Iron Mining Company.[41]

After its organization in 1901, the United States Steel Corporation acquired from year to year numerous small mining properties. Within a year from its organization it had accumulated by fee or lease, it was estimated, some seven hundred million tons of iron ore in the Lake Superior region, by far the larger part on the Minnesota ranges. The Minnesota tax commission in its first report, that of 1908, gave out as the result of careful listing and estimates the ton-

[40] Mussey, *Combination in the Mining Industry*, 117–119, 120, 123, 139; Van Brunt, *Duluth and St. Louis County*, 1: 408–412; 2: 576–578; James H. Bridge, *The "Carnegie Millions and the Men Who Made Them"; Being the Inside History of the Carnegie Steel Company*, 257–268 (London, 1903); Commissioner of Corporations, *Report on the Steel Industry*, part 1, pp. 2, 12, insert at 107; Carnegie's testimony, in *Steel Corporation Hearings*, 3: 2351; *Duluth Daily News*, 1892: August 4, p. 4; 5, p. 4; 7, p. 2. It is understood that Carnegie was at first not in favor of large acquisitions of ore lands in Minnesota, but that he gave way at length to Oliver's persistence.

[41] Van Brunt, *Duluth and St. Louis County*, 1: 412; Commissioner of Corporations, *Report on the Steel Industry*, part 1, pp. 2, 12, insert at 107.

AN OPEN PIT MINE

AN UNDERGROUND MINE
[From photographs taken in the Fayal mines, Eveleth, in 1915, in the museum
of the Minnesota Historical Society.]

nage owned by the United States Steel Corporation in Minnesota (the Oliver Iron Mining Company) to be 912,768,830 tons, out of a total of 1,192,509,757 tons.[42]

Another great amount of tonnage had been acquired by a notable personage in Minnesota history and not many years later this became a matter of concern to the steel corporation. Readers of this history have noted the career of James J. Hill as a buyer, builder, and administrator of railroads. On June 2, 1897, the Great Northern Railway Company, of which Hill was president, bought the bankrupt Duluth and Winnipeg Railroad, mentioned above, which was later merged into the division of the Great Northern called the Eastern Railway of Minnesota. Some ten or twelve thousand acres of land held by subordinate corporations were acquired by this purchase.

From the mouth of the Swan River, a tributary of the Mississippi in Aitkin County, ran a lumberman's railroad — the Duluth, Mississippi River, and Northern — some forty miles northeastward toward Hibbing and the Mahoning Mine. It crossed the Minnesota Eastern at nearly right angles at Swan River station, some sixty miles from Duluth. This logging road belonged to Ammi W. Wright and Charles H. Davis, lumbermen of Saginaw, Michigan, who had bought large tracts of pine lands and had now cut off the timber and sold the stumpage. A son of Hill, James N. Hill, who was on the directorate of the Eastern Railway Company of Minnesota, learned that Wright and Davis were prepared to sell their cut-over lands and with them the railroad. He conceived the idea that if this piece of road were added to the Minnesota Eastern and substantially rebuilt, a good business might be done hauling iron ore.

At James N. Hill's suggestion, his father went up to the region for the first time and saw the Mahoning Mine on the

[42] Minnesota Tax Commission, *Reports*, 1908, p. 122; Abraham Berglund, *The United States Steel Corporation: A Study of the Growth and Influence of Combination in the Iron and Steel Industry*, 82 (New York, 1907); Com-

railroad property in operation. As the elder Hill says, he
"knew nothing about iron ore," but he thought it important
to get the transportation of the ore and authorized his son to
take the matter up with Wright and Davis. Within a short
time James J. Hill met Wright and Davis in Chicago and,
after a brief negotiation, bought of them on January 27,
1899, their railroad and about twenty-five thousand acres
of land on the Mesabi Range for $4,050,000. As they were
paid for from his own funds, they might have become and
remained his individual property, but it was not Hill's pleasure to hold that property as his own. As the head of the
Great Northern system for many years, he conceived that it
would be the proper thing, or at least the generous course,
to share with its stockholders, who had sustained and trusted
him, any profit resulting from a transaction related to it.[43]

As the Great Northern Railway Company could not
legally hold more lands than were necessary to its operations, except government and state grants, Hill's purpose was
effected by some ingenious financiering. As a first move, on
October 20, 1899, the Hill interests in the Wright and Davis
properties, except the railroad, which had been sold to the
Eastern Railway of Minnesota on May 1, were placed in
trust with the Lake Superior Company Limited, which had
been organized on July 25, 1899, under the laws of Michigan.
The company was authorized to deal in mineral lands, to

missioner of Corporations, *Report on the Steel Industry*, part 1, pp. 40, 204;
Investigation of United States Steel Corporation, part 1, p. 80 (62 Congress,
2 session, *House Reports*, no. 1127 — serial 6138). The latter report is also
in *Steel Corporation Hearings*, vol. 8.

[43] Hill's testimony in *Steel Corporation Hearings*, 4: 3152, 3153, 3155,
3160, 3171, 3228, 3239, 3240; G. R. Martin, vice president of the Great Northern
Railway Company, to the author, February 18, 1927, and George H. Hess, Jr.,
comptroller of the company, to Martin, February 15, 1927, Folwell Papers;
Joseph G. Pyle, *The Life of James J. Hill*, 2: 217–222 (Garden City, New
York, 1917); Van Brunt, *Duluth and St. Louis County*, 2: 540, 543, 548;
Railroad and Warehouse Commission, *Reports*, 1897, pp. 143, 152, 156. On
Hill's railroad activities, see *ante*, 3: 451–462.

On January 7, 1907, in the course of an interview, Hill, unrolling a long
map, said to the author: "There, Mr. Folwell, this map shows ore land worth
$600,000,000, more or less. All of this I could have kept as my own, but I

mine and market ores, to lease lands and mines, and to
acquire securities and hold them in trust. The membership
consisted of James J. Hill, two of his sons, and a fourth
person. The company eventually paid Hill his purchase
money with five per cent interest, held the property some
seven years, and disposed of the income as directed by the
Great Northern board.[44]

Hill's sight of the Mahoning Mine made a deep impression
upon him and his views on the subject of iron ore rapidly
expanded. Under his initiative the Lake Superior Company
acquired parcels of land on and along the Mesabi Range until in the course of about seven years the holdings of the company by fee or lease reached 65,091.40 acres. As the state
law forbade corporations, other than those organized for the
operation of railroads, canals, or turnpikes, to hold more
than five thousand acres of land in the state, a plan, for
which there was abundant precedent, was adopted, that of
causing the organization of subsidiary corporations, each of
which could lawfully own five thousand acres. As the law
allowed mining corporations to acquire the stocks of other
mining corporations, the Lake Superior Company, by buying the stocks of the auxiliaries, had absolute control of the
lands, leaving these subsidiary companies to function as mere
dummies to hold the technical titles.[45]

The consummation of Hill's purpose was advanced by a
further transfer of the properties. It was deemed that an

have turned it over to the stockholders of the Great Northern Railway Company.
No man cares less for money than I do. I have enough for myself and my
family; why should I burden myself with all this wealth?" This interview
is recorded in the author's notebooks, 3: 134.

[44] General Laws, 1887, p. 323, as amended by Laws, 1899, p. 130; Hill's
testimony, in Steel Corporation Hearings, 4: 3162–3172; Hess to Martin, February 15, 1927, Folwell Papers. In his testimony before the investigating
committee, Hill said, "I always had a rule that if I could make money for
myself in a transaction connected with the company, I could make it for
the stockholders."

[45] Commissioner of Corporations, Report on the Steel Industry, part 1, p.
260; Great Northern Iron Ore Properties, Reports, 1907; 1911, pp. 1, 8;
General Laws, 1887, p. 323, as amended by Laws, 1899, p. 130; General Laws,
1876, p. 46, as amended by General Laws, 1881, p. 47.

(

agency more flexible and permanent than the Lake Superior Company for holding them and distributing the income and profits was desirable. On December 7, 1906, as previously authorized by the directors and shareholders of the Great Northern Railway Company, all the lands mentioned were transferred in trust by stock deliveries to an unincorporated association named the " Great Northern Iron Ore Properties." The trustees were Louis W. Hill, James N. Hill, Walter J. Hill, and E. T. Nichols. The final act was the issue, on the same date, and the distribution of " certificates of beneficial interest " to the holders of 1,500,000 shares of stock in the Great Northern Railway Company, to each as many certificates as he held shares. These certificates were, and are, independent securities bought and sold on the market separately from Great Northern stock. It may be assumed that Hill's choice of beneficiaries was altogether agreeable to the Great Northern shareholders of the time, since they and not a far greater number of future shareholders were the preferred objects of Hill's generous forbearance. The amount distributed to the holders of the certificates from September 16, 1907, to December 28, 1925, was $56,250,000.[46]

This remarkable transaction was probably expedited in anticipation of another equally extraordinary. From sources best known to himself, Hill had learned that on the demised lands lay vast quantities of good iron ores; they might amount to hundreds of millions of tons. The United States Steel Corporation pursued the ostensible policy of acquiring by purchases of fees or by leases a controlling interest in the Minnesota mines, whether to enjoy a monopoly or — it has been much disputed — to make sure of a sufficient supply for a long time of ores to feed its numerous and costly

[46] Hill's testimony in *Steel Corporation Hearings*, 4: 3173–3176; a printed circular from the Great Northern Iron Ore Properties to the "Holders of Certificates of Beneficial Interest," December 7, 1906, a copy of which is in the Folwell Papers; Great Northern Iron Ore Properties, *Reports*, 1911, p. 1; 1925, p. 4.

furnaces and its affiliated manufacturing plants. It may be assumed that previous overtures had been made toward the purchase of the Hill interest; if so, they were without result. So eager was the great corporation to control the ore supply or prevent the appearance of a dangerous competitor that, by promise of an inordinate rental, it obtained a lease of 39,296 acres from the trustees of the Great Northern Iron Ore Properties to the Great Western Mining Company, a convenient subsidiary of the Steel Corporation. The indenture of lease was dated January 2, 1907, but, awaiting the guaranty of the Steel Corporation, it was not effective until August.

The agreement bound the lessee — the Steel Corporation in fact — to make immediate explorations of the lands and to mine and ship definite minimum quantities of ore: 750,000 tons in 1907 and thereafter amounts increasing annually by 750,000 tons until 1917; in that and following years the minimum would stand at 8,250,000 tons. If in any year the full amount of ore was not mined, the full royalty was to be paid, but the lessee was to be allowed certain credits in the years when its shipments exceeded the minimum. For this privilege the Steel Corporation agreed to pay in 1907 a royalty of eighty-five cents for every ton of dried ore containing fifty-nine per cent of metal, to ship the whole output over the Great Northern Railway to its docks at Superior, Wisconsin, and to pay eighty cents per ton freight. The lease had no term and might run until all the ore on the leased lands should be exhausted. The aggregate amount of ore to be mined and shipped, in the absence of explorations and drillings, was a matter of estimate; both parties believed it to be very great. The Steel Corporation reserved the right to cancel the lease in 1915, upon giving two years' notice of its intention to do so. The freight rate was the same as that of the other ore roads from the mines to the lake, but the royalty was nearly double the average at the time, which was forty-four cents a ton for the same grade of ore, as estimated by a high authority; and the royalty was to be increased 3.4 cents a ton each year, so that, for fifty-nine per cent ore, in 1910 it would stand at $0.952, and in 1915 at $1.122, when the combined royalty and transportation would be $1.922. In 1911 the Steel Corporation gave notice of its intention to cancel the lease, and on December 31, 1914, it surrendered the property.[47]

The explanations of this extraordinary transaction are various. It was a "tantalizing enigma" to the chairman of the committee appointed in 1911 by the United States House of Representatives to investigate the Steel Corporation. It was the opinion of Hill that it was no more than ordinary business prudence on the part of the corporation to secure all the rich ore it could get. With an investment or capitali-

[47] Commissioner of Corporations, *Report on the Steel Industry*, part 1, pp. 47, 48, 260–263, 318–322; Hill's testimony in *Steel Corporation Hearings*, 4: 3154, 3203–3205; Hess to Martin, February 15, 1927, Martin to the author, March 17, April 20, 1927, Folwell Papers; Great Northern Iron Ore Properties, *Reports*, 1907; 1911, p. 15; *Investigation of Steel Corporation*, 90 (serial 6138). A lease of the Hill properties was no sudden conception on the part of the Steel Corporation. On May 6, 1902, at a meeting of the executive committee of the corporation, a member said, "I think we ought to buy Mr. Hill's ores." The chairman, Gary, thought the corporation had enough low-grade ore. On May 20 the president, Schwab, said: "I believe we must make some arrangement with Hill. We have depended upon his assurances that he would let us have the properties, and we are now giving him a million tons of ore every year down his road. I think Mr. Hill ought to give us the leases of all his properties, subject to a contract with him by which we would guarantee him a certain minimum of traffic over his road. All he wanted was the traffic. He does not want any royalty." The chairman said, "I think you will have to pay a small royalty." See the report of Farquhar J. MacRae to the investigating committee, February 12, 1912, in *Steel Corporation Hearings*, 6: 3799–3801.

A printed copy of the lease, 1029 pages, quarto, is in the office of the Great Northern Iron Ore Properties in St. Paul. Articles 3 to 8 are printed in *Steel Corporation Hearings*, 4: 3247–3253. The royalty of eighty-five cents a ton was fixed for ore containing fifty-nine per cent of metal after drying. A sliding scale of royalties was provided for ores richer or leaner in iron, and these also were subject to the same annual increase of 3.4 cents. In 1907 the royalties ranged from $.368 to $1.1874. Fifty-nine per cent dry was approximately equal to fifty-three per cent natural. In regard to the absence of explorations before the lease, see the testimony of Joseph Sellwood and Thomas F. Cole in *Steel Corporation Hearings*, 7: 5434, 5499, and *Investigation of Steel Corporation*, 90 (serial 6138.) In regard to the estimates of tonnage covered by the lease, see Cole's testimony in *Steel Corporation Hearings*, 7: 5450, 5498, 5499. Cole, who was made president of the Oliver Iron Mining

zation of fifteen hundred million dollars, a twenty or twenty-
five years' supply of ore, which was what the corporation
had before it leased the Great Northern properties, was not
enough. When that supply was exhausted the plants of the
corporation would be worth what they would bring as scrap
iron. The leased ores would extend the period ten years and
that, said Hill, was "rather a short life." The United
States commissioner of corporations, in his report of July
1, 1911, on the steel industry, gave as "the only reasonable
explanation" of the extremely high royalty and the high
minimum requirements of the lease the desire of the corporation to prevent the Hill ores from falling into the hands of
competitors in the iron and steel business. The investigating committee, or rather a majority of five members, quoted
the commissioner's opinion with approval and expressed its
conclusion that the Steel Corporation complied with Hill's
"inexorable demand" and "paid the inconceivable price"
to secure its "absolute and long-coveted monopoly" of
iron ore.[48]

Company upon the organization of the Steel Corporation, said to the investigating committee, "Our engineers felt, like we all felt, that there was a possibility
of a tonnage amounting to; well, up to 250 million tons . . . on those lands."
The estimates of Hill's engineers are not known. His own guesses are
variously reported. See *Hearings*, 4: 3200, 3206, 3236, 3239, 3241. The commissioner of corporations, in his *Report on the Steel Industry*, part 1, p. 263,
states that Hill had been quoted as saying that "'experts have figured it from
400,000,000 to 600,000,000 tons, but it would not be surprising if operations
would uncover 1,000,000,000 tons.'" Berglund, in his *Steel Corporation*, 80,
says that Hill's holdings "which the Steel Corporation recently leased have
been estimated to contain as much as 500,000,000 tons."
  For a widespread belief that the cancellation of the Hill lease was due
to the fact that the United States Steel Corporation did not need the Hill ores
after its purchase in November, 1907, of the great properties of the Tennessee
Coal, Iron, and Railroad Company in Alabama, Georgia, and Tennessee, no
evidence has been found. There was probably some connection between the
two events. For accounts of that purchase see *Investigation of Steel Corporation*,
part 1, pp. 161–209 (serial 6138) ; Gary's account in *Steel Corporation Hearings*, 1: 125–150; *Absorption of the Tennessee Coal & Iron Co.* (60 Congress,
2 session, *Senate Reports*, no. 1110, part 2 — serial 5383; printed also in
Steel Corporation Hearings, 2: 1119–1144) ; Commissioner of Corporations,
Report on the Steel Industry, index, under Tennessee Coal, Iron, and Railroad
Company; and *Steel Corporation Hearings*, general index, under the same entry.
  [48] *Investigation of the Steel Corporation*, part 1, pp. 92–94 (serial 6138) ;
Steel Corporation Hearings, 4: 3196, 3203, 3204, 3226; Commissioner of Corpora-

The lease of so great a property to the United States Steel Corporation aroused a keen interest in the Minnesota legislature of 1907, at least in the House, which on January 15 appointed a committee to investigate and report on the propriety and legality of the transaction. On February 15 and 16 the committee subjected James J. Hill to a rigorous examination with the apparent expectation of disclosing that the Great Northern Railway Company, and not Hill personally, had in fact illegally bought the Wright and Davis lands. The questioning took a very wide range and elicited much interesting, though irrelevant, gossip. Hill gladly related how, with but slight knowledge of the possible amount of iron ore on the still unexplored lands, he had bought the land and the railroad to get the hauling of freight; how he had used the Lake Superior Company as a convenient agency for bestowing the proceeds of the purchase upon the stockholders of the Great Northern; how he had signed the lease and Gary had signed on behalf of the Steel Corporation. He had had no full estimates by experts of the amount of ore that might be developed, but, he said, " if there are 500,000,000 tons of ore there I shouldn't be surprised." [49] According to the best available record, the amount of ore shipped from the lands during the term of the lease was

tions, *Report on the Steel Industry*, part 1, p. 322; Martin to the author, March 17, 1927, Folwell Papers. On Hill's " inexorable demand " see *Hearings*, 4: 3242: " I told them . . . the price they could have it at," said Hill, " and it was a loss of their time and a waste of mine to ask for any other figure." Thomas F. Cole defended the lease with its surrender clause, considering it as a business proposition: " We felt that it would be wise to secure that ore territory," he said, " explore it thoroughly, and be guided by the result of those explorations as to whether the lease would be held beyond the 1915 period or not." See *Hearings*, 7: 5450. In 1911 the freight rate was reduced to sixty cents a ton. The commissioner of corporations, in his *Report on the Steel Industry*, part 1, p. 379, cites the following from a letter from the secretary of the Minnesota tax commission, dated May 12, 1909: " They [the United States Steel Corporation] now control at least 80 per cent of the present known tonnage in the state."

[49] *House Journal*, 1907, vol. 1, pp. 49, 268; *Daily Pioneer Press*, 1907: February 15, pp. 1, 3; 16, p. 1. The *Minneapolis Journal*, 1907: February 15, p. 14; 16, p. 7, gives a cynical account. The printed copy of the lease does not show Hill as a signatory; it was signed by the officers of five land companies and twelve iron mining companies.

26,573,808 tons, on which the royalty was $30,310,716 and the freight charges, $14,863,509 — a total of $45,174,225.[50]

THE FUTURE OF THE ORE DEPOSITS

In the territorial years and the early years of statehood it was fondly believed that the pine forests of Minnesota would furnish an abundant supply of lumber for building, fencing, and all other purposes forever and a day. The state is not fourscore years old and nearly all that " inexhaustible " pine has disappeared; Minnesota is now a large importer of forest products. This mistake cannot take place in regard to iron ore. The area where ore is geologically possible is so small in comparison with the whole surface of the state that it would be ridiculous to apply the term " inexhaustible." [51] Forests can be planted and replanted for centuries; mines when exhausted have no future. But the question, How long can the Minnesota iron ore deposits hold out? is an alluring and serious one. It frequently comes up in the form of a problem: given 1,500,000,000 tons of available ore and an annual decrement of 30,000,000 tons, in how many years will the mines be exhausted? The obvious quotient is fifty years.

The matter is not so elementary, however. The dividend is far from being constant. In the first decade of Minnesota mining, sixty per cent dried ore only was considered worth winning; in the next, the figure dropped to fifty-five per cent; now fifty-one and one-half per cent natural ore is the common market standard of richness. As furnaces and smelting processes have undergone many improvements, it may be expected that others will follow to render the reduction of much leaner ores economical. It is already, although not generally, known that laboratory experiments have been

---

50 Great Northern Iron Ore Properties, *Reports*, 1914, p. 9.

51 On both the Mesabi and Vermilion ranges the ore beds occupy but a minute fraction of the iron-bearing formation. Leith, *Mesabi District*, 206; Van Hise and Leith, *Lake Superior Region*, 137.

made that promise the evolution of an electric process that will entirely supersede the present blast furnace. As already noted, lean ores are now raised to market standard by beneficiation.[52]

There may be another increment to the dividend. There lie in Minnesota millions upon millions of tons of iron ore now absolutely unavailable on account of a deleterious chemical admixture in an oxide of titanium, one of the rare metals for which but few uses have been discovered. Iron expensively produced from this ore containing a very small percentage of titanium is of superior quality; but the smelting of titaniferous iron ore in existing furnaces has been proved virtually impossible. It is by no means unreasonable to believe that some day chemistry will extort the secret of a jealous nature and render these ores, now despised and rejected, as desirable as any. They occur in enormous masses in a rock formation called by the geologists the "Duluth gabbro," running along or parallel to the north shore of Lake Superior all the way from Duluth to Pigeon Point. Analyzed samples show a percentage of iron ranging from twenty to fifty-four, with an average of forty-three. The United States geological survey in 1911 estimated roughly that, counting all lean and refractory ores and excluding "available" ores, the tonnage of the iron formations in Minnesota, except the Cuyuna, to a depth of 1,250 feet for steeply dipping beds and 400 feet for those of the Mesabi district, is 173,000,000,000 tons, of which 31,025,000,000 contain thirty-five per cent or more of iron. Minnesotans need not lose sleep for fear of a collapse of the mining industry in the near future.[53]

[52] Van Hise and Leith, *Lake Superior Region*, 493.

[53] Winchell, *Iron Ores of Minnesota*, 123, 135, 142–144, 162; Van Hise and Leith, *Lake Superior Region*, 31, 492, 494, 561; Thomas M. Broderick, *The Relation of the Titaniferous Magnetite Deposits of Northeastern Minnesota to the Duluth Gabbro*, 683 (Lancaster, Pennsylvania, 1918). The estimate of the tonnage of iron-bearing formations exclusive of "available" ores for the whole Lake Superior region is 467,450,000,000 tons, 67,640,000,000 tons of thirty-five per cent and over. The Lake Superior region, which includes

The divisor of the ore problem is also fluctuating. The increase of population and the discovery of new uses for iron and steel add to it and lower the time quotient. Other considerations tend to lower the divisor, among them the introduction of new metals, notably of aluminum and its alloys, the employment of concrete in place of steel for bridges, and the use of scrap iron in the manufacture of steel. Paper containers for storing and shipping a great variety of products have lessened the use of nails. If ever, and it may be expected, a cheap method of preventing the rusting of iron and steel shall be invented, the demand for iron ore will be materially decreased.

THE ORIGIN OF THE MINNESOTA ORES

There must have arisen in the minds of thoughtful readers the interesting query, Where did the ores of the Lake Superior region come from? On this question the historian may not presume to have any opinion of his own; he will do well if he can put into simple language the substance of the best argued of the theories worked out by the distinguished geologists who have studied the problem. It is commonly known that native iron has been found only rarely. In some far-off geologic age a vast Huronian sea covered large portions of the Lake Superior region. On leveled portions of its bed was deposited a mud consisting chiefly of silica in composition with iron oxide to the amount of about twenty-five per cent. This primeval sediment, hardened into rock many hundreds of feet in thickness, called by geologists "ferruginous [that is, iron-bearing] chert," was the original of all the iron ore beds. In this combination the most useful of all metals would have remained valueless. There was too much silica and it was bound to the iron by a bond as

parts of Michigan, Wisconsin, Minnesota, and Ontario, lies between latitudes 44 and 49 degrees and longitudes 84 and 95 degrees. The iron-bearing districts cover not much more than two per cent of the region, perhaps thirty-six hundred square miles.

powerful as it was mysterious. To break up this union and liberate the iron it was necessary to reduce — to eliminate — the silica. This was effected mainly in "Nature's great concentration mill." Nature's work went on tardily through long geologic ages, during which the lands of the region were raised out of water, were sunk and raised again, were tilted, squeezed, and, in places, folded, and were invaded by volcanic upthrusts until at length the rocks were established as they now appear. These convulsions left the iron-bearing chert seamed and cracked and in places shaped into troughs as if in preparation for the concentrating process, so simple that it was for a long time doubted. Silica is slowly soluble in water, especially in ground waters. Those settling into the shattered chert and flowing through its crevices slowly dissolved out the silica and left the iron ore more or less pure. The silica was simply leached out of the chert. But Nature never carried her process to perfection. The richest iron ores she has left us hold so much silica that only the fierce heat of the blast furnace, aided by a limestone flux, can break its bond with the metal. In a later geologic time glaciers coming down from the north scoured off great quantities of ore and, as they melted away, left the mantle of " glacial drift " that miners have to strip or dig through. The whole matter is now clear, unless some reader singularly inquisitive desires to know where the waters of the Huronian ocean picked up the iron it deposited in the original sedimentary mud. Further this deponent saith not.[54]

The Loss of the Mountain Iron Mine Property

The act of Congress of March 3, 1849, creating the Territory of Minnesota, provided that when the lands should be surveyed sections 16 and 36 of every township should be reserved for the support of schools. The enabling act of

[54] Van Hise and Leith, *Lake Superior Region*, 462, 499–518, 530–570; Leith, *Mesabi District*, 17, 41–45, 60, 237–272; Frank F. Grout and T. M. Broderick,

February 26, 1857, offered the same numbered sections for the same purpose and provided further that, if either of them, or parts of them, should have been sold or otherwise disposed of, other equivalent lands would be granted. The state constitution framed in that year and put into effect on May 11, 1858, formally accepted the school grant. The intended operation of the indemnity clause was to save the state from loss where preëmptors before surveys or homesteaders thereafter had in good faith settled on school sections. As such cases multiplied the state auditor, as land commissioner, from time to time made applications for indemnity lands by filing descriptions in the state land offices.[55]

On February 9, 1884, William W. Braden, the state auditor, filed in the Duluth land office a list, numbered 9, of certain lieu lands desired by the state. The land office officials — the register and the receiver — appended to the list their certificate that the selections were correct. The list was filed in the general land office, where, on March 25, 1884, it was "posted in tract books." The lands were accordingly withdrawn from the market. In the ordinary course of business the tracts listed would have become the property of the state. Four years later, on January 26, 1888, Braden sent to the land office at Duluth a new list of indemnity lands, numbered 12, with a simultaneous relinquishment of all

The Magnetite Deposits of the Eastern Mesabi Range, Minnesota, 40–47; John W. Gruner, Contributions to the Geology of the Mesabi Range, with Special Reference to the Magnetites of the Iron-Bearing Formation West of Mesaba, 45–67 (University of Minnesota, Minnesota Geological Survey, Bulletins, nos. 17, 19 — Minneapolis, 1919, 1924); Winchell, Iron Ores of Minnesota, 103–111, 391–399. On pages 224–257 Winchell gives eighteen theories of the origin of iron ores, with a list of advocates, more than a hundred in number. See also Winchell, Geology of Minnesota, 4: 359–364, 546–549; 5: 990–999. In the preface to this volume, p. xx, Winchell says that the investigation of the Mesabi district was incomplete at the time of publication. On the effect of glaciers, see United States Geological Survey, Reports, 1899–1900, part 3, p. 329. According to J. R. Finlay, reporting to the federal bureau of mines, in State Auditor, Reports, 1917–18, p. lv, in one section of an ore formation on the Mesabi, which had been leached from top to bottom, "we find about 400 feet of ore made from about 700 feet of formation."

55 Minnesota constitution, article 2, section 3. The constitution and the organic and enabling acts may be found in any issue of the Legislative Manual.

lands included in eleven previous lists, list number 9 included. The reason given was that the old lists did not comply with instructions issued by the general land office, and
a substitute list was made to conform with those instructions.
On March 15, 1888, the commissioner of the general land
office accepted the new list and the lands described became
the property of the state for school purposes.[56]

In the early winter of 1897 Robert C. Dunn, the state auditor, in his official report for the biennium 1895–96, the first
years of his service, revealed to the legislature that the state
had suffered a loss of twelve million dollars of its school
fund by reason of a " serious error of judgment or a grave
mistake." The gravamen of the statement was that Braden
in his substitution of list number 12 for previous lists of lieu
lands had omitted three forties in township 58, range 18, on
which the Mountain Iron Mine had been thereafter opened.
Here was a capital opportunity for Representative Donnelly
to employ his talent for the investigation of corrupt practices, real or imaginary. As soon as the House was organized, he introduced, on January 12, 1897, a resolution for
the appointment of a joint committee of fifteen representatives and seven senators to inquire into the relinquishment
of the lands, with power to compel testimony. Two days
later the House amended by reducing the numbers to seven
and four, respectively, and passed the resolution by a unanimous vote. The Senate concurred and the committee was
appointed.[57]

The reason for the delay is not known, but it was not until
April 6 that the committee's elaborate report came up in the

---

[56] " Report of the Joint Committee of the Two Houses, Appointed to Investi-
gate the Question of the Right of the State to Certain Lands Known as the
'Mountain Iron Mine Property,' Situated in St. Louis County, Minnesota,"
in *House Journal*, 1897, appendix, 75, 79; Matthias N. Orfield, *Federal Land
Grants to the States, with Special Reference to Minnesota*, 232 (University of
Minnesota, *Studies in the Social Sciences*, no. 2 — Minneapolis, 1915).

[57] *Executive Documents*, 1896, vol. 1, pp. 344–346; *House Journal*, 1897,
pp. 35, 55, 60; *Senate Journal*, 50, 71; Woodbridge to the author, November 29,

House and it did not come up for final disposition until
April 13. It was signed by all but one of the members of
the committee. The principal conclusions were: (1) that
the state had acquired title to the forties when list number 9
was filed and posted in the tract books; (2) that the state
auditor had no power to relinquish them; (3) that evidence
taken tended to show that the state auditor knew that the
lands relinquished were mineral lands of great value; and
(4) that the state ought to recover possession. The committee's recommendation was that a joint committee of four
from the House and three from the Senate be appointed,
with power to institute such proceedings as should be found
necessary, to employ counsel, and to demand that the occupants of the lands surrender them to the state and pay over
the profits that they had derived from them. As might have
been expected, neither house was disposed to invest Donnelly,
with his temperament and prejudices, with the conduct of a
judicial inquiry and probable litigation. After an adjustment of differences over a bill in conference, the houses
agreed to appoint the governor, the state auditor, and the
attorney-general a committee to make a thorough investigation of all the facts pertaining to the rights of the state in the
premises, with power to employ counsel to assist in the investigation and the resulting litigation. An appropriation of
ten thousand dollars was made.[58]

Soon after the adjournment of the legislature of 1897,
the members of the committee, Governor David M. Clough,
Attorney-General Henry W. Childs, and Auditor Robert C.
Dunn, met and employed W. P. Warner and Henry C. Belden
as their counsel. The result of consultations, as stated by

December 1, 1926; *Minneapolis Tribune*, 1897: January 13, p. 2; 15, p. 2;
16, p. 6; *Daily Pioneer Press*, 1897: January 13, p. 1; 29, p. 6; 30, p. 3. The
issue of the latter paper for January 15, p. 1, gives the substance of Donnelly's
speech reviewing the history of the affair.

[58] See *ante*, 3: 223; *House Journal*, 1897, pp. 384, 869, 987, 1018–1021, 1181,
appendix, 106; *Senate Journal*, 872, 904, 927, 936; *Laws*, 1897, p. 580; and
Minneapolis Journal, 1897: April 6, p. 10; 14, p. 12.

the attorney-general in his report for the biennium 1897–98, was that in the opinion of the able counsel the state had no rights. The state acquired no title by the filing of lists of indemnity school lands. Such lists were mere *ex parte* applications on behalf of the state, which the secretary of the interior might allow in whole or in part or might reject altogether. His order only conveyed title. The state had never owned the Mountain Iron Mine forties. Such being the legal situation, further investigation would have been absurd. The state had no interest in pushing a futile inquiry into the question whether or not Auditor Braden, in relinquishing the Mountain Iron Mine lands, had committed " a serious error of judgment or a grave mistake." Braden had died in California on March 11, 1897, while the Donnelly committee was still at work. As a citizen, as a regimental captain, and in public office his record was otherwise stainless.[59]

THE OWNERSHIP OF LAND UNDER PUBLIC WATERS

Situated on divides of land, the Minnesota iron ranges did not abound in lakes, so numerous in most parts of the state. Where they occurred as mere ponds, mining claims covered them without question. There were a few large enough to be meandered by the government surveyors, and it was commonly believed that the rights of riparian owners extended over the water and all beneath it. The mining companies were not advised to the contrary by lawyers and they began, or prepared to begin, operations into and under

[59] State Auditor, *Reports*, 1897–98, p. 38½; Attorney-General, *Reports*, 1897–98, p. 35; Edward T. Young to the author, April 4, 1914, Folwell Papers. In an interview with the author on January 12, 1914, Samuel G. Iverson said: " His [*Braden's*] character made him incapable of wrong. He could have enriched himself in various ways. . . . He left only a small fortune, possibly $50,000. He died of a broken heart sorrowing over the error in his office." This interview is recorded in the author's notebooks, 7: 106. Iverson was state auditor from 1903 to 1915 and had been employed in the offices of the state auditor and the state treasurer for fifteen years before. Orfield, in his *Federal Land Grants*, 229–234, appears to overrate the *ex parte* testimony taken by the joint legislative committee. See also the *St. Paul Dispatch*, March 11,

lakes. On April 24, 1903, application was made to the state land commissioner for prospecting mineral leases on land lying beneath the water of Longyear Lake in township 58, range 20, near Chisholm. The commissioner issued the leases, but, uncertain about his powers in the matter, he brought it to the attention of the legislature of 1905, which gave it no consideration. In 1907 a bill declaring all minerals and mineral lands under public meandered lakes and rivers to be the property of the state was passed by the House but was lost in the Senate. Two years later, however, a similar bill became a law.[60]

On September 4, 1909, the attorney-general brought suit against the owners and lessees of land abutting on Longyear Lake. The owners on October 1, 1908, had granted a mining lease to the White Iron Lake Iron Company, which in turn had entered into a lease with the Euclid Iron Mining Company. The complaint alleged that the defendants had built up an embankment inclosing a portion of the lake, had stripped off the soil, and had removed a quantity of iron ore, which they had no right to do. In reply the defense alleged that the legislative act was void because it was in violation of both the state and the federal constitutions and, as fact, that Longyear Lake was not a public navigable water. The district court decreed that the defendants were entitled to judgment and to recover their costs and disbursements. It was the opinion of the court that Longyear Lake was not a public water and that, if it were, the riparian owners, rather than the state, had title to the soil. On September 23, 1913, an appeal was taken to the state supreme court, but a year passed before that tribunal, on September 11, 1914, ren-

1897, p. 5; the *Saint Paul Globe,* March 12, 1897, p. 8; and an editorial in the *Martin County Sentinel,* March 19, 1897, p. 8. It is notable that Donnelly's paper, the *Representative,* had practically nothing to say in regard to the investigation.

60 State Auditor, *Reports,* 1903–04, pp. xxxv–xxxvii; 1905–06, p. lv; 1907–08, p. xxxi; *House Journal,* 1907, pp. 548, 1654; 1909, pp. 231, 713, 769; *Senate Journal,* 1907, pp. 1442, 1488; 1909, pp. 319, 343, 487, 561; *Laws,* 1909, p. 48.

dered its decision reversing the decree of the court below, without dissent. It was considered that Longyear Lake, a meandered water of some one hundred and fifty acres in area, although not technically navigable for traffic, was a public water useful for boating, bathing, fishing, and other public purposes. The question of the title to the soil under water was elaborately discussed and numerous authorities were cited. It was held that in the United States each state determines for itself the question of the ownership of land under its public waters. The title to land under water belongs to the states, " and if the riparian owner has acquired it at all it is by the favor or concession of the state." The state of Minnesota is the owner of all the soil under all public waters beyond low-water mark, not as an absolute proprietor, but in trust for public purposes. Riparian owners have the right of access, the rights to accretions and relictions, and the right of wharfing out subject to public regulation. They may improve, reclaim, and occupy the surface of the submerged land out to the point of navigability, subject to the control of the state. As no appeal has been taken, such is now established law. The effect of the decision in the particular case was of little account, but its application to the ten thousand lakes of Minnesota is of importance.[61]

The Growth and Development of the Mining Communities

The iron ore mining industry, beginning in 1884 in the Vermilion district and greatly increased after 1892 by the Mesabi developments, rose in twenty-eight years thereafter to be the third in importance in the state. According to the census of 1920, Minnesota ranked eighth in the whole country in the value of its mining products, and in the value of

[61] State v. Eliza Korrer and others, 127 Minnesota, 60–78; paper book of the case in the state library, bound in Cases and Briefs of the Supreme Court, April term, 1914, calendar no. 4. The auditor in his Reports, 1913–14, pp. xxiii–xxix, gives a brief history of the case.

iron ore produced it led all other states.   There were 89
enterprises producing iron ore, operating 141 mines, and
employing 17,422 persons, to whom more than thirty-one
million dollars were paid in wages and salaries.   The capital invested, ore lands not included, was $304,386,006 and
the value of the products was $128,377,174. Taxes amounted
to $26,013,086 and royalties and rents, to $17,532,030.
Practically all the enterprises were owned or controlled by
corporations, only two small concerns excepted.[62]

The effects of the mining development upon the settlement and population of St. Louis County had no precedent
in Minnesota history. The population of that county, the
area of which is 6,503 square miles, was 4,504 in 1880; in
the next decade it was increased nearly tenfold, reaching
44,862; from 1890 to 1900 it was nearly doubled, reaching
82,932; and in the next decade the number was again nearly
doubled, for the census reported 163,274 in 1910.   The rate
then moderated, the county having a population of 206,391
in 1920, of which 98,917 were residents of the city of Duluth. The growth of mining towns was greater in rate than
that of Duluth, whose population in 1900 was 52,969. For
example, Chisholm, which had no population in 1900, numbered 9,039 in 1920; Eveleth increased in the same period
from 2,752 to 7,205; Hibbing, from 2,481 to 15,089; and
Virginia, from 2,962 to 14,022.[63]

The rapidly advancing communities were naturally desirous to enjoy not only the comforts and luxuries of older
places, but also the cultural advantages. An economic situation made it possible for them to obtain all these with surprising expedition.   Like municipalities in general, they
had the right of local taxation for schools and public im-

[62] *United States Census*, 1920. *Minnesota State Compendium*, 170–173. See
also Victor S. Clark, *History of Manufactures in the United States, 1860–1914*,
552–554 (Washington, 1928) for brief comment on the growing importance
of the iron trade of Minnesota.
[63] *United States Census*, 1920, *Minnesota State Compendium*, 12, 25, 48, 53.
In 1920, of the 71,313 foreign-born residents of St. Louis County, 56,053 were

provements. As the valuations of mining properties were fixed by the state tax commission, local assessors could not, through infirmity of judgment or otherwise, reduce them. Here was a source of large revenue for public objects without burden to the average citizen. The towns supplied themselves in rapid succession with waterworks, sewers, fire protection apparatus, electric lighting, intercity street railroads and omnibus lines, cement pavements, community houses, parks, and libraries, all generously planned. Expenditures for schools of all grades were lavish beyond comparison. Chisholm expended $275,000 for a high school building, $300,000 for a grade school building, and $650,000 for a community building. In Virginia a technical high school was built, and later enlarged, at a total cost of $1,089,000. The city of Hibbing outdid all the towns on the Mesabi Range, putting $350,000 into a building for its grade schools and $3,800,000 into one for its high school and junior college. Few college buildings anywhere compare favorably with this structure and its equipment. It has its chemical and physical laboratories, its kitchen and cafeteria, its gymnasium and swimming pool, and a splendid auditorium.[64]

The legislature of 1921, in response to agitation by people in the southern part of the state against the lavish expenditures of the mining towns, limited the general tax levy in cities and villages to one hundred dollars per capita and the school tax levy to sixty dollars per capita. The legislature of 1929 amended the act of 1921 by providing that the general tax levy should not exceed eighty dollars per capita

natives of six countries: Finland, 17,342; Sweden, 12,239; Jugo-Slavia, 8,563; Norway, 7,188; Canada, 6,812; and Italy, 3,909. Lawrence A. Rossman, in *The Iron Ore Industry*, an article printed on four loose sheets, a copy of which is in the Folwell Papers, states that the number employed in mines in St. Louis County fell from 15,200, the average number from 1910 to 1920, to 9,225 in 1926, as a result, among other causes, of improvements in mining methods and machinery. This paper was read before the Engineers' Club of Minneapolis on February 21, 1927. Although a careful study, it is written candidly from the mine owners' point of view.

[64] Van Brunt, *Duluth and St. Louis County*, 509, 570, 605.

in 1930 and 1931, seventy-five dollars in 1932, and seventy
dollars in 1933.[65]

THE TAXATION OF MINING PROPERTIES

The reader will easily recall the generous action of the
legislature of 1881 in its extra session to encourage the then
unborn mining industry by imposing the nominal tax of one
cent per ton on iron ore mined, shipped, or disposed of,
in lieu of all other taxes and assessments. It was not until
fifteen years later, on May 19, 1896, that an attorney-general
discovered that such a tax was in violation of the state constitution, which required that all taxes on property be uniform. In that year mining properties were assessed like other
real estate and the legislature of 1897 repealed the tax of
one cent per ton. The ad valorem tax has been levied and
collected ever since.[66]

After the development of the Mesabi mines had run the
yearly output of ore into tens of millions of tons, complaints
were heard that mining properties were not taxed as heavily
as their peculiar nature warranted and demands were frequent for heavier impositions. The matter was not taken
up seriously by the legislature until 1907, when it appointed
a joint committee to investigate the best method of taxing
the ore and ore lands of the state. To enlarge their knowledge, the members of the committee traveled the whole length
of the two ranges and found a string of prosperous villages
surrounded by an absolute wilderness. The conclusions from
their observations were that a tonnage tax, whether flat or on
a sliding scale, was impracticable and that a well-admin-
istered property tax on an ad valorem basis would be the
only advisable one. The House resolved that $225,000,000
would be a fair valuation of the ore lands, which was not a

[65] *Laws*, 1921, p. 646; 1929, p. 206.
[66] See *ante*, p. 11; Attorney-General, *Reports*, 1895–96, p. 186; *General Laws*, 1897, p. 41.

very bad guess, and adopted a motion to transmit a copy of the committee's report to the governor to be filed with the Minnesota tax commission, created by the same legislature, as soon as it should be appointed.[67]

Governor Johnson appointed Professor Frank L. McVey of the University of Minnesota and two able colleagues as members of the Minnesota tax commission. They attacked their problems at once with remarkable vigor and discretion. Their first undertaking in regard to mining property was to obtain, by means of a questionnaire, from mine owners and lessees descriptions of properties and estimates of tonnage held and operated by them, operating costs, records of shipments and sales, and other pertinent information. The footings showed an aggregate of 1,192,509,757 tons of iron ore, valued at from eight to thirty-three cents per ton in the ground, the average being fifteen and six-tenths cents, with the total valuation placed at $186,204,002. The increase in valuation over that of 1906, the previous year, when it was $63,024,332, was creditable alike to the efficiency of the commission, invested with power to modify and determine assessments on the several properties, and to the willing coöperation of mine owners. In the following year, 1908, the commission revised its tables, corrected errors, and reduced the total valuation to $176,340,749 on a tonnage greater by 1,219,202 tons. From this time the amount of assessable tonnage increased from year to year by the opening of new mines and by larger estimates for old ones, and after 1914 by a few millions of tons from the Cuyuna Range, reaching its peak of 1,468,574,970 tons in 1914; but the crest of valuation was not reached until 1918, when there was an increase over 1914 of $23,363,242 for 37,863,673 fewer tons of ore.[68]

[67] Senate Journal, 1907, pp. 46, 106–110, 866–870; House Journal, 70, 120–122, 134, 151, 945–949, 1857, 1864.

[68] Laws, 1907, pp. 576–584; Minnesota Tax Commission, Preliminary Report, 7, 37, 41 (St. Paul, 1907); Reports, 1907–08, pp. 130–133; 1925–26, p. 46.

In its first biennial report, that of 1908, the tax commission recommended a tonnage tax on iron ore, believing it would be as easy to administer and would establish " automatically a rough system of justice . . . much nearer equality than any system of assessment is likely to develop." After the veto by Governor Johnson on April 20, 1909, of a tonnage tax bill, the commission remained silent on the subject and devoted its best efforts toward administering the ad valorem tax as effectively and fairly as possible. But agitation was kept up by newspapers and other agents and bills were introduced in successive legislatures. The heritage argument was the one most frequently employed: that such a natural deposit belonged to the whole state and that the present private owners had no right to exhaust it and leave nothing but holes in the ground to future generations. In 1919 a bill was passed for a royalty tax on ore, which Governor Burnquist vetoed as unfair and inadequate.[69]

To the session of 1921 Governor Preus proposed a " severance tax," which was regarded as a new name for a tax on tonnage. There was a lively sentiment in favor of exacting from lucky mine owners a large contribution to compensate future generations for their lost heritage. A tax was proposed, with a new name, that would secure the heritage and be distinguishable from a tonnage tax. An act was passed submitting to the electors an amendment to section 1 of article 9 of the state constitution, creating a new tax, the rate to be fixed by the legislature, on the " business of mining " and giving it the new name " occupation tax." A precedent for such taxes had been found in federal revenue acts and in the practice of a number of southern states. Of the proceeds to be derived from the tax, fifty per cent was to go into the general revenue fund of the state, forty per cent into the permanent school fund, and ten per cent into the

[69] Minnesota Tax Commission, *Reports*, 1907–08, p. 142; 1909–10, pp. 74–89; 1911–12, pp. 86–100; *House Journal*, 1911, p. 314; 1913, p. 78. See *ante*, 3: 289, 307.

permanent university fund. In anticipation of the ratification of the amendment the same legislature passed an act imposing a tax " equal to 6 per cent of the valuation of all ores mined or produced," in addition to all other taxes. After a litigation lasting two years, the Supreme Court of the United States, on May 7, 1923, sustained the constitutionality of the act. It took effect from the date of its passage in 1921. In the first five years in which the occupation tax was levied, $16,981,534 were assessed, approximately eleven cents per ton. In the same period the ad valorem taxes on mining properties amounted to $93,559,109, sixty-nine and one-tenth cents per ton of ore mined.[70]

The new tax on the mining business imposed upon operators of leased mines did not require owners of the fee to pay a tax on their part of the business. To remedy this discrimination, the legislature of 1923 provided by law for a tax of six per cent on the amounts of money or values received by the owners of mining lands for permission granted by them to carry on mining thereon, the income to go into the general revenue fund. As in the case of the occupation tax, opposition promptly arose against the royalty tax and a test case was carried to the United States Supreme Court. By a decision rendered on June 7, 1926, the validity of the law was sustained. For the years 1923, 1924, and 1925, the total amount of taxes assessed was $2,768,744, being six per cent of $46,145,740, the amount of royalties received by persons subject to the royalty law. The average of the tax per ton of ore for the three years, as estimated by the tax commission, was $.447. With ore worth $3.00 at the mouth of the mine, the tax per ton would be $1.34. Operating together, the ad valorem tax and the super occu-

[70] See *ante*, 3: 307–309; *Laws*, 1921, pp. 274–277; Oliver Iron Mining Company *et al. v.* Lord *et al.*, 262 *United States*, 172–181; and Minnesota Tax Commission, *Reports*, 1925–26, p. 98. The act passed in the session of 1921 stipulated that all taxes collected under its provisions be credited to the general revenue fund. The legislature of 1923 passed an amendment providing that the proceeds be apportioned to the general revenue fund and the permanent school and university funds in accordance with the constitutional amendment.

pation and royalty taxes exact over twenty per cent of the annual value of the iron output. As the tax commission remarked, the "mining industry is not lightly taxed." [71]

It would be fruitless to reopen the question of the validity or the justice of the super taxes. There remains, however, an unanswered question, whether the rate of those taxes has been judiciously chosen and whether it has not been placed so high as to defeat in some degree their intended operation. Already mines of low-grade ore have been closed and the output of high-grade mines has been unduly stimulated, thus hastening their exhaustion.

Advocates of the super taxes have always assumed, and opponents have acquiesced in the theory, that Minnesota, or at least the Lake Superior region, would control the American iron ore market indefinitely so that those taxes would be shifted to furnace men, who in turn would exact them from consumers of iron and steel. The assumption is already in question; it is alleged that furnaces east of the Alleghenies can obtain ore cheaper from South America and that iron and steel are being imported from Germany, Belgium, and India. But it is not to be expected that any Minnesota legislature will abate the rates on the super taxes until it shall have been very clearly proven that they are injurious to the mining industry and disappointing in results. [72]

According to the heritage theory, the whole income from the extra taxes should form an endowment to compensate

[71] Laws, 1923, pp. 258–260; 1925, p. 461; 271 United States, 577; Minnesota Tax Commission, Reports, 1925–26, pp. 103–108.

[72] Minnesota Tax Commission, Reports, 1925–26, pp. 47, 51; Rossman, Iron Ore Industry. At the instance of eastern producers of pig iron, the tariff commission carried on an investigation into that business beginning in 1922. On February 2, 1927, the commission reported to the president that, in its judgment, the tariff on pig iron ought to be raised from seventy-five cents a ton to $1.12½ to place the American producers upon an economic equality with foreign, especially British-Indian, producers. On February 23, 1927, the president by proclamation put the recommendation into force. See the United States Tariff Commission, Iron in Pigs: Report of the United States Tariff Commission to the President of the United States (Washington, 1927). The New York Times, May 29, 1927, section 2, p. 18, states that since the new rate had been in effect the import of pig iron had fallen off eighty-seven per cent of the amount imported in the like period in 1926.

posterity for the loss of the heritage. But it pleased the legislature to divert one-half of the occupation tax to the general revenue fund and to plump the whole royalty tax into that fund. Was that an honest thing for trustees to do?

THE LEASING OF STATE ORE LANDS

The main iron ore deposits of Minnesota were found on lands that had been a part of the public domain of the United States and had passed into private hands by purchases at the public sales, by homesteading, and by the location of scrip. The state was owner by gift of Congress of two sections of land in every township, of what swamp lands there might be left after grants to railroads, and of scattered tracts that had been located under the second congressional grant to the state for a state university. Account has already been made of the policy adopted in 1889 of reserving state lands supposed to contain iron or copper deposits and leasing them to private operators paying a royalty for ore mined and shipped. In a little over a year 225 one-year leases and 6 fifty-year contracts were issued. Thereafter leases ran up year by year into thousands, and contracts, into hundreds in number. The peak was reached in the fiscal year 1901–02, at the end of which 3,272 prospecting leases and 550 mining contracts had been issued, but only 262 leases and 211 contracts were then in force. In the biennial period 1903–04, there were 733 permits taken out, but only 72 leases resulted. Better luck attended 781 seekers for ore in the next two-year period, 1905–06, as 361 obtained leases. The lease of the Hill properties to the United States Steel Corporation on January 2, 1907, awakened the legislature of that year to a realization that state ore properties might be valuable assets to be held for further disposition. It repealed the act of 1889 and put a stop to permits and leases.[73]

[73] *Laws*, 1889, pp. 68–73; 1907, p. 14; State Auditor, *Reports*, 1889–90, p. 13; 1901–02, p. xxv; 1903–04, p. xxxv; 1905–06, p. li; 1925–26, p. 57.

Ten years passed without legislation. After the title of the state to ore lying under meandered lakes had been tardily sustained by the courts, the legislature of 1917 authorized a board consisting of the governor, the attorney-general, and the state auditor to issue permits and leases for removing ore so situated. The royalty was fixed at a minimum of fifty cents per ton. But two leases were taken out at the price. Four years later, in 1921, a new act was passed, amounting almost to a code, for the handling of ore on the plan long in use for the disposal of timber. The state auditor, treasurer, and attorney-general were authorized, after advertisement, to open sealed bids for leases on the second Monday in January and August in each year and to award leases to the bidders offering the highest royalties. In the years that have followed but five leases have been taken out and four of them have been canceled. On May 1, 1926, out of the whole number of leases issued, 879, but 66 remained in force. Of these, 29 have either no ore or only a little of low grade. The tax commission stated that the remaining 37 mines contain 138,055,820 tons of merchantable ore, of an assessed value of $28,461,002. Up to the same date the total output of the state mines was 67,745,947 tons, more than half from three mines and nearly forty per cent from one, the Missabe Mountain Mine near the village of Franklin, the lease held by the Oliver Iron Mining Company. With this exception, none of the great deposits were found on state lands. The whole amount received by the state for royalties to 1926 was $17,462,317.05, and a half million ($499,615.77) was received as fees for permits and leases. These moneys have gone into the permanent school, swamp, and university funds in proportion as derived from their respective lands.[74]

[74] *Laws*, 1917, p. 137; 1921, pp. 630–640; State Auditor, *Reports*, 1925–26, pp. 25, 27; Tax Commission, *Reports*, 1925–26, p. 55; *Mining Directory of Minnesota*, 1926, p. 111.

II. THE UNIVERSITY OF MINNESOTA

IN THE large illustrated volume entitled *Forty Years of the University of Minnesota,* edited by E. Bird Johnson, may be found the annals of the university from its reorganization in 1868 up to 1910, recorded with fidelity and in excellent literary form. A sufficient account of a previous chaotic period of eighteen years, beginning with the statutory creation of the institution by the legislature of 1851, is prefixed. That is mostly a pitiful story of how, as the result of a series of errors and blunders, next to nothing was accomplished and a great debt was accumulated. The very corporate existence of the university was threatened, but the institution was at length " extricated " by the good judgment, foresight, and enterprise of John Sargent Pillsbury.[1] The following pages treat merely of certain topics that have been omitted from the volume mentioned or that call for fuller treatment on the basis of information later available or supplied from the author's personal knowledge.

THE MINNESOTA PLAN OF ORGANIZATION

The act of the legislature of February 18, 1868, reorganizing the university, provided for a central college of science, literature, and the arts and associated colleges of agriculture and mechanic arts, law, and medicine, as well as for a department of elementary instruction. A report made by a committee on organization was " accepted and adopted " by the board of regents on May 7, 1869, and the plan outlined became the organic law of the university, though not in statutory form. Although it never became operative, a brief account seems worthy of insertion here to show the

[1] Johnson, *University of Minnesota,* 17–31 (Minneapolis, 1910).

situation at the time when the college work was about to begin and the expectation of the governing board, so far as it had any understanding or appreciation of the plan.[2]

The intention of the legislature, the committee said, was not "to establish a college of the old style, simply giving exclusive attention to the fitting of men for the professions of law, medicine and theology." It desired to give the old course "an honorable place" and to give equal prominence to studies "calculated to fit men for the pursuits of agriculture and the various departments of the mechanic and manufacturing arts." The grand divisions of the institution had been determined by the legislature in the charter of 1868. The department of elementary instruction had already been organized in the "preparatory department," opened in 1867; the departments of law and medicine were left to the more distant future. There were left to be organized the department of science, literature, and the arts — often later called "the academic department" — and the college of agriculture and the mechanic arts. The plan of the committee on organization provided for four courses of study in the academic department: classical, Latin-German, scientific, and selected. No attempt was made to describe any of the courses in detail, but the requisites for admission were carefully scheduled. This arrangement was an early forecast of the "elective system." In the college of agriculture and the mechanic arts there were to be arranged general and

[2] *General Laws*, 1868, pp. 1–6; Minutes of the Proceedings of the Board of Regents of the University of Minnesota, B 1: 22. The minutes are in two manuscript record books in the office of the comptroller of the University of Minnesota. The volume containing the records from 1860 to February, 1868, is marked "A 1," and that including the records from March, 1868, to 1904, "B 1." A copy of the *Report of the Committee on Organization Made to the Board of Regents of the University of Minnesota, May 7, 1869,* is in the library of the Minnesota Historical Society. It was without doubt written by the Reverend W. W. Washburn, principal of the preparatory department. It was signed by him and by Regents Mark H. Dunnell and Avery A. Harwood. It is an able document, showing a knowledge of the general situation of the western state universities, familiarity with that of Michigan, and an appreciation of the demands of the Morrill bill of 1862. On this bill, see *post,* p. 78.

special courses. The general courses were to extend over two years and were to be substantially identical with the scientific course in the academic department. Then were to follow two-year special courses severally in agriculture, civil engineering, mining engineering and metallurgy, mechanical engineering, chemistry and mineralogy, and natural history and geology, and also a short course in agriculture.[3]

The charter of 1868 had included "military tactics" in the department of agriculture and the mechanic arts. The committee recommended, however, that the regents establish a separate military department and open in it courses in military engineering and military tactics, in the expectation that the United States government would appoint a competent person to have charge of the department. In regard to practice in military tactics, it was suggested that the board provide some plan "as soon as the number of students shall make it desirable, or as soon as there shall be a demand for such instruction."[4]

Excellent principles were laid down for the constitution of the faculty. All the men were to possess scholarship, eminent ability to teach attested by experience, unexceptionable moral character, and gentlemanly and courteous manners. If it should be necessary while the institution was new to employ young men, they were to be men of marked ability and energy, to whom classroom work had not become irksome drudgery. It was desired that such men should not be required to give their whole time to teaching, but should be allowed a part of each day for study and research.

[3] Committee on Organization, *Report*, 4, 6–9, 13–20. The proposition to base all the special courses of the last two years upon a common scientific course anticipated an element of the plan of organization that came to be known as "the Minnesota plan."

[4] *General Laws*, 1868, p. 2; Committee on Organization, *Report*, 8, 17; Board of Regents, Minutes, B 1: 29, 31. The military policy was adopted by the regents in July, 1869, and a month later they elected a major general of the United States Army, retired, to take charge of the military department at a full professor's salary. In September all the men students were required to take military drill, a practice that has been continued to the present. President's report, in Board of Regents, *Reports*, 1870, p. 39.

Resident and nonresident professors were to be employed and assistant professors and tutors were to be provided as needed. It was estimated that for the full equipment of the two colleges nineteen resident professors would be required to teach the following subjects: (1) mathematics; (2) astronomy; (3) civil engineering; (4) physics and industrial mechanics; (5) mining and metallurgy; (6) geology and paleontology; (7) zoölogy and comparative anatomy; (8) botany, horticulture, and arboriculture; (9) practical and theoretical agriculture; (10) general and agricultural chemistry; (11) veterinary science; (12) analytical chemistry and determinative mineralogy; (13) French language and literature; (14) German language and literature; (15) Greek language and literature; (16) Latin language and literature; (17) rhetoric and English language and literature; (18) history and social science; and (19) moral and intellectual philosophy. Seven nonresident professors were to teach: (1) physiology, hygiene, and physical culture; (2) physical geography and climatology; (3) history of education and theories and methods of instruction; (4) science of language and comparative philology; (5) entomology, with special reference to insects injurious to vegetation; (6) architecture; and (7) social science. It was recommended that for a time certain related subjects be combined to reduce the number of professors to be elected at an early day to thirteen and that for the first college year about to begin six should be employed — professors of (1) mathematics; (2) rhetoric, English language and literature; (3) Greek; (4) Latin; (5) German; and (6) chemistry. The professor of chemistry was to teach agriculture for the time being.

After disposing of the framework of the plan, the members of the committee took up a number of questions more or less debatable. In the department of agriculture they proposed some system of voluntary labor by students, "to foster a taste for agricultural pursuits." They deplored the "tendency of American youth to leave the paths of honest, patient industry, and seek a precarious livelihood in the already overcrowded professions," turning their backs upon " one of the most healthful and independent occupations in which man can engage." The students in agriculture should therefore pass a part of each day in labor, in company with their fellow students, under the direction of their instructors. The committee was opposed to the adoption of a dormitory system, except in the agricultural department, where manual labor was to be carried on. It was deemed desirable that students should obtain lodging and board with families of St. Anthony.

Under the heading "Ladies' College," the committee discussed at length the subject of coeducation, "one of the most vital connected with the organization of the University." The charter was silent on the subject of the education of women and the legislature had issued no mandate. But the actual or prospective admission of "ladies" at the universities of Michigan, Wisconsin, and Iowa indicated a change in the attitude of the public on the subject. "Female education is a demand of our advancing civilization and Christianization," said the committee. That point was settled, but the question as to the manner in which the demand should be met — what should be the character of the "Ladies' College" — was one to be carefully considered.

Three plans were mentioned. The first, a plan for two separate institutions in different places, was disposed of briefly with the remark that a duplication of the university was impracticable. The second plan, to admit both sexes to the one institution on the same conditions, to pursue the same courses of study, was discarded because it took no account of the special sphere and needs of women; women would better spend their time on modern languages and art than on higher arithmetic and Greek, said the committee. There remained a third, which would combine the advantages of the two rejected plans. This was to establish two institutions " in juxtaposition," under the same governing board and faculty, with " a common library, laboratory, museum, &c." The " Ladies' College " should be a distinct department of the university. For it there should be a separate building suitably fitted and furnished for recitation rooms, musical instruction, and instruction in various branches of art, such as painting and drawing. It should contain an art gallery hung with copies of the old masters and of the works of eminent modern artists and should be supplied with engravings illustrating every variety of excellence. The faculty of the " Ladies' College" should be composed in part of women and there should be a preceptress to have general oversight in regard to studies and to attend to the less important cases of discipline. The dormitory system having been rejected, no provision was suggested for the board and lodging of the ladies. It was considered that there was no system " so detrimental to sound morals and a healthy sentiment as this of shutting young women up in cloistered dormitories away from common society." It was safer and better for the young ladies to reside in the families of the university city, where a good understanding between them and the faculty and a strong moral and religious influence might prevail.

The committee on organization deemed its outline sufficient as a foundation upon which to build the institution and closed its report with the fervent benediction that " with man's best endeavor, and the smiles of Heaven, there shall rise here a temple of learning which shall be an honor and a blessing to the people of this commonwealth for ages to come." [5]

When the doors of the university were opened in September, 1869, there was no other thought, idea, or plan than that an American state university of the traditional type

[5] Committee on Organization, *Report*, 20, 23–38. The regents took no notice of the proposition for the " Ladies' College " or of that for a separate building for women, and they have not yet recognized a separate education for women.

would be developed; but there was presently proposed, entertained, and adopted a plan diverging from that pattern, which, having grown up with the country, was generally believed not to need or to be capable of improvement. The plan was a pet scheme of the president of the university, who was ignorant of the plan adopted in May, 1869. He had been called to the position from a professorship in an Ohio college held for a short time. Before that he had been for four years employed in a large flour-milling business and with incidental concerns such as cooper shops, a sawmill, a country store, a post office, and a considerable landed property — this after three and a half years of service as an officer of volunteer engineers in the Army of the Potomac. Before the war he had been an academy teacher and a college tutor, with the ambitious title of " adjunct professor of mathematics," dividing a four-period day about equally in teaching that subject and " the classics " with much enthusiasm. A year and more of study in a German university and in European travel, after the usual common school, academy, and college courses, constituted his education. Partly from observation, in greater part perhaps from association with a friend who had spent many years in study abroad, he had become convinced that the American college system was capable of improvement. The main defect, as he saw it, was that the college suppressed the development of secondary education by absorbing a large part of it and thus discouraging the expansion of the preparatory schools by covering the whole field belonging pedagogically to that education. The natural tripartite division of schools into those for children, youths, and adults had not been clearly recognized in America.

In his inaugural address, delivered on December 22, 1869, the president unfolded his plan, but only briefly, so as not to excite alarm, and it probably was not noticed. In the following April it was laid before members of the faculty with a request for their several opinions. No objections were heard from them. It was also sent to some, probably to all, of the regents. At a meeting of the board of regents on June 28, 1870, the president of the university was " introduced to the Board . . . and requested to present for consideration such matters as he deemed proper." He took the occasion to lay before the regents his plan of organization. It was referred to the executive committee of the board, which reported at once that it had examined the plan and recommended its adoption. It was adopted unanimously by the nine regents present, to the president's surprise. The substance of the plan was to detach the first two years of college work and merge them with two years of preparatory work into a so-called " collegiate department." In this day the better term "junior college" would be used. Some assortment of studies was presumed, as well as the emancipation of the upper classmen in the university proper from the constraints of school discipline.[6]

It is now easy to see that the project was a premature romance. It was one to be agitated in reviews, magazines, and newspapers, dallied with in educational conventions, timidly proposed to college faculties, referred to committees, re-

[6] Copy of a letter from the president to members of the faculty, April 12, 1870, Folwell Papers; Board of Regents, *Reports*, 1869, p. 7; 1870, pp. 6, 26–35; Board of Regents, Minutes, B 1: 36. The president's inaugural address may be found in his *University Addresses*, 35–38 (Minneapolis, 1909). It was also published in a pamphlet entitled *Addresses at the Inauguration of William W. Folwell as President of the University of Minnesota, Wednesday, December 22, 1869* (Minneapolis, 1870). An early and interesting presentation of the plan, made in an address before the Minnesota State Teachers' Association at Mankato on August 24, 1870, is in the *Minneapolis Daily Tribune*, August 28, 1870, p. 3. For a similar exposition see "The Minnesota Plan," in the author's *University Addresses*, 77–127. Another explanation of the plan is given in the report of the president of the university, in Minnesota Superintendent of Public Instruction, *Reports*, 1870, pp. 127–144. The diagram on page 144, with variant details, was used on many occasions to illustrate the plan.

The excellent report of the committee on organization adopted on May 7, 1869, was not made known to the president upon his arrival, and he neither saw nor heard of it until nearly sixty years later, when it was found in a bound volume of early university papers that had belonged to Professor Gabriel Campbell of Dartmouth College, who had probably coöperated with

ported on and recommitted, and, after some decades, adopted, with misgivings, " in principle." When President Goodnow of Johns Hopkins University in 1925 presented the same plan, he said that no American university was in so favorable a position as Hopkins to strike out a new path, and, referring to Bunyan's Christian, who found lions in the way, he proposed to " go forward notwithstanding the lions. . . . Probably we shall hear the lions roar. But they will do us . . . no harm." [7]

A circular announcement gave notice that the plan would be in effect at the opening of the next college year, 1870–71. With but 225 students then in attendance — all but a handful " preparatories " — it made a small show in fact. Four faculty members — three of them graduates of New England colleges and one a graduate of the University of Michigan — although they had not protested against the plan as proposed, did not like it and quietly made known their views to members of the board of regents. In March, 1872, a regent sympathetic with the plan, by a resolution asking for the opinions of the several members of the faculty in writing, proposed to reopen the whole question. Without objection the resolution was agreed to. The four professors filed their opinions in dignified but very emphatic form. The other three professors approved the plan. Manuscript copies

Washburn in drafting the report. Had it been revealed to him he might have sought and obtained modifications embodying his advanced views, and this chapter of university history would then happily have been shortened.

It was the original policy of the board of regents to conduct directly all the affairs of the university except the teaching of the classes. The president of the university was merely chairman of the faculty. In 1872 he was made a member ex officio of the board, without a vote, and corresponding secretary, according to his wishes. See *General Laws*, 1872, pp. 55–57. The conception of employing the president as general manager came later and was adopted piecemeal. The regents hired and discharged teachers according to their judgment and all contracts expired at the close of each college year. In April, 1871, standing committees were authorized to request the president of the university to confer with them. A committee of three regents was appointed to visit the university at least once in each term and to report severally in writing on the condition and progress of the work in the various departments. Board of Regents, Minutes, B 1: 50.

[7] *Johns Hopkins Alumni Magazine*, 13: 242 (March, 1925).

of all the contributions were distributed to the several members of the board.

The principal objections to the plan were (1) that it was not in harmony with the time-honored American system of education, never to be changed, and (2) that the high schools would never carry their instruction up to the junior year of college; that they would was a " vain and illusory " hope. There were criticisms of inferior importance that were soon lost sight of when the main questions came up: the plan would degrade freshmen and sophomores and unduly exalt preparatory students by merging the two groups in a single department, and there would be confusion due to novel nomenclature. The suggestion was added that, by demanding what was impossible of high schools, it was probably intended to encourage the multiplication of denominational secondary schools, those of one denomination in particular.[8]

The main objections were well worthy of serious consideration by the board. On July 16, 1872, it gave a whole day to a hearing, allowing the president of the university all the time he wanted for an exposition and a defense. He challenged the contention that the American college was so admirable and so firmly intrenched that it would never be supplanted and he was ready with proofs to sustain the challenge. In February, 1870, he had given wide circulation to a printed prospectus of the plan as then proposed. To this he had received numerous replies, all, as he now remembers, favorable. These he placed before the board with such comment as seemed appropriate.

The most important of the collection must here be briefed. President Noah Porter of Yale College, with the concurrence of Professors Daniel C. Gilman, afterwards president of Johns Hopkins University, William D. Whitney, James Hadley, George F. Barker, William H. Brewer, and Thomas

---

[8] Board of Regents, Minutes, B 1:56. Manuscript copies of the opinions of the seven professors are in the Folwell Papers.

R. Lounsbury, praised the plan for its adaptation to the wants of a new state and for " its just recognition of the value of literary, scientific and professional culture." President Mark Hopkins of Williams College said, " The general plan seems to me judicious." President Andrew D. White of Cornell University found the plan interesting and, in view of the situation, excellent. President Henry S. Frieze of the University of Michigan saw no deficiency in it and was convinced that America would never have a university until some one of its institutions should adopt such a course. President Henry Morton of the Stevens Institute of Technology wrote, " I can heartily approve of your course." President Daniel Reed of the University of Missouri said, " Your plan meets my entire approval." President James B. Angell, then of the University of Vermont, wished " the highest measure of success " to the " praiseworthy effort." President John M. Gregory of the Illinois Industrial University most heartily approved of a plan that had for its aim " to hold fast all that is good in the past, while you gain all the new good the present offers." Professor Andrew P. Peabody of Harvard University expressed his sincere and gratified interest in the plan. Professor William D. Wilson of Cornell University approved " in general without reserve." Professor Asahel Kendrick of the University of Rochester said, " The general plan seems to me unexceptionable and excellent." Professor Asa Gray of Harvard University wrote, " I can say in general, that your plan seems to me well considered, and we wish you every success." Professor James R. Boise of the University of Chicago wrote, " Your views appear to me to be enlightened and liberal." William T. Harris, then superintendent of schools in St. Louis and later United States commissioner of education, found the views and plans " very catholic and very practical."

The board listened patiently to the president's address and excused him until half past two o'clock. The record shows that, on the motion of General Sibley, a resolution was adopted that, after full consideration, it was the judgment of the board that it was "not expedient to make any radical change or modification in the settled policy of the University." An additional and superfluous resolution asked the full and hearty coöperation of the faculty in carrying out that policy. What else could those regents do? Against the objections of half of their faculty they had before them the approval, in most cases flattering, of thirteen distinguished presidents of universities and colleges, of twenty eminent professors, most of whom were from old and famous colleges, and of eleven other persons whose opinions were entitled to consideration. One thing these concurrent testimonials settled: that the American college was not regarded as perfected and final and that the development of the genuine university in America awaited the development of the genuine secondary school.[9]

The other main objection to the plan — that the American high schools would not and could not be expanded into full-orbed secondary schools and take over the secondary work to be dropped by the colleges — was not touched by the formidable catena of opinions. Apparently it was the hope of the admirers of the plan that in a new state in the West the evolution might presently take place. That hope, as the venerable Professor Jabez Brooks had said, was a "vain and illusory" one. It was not until 1890 that the last subfreshman work could be discontinued in the university, by the operation of a policy that will be explained on a later page. The high schools of the state had then become active and cordial feeders of the university up to the freshman line. Up to the present time only a beginning, but a promising one, has been made in the expansion of high schools to take over

[9] Board of Regents, Minutes, B 1: 63. Manuscript material used in defense of the plan is in the Folwell Papers. The testimonials as briefed may be found on pages 9–13 of a pamphlet, without title, dated June 25, 1872, and addressed to the board of regents, also in the Folwell Papers. This

two years of college work. The junior college movement, spreading widely in the South and the West, advances but slowly in Minnesota. The author may well refrain from any definite prophecy, but he may modestly suggest that his dreams will come true and the genuine American university, resting upon the genuine normal secondary school, will appear. It is daybreak now.

The Minnesota plan had a book existence of fifteen years, from 1871 to 1885. Such small beginnings had been made of professional schools that the university really consisted only of the college of science, literature, and the arts and the collegiate department. The institution was in fact an American college with preparatory classes. The operation of the plan was very much like that of the fifteenth amendment of the Constitution of the United States. Cyrus Northrop assumed the presidency of the university in September, 1884. At the close of the school year then begun, upon his suggestion all existing departments of the university were placed in charge of the one general faculty. That gave the plan a quiet coup de grace. The author has no regrets that it began and ended as it did. President Northrop had his ideals, but they did not include experimentation in the organization of education and he had need of all his time and strength to guide the regents in the opening of the professional schools soon to take place.[10]

THE HIGH SCHOOL BOARD

In the territories successively formed out of the Territory Northwest of the Ohio River under the Ordinance of 1787

pamphlet contains the president's "orderly statement of the plan itself, of the conditions which seemed to justify its adoption, and of some facts and opinions which might, upon occasion, be adduced in defense of it." The vote on the question to continue the plan in operation stood: ayes, 7 — Austin, Bryant, Nicols, Wilson, Gibson, Harwood, and Sibley; nays, none; not voting, one — Pillsbury; absent, one.

[10] Johnson, *University of Minnesota*, 65; Leonard V. Koos, *The Junior College*, 2: 605–620, 653 (University of Minnesota, *Research Publications, Education Series*, no. 5 — Minneapolis, 1924); University of Minnesota, *Presi-

the various religious denominations promptly located their colleges as centers of influence and expansion. As there were for many years few or no fitting schools, the colleges organized their own preparatory departments. Some of the most useful work ever done by them was in these preparatory departments. They served to spread the influence of the particular denomination represented by them and they set an example and a standard of good scholarship for the fitting schools, public and private, as they were gradually established.

On February 19, 1851, Congress " set aside and reserved " two townships in Minnesota for the use and support of a university. In harmony with this act the state legislature on February 25 incorporated the University of Minnesota and made it the duty of the regents to establish a temporary preparatory department. In November of the same year the school was opened. Through a lamentable change of policy it was closed in the spring of 1855.[11] Twelve years ran by in which no school was kept. The special board of regents created to extricate the institution from the morass in which it was floundering was authorized to open a school and did so on October 7, 1867, with a sufficient corps of capable teachers. The reorganization act of February 18,

dent's Reports, 1924–25, pp. 85–88 (Bulletins, vol. 28, no. 52); Rodney M. West to the author, August 20, 1926, Folwell Papers. In the year 1924–25 there were eighty-eight entrants from junior colleges of Minnesota, and one each from those of Iowa, Missouri, and Texas. Sixty-eight came from Minnesota teachers' colleges and normal schools to enter the junior class. A much larger number were received from certain private colleges offering but little, if any, work above the sophomore year. In 1920 the college of science, literature, and the arts was subdivided into senior and junior colleges, with an assisting dean for each. For a sympathetic yet critical account of the operation of the plan, see Willis M. West, " The University of Minnesota," in John N. Greer, The History of Education in Minnesota, 112–116 (United States Bureau of Education, Circulars of Information, no. 2 — Washington, 1902).

11 United States, Statutes at Large, 9: 568; Minnesota Territory, Laws, 1851, pp. 9–12; reports of the territorial board of regents, in House Journal, 1853, p. 225; 1856, appendix, 16; Johnson, University of Minnesota, 21. All the United States and Minnesota laws relating to the University of Minnesota were compiled by a committee, Professor James Paige, one of its mem-

1868, which is by many mistaken for the original incorporation of the university, contained a provision for a department of elementary instruction. Either ill advised or not advised at all, the regents in the summer of 1869 decided to open the university proper and elected a president, seven professors, and one tutor. This learned faculty was for many years doing the elementary teaching that properly belonged to preparatory schools.[12]

The high schools of the state, slowly developing their own work, were not in condition to prepare students for the university and some of them did not consider it their function to do that; and yet there was much criticism of the university for doing so much preparatory school work. The situation in Minnesota was not peculiar. The 118 colleges of nine northwestern states, excluding Minnesota, in 1874 had 14,410 preparatory students and 8,329 college students. Only one of ten state universities, Michigan, had dropped its preparatory classes. There were few or no private fitting schools. The only possible resort was to the public high schools; but they were the organs of independent school districts, outside the state system. How to enlist them in recruiting for the university was a problem that the regents and the faculty had much in mind and no one of them was more interested than the president of the university, whose plan of organization called for an early and cordial affiliation of the high schools with the university. In reports, addresses, and newspaper articles, high school boards and their faculties were appealed to for friendly coöperation in a state system of public instruction in which the high schools should be an integral part. "The university begins wherever the high schools leave off," was a slogan often sounded. Neither logic nor rhetoric had much effect.

bers, doing most of the actual work, and were published by the university in March, 1920, in a volume entitled *Laws and Regulations Governing the University of Minnesota.*

[12] Board of Regents, *Reports*, 1868, pp. 7–9; 1869, pp. 6–8; *General Laws*, 1867, p. 9; 1868, pp. 1–6.

In his report of December 23, 1869, the president of the university made the suggestion that some legislation might be desirable to enable high schools to provide preparatory instruction. In his annual report of 1873 to the state superintendent of public instruction, the president said that the state must organize, or encourage others to organize, " preparatory schools of high and uniform grade, open to all the people." In 1874 he stated to the board of regents his conviction that the high schools " ought to be enabled " to take up the work of preparing for the university, admitting students from the adjacent county or counties free of tuition without burdening the local taxpayers. Superintendent Burt in 1875 suggested, but was not ready to advocate, granting state aid to the principal county high schools that would admit rural students free. A bill, drawn by the president of the university, to grant aid out of the state treasury to high schools that would voluntarily undertake to prepare students for the university was introduced into the legislature of 1876. The bill passed the Senate and was recommended for passage by the House committee on education, but it did not become a law.[13]

On August 30, 1877, the Minnesota State Teachers' Association in convention at Mankato adopted resolutions prepared by the president of the university recommending that boards of education in cities and in the larger villages offer courses of studies preparatory to the university and that the legislature be asked to make an appropriation to

[13] Superintendent of Public Instruction, Reports, 1875, p. 45; president's reports, in Board of Regents, Reports, 1869, p. 22; 1874, p. 32; 1875, pp. 45–50; in Superintendent of Public Instruction, Reports, 1873, pp. 86–88; 1874, p. 88. In his report for 1874–75 the president of the university defended the policy of the institution. For examples of extreme newspaper criticism, see an article entitled, " The State University: A Swindle, or What? " in the St. Paul Daily Dispatch, February 13, 1875, p. 2, and a communication in the same paper, March 2, 1875, p. 3, echoing the points made in the earlier article. For a history of the education bill (Senate file 305), see Senate Journal, 1876, pp. 204, 311, 451, and House Journal, 354, 388, 429, 454. The bill was passed in the Senate by a vote of 21 to 7. Among the nays were William Pitt Murray and Knute Nelson. In the House it was " lost in the shuffle " on the last night of the session because the person most interested, feeling too confident, went home at bedtime.

pay the tuition of students from the country attending city high schools. In his annual report for 1877 to the board of regents the president revived the plan for state aid to high schools for preparatory work by including a memorandum that had been laid before the legislature of 1876. The regents, advised by Superintendent Burt, were willing that another experiment be made. A bill was introduced and was passed by two-thirds votes in both houses. The essential feature was a grant of four hundred dollars to any high school, properly equipped, that would admit students of both sexes from any part of the state and prepare them for the university without charge for tuition. A high school board, consisting of the state superintendent of public instruction, the president of the university, and a third member to be appointed by the governor, was charged with the distribution of a fund that was not to exceed nine thousand dollars. A modest but promising beginning was made in the school year of 1878–79, but a ruling by the state auditor that the appropriation was not in fact annual caused a suspension of operations in the following year. The idea of an affiliation of the high schools with the university was now familiar, however, and was widely approved. A bill "for the encouragement of higher education," which was in the same essential terms as that of 1878, was sponsored by Senator Horace B. Wilson, who had been state superintendent of public instruction from 1870 to 1875, and was passed by the legislature of 1881 by unanimous votes of both houses. The annual appropriation was fixed at twenty thousand dollars.[14]

The operation of the scheme answered reasonable expectations. In the year 1882 thirty-nine high schools came under the supervision of the board, fifty-three in the year

[14] *Pioneer Press* (St. Paul and Minneapolis), September 1, 1877, p. 2; report of the president, in Board of Regents, *Reports*, 1877, p. 39; *General Laws*, 1878, p. 154; 1881, p. 186; *Senate Journal*, 1878, pp. 131, 220, 261, 280; 1881, pp. 17, 67, 185, 415; *House Journal*, 1878, pp. 427, 516; 1881, pp. 274, 411, 442, 564; Johnson, *University of Minnesota*, 38–41.

following, and fifty-six in the third year. The effect in filling up the university soon became apparent and the steady expansion due to the beneficent operation of the act has continued to the present time. In the year 1924–25 there were enrolled in the university 1,787 entrants from 224 Minnesota high schools.[15]

THE AGRICULTURAL COLLEGE OF MINNESOTA

On April 20, 1858, Justin S. Morrill, representative in Congress from Vermont, addressed the House in advocacy of his bill to donate almost six million acres of public lands to be apportioned among the several states for the endowment, support, and maintenance of colleges in which the leading object should be " to teach such branches of learning as are related to agriculture and the mechanic arts." Three-fourths of the arable land of the country, he said, was being exhausted; to feed the increasing population its fertility must be restored. The great desert lying between the ninety-eighth degree of longitude and the Rocky Mountains placed a limit upon the extension of settlement. There was pressing need of special schools similar to those existing in Europe, in which farmers could be liberally educated and experimentation in the application of science to agriculture could be carried on. Farming should become "a learned, liberal, and intellectual pursuit." Morrill in his speech placed little emphasis upon the "mechanic arts," a phrase

[15] University of Minnesota, *President's Reports*, 1924–25, pp. 73–79. The reports of the state superintendent of public instruction for the years from 1881 to 1919 contain reports of the activities of the high school board. In 1919 the functions of the board were assumed by the state board of education, consisting of five members appointed by the governor with senatorial consent and a commissioner of education elected by them as their executive officer and secretary. See *Laws*, 1919, pp. 355–359. A reason for this merger was the great extension of state aid to graded, rural, and agricultural schools. In the year 1926, the amount of state aid to high and elementary schools was $4,725,559.71. See Minnesota Board of Education, *Minutes*, May 19, June 2, 1919, for the organization of the high school board. For much information in regard to the origin of the board and its operation until 1899, see Albert W. Rankin, "High Schools," in Greer, *Education in Minnesota*, 73–93.

that seems to have been tagged on for good measure. It was a farmers' bill.[16]

As is well known, the Morrill bill was vetoed by President Buchanan on February 24, 1859. His principal and, if valid, sufficient objection was that the act would be unconstitutional. The power granted to Congress to " dispose of " the property of the United States was not a power to give it away. The superfluous objections were: (1) the government needed the revenue that would come from the sale of the public lands; (2) the gift to the states for education would be a precedent for further appropriations for state purposes, and as a result " the character of both governments " — state and federal — would be " greatly deteriorated "; (3) speculation in the scrip by wealthy individuals would be injurious to the new states; (4) the federal government had no power to follow the grant into the states and compel the execution of the trust; and (5) the establishment of colleges sustained by the federal government would discourage existing colleges engaged in teaching agriculture.[17]

But the idea of devoting a great portion of the remaining public lands to the rescue of a decadent agriculture by the education of farmers and the application of science to farming was in the air. Morrill reintroduced his bill in the session of 1860, but an adverse report of the committee on public lands, to which it was referred, blocked its progress. In 1861 Congress had matters to provide for of even greater moment than the relief of the suffering farmers. The measure went over to the session of 1862, when the Morrill bill, with some modification, was brought into the Senate by Wade of Ohio. Against lively but futile opposition it was passed and the House concurred by a large majority. As passed the act granted to each state 30,000 acres of public

[16] *Congressional Globe*, 35 Congress, 1 session, pp. 1692–1697.

[17] James D. Richardson, *A Compilation of the Messages and Papers of the Presidents, 1789–1897*, 5: 543–550 (53 Congress, 2 session, *House Miscellaneous Documents*, no. 210 — serial 3265) ; Constitution, article 4, section 3.

land, either " in place " or in scrip, for each member of
its delegation in Congress. Minnesota, with her two senators
and two representatives, thus became the trustee of the proceeds of 120,000 acres for the support of a college of agriculture and mechanic arts.[18]

It was not necessary in Minnesota to create a new college
to be the beneficiary of the national bounty for agriculture.
Washington was a long way from Minnesota in those days
but there was one citizen whose ear was attuned to radia-
tions from the Capitol. That was Colonel John Harrington
Stevens, whom the reader may remember as the pioneer
settler in 1849 on the west side of the Mississippi at the
Falls of St. Anthony, the first housebuilder and the first
farmer there. In the course of five years his farm had been
cut up into town lots and the nucleus of Minneapolis had
been established on the terrain. A pioneer by nature " and
more so by practice," Stevens sought for a new home and a
new sphere of activity. He found them on May 21, 1855,
on the prairie west of the Big Woods, where the village of
Glencoe was later built. The next year he moved his household and its gear, established a new home, resumed farming
on his new claim, and entered into the public affairs of his
village and county, which were rapidly filling up in that
boom year. His neighbors sent him to the state House of
Representatives for the session of 1857–58.[19]

[18] *Statutes at Large*, 12: 503–505; 36 Congress, 1 session, *House Journal*,
part 1, p. 180 (serial 1041); *Congressional Globe*, 793, 1023. For the history
of the bill passed in the second session of the thirty-seventh Congress, see
the indexes of the House and Senate journals under " S. 298 " and of the
Congressional Globe under "Public lands, S. 298." The vote on the final
passage was 32 to 7 in the Senate and 89 to 25 in the House. Senator Rice
voted "yea," Wilkinson, " nay," and Representatives Aldrich and Windom,
both "nay." See *Senate Journal*, 628, and *House Journal*, 880. Objection
was made to the location of scrip in one state by another. Donaldson, in
his *Public Domain*, 229–231, 1250, gives statistics for grants of 9,600,000
acres to thirty-eight states and the amounts severally derived from these grants
to June 30, 1883, by forty-two colleges.

[19] See *ante*, 1: 428, 432; Return I. Holcombe, in *Minnesota in Three
Centuries*, 3: 100 (New York, 1908); John H. Stevens, *Personal Recollections
of Minnesota and Its People, and Early History of Minneapolis*, 233, 265–268,
382 (Minneapolis, 1890); and Warren Upham and Rose B. Dunlap, *Minne-*

The villagers of Glencoe would have been out of the fashion of the time if they had not aspired to establish a seat of learning, a college or a university, in their place of great expectations. It is as good as certain that Stevens got wind of the great project launched in the winter of 1858 by Morrill. He lost no time in drafting a bill for the establishment of an agricultural college at his home town. Without serious opposition it became a law on March 10, 1858. It prescribed courses of instruction for the college, including an "English and Scientific course, Natural Philosophy, Chemistry, Animal and Vegetable Anatomy and Physiology, Geology, Mineralogy, Veterinary Art, Mensuration, Leveling and Political Economy, with Bookkeeping and the Mechanic Arts that are directly connected with Agriculture." There were to be two scholastic terms, a long summer term from April to October and a short winter term from December to February. The pupils — boys, of course — were to perform manual labor in the first term of each year for not less than three hours nor more than four hours daily. Tuition was to be forever free and if more students applied than could be accommodated admissions were to be apportioned among the counties. The government of the college was vested in a board of education, equivalent to a board of regents, of twelve members, to be elected by the State Agricultural Society at its annual meetings in classes to serve for three years. The board of education was authorized to appoint a board of instruction, that is, a faculty, and to designate one of the professors as president of the college.[20]

The years following the business cataclysm of 1857 were no time to expect legislative appropriations for a college out

sota Biographies, 1655–1912, 742 (Minnesota Historical Collections, vol. 14 — St. Paul, 1912).

[20] General Laws, 1858, pp. 42–45; House Journal, 323, 373, 460–408, 430; Senate Journal, 279, 287. The vote in the House was 57 to 3, and in the Senate, 22 to 7. For comments on the establishment of the college, see the Glencoe Register, 1858: February 19, p. 2; May 1, p. 2; 15, p. 2; and Martin McLeod to Stevens, February 26, March 4, 15, April 4, 1858; William S. Chapman to Stevens, February 26, March 5, 11, 1858; and the Reverend J. J. Hill to Stevens, March 20, 1858, in the Stevens Papers. Letters from

west of the Big Woods. The period was equally unfavorable for gathering private contributions, but the enterprising citizens of McLeod County early in 1858 raised three thousand dollars or more to pay for a half section of land as a site for the college and an experimental farm. Subscriptions for building came in tardily, but by February, 1861, ten thousand dollars were accumulated. A contract was drawn for a building and would have been signed had not Governor Ramsey been absent from a meeting.[21] He was in Washington offering President Lincoln a regiment of infantry — the First Minnesota — for the defense of the insulted nation. Like many another brave enterprise, the college at Glencoe lay asleep while the Civil and Indian wars went on. During the Indian uprising Stevens, as brigadier general of militia, was in command of a long stretch of the frontier against the raids of the Sioux. His resolution and vigilance in stopping the headlong flight of settlers, turning them back to their farms and villages, and organizing them for self-defense have been greatly and justly praised. Probably his considerable experience in the Mexican War, although he had been in a staff department, qualified him for the duty.[22]

McLeod to Stevens, dated January 1 and 20, 1857, in the Stevens Papers, indicate that Stevens and McLeod had been thinking of a university at Glencoe in that year.

The State Agricultural Society was incorporated in 1860. At a meeting on March 5, 1860, the society elected a board of education for the state agricultural college, with Stevens as president. See *Laws*, 1860, pp. 143–145; Darwin S. Hall and Return I. Holcombe, *History of the Minnesota State Agricultural Society*, 49, 54 (St. Paul, 1910); and the *Glencoe Register*, March 24, 1860, p. 1. In the *Glencoe Register*, June 12, 1858, p. 2, is a toast given by Charles Hoag at the opening of the Nicollet House: "He [Stevens] has left us to lay the foundation of another county, and ere long the classic walls of the State Agricultural College at Glencoe will speak the praises due to Col. John H. Stevens, its founder."

[21] Sibley's special message, June 15, 1858, in *House Journal*, 1858, p. 672; Hall and Holcombe, *Agricultural Society*, 66; *Glencoe Register*, April 16, 1859; April 20, 1861; *Pioneer and Democrat* (St. Paul), February 6, 1861; McLeod to Stevens, January 23, March 24, 1859, Stevens Papers.

[22] See *ante*, 2: 76, 159, n.; Miller to Stevens, June 25, July 22, 1863, Stevens Papers; Charles S. Bryant and Abel B. Murch, *History of the Great Massacre by the Sioux Indians*, 211 (St. Peter, 1872); and Charles E. Flandrau, "The Indian War of 1862–1864, and Following Campaigns in Minnesota," in *Minnesota in the Civil and Indian Wars, 1861 65*, 739 (St. Paul, 1891).

The Morrill bill became a law on July 2, 1862. The Minnesota legislature of 1863, by joint resolution of January 27, accepted the grant with its conditions that the moneys derived from the sale of the lands should constitute a perpetual fund to " remain forever undiminished " and that the interest thereof should be " inviolably appropriated " to the purposes of the act. The state was pledged to keep the fund invested in stocks of the United States or of the states, or in some other safe stocks yielding not less than five per cent on the par value thereof. As there were millions of acres of public lands of the United States in Minnesota, the obvious policy of taking the actual land and not scrip was adopted. Since title could not vest in the state until after the lands had been located and the approval of the general land office had been obtained, there was no need of immediate action in regard to their disposition.[23]

The various boards of the agricultural college and their moving spirit were not forgetful of its interests and easily procured from the legislature of 1865 a revamp of the creative act of 1858. The new act declared it to be the design of the institution, under the new name " Agricultural College of Minnesota," to fulfill the conditions of the Morrill Act; and for that purpose the college was to be " a high seminary of learning, in which the graduates of the common schools of both sexes, can commence, pursue and finish a course of study terminating in thorough theoretic and practical instruction in those sciences and arts which bear directly upon agriculture and kindred industrial pursuits." The course of

[23] Minnesota, *General Laws*, 1863, p. 262; United States, *Statutes at Large*, 12: 503–505. In the whole history of the country land speculators probably never had fatter pickings than when the Morrill Act threw nearly eight million acres of public land scrip on the market. For examples of the amounts derived by some states obliged to accept scrip, see Donaldson, *Public Domain*, 230. Connecticut received $135,000 for 180,000 acres of scrip; Maine, $116,359 for 210,000 acres; New Jersey, $116,000 for 210,000 acres; Rhode Island, $50,000 for 120,000 acres; Delaware, $83,000 for 90,000 acres; Illinois, $319,494 for 480,000 acres; Indiana, $212,238 for 390,000 acres; and Pennsylvania, $439,186 for 780,000 acres. Minnesota, taking its portion " in place," realized $563,183.11 for 94,439.28 acres. The

instruction was to be similar to that provided for in the act of 1858, with the addition of mathematics, civil engineering, entomology, rural and household economy, horticulture, history, and moral philosophy. The application of science and the mechanic arts to practical agriculture was especially enjoined. Students were to be required to labor from two to four hours daily and were to pay tuition until appropriations should be sufficient to dispense with it. The board of education elected by the State Agricultural Society was replaced by "the Agricultural College Board," to consist of the governor, the secretary of state, the president of the State Agricultural Society, and four members to be elected by the legislature in classes to serve for four years. It was made the duty of the agricultural college board to choose a president as executive officer of the college, professors, superintendents, and employees and to prescribe their duties and fix their compensations. The secretary of the agricultural college board was to be a member of the faculty and its secretary. An appropriation of five thousand dollars was made for the current year. The act made a specific appropriation of the income from the Morrill grant to the Agricultural College of Minnesota.[24]

Because of delays due to "conflicting claims," not explained by the state auditor in his reports, the title to the lands was not perfected until March, 1867.[25] The legislatures were in no haste to make appropriations for buildings for a superfluous agricultural college in a state where millions of acres of virgin soil awaited the plow. In 1867 the

act provided that as a substitute for land at the usual price, a smaller number of acres might be selected from land that had been raised to double that price in consequence of railroad grants. Because of this provision, by 1870 only 94,119.28 acres were selected in Minnesota from seventeen counties. Of these, nearly 38,000 acres were located in Freeborn, Sibley, and McLeod counties. See State Auditor, *Reports*, 1870, p. 43; 1913–14, p. 11. For an account of the disposition of the agricultural lands and the progress of the institutions endowed up to 1874, see *Agricultural Colleges* (43 Congress, 2 session, *House Reports*, no. 57 — serial 1656).

[24] *General Laws*, 1865, pp. 26–31.
[25] State Auditor, *Reports*, 1865, p. 22; 1866, p. 30; 1867, p. 17.

special board of regents of the University of Minnesota was concluding its extrication of the institution from the swamp of indebtedness in which it had been floundering for ten years and in October the preparatory department was opened. The regents and others could not have been indifferent to the advantages of combining the two institutions. The university had a large building in which the agricultural college could be at once accommodated and could begin its work. As required by law, a school had actually been opened. One strong institution would do more for education than two weak ones contending with one another for the annual appropriations at St. Paul. The project for a combination came before the legislature of 1868 in a bill to reorganize the University of Minnesota and " to establish an Agricultural College therein." There was earnest argument for and against the bill, but it was passed by a sufficient majority.[26]

The smothering of the Agricultural College of Minnesota at Glencoe was less strenuously opposed because Colonel John H. Stevens, having been less successful in his ventures and investments at that place than he had hoped to be, had resumed a residence in Minneapolis. He had no more heart to " boost " for Glencoe.[27] The legislature found a convenient means to mitigate the disappointment of the Glencoe villagers. In 1861 all the swamp lands in McLeod County,

[26] *Ante*, pp. 60, 61, 73; *General Laws*, 1868, pp. 1–6; *Senate Journal*, 70, 89, 116, 148; *House Journal*, 141, 156, 165. The vote in the Senate was 16 to 2; in the House, 31 to 3. For accounts of the controversy over the bill, and its passage, see Johnson, *University of Minnesota*, 30; John S. Pillsbury, *An Address Delivered before the Alumni of the University of Minnesota, June 1st, 1893; Being a Sketch of the Growth and Development of the University for the Thirty Years in Which He Has Been a Regent*, 19–21 (n. p., n. d.) ; the *Saint Paul Daily Press*, 1868: February 4, p. 1; 12, p. 1; 13, p. 1; and the *Saint Paul Daily Pioneer*, February 2, p. 1; 9, p. 1. The issue of the latter paper for February 18, p. 2, contains a two-column protest by Lyman C. Dayton against combining the two institutions. Governor Marshall and the special board of regents, in their reports to the legislature, strongly recommended the passage of the measure. *Executive Documents*, 1867, pp. 11, 344; Special Board of Regents, *Reports*, 1868, p. 9.

[27] For biographical sketches of Stevens, see Upham and Dunlap, *Minnesota Biographies*, 742, and citations; Charles E. Flandrau, *Encyclopedia of*

nearly five thousand acres, had been bestowed by the legislature on the agricultural college at Glencoe. When the
Morrill grant was transferred to the university, the legislature of 1868 by a separate act made a gift of that swamp
land to the Stevens Seminary at Glencoe. The *McLeod
County Register* of June 11, 1868, comforted the townsmen
by saying that the grant to the seminary " is really of more
benefit to us than the college grant itself, the way it was always likely to be conducted." Another consideration probably had its effect in reconciling them to the loss of their
college. But 1,120 acres of agricultural college land had
been sold, for which $5,600 had been received; large sales
at the price asked were not to be expected in the immediate
future. The income of interest on the invested fund would
not go far toward supporting a college for which appropriations for buildings and equipment would have to be sought
from grudging legislatures.[28]

THE SCHOOL OF AGRICULTURE

If the friends of the university who in 1868 brought the
state agricultural college into camp could have foreseen the
twenty years of anxieties and annoyances that were to beset
them they might well have been content to leave that institution at Glencoe. Of those troubles but a bare outline can

Biography of Minnesota, 1: 484 (Chicago, 1900) ; and Daniel S. B. Johnston,
"Minnesota Journalism in the Territorial Period," in *Minnesota Historical
Collections*, 10: 328 (part 1). In his *Personal Recollections* Stevens seems to
have remembered everybody but himself. He lived in Minneapolis until his
death on May 28, 1900, her most conspicuous citizen. He was principally
engaged in editing agricultural newspapers and later in writing a history
of his city and his very valuable *Personal Recollections*. His statue in bronze
stands near his home in the small park at the junction of Portland Avenue
and Eleventh Street.

[28] *General Laws*, 1861, p. 199; *Special Laws*, 1868, p. 404; State Auditor,
Reports, 1867, p. 17; 1870, p. 28. The exact number of acres granted was
4,684.17. In an article in the *St. Paul Dispatch*, July 14, 1926, p. 1, the
statement is made that Liberty Hall, editor of the *Glencoe Register*, made
the suggestion that the college be given up on condition that the swamp lands
be retained. The article states also that the fund resulting from the sale
of the lands of the original grant amounted to approximately fifty thousand
dollars.

be attempted here. The university historian, Johnson, has expressed the opinion that the members of the first board of regents appointed under the act of 1868, or at least a majority of them, were " exceedingly skeptical of the possibility of agricultural education " and therefore contented themselves with buying for the experimental farm a tract of land of inferior quality, a quarter of a mile east of the campus on the main road to St. Paul. Such may have been the minds of the regents, but the inference ought not to have been drawn that they were content to do " as little as they felt they could do " for education in agriculture. They did then and ever afterwards all they knew how to do with the means at their disposal and the counsel they obtained. There were no precedents and no agricultural pedagogy had been developed. The regents considered that the university was fulfilling all the requirements of the Morrill Act for a college of agriculture and the mechanic arts. They provided for instruction in branches of learning related to agriculture and the mechanic arts without excluding other classical and scientific studies and they insisted religiously upon subjecting all the men students to military drill to save the land grant.[29]

On December 23, 1869, the board elected as professor of agriculture that eminent citizen of St. Paul, Colonel Daniel A. Robertson, a devotee of agriculture and horticulture and one of the promoters of the Patrons of Husbandry. As no individual students applied for instruction, Colonel Robertson could do little more than give occasional lectures to the student body. After less than a year's service he resigned.[30] From that time until the close of the school year 1873–74 it was deemed sufficient to leave the subject of agriculture in the hands of the professor of chemistry. During this period

[29] Johnson, *University of Minnesota*, 30; Board of Regents, *Reports*, 1868, p. 9.
[30] Board of Regents, Minutes, B 1: 33; report of the president of the university, in Superintendent of Public Instruction, *Reports*, 1870, pp. 127, 142; Upham and Dunlap, *Minnesota Biographies*, 648.

the course of instruction in agriculture as published coincided with the scientific course for the first two college years. For imaginary upper classmen there was provided a generous program of studies in seven sciences, with a fine catena of practical applications. To insnarc any possible seekers for agricultural enlightenment, notice was given that any person apparently competent to receive the instruction might join the upper classes after passing an examination.[31]

In the year 1874 the regents thought the time had come to fill the chair of agriculture with a well-educated and qualified expert. They called into service Charles Y. Lacy, an agricultural alumnus of Cornell University, twenty-four years of age, and put him in charge of instruction and of the experimental farm. They were just completing the first agricultural building on the campus, a building of moderate size but well proportioned and well built, with one wing for a chemical laboratory and another for a plant house, both well equipped. It was hoped that this physical demonstration would call in students to pursue agricultural studies in good faith. There were plenty of men students who would gladly work on the farm for customary wages, but hardly one of them would suffer himself to be enrolled as a student of agriculture. In his first year Lacy had no student of college rank. In the next, 1875–76, there were three students, two of whom dropped out at the end of the winter term. In the third year there were two students, one of whom escaped. In the fourth year there was one special student.[32]

It did not take Assistant Professor Lacy long to discover that the twenty-five acres of the experimental farm that had been broken were " of a sandy nature," exhausted by cropping, and that the remaining area would produce nothing but marsh hay until it was drained. A larger and better farm

[31] Board of Regents, *Reports*, 1870, p. 42; 1871, pp. 17, 23; 1872, p. 5.
[32] Board of Regents, *Reports*, 1874, pp. 5, 8; 1875, p. 8; 1876, p. 40; 1877, p. 57; 1878, pp. 31, 45. In the University of Minnesota *Calendar*, 1876–77, facing page 87, is a sketch of the agricultural college building, and the floor plans are given on pages 89 and 90.

was necessary, he advised the regents, especially if experiments in stock raising were to be undertaken. During his term of service the industrious professor carried on experiments in series in field, garden, and nursery culture, surprisingly numerous considering his small area of cultivation. He made creditable displays of produce at the state fairs. After the board of regents, on January 13, 1880, had declined by a tie vote to increase his salary from twelve to fourteen hundred dollars, he was content to resign during the summer of 1880 to engage in sheep ranching in Montana.[33]

From the date of Lacy's resignation until the winter of 1881 the professorship was vacant, while the regents sought with diligence to find the right man for the place. The farm was in the charge of a capable graduate of the academic department, who, as the son of an actual farmer, was accustomed to labor and farm practice. Under the circumstances, he had no ambition to become a professor of agriculture. In this interval the Chicago, Milwaukee, and St. Paul Railroad Company ran double freight tracks diagonally through the farm, a considerable fraction of which had been cut off in a previous year by the opening of University Avenue. The farm was now cut into four parts of unequal area. The regents, who had not appreciated Lacy's counsel, now saw that it was imperative to discover and acquire a new farm. The legislature of 1881 gave them permission, probably superfluous, to sell the old farm and to use the proceeds to buy a new one. The selection of the new farm was a matter of difficulty. A neighboring location was obviously desirable; a distant one implied dismemberment, partial at least, sooner or later. The result of a comparison of the sites offered was the purchase of a quarter section in Ramsey

[33] Lacy's reports, in Board of Regents, *Reports,* 1874, pp. 127, 129; 1875, pp. 78–99; 1876, pp. 41–52; 1877, pp. 58–69; 1878, pp. 56–79; 1879–80, pp. 83–85; Board of Regents, Minutes, B 1: 189; Lacy to the author, August 30, 1926, and attached thereto a copy of a letter from Lacy to D. D. Mayne, undated, Folwell Papers.

County on the Como road, distant some three miles from the university campus.[34]

A year of inquiry, correspondence, and scrutiny of testimonials ended in the selection of Edward D. Porter as professor of theoretical and practical agriculture. He was a native of Vermont, had been graduated from the University of Pennsylvania, and had held the chair of agriculture in Delaware College, Newark, Delaware — the land-grant college of that state — for several years. At fifty-two he was still young in spirit, alert, widely informed, and perhaps too versatile and too industrious for the best success. The story of his multifarious engagements during the eight years of his service, managing a model farm, conducting a multitude of farm and garden experiments, superintending the erection of buildings, making numerous addresses, attending to a voluminous correspondence, and, in his last two years, directing the experiment station established under the Hatch Act of 1887 must be put aside for some account of his efforts to discover and gather in students desiring to learn agriculture in a college in order to practice it on the farm.[35]

Finding no pupils enrolled in his department, Professor Porter readily fell in with a plan of lecture instruction that for some years had been advertised to no purpose. The president of the university had never been content with the assumption that merely by teaching sciences related to agriculture could the demands of the land-grant act of 1862 be fulfilled. He believed that a line of instruction strictly professional in agriculture might be attempted. On April 20, 1874, he laid before the board of regents a plan for free professional instruction in agriculture to last about one hun-

[34] Board of Regents, Reports, 1879–80, p. 9; 1881–82, pp. 8, 12; General Laws, 1881, p. 116. The tract consisted of all but five acres of the northwest quarter of section 21, township 29, range 23 west. Ninety-three adjoining acres were purchased soon afterwards.
[35] Board of Regents, Minutes, B 1: 211, 213, 217; Upham and Dunlap, Minnesota Biographies, 609; University of Minnesota, Department of Agriculture, Reports, 1887–88, pp. 48, 54. For the Hatch Act, see United States, Statutes at Large, 24: 440.

dred days, between November and March, and to be given in part by members of the university faculty and in part by lecturers of distinction in different specialties who were to be called in. Each lecturer would cover his field more or less completely. The class was to be composed of young men engaged, or about to engage, in farming. No examinations were to be exacted for admission and any persons interested might attend. It was hoped that on this plan a college of agriculture might be developed in a manner similar to that in which law and medical schools had grown up. Professor Lacy had favored the project and had advertised it year after year, but no young farmers had responded.[36] Porter hopefully announced the opening of the "Farmers' Lecture Course" for February 28, 1882. The newspapers gave wide publicity to the venture. The United States commissioner of agriculture, George B. Loring, came out and delivered the opening address, which is a valuable paper today. Some of the papers read in the sessions that followed were on "The Cow," "Farmers' Orchards," "The Culture and Management of Our Native Forests," "Market Gardening," "Farmers' Gardens," "Fruit Culture of the Northwest," and "The Birds of Minnesota" — all valuable and thoroughly interesting; but they did not form a course of instruction. More than two hundred and fifty persons attended, but few were apprentices to farming.[37]

[36] Board of Regents, Reports, 1874, pp. 33–36, 130; 1881–82, pp. 90, 91. The University Calendar, 1874–75 to 1879–80, contains announcements of the lecture course. In the Folwell Papers are some twenty letters written in the summer of 1874, generally commendatory of the farmers' lecture plan. Among them are letters from Andrew D. White, president of Cornell University; John M. Gregory, president of the Illinois Industrial University, now the University of Illinois; A. S. Welch, president of the Iowa State Agricultural College; D. C. Gilman, president of the University of California and later, of Johns Hopkins University; and Professors William H. Brewer of Yale College, George H. Cook of Rutgers College, W. W. Daniells of the University of Wisconsin, and Edward H. Twining of the University of Missouri.

[37] Porter's report, in Board of Regents, Reports, 1881–82, pp. 93, 95–212. A letter from Porter to Pillsbury, December 3, 1881, in the Folwell Papers, contains a prospectus of the farmers' lecture course of 1882. A copy of the program for 1883 is attached to the letter.

The approval of the Farmers' Lecture Course in 1882 was so cordial that Porter announced a second course of four weeks beginning on January 16, 1883, with a long list of distinguished speakers. The leading course — it amounted to a course — was given by Professor William H. Brewer of Yale College, on the "Principles of Stock Breeding," a subject upon which he was a well-known authority. All the other papers were on single topics relating to farm, garden, and forest. Three hundred and eight attendants were registered and satisfaction was general. For 1884 Porter took a wide departure from the idea of the lecture plan and engaged the well-known culinary expert, Juliet Corson of New York, to give a course on the "Principles of Domestic Economy and Cookery." It turned out to be simply a course in cookery. The lectures were illustrated by actual demonstrations with portable apparatus on the platform. They were exceedingly popular. Over eleven hundred persons — very few of them men — attended. So, diverted from its true purpose, ended the Farmers' Lecture Course. Had the original plan been held to, it is doubtful whether enough actual or prospective young farmers would have attended to form classes. There was an incidental outcome, however, of no little moment. Porter, observing that, of all the attendants at his courses, at least three-fourths came from homes inside a circle of a twenty-mile radius, conceived the idea of carrying his lecture instruction outside that limit. Authorized by the regents, he organized and conducted or attended thirty-one farmers' institutes at as many places in the year 1886. Such was the beginning of the long series of farmers' institutes carried on with great success by Oren C. Gregg.[38]

In an annex to the large farmhouse built according to Porter's liberal views was a series of chambers for lodging

[38] University of Minnesota, Department of Agriculture, *Reports*, 1883–86, pp. 32–37, 140–435. The Corson lectures, separately paged, are printed as an appendix to this report.

workmen. He found an established custom of giving employment to men students and willingly followed it, treating the
young men as apprentices rather than as mere laborers. He
soon conceived the idea of a training school and in April,
1886, he issued a circular announcing a school of practical
agriculture to open on May 1 and continue until November
1. That year he had ten students in his class.[39]

The experience of the first year convinced Porter that his
school of practical agriculture might be enlarged into a more
liberal school to include some general studies and applied
science. He was aware that such a school on the experimental farm would meet the wishes of influential farmers. To
obtain consideration of the scheme by the regents and, if
possible, their approval, he secured the adoption of a resolution at a meeting on April 1, 1887, for the appointment
of an advisory board of seven members — " practical farmers " — to make any recommendations of policy they might
be pleased to. On April 7 the members were appointed and
Porter was directed to confer with the advisory board with
regard to the establishment of an industrial school of agriculture. A week later, on April 13, the board submitted a
report in the form of four resolutions, drafted, it may be
assumed, by the interested professor. The substance of it
was that the proposition to establish a school of agriculture
on the experimental farm offered " the best possible solution
of the problem of agricultural education in Minnesota " and
that an appropriation of money for the purpose should be
made. It was voted on the spot to establish the school and
the executive committee was authorized to expend ten thousand dollars for the erection of a building.

[39] See Department of Agriculture, *Reports*, 1883–86, pp. 23–25, and the
map facing page 22, for the plan of the new farm and buildings. The original announcement of the school of practical agriculture is given on page 27.
Porter presented no formal reports for the years 1883–84 and 1884–85. He
was employed in the management of the state exhibit at the World's Exposition in New Orleans in 1884–85. Though he gave a year's time to this work,
he received no compensation for his services. Department of Agriculture,
Reports, 1883–86, pp. 20, 119.

The university *Catalogue* for 1886–87, containing announcements for the following year, gave notice of a "New School of Agriculture" to open in the spring of 1888. The course of studies would extend over two terms of five months each and would include arithmetic, penmanship, bookkeeping, composition, practical mensuration, surveying and leveling, botany, chemistry, physiology, and veterinary science. More definite announcement was to follow. But none followed and the "New School of Agriculture" did not open in the spring of 1888.[40]

The appropriation of the small sum of ten thousand dollars toward the establishment of the school recommended by the advisory board indicated that the regents at the time had no great degree of confidence in the experiment. Later they, or some of them, took up the matter more seriously; they had good reason to do so. The Granger movement of the seventies had made a large body of farmers "class conscious" and the number was vastly increased by the crusades of the Farmers' Alliance during the eighties. Farmers demanded a higher place in the social order and a larger share of the national income and of the benefactions dealt out by Congress. The Minnesota farmers became critical of the use of the land grant for agricultural colleges. They observed that the separate colleges, such as those of Iowa and Michigan, were apparently doing more than the agricultural element of the Minnesota state university for the farmer. The regents were charged with diversion of the land-grant fund. Violent attacks were made upon the regent most influential and most responsible for the policy. Demands were made for the segregation of the agricultural college. The legislature of 1887 created a joint committee to make an investigation of the university and a bill was prepared to separate the university and the agricultural college. The violence of

[40] Board of Regents, Minutes, B 1: 293–298; Johnson, *University of Minnesota*, 57; University of Minnesota, *Catalogues*, 1886–87, p. 79; Department of Agriculture, *Reports*, 1887–88, p. 37.

the attack was presently mitigated by a powerful address made by President Cyrus Northrop before the Minnesota State Horticultural Society on January 19, 1887. He rehearsed the whole story of the incessant endeavors to develop the agricultural department as such and claimed that the conditions of the land-grant act had been honestly fulfilled. The report of the investigating committee, submitted late in the session, completely exonerated the regents from the charge that they had stolen the agricultural college land grant from the farmers and from minor allegations of corrupt management of university lands and timber.[41]

That storm had blown over, but it was well understood that another tempest would follow; and it did. The regents saw what the situation called for: they must ignore Morrill's expectation that colleges of agriculture would educate farmers for "a learned, liberal and intellectual pursuit," and must give the farmers what they wanted. The Reverend David L. Kiehle, superintendent of public instruction and regent by virtue of his office, appears to have taken up the study of the situation earnestly and to have enlarged his information by travel and correspondence. He could not have found anything to be imitated, but he got an idea. He contributed to *Farm, Stock, and Home* for February 1, 1888, a plan for a school of agriculture on the experimental farm, roughly similar to Porter's plan, with a novel and meritorious amendment. Instead of two terms in the year, one term of five winter months was proposed. During those months farm boys could generally be spared from farm work.

On March 6, 1888, President Northrop, for a committee of the board of regents, submitted to the regents the Kiehle curriculum, with slight modifications from the magazine

[41] Cyrus Northrop, " Agricultural Education," in his *Addresses, Educational and Patriotic*, 393–417 (Minneapolis, 1910) ; Pillsbury, *Address before the Alumni*, 29–31; David L. Kiehle, *Education in Minnesota*, part 1, p. 73 (Minneapolis, 1903). On Senate file 618, a bill to reorganize and provide for the endowment and regulation of the Agricultural College of Minnesota, see *Senate Journal*, 1887, pp. 455, 562, 585, 677. The bill was indefinitely postponed and it never reached the House. In the Folwell Papers is a printed

announcement. There were to be three courses — a literary
and business course, a scientific and manual training course,
and a lecture course. The literary and business course was
to include (1) language and composition, (2) business arithmetic, (3) penmanship and bookkeeping, (4) descriptive
and physical geography, (5) United States history, (6)
civil government, and (7) political economy; the scientific
and manual training course was to comprise (1) shop work,
(2) chemistry, (3) mineralogy and composition of soils,
(4) botany, (5) physiology, and (6) natural philosophy;
and the subjects of the lecture course were to be (1) farm
management, (2) soils, (3) plants, (4) stock, (5) farm
hygiene, (6) farm architecture, (7) farm homes, and
(8) veterinary science. The report was adopted on the
same day and the regents " assigned " Professor Maria L.
Sanford, against her desire, to the principalship of the
school, but the arrangement proved impracticable and another very satisfactory selection was made.[42]

In the university *Catalogue* issued in the summer of 1888
the " School of Agriculture " was duly advertised to open
on October 18. The tabulated curriculum conformed to the
Kiehle scheme as adopted by the regents, with modifications.
Although a good common school education was required
for admission, notice was given the following year that for
applicants not prepared in arithmetic, penmanship, botany,
and physiology special classes would be formed, and that any
students defective in arithmetic, grammar, United States

copy of the bill. The effort to separate the college of agriculture and
mechanic arts from the university was renewed in the legislature of 1889.
The bill of 1887, or a similar one, was brought up in the Senate but it
failed to pass. The proceeding came to a sudden end when John S. Pillsbury
proposed at a meeting of the regents with a committee of the legislature
to make a gift of $150,000, if he could be assured that the agricultural
college would not be moved. The gift was accepted and by concurrent
resolutions the solemn assurance of the legislature was given that the unity
of the agricultural college with the university should be permanent. Johnson,
University of Minnesota, 62; *Senate Journal*, 1889, pp. 366, 644, 711, 743,
828, 875; *House Journal*, 1127.

[42] David L. Kiehle, " Education Applied to Agriculture," in *Farm, Stock,
and Home*, 4: 83 (February 1, 1888) ; Board of Regents, Minutes, B 1: 309, 327.

history, and geography would have to take another year to obtain the certificate of graduation. In 1890 a regular preparatory year was added for those elementary studies. Such was the curriculum of instruction that the agricultural department of the University of Minnesota, with a plant worth five hundred thousand dollars, offered to the Minnesota farmers. If they had asked for a kindergarten at the time it would have been conceded. Board and room in the fine new school building were to be furnished at cost and were not to exceed three dollars a week.[43]

With these liberal attractions but 47 young men were allured into the school the first year. In the year 1889–90 that number was raised to 78 and in the next year the enrollment was 104. In the year 1891 a course in dairying was instituted and in that year the enrollment was 115. In the next two years 144 and 203, respectively, were enrolled. In the year 1894–95 the admission of women to a summer school raised the total attendance to 372.[44]

The purpose of this section has now been accomplished. It should be apparent that the failure of the university for twenty years to develop the agricultural department was due to the simple fact that there was no demand for school education in agriculture. Minnesota had been and was still a one-crop state. The farm boys who wanted " education " went to the high schools where tuition was free and then

[43] University of Minnesota, *Catalogues,* 1887–88, p. 77; 1888–89, pp. 87–89; 1889–90, p. 94; 1890–91, pp. 106–113. In a letter from Mrs. J. D. Scofield, dated at Oak Grove Farm, March 27, 1895, the claim is made that the Kiehle curriculum of the school of agriculture was originally arranged by a committee of the Minnesota State Grange. A copy of this letter is in the Folwell Papers. Regent Pillsbury stated informally to the board of regents on December 18, 1888, that from the proceeds of the sale of the old farm a new farm of 245 acres had been bought and that the buildings erected and the stock, apparatus, and implements purchased were worth, in the aggregate, $500,000. See Board of Regents, Minutes, B 1: 335. In his *Address before the Alumni,* 29, Pillsbury used the more modest sum of $350,000. But times had changed.

[44] The enrollment figures are given in the university catalogues for the years mentioned. It was not until the fall of 1897 that women were admitted to the regular winter course in the school of agriculture. President's report, in Board of Regents, *Reports,* 1897–98, p. 52.

took the old college courses. To draw in a handful of students the school of agriculture was obliged to offer not only free instruction, but very cheap board and lodging and a twelve months' course of study in two winter terms, spread very thinly over a great number of subjects reaching down into the common school branches. And then years were to pass before success was assured!

The need and the desire for education in agriculture in its numerous specialties came slowly in Minnesota, but they came. To some future historian must be left the task of relating the remarkable expansion of the school of agriculture on the farm after the period ending in 1910, covered by Johnson in his history, its service in fitting many of its pupils for admission to the full four-year course of the college of agriculture proper, and the continuation of large numbers of the college graduates in advanced studies. In the year ending in 1925 the enrollment in the school of agriculture in St. Paul was 400 and that in the college of agriculture was 761. In the twenty-year period then ending, 273 students had taken degrees for advanced work in the agricultural group. The agricultural department of the University of Minnesota holds an acknowledged eminence in the group of institutions endowed by the land grant of 1862.[45] On a separate campus, adjacent to the permanent grounds of the State Agricultural Society, splendidly wooded, with a great array of buildings and ample experimental farm and gardens, the comprehensive "department of agriculture," virtually controlled by a committee of regents, has all the advantages of a separate institution and enjoys the prestige of a university status.

THE DOUBLE UNIVERSITY LAND GRANT

The double university grant by Congress to Minnesota was exceptional. Beginning with the admission of Ohio in 1802,

[45] University of Minnesota, *President's Reports*, 1924-25, pp. 65, 68; *Minnesota Alumni Weekly*, August, 1926, p. 27.

the public land states as they were successively admitted had been granted seventy-two sections of land for the use and support of universities or, as otherwise phrased, "seminaries of learning." The bill for the enabling act of Minnesota, introduced in the session of 1856 by Henry M. Rice, departed from the norm by setting apart and reserving seventy-two sections of land for the use and support of a *state* university, to be selected by the governor of the state. There was no reference to a previous reservation of the same amount to the territory obtained by Sibley in 1851.[46] As the novel phraseology was not remarked upon in the debates it is safe to assume that Congress understood that it was merely confirming the territorial grant to the new state. Had it been understood at that time that the enabling act doubled the university grant, that construction would certainly have appeared in the constitutional conventions that began their sessions on July 13, 1857. It was not so understood. In the Democratic body repeated statements were made that the enabling act merely confirmed the reservation that had already been made to the territory. No other idea was suggested. The same construction ran through the debates in the Republican wing. Near the close a lawyer member, Billings, thought he saw in the enabling act a separate additional grant. He was immediately corrected by North, who said, "They mean the same thing precisely, and apply to the same land," and by Secombe, who said that the en-

[46] See *ante*, 1: 390; 4: 73. The enabling act may be found in any issue of the Minnesota *Legislative Manual*. In his *Address before the Alumni*, 21, Pillsbury said: "The University is indebted to Hon. H. M. Rice . . . by whose influence was secured a grant of 72 sections of land for a State University. . . . Mr. Rice was a member of the Territorial Board of Regents, and was conversant with the hopeless condition of the Territorial University." In his "History of the University of Minnesota," in *Minnesota Historical Collections*, 12: 61, John B. Gilfillan states that Rice, as the Minnesota delegate in Congress and a regent of the university, "succeeded in having a clause embraced in this [*the enabling*] act, making a second reservation, granting to the State seventy-two sections of land for the use and support of a State University. This was entirely independent of the former grant to the Territory."

abling act was merely carrying out the intended grants that
had been promised previously to the schools and the university.[47]

It is not known that the territorial board of regents in its
remaining years of tribulation thought of getting possession
of a second university grant bestowed by the enabling act.
That idea dawned upon the state board of regents that succeeded the territorial board on February 14, 1860. On
April 5, at its first meeting, it adopted a "memorial" to
Governor Ramsey asking him to provide for the selection of
the two townships of land for the *state* university incorporated
by the last legislature. In the memorial it was maintained
that the enabling act made no reference to a territorial university, but prescribed for a future state university. It was
the intention to give Minnesota a grant for a state university
free from all connections with territorial organizations and
not "to turn over the debts and prospectively encumbered
lands of an old and badly managed territorial institution."
The correspondence of Governor Ramsey with the general
land office has not been found, but it is well known that his
selections were not approved.[48]

[47] *Congressional Globe*, 34 Congress, 3 session, 517–519; Minnesota Constitutional Convention (Democratic), *Debates and Proceedings*, 438, 454–460
(St. Paul, 1857); (Republican), 482–498 (St. Paul, 1858). For remarks
by Sibley, Emmett, Norris, Brown, and Sherburne, see *Debates and Proceedings* (Democratic), 456–459. For the passage between Billings and North
and Secombe, see *Debates and Proceedings* (Republican), 489.

[48] Board of Regents, Minutes, A 1: 1, 2, 19. The memorial is on pages
14–16. On page 4 is a second communication from the board to Governor
Ramsey asking him to ascertain whether the regents had the right to "dispose
of the lands reserved for the uses of a Territorial institution for the purpose
of liquidating the indebtedness incurred by the Territorial Regents." It is
remarkable that, although this board, at that time called the "state board,"
set up the theory that its university was an absolutely new creation, it presently considered itself as receiver of the assets of the territorial board. It
obtained the records and seal of that board. The state board leased lands
and collected rents and moneys due for stumpage. On June 30, 1860,
Governor Ramsey appealed to the commissioner of the general land office
for a liberal construction of the enabling act in behalf of the university,
whose territorial grant had been "virtually absorbed by the action of the
Territory, leaving the State nothing but an inheritance of debt." For further
action with regard to liabilities and assets of the territorial board, see Board
of Regents, Minutes, A 1: 1, 2, 6, 9, 20, 22, 26, 30, 36.

The special board of three regents appointed by the legislature of 1864 to extricate the university from the burden of debt incurred by the territorial board of regents in the years before the panic of 1857 evidently thought it just and proper to renew the claim for a second university grant. At its first meeting, on March 16, 1864, the special board adopted a resolution to request Henry M. Rice to act for them in obtaining title to the lands donated by the enabling act. No record has been found of any intervention by him. Other efforts proving futile, the regents concluded that to secure the state's claim it must be more forcibly presented at Washington. To remove doubt as to their power, they obtained from the legislature of 1867 authority to employ counsel to prosecute the claim "upon a contingent compensation in land or money." [49]

The attorney employed, who had had "wide and successful practice before the Department [of the Interior]," was not able to induce the secretary to reverse the rulings of his predecessors. He could only suggest an appeal to Congress for the desired relief. A bill introduced in the session of 1868 was passed by the Senate. It came up in the House late in the session, was referred to the committee on public lands, and appeared no more. [50]

In February, 1869, Ramsey introduced in the Senate a bill to allow the Minnesota grant. It was referred to the committee on public lands and ordered printed, but it did not appear again. In March, Eugene M. Wilson, representative from the second Minnesota district, reintroduced in the House the bill that had failed the year before. It was reported from the committee on public lands on January 19, 1870, and was recommitted, to lie in the committee's file case for

[49] Laws, 1864, pp. 61–64; 1867, p. 179; Board of Regents, Minutes, A 1: 45. The minutes of the special board are recorded in the same book with those of the state board.

[50] Pillsbury, Address before the Alumni, 22; William R. Marshall, Message, January 7, 1869, p. 12; Congressional Globe, 40 Congress, 2 session, 2329, 3240, 3721, 4490; Board of Regents, Minutes A 1: 89. At the last

the next five months. During this time the able attorney
for the regents was diligently enlightening members upon
the equity of the measure. On June 22 Wilson reported the
bill from the committee with the recommendation that it pass.
He made a brief explanation, insisting that a mere legal
point was involved. An Ohio member replied that, nevertheless, it gave Minnesota a double university land grant and
asked for a vote. It stood: yeas, 84; nays, 75; not voting,
71. A fuller vote and a larger majority would have indicated a keener appreciation of the justice of the Minnesota
claim.

The bill came up in the Senate two days later. Senator
Ramsey, presuming that the Senate would immediately con-
cur, as it had passed the very same bill two years before,
said, "I suggest . . . that we had better pass that bill
now." He made no appeal for it. Because of the absence
of Senator Williams of the committee on public lands, who
had the bill in charge, it went over to the next day. Williams
stated in explanation of the bill that the grant made in the
Minnesota enabling act was a distinct transaction from the
reservation of February 19, 1851, and was converted into a
donation by the act of March 2, 1861. He did not know the
motive or the policy of the legislation. "We take the law
as we find it," he said. Another senator said that the act
would give Minnesota more than her share, but that the purpose was excellent and that the mistake, if there was one,
was on the right side. The Senate then passed the bill without division. The surmise may be ventured that senators and
representatives had come to the conclusion that the offer
made in the enabling act and its acceptance by Minnesota
concluded a contract. Congress had made a bargain and, al-

meeting of the special board of regents, on February 29, 1868, Governor
Marshall was requested to go to Washington at the expense of the university
to prosecute the claim to the second land grant. The governor made the
journey and drew up a "petition" to Congress, which was presented to the
Senate by Senator Ramsey on April 23, 1868. A copy of the petition is in
the Folwell Papers.

though it was a bad bargain made through an undetected finesse, it ought to be fulfilled. In a single paragraph the act directed the commissioner of the general land office to approve and certify seventy-two sections mentioned in the enabling act, without taking into account the reservation of 1851.[51]

It was to be expected that in ordinary course the able attorney at Washington whose influence had so greatly contributed to winning from a reluctant Congress nearly half a million dollars' worth of land more than other neighboring states had been granted would be promptly and generously rewarded for his labors. The treasurer of the regents seems to have been instructed to ascertain the amount of the fee, apparently in cash. On June 26, 1872, he reported verbally that Henry B. Beard, the attorney in question, would probably visit the university in August or September. On September 3, 1872, Beard presented in person a statement of his claim. Upon the report of a committee appointed to confer with him the board voted to convey to him three sections of land. The matter rested until December 23, 1873, when a prominent Minnesota lumberman came before the board with a written statement indicating that Beard had made an assignment of the three sections. The question came up as to how the three sections should be selected from university lands at large. Would the regents select them or would they leave Beard or his assignee to pick them out? The board, upon motion, agreed to this equitable arrangement: the president and treasurer might select one quarter section, the assignee another, and so on alternately until

[51] See *ante*, 3: 16; 41 Congress, 2 session, *Senate Journal*, 885, 1009 (serial 1404); *House Journal*, 164, 1064 (serial 1410); *Congressional Globe*, 40 Congress, 3 session, 1406; 41 Congress, 1 session, 248; 41 Congress, 2 session, 576, 4685, 4804, 4829; *Statutes at Large*, 16: 196. See *Minnesota State University* (41 Congress, 2 session, *House Reports*, no. 4 — serial 1436) for the argument that the enabling act was in the nature of a compact. On page 22 of his *Address before the Alumni* Pillsbury appears to award the principal credit for obtaining the passage of the bill to Henry B. Beard, the able attorney of the lobby.

the twelve quarter sections should be selected; or the assignee might make the selections and pay the difference between their value and the average value of the tracts selected from. The selections were probably made in the winter of 1874, for on April 22 of that year the regents instructed their president and treasurer to convey to Beard three sections of land. On April 29 the deed was executed and delivered. Two years later the transaction was legalized by action of the state legislature.[52]

These protracted maneuvers resulted in the transfer of three sections, 1,920 acres, of the best pine-timbered land owned by the university. A government commission found the value of Minnesota pine lands in 1872 to range from five to ten dollars an acre, increasing at the rate of twelve per cent a year. No algebra is needed to demonstrate that the regents paid liberally, for the times, for the services of their attorney.[53]

THE COLISEUM [54]

From the time of the reorganization of the university for college work under the charter of 1868 the regents of the university have ever insisted upon requiring the men students to study "military tactics" to conform to the Morrill Act and hold on to the land grant of 1862. The first president of the university, who had served as an officer of volunteer

[52] Board of Regents, Minutes, B 1: 59, 68, 97, 99, 101; Johnson, *University of Minnesota*, 90; *Laws*, 1876, p. 110. In an interview with the author, Thomas B. Walker stated that Beard got $2.50 an acre for his land. This interview is recorded in the author's notebooks, 9: 38. In the Folwell Papers, accompanying a letter from Ray P. Chase, state auditor, to the author, September 25, 1926, is a copy of the deed of the regents to Beard, conveying 1,914.59 acres of land in 22 parcels in Itasca and Cass counties. It was understood at the time that a grant of land by sections meant a grant of " an amount of land equal to so many sections."

[53] In regard to the value of Minnesota pine lands in 1872, see *ante*, 1: 477, and record of interviews with Nathan Butler, in the author's notebooks, 4: 39; 9: 46.

[54] This title, used by the newspapers of the time, does not conform to the better English spelling, "colosseum," given by Webster's Dictionary.

engineers in the Army of the Potomac for three years and a half, placed a high value on military exercises for their gymnastics, their training in teamwork, and their inculcation of honor and loyalty to country. Outdoor drills were impracticable in the latitude of Minnesota for five months of the college year and foul weather often interfered during the other four months. The commandants of cadets, supported by the president, made repeated appeals to the regents to provide a drill hall, even if it should be one of the cheapest construction. The regents were willing enough to build a drill hall, none more so than General Sibley, their president; but they deemed it unwise to ask for an appropriation for that particular purpose when needs were so many, especially after the hard times following the financial depression of 1873. But when better times came and the work done at the university was giving general satisfaction, the board gained courage to ask for appropriations to meet and carry on its expanding activities.

On April 8, 1880, the president of the university was ready with a scheme for a group of buildings and a proposition that the legislature be asked to make an appropriation of fifty thousand dollars a year for six years. The regents thought the demand so great that it would meet opposition and they cut it to thirty thousand dollars a year. It was their opinion that this large sum would provide all the buildings that the university would need in their time. The legislature of 1881 made the desired appropriation and specified the buildings, six in number, to be erected out of it. On January 4 of that year the state Capitol, lately rebuilt, was so much damaged by fire that it was necessary to rebuild it a second time. The university building program was automatically postponed and three years of patient waiting passed before it could be resumed. The military building, although not first on the authorized list, was selected to be first undertaken. The president of the university prepared a rough plan modeled on one of a building he had seen at

Cornell University, which had cost twelve thousand dollars. The sketch showed a simple one-story structure open to the roof, rectangular in shape with small annexes on the long sides. It might have cost ten thousand dollars according to the prices of the time. The drawing was handed to a Minneapolis architect of good education, whose work had given evidence of talent.[55]

In the decade ending in 1880 Minneapolis had grown from a small city of 13,066 inhabitants to one of 46,887. In the five years following the footing was raised to 129,200. That was a veritable boom period in business and one of great elation in the social, intellectual, and even spiritual life of the place. In 1883 the Minneapolis Society of Fine Arts was incorporated and not long afterward, the Philharmonic Association.[56] The leader of the musical movement was David Blakeley, owner and editor of the *Minneapolis Tribune* and a musician and conductor of choruses. He and his associates became desirous to have the people of Minneapolis, St. Paul, and the neighboring communities exposed to the compositions of the great masters of classical music. He learned that the Chicago Symphony Orchestra, which had been trained to great excellence by Theodore Thomas, might be brought to Minnesota for a series of concerts. But there was no concert hall in either of the Twin Cities large enough for the audiences that might be expected and that would be necessary to finance the venture.

To Blakeley must be credited the conceit of having the university drill hall enlarged and arranged into a concert hall. He communicated the idea to the architect, Leroy Sunderland Buffington, and obtained the tacit consent of the building committee of the regents, local members, to an experiment in college architecture. The president of the university was not consulted; he had resigned and was merely

[55] Board of Regents, *Reports*, 1881–82, p. 9; *General Laws*, 1881, p. 225. On the burning of the Capitol, see *ante*, 3: 138.
[56] *United States Census, 1880, Population*, 420; Minnesota Secretary of State, *Reports*, 1883, p. 8; 1884, p. 10; 1885, appendix, 26.

holding over while the regents were looking for a successor. When General Sibley was informed of the plan he said that it could not possibly be seriously considered. It was not sanctioned by the board nor even discussed. Taking the simple rectangular sketch with its slight annexes on the long sides, the ingenious architect expanded one annex, the front one, into a vast semicircle of an eighty-five foot radius. In this area he included the customary amphitheatrical divisions of parquet, dress circle, and balcony. The rear annex was boxed out to include a large semicircular stage, a broad *foyer* around it, and numerous dressing rooms. The extreme dimensions were: depth, 160 feet; width, 170 feet; and height, 80 feet. With the exception of the steel columns and trusses that supported the roofs, the construction was wholly of wood, including the ceilings and wall linings of clear white pine without paint. Windows and a skylight thirty feet in diameter lighted the theater by day and electricity illuminated all parts by night. The cost of the building was $56,127.58, not including lighting, which was more than four times what an ample drill hall need have cost.[57]

The transformed and glorified drill hall was first put into public use on May 29, 1884, when the commencement of the year took place. On June 10 the great musical festival began. The leading attractions were the Theodore Thomas Symphony Orchestra of Chicago, Christine Nilsson, a star of the concert stage at the time, the St. Paul Choral Society, and the Minneapolis Philharmonic Association. The *Minneapolis Tribune* of the following morning, in an editorial headed " Successfully Opened," said: " The University Coliseum proved to be admirably adapted to great musical gatherings. . . . Its vast dimensions, its commodious arrangements, its safety, accessibility and excellent acoustic properties unite to make it one of the most complete auditoriums in the country." All the

[57] For the cost of the building, see Board of Regents, *Reports*, 1883–84, p. 34; 1885–86, p. 26.

THE OLD MAIN BUILDING

THE COLISEUM

[From photographs in the museum of the Minnesota Historical Society.]

concerts were admirable; the audiences were large — estimated at five thousand or more at each performance — responsive, and representative of all parts of the state. The matinee of June 12 was dramatically interrupted. A chorus of one thousand children in gay uniforms of red, white, and blue were seated back of the orchestra. While they were singing their part, a heavy shower of rain was falling. Later, in an interval between numbers, a blinding flash of lightning accompanied by a terrible thunderclap struck the central flag staff. Nobody was seriously hurt, however, and the damage to the building was nominal. Fragments of broken glass from the skylight fell on the parquet, the audience rose, and a stampede seemed imminent. Thomas had the coolness to start his musicians playing a lively overture; the people resumed their seats and the concert proceeded.[58]

After the great concerts the floor of the parquet was leveled and, with the chairs piled back, it made an excellent drill hall for squad and company movements. As no heating apparatus had been provided the hall was useless for seated gatherings except in summer weather. It served well for the annual commencement, the president's receptions, and the student balls. During its lifetime occasional use was made of it by musical societies. A state encampment of the G.A.R. and a Grant memorial service were conveniently accommodated. At nine o'clock in the evening of August 9, 1894, a fire starting from an unknown source totally consumed the structure in a single hour. In an editorial article headed "Vale Coliseum," the *Minneapolis Tribune* — under changed management — said it was an ungainly eyesore wthout classic outlines and its loss was not to be regretted; if the insurance was fifteen thousand dollars that was all it was worth. Two years later the present armory and gym-

---

58 *Pioneer Press*, 1884: May 30, p. 6; *Minneapolis Tribune*, 1884: June 11, p. 4; 13, p. 4. An announcement of the "Great State Musical Festival," accompanied by a sketch of the floor plan of the Coliseum, is in the *Tribune*, May 10, 1884, p. 9.

nasium, ample in dimensions for the time and well equipped, was erected.[59]

THE MAYO FOUNDATION

When the framers of the state constitution confirmed the location of the University of Minnesota as established by existing territorial law, " at or near the Falls of Saint Anthony," they had no other idea than that the twenty-seven and a fraction acres of campus on the southeastern verge of the city of St. Anthony and the stone building, when completed, would be the permanent and adequate seat of the university. They could not have imagined the amplifications that were to take place: successive enlargements of the campus to embrace some 120 acres; the purchase in separate parcels of some 420 acres in Ramsey County, still " near," though not adjacent to, the Falls of St. Anthony, for the department of agriculture; the establishment of schools of agriculture at Crookston, Morris, Waseca, and Grand Rapids, with large farms about them; the fruit-breeding station at Zumbra Heights; and the forestry station at Cloquet; the creation of a general extension division, including extension courses of study in selected cities, state-wide correspondence courses for home study, and community service, the last embracing lyceum, lecture, drama, and motion picture branches; the erection of the Minnesota Hospital and Home for Crippled Children near Minnehaha Falls, endowed to the amount of a million and a half dollars by William Henry Eustis; and, most memorable of all expansions, the annexation on June 9, 1915, of an institution which, with the graduate department of the medical school of the university, constitutes " the most effective working graduate school of medicine in the world and one of the best, if not

[59] *Minneapolis Tribune,* 1894: August 10, p. 1; 11, p. 4. The most serious loss was that of a collection that had been made for the state educational exhibit at the World's Fair. It had cost several thousand dollars and was reserved as a nucleus of an educational museum. Insurance of nineteen thousand dollars was collected. Johnson, *University of Minnesota,* 204, 248.

the best, organized, manned, and most productive departments of medical research." [60]

In 1845 William Worrell Mayo, a well-educated young Englishman of twenty-six years, came to New York. He was employed for a time as instructor in physics and chemistry in the Bellevue Hospital Medical College in that city. Later he went west, studied medicine under a preceptor in Lafayette, Indiana, and obtained his M.D. degree from the University of Missouri in 1854. The next year he came to Minnesota and, after various adventures, settled in Le Sueur. He was practicing there at the time of the Sioux Outbreak and joined Flandrau's company on its way to New Ulm, where he remained until after the battle of August 23, 1862, as one of the volunteer medical staff. The year following he moved to Rochester, in Olmsted County, where he lived until his death on March 6, 1911. In 1871 he took a graduate course in the Bellevue Hospital Medical College to enlarge his professional knowledge and was granted an *ad eundem* degree. He soon became a leading medical practitioner in his own county and counties adjacent and performed numerous surgical operations, many of them daring for the time. [61]

[60] Johnson, *University of Minnesota*, 91; *Laws*, 1851, p. 11; Louis B. Wilson, director of the Mayo Foundation, in University of Minnesota, *President's Reports*, 1924–25, pp. 144, 148; Board of Regents, Minutes, B 1: 223, insert. On December 22, 1881, the president of the university submitted to the board of regents a statement in which he recommended that the university be moved. It was his judgment that the university campus was too small in area, ill shapen, likely to be dismembered by railroad tracks, and surrounded by undesirable structures. Regent Tousley said, "What Mr. Folwell says on this matter is absolutely true." The matter was referred to a committee, but on account of local opposition it made no report. Some hundred acres on the south shore of Lake Minnetonka were thought of. Although the state has expended more than half a million dollars on successive enlargements of the campus since that time, it is still too small.

[61] Biographical sketches of Dr. William W. Mayo may be found in *Sketch of the History of the Mayo Clinic and the Mayo Foundation*, 1–4 (Philadelphia, 1926); *History of Winona and Olmsted Counties*, 1037–1039 (Chicago, 1883); Joseph A. Leonard, *History of Olmsted County*, 160 (Chicago, 1910); Salmon A. Buell, "Judge Flandrau in the Defense of New Ulm during the Sioux Outbreak of 1862," in *Minnesota Historical Collections*, 10: 809 (part 2); the *Duluth Herald*, March 8, 1911, p. 9; the *Rochester Daily Post and Record*, March 6, 1911, p. 5; and the *Olmsted County Democrat*, June 4, 1915, p. 2.

The Right Reverend Thomas Langdon Grace was the Roman Catholic bishop of St. Paul from 1859 to 1897. Not long after the close of the slaveholders' rebellion he wished to establish in southern Minnesota an " academy," that is, a high school, for girls. Mother Mary Alfred Moes, who was released through ecclesiastical comity from service in a community in Illinois, came to Minnesota to found the school at Owatonna. Twenty-five sisters of her order later joined her and on December 8, 1877, " The Congregation of our Lady of Lourdes, Sisters of Saint Francis, Rochester, Minnesota," was formally dedicated. The sisters erected a building costing twenty thousand dollars on land, given by the local parish, worth twenty-five hundred dollars. The academy prospered and might have continued its appropriate work of education as its only service but for a diversion no one would have expected.[62]

On August 21, 1883, a tornado of extreme violence struck Rochester at seven o'clock in the evening. In a quarter of an hour three hundred dwellings were leveled, ninety-seven persons were wounded, and thirty-five were killed in the city and vicinity. The city council promptly provided for an emergency hospital and put Dr. Mayo in charge. Under the direction of their superior, Mother Alfred, the sisters were helpful in caring for the wounded. It was probably in the course of these ministrations that Mother Alfred caught the idea of diverting the labors of her community in part, at least, from education to the relief and care of the sick, especially of surgical patients.

[62] Upham and Dunlap, *Minnesota Biographies*, 270; Sister M. Anastasy to Miss Elizabeth Chute, June 10, 1927, and accompanying memorandum, Folwell Papers; address of the Right Reverend Patrick R. Heffron at the commemoration of Mother Mary Alfred Moes, February 12, 1920, at Rochester, in the *Teresan News-Letter*, August, 1920, a publication of the College of Saint Teresa at Winona; *The Sisters of Saint Francis of the Congregation of Our Lady of Lourdes*, 4, 7–11. The latter publication was printed as a souvenir of the commemoration of Mother Mary Alfred. The memorial tablet unveiled at the commemoration records the birth of this remarkable character in Metz, Alsace, on November 1, 1829, and her death in St. Paul on December 18, 1899. The sisters' academy is still in existence.

Some time after the closing of the temporary hospital Mother Alfred made a proposal to Dr. Mayo that the sisters would open a permanent hospital if he would take the medical superintendence. He thought favorably of it and in 1885 selected a tract of fourteen acres of land as a site. Four years ran by before the project took form. On October 1, 1889, St. Mary's Hospital was opened in a building which, with the grounds, cost seventy-five thousand dollars. Both before and after the opening there was distrust of and opposition to the enterprise. Some of the sisters were not in favor of it, Catholic and Protestant citizens did not like the combination, and several Protestant ministers spoke against it and counseled their congregations to beware of it. Dr. Mayo and Mother Alfred, however, held to their purpose and friends rallied to their support. In its first year St. Mary's cared for three hundred patients. Dr. Mayo was seventy years old when the hospital was opened and was intending to retire from active practice. He was soon to be aided in and later to be relieved of his superintendence of St. Mary's.[63]

Dr. William W. Mayo had two sons, William James, born in 1861, and Charles Horace, born in 1865. There was nothing out of the ordinary in their childhood. As boys they passed through the Rochester grade school and high school and studied in Sanford Niles' Academy in Rochester. Both chose medicine as their profession. The elder brother obtained his M.D. degree at the University of Michigan in 1883 and the younger received his from Northwestern University in 1888. In their vacations both clerked in drug stores, helped their father in his office, and assisted at some operations.

When St. Mary's Hospital was opened none of the Rochester physicians were disposed to join in the doubtful venture

[63] *Rochester Post,* August 24, 1883, p. 2; October 4, 1889, p. 2; *Mayo Clinic and Foundation,* 12–14; Holmes, in *Minnesota in Three Centuries,* 4: 214–216; Leonard, *Olmsted County,* 158, 217. Dr. W. W. Mayo was a state senator in 1891 and 1893.

and become members of the hospital staff. That was accordingly made up of the three Mayos, father and two sons, with five sisters from the convent as helpers. Dr. William J. Mayo had been in general medical practice since his graduation and his brother had practiced for less than two years. Neither had served as a hospital interne and both had everything to learn about hospital administration; but under the guidance of their experienced father they rapidly acquired the necessary technique of nursing and dressing. For the first two years there was no trained nurse to relieve the three surgeons.

St. Mary's Hospital was planned to receive and care for all kinds of patients except those with contagious diseases, but it was soon obliged to give preference to surgical cases. The hospital had a proper operating room and facilities for the reception of patients awaiting operations and for their observation and treatment afterward. Within three months after the opening of the hospital fifty-nine operations had been performed and during the next year there were one hundred and sixty. Physicians of a widening vicinity began to send in surgical cases too serious to be handled in private houses.[64]

It may be presumed that the Mayo brothers, who had inherited an interest in medicine, inherited also the gifts essential to success in surgery — a keen eye for observation, manual dexterity, courage, sound judgment, and a sense of responsibilty. Opportunities added the practice that makes perfect. The number of operations increased from year to year and in 1904 reached 3,131, all performed by the two surgeons and their assistants. Physicians and surgeons, always welcome, impressed with the preliminary observations as well as with the operations, came to speak of the "Mayo Clinic" as if it were an institution. The convenient title was assumed for the business partnership as if it were a firm name.

[64] Leonard, *Olmsted County*, 160; *Rochester Post*, October 4, 1889, p. 2; *Mayo Clinic and Foundation*, 6–18, 22.

In 1905 began an expansion of the Mayo Clinic which is still going on but which, for the present purpose, will be closely followed only for a decade. In that year a third operating room was opened and an assistant surgeon placed in charge. The number of operations for the year rose to 3,836, and from year to year thereafter the number of surgeons, operating rooms, and operations increased steadily. In 1914 there were 11,933 operations.[65]

From the beginning the Mayos had considered general diagnosis — the detection of diseases from obvious physical conditions, such as the pulse, the temperature, the color of the skin, and so forth — of capital importance and carried it on in ways as old as Galen. It was not until 1905 that they were able to command the space and employ an expert for a laboratory where, by chemical analyses, the microscope, and the Roentgen ray, or "X ray," apparatus, diagnosis could be extended far beyond that possible with the unaided eye, hand, and ear. The result was an avalanche of people resorting to Rochester to be examined and told what ailed them. To accommodate the increasing throngs and to house the laboratories, a special clinical building was erected with waiting, registering, consultation, record, and minor-treatment rooms. During the daily clinic hours expert clerks registered the arrivals and assigned them to the appropriate departments for preliminary examinations. The opening of the laboratories and the consequent influx of people with nearly all kinds of diseases, real or fancied, for diagnosis was followed by an expansion of the clinic, first in the field of general medicine and later in that of particular diseases. Numerous additions were made to the staff, now occupied not merely with diagnoses, but also with the treatment of patients who remained in the hospitals of Rochester.[66]

As the numbers of patients resorting to the clinic for diagnosis, operations, and treatment in the hospitals multi-

[65] Mayo Clinic and Foundation, 19, 31, 117. Pages 71 to 91 contain an account of the development of special laboratories.
[66] Mayo Clinic and Foundation, 51-54, 71-73.

plied, there was an increasing need for assistants to the surgeons at the operating tables and for internes in the hospitals. There was no difficulty in recruiting them from graduates of medical schools. They naturally formed a group, partly for social reasons but also for mutual stimulation in their studies. The chiefs of the clinic arranged a three-year course for them to follow: a year of pathology, another of clinical diagnosis, and a third of surgery or internal medicine, and called the young men "Fellows of the Mayo Clinic." There were thirty-six fellows in 1912. Probably without seriously planning it, the Mayos had built up an incipient graduate medical school. But the clinic had no standing as an educational institution; it could confer no degrees and award no honors. It chanced that a large proportion of the fellows were graduates of the medical school of the University of Minnesota, and some of them were promoted to the staff. Some of them must have understood that the title "fellow" traditionally belonged to university men working in advanced studies and aspiring to higher degrees or other marks of distinction and was therefore a misnomer.[67]

Dr. William J. Mayo was appointed a regent of the university in 1907. As the graduate work was developing at Rochester it was an easy matter for him to inquire why the university might not extend its authority over it, hold examinations, confer degrees, and thus give the clinic a university status. At any rate, it is of record that he did. The idea of an affiliation between the two institutions had been entertained by members of the university faculty and a correspondence was initiated in February, 1914. An obstacle was at once encountered. The Mayo Clinic was not a corporate body with which a contract could be conveniently made. The obstacle was removed at the suggestion of President George E. Vincent. On February 8, 1915, the "Mayo Foundation for Medical Education and Research" was duly incorporated

[67] *Mayo Clinic and Foundation*, 141–143.

under the laws of Minnesota. In anticipation of an arrangement to be made, the Drs. Mayo as " founders " on February 9, 1915, placed in the hands of three trustees interest-bearing securities to the sum of $1,500,000. The contemplated merger was effected on June 9, 1915, by a contract in which the board of regents of the University of Minnesota engaged to appoint professors and instructors to carry on at Rochester a part of the university's graduate medical instruction and research. The foundation on its part undertook to furnish rooms, furniture, instruments, apparatus, and medical and surgical supplies for its part of the graduate instruction and research and also to pay the salaries of the Mayo Foundation professors and instructors and the wages of all nonprofessional employees. The foundation further agreed that if the contract should not have been terminated before September 21, 1921 — six years — the whole endowment should vest in the university. The regents thereupon appointed six Mayo professors, eleven associate professors, and the same number of assistant professors. The annexation thus took legal effect.[68]

The innovation met with slight approval from the medical faculty of the university, and some members opposed it violently. With such a body of experts as composed the Mayo faculty, with such facilities for instruction and research as the foundation could offer, with unlimited clinical opportunities, and with a large number of paying positions for graduate students, they foresaw the emigration of their alumni to Rochester. There was lively opposition to the proposed affiliation by many alumni of the university, who regarded it as an abnormal alliance of public and private agencies. A bill forbidding the regents to delegate any of the teaching functions of the university to any person, firm, or corporation not under their exclusive control was passed by the state Senate by a vote of 36 to 31. It reached the House on the last day but one of the session and no action was

68 *Mayo Clinic and Foundation*, 144, 146–149, 158–170.

taken. The regents listened patiently to protests and remonstrances, took time for deliberation, and decided by a vote without a nay that it was the duty of the university and the state to accept the offered endowment, apply it to the high purpose of advancing medical science and skill, and thus promote the health and comfort of the people.[69]

The scheme went into actual effect with the beginning of the college year 1915–16 and the results of the year's experiment were gratifying to the regents and the founders, but not to some of the persons who had opposed the affiliation in 1915. At their instance a bill was introduced into the state Senate on March 8, 1917, requiring the regents of the university to dissolve the agreement with the Mayo Foundation. On April 5 the committee on education reported the bill favorably, but it did not reach a test vote. While there was at no time the least danger of its passage, undue alarm and apprehension were excited. The Twin City newspapers published numerous articles and editorials denouncing the bill. A number of these were reprinted and distributed to the members of the legislature. On the evening of March 23, Dr. William J. Mayo made an address at a public hearing in the Senate chamber, which, loudly applauded, gave the bill its coup de grace.

The attack was not without result, however. The Mayo brothers, desirous of placing their donation out of danger of such attacks and of proving their good faith, were willing

[69] Mayo Clinic and Foundation, 147; Senate Journal, 1915, p. 1405; House Journal, 1769; Minneapolis Morning Tribune, February 9, 1915, p. 1; June 10, 1915, p. 1; Olmsted County Democrat, June 11, 1915, p. 4. The Minneapolis Journal, March 23, 1915, p. 11, and the Minneapolis Morning Tribune, May 12, 1915, p. 1, contain accounts of an open hearing before the executive committee of the board of regents and lists of objections to the plan. Objections offered orally or in print were such as these: The Mayo Foundation could not be separated from the Mayo Clinic, which was commercial in character and a finite body. The Mayos were making no gift, but were merely using the board as their agent. They were already conducting a graduate medical school at Rochester and had no need to dismember the university medical graduate school. The university ought not to grant to a private corporation the right of teaching as a special privilege. The Mayo firm was securing scholastic powers, the sponsorship of the university, and the state's

to make concessions to objectors, especially to those who opposed the permanent location at Rochester. They therefore, on July 2, submitted a new proposition, which the regents, on September 13, 1917, accepted and ratified by contract. The surgeons legally cancelled their trusteeship of their endowment fund and gave the augmented sum of $1,656,072 outright to the university, with the following conditions: first, that the principal sum should be allowed to accumulate until it should reach two million dollars; second, that the foundation should be known as the " Mayo Foundation for Medical Education and Research "; third, that the fund should be kept forever invested, the income to be used for graduate medical and surgical instruction and research under the direction of the university; fourth, that Rochester, Minnesota, should be the place for carrying on such instruction, provided, however, that at any time after the lapse of twenty-five years, which would be in 1942, the board of regents, by a vote of three-fourths of all the members at a regular meeting might give notice of a proposition to discontinue work at Rochester in whole or in part, and at the expiration of three years thereafter might by the same vote cause the whole net income of the foundation fund to be expended for work carried on at, or directed from, the University of Minnesota at Minneapolis or other places, including Rochester; fifth, that the endowment fund should be kept invested in federal, state, county, or municipal securities, unless in particular cases otherwise ordered by a unanimous vote of the regents. The obvious effect of this contract was to

guaranty of their privilege without any contribution to the revenues of the university.

The controversy, which took on an acrimonious character, may be followed in the issues of the *Minnesota Alumni Weekly* of the spring of 1915. Records of the action of the board of regents in the spring and summer of 1915 on the proposed affiliation are in Board of Regents, *Minutes*, 1914–15, pp. 90a, 112, 125–133, 156, 175, 179. Dr. Richard O. Beard of Minneapolis has a collection of forty-five letters, all dated in March and April, 1917, from presidents of universities and deans and professors of medical colleges, warmly commending the affiliation of the Mayo Foundation and the University of Minnesota and deprecating its termination.

substitute for a quasi affiliation of separate institutions a branch of the medical department of the university at Rochester, with an ample endowment to secure its indefinite existence and usefulness.

On the same date the Mayo brothers, by an instrument in writing, donated to the university all the facilities of the Mayo Clinic reasonably necessary for graduate teaching and research and promised to give opportunities for clinical study in the hospitals at Rochester controlled by them. They further promised to pay all the salaries, stipends, and wages of the persons on the Mayo Foundation until the endowment should by additions from income amount to two million dollars, the regents to furnish annual budgets.[70]

From a published résumé of the educational work of the Mayo Foundation for its first ten years, from 1916 to 1925 inclusive, it appears that a definite plan was adopted and pursued for graduate medical instruction. From a large number of applicants, a small number of well-qualified men who had had at least one year's hospital residence were admitted from year to year on probation for six months. Those then found "desirable" were appointed as fellows for a year, including the probation time already spent at the foundation. Reappointments of desirable fellows were made from year to year for four years, to make the full time of service five years. No regular classes of students were formed, but seminary and conference groups assembled according to convenience. Lectures by members of the faculty or eminent men from abroad covered essential parts of the several specialties. All students were placed in small groups under individual instructors in the laboratories and at clinics; in most cases but three students were thus associ-

[70] Senate Journal, 1917, pp. 563, 1184, 1189. For newspaper accounts relating to the bill, Senate file 707, see the Minneapolis Morning Tribune, 1917: March 23, p. 1; 24, p. 11; 26, p. 1; 28, p. 1; 31, p. 14; April 2, p. 4; 3, p. 8; 5, p. 1; the Minneapolis Journal, 1917: March 9, p. 15; 24, p. 4; 25, section 2, p. 3; 26, p. 6; 27, p. 13; 28, p. 1; 30, p. 1; the St. Paul Pioneer Press, 1917: March 25, section 2, p. 1; 26, p. 10; 29, p. 1; 30, p. 5. The regents' acceptance of the offer is in the Morning Tribune, 1917: September 14, p. 11. See Board of Regents, Minutes, 1916–17, pp. 178–184, for proposed new

ated. Unless engaged in special research, every student was required to make a careful study of from a thousand to twelve hundred cases a year and to make reports thereon. Every student aspiring to a graduate degree was required to prosecute a piece of original investigation and to submit a thesis thereon.

In the ten-year period 641 different students were registered. Of that number, 493 received their stipends from the Mayo Clinic, 61 from the Mayo Foundation, and 76 from the army and navy and from other institutions, such as the Rockefeller Foundation. All the fellows were enrolled as graduate students of the University of Minnesota. Candidates for degrees were examined orally, man by man, by committees of the graduate school at Minneapolis. The board of regents awarded degrees to those who passed the examinations successfully, and the president of the university conferred the diplomas. Not all the 641 students received degrees; many were obliged to give up their opportunities. Of those remaining it is reported with apparent satisfaction that "a fairly large percentage failed of recommendation." The whole number of degrees conferred was 106, six of them the degree of doctor of philosophy and one hundred that of master of science. The latter is a qualified degree for particular subjects, such as master of science in surgery, in pediatrics, in ophthalmology, and so forth, much desired by persons already doctors of medicine, expecting to specialize in practice. The total of expenses of the foundation for the decade was $2,194,166.25, all paid by the Mayo Clinic, except $243,882.92 derived from the income of the Mayo Foundation fund.[71]

agreements for affiliation, and a letter from the president of the board, Fred B. Snyder, to the regents, explanatory and highly commendatory. See the *Minutes*, 1916–17, pp. 27–52, for the vote on the acceptance of the gift and the new agreements made. The agreements may also be found in *Laws and Regulations Governing the University of Minnesota*, 391–411. The newspaper articles distributed among the legislators were printed on six broadsides with the title *Editorial Comment on the Mayo Foundation;* a copy is in the Folwell Papers.

[71] *Mayo Clinic and Foundation*, 154–158.

The reader will desire to know something of the later history of the Mayo Clinic as one of the outstanding institutions of the state. For years all the physical properties, moneys, and good will of the clinic had been the property of the Mayo brothers as partners. As the income of the clinic mounted into large sums, they began to think less of a business profit and to regard the clinic as an institution existing for the nobler purpose of the general good of the community and, at length, of humanity. To serve the higher purpose they resolved to convert their partnership, terminable on the death of either, into a corporation having a species of legal immortality. On October 8, 1919, with seven other persons, they executed a certificate of incorporation of " The Mayo Properties Association," to last for thirty years and as much longer as the laws of Minnesota might allow. In article 2 it is declared that the general purpose of the corporation shall be " to aid and advance the study and investigation of human ailments and injuries, and the causes, prevention, relief and cure thereof, and the study and investigation of problems of hygiene, health and public welfare, and the promotion of medical, surgical, and scientific learning, skill, education and investigation, and to engage in and conduct and to aid and assist in medical, surgical, and scientific research in the broadest sense." [72]

On the date mentioned, October 8, 1919, William J. and Charles H. Mayo by deed of gift conveyed to the Mayo Properties Association " all the real estate owned and used in connection with the Mayo Clinic and all equipment, materials, furnishings, supplies, clinical material, case records, specimens, library and other personal property in the Mayo Clinic together with all its securities, moneys, book accounts, and evidences of indebtedness." The gift was subject to the contract of September 13, 1917, with the regents of the university, binding the Mayo Clinic to furnish such facilities

[72] *Mayo Clinic and Foundation*, 117, 127–132.

as might be necessary for graduate instruction and research. It was a condition of the deed that the properties conveyed should forever be kept and administered, and the business transacted, at Rochester, Minnesota.

It needs to be understood that the Mayo Properties Association did not absorb the Mayo Clinic. That institution remained and still remains as a " going concern." To it the Mayo Properties Association, as a proprietary company, leases the clinic plant and equipment, the rental to be the whole net income of the clinic as operated under the lease and to be added to the association's endowment fund. It is a condition of the deed of gift that when the endowment fund of the association shall amount to ten million dollars the income may be added to the two-million-dollar fund of the Mayo Foundation; but the endowment fund itself is to be carried in perpetuity for the protection of the foundation and its contract with the university, the ultimate beneficiary to be a class A medical school in the United States to be selected by the association when it shall be " demonstrated " that the ideals of the clinic can be so best carried out.[73]

The status of the Mayo Clinic as a leased property made necessary, or at least convenient, a change in its administrative organization. The control was vested in a governing board of the same persons principally as the incorporators of the association, a board analogous to a board of regents or trustees of a university or college. There is a faculty composed of surgeons and physicians, most of whom have been on the clinic staff for five years or more. They meet annually, elect their own officers, and nominate an executive committee, which has charge of all professional activities.[74]

Under the continued supervision of the Mayo brothers, and it may be presumed at the desire of the staff, the Mayo Clinic is carrying on its beneficent work. In the year 1928 the whole number of registrants was 76,390 and the surgical

73 *Mayo Clinic and Foundation*, 117–122.
74 *Mayo Clinic and Foundation*, 122.

operations numbered 27,379, an average of 75 a day. Continually increasing numbers of people from far and near resort to it merely for diagnosis of their ailments. Some of the pilgrims are sent home with counsel to be careful of their habits, under the advice of their family physicians; some needing minor medical treatment receive it at once; and others are sent to one of the Rochester hospitals for observation and medication as needed. It may properly be said here that none of the Rochester hospitals are owned by the Mayo Clinic and the Drs. Mayo have no financial interest in them or in the hotels. On December 31, 1928, there were sixteen hundred hospital and convalescent beds available, St. Mary's Hospital having the largest number, six hundred.

The published contributions of the members of the clinic may be found in all leading medical journals. The whole net income is now sacredly devoted to the promotion of medical, surgical, and scientific learning, skill, education, and research for the good of mankind. There will be no brighter pages in the history of Minnesota than those that record and illustrate the work of the Mayo Clinic and its founders. Rochester, Minnesota, is "the surgical Mecca famous the world over." [75]

THE EUSTIS TRUST

Since the preceding pages were written, events unlooked for have become a part of university history. One of them illustrates how a university whose primary function is to enlarge knowledge, including that of the laws of health and the means of healing diseases, may become the custodian and trustee of private endowments for charity.

In October, 1881, William Henry Eustis came to Minneapolis to live. He was born of English parents on July 17, 1847, in Jefferson County, New York. He attended local

[75] A. J. Lobb to the author, February 19, 1929, Folwell Papers. Matthew O. Foley, *The Mayo Clinic and Its Work*, 8. This pamphlet is a revision

schools and in 1873 was graduated from Wesleyan University, Connecticut, and the next year, from Columbia Law School. He became a partner in a law firm in Saratoga Springs, New York, in 1875, and continued in practice there for five years. In 1881 he traveled in Europe for a few months and then moved to Minneapolis. The late completion of his education at twenty-nine was due to a hip disease that he contracted at the age of fifteen, which caused the loss of years of time from school; but it did not prevent private study and extensive reading. He recovered sufficiently to walk with a cane, which he replaced by crutches in his last years. The affliction that enforced a regular and temperate regimen of life kept his intellect clear and strong and was a background for his never-failing cheer.[76]

The early eighties were a boom period in Minneapolis. From 1880 to 1885 its population swelled from 46,887 to 129,200.[77] It may be presumed that some successful deals in real estate during those years diverted Eustis from ordinary law practice. Indeed, throughout the rest of his career he was better known as a dealer in city property and an owner of rent-paying buildings than as an attorney. Private affairs, however, did not consume all his time and energy. An earnest Republican, he took a full share in party affairs and activities. He served as mayor of Minneapolis in 1892 and 1893 and in 1898 he was the Republican candidate for governor, but was defeated by John Lind with his following of Scandinavian admirers. He withdrew from active politics after 1900, and for many years his private affairs occupied most of his time, but frequently clubs and societies made demands upon him for addresses, which were always full of wisdom and counsel. There was much of charm in his

of an article in *Hospital Management*, September, 1923. See *Mayo Clinic and Foundation*, 22–30, for descriptions and illustrations of the hospitals.

[76] Alonzo Phelps, *Biographical History of the Northwest*, 122 (*American Biography of Representative Men*, vol. 4 — Boston, 1890); *Minnesota Alumni Weekly*, December 8, 1928, p. 212.

[77] See *ante*, 3: 480.

delivery, which was impressive when he rose to an impassioned strain.[78]

Eustis did not marry. As the years crept on toward the fourscore mark, he considered personally making a disposition of his accumulated wealth — " mostly unearned increment," he said facetiously to the author — instead of leaving it for executors to distribute. His main purpose was readily determined. For years he had had in mind the endowment of an institution for the care and cure of crippled children. After much consideration as to what agency would best conserve and manage a trust, he decided to ask the board of education of Minneapolis and the board of regents of the university to become his trustees. In March, 1923, he bought sixty-five acres of land fronting on the parkway along the west bank of the Mississippi. Twenty-one acres of the property he at once deeded to the Minneapolis board of education as the site of the Michael J. Dowling School, to be devoted to the care and education of crippled children.[79]

On June 14, 1923, Eustis, in a letter to the board of regents, submitted a proposition, which apparently had already been discussed, to deed to the board forty-four acres of land worth one hundred thousand dollars and, on or before July 1, 1927, interest- and dividend-bearing securities worth nine hundred thousand dollars, to be held by the regents in trust for the erection and endowment of a hospital and a convalescent home or homes for crippled children. He stipulated that the convalescent home be located on the river bank site, but that the hospital for clinical and surgical work might, in the discretion of the board, be built on the university campus. Medical service and the use of all equipment should be free to needy crippled children. It was

[78] See *ante*, 3: 244, 256; *Minnesota Alumni Weekly*, December 8, 1928, p. 212.

[79] Board of Regents, *Minutes*, June 19, 1923, p. 520; *Minneapolis Journal*, June 14, 1923, p. 1; November 30, 1928, p. 1; *Minneapolis Tribune*, November 30, 1928, p. 10. The sum of fifty thousand dollars was raised by citizens of the state for the building of the Dowling School, and the legislature appropriated the same amount.

his pleasure that his name should not be used in the title of the institution, and he suggested that of " Minnesota Hospital and Home for Crippled Children." Following the letter the minutes of the board read, " Voted to accept the gift in trust upon the terms and conditions expressed in the foregoing letter." [80]

On December 22, 1924, with the concurrence of the regents, Eustis changed the form of his endowment from " promised securities " to a major interest in his Flour Exchange and Corn Exchange buildings, thereby increasing his gift to $1,500,000. In 1926 he again enlarged it by deeding his remaining interest in the buildings. The rentals were also added to the endowment. In his report for the year ending on June 30, 1928, the comptroller of the university stated that the Eustis trust fund amounted to $2,122,749.26.[81]

On November 10, 1928, the corner stone of the Minnesota Hospital for Crippled Children was laid with impressive ceremony on the extended university campus near the intersection of Seventeenth Avenue and Delaware Street. Dr. Charles H. Mayo, of Rochester, in the principal address remarked that Eustis would be honored forever, not only as a benefactor of children but also as a great contributor to education and scientific progress. " He thought," said Dr. Mayo, " of the future of education in Minnesota when he stipulated that this hospital, his gift to unfortunate children, should be located at the University, the center of education in the state." It appeared from other addresses that it was the expectation that the hospital would be conducted " on the highest order," and that Eustis had left to the discretion of the regents the modification of details regarding its use.[82]

[80] Board of Regents, *Minutes*, June 19, 1923, p. 520; *Minneapolis Journal*, June 14, 1923, p. 1.

[81] Board of Regents, *Minutes*, January 23, 1925, p. 401; April 1, 1926, p. 162; Comptroller, *Reports*, 1928, p. 138 (University of Minnesota, *Bulletins*, vol. 31, no. 57).

[82] *Minnesota Alumni Weekly*, December 1, 1928, p. 195. The children's hospital forms a wing of the addition to the Elliott Memorial Hospital recently erected at a cost of nearly a million dollars.

The occasion was saddened by the absence of the donor, who was not well enough to attend. His illness, essentially a heart trouble, rapidly advanced beyond medical control and on the afternoon of November 30, Thanksgiving Day, William Henry Eustis died peacefully in his rooms at the Radisson Hotel, where his home had been for many years. The newspapers of the next day contained obituary notices and numerous eulogies. There was general mourning in Minneapolis.[83]

THE REVOLUTION OF 1928

In a previous volume of this work brief mention has been made of an act passed by the legislature of 1925 " in relation to the organization of the state government," which provided for the creation of a commission of administration and finance. This commission was given " power to supervise and control the accounts and expenditures of the several officials, departments, and agencies of the state government and of the institutions under their control; the making of all contracts . . . the purchase, rental, or furnishing of all property, equipment, supplies, or materials . . . the construction and erection of all buildings and structures by or for the state or any such department, agency, or institution." The commission was empowered also " to determine the classes, grades, and titles of the employes of the various officials, departments, and agencies of the state government and the institutions under their control" and to establish salary scales for the various classes. The commission was to consist of three members to be appointed by the governor with the consent of the Senate, and any member might be removed by the governor " without cause." The governor was authorized to make a survey of the various departments, agencies, and institutions, " to the end that greater efficiency and economy " might be secured.

[83] *Minneapolis Tribune*, November 30, 1928, pp. 1, 10, 11; *Minneapolis Journal*, November 30, 1928, pp. 1, 18.

The act required every department, official, or agency to submit, not later than the first day of September preceding the convening of the legislature, estimates on prescribed forms for all desired receipts and expenditures for each year of the succeeding biennium. These estimates were to be subject to approval, disapproval, or alteration by the commission. The governor was charged with submitting to the legislature the consolidated budget, with his recommendations in detail of the amounts to be appropriated for the several departments, officials, and agencies. For the greater check and control of the departments, officials, agencies, and institutions, it was provided that no appropriation should be available for any quarterly period of a fiscal year until after estimates should have been submitted for each activity during the quarter and approved by the commission. The act took effect in regard to appointments upon its passage, on April 25, 1925, and in other respects, on July 1, the beginning of a fiscal year and a biennium.[84]

The University of Minnesota was nowhere mentioned in the law, but it was at once understood that the new commissioners would presume that it was one of the institutions under their control. The regents deemed it their duty to enter protest against such control. In a communication to the commission, dated June 29, 1925, three days before the law took general effect, the regents gave notice that they would submit budgets for pre-audit, but with the express understanding that their acquiescence, not only as to budgets, but as to any rule, regulation, or demand by the commission, was not to be construed as a waiver of the constitutional rights of the university. On July 9, 1925, the estimate for the quarter beginning on July 1 was submitted by the comptroller of the university, and quarterly estimates were regularly furnished for three years. The first biennial budget of the university requirements for the years 1927 and 1928 was submitted on November 24, 1926. The gross amount asked

[84] See *ante*, 3: 321, and *Laws*, 1925, pp. 756–773.

for was $7,491,446. The commission disapproved items to the amount of $691,446.[85]

It was not merely the reduction in the amount of the university budget that aroused adverse criticism and further protest by the board of regents, which were voiced in the report of the president of the university for 1926–27 and approved by the board. The policy of the act of 1925 was also challenged. Control of the financing of the institution by the commission, said the president, would reduce the regents to a mere advisory organ to a superboard without skill or experience in the management of a university. Objection was made to turning over to the commission the control of university funds derived from the federal government, of the income from trust funds for specific purposes, and of fees from students. The suggestion was renewed that the university, under the state constitution, was, or ought to be, immune from control by any commission created by law.[86]

The commission was composed of very able, fair-minded citizens who had no desire to control and manage the vast and multifarious affairs of a great modern university, except so far as that duty was required of them by law. Friendly conversations took place in which the governor participated, and an understanding was reached that on some convenient occasion the controversy should be taken to the courts. Such an occasion was at hand.

For some years retired members of university faculties had enjoyed peace and comfort through the Carnegie retiring allowances. According to notice given, the trustees of the

[85] The author to William T. Middlebrook, comptroller of the university, December 16, 20, 1928, with replies interlined, Folwell Papers; Board of Regents, *Minutes*, 1924–25, p. 519; State of Minnesota on Relation of University of Minnesota and the Board of Regents of the University of Minnesota v. Ray P. Chase, State Auditor, *Record*, 13 (Minnesota Supreme Court, no. 26,800). This will be cited hereafter as *Record*.

[86] University of Minnesota, *President's Report*, 1926–27, pp. 16–23 (University of Minnesota, *Bulletins*, vol. 30, no. 88). Federal aid for the year amounted to $293,633.31; students' fees, to $1,045,348.83; the Mayo endowment, to $2,129,645.76; the Eustis endowment, to $2,121,800.00; the Murphy endowment, to $410,444.00; and sundry trust fund investments, to $400,027.00. See *Comptroller's Report*, 1927–28, pp. 8, 10, 42, 67, 73 (University of Minne-

Carnegie Foundation ceased to grant allowances to college and university teachers employed after November 17, 1915. Within a few years thereafter colleges and universities, said to be 132 in number, made provisions for pensioning their faculty members of advanced age after long terms of service. Positions in such institutions were desirable, and some resignations from the faculties of the University of Minnesota took place. With such competition it was obvious that some kind of pension system was necessary. A faculty committee labored for two years upon a scheme, which it is unnecessary to describe here, for so-called "staff insurance" against death, disability, and old age for teachers and employees. The board of regents, by resolution, approved the plan on June 8, 1926, and in a quarterly budget estimate for the period from July 1 to September 30, 1927, asked for forty-five thousand dollars to put it into operation. The commission denied the request because it would increase the expenses of the state, especially if the plan should be extended — and it was probable that it might be — first to other state educational institutions and later to all state employees.[87]

On July 19, 1927, the regents voted an appropriation of forty-five thousand dollars, from funds claimed to be rightly under their control, to put the insurance plan into effect. To perfect some of the details of the plan, on August 2 they employed Charles H. Preston and Company, reputed experts in insurance business. That company presented a bill of fifty dollars for its services. Three days later, on August 5, the university comptroller, as authorized, demanded of the state auditor a warrant on the state treasurer for its pay-

sota, *Bulletins*, vol. 31, no. 57). In a letter from President Coffman to the regents, September 8, 1926, in Board of Regents, *Minutes*, 1926–27, pp. 281–289, statements in his report for 1926–27 are anticipated. "Apparently," said the president, "the commission is of the opinion that the university should operate on a fixed budget. . . . It spells mediocrity and stagnation for the university."

[87] *President's Report*, 1925–26, p. 39 (University of Minnesota. *Bulletins*, vol. 29, no. 53); Board of Regents, *Minutes*, 1926–27, pp. 285–287; *Record*, 17–20.

ment. The auditor at once declined to issue the warrant because the expenditure had not been approved by the commission of administration and finance. On September 28, 1927, the regents in a regular meeting directed their executive officers to bring suit against the auditor.[88]

The prosecution began in the form of a petition, dated October 17, 1927, to the district court of Ramsey County for a writ of mandamus commanding Ray P. Chase, state auditor, to draw his warrant for the payment of the fifty dollars claimed. The petition alleged that the University of Minnesota, a corporation created by the legislature of 1851 and confirmed and perpetuated by section 4 of article 8 of the state constitution, had full and exclusive control of university property and moneys. It was set forth in detail that the value of the property of the university was $30,500,000 and that the income from all sources for the year 1927–28 was $2,208,000, exclusive of state appropriations. It was denied that the commission of administration and finance had any authority to supervise, control, or disallow the expenditures of the university and, in particular, to forbid the state auditor to draw his warrant for the fifty-dollar claim.[89]

The answer to the university petition, made by the attorney-general and dated December 2, 1927, in form on behalf of the state auditor, in fact on behalf of the commission of administration and finance, admitted all allegations of historical facts in the petition and asserted that, under the act of 1925, the commission alone had authority " to supervise and control the expenditure of any and all moneys in the state treasury available for the support, maintenance and operation of the university, or for the use and benefit thereof." Notable allegations were those that the public institution created in 1851 and perpetuated by the constitution in 1857 was not and is not a corporation, and that the univer-

[88] Board of Regents, *Minutes*, 1927–28, p. 45; *Record*, 34–35.
[89] *Record*, 3–16; *Laws*, 1851, p. 142; 1927, p. 670.

sity authorities for sixty-five years had at all times recognized the power of the legislature to reorganize the institution, to change its board of regents, and to direct the actions of the regents. More than forty instances were cited.[90]

The case was heard in the district court of Ramsey County on December 3 and 10, 1927, and was decided on February 8, 1928, by an order that a writ of mandamus issue commanding the state auditor to draw his warrant for the payment of the fifty-dollar voucher. The order was accompanied by an elaborate memorandum of the considerations upon which it was founded. The sober recital of facts and legal principles in the memorandum, supported by numerous cited authorities, was enlivened by occasional *obiter dicta* of impressive character. Following a statement that the act of 1925 clothed the governor with power to appoint the commission of administration and finance, with senatorial consent, arbitrarily to remove any member at any time " without cause," and to review the orders and rulings of the commission under certain circumstances, the remark was made that "no such power was conceded by the people to Czar or Iron Chancellor, nor asserted by such." Referring to the assertion of the commission that it had authority to supervise and control the finances of the university, the court said that the ultimate control of the institution would be "not by a board with special knowledge of the needs of an educational institution, but by a commission with many interests to look after and with a necessarily limited knowledge of the needs of an educational institution; not by a board with no conflicting duties, but by a commission with state-wide duties; not by a board with continuity of office, but by a commission likely to change whenever a new governor is elected; not by a board that will have continuity of policy, but by a commission whose policies will change as the governor changes; not by a board which will formulate policies in the sole interests of the educational institution, but by a com-

[90] *Record*, 22–30.

mission which will formulate policies with a view to many diverse interests; not by a board that will be free from political influences, but by a commission whose outlook is necessarily political; not by a board in whom private individuals will have such confidence that they will make gifts to the institution, but by a commission which will be recognized as necessarily participants in politics." Another dictum, emphasized by italics, was that *"The tendency to sacrifice established principles of constitutional government in order to secure centralized control and high efficiency in administration may easily be carried so far as to endanger the very foundations upon which our system of government rests."* [91]

It was understood that an appeal would be taken to the state supreme court so that an end could be put to the controversy forever. Notice of appeal was given by the attorney-general on February 27, 1928, and service was acknowledged on the same day. On June 7 the case was argued before the supreme court, which on July 27, 1928, filed its decision, closing curtly, " Judgment affirmed." The essential memorable point of the argued decision was that the state constitution adopted in 1857, by declaring the existing (territorial) university to be the university of the state of Minnesota and by perpetuating to the said university all rights, immunities, franchises, and endowments, perpetuated the then existing institution as a corporation of which " the regents were both the sole members and the governing board." " So we find," said the court, " the people of the state, speaking through their constitution, have invested the regents with a power of management of which no legislature may deprive them." The admitted notorious fact that for seventy years " the legislature, beginning as early as 1860, has taken all manner of liberties with university management " and the acquiescence of the university therein did not annul the will

[91] *Record,* 38–101.

THE REVOLUTION OF 1928

of the people declared in plain and unmistakable words in
the constitution.

The implications of a favorable decision of the case must
have been understood by the university lawyers, and the regents may have been prepared for a decree that might nullify their very existence as a legitimate governing board.
The newspaper announcement astonished the public. The
court held that the university that had been perpetuated was
that which had been established by the legislature of 1851
and which was doing business, if not keeping school, while
the constitutional conventions were sitting — a university
governed by a corporate board of regents elected by the legislature. It was obvious that the regents in 1928 were not successors in office to those originally elected in 1851.[92]

That a university with more than twenty-five thousand students should be left without a regency to govern and manage
it was not to be thought of, but the question of how to legitimate the existing regency was a puzzle. The problem was
happily solved by the attorney-general. In a letter to Fred
B. Snyder, president of the board of regents, on August 17,
1928, he stated that, under the decision of the supreme court,
the organization of the board was controlled by the law
of 1851, and the legislature could not change it. Regents
must be elected by the legislature. But the same law provided that whenever there should be a vacancy in the board
of regents of the university from any cause whatever, it
should be the duty of the governor to fill it by appointment.
The regents in office in 1928 had been appointed according

[92] *Record*, 106; 175 *Minnesota*, 259–275; Constitution, article 8, section 4.
The court remarked that the real issue of the suit was between the regents
and the governor. The author attended the session. An article by Everett
Frazer, dean of the law school, in the *Minnesota Alumni Weekly*, October
13, 1928, p. 73, gives an excellent résumé of the case. The attorneys for the
university were Charles W. Bunn of St. Paul and Dean Frazer. Attorney-
General G. A. Youngquist conducted the defense. For an exhaustive discussion of the advantage of the independent control of university income by
a permanent governing board as compared with control by a legislature or
a finance commission, see *President's Report*, 1927–28, pp. 5–16 (University
of Minnesota, *Bulletins*, vol. 31, no. 56).

to that law, but an election must take place at the meeting of the next legislature in 1929. In the same letter the attorney-general advised the board to conform to the law of 1851 and, by resolution, to designate the president of the university as chancellor. Accordingly, on August 17, 1928, President Lotus D. Coffman was authorized to act as chancellor of the university, which title he now holds.[93]

In the spring of 1929 the legislature bestirred itself to provide for a joint nominating committee, which, according to the law of 1851, submitted the names of twelve persons for membership on the board of regents. On the afternoon of April 3 the Senate and the House met in joint session for the purpose of voting. Two additional lists were submitted by Representatives Youngdahl and Stockwell, respectively. The legislators were also privileged to vote for any person of their choice. The result of the vote was the election of nine former members of the board — Egil Boeckmann, Julius A. Coller, Samuel Lewison, William J. Mayo, George H. Partridge, Fred B. Snyder, J. E. G. Sundberg, John G. Williams, and Bess M. Wilson — and of three new members — W. H. Gemmell, A. J. Olson, and L. O. Teigen. These twelve constitute the " governing board " of the University of Minnesota at the present time.[94]

[93] Laws, 1851, p. 142; Board of Regents, Minutes, 1928-29, p. 253.
[94] House Journal, April 3, 1929, pp. 2, 14-23.

III. PUBLIC EDUCATION

The Establishment of the Public School System

ARTICLE 3 of the "Ordinance for the government of the territory of the United States northwest of the river Ohio," commonly called the Northwest Territory, begins with the words, "Religion, morality, and knowledge, being necessary to good government and the happiness of mankind, schools and the means of education shall forever be encouraged." In furtherance of this obligation, Congress in 1802 granted to the state of Ohio, the first to be carved out of the Northwest Territory, upon its admission to the Union, one section — 640 acres — of public land in each township for the support of schools. Similar donations were made to Indiana, Illinois, Michigan, and Wisconsin as they severally came into the Union. To Minnesota, when it was made a territory, the customary grant was generously doubled. Delegate Sibley must be credited with obtaining this munificent reservation, which he says could not "have been secured if the impression had not been general in Congress that the soil and climate were alike unsuited to the production of cereals and vegetables, and the land therefore of little value." The delegate seems not to have exerted himself to remove that impression.[1]

The people of the new territory were not indifferent to the value of school education and to the munificence of the federal government. In his message to the first territorial legislature, which convened on September 3, 1849, Governor

[1] Donaldson, *Public Domain*, 155, 224, 228; Nathaniel West, *The Ancestry, Life, and Times of Hon. Henry Hastings Sibley, LL.D.*, 122 (St. Paul, 1889); United States, *Statutes at Large*, 9: 408. The land ordinance of 1785 provided that there should be reserved "the lot No. 16, of every township, for the maintenance of public schools, within the said township." Orfield, *Federal Land Grants*, 37.

Ramsey expressed his expectation that the subject of education would receive the "earliest and most devoted care" of that body. On October 9 Martin McLeod, chairman of the Council committee on schools, submitted a memorable report. "The strength and true glory of the commonwealth," it reads, "must rest at last on the intelligence and virtue of its citizens. . . . The diffusion of knowledge is . . . one of those great purposes for which all should be taxed for the common good. . . . Man should be educated for eternity." In particular, "the sublime truths and precepts of Christianity should be impressively urged, and clearly explained, as presented in the Bible, and as taught and illustrated by its Divine Author." While common schools should be the primary concern, higher education should be kept in view in all legislation. The bill that was passed authorized county commissioners to levy a tax of one-fourth of one per cent for the support of schools. Any township having five resident families was declared a school district, and the school funds were to be apportioned according to the number of pupils in each district. District clerks were required to make a census of all persons in their districts between the ages of four and twenty-one.[2]

Governor Ramsey repeated to the next legislature, that of 1851, his exhortation of 1849 and, as if such argument was still necessary, he asserted that "the principle that society is bound to provide for its members, education as well as protection, is the most important that belongs to modern philosophy. This indeed lies at the foundation and constitutes the platform of our republican system." That legislature passed a notable act for St. Paul. It provided that school district number 2 should be the "St. Paul Institute," to be governed by six elected trustees. Its primary department was to be a free common school, to which might be added a normal school and a department of literature,

[2] *Council Journal*, 1849, pp. 13, 68–70, 113, 132, 160; *House Journal*, 144, 149, 162; *Laws*, 41–43.

science, and arts. The trustees were authorized to confer
degrees and grant diplomas such as those given by colleges
and universities. Such was the first university charter
granted by a Minnesota legislature. Premature and impracticable as it was, it reveals a hope and an aspiration that
did honor to the infant capital city.[3]

During the remaining years of the territorial period the
Minnesota schools were conducted on the neighborhood
district plan, to which the people had been accustomed in
the older states from which they had emigrated. In the bifur-
cated constitutional convention of 1857 the question of the
unit of school administration came up, to be immediately
subordinated to and confused with the matter of handling
the school lands reserved by Congress. In the Republican
assemblage, which was the first to take up school matters, a
motion to amend the report of the committee on educational
interests by substituting a township system for the district
unit prevailed. A proposition to intrust the disposal of the
school lands to the authorities of the several counties, debated
at length, received but five votes in its favor. The adoption
of a judiciously framed substitute for the elaborate report
of the committee left the whole subject of the school system
and the school lands to the legislature.[4]

The committee of the Democratic body brought in a report
containing a section beginning, " The proceeds of lands . . .
granted by the United States for the use of schools within
each Township in this State shall remain a perpetual fund."
The debate had not gone far before William Pitt Murray
asked what might be the meaning of that sentence. Willis
A. Gorman replied that it meant that each township should
have control of the particular sections within its limits and

[3] *Council Journal*, 1851, p. 15; *Laws*, 12. In 1852 the legislature required
district schools to be in session for three months in the year in order to
share in the apportionment of county school funds. Minnesota Territory,
Amendments to the Revised Statutes [of 1851], 32 (St. Paul, 1852).

[4] *Debates and Proceedings* (Republican), 231, 235–237, 249, 250–258. See
page 234 for Representative Lyle's substitute for the report of the committee.

that there should not be a common resulting fund. That
policy he opposed in an able speech. Sibley defended it.
He was not in favor of a magnificent school fund in the control of a board of commissioners in St. Paul. In less than
a quarter of a century but little would be left of it. Sibley's
counsel prevailed and the clause remained unchanged. The
conference committee that patched together the articles
threshed out in the two convention bodies incorporated the
Democratic draft almost entire, but modified the clause
quoted above by adding to the words, " shall remain a perpetual fund," the three words, " to the state." A separate
section of the constitution required the legislature to establish an efficient system of public schools in each township
in the state.⁵

The first state legislature, elected in October, 1857,
opened its adjourned session on June 2, 1858. Governor
Sibley in his inaugural message reminded the lawmakers
of the provision in the constitution that the fund to be derived
from the congressional grant for schools must " forever be
preserved inviolate and undiminished." The fund, he said,
was " a sacred gift," and, " if wisely fostered," the state
would " possess ample means for all time to come for the
education of her children." He made no suggestion in regard
to the unit of school land administration. The session was
a busy one. Much time was devoted to inventing a process
for extracting from the state treasury ten thousand dollars
for postage and stationery constructively used by the legislators. But school matters were at length taken up. On July
28 a House bill for the organization of common schools,
which had been previously reported, was considered in committee of the whole. It was not until August 11, the last
day but one of the session, that a vote on its passage was
reached. There was but one vote in the negative. The Senate
passed the bill with but two nays. It provided for township

⁵ *Debates and Proceedings* (Democratic), 437–444, 464, 595–600, 614, 617,
632, 664.

boards of education, with power to subdivide the townships into districts and to employ teachers and collect taxes to pay them.[6] A companion bill providing for the sale of the school sections in each township, the holding of the invested proceeds in the town treasury, and the pledge of all the property of the township for its safe-keeping was passed on the same day with trifling opposition. Both bills went to Governor Sibley on August 12 and would have become law had he not put an emphatic veto on them.[7]

At the opening of the legislative session of 1860 Governor Sibley in his retiring message informed the legislators that many sections of school lands were being trespassed upon and that the timber on them was being destroyed. Governor Ramsey in his inaugural message urged that the lands be protected from depredation and advised that they should not be sold immediately at a sacrifice. The situation was not changed by that legislature, however.[8]

The third state legislature, that of 1861, took up the subjects of schools and school lands with energy and enacted a school code of sixty-nine sections. Every township was made a school district. The town supervisors were made school trustees ex officio. The town clerks and treasurers were also to act as school officials. The town boards were to employ teachers for the schools of the subdistricts and to appoint town superintendents to examine teachers and visit the schools. It is perhaps unfortunate that a township plan could not have been given a trial. The people of that day, however, preferred the old neighborhood plan and the legislature of 1862 restored it. It has remained in operation to the present time.[9]

[6] See ante, 2: 30–33; House Journal, 1857–58, pp. 600, 607, 924, 939, 1080; and Senate Journal, 731.
[7] House Journal, 1857–58, pp. 1058, 1082; Senate Journal, 731; Daily Pioneer and Democrat (St. Paul), 1858: August 15, p. 2; 21, p. 2. See the House Journal, 927–929, for proposed plans for the sale of school lands.
[8] Henry H. Sibley, Message, December 7, 1859, p. 18; Alexander Ramsey, Message, January 2, 1860, p. 20.
[9] General Laws, 1861, pp. 54–73; 1862, pp. 18–30; Sanford Niles, "The

Sibley's veto of the absurd bills of 1858 left the administration of the school lands in the air until three years later. By that time the idea of the lands being held and the funds handled by the townships had become ridiculous. Governor Ramsey in his message to the legislature of 1861 voiced what was probably the better sentiment. These lands, he said, are "the noble heritage of which Providence has made us the trustees for their [*our children's*] benefit." Moved by the governor's fervent appeal to place the lands in the hands of the state, the legislature passed an act providing for a state board of commissioners of school lands, with power to sell or lease land and invest the resulting fund. The board was to consist of the governor, the attorney-general, and the state superintendent of public instruction. The life and work of that board was cut short by a legislative act of 1862, mentioned in an earlier volume, which established a state land office and made the state auditor the commissioner of all public lands, including the school lands. The policy of reposing so vast an interest in a single official, who was already burdened with duties and whose principal duty was inconsistent with that trust, has not been so beneficent as to exclude the surmise that the earlier policy might have been more so. The legislature of 1862 did not follow Governor Ramsey's counsel in regard to the minimum price at which the school lands should be sold and the payments made. He suggested a price of eight dollars an acre, one-fourth of the purchase price to be paid in cash and the remainder to run for thirty years or more at seven per cent interest. The legislature made the minimum price five dollars an acre, fifteen per cent to be paid at the time of purchase and the remainder to run for twenty years. The legislature apparently desired to stimulate early sales, which Governor Ram-

Common Schools," in Greer, *Education in Minnesota*, 23. For outlines of a proposed school law for Minnesota by Benjamin F. Crary, see Superintendent of Public Instruction, *Reports*, 1861, pp. 157–179. This model law, with a few important changes, was followed closely by the legislature.

sey clearly did not desire. Pine lands were to be paid for in full.[10]

The Development of High Schools

When Governor Sibley in his message of June 3, 1858, suggested that the income from the congressional school land grant would, if preserved inviolate and undiminished and wisely managed, be ample for the schooling of all the children of the state for all time to come, he doubtless had in mind conditions in his early days, when higher education was obtained, like his own, from private teachers or in private institutions and only elementary schooling was expected of public schools. But in older states advances had been made toward higher education in public schools, and, as we have seen, Martin McLeod had declared that all school legislation in Minnesota should have high schools and academies in view. The forward movement in Minnesota began in some of the villages and cities created by special legislative charters in territorial days. In general such municipalities were made, by separate acts, single "special school districts," with school boards empowered to manage all the schools of the districts. The boards were authorized to build schoolhouses, to employ teachers, to make rules and regulations, and, in some cases, to levy taxes for school purposes. In the larger places "union schools" were soon organized, in which higher grades were formed for pupils who had got beyond the common school branches. To have those pupils schooled in their home communities was satisfactory to parents and at length the public was reconciled to the policy. High schools were thus quietly developed

---

[10] See *ante*, 3:500; Ramsey, *Message*, January 9, 1861, pp. 14–19; and *General Laws*, 1861, pp. 79–94; 1862, pp. 18–30, 121–132. For the proceedings of the meeting of the state board of commissioners of public lands and the state board of commissioners of school lands on April 1, 1861, see State Auditor, *Reports*, 1861, pp. 19–25. The commissioners were Alexander Ramsey, Gordon E. Cole, and Edward D. Neill.

and they became an accepted part of the public school system.[11]

There were villages and, later, cities, however, that were organized under general incorporation laws of various dates. As some of them increased in wealth and population, the residents desired for their children school advantages equal to those of the special districts. An act of 1865 authorized any city, town, or village to organize as " an independent school district " and to elect a school board empowered to manage the schools in all respects, to establish grades, and to employ teachers. The right to establish high schools in independent districts was questioned, but it has never been legally challenged in Minnesota. High schools multiplied but slowly while the state was young and poor, but with growing prosperity and the additional stimulation of state aid, they have increased rapidly. In 1928 there were 256 high schools, 210 " high school departments " in graded schools, and 66 junior high schools in the state.[12]

School Taxes

The legislature of 1862 firmly established the district system of public schools, which includes all the public schools of the state except the normal schools and the univer-

[11] See ante, 1:161; Sibley, Message, June 3, 1858, p. 11; Council Journal, 1849, p. 69; General Laws, 1865, pp. 37–46; Amendments to the Revised Statutes [of 1851], 33, and House Journal, 1859–60, p. 697. St. Paul and Minneapolis furnish examples of special school districts. See Kiehle, Education in Minnesota, part 2, p. 59, for the substance of the original acts. Under a charter adopted in 1900, since amended, the public schools of St. Paul are managed by a member of the city council designated by the mayor as commissioner of education. The council reserves the supreme direction, levies the school taxes, and appropriates the proceeds. St. Paul still constitutes a special school district. See Special Laws, 1856, pp. 91–93; 1868, pp. 319–322; City of St. Paul, Charter, 1900, pp. 71–75; 1905, pp. 114–121; 1920, p. 88. See Superintendent of Public Instruction, Reports, 1877, pp. 45–51, for a history of the evolution of the public high schools in older states. An unpublished doctoral dissertation by Hugh Graham on "The History of Secondary Education in Minnesota" (University of Minnesota, 1929) was not available when this chapter was written.

[12] General Laws, 1865, p. 37; Superintendent of Public Instruction, Reports, 1878, p. 18; Department of Education, Financial Statement and Public School Statistics, 1927–28; Kiehle, Education in Minnesota, part 1, pp. 94–99; Rankin,

sity; it also confirmed the policy of merging the proceeds of
the lands granted by Congress for the support of schools
into a " permanent school fund," to remain forever undiminished and to be administered and conserved by state officials.
Probably no later legislature has failed to make some
enlargement or modification of the school laws. The purpose
of this history will be better fulfilled by an account of the
salient modifications without adherence to order of time,
than by a catalogue of the statutes and rulings.

The financial support of the public schools has ever been
by taxation, local or general. The basic local tax is the
district school tax. The prevailing reason for adherence to
the traditional district system is doubtless the desire of the
people to fix in primary assemblage the amount of the common school taxes, instead of leaving that duty to a board of
a larger jurisdiction. Accordingly, the district school tax
for a common school district has always been voted at the
annual school meeting by the legal voters of the district.
If, however, the meeting fails to levy a tax sufficient to maintain a school for five months, the district board is required by
law to do so. There are separate levies for the support of the
schools and for acquiring school grounds and erecting and
furnishing buildings. The latter is often spoken of as a
special school tax. The rate of the district school tax has
always been limited by law. At the present time the limit is
thirty mills for the support of common schools in common
school districts and ten mills for other purposes, such as
the purchase of school sites and the erection and equipment
of buildings. In independent districts the boards of education levy the taxes, and the only restriction is that not more
than eight mills may be levied for school grounds and build-

in Greer, *Education in Minnesota*, 69–93. See Superintendent of Public
Instruction, *Reports*, 1878, p. 19, for a table of twenty-four special and thirty-
eight independent districts. All the reports of Superintendent David Burt
are of exceptional value. In 1876 ten larger cities had schools graded from
the primary department to the graduating class of the high school. Superintendent of Public Instruction, *Reports*, 1876, p. 74.

ings. In special districts the district school taxes are levied by the school boards, according to the special laws creating them.[13]

The act of the first territorial legislature authorizing a district school tax provided also for the levy of a county school tax and fixed the rate at two and one-half mills. That rate was reduced to two mills in 1862, and in 1875 to one mill, where it still remains. For thirteen years the amounts collected were divided among the districts in proportion to the number of children of school age and were devoted to the payment of teachers' salaries. An act of 1873 changed that principle of distribution and required that the amounts collected from the several districts be returned to them, thus converting the county school tax into an additional district tax and depriving the poorer districts of aid from the richer ones. This illiberal policy has been continued to the present time.[14]

Another general school tax is the state school tax, which was first levied in 1887, after many fruitless appeals to the legislature. Various considerations combined to secure the legislation providing for this tax, among them the need of aid for poorer districts, long deprived of help from the county school tax, and an increasing desire for the improvement of the schools. The act passed in 1887 provided for a levy of a state school tax on all the taxable property of the state at the rate of one mill. The same act provided for the application of the rational principle of distributing the fund to districts maintaining a school for four months according to the number of " scholars " actually attending school for thirty days. Within a decade this tax added more than

---

[13] *General Laws*, 1862, pp. 17–30, 132; *Laws of Minnesota Relating to the Public School System*, 1927, pp. 30, 35, 67. An act of 1921 provided that district schools must be maintained for six months in the year in order to share in the apportionment of the state fund, and an act of 1923 fixed the minimum school year at seven months. *Laws*, 1921, p. 770; 1923, p. 463.

[14] Minnesota Territory, *Laws*, 1849, pp. 41–43; *General Laws*, 1862, p. 28; 1873, p. 65; 1875, p. 59.

half a million dollars to the current school fund of the state. Some rural districts were so much enriched by the state one-mill tax that, instead of employing better teachers at good salaries, they neglected to vote the district school tax. An act of 1891 checked that neglect by providing that no district should receive more than the amount of the district tax.[15]

THE PERMANENT SCHOOL FUND

The congressional land grant for schools took legal effect upon the admission of Minnesota to the Union on May 11, 1858. The short-lived board of commissioners of school lands created in 1861 took only some preparatory steps toward selling lands. Selling began in 1862, when the state auditor became commissioner of public lands, and in that year the amount realized from the sale of lands was $242,531, which was placed to the credit of the permanent school fund. The income in that year was $12,232, which was divided among the several counties for the benefit of the 32,560 pupils enrolled. At the end of the last fiscal year of the century, July 31, 1900, the permanent school fund amounted to $12,546,599, the income from which was $658,256. The school enrollment for that year was 399,207. In the fiscal year ending on June 30, 1929, the permanent school fund was $54,358,617; the income, $4,093,838; and the school enrollment, 553,336.[16]

Since 1889 the permanent school fund, also called the "school endowment fund," has been increased by rentals from mining lands on school sections and by royalties on iron mines. Large increments will continue, but the fund will not reach hundreds of millions of dollars, as many

[15] General Laws, 1887, p. 97; 1891, p. 185; Superintendent of Public Instruction, Reports, 1886, p. 32.

[16] State Auditor, Reports, 1861, pp. 19–25; General Laws, 1862, p. 122; Superintendent of Public Instruction, Reports, 1899–1900, pp. 3, 214. The statistics for 1929 were obtained from the offices of the state auditor and the state department of education.

people have fancied it would. Since 1907 the fund has been augmented annually by one-half of the interest accruing from the state swamp-land fund. To what amount the school fund might have been swelled had the timbered sections been judiciously reserved and sold, with or without the timber, and actual trespass and theft been fully paid for, cannot be conjectured. It would have been impossible to conceive of retaining any sections for permanent forest reserves in a generation when trees were thought of as encumbrances to be joyously cut down. An amendment to the state constitution, proposed in 1913 and ratified in 1914, authorized the legislature to set apart school lands better adapted to the production of timber than to agriculture as " state school forests " and to provide for their management on forestry principles.[17]

The record of the state in preserving the school fund is creditable. An act of 1862 provided that the proceeds of the sales of the school lands should form a perpetual fund never to be reduced by any costs, fees, or charges whatever. The same act charged the state auditor, as commissioner of the state land office, with the selling of the lands for not less than five dollars an acre and required him to credit the proceeds to the permanent school fund. The state treasurer was made the custodian of the fund. The investment of the fund seems to have been left to the discretion of the two officials, who were, of course, placed under bonds and required to make annual reports of their transactions. It was not until 1875 that legislative action was taken to control investments. In that year the legislature submitted to the electors an amendment to article 8 of the state constitution requiring

[17] *General Laws*, 1889, pp. 68–72; 1907, p. 543; 1913, p. 90; William Anderson, *A History of the Constitution of Minnesota*, 183, 233, 236, 284 (Minneapolis, 1921). After over half of the swamp lands donated by Congress to the state had been given to railroads, an amendment to article 8, section 2, of the constitution, adopted in 1881, devoted one-half of the invested swamp-land fund to the permanent school fund. An act of 1907 gave effect to the amendment. See Samuel G. Iverson, " The Public Lands and School Fund of

the enactment of laws suitable for the safe investment of the school fund. It was ratified on November 2, 1875. It provided for the investment of the fund in bonds of the United States, of Minnesota — with the exception of those issued before 1860 — or of such other states as might be selected.[18]

In the decade from 1880 to 1890 the population of Minnesota increased almost sixty per cent. In some counties there was urgent need of new or enlarged school and other public buildings. The interest on bank loans was still high and the interest on government and state loans had declined. The question arose, Why not accommodate the needy counties and school districts with properly secured loans from the school fund? It came up in the legislature of 1885 in the form of a bill to submit to the electors another amendment to article 8 to authorize loans from the school fund to counties and school districts " to be used in the erection of county and school buildings." The bill was carefully drawn to meet expected objections. It stipulated that no loan should be made that exceeded in amount three per cent of the assessed valuation of the real estate of the county or district. Loans were to be made only upon application approved by a board of investment, to consist of the governor, the state auditor, and the state treasurer. County auditors were required to " levy and extend " a tax fifty per cent in excess of the amount necessary to pay the interest or the principal of such loans. The interest rate was made five per cent. The bill was passed and the amendment was ratified at the general election of 1886 and was put into effect by statute in 1887.[19]

Minnesota," in *Minnesota Historical Collections*, 15: 307–311, for an estimate of the increase of the permanent school fund to two hundred million dollars.

[18] *General Laws*, 1862, pp. 121–132; 1875, p. 20; Anderson, *History of the Constitution*, 233, 278.

[19] *United States Census*, 1890, *Population*, 2; *General Laws*, 1885, p. 5; 1887, pp. 310–312; *Senate Journal*, 1885, pp. 257, 333; *House Journal*, 380, 516, 676; Anderson, *History of the Constitution*, 182, 234, 281.

The demand for loans was not extravagant and the policy was generally so satisfactory that its extension to municipal bodies — towns, cities, and villages — was soon proposed. Another amendment to article 8, submitted in 1895, ratified in 1896, and put into effect in 1897, authorized the investment of the permanent school and university funds in the bonds of any county, school district, city, town, or village issued for the purposes and within the limits prescribed by statute. No loan was to be made that would raise the bonded debt of a municipality to an amount greater than seven per cent of the assessed valuation of its taxable real property. The interest rate was not to be lower than three per cent. Protest was immediately heard against the " seven per cent limit," and identical amendments to raise it were submitted in 1899 and 1901. Both received in their favor large majorities of the votes cast on them, but not majorities of all the votes cast at the elections, as required by the constitutional amendment of 1897. Better fortune attended the submission of an amendment of the same tenor proposed by the legislature of 1903, which was ratified the following year by a large majority. The seven per cent limit was raised to fifteen per cent, and a large increase in loans from the school fund followed.[20]

It is generally assumed that the farmers of the country have from early times been at a disadvantage as compared with the classes engaged in industry and commerce. The marketable surplus of their products has been sold abroad in competition with the products of cheap foreign labor, after deductions have been made for transportation and

[20] *General Laws*, 1895, p. 13; 1897, p. 90; 1903, p. 33; 1905, pp. 3, 18; Anderson, *History of the Constitution*, 235, 251, 281, 282; State Auditor, *Reports*, 1925–26, p. v. At the close of the fiscal year 1926 the amount of loans to municipalities from the permanent school fund was $22,880,608.56, a little over one-half of the whole fund then accumulated, $44,743,793.32. In the Folwell Papers is a blank, dated April 17, 1928, and entitled " Application for Loan," prepared by the attorney-general, which indicates the evidence required as to the legitimacy of the municipal bonds and the purposes for which they could lawfully be issued.

handling. The farmer has bought his groceries, his clothing, and his implements and machinery in home markets protected by tariffs against competition from abroad. Movements toward reducing this handicap form a large part of the economic history of the country. Wishing to provide some relief for the Minnesota farmer, the legislature of 1915 submitted another amendment to article 8, which was ratified in November, 1916. It authorized loans from the school fund secured by first mortgages on improved and cultivated farm lands in the state. No loan was to exceed thirty per cent of the cash value of the mortgaged land, and the interest rate was not to be lower than three per cent. Expectations in regard to this constitutional aid to agriculture have not been met. No appropriations have been made for the expenses of administration and no serious applications have been made for loans.[21]

STATE AID FOR SCHOOLS

To the support of schools by school taxes — district, county, and state — a recent addition of importance must be noted. As elsewhere related, the legislature of 1878 enacted a law granting the sum of four hundred dollars annually from the general revenue fund of the state to each of such high schools as would undertake to prepare students for the university and give the instruction free to students residing outside their several districts. The operation of the act was satisfactory, and high schools in slowly increasing numbers performed the duty and accepted the bonus. Such was the beginning of "state aid." Although in all probability the possibility that state aid might be extended to other schools had been thought of earlier, the next step was not taken until 1895, when an act was passed granting aid to the amount of two hundred dollars to graded schools

[21] *Laws*, 1915, p. 549; 1917, p. 13; Anderson, *History of the Constitution*, 236, 284; interview with Matt J. Desmond, deputy auditor of state, memorandum in Folwell Papers, April 17, 1928.

the equipment and general efficiency of which might be approved by the high school board. Two years later fifty dollars a year were allowed to common schools approved by county superintendents. State aid for schools, thus launched, was soon to be under full sail. An act of 1899 provided for aid to public schools in four classes — high, graded, semigraded, and rural — that fulfilled prescribed conditions as to grounds, buildings, equipment, and teaching forces. An approved high school was awarded eight hundred dollars a year; a graded school, two hundred dollars; a semigraded school, one hundred dollars; and a rural school, seventy-five dollars.[22]

The beginning was modest. In 1901 the state treasurer paid out but $142,649.57 for state aid for schools. But the number of schools of the several classes qualifying for aid increased from year to year, and the legislatures became more liberal. In 1909 the amounts of aid to schools in each of the four classes were raised. Approved high schools were allowed not more than $1,750 each; graded schools, $600; semigraded schools, $350; and rural schools, $100. In the year following the sum of $870,084 was disbursed. In 1913 the maximum aid to high and graded schools was increased to $2,200 and $750, respectively. In the next year the total of payments was $1,984,076. In 1921 state aid passed the three-million mark and in 1927 it rose to $6,304,227, a sum equal to about one-ninth of the total school expenditure for the year, $54,264,674. Without doubt the purposes of state aid as scheduled by the legislature of 1921 — the equalization of educational opportunities, the establishment of generally accepted standards for schools, and the stimulation of educational progress — have been reasonably fulfilled.[23]

[22] See *ante*, p. 76; *General Laws*, 1878, p. 154; 1895, p. 451; 1897, p. 483; 1899, pp. 468–477; Albert W. Rankin, " The State Aid Imbroglio," in *School Education*, vol. 37, no. 1, p. 9 (September, 1917) ; and Rankin, in Greer, *Education in Minnesota*, 76–86.

[23] Superintendent of Public Instruction, *Reports*, 1901–02, pp. 28, 118–120; 1909–10, p. 256; 1913–14, p. 27; *General Laws*, 1909, p. 381; 1913, p. 427;

Legislatures have been advised to levy a state tax for state aid instead of making appropriations from the general revenue fund, but as yet no legislature has been pleased to take such action. Taxes, which are a lien on every man's property, have immemorially been offensive; appropriations may be scaled down or cut off altogether. The proposition of one superintendent that the state assume the cost of all public schooling is not likely to be seriously entertained.[24]

TEXTBOOK LEGISLATION

Wherever instruction is given and textbooks are used it is virtually necessary that all the pupils in a class have the same books. That all the schools of a community, county, or state should have uniform sets of books is not so necessary, but it is obvious that uniformity may be pecuniarily economical. This consideration has led to a number of experiments in Minnesota. During the territorial period the books known to teachers and parents in the communities from which they had migrated seem to have been used in great variety. The

1919, p. 43; 1921, p. 766; 1927, pp. 544, 547; State Treasurer, *Reports,* 1921–22, p. 57; Department of Education, *Financial Statement and State Aid to Public Schools,* 1927–28, pp. 29, 30; James M. McConnell, "The Cost of Elementary and High School Education and Sources of School Support," in *Minnesota Municipalities,* 12: 104–109 (March, 1927); Department of Education, *Educational Directory of Minnesota,* 1927–28, p. 3; *Laws of Minnesota Relating to the Public School System,* 1927, p. 71. The legislature of 1919 appropriated $1,070,193 for deficiencies of 1915 and 1916. The *Laws* of 1927 provided for the issue by the state auditor of "certificates of indebtedness" to the amount of $1,786,758.83, part of which was to be used for deficiencies of 1923 and 1924. An act of 1927 authorized the state auditor to transfer money from the current school fund, to the amount of $500,000 if needed, to pay state aid in full. Up to 1922 high schools receiving state aid were required to admit and instruct, free of tuition, pupils from any part of the state preparing for the university. An act of 1921 provided for the payment of seven dollars a month from the state treasury for the tuition of every nonresident high school pupil. In the year ending on June 30, 1927, tuition of nonresident pupils in state high schools was paid for 18,500 persons; the total amount paid was $1,083,401, a little less than sixty dollars per pupil.

[24] Superintendent of Public Instruction, *Reports,* 1915–16, p. 22; 1917–18, p. 12. The act of 1919 creating the state board of education called for an investigation of "the administration of funds appropriated by the legislature for public school aid" and for recommendations for the "modification and unification of laws relating to the state system of education." No appropriation was made for expenses, but investigations were conducted by the staff of the department of education. Its report had the unanimous approval

first state superintendent of public instruction, Edward D. Neill, in accordance with the law creating his office, recommended a list of textbooks for general use, but suggested that the legislature should provide for a commission to select a list of books and to secure compulsory uniformity. The legislature preferred to impose those duties upon the state normal board, which it authorized to select a list of books to be used in all the public schools for five years. On April 17, 1861, that board gave effect to the law by publishing its selections.[25]

There seems to have been a willing conformity with the law and reasonable satisfaction with its operation during the five-year period ending in 1866. From 1862 to 1867 the duties of state superintendent were discharged by the secretary of state. The legislature of 1867 reëstablished the office and Governor Marshall appointed Mark H. Dunnell superintendent. In his first annual report Dunnell argued forcibly for uniformity of textbooks and for low prices for them, and declared that there was " an overwhelming necessity" for immediate action. The indefatigable book agent, he said, was at his work in Minnesota. Moved by Dunnell's counsel, the legislature of 1868 provided for a textbook commission, to consist of the superintendent of public instruction, the principal of the preparatory school of the University of Minnesota, and the secretary of state, to select a list of books for use in the public schools for a five-

of the board. The document is of much historical interest, although the following legislature did not enact the recommendations made therein for a revision and codification of the general statutes of 1913 and subsequent laws. A proposed bill for a law relating to state aid, however, was closely followed as a model for an act passed by the legislature of 1921. The legislature of 1925 reduced the amount of aid to high schools to $900; to graded schools of eight school years, to $500; and to graded schools of six school years, to $400. *Laws*, 1919, pp. 355–358; 1921, pp. 763–772; 1925, p. 584; Department of Education, *Reports*, 1919–20, pp. 13–15; *Report of the State Board of Education upon the Revision of State Aid*, 2, 4, 8–15, 24–30 (1920).

[25] Niles, in Greer, *Education in Minnesota*, 54, 55; David L. Kiehle, "Department of Public Instruction," in Greer, *Education in Minnesota*, 10; *General Laws*, 1861, p. 71; Superintendent of Public Instruction, *Reports*, 1860, pp. 10, 34; 1861, p. 42.

year period. A list prepared after much deliberation was published on August 6, to be in effect on October 1, 1868.[26]

The books thus selected and imposed upon the schools may have been generally satisfactory, but the prices allowed and exacted were not. An act of the legislature of 1873 enjoined the commissioners not to change textbooks for the next three years if the books then in use could be procured and sold at a reduction of thirty per cent. The publishers, however, refused to make the reduction. The contracts expired on October 1, 1873, and for four years all publishers and dealers in schoolbooks were at liberty to sell their books; and parents, advised, as some of them were, by teachers exposed to temptation, could buy such books as they pleased. In his report to the legislature of 1874, the state superintendent, Horace B. Wilson, protested vigorously against uniformity of textbooks, citing unfortunate experiences in other states and quoting a high educational authority to corroborate his statements. Governor Austin brought the matter to the attention of the same legislature. Persons thoroughly informed, he said, had told him that the cost of schoolbooks in the state was $250,000 and that it was increasing at the rate of ten per cent a year. They had assured him that the average profit of the publishers was one hundred per cent and that a convention of the craft had irrevocably fixed the prices.[27]

The response of the legislature of 1874 was a joint resolution, which declared in its preamble that a schoolbook ring was holding a monopoly of American textbooks and selling at prices sixty per cent above cost and reasonable profits. Schoolbooks as good as those in use in Minnesota were published abroad, especially in Great Britain, at much lower prices. It was therefore resolved to demand of Congress that

[26] General Laws, 1867, p. 7; 1868, p. 10; Superintendent of Public Instruction, Reports, 1867, pp. 57–61.
[27] General Laws, 1873, p. 78; Superintendent of Public Instruction, Reports, 1873, pp. 25–40; Horace Austin, Message, January 9, 1874, p. 8.

it repeal the import duties on such books and pass a law providing that combinations between publishers and copyright-holders should result in the forfeit of copyright privileges. Free trade in schoolbooks went merrily on. Publishers and dealers, by making low prices for the introduction of new books and liberal terms of exchange for old ones, stimulated sales. It was not long before seven different readers, six geographies, and countless arithmetics and grammars were in use. Numerous book agents were in the field and they were industrious. Changes in books took place " in some dark way that nobody can explain." [28]

Ignatius Donnelly was in the state Senate in the mid-seventies. Some years before, while a representative in Congress, he had originated the movement that resulted in the establishment of the national bureau of education and, in one of his delicious passages, had aired a dream for a national university. It was now to his taste and interest to appear on the field as the champion of the people against the schoolbook ring. Among the bills introduced by him was one providing that the books be written by scholars employed by the state, printed by the boys in the state reform school, and furnished at cost to the schools. This bill may have been merely a play to the gallery. A more serious proposition of Donnelly's, to provide for a textbook commission to receive bids and enter into contract for textbooks, was twice passed by the Senate, only to be defeated in the House.[29]

While the matter hung in suspense, an enterprising book-seller, a very reputable citizen of St. Paul, laid before the legislature of 1877 a novel and alluring proposition. He offered to sign a contract to furnish textbooks to the common schools for fifteen years at one-half the prices of the time. The proposition was not seconded by the state superintendent,

[28] *General Laws*, 1874, p. 298; Superintendent of Public Instruction, *Reports*, 1874, p. 56; 1875, p. 33.
[29] See *ante*, 3: 12; Everett W. Fish, *Donnelliana: An Appendix to " Caesar's Column*," part 1, pp. 83, 85–87 (Chicago, 1892) ; and the *Saint Paul Pioneer*, 1874: February 17, p. 2; 1875: February 28, p. 2.

David Burt, but it found favor with the legislature of 1877. A bill drawn to put it into effect was promptly passed by the Senate and, after fruitless opposition, by the House. The act authorized the governor, the secretary of state, and the attorney-general to enter into contract on behalf of the state with Daniel D. Merrill for the supply of textbooks to the common schools for a term of fifteen years. Merrill was to give his bond in the sum of twenty-five thousand dollars, conditioned upon the faithful execution of the contract. The selection of the books was made the duty of a commission consisting of Superintendent Burt, Sanford Niles, and William Benson. The books were to be equal in matter, size, and manufacture to certain books, severally named, then in use. The prices to be paid for a speller, four readers, two grammars, three arithmetics, two geographies, and a history were specifically stated, and they were, on the average, half of those of the old books. District clerks were charged with calling for books, delivering them to parents, and collecting the money. To enforce compliance with the law, it was provided that no school district should receive its share of the state school tax until the county superintendent should have certified that the state books had been introduced in the schools of the district. A revolving fund of fifty thousand dollars was created to put the law into operation. The act did not apply to the twenty-nine special school districts then in existence. Governor Pillsbury signed the bill with reluctance, believing that the situation warranted the experiment.[30]

[30] *Minneapolis Tribune*, February 7, 1877; *Pioneer Press* (St. Paul and Minneapolis), February 6–21, 1877; *Saint Paul Daily Dispatch*, February 6–21, 1877; *General Laws*, 1877, pp. 155–159; Superintendent of Public Instruction, *Reports*, 1877, p. 88. For an account of the "machinery of the scheme" and a general severe criticism, see the report of a speech of Horace B. Wilson, former superintendent of public instruction, to the House of Representatives, in the *Pioneer Press*, February 21, 1877, p. 5. An editorial in the *Tribune*, February 13, gives five objections to the bill. The *Pioneer Press* supported the bill for the reason that one clause of it would, if enforced, break down the system of public robbery by the publishers' ring. The *Dispatch*, in editorials of February 13 and 19, considered the bill the only reasonable

The act was legally in effect after February 23, 1877, but its actual operation was delayed for a year because of the tardy selection of books and because the act had put no money in the treasury for the revolving fund. The contractor had not obtained definite tenders beforehand, and when the contract was to be awarded he was not embarrassed with a flood of competitors. It was not until May 17 that he was ready to lay before the commission a geography. On August 7 he submitted a speller and another geography and at later sessions in August and in November other books were offered. It was not until January 19, 1878, that the selection was complete. Signed by a majority, the list was laid before the legislature on January 31.[31]

The legislature of 1878 had been in session but a few days when a bill was introduced into the Senate to amend the contractual act of 1877 so as to simplify its operation and secure readier compliance. Then set in " a battle the most desperate and prolonged ever seen in our Legislature since Minnesota became a state." It was opened by a communication from Merrill to the governor, attacking the state superintendent of public instruction for alleged unfair and unjust criticisms of the system in his annual report for 1877, to which the superintendent made reply. Senator Donnelly naturally took the lead in advocacy of the bill. His first step — a mere gesture — was to move a reference of the whole subject to the committee on the insane. On February 6 he made his great speech, which abounded in denunciation of the schoolbook ring as a combination dominating the whole country from Maine to California and taking millions of dollars out of the hands of the people. Its agents,

means of destroying the odious school monopoly. Two letters, signed " Dion " and " One of the People," in the *Dispatch*, February 13, 1877, p. 2, denounce the measure vigorously.

[31] John S. Pillsbury, *Message*, January 11, 1878, p. 34; Superintendent of Public Instruction, *Reports*, 1877, pp. 73–95. The *Senate Journal*, 1878, appendix, 1–48, gives the proceedings of the commission, an argument of the majority in favor of their conclusions, and replies to objections of Superintendent Burt to some of the books.

said Donnelly, had been at work all over the state; they were filling the hotels and lobbies at St. Paul and paying out money for votes. The senator's eloquence was unnecessary; the very next day the Senate passed the bill with a comfortable majority.[32]

A few days later, while the debate was going on in the House, with the friends of the bill providing most of the oratory, an episode occurred that caused suspicion and delay. On February 16 Representative Brandt from Brown County rose in his place and displayed a fifty-dollar United States note, which he stated had been paid him to secure his vote on a pending amendment, the substance of which was to allow school district boards the option of taking or leaving the state textbooks. If adopted and finally passed, it would have rendered the Merrill contract a nullity. A committee of investigation was at once appointed, and on February 21 it reported, without opinion or recommendation, the testimony it had taken. Brandt testified that he had intended to vote for the amendment; when he had been offered the money he had decided to take it and to expose the infamy. Liberty Hall of Glencoe swore that after Brandt had assured him that he would vote for the amendment, he (Hall) had given Brandt the money to secure the latter's political support in the future. The House refused to arrest Hall or to thank Brandt for his revelation.[33]

[32] *Senate Journal*, 1878, pp. 40, 83, 102; *Anti-Monopolist* (St. Paul), 1878: January 24, p. 4; 31, p. 7; February 7, p. 1; 14, p. 5; March 14, p. 1; *Tribune*, 1878: February 5, p. 2; 7, p. 1; *Pioneer Press*, 1878: January 23, p. 4. Superintendent David Burt's reply to Merrill's attack is printed in the *Daily Globe* (St. Paul), January 23, 1878, p. 3. A pamphlet by Superintendent Burt, *Concerning Those Books* (Winona, n.d.), gives adverse opinions of four college professors, three principals of normal schools, and eight county superintendents. See also a sixteen-page pamphlet by George P. Quackenbos, *To The Legislators and Teachers of Minnesota* (New York, 1878), and an eight-page pamphlet by an unknown author, *A Reply to the Assault of Mr. Quackenbos upon One of His Numerous Critics in Minnesota* (n. p., n. d.). For resolutions of the Minnesota Teachers' Association condemning the Merrill books, see Niles, in Greer, *Education in Minnesota*, 64. The bill was passed in the Senate by a vote of 22 to 16.

[33] *House Journal*, 1878, pp. 201, 271, 484. For daily reports of the Brandt bribery investigation, see the *Tribune*, February 18–22; the *Pioneer*

When it became apparent that the bill would be passed, opponents undertook to discredit the measure and possibly at length to annul it by securing its reference to a vote of the people. The House adopted an amendment providing that it should not take effect until after two-thirds of the people had voted upon it in the affirmative. In the Senate Donnelly — for he had got scared — obtained a favorable vote for two submissions, one in 1883 and the other in 1888. A conference committee, however, arranged that the act should be in operation immediately after its passage, but that at the general election of 1880 the question of its continuance should be submitted to the people, and, if a majority of electors " present and voting " should vote against continuance, both the original act of 1877 and the supplementary act should cease to be in force. At the general election of 1885 the same question was to be submitted again, and, if two-thirds of those voting on the question should vote against continuance, the contract with Merrill should cease to be in effect. In both cases no vote was to be taken in the special school districts.[34]

The " desperate battle " in the legislature of 1878 was, as will have been observed, over the question of continuing or nullifying the Merrill contract. The new provisions of the supplementary act, aside from the provision for submission to the people, were easily agreed to. The period of one year allowed by the original act for putting the new system into operation was extended to two years. District clerks were required to give bonds for faithful performance of their duties under the act, and if any of them should fail to make requisitions for books by March 15, the director or the treasurer of the district might perform the duty. The electors of a school district at an annual meeting might

Press, February 16–26; and the Daily Globe, February 17–26. For the testimony in full, see the Globe, February 22, p. 1.

[34] House Journal, 1878, pp. 490, 494; Senate Journal, 306, 355, 413, 421; General Laws, 67–70. The amended bill was passed by a vote of 54 to 44 in the House, and by a vote of 23 to 12 in the Senate.

designate an agent to sell the books under bond at a ten-per-cent commission. County superintendents were required, upon receipt of the requisition of any district, to file a copy with the county auditor. The auditor was to compute the total cost, add five per cent for transportation of the books, and notify the county treasurer, whose duty it was to retain the amount from any moneys derived from taxation belonging to the district. The amount retained was to be merely a lien upon the district's share of the state school tax.[35]

The new act was so far effective that in the course of the year 1878 nearly one-third of the common and independent school districts had put the state books into use. The measure, so much despised by some of the school men, found the public patiently tolerant. Upon the referendum of 1880 a slight majority of votes cast on the measure were against the continuance of the contract, but it was far from being a majority of the electors " present and voting." Governor Pillsbury in his message assured the legislature of 1881 that, in spite of crude provisions and reluctant support, the new system was gaining ground. He stated that 731,747 books had been supplied at a cost of $173,951; at the old prices they would have cost $414,757. He had been assured by competent judges that the state books were " fully equal, if not superior, to any class of school books " then in use, and he hoped for the hearty coöperation of all persons.[36]

The financial saving no doubt did much toward securing the desired coöperation; but further legislation was found necessary. An act of 1883 required county superintendents to ascertain and report the kinds and numbers of books needed in the several districts. County commissioners were authorized to appoint agents to sell the books at a price to

[35] *General Laws*, 1878, pp. 67–70.
[36] Superintendent of Public Instruction, *Reports*, 1878, p. 82; Pillsbury, *Messages*, January 9, 1879, p. 7; January 6, 1881, p. 9; Secretary of State, *Reports*, 1880, p. 42. Out of 3,794 districts, 1,202 had ordered state books to the value of $33,293.55. The vote cast for continuance was 44,739, and against it, 45,465; the whole number voting at the election was 120,630.

be fixed by the superintendent of public instruction. The
agents were to receive eight per cent of the amount of the
sales. School officers who neglected to perform any of their
duties under the act were liable to a fine of from twenty-five
to one hundred dollars, or to imprisonment for from thirty
to ninety days. The Merrill Act was now air-tight. The
school men grumbled, but the law remained in operation
until August 25, 1892, the end of the fifteen-year term.
Minnesota was poor territory for agents of schoolbook publishers, although they were free to offer their products to the
schools in the special districts. The pedagogical shortcom-
ings of the Merrill books were not so detrimental as to call
out loud complaints. Good teachers easily supplemented
their defects; poor teachers could not have profited much
from better texts. The pecuniary savings must have been
considerable, but that they amounted to the handsome total
of $2,839,965, as estimated by Donnelly's political arith-
metic, may be doubted. His biographer says the state was
"that much better off from Governor Donnelly having lived
in it." [37]

A St. Paul bookseller brought suit against the contractor
for damages to the amount of $150 for books in his stock
rendered unsalable by the Merrill Act, and $8 for old books
that his children could no longer use. The state supreme
court declined to question the legislative policy of the law,
and held that the plaintiff had no case against Merrill. [38]

It was not to be expected that upon the expiration of the
Merrill contract in 1892 publishers of schoolbooks would be
allowed to resume sales, with piratical incidents, direct or
indirect to individual parents. Some form of regulation
was sure to be established. The very next legislature, that
of 1893, permitted publishers and dealers in schoolbooks

[37] *General Laws*, 1883, pp. 38–40; Fish, *Donnelliana*, part 1, p. 86. The
act of 1883 repealed the absurd clause in the act of 1878 providing for a
referendum in 1885.

[38] Joseph C. Curryer *v.* Daniel D. Merrill and others, 25 *Minnesota*, 1–8.

to sell after depositing with the state superintendent sample copies of their books and lists of the prices to be charged. School boards were authorized to contract for books for periods of not less than three years nor more than five, to pay for the books out of district funds, and to sell them at cost. The act contained the further provision that school boards, when so directed by a majority of votes at an annual school meeting, should furnish the books to the pupils free. The claim had already been heard that a school system that paid teachers and provided buildings at public expense might as well supply the textbooks in the same manner. The free textbook policy was acceptable enough to induce half of the districts of the state to adopt it immediately, and by the end of a decade it had become the general custom, with only lingering exceptions.[39]

Experience showed, however, a need of more rigorous regulation of sales, whether to boards or individuals. An act of 1911 introduced the principle of inviting competition, but it required publishers to obtain licenses before selling. That act so fully remedied defects in the system that, with occasional modifications in details, it has ever since remained in force. To obtain a license to sell school textbooks in Minnesota, an applicant must deposit in the office of the state superintendent samples of books, accompanied by verified lists showing the usual list prices and the lowest wholesale prices obtained anywhere in the United States; must file a written agreement to furnish the books, which shall be equal in every respect to the samples on deposit, anywhere in the state at stipulated prices; and must furnish a bond of not less than two thousand nor more than ten thousand dollars, which shall be approved by the attorney-

[39] *General Laws*, 1893, p. 125; Superintendent of Public Instruction, *Reports*, 1893–94, p. 18; 1903–04, p. 190. Superintendent Kiehle strongly recommended that textbooks be furnished to pupils free of charge. See Superintendent of Public Instruction, *Reports*, 1885–86, p. 28; 1889–90, p. 17; 1891–92, p. 15. In 1904 textbooks were supplied free in 5,123 districts and were sold at cost in 872.

general. To make a sale or an offer to sell before obtaining a license is a gross misdemeanor, punishable by a fine of not less than five hundred nor more than two thousand dollars. County superintendents are especially charged with initiating prosecutions. It is not agreeable to record that the legislature thought it necessary to provide for a penalty of a fine of five hundred dollars or imprisonment for thirty days, or both, for a state superintendent or any member of his force who should be convicted of receiving any gift or favor from a licensee. Nor is it pleasant to add that a fine of from fifty to two hundred dollars awaits any teacher, county or city superintendent, or member of a school board convicted of being interested in the sale of school textbooks in his district. School boards are authorized to buy books and lend them free when they think it advisable or when they are directed to do so by school meetings.[40]

COMPULSORY EDUCATION

Illiteracy is obviously so great a handicap to citizens, whether or not they are electors, that modern states, to reduce it, or, if possible, to obliterate it, have established schools supported in whole or in part by taxation. From the first day of its existence Minnesota has pursued that generous policy, offering to every child within its borders free instruction, not merely in the elementary branches of knowledge, but also in many higher branches and, in late years, in numerous vocations. For a generation it was assumed that without question all parents and guardians would appreciate the policy and would give their children the full benefit of it, without exhortation, certainly without compulsion. Experience and statistics at length showed that assumption to be too liberal. The annual lists of schoolable children taken in the districts gave large totals, far in excess of the numbers

[40] *General Laws*, 1911, pp. 61–64; *Laws of Minnesota Relating to the Public School System*, 1927, p. 78.

of children in actual attendance. The state superintendent of public instruction, in his biennial report for 1883–84, called attention to the large number of children out of school and recommended remedial legislation. The legislature of the following year, 1885, thus advised, passed a bill entitled " An act requiring the education of all healthy children." In general the measure required every parent, guardian, or other person in charge of a child between the ages of eight and sixteen to send him to a public or private school having a competent teacher, for twelve weeks in the year, six weeks to be consecutive. In cases where the parent was too poor to clothe the child or the child was too infirm in body or mind to attend, where he was being taught at home or had already acquired the ordinary school branches, or where there was no school within two miles of the home, school boards might grant excuses. Disobedience of the law was made a misdemeanor punishable by a fine of from ten to twenty-five dollars for a first offense and from twenty-five to fifty dollars for a subsequent offense, to be imposed by a court of competent jurisdiction. It was made the duty of school directors and presidents of boards of education in particular to ascertain cases of negligence and secure prosecutions.[41]

The loosely drawn act of 1885 served as an expression of sentiment and little more. In 1899, at the suggestion of the state superintendent, an act was passed that could be effective only in cities and large villages. It authorized school boards to appoint truant officers with power to arrest truants, to take them to school, and to file complaints against parents or guardians neglecting their duty. The penalty for such neglect was raised to a fine of not more than fifty dollars or imprisonment for not more than thirty days. The act prescribed no definite procedure for its enforcement. An act of 1901 provided that incorrigible

[41] Superintendent of Public Instruction, *Reports*, 1883–84, p. 32; *General Laws*, 1885, p. 261.

children might be brought before a justice of the peace and, upon conviction, might be committed to the state training school at Red Wing. No instance of such incarceration has been found. A decade now ran by with no change for the better.[42]

In three successive biennial reports John W. Olsen, the state superintendent, laid the matter before the legislature. The statistics, he said, showed that large numbers of rural and village children were out of school more than half of the time. School boards would not prosecute neighbors, nor would they appoint truant officers. It was not poverty that kept children out of school. One county superintendent reported that many wealthy farmers, some of whom were school officers, were the worst offenders. The compulsory law was a dead letter. In cities the law was somewhat better obeyed. The superintendent recommended the appointment of nonresident truant officers and the taking of an exact census of school children in all districts.[43]

The legislature of 1909 undertook to put teeth into the compulsory law. An act was passed requiring school boards to furnish to the principal teachers of their districts at the opening of the school year lists of all excuses granted. After five days the principals were to report to the county superintendent of schools the names of all absent children not excused. The county superintendent was then to report all such cases to the county attorney, who was to warn the parents concerned to put their absent children in school. Should any parents neglect to do so, the county superintendent was required, upon request of the county attorney, to file criminal complaints and the county attorney would conduct prosecutions. To stimulate the activity of officials, it was provided that neglect by a school officer or county superintendent to perform his duty should be a misdemeanor

[42] Superintendent of Public Instruction, *Reports*, 1887–88, p. 23; 1889–90, p. 16; 1897–98, p. 39; *General Laws*, 1899, pp. 248–250; 1901, p. 202.

[43] Superintendent of Public Instruction, *Reports*, 1903–04, p. 22; 1905–06, p. 15; 1907–08, p. 22.

punishable by a fine of not more than ten dollars or by imprisonment for not more than ten days. It is not known that any one of them suffered pecuniarily or otherwise.[44]

Olsen's successor, who took office on January 1, 1909, was not content with the legislation of that year. The law, he said, could still be evaded; it did not secure regular and complete attendance. Procedure in cases of neglect was complicated and tedious. Private and parochial schools gave trouble. He made seven recommendations for amendments. The legislature of 1911 was not pleased to adopt all the recommendations of the superintendent, but it made some notable changes. The schedule of grounds for excuses was modified by the omission of the poverty item, by the requirement of an eight-grade education, and by a clause permitting pupils over fourteen years of age to be out of school from April 1 to November 1 when they were needed to help about the home. Children might be kept out of school also on days when religious instruction was given under church authority. To aid in the enforcement of the law, the commissioner of labor was authorized to have his deputies throughout the state examine excuses and revoke any that were found to be insufficient. A more important amendment was one requiring school boards to have a complete annual census of all children between the ages of six and sixteen made by their clerks or other appointees between July 1 and September 1. The record was to show the name and the date of birth of each child and the name and address of the parent or guardian. One copy was to be sent to the principal teacher of the district and another to the county superintendent of schools. That there might be a complete census of all children of school age in the state, the act required also that every principal or other person in charge of a private or parochial school should make the same reports concerning attendance that were required for

[44] *General Laws*, 1909, pp. 476–478.

public schools. The census requirement seems to have been lightly regarded. The legislature of 1913 tightened it by passing an act directing that state aid be withdrawn in any district in which the census was not taken and reported.[45]

The Minnesota Commission of Public Safety, in the exercise of its elastic powers, in 1917 caused an investigation to be made to ascertain to what extent foreign languages were in use in the schools of the state. It was found that a considerable number of private and parochial schools were "using a foreign language wholly or in part as a medium of instruction, and that some 10,000 children receiving their education in these schools were brought up as aliens and foreigners." The state superintendent advised the commission to issue an order forbidding the use of any language other than English as a medium of instruction, except in the study of another language, but that plenipotentiary septemvirate was content to leave the matter to the legislature. An act of 1919 provided that "a school, to satisfy the requirements of compulsory attendance, must be one in which all the common branches are taught in the English language, from textbooks written in the English language and taught by teachers qualified to teach in the English language." Instruction in foreign languages might be given, but for not more than one hour in each day.[46]

Public school administration entered upon a new era with the creation in 1919 of the state board of education. In its first report the board was constrained to state that large numbers of children were out of school and that larger numbers attended only irregularly. Enforcement of the

[45] Superintendent of Public Instruction, *Reports*, 1909–10, pp. 18–20; *General Laws*, 1911, pp. 483–486; 1913, p. 793. The section of the law of 1911 requiring reports from private schools has not been conformed to by the parochial schools except for a brief period and the section apparently provides no means of enforcing it. Interview with Commissioner J. M. McConnell, memorandum in Folwell Papers, June 13, 1928.

[46] Superintendent of Public Instruction, *Reports*, 1917–18, pp. 6, 26; *Laws*, 1919, p. 337; Minnesota Commission of Public Safety, *Report*, January 1, 1919, pp. 23, 162.

attendance law, said the board, was difficult on account of neighborhood relations. Effective enforcement could be had only by giving the state department of education state-wide powers similar to those of the department of labor in the administration of the child labor laws. Local agencies would always be ineffective. The legislature of 1921 was not disposed to expand the powers of the state department as advised, but merely passed an act requiring every school board to investigate cases coming to its knowledge of children unable for various reasons to attend school, and to report to the county auditor. After proper investigation, the county board was authorized to furnish such relief in each case as would enable the child to attend school during the entire year.[47]

In 1927 the commissioner of education, aided by the attorney-general, published a compilation of all the school laws of the state then in force in a volume of 165 pages of fine type. Printed in the same type as the state laws or the decisions of the supreme court, they would make a very bulky volume. The chapter on " Compulsory Education — Child Labor " fills seven and a half pages of fine print.[48] It would seem strange that in a period of enlightenment so drastic a code should be needed to compel parents to give their children the full benefit of the free public schools. Some reasons for their reluctance have already been suggested. To these may be added the well-known fact that from ancient times the school has been regarded as a species of prison and the schoolmaster, as a tyrant. Literature abounds in the likes of Squeers and Dotheboys Hall. Short-sighted parents have for long tolerated truancy. Back of all is the immemorial sentiment that the rearing of children is an original parental prerogative that the state has no right to take away. Such is the conviction of numerous citizens

[47] *Laws,* 1919, p. 355; 1921, p. 668; Department of Education, *Reports,* 1919–20, pp. 7, 11.
[48] *Laws of Minnesota Relating to the Public School System,* 1927, pp. 84–91.

who believe that secular instruction ought not to be separated from religious instruction, and that both should be given under ecclesiastical direction. In cities and large villages it is practicable for such good citizens to maintain parochial schools while paying their taxes, more or less willingly, for the support of the public schools. Many citizens prefer to have their children taught in private schools, often high-priced, in order that they may be separated from children of the industrial classes. It is difficult to enforce any law when indifference to it is frequent and opposition strong, as, for example, the Sunday laws, the common violation of which is tolerated by all, and the Volstead liquor law, passed to enforce the eighteenth amendment to the national Constitution.

Consolidated Schools

The attachment of the people of Minnesota, especially the rural residents, to their inherited system of small neighborhood school districts, with the schoolhouse within easy walking distance of the home, had persisted from the beginning of the organized existence of the state. Efforts in the constitutional conventions to establish township or county units were fruitless. Repeated recommendations of state superintendents made no impression upon legislatures. At the beginning of the present century a plan, probably imported from some older state, to mitigate the disadvantages of small and isolated schools was much talked about. In response to a popular desire for an experiment, the legislature of 1901 passed an act to authorize two or more school districts to be united into a single independent district. The union was to be effected by a petition addressed to the county superintendent of schools and signed by a majority of the freeholders in each district, and by an affirmative vote of a majority of the legal electors in the several districts. The school board was given authority to provide transportation for pupils. An act of 1903 authorized the consolidation of

AN EARLY SCHOOL

A CONSOLIDATED SCHOOL

[From photographs in the museum of the Minnesota Historical Society. The upper picture shows the first schoolhouse at Ross, Roseau County. The lower picture was taken at Saum, Beltrami County, about 1912.]

rural schools with districts maintaining high or graded
schools. Under these acts twelve small districts were merged
into five consolidated school districts. An act of 1905 provided for changes in procedure and gave the new schools
the rank of graded schools.[49]

The consolidated schools thus inaugurated gave much
satisfaction and were commended by state superintendents.
They were " a big improvement." But they did not multiply.
At the end of a decade but nine experiments survived. The
schools were not cheap, transportation was difficult, and state
aid was inadequate. To remedy these deficiencies and to
simplify procedure, a carefully prepared bill was laid before
the legislature of 1911. It was passed without serious opposition. It provided that two or more school districts of any
kind might be merged into a single consolidated school district by a majority vote of the electors of the whole area.
In districts containing not less than twelve sections, schools
complying with certain requirements might receive state aid.
Three classes of schools were recognized: Class A schools
were to receive aid to the amount of $1,500 annually; class B
schools, $1,000; and class C schools, $750. Schools of all
three classes were to receive aid in the construction of buildings equal to twenty-five per cent of the cost. School boards
were given authority, and in cases in which schools received
state aid they were obliged, to provide for the transportation
of pupils living more than two miles from the school, or to
pay for the room and board of those whose attendance could
thus be more economically and conveniently provided for.[50]

---

[49] See ante, p. 139; General Laws, 1901, p. 432; 1903, p. 412; 1905, pp.
511–514; and Superintendent of Public Instruction, Reports, 1903–04, p. 12.
See pages 415–433 of this report for an article by Superintendent Olsen
entitled " Consolidation of Rural Schools and Transportation of Pupils at
Public Expense," reprinted with additions from his report for 1901–02. The
article includes a history of the movement in other states. See Minnesota
Public Education Commission, Report to the Governor, December 1, 1914,
pp. 18–20, for warm commendation of the " county unit" plan.

[50] Superintendent of Public Instruction, Reports, 1907–08, pp. 11, 133;
1909–10, p. 12; 1911–12, p. 33; Senate Journal, 1911, pp. 265, 552–554, 1225,

The act of 1911 was recast by the legislature of 1915 with
desirable changes of detail. State aid was adjusted to the
grade of the school, to the length of the school year, and to
the number of departments in the school. Transportation or
boarding of pupils living at a distance was made mandatory.
The biennial report of the state superintendent for 1915–16
was highly commendatory of the consolidated schools, which
in 1916 numbered 170. The instruction given was good,
it was reported, especially in the grades, and the influence of
the schools upon rural life was beneficial. The excellent
modern buildings furnished opportunities and centers for
community affairs, lectures, music, plays, literary societies,
parents' meetings, and farmers' clubs.[51]

Later legislation has not changed the general plan of the
consolidated schools. At the present time they number 385
in 79 counties, with 101,417 pupils in attendance. The
evolution of the consolidated schools in Minnesota has not
been without vicissitudes. There have been a few complete
failures due to the shifting of populations and delinquencies
in the payment of taxes. There have been disappointments
due to extravagant expectations and to premature opening
of high school work with too few teachers. But the large
and steady multiplication of consolidated schools indicates
that they have been generally satisfactory and successful.[52]

RELIGION IN THE SCHOOLS

It is a matter of common knowledge that where common
schools existed in the United States in early times, although

1271, 1274; *House Journal,* 166, 298, 1614, 1760; *General Laws,* pp. 268–272.
The law is often called the "Holmberg Act." An act of 1921 provided for
the payment by the state of forty per cent of the cost of buildings, but not
over six thousand dollars in each case. The law is still in force. See *Laws,*
1921, p. 765, and *Laws of Minnesota Relating to the Public School System,*
1927, p. 75.

[51] *Laws,* 1915, pp. 336–340; Superintendent of Public Instruction, *Reports,*
1915–16, pp. 35, 172.

[52] James M. McConnell, *Address to the Minnesota School Board Association on School Consolidation in Minnesota,* 10 (St. Paul, 1928); Department
of Education, *Educational Directory,* 1928–29, p. 3. The following publica-

scholastic in purpose, they were expected to inculcate the Christian morality accepted in their several neighborhoods. Schools began the day with a Bible reading, often accompanied by a prayer or a hymn. Invocations and benedictions opened and closed the public exercises and exhibitions. The schools were just as Christian as their communities. A tardy restriction of this custom resulted through a change in the composition of the population, brought about by the immense increase of foreign immigration that set in about the middle of the nineteenth century. In 1870 more than one-third of the people of Minnesota were foreign born.[53] Large numbers of them had settled in communities. In their European homes they had been taught their religion, either Catholic or Protestant, in their schools. When public schools were organized in the new communities, the teachers, Catholic or Lutheran, following old-country custom, conducted familiar forms of worship and taught doctrines of religion. For this they had American precedent. The isolated foreign-born communities were, however, few in number. In the rapidly filling counties of the frontier there was a mixture of native and foreign-born people and their children in the schools. Catholics could not tolerate the reading of the King James translation of the Bible; Protestants would have no other. Doctrinal instruction was, of course, impracticable. The reasonable and practical treatment of the *impasse*, it was thought, was to relieve the public schools of religious observances. That sentiment culminated in an act of the legislature of 1877 submitting to the electors an amendment to the state constitution, which was ratified at the general election in the same year. It forbade the appropriation of any public money or property " for the support of schools wherein the

tions of the department of education relate to consolidated schools: *Consolidation of School Districts and Transportation of Pupils (Bulletins*, no. 22 — n. d.) ; E. M. Phillips, *Manual for Consolidated Schools in Minnesota (Bulletins*, no. 52 — September 1, 1914) ; and C. C. Swain, *Manual for the Organization and Administration of Consolidated Schools in Minnesota (Bulletins*, no. 61 — July 1, 1916).

[53] *United States Census*, 1870, *Population*, 299.

distinctive doctrines, creed or tenets of any particular Christian or other religious sect are promulgated or taught." [54]

Instruction in morals and manners had been considered from earliest times a proper function of schools. It had been the general belief that they could be taught only upon a foundation of religion. The ultimate sanction of morality, it was believed, was in the doom of the judgment day. With the exclusion of the Bible from the school, many good people were fearful of a decline in morals and an increase in crime. There were others, however, who conceived that right conduct could be taught and inculcated by purely secular agencies and that the school might become a nursery of good behavior. That sentiment found expression in an act of the legislature of 1881, passed by large majorities in both houses. It authorized, but did not require, teachers in public schools to give instruction in the "elements of social and moral science, including industry, order, economy, punctuality, patience, self-denial, health, purity, temperance, cleanliness, honesty, truth, justice, politeness, peace, fidelity, philanthropy, patriotism, self-respect, hope, perseverance, cheerfulness, courage, self-reliance, gratitude, pity, mercy, kindness, conscience, reflection and the will." Teachers might give short oral lessons every day and require pupils the following morning to give illustrations, which they were to put into practice in their daily conduct. [55]

The state superintendent made a favorable reference to the act in his report for 1881, and the state normal board instructed the principals of the normal schools to make provisions for preparing teachers to give instruction in the several subjects. The act was duly printed in the session laws and was carried into the *General Statutes* of 1894. The *Revised Laws* of 1905 reduced it to a single sentence: " The teachers in all public schools shall give instruction in morals,

[54] *General Laws*, 1877, p. 23; 1878, p. 15.
[55] *General Laws*, 1881, p. 200.

in physiology and hygiene, and in the effects of narcotics and stimulants." The state superintendent, in successive reports, argued that morals could be taught in schools, while religion might be left to the family, and he urged conformance to the law of 1881. It may safely be assumed that the great majority of Minnesota teachers did not know that there was such a law, but that they went on silently teaching good behavior by example and casual precept. The act of 1881 was nothing more than a pious gesture, creditable to the good intentions, if not to the intelligence, of the legislature.[56]

The constitutional amendment of 1877 excluding from the public schools the teaching or promulgation of the distinctive doctrines, creeds, and tenets of any religious sect appears immediately to have been understood to prohibit the reading of the Bible in any version in the schools. On various occasions the attorney-general so ruled. In particular, in response to an inquiry from the state superintendent in 1895, the law officer of the state advised him that the opening of a public school with Bible reading or prayer, however frequently it might have been indulged in, was in violation of the constitution. It was not until 1927 that the matter came up for judicial determination. The supreme court ruled that it was not unconstitutional for a teacher to read in school extracts from the Old Testament of the King James version of the Bible. The use of schoolhouses for Sunday schools and divine worship under an act of 1907 seems not to have been considered a violation of the constitution. No objection has been heard against the giving of a few lectures from year to year in the English department of the state university on the place in and the influence of the King James version of the Bible upon English literature.[57]

[56] Superintendent of Public Instruction, *Reports*, 1881–82, p. 19; 1883–84, p. 24; 1885–86, p. 31; 1887–88, p. 12; 1891–92, pp. 23–26; *General Statutes*, 1894, p. 1053; *Revised Laws*, 1905, p. 274.

[57] Attorney-General, *Reports*, 1895–96, p. 111; *General Laws*, 1907, p. 636; Max Kaplan *v.* Independent School District of Virginia and others, 171 *Minnesota*, 142–157.

An unexpected consequence of the constitutional amendment of 1877 prohibiting sectarian teaching in the public schools was to give added importance to existing parish schools with, where circumstances favored it, an increase in their number. The support of parish schools by citizens who were also paying taxes for public schools became, except in a few large places, a heavy burden. In many parts of the country the idea of a school organization that would provide free schooling for all children and at the same time allow churches to teach religion in school buildings had been thought about and talked about, and a few experiments had been ventured. It remained for Minnesota to become the arena of an experiment that was widely advertised at home and abroad.[58]

The Faribault Plan

On Saturday, August 22, 1891, the school board of Faribault was in session to take action on matters pertaining to the schools, which were to reopen a week from the following Monday. After the routine business had been disposed of, the Reverend James J. Conry, pastor of the Roman Catholic Church of the Immaculate Conception, made the unexpected statement that his parochial school would not reopen. He did not need to say that as a result the Faribault school board would be legally required to make immediate provision for some 150 pupils for whom no school rooms had been made ready and no teachers had been employed. The amiable and respected priest, however, was ready with a plan to relieve the situation, which he put into writing on August 26. That his Catholic children might have the benefit of American training for American citizenship, that the " renown " of the city might be enhanced, and that the city's school funds might be increased by the additional enrollment, he would

[58] See Maurice F. Egan, *Recollections of a Happy Life,* 145 (New York, 1924), for the great increase of interest in Catholic parish schools in the eighties and the superior advantages claimed for them.

lease the parochial school grounds and building to the school board for educational purposes at a rent of one dollar. The plan was discussed in two meetings held on that and the following day and was unanimously adopted, but not until after certain implications and conditions had been considered and agreed to. It was agreed, of course, that the city superintendent should have supervision of the new school. The teachers of the disbanded parochial school, three Dominican sisters, were to be employed, after obtaining certificates from the county superintendent, and were to be paid proper salaries. They were to serve full time, to conform to the regulations of the board, and to attend teachers' meetings. They were to use the same textbooks that were in use in the other public schools. No religious ornaments or emblems were to be displayed in the school rooms. The sisters might retain the customary uniform of their order. The term of the contract was understood to be one year, with the expectation of a renewal.[59]

The arrangement went into effect. It was news to the press in the state and elsewhere and it was given wide publicity. The logic of the situation at Faribault seemed to justify the action and disarmed, or at least suspended, opposition. The priest in charge of the parochial school had suddenly found it impracticable to continue it in operation; as a patriotic citizen he had turned his children over to the public school that they might be trained for American citizenship. The school board had simply performed an obvious duty. The *Faribault Republican* on September 16, 1891, quoted from a communication in the *Christian Union* from a former Minnesota journalist in which it was stated that Father Conry had wished to secure for his people the

[59] *Faribault Democrat*, August 28, 1891, p. 3; *Faribault Republican*, September 2, 1891, p. 3; *Minneapolis Tribune*, August 31, 1891, p. 4; interview with Willis Mason West, superintendent of schools at Faribault in 1891, memorandum in Folwell Papers, May 15, 1928; proceedings of the board of education of Faribault, August 22, 26, 27, September 5, 1891, transcript in Folwell Papers, August 4, 1928.

superior advantages of the public schools and had undoubtedly acted with the consent of Archbishop Ireland; the
incident was significant of more important things in the future.
All was quiet in Faribault and might have remained so
indefinitely but for another incident.

The public schools of Stillwater in Washington County
did not reopen until October 5 on account of an epidemic
of diphtheria. At a meeting of the school board on October
13 the Reverend Father Corcoran and three representative
parishioners submitted a proposition, apparently unexpected,
to grant to the school board the use of the building and
grounds of St. Michael's School for school purposes at a
rent of one dollar for a year. The proposition was accepted
and went into immediate effect. The news of the Stillwater
incident spread like a prairie fire. The state superintendent,
bombarded with inquiries, lost no time in visiting Faribault
and, after making a personal inspection, in issuing a circular
letter. After stating the duty of school boards to provide
nonsectarian instruction for all the school children of their
several districts and adding some superfluous corollaries, he
concluded that the Faribault board had acted intelligently
and that the experiment, if found unsatisfactory, might be
amicably discontinued at the close of the year.[60]

A Protestant minister of Minneapolis, well known for
radical views and boldness of utterance, denounced the
arrangement in a sermon on October 11 as a "tiger's claw
within a velvet paw," a "Jesuit 'wooden horse,'" and
"a modified Poughkeepsie plan." A few days later he
visited the two cities and published his observations. He
did not like the Pope's picture over a teacher's desk at Faribault, nor Catholic paraphernalia in a room at Stillwater.
There was one Catholic on the school board at Faribault and
there were two on that at Stillwater. Both boards had com-

[60] Stillwater Daily Gazette, 1891: September 19, p. 3; October 6, p. 3; 14,
pp. 2, 3; 15, p. 2; 21, p. 2; December 23, p. 3; Minneapolis Tribune, 1891:
October 6, p. 4. For Kiehle's circular and editorial comment, see the Minneapolis Journal, October 21, pp. 4, 7.

mitted treason to the constitution, said the minister. In
Thanksgiving Day sermons Protestant clergy in St. Paul and
elsewhere condemned the plan more or less emphatically.[61]

On Monday, December 7, the conference of Protestant
ministers of Minneapolis held one of its appointed meetings.
A delegation of Protestant ministers from Stillwater appeared
and through one of their number informed the conference that
the school at that place, supported by public funds, was
" a Roman Catholic school pure and simple." As the sister
teachers under the rule of their order could hold no earthly
possessions, their church was making some two thousand
dollars a year out of the arrangement. It was a case of the
Catholic camel getting its nose under the canvas of American
free institutions, said the spokesman. A report of a committee previously appointed stated that the movement was
not suddenly originated by a few priests of liberal views,
but that it was " a part of a wide-spread scheme in progress
for years." The plan had been in operation in Poughkeepsie,
New York, for eighteen years. It was now going on in
fifteen or twenty districts in Stearns County, where the
children were taught by Benedictine sisters. A resolution
that the arrangements at Faribault and Stillwater were in
violation of the constitution was unanimously adopted. The
mover of the resolution said that the movement was the most
subtle and dangerous attack ever made by the Roman
hierarchy.[62]

Archbishop Ireland evidently had this deliverance of the
Minneapolis ministers in mind when he dictated an interview published in the *New York Herald* a few days later, in

---

[61] *Minneapolis Tribune,* 1891: October 12, p. 5; 24, p. 5; 26, p. 5; *St.
Paul Dispatch,* 1891: October 26, p. 5; *Faribault Democrat,* 1891: October
23, p. 3; *Minneapolis Journal,* 1891: December 7, p. 1. The *Minneapolis
Tribune,* October 26, p. 5, contains a report of an address of the Reverend
Gulian L. Morrill in Century Hall the previous day representing the extreme
Protestant position.

[62] *Minneapolis Journal,* December 7, 1891, p. 1; *Minneapolis Tribune,*
December 8, 1891, p. 5. For the favorable view taken by the Unitarian minister of Minneapolis, see the *Minneapolis Times,* January 18, 1892, p. 6.

which he was reported to have said that " Protestant ministers who strive, by warlike rhapsodies, to prevent the Catholic church from guarding the faith of its children, would be better employed in guarding the Protestant faith of Protestant children by adopting some method of giving to them some religious instruction in the public schools before or after school hours." On January 4, 1892, a committee of the Minneapolis conference reported a draft of an address to the archbishop in reply to his compliments. The conference was averse to engaging in a controversy with the prelate and appointed a committee to ask the state superintendent of public instruction to make an official investigation and to take such action as might be found appropriate. The superintendent, a former Presbyterian clergyman, said in reply that the conduct of school affairs rested in the hands of the school boards of the respective districts. His only function, he said, was to apportion the school funds. He had not been advised by the attorney-general as to whether or not he had power to decide the question of the right of a district to its share of the fund. It was his belief that in Faribault the former parochial school had been made an integral part of the public school system; he therefore cordially approved the action. As to the arrangement at Stillwater, he was not well informed.[63]

The industrious committee of the Minneapolis Protestant ministers then asked the attorney-general to rule upon two questions: (1) Who was the proper person to decide whether or not a school was public or parochial? (2) How might the payment of public money to a parochial school masquerading as a public school be stopped? The law officer of the state gave no opinion of his own, but he suggested that those who wished for the information might petition the district court to enjoin the county auditor from apportioning school money

[63] *Minneapolis Tribune,* 1891: November 3, p. 8; December 22, p. 3; 1892: January 5, p. 5; *North-Western Chronicle* (St. Paul), 1891: December 25, p. 8; *Minneapolis Journal,* 1892: January 4, p. 1; *Faribault Democrat,* 1892: January 22, p. 3; February 5, p. 3.

to a district believed and alleged to be unqualified to receive
it. Having failed to find a way to put an immediate end to
the misalliances at Faribault and Stillwater, except by a
litigation that somebody must pay for and that would be
uncertain as to results, the Minneapolis ministers were constrained to let the experiments go on. They were not obliged
to exercise their patience for a long time, however.

The experiment at Stillwater was discontinued by common consent at the close of the year. That at Faribault went
on through a second year, but its fate was decided soon after
the beginning of that year. At the annual school meeting
held on October 1, 1892, the question as to whether or not
the alliance between the Catholic school and the public school
system ought to continue was made a definite issue. There
were two tickets — one containing the names of two members
of the old board and Father Conry, supporters of the combination, and the other, those of three citizens opposed to it.
There was great excitement at the polls and the number of
ballots cast was without precedent at a school meeting. By a
majority vote of sixty-five per cent the alliance was disapproved. As the contract had been renewed for a second year,
which had already begun, it was reasonable and proper that
it should be allowed to run. In the summer of 1893 the new
board, contrary to expectation perhaps, arranged for the
leasing of the Catholic school for a third year. As the time
drew near for the opening of the new year, one of the
Catholic sister teachers was assigned to another public school
and two Protestant teachers were placed in the former
Catholic school. On September 8 Father Conry gave notice
to the board that the arrangement was not satisfactory. The
board, as it had probably been expected to do, refused to
change the assignments and resolved to cancel the lease. Such
was the end of the " Faribault plan." [64]

[64] *St. Paul Dispatch*, 1892: February 1, p. 3; *Minneapolis Tribune*, 1892:
February 1, p. 3; *Faribault Democrat*, 1892: February 5, p. 3; *Faribault
Republican*, 1891: October 7, p. 3; 1892: March 9, p. 2; October 5, p. 3;

The protest of the Minneapolis Protestant ministers was but an inconsiderable storm cloud compared with the tempest that swept over Catholic quarters far beyond the borders of Minnesota. According to the newspapers, the Roman Catholic priest at Faribault, having observed that the public schools were training children for American citizenship, desired to obtain that training for the children of his parish. He may have meditated upon the matter for a long time, but it was not until a few days before the beginning of a new school year that he dramatically notified the school board of his wish to merge his parish school with the public school system of the city. Whether or not the theory voiced by the Protestant ministers, that a deep-laid scheme had been concocted by the Roman hierarchy to be unfolded in some selected community at a favorable moment, had any basis of truth, the Faribault priest must have been aware that his action would not be offensive to his ordinary, Archbishop Ireland.

On July 10, 1890, Archbishop Ireland had read before the convention of the National Education Association in St. Paul a paper entitled " State Schools and Parish Schools," in which he declared that he was a friend and advocate of state education and that he " would fain widen the expanse of its wings until all the children of the people find shelter beneath their cover." After making a suggestion, which he did not elaborate, that the state pay parish schools for secular instruction given by them, he outlined the plan already in operation in Poughkeepsie and other places. In Poughkeepsie the school board rented the parish school buildings from nine o'clock in the morning until three o'clock in the afternoon. The school was in every particular a public school. No positive religion was taught during school hours. Catholic teachers who were competent, industrious, and loyal held their

1893: September 13, p. 3; proceedings of the board of education of Faribault, May 13, 17, June 24, July 14, September 9, 11, 30, 1893, transcript in Folwell Papers, August 4, 1928.

positions and were free to teach religion in the school buildings out of school hours.[65]

It may be believed that the patriotic priest at Faribault
knew the sentiments of the archbishop. He needed no instruction when opportunity was discovered. Beyond question, the
archbishop gave the experiment his immediate and cordial
approval. It was not long, however, before he was obliged
to defend it against attacks from numerous quarters. The
interview published in the *New York Herald* was a reply to
critics, whom he told, after explaining the plan, that under it
a multitude of Catholics might give their children free secular
schooling in company with the children of their fellow citizens. The state would teach what was necessary to the state
without hindering the church's teaching. Catholic conscience
would be satisfied. There was no union of church and state.
He reminded his critics that, according to the letter of 1875
from Rome, Catholic children might be allowed by their
bishops to attend public schools.[66]

The apology did not silence the clamor. The Catholic
organ of St. Paul, the *North-Western Chronicle*, strove to
moderate the " fierce controversy," in which the archbishop
was "reviled by the [Catholic] press as an enemy of the
church and a destroyer of the faith." Early in the winter of
1892 the archbishop departed for a stay of some months in
Rome. After some delay, he was heard before the Sacred
Congregation of Propaganda in " a masterly argument " in
defense of his position. The decree of the congregation was
tolerari potest, that is, " It can be allowed." The Jesuit organ,
Civilta Cattolica, displeased with the decision, appears to
have questioned the import of the phrase. The archbishop
wrote to the prefect of the Propaganda asking if the phrase
did not mean " It *is* fully allowed." In the reply, which was

---

[65] *North-Western Chronicle*, July 11, 1890, p. 1. Archbishop Ireland's
address is included in his *The Church and Modern Society: Lectures and
Addresses*, 1: 217–232 (New York, 1903).

[66] *North-Western Chronicle*, December 25, 1891, p. 8.

in the affirmative, it was requested that the controversy over the Faribault plan should cease. Upon his return to New York, on July 8, 1892, the archbishop declined to talk on the subject, saying the Pope had requested that the controversy be closed. A dispatch of July 12, 1892, from Washington to St. Paul stated that, on being asked to state plainly whether the Pope had approved or had merely tolerated the Faribault plan, the archbishop replied that " his holiness approved the trial of the Faribault system and hoped for its success." [67]

The belief that religion ought to be formally taught to children in their school years survived and is still held by many. In deference to that sentiment, the compulsory education law was amended in 1923 to permit children to be excused from school for not more than three hours a week to attend a school for religious instruction maintained by a church or an association of churches. Such schools may not be kept in a public school building. They cannot, of course, be maintained in small and scattered communities. Statistics

[67] *North-Western Chronicle,* 1892: January 15, p. 4; February 12, p. 4; May 13, p. 1; June 10, p. 4; July 15, p. 1; October 28, p. 7; 1893: April 28, p. 4; *Faribault Democrat,* 1892: May 13, p. 2; *Pioneer Press,* 1892: July 12, p. 4; *St. Paul Dispatch,* 1892: July 12, p. 1. The acrimonious spirit of the controversy is revealed in John A. Mooney, " The Catholic Controversy about Education," in the *Educational Review,* 3: 237–253 (March, 1892), criticizing two pamphlets published by the Reverend Thomas Bouquillon of the Catholic University of America. In the April issue of the same periodical (3: 365–373), Dr. Bouquillon replies to Mooney. The *North-Western Chronicle,* May 13, 1892, p. 1, contains a reply to Mooney by the Very Reverend Thomas O'Gorman, a professor in the Catholic University. The *North-Western Chronicle,* July 8, 1892, p. 4, quotes Bishop Bernard J. McQuaid of Rochester, New York, as stating that the Faribault plan had thrown back the settlement of the school question a quarter of a century. The statement of the *North-Western Chronicle,* March 11, 1892, p. 5, that a four-column article in the *Moniteur de Rome* defending Ireland had been " inspired, if not dictated by the pope," may be taken *cum grano salis.* Observant of proprieties, Archbishop Ireland refrained from giving to the press his memorial to the Propaganda. As part of the official *ponenza,* or brief, of the secretary of the Propaganda, it was a confidential document. The *North-Western Chronicle,* March 3, 1893, p. 4, and the *Pioneer Press,* February 27, 1893, p. 4, state that it leaked out in Rome, that it was translated from Italian to English and printed in pamphlet form, and that a copy was sent to a private residence in New York City, to be " scooped " by the *Herald* reporter. The question was revived in 1928, when John Hearley, in a preface to an anonymous article entitled " The Catholic Church and the Modern Mind," in the *Atlantic Monthly,* 141: 14 (January, 1928), stated that a number of modern-minded Catholic clergy-

to show the results of the amendment are lacking, but casual accounts indicate that they have been satisfactory.[68]

STATE SUPERVISION OF SCHOOLS

A study of the subject of state supervision of schools leaves the impression that for a long time the people of Minnesota wanted as little of it as possible and that they later grudgingly tolerated its expansion as school funds requiring guardianship increased. The ambitious legislature of 1851, which wrought out the code of that year, could not have expected the devotion of much time and labor by a territorial superintendent on a salary of one hundred dollars a year. The brilliant Neill held the office for two years, and three successors held it one year each. Governor Gorman said in his message of 1856 that the superintendent had resigned and that he had not found anybody who would take the office at one hundred dollars a year. In 1857 a St. Paul lawyer accepted the position, and he probably held it until the close of the territorial period.[69]

One of the school bills vetoed by Governor Sibley on August 12, 1858, provided for a state superintendent of schools to have a check on the proposed sale of the school lands by the townships. There was no session of the legislature in 1859. That of 1860 made the chancellor of the university, as elected by the board of regents, state superintendent. On April 5 of that year Edward D. Neill was elected

men " recalled the late Archbishop Ireland's opposition to the existing parochial-school system and declared that time had ' proved Ireland right.' " The February issue of the same magazine (141: 159–166) contains a second article by the anonymous Catholic writer, on " The Heresy of the Parochial School," which indicates a continuing division of sentiment on the question in church ranks. The March number (141: 395) contains a reply to Hearley's statement by the Right Reverend Humphrey Moynihan, for many years secretary to Archbishop Ireland, to the effect that the prelate did not wish to destroy parochial schools, but desired rather to perpetuate and strengthen them by an amicable affiliation with the public schools. Monsignor Moynihan states further that " Rome's ' Tolerari Potest ' vindicated the Archbishop."

[68] Laws, 1923, p. 76.
[69] Revised Statutes, 1851, pp. 30, 144–198; Kiehle, in Greer, Education in Minnesota, 9; Willis A. Gorman, Message, 1856, p. 5.

to the two offices. In the following year, 1861, that arrangement was upset by an act providing for the election of a state superintendent by the legislature in joint convention and authorizing a salary of one thousand dollars. Neill was elected by a vote of 55 to 6. The popular official continued in office until midsummer, when he resigned to become chaplain of the First Minnesota Regiment. He was succeeded by Benjamin F. Crary, who, after a year's service, resigned to become chaplain of the Third Minnesota Regiment.[70]

The Civil War period was one in which the legislatures were sensitive to demands for economies in public expenditures. The legislature of 1862 considered the state superintendency an office that could be dispensed with and devolved the duties upon the secretary of state, allowing him no additional compensation. The duties of the position were discharged by the secretaries under protest until April 1, 1867, when, under an act of that year, Mark H. Dunnell became superintendent of public instruction. From that time until 1919 the office was held by eight superintendents, to each and all of whom Minnesota owes much for faithful and intelligent services, for which their " pay " was a meager compensation. In 1913 the long title was happily shortened to " superintendent of education." Throughout the period the primary duty of the superintendent was the annual apportionment of the income from the invested school funds and the state school tax to the counties. For that purpose he was early authorized by law to require uniform records and reports from county superintendents, principals, teachers, and school officers, to impose upon them a uniform system of accounting, and to supervise and examine the accounts and records of all public schools. To those grave responsibilities there were added from time to time others, such as the classification and standardization of schools according to law, the

[70] See *ante*, p. 139; *General Laws*, 1860, p. 209; 1861, p. 72; *House Journal*, 1861, p. 416; West, in Greer, *Education in Minnesota*, 97; and Upham and Dunlap, *Minnesota Biographies*, 148.

regulation of the examination of teachers throughout the state and the issue of certificates to the competent, the licensing of dealers in textbooks, the establishment of specifications for school buildings, and the approval of all building plans. The superintendent was throughout the period a regent of the university and a member and secretary of the state normal school board ex officio.[71]

A function that would seem naturally to belong to a superintendent, the critical and directive supervision of the schools themselves, was not imposed upon him, but grew up tardily as an incident of state aid. The act of 1878 creating the high school board, which granted money from the state treasury to high schools that would volunteer to prepare students for admission to the university, provided that no school should receive the money until it had been inspected by a member of the board or a competent appointed inspector. As it was impracticable for the members — the governor, the state superintendent of public instruction, and the president of the university — except in occasional instances, to devote much of their time to inspecting schools, in 1881 members of the university faculty were employed as inspectors without additional compensation. This economical arrangement was continued for many years, until the number of schools became so large that the work of inspection took too much of the professors' time. Objections were heard also that the university was enjoying an unfair advantage through the visitations of its faculty. In 1893 the high school board was authorized by law to employ a salaried inspector and an appropriation was made for his pay and expenses. The first appointee was George B. Aiton, a graduate of the university and an experienced high school principal. It was the good fortune of the state to retain his services for more than twenty years. In his first year he formulated the minimum qualifica-

[71] General Laws, 1862, p. 29; 1867, p. 7; 1913, p. 796; General Statutes, 1913, p. 642. For a list of the superintendents of public instruction, see Legislative Manual, 1929, p. 81.

tions that a high school should possess as to teachers, buildings, library apparatus, and a foundation of efficient graded classes, in order to entitle it to state aid. The annual visitations and examinations of the inspector and his generous and kindly counsel stimulated the high schools to increase their efficiency, and before long they formed a system of secondary schools that was highly appreciated at home and in other states. It was a part of the inspector's duty to visit graded schools aspiring to high school rank. His counsel enabled many of them to succeed and thus to swell the number of high schools in the state.[72]

State aid to schools other than high schools was implicit in the act of 1878, but it was not until 1895 that it was granted to qualified graded schools. Two years later it was conceded to the rural schools. The high school board was authorized to appoint an inspector of graded schools and was fortunate in the selection of Albert W. Rankin. The inspection of the rural schools was left to busy county superintendents, who were often incompetent and indifferent.[73]

Up to the beginning of the present century the common school system had been augmented only by the establishment of high and graded schools in towns. By that time there had grown up a belief that schools could and ought to give instruction, not only in the elementary branches of learning necessary to general society, but also to those needed or desired by certain great classes. The demand for agricultural schooling was perhaps loudest. The increase in school endowments and the development of a new pedagogy as a result of better laboratory facilities and methods seemed to make specialized instruction more feasible than it had been before. The long and interesting story of the really romantic experiments made in Minnesota cannot be undertaken in this history. They

[72] General Laws, 1878, p. 154; 1881, p. 186; 1893, p. 213; Rankin, in Greer, Education in Minnesota, 80; Upham and Dunlap, Minnesota Biographies, 6.
[73] General Laws, 1895, p. 451; 1897, p. 483; Superintendent of Public Instruction, Reports, 1895–96, pp. 29, 33, 72.

include the establishment of agricultural departments in high schools; of general industrial training expanded out of manual training after the passage of the Smith-Hughes Act of Congress of 1917; of commercial training departments in high schools; of home economics courses developed out of cooking and sewing; and of teachers' training courses in high schools. Evening schools were established after the revelations of excessive adult illiteracy by the draft for the World War; and junior colleges, which are still few in number, were opened in response to a widespread desire for the extension of secondary education to its normal scope near the homes of the people. Other recent extensions of the school system have been the requirement by law of instruction in physical culture and health in all public schools and the provision for the instruction in separate schools of deaf, dumb, blind, crippled, and subnormal children. All these innovations added to the duties and responsibility of the state superintendent and, as far as state aid and inspection were concerned, to those of the high school board. The school system had become complex and unbalanced.[74]

In December, 1912, the Minnesota Educational Association in convention instructed its committee on legislation to present to the legislature of 1913, about to assemble, a bill for the appointment of a state school committee to study the school situation and to draft a revised school code. The legislature responded by authorizing the appointment of a public school commission of seven members. The selection was most happily made and the commissioners' study was extensive and thorough. Their report, dated December 1, 1914, laid empha-

[74] *Laws*, 1917, p. 305; 1923, pp. 464, 482; 1927, pp. 54, 386; Superintendent of Public Instruction, *Reports*, 1915–16, p. 55. In the year ending July 31, 1927, there were, connected with high schools receiving state aid, 65 agricultural departments, 185 general industrial departments, 151 in commercial training, 266 in home economics, and 98 in teacher training. In the same year there were 18 classes for the deaf, 18 for those with defective speech, 21 for the blind, 12 for crippled children, and 196 for subnormal children. Department of Education, *Financial Statement and Public School Statistics*, 1927–28.

sis upon the unification of the system. To that end they recommended the creation of a state board of education and the transfer to it of all the duties and powers of the high school board, the normal school board, the state library commission, and the board for the special schools for the deaf and the blind. But for " constitutional difficulties," they would have recommended that the control of the state university be put in the hands of the new board. For the greatly needed improvement of the eight thousand rural schools, the commissioners recommended that the small neighborhood districts be grouped into county units and that the schools, when not consolidated, be controlled by an elective county school board. The distribution of state aid in amounts to be fixed by law was to be devolved upon the state board.[75]

The legislature of 1915 was in no mood to entertain the recommendations of the commission and that of 1917 was equally indisposed to radical school legislation. The program of the commission was more acceptable to the House and the Senate in 1919. With but slight opposition an act was passed establishing a state board of education of five citizens, placing under its direction and control all the state educational institutions except the normal schools and the university, and empowering it to administer and enforce all the school laws. For the latter purpose the board was required to elect a commissioner of education for a term of six years as its "executive officer." The act specifically charged the commissioner with safeguarding the school funds. It made him responsible for the administration of the department of education and gave him the privilege of nominating all its officials and employees. The five citizens who were appointed and who on August 1, 1919, organized the state board of education have ever since given their devoted service in the great department committed to their care. The election and

[75] *General Laws*, 1913, p. 848; Public Education Commission, *Report*, December 1, 1914, pp. 7, 11, 15, 18, 22–26. On page 10 is a map showing the number of schools of the several classes.

reëlection of James M. McConnell as their executive officer
have been amply justified. A staff of competent and experienced directors and supervisors now maintains a moderated
and benign oversight of all public school management and
instruction and a check on the disbursement of the vast school
funds.[76]

[76] *Laws*, 1919, pp. 355–359; Department of Education, *Educational Directory*, 1928–29, p. 4 Adequate supervision of the thousands of rural schools
awaits the grouping of them into county or other large units.

IV. CHIPPEWA INDIAN PROBLEMS

EARLY EFFORTS TO CONCENTRATE THE CHIPPEWA

THE present work ought not to close without further account of a people who, at the time of the white man's appearance in Minnesota, occupied more than half the area of the state. Mention has frequently been made in the preceding volumes of the Chippewa or Ojibway Indians, of Algonquian stock, who in early times extended themselves westward and southwestward beyond Lake Superior and at length drove the Sioux beyond the Mississippi. Account has also been made of the effort of the government in 1825 to confine the Chippewa to the north of a line stretching diagonally across the state from a point near Stillwater to another near Moorhead, passing not far from St. Cloud, Alexandria, and Fergus Falls. The expectation of some statesmen that the Mississippi would become and would remain the utmost limit of settlement and that aborigines might continue their occupancy of the regions beyond vanished with the admission of Missouri as a state in 1821.[1]

The first inroad upon Chippewa hunting grounds was made in 1837, when the United States acquired the territory between the St. Croix and the Mississippi from the line of 1825 up to the latitude of the mouth of the Crow Wing River. The next major encroachment was deferred until

[1] *Ante*, 1: 80–84, 147. This chapter will be better understood if the reader will observe and bear in mind that the Chippewa of Minnesota lived in four great divisions, each containing a number of bands. Before any cessions were made, one division held the northeastern part of the state, mostly north of Lake Superior. Grouped with a number of Wisconsin bands, the bands of this division were known as "the Chippewa of Lake Superior." In the extreme northwestern part of the state lived the Red Lake and Pembina bands. The great central area was held by "the Chippewa of the Mississippi," whose principal villages were located on the small lakes near that stream, and by the Pillager and Winnibigoshish bands, most of whom lived about the large lakes that form the headwaters of the Mississippi.

1854, when the "triangle" north of Lake Superior, with its base on the line of the Swan and Vermilion rivers, was ceded by the Chippewa of Lake Superior. The expectation at the time was that copper and at least one of the precious metals would be found in the ceded area. In the year following, by a treaty of February 22, 1855, the Chippewa of the Mississippi and the Pillager and Winnibigoshish bands gave up their rights of occupancy to a great central tract stretching from the Swan River to the Red and from the mouth of the

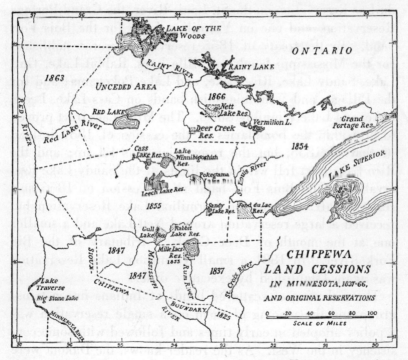

Crow Wing to Rainy River. A fourth great Chippewa cession took place when a tract of about six thousand sections of land in the northwest corner of the state was acquired from the Red Lake and Pembina bands by a treaty of 1863, and in 1866 the United States extinguished the title of the Bois Fort band of the Chippewa of Lake Superior to a tract of some three thousand sections west of the cession of 1854.

After this fifth principal cession the Minnesota Chippewa possessed only their reservations and a large unceded area held by the Red Lake and Pembina Indians east of their cession of 1863.

The reservations originally provided for in the various treaties for the cession of Chippewa lands were usually so located as to include the principal villages of the scattered bands. Thus under the treaty of 1854 the Chippewa of Lake Superior acquired three reservations in Minnesota, the Fond du Lac Reservation on the St. Louis River, the Grand Portage Reservation, and one on Vermilion Lake for the Bois Fort band. By the treaty of 1855 reservations were established for the Mississippi bands on Mille Lacs, Rabbit Lake, Gull Lake, Sandy Lake, Rice Lake, and Lake Pokegama; and for the Pillager and Winnibigoshish bands on Cass Lake, Leech Lake, and Lake Winnibigoshish. The Mille Lacs tract proved to be within the boundaries of the cession of 1837 instead of that of 1855, but the reservation was set up; and the Rice Lake tract fell within the limits of the Sandy Lake Reservation. The Bois Fort band in its cession of 1866 surrendered all claim to the Vermilion Lake Reservation but received a large reservation around Nett Lake and a smaller one at the mouth of Deer Creek, a tributary of the Big Fork River. In 1881 a small Vermilion Lake Reservation was again established by executive order.[2]

The gathering of scattered bands of Indians into a tribal group and the placing of them on a single reservation was a policy adopted in early times and followed with some consistency in the West. As the reader knows, the Dakota were segregated on their ill-shaped reservations along the upper

[2] Ante, 1: 160, 306; Charles C. Royce, Indian Land Cessions in the United States, 802, 804, 828, 840, 844, maps 33, 34 (Bureau of American Ethnology, Eighteenth Annual Report, part 2 — Washington, 1899) ; Newton H. Winchell, The Aborigines of Minnesota, 619, 624–627, 629, 631 (St. Paul, 1911) ; Statutes at Large, 13: 667–671, 689–697; 14: 765–768. The Red Lake and Pembina treaty of October 2, 1863, was amended by a treaty of April 12, 1864, without change as to the area of cession. For Chippewa cessions for the Winnebago and the Menominee in 1847, which are not important here, see ante, 1: 308–321. The original Vermilion Lake Reservation was never located.

Minnesota River under the operation of the treaties of 1851, and in 1855 the scattered bands of Winnebago were finally located on their Blue Earth Reservation. The Indian office and friends of the Indians believed that the concentration of the Chippewa bands residing on the eight reservations assigned to them in 1855 would be desirable. A concentration treaty was negotiated at Washington on March 11, 1863, in which the Mississippi bands agreed to abandon their five scattered reservations in exchange for a single greater reservation surrounding the three reservations occupied by the Pillagers and allied bands at Cass, Leech, and Winnibigoshish lakes. The Chippewa were represented at the negotiation by Henry M. Rice, who had finished his term in the United States Senate on March 3. The concessions that he obtained for his trustful clients show that he knew what things would be most beneficial to them: land prepared for planting, oxen, farm implements, a sawmill, carpenters, blacksmiths, farm laborers, and a physician. An extraordinary provision was that for the appointment by the president of a board of visitors to attend the annual payments, to inspect the fields and gardens, and to report thereon, as well as on the qualifications and moral deportment of all persons lawfully resident on the reservation.[3]

The president appointed Henry B. Whipple, Episcopal bishop of Minnesota, Thomas L. Grace, Roman Catholic bishop of St. Paul, and Thomas S. Williamson, a retired Dakota missionary, as members of the board of visitors. They attended the first payment made under the treaty, in October and November, 1863. In its report to the commissioner of Indian affairs the board stated that the Indians were not pleased to receive the larger proportion of the money due them in paper instead of coin. The visitors approved of the general provisions of the treaty and urged an

[3] *Statutes at Large*, 12: 1249–1255. Rice saw to it that along with oxen went log chains and along with axes, grindstones. He gave minute specifications for chiefs' houses. The Dakota treaties of 1851 and the Winnebago treaty of 1855 are discussed *ante*, 1: 271–304, 318–320.

early appropriation of money to complete the concentration of the Indians. The new reservation, they said, was remote from white settlements, its numerous lakes abounded in fish and wild rice, and there were groves of sugar maple and pastures. But the Indians were not content with the treaty that Rice had made for them. At bottom they did not like to leave their old homes and the white man's allurements, whisky in particular, and move to a far-off wilderness to live with the barbarous Pillagers. The principal reason they put forward for their discontent was that the new reservation was lacking in good farming land, which was probably true. Minor objections may be neglected here for a reason that will presently appear.[4]

The willing consent of the small bands was so much desired by the Indian office that it was deemed advisable to make such changes as they might desire. Accordingly, Chief Hole-in-the-Day and another were brought to Washington in May, 1864, and a new treaty was negotiated with them as representatives of all the Indians concerned. In form it followed closely the treaty of March 11, 1863. The principal change was the addition of a large area to the western end of the reserve and of a trumpet-shaped piece extending to the Red Lake River, much of it good farming land. The Senate ratified this treaty with an amendment, which is not important here, on February 9, 1865. According to a provision of the treaty, the small bands were not obliged to move to the new reservation until three hundred acres of land had been cleared and prepared for planting, a new agency and a sawmill built, and roads opened; and the Mille Lacs Indians, as a reward for previous good conduct, were accorded the further privilege of remaining on their old reservation so

---

[4] *Ante*, 3:22–26; Indian Office, *Reports*, 1863, pp. 328–331, 341–346. This series of reports is described *ante*, 2:111, n. 3. The visitors did not fail to remind the commissioner of the radical faults of the Indian system: the policy of treating the Indians as independent powers, the lack of government by law, and the need of individual ownership of land.

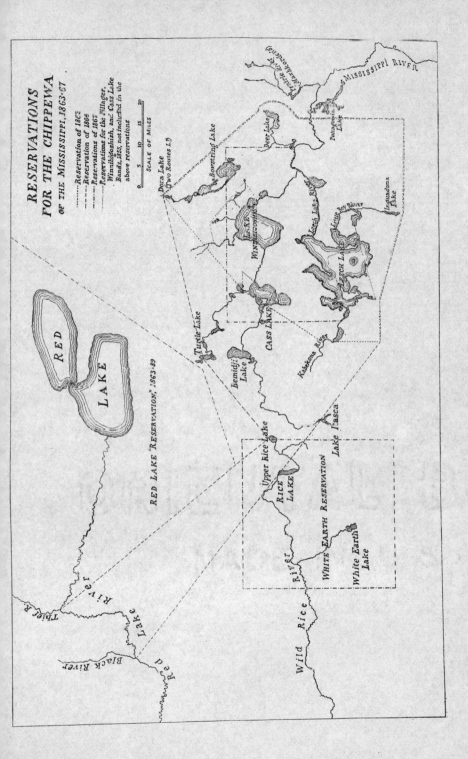

RESERVATIONS
FOR THE CHIPPEWA
OF THE MISSISSIPPI, 1863-67.

········· Reservation of 1863
– – – – Reservation of 1864
—··—··— Reservations of 1867
··········· Reservations for the Pillager,
　　　　　 Winnibigoshish, and Cass Lake
　　　　　 Bands, 1855, not included in the
　　　　　 above reservations

SCALE OF MILES

0   5   10   15   20

MISSISSIPPI RIVER

Potagomigan Lake

Deer Lake

Bowstring Lake

Dora Lake
(Two Routes L?)

Inguadona Lake

LAKE WINNIBIGOSHISH

Leech Lake River

Little Boy River

LEECH LAKE

Turtle Lake

CASS LAKE

Kabekona River

Bemidji Lake

RED LAKE

RED LAKE "RESERVATION," 1863-69

Thief R.

Black River

Red Lake River

Lake Itasca

Upper Rice Lake

RICE LAKE

WHITE EARTH RESERVATION

White Earth Lake

Wild Rice River

long as they did not molest the whites. Although Congress made an appropriation for carrying out the provisions of the treaty, but few Indians moved, and the fair scheme for a greater Chippewa reservation did not materialize. The Indians remained on their old reservations wondering what the Great Father would do next. They had not long to wait for the presentation of a concentration plan which, it was believed, would be more alluring.[5]

On March 19, 1867, a treaty was negotiated at Washington with ten chiefs of the Chippewa of the Mississippi. In the principal article the Indians ceded their treaty rights to the reservation assigned to them in 1864, with the exception of a considerable area adjoining the Cass Lake, Leech Lake, and Lake Winnibigoshish reservations, and accepted an additional tract of thirty-six townships including White Earth and Rice lakes. When located and surveyed, this new reservation extended from township lines 141 to 147 and from range lines 37 to 42. The White Earth Reservation was believed to be an ideal country for the Indian. The two tiers of townships on the west were beautiful rolling prairie, with a deep soil of rich loam on clay subsoil. The two eastern tiers of townships were well timbered with pine, sufficient for the uses of the residents for an indefinite time. The two intermediate tiers were mingled timber and prairie, most desirable for the settler. Every township was dotted with lakelets and all parts of the reservation were drained by rivulets running either to the Crow Wing or to the Red River. The region has ever been regarded as one of the most charming parts of the park region of Minnesota. To encourage removals to the new reservation the government undertook to furnish clothing and provisions to newcomers, to aid them in erecting houses, and to assist them in opening farms by furnishing them cattle, horses, and farming implements. A sawmill, a gristmill, and a schoolhouse were to be erected

[5] *Ante*, 3: 26, 29; *Statutes at Large*, 13: 560, 693–697.

and free schooling was to be provided for ten years. A further provision of the treaty intended to stimulate removals to White Earth was that which promised to every Indian who should clear and cultivate ten acres of land a certificate of ownership of forty acres, a process that might be repeated until he should be the owner of one hundred and sixty acres. These farms were to be exempt from taxation and from attachment for debt and were to be inalienable without the consent of the secretary of the interior, and with his consent they could be alienated only to a member of the Chippewa tribe.[6]

The Chippewa of the Mississippi, then 2,166 in number, still on their old reservations along the shores of the Great River and the lakes traversed by it, were in no haste to move to an unknown region and turn to farming. A limited number reached White Earth the year after the treaty was made and additional numbers dribbled in from time to time. In 1872 Agent Edward P. Smith reported the average population at 550. In that year an agency was established at White Earth, which became the center of government operations. In 1875 Smith, then commissioner of Indian affairs, gave the number of residents as about eight hundred, who were supporting themselves in comfort by agriculture. They had houses, farms, stock, farm implements, sawmills and gristmills, churches with pastors, and three schools. He quoted from a report of the assistant secretary of the board of Indian commissioners, who said, "No good reason appears why

[6] *Statutes at Large,* 16: 719–723. A part of the western extension of the reservation of 1864 was not ceded because it fell within the new White Earth Reservation. The main reservation from the cession of 1867 together with the three reservations assigned to the Pillager and Winnibigoshish bands still constituted a solid area of Indian land surrounding Cass Lake and Lake Winnibigoshish and nearly surrounding Leech Lake. To this area considerable additions were made by executive orders in 1873 and 1874, one of the additions being a tract embracing White Oak Point on the Mississippi, to which the Sandy Lake and Rabbit Lake bands had been removed in 1867 on the supposition, apparently, that it was in the reserved area. The White Earth Reservation was enlarged by executive order in 1879 but the addition was restored to the public domain in 1883. Charles J. Kappler, ed., *Indian Affairs, Laws and Treaties,* 1: 851–854 (Washington, 1904); Indian Office, *Reports,* 1872, p. 209. See the maps on pages 233, 257, *post.*

these Indians should much longer need the care of the General Government." [7]

The year 1876 was marked by a great accession to the Indian population on the White Earth Reservation, raising the total to 1,427. Not many of the newcomers were Chippewa of the Mississippi from their old reservations. The increment was made up mostly of Pillagers who had been squatting about Otter Tail Lake, where they had become a source of annoyance to settlers, and of Pembina Indians, who had continued to occupy their old haunts in the Red River Valley after the cession of 1863. Both these bodies were still wild Indians and years passed before they ceased to wander about and settled down on the reservation to live off the land. The agent reported a marked progress in farming by the Indians on the reservation in 1876. Two years before it had taken five men to run a breaking team of three yokes of oxen, three to drive and two to hold the plow; now two men were doing the same work. He had a school in session eight months during the year, with four woman teachers. The mission of the Protestant Episcopal church was prospering under the general charge of the Reverend Joseph A. Gilfillan, with the Reverend John Johnson (Enmegahbowh) in charge of the church, composed mostly of the people he had brought with him from Gull Lake in 1868. The Roman Catholic mission was in charge of the Reverend Ignatius Tomazin, whose church was made up mostly of French mixed-bloods. After a period of friction between the two leaders, they had apparently found a way to work harmoniously. [8]

During the next decade the affairs of the Chippewa on the White Earth Reservation showed steady, if not very rapid, progress. The number of farms increased. Some of them were large and were supplied with harvesting ma-

[7] Indian Office, *Reports*, 1867, p. 397; 1868, p. 301; 1870, p. 305; 1871, p. 588; 1872, p. 210; 1875, p. 53; Winchell, *Aborigines of Minnesota*, 670.
[8] Indian Office, *Reports*, 1871, p. 592; 1875, pp. 53, 298; 1876, p. 84; 1878, p. 81. The removal of the Otter Tail and Pembina bands to the White

chinery, but the agent stated that three-fourths of the crops were raised by mixed-bloods. In 1879 a fair managed entirely by Indians was held and a very creditable display of Indian products, agricultural, mechanical, and domestic, was made. The agent said that but few fairs anywhere could present a greater variety of domestic products, or products of superior quality and workmanship. The schools were well attended. In 1884 the agent reported the population of the reservation as about eighteen hundred. There was little crime and not much drunkenness, and the Indian police handled with discretion the few complaints made of wrongdoing or disorder. The large attendance at the services of the mission churches may have been due in great part to the prominence given to ritual, music, and vestments in the Episcopal and Catholic churches. Fortunately no other denomination came on the ground to distract and divide. It is not too much to say that the advance made in civilization in the period in view, from 1877 to 1886, was due, more than to any other agency, to the devoted labors of the missionaries and their helpers and converts. Bishop Whipple said in 1886, " There is not in the State a more orderly Christian community than the Indians of the White Earth Reserve." [9]

THE NORTHWEST INDIAN COMMISSION, 1886

When the White Earth Reservation was planned it is probable that there was an expectation, a hope at least, that some

Earth Reservation had begun in 1874, in accordance with congressional legislation. The expenditure of twenty-five thousand dollars appropriated for the relief of the Chippewa on the White Earth Reservation in May, 1872, was made contingent upon the consent of those Indians to the establishment of the Otter Tail Pillagers on the reservation; and in 1873 twenty-five thousand dollars were appropriated for the purchase from the Mississippi Chippewa of one township in the reservation as a home for the Pembina band. See the map on page 233, post. Additional appropriations were made to meet the expenses of removal. Statutes at Large, vol. 17, pp. 189, 539; vol. 18, part 3, pp. 173, 174; Indian Office, Reports, 1874, p. 195; 1875, pp. 53, 298; 1877, p. 129.

⁹ Indian Office, Reports, 1878, p. 78; 1880, pp. 103–105; 1884, p. 103; 1885, pp. 114–116; 1886, pp. 168–170; commissioner of Indian affairs to the

day all the Chippewa of Minnesota would be gathered there. Its area of eight hundred thousand acres would provide a farm of more than one hundred and sixty acres for every Chippewa family in the state. The concentration idea was much favored by friends of the Indians. President Grant's board of Indian commissioners appointed in 1869 laid out a charming scheme for collecting the Indian tribes in small contiguous reservations to be included in bigger ones. When the Indians should be civilized the small reserves would be counties within the large reservation states. Chippewa agents, contrasting the wretched conditions of the Indians on the old reservations with the comfort and prosperity of their wards at White Earth, from year to year urged the removal of some or all Minnesota Chippewa to that center.[10]

The emergence of new circumstances at length took the matter out of the field of conjecture and debate. In the early eighties a tide of home-seekers, native and foreign born, swept down the valley of the Red River and converted it into a vast wheat field. To these farmers it seemed absurd that fewer than two thousand Indians and half-breeds should be holding eight hundred thousand acres of land, half or more of which was ready for the breaking plow. In the summer of 1885 an assemblage of settlers adopted a resolution demanding the opening of the White Earth Reservation to white settlement. On the east of the reservation the enterprising lumbermen of Minneapolis had extended their operations into the forests of Hubbard County and it was no secret that they would be pleased to push their logging crews into the fine stands of pine in the eastern townships of the reserve. These suggestions of intrusion upon a tract supposed to have been dedicated to the Chippewa for all time gave alarm.[11]

secretary of the interior, January 14, 1886, in 49 Congress, 1 session, *Senate Executive Documents*, no. 44, p. 5 (serial 2333).
    [10] Indian Office, *Reports*, 1869, p. 49; 1873, p. 182; 1876, p. 84; 1878, p. 82; 1882, p. 98. The reservation contained 796,672 acres of land.
    [11] Edward V. Robinson, *Early Economic Conditions and the Development of Agriculture in Minnesota*, 63, 85, 115, maps (University of Minnesota,

No person was more willing or better qualified to voice a protest against the opening of the reservation to white settlement than Bishop Henry B. Whipple. He had come to Minnesota in the summer of 1859. Within ninety days he made a visit to the Chippewa band at Gull Lake. Thereafter from year to year he visited the Chippewa country, sometimes making tours of five hundred miles. He had become the friend of many of the leading men and through his ministrations had endeared himself to hundreds of individuals. The Episcopal mission at White Earth under the Reverend Joseph A. Gilfillan was a darling project.[12] Immediately after the meeting of the settlers in the summer of 1885 he wrote a protest to every senator and representative in Congress and to heads of bureaus in Washington. Early in October he went to Washington and had the chief justice of the United States introduce him to President Cleveland, who received him, as Bishop Whipple said, "with a frank, warm, earnest heart," listened to his explanation of the situation and to his appeal for the preservation of the White Earth Reservation as a home for the Chippewa of Minnesota, and at the close of the interview asked the bishop to put the substance of his statements into writing. Accordingly, on October 14, 1885, Bishop Whipple wrote from Faribault the following letter to the secretary of the interior:

I respectfully suggest that you should call the chiefs of the Chippewas to Washington at as early a day as consistent.

(1) They have suffered very great wrongs by the building of dams on the Mississippi.

(2) They own large tracts of valuable pine land, which is year by year injured by fire.

Studies in the Social Sciences, no. 3 — Minneapolis, 1915); 49 Congress, 2 session, Senate Executive Documents, no. 115, p. 53 (serial 2449).

[12] Henry B. Whipple, Lights and Shadows of a Long Episcopate, 29 (New York, 1900); George C. Tanner, Fifty Years of Church Work in the Diocese of Minnesota, 1857–1907, 299–301, 511–515 (St. Paul, 1909). It was Tanner's hope to prepare a history of the Protestant Episcopal mission to the Chippewa. Unfortunately the hope was not fulfilled. The final chapter of his book contains a table of contents of the contemplated work that will be indispensable to the future historian, and the present reader may find it useful.

(3) The Indian annuities have expired, or will soon.

(4) They have little or no funds for civilization.

(5) The Leech Lake, Cass Lake, Winnibagoshish, Oak Point, Sandy Lake, and Mille Lac Indians cannot be protected where they are or led to civilization.

(6) There is abundant land at White Earth of the best quality. The White Earth Indians will for a fair consideration give all that is needed for the other Chippewas.

(7) Great care must be taken to secure only those chiefs who can control their people and whose influence is on the side of civilization.

I do not believe that it is possible for a commission to make a treaty in the Indian country. It can be done at Washington.

I respectfully suggest that great care shall be taken to select proper representatives of the different bands, as well as the interpreters who are to accompany them. If you can do this, you will, I am sure, under God be the instrument of saving this poor race.

The following memorandum was attached to the letter:

(1) No almshouses for able-bodied men to graduate savage paupers.

(2) All funds except for aged, infirm and sick, widows and children, to be expended as rewards for labor.

(3) Provision for schools in each settlement.

(4) Lands to be given on actual settlement in severalty and inalienable.

(5) Provision for police administration of law.

(6) White Earth Reservation to be kept for their inheritance forever.[13]

The secretary of the interior, L. Q. C. Lamar, put the bishop's letter into the hands of the commissioner of Indian affairs, J. D. C. Atkins, whose report on it, made to the secretary on January 14, 1886, showed that he had made a long and careful study of the Chippewa situation in Minnesota. He found the residents on the White Earth Reservation living in plenty and comfort, while those on the old reservations were in a deplorable condition of poverty and barbarism. Fifteen hundred others were wandering about

[13] Whipple, *Lights and Shadows*, 314; 49 Congress, 2 session, *Senate Executive Documents*, no. 115, p. 53 (serial 2449). Whipple's letter is in 49 Congress, 1 session, *Senate Executive Documents*, no. 44, p. 6 (serial 2333). In the *St. Paul Pioneer*, January 12, 1869, is a letter from Whipple in which he sharply criticizes the treatment of Indians by the United States.

exposed to the white man's allurements. Consolidation on White Earth was necessary to save the Chippewa. The commissioner did not, however, approve of the bishop's suggestion that a delegation be brought to Washington. He would send out a commission of men familiar with the history and surroundings of the Indians and known to be interested in their welfare. The bishop's plan may have been the wiser one. The secretary gave the report a favorable indorsement and laid it before President Cleveland, who, on January 25, 1886, transmitted the papers to both houses of Congress with a request that "the matter . . . have early attention, consideration, and action." The executive's appeal seems to have made little impression. Both houses ordered the papers printed and referred them to their committees on Indian affairs. But somebody was sufficiently interested to see to it that an item was included in the Indian appropriation bill of the year, which was approved on May 15, authorizing the secretary of the interior to negotiate with the Chippewa Indians of Minnesota for a modification of treaties, a change of reservations, and an adjustment of claims.[14]

When the commissioners were appointed to conduct the negotiations authorized in the act of May 15, 1886, Bishop Whipple, of course, was named one of them. The other two were Charles F. Larrabee, an experienced official of the Indian office, and John V. Wright of Tennessee, a former representative in Congress and a judge, who was elected chairman. Their special instructions from the commissioner of Indian affairs were dated July 27, 1886. The chief duty laid upon them was to negotiate for the removal of all the Chippewa of Minnesota, except the Red Lake Indians, to the White Earth Reservation and for their consolidation there as a single people; next to that in importance was to procure the cession of the old reservations for a just compensation.

[14] 49 Congress, 1 session, *Senate Executive Documents*, no. 44 (serial 2333) ; *Congressional Record*, 863, 923; *Statutes at Large*, 24: 44.

The season was far advanced and the commissioners lost
no time in meeting in St. Paul and hastening on to White
Earth. On August 5 they met in general council the chiefs,
headmen, and nearly all, if not all, the principal men on
that reserve. Obviously the first task of the commission was
to ascertain the sentiment of the White Earth Indians in regard to a great accession of less civilized Chippewa to their
numbers. After prayer by Bishop Whipple, Colonel Timothy
J. Sheehan, Indian agent at White Earth, introduced the
commission severally to the council. " I want you," he said,
" to have the utmost confidence in them. They will stand
between you and the ' pine ring ' and all the bad speculators
of the Northwest. . . . You will never again get such a
commission, in our day."

In his opening address Judge Wright, the chairman, said:
" The Great Father thinks that if all your tribes were together
it would make you strong and make you happier. . . .
You have a good country . . . one of the richest countries I have seen in any part of the United States. You
are better off now . . . than thousands of white men
in the country where I live. . . . I might say half of
the people of Tennessee work upon other men's land and
barely make a support for themselves and their families.
You have good homes here. . . . We want you to keep
these homes . . . and be a strong, prosperous, and happy
people." Larrabee told the Indians of the passion of
white men to get Indian lands. " We have sixty millions of
people in this country," he said, "and it will only be a short
time before there will be one hundred million. . . . The
pressure for Indian land is terrible." Bishop Whipple
spoke of his twenty-seven years' acquaintance with the
Chippewa and of his action in the previous summer to stop
the movement to open the White Earth Reservation. He
read the letter he had written to the Great Father and told
them how the Great Father had advised the Great Council to

take action and how the Great Council had provided for a commission to preserve White Earth and to bring the people on the other reservations there. He said to them: "When . . . the Secretary of the Interior . . . told me . . . that the only object of the Government was the salvation of the entire Ojibwa Nation, I said it may be that God will crown with success all the labors of the friends of the Ojibwas, and I can see it accomplished before I go to the other home." White Cloud, the chief spokesman of the Indians, thanked the bishop for the kind feeling he had expressed and for his comforting words.

The commissioners found it difficult to confine attention to their first inquiry, whether the White Earth residents would or would not welcome the other Chippewa if they should be brought from their old reservations. As White Cloud said, "the Indians will fly off the track and talk about something else." At one point White Cloud made the acute suggestion that delegations from the various Chippewa bands be invited to come to White Earth and see the country to which they were asked to move. A great many of those people, he said, had never seen a spear of wheat and did not know how it looked. It was explained by the bishop that the commission had no money to bring the Indians there. A delay for Congress to furnish more money would give the enemies of the Indians opportunity to prevent consolidation and that would mean the opening of White Earth and the destruction of the Indians there.

It appeared in one of the early sessions that the Indians in their separate deliberations had found the "money matter" the most difficult question. Apparently they desired that the commission name some gross sum that they might expect to receive and wanted to be sure who would be the final beneficiaries. Bishop Whipple explained to them that the government would get for them the full value of the lands to be sold. He told them that the commission proposed that

" this land — that is, the pine lands " should be appraised
at its value and sold to the highest bidder. The money realized from the sale would " amount to a very large sum;
very much more for the Indians than they could possibly get
if they named any fixed sum . . . and more than Congress would appropriate under any circumstances " for
their land. The money received for the land would be put
into the United States treasury and kept there, and for every
one hundred dollars, five dollars would be paid every year
forever to the Chippewa nation — " one people . . . all
equally dear to each other, and all equally dear to the
Government."

The principal objection made to bringing a large body of
uncivilized Indians to White Earth was that the reservation
would be filled up with paupers. For this the commissioners
were ready with the statement that the Great Father would
make them rich the moment they arrived. In addition to
the allotments of land elsewhere described, every head of
a family would receive a comfortable hewed log house, a
cookstove, a yoke of oxen, a cow, a plow, a wagon, an ax, a
hoe, a spade, a hand rake, a scythe, and a pitchfork. He
would have five acres of his allotment broken for him and
would be given seed for a first crop. Every man of eighteen
or over, as soon as he should have begun in good faith the
cultivation of his allotment, would receive the same outfit.
The government would furnish food to every individual
Indian coming to White Earth until he should be able to
support himself, but not for longer than two years. The
daily ration would be a pound and a half of beef or half
a pound of bacon, half a pound of flour, and half a pound
of corn; and for every hundred rations four pounds of coffee,
eight pounds of sugar, and three pounds of beans would be
supplied. The United States would furnish free such carpenters, farmers, blacksmiths, physicians, and clerks as
might be necessary. The Indians coming to live on White

Earth would be, not paupers, but rich people the moment they arrived. The commissioners seem to have anticipated an objection of the Indians that bad white men would obtain residences on the reservation by marrying Indian women or by getting employment under the government. In the draft agreement it was therefore provided that no Indian woman should be married to a white man unless her chief, the agent, and one of the white missionaries should certify to his moral character and fitness to live on the reservation and that all government employees must be married men living with their families.

There was another consideration, about which little was said in the councils but which perhaps more than any other brought the majority over to the agreement. Under the treaty of 1867, which established the White Earth Reservation, an Indian who should clear and cultivate ten acres of land might have a certificate for forty acres and, after three repetitions of the process, might become the owner of a farm of one hundred and sixty acres. It is not known how many individuals had fulfilled the conditions, but probably the number was not great. The proposed agreement offered to bestow immediately upon all the White Earth Indians the same land grants as those to be enjoyed by the Indians coming from the old reservations, that is, one hundred and sixty acres to every head of a family, eighty acres to each single person of eighteen or over and to every orphan child under eighteen, and forty acres to every other person under eighteen. An Indian having four children would at once become possessed of three hundred and twenty acres. What was perhaps still more alluring to some was the statement made in council that "every Indian on the White Earth Reservation shall have the same advantages to begin his career of civilization — the young men, with a wagon, cattle, plows, &c. — as these men who come here" — a statement not completely in accord with the text of the agreement.

The council lasted six days, no small part of the time being used by the Indians for private consultations. The commissioners listened with great patience and good humor to the queries and objections, many of them trivial and much like those occasionally heard in the councils of the Great Father. The influence of Bishop Whipple, acquired by an intercourse of nearly thirty years, was exerted with discretion and eloquence. At one point White Cloud broke out: " You are the man who took us from the dust. You are the man who shook the dust away from us. You are the man that put us again on our feet. . . . You took us by the hand and placed us here. . . . From year to year when we see the actions of the whites, how they are looking upon our land with covetous eyes . . . you, Bishop Whipple, still stand by us and uphold us." It was this chief who, with prophetic insight, secured a promise that no pine lands, but only agricultural lands, should be allotted. The tedious debate ended in a love feast, slightly marred by the morose utterance of one Indian, " We think that we have done a great thing for our Great Father in selling him some of our possession, that he may give it to those whites who are clamoring for land." On August 11 the agreement was signed by all the Indians then present.[15]

On August 30 the commissioners met the representatives of the Pillager bands in general council at the Leech Lake agency. In long addresses they dwelt upon the comfort and wealth that awaited the Indians at White Earth — the farms, cattle, tools, and wagons, the land ready broken, and food for all until they should be producing for themselves. " I see over there at White Earth," said Bishop Whipple, " such a future as no Indian has ever had on this continent." The

15 49 Congress, 2 session, *Senate Executive Documents*, no. 115, pp. 1, 3, 12, 39–41, 50–82 (serial 2449). This document includes, among other papers relating to the subject, the report of the Northwest Indian Commission to the commissioner of Indian affairs, December 1, 1886; the agreements with the several bands of Chippewa; and the proceedings of the councils with the Indians. It will be cited hereafter as *Northwest Indian Commission Report*. The treaty of 1867 is in *Statutes at Large*, 16: 719–723.

Indians were told that they were not to be robbed of their country, but that the Great Father would take in trust the land they left, would sell it, especially the timbered land, at the highest prices obtainable, would put the money in his treasury, and would pay them and their children what the white man calls "interest," five hundredths of the principal sum every year forever.

There was immediate opposition to leaving their homes, especially from a body of older men who were known as the "Smokers." Said one of them, "The Great Spirit put us here on this land to live. . . . the Great Spirit has also put this beautiful lake here. . . . we do not wish to leave what the Great Spirit has given us; we do not wish to leave the home that our Great Father has given us here." This local opposition was inflamed by letters and messages from enemies of consolidation. Fortunately there was another body of Pillagers, young men, called the "Working party," which was willing to entertain the proposals of the commission. These were rehearsed in detail from day to day. Colonel Sheehan came up from White Earth and appealed to the Pillagers not to listen to "the evil men who are trying to poison your minds." "Whatever these commissioners offer you," he said, "I believe from the bottom of my heart it will be for your good, and I beg of you to accept it. I know the intriguers, the whisky men, and the pine ring men. . . . I know them." Very little objection was made to the personnel of the commission, but one of the Indians said that they would like to leave the whole affair to their great friend, Rice. Another proposed that a delegation of chiefs, braves, and young men be sent to Washington to ask for the money already due them and that Father Aloysius Hermanutz, the Roman Catholic missionary at White Earth, be allowed to take them down. They would pay their expenses out of their own money.

A Chippewa Birch Bark and Grass Wigwam

Graves of Chippewa Medicine Men and Chiefs
[From photographs taken at Leech Lake in 1896, in the museum of the
Minnesota Historical Society.]

It is probable that a sufficient majority of these Indians would have been brought over by the attractions at White Earth, the eloquence of the commissioners, and their reminders that game, fish, and wild rice were not so plentiful as they had been about the beautiful lake; but an increased majority was secured by some minor considerations. In the councils the Indians repeatedly mentioned large and indefinite sums of money that the government had promised them but had never paid. The commissioners agreed that an examination of all claims should be made and that all found justly due should be paid.[16]

Some of these claims arose out of the great reservoir project undertaken by the government shortly before for the improvement of navigation on the upper Mississippi. An account has already been given of the " break " in the limestone rock a few hundred feet above the Falls of St. Anthony on October 4, 1869, threatening the destruction of that cataract. Soon after that event the water power companies at the falls instituted an investigation to determine the feasibility of a system of dams at the upper sources of the Mississippi to hold back the spring floods and thus simplify the preservation of the falls, and a few years later another investigation, directed by a member of the corps of engineers, was made and reported upon. On June 18, 1878, Congress directed the secretary of war to cause an examination to be made to determine the practicability and cost of a system of reservoirs. In conformity with this act, a survey was made by Captain Charles J. Allen of the corps of engineers. His recommendation for dams at Lake Winnibigoshish, Leech Lake, and Pokegama Falls was accepted, funds were appropriated for the carrying out of the project, and in 1882 work was begun. The three dams were com-

---

[16] *Northwest Indian Commission Report*, 16, 95–112. A brief sketch of the career of Father Aloysius is given *post*, p. 324.

pleted in 1885. A fourth dam, on the Pine River, was finished in 1887.[17]

In the act of Congress of March 3, 1881, making an appropriation for the construction of the dams, the secretary of the interior was directed to estimate any damages that might be done to the property of friendly Indians; for such damages the Indians were to be reimbursed, but not in excess of ten per cent of the total amount appropriated for the reservoir project. On October 6, 1881, a commission of three citizens, appointed on August 11 of the same year to estimate such damages, reported the total sum of $15,466.90, which was approved by the department of the interior. The Indians would not touch a dollar of it, the award being in their judgment altogether inadequate. There was much indignation in the villages and some foolish young men talked of driving off the surveying parties. A rumor of an outbreak spread, but if there was any danger it was put to rest by a very judicious letter from White Cloud at White Earth to a local chief. At the urgency of Bishop Whipple the secretary of the interior on December 22, 1882, appointed a second commission, consisting of General Henry H. Sibley, ex-Governor William R. Marshall, and the Reverend Joseph A. Gilfillan. Nothing could be done in the winter of 1883 and a long illness of General Sibley delayed action still further. He was at length obliged to resign and on September 21, 1883, Russell Blakeley of St. Paul was appointed in his place.[18]

It was not until November 10, 1883, that the commission could meet the bands of Leech Lake and Lake Winnibigoshish in the agency building at Leech Lake. The Indian

[17] *Ante*, 3: 336–346; Chief of Engineers, *Reports*, 1870, pp. 282–289 (serial 1447); 1875, part 2, pp. 434–441 (serial 1676); 1880, part 2, pp. 1590–1600 (serial 1954); 1882, part 2, pp. 1763–1770 (serial 2012); 1885, part 1, p. 272 (serial 2370); 1887, part 1, p. 224 (serial 2534); United States, *Statutes at Large*, 20: 162; 21: 481; 22: 203.

[18] *Statutes at Large*, 21: 481; Indian Office, *Reports*, 1883, p. lviii; *Damages to Chippewa Indians*, 1–3, 6–12, 17, 21 (48 Congress, 1 session, *House Executive Documents*, no. 76 — serial 2200).

spokesmen had evidently reached an understanding beforehand and were unanimous in their demands. This was their
country, they said; it was their right to say what the Great
Father should pay for the injuries to their people. The dams
would utterly destroy all their means of living — their rice
fields, their cranberry marshes, their meadows, and their
sugar bushes. They must have $250,000 every six months.
They refused to give any definite information as to amounts
or values of crops and other property that would be damaged.
The commissioners found it impossible to arrive at any reasonable conclusion with the Indians and had to depend upon
a small body of desultory evidence and such general information as they could pick up. They concluded, however,
that the damages would probably be great and estimated them
at $26,800 a year without term. As if to suggest the best way
out of the matter, they tacked on to their report a suggestion
that all these Indians ought to be moved to White Earth.
The commissioner of Indian affairs and the secretary of the
interior approved the award and recommended a settlement
of $10,000 for property destroyed during the prosecution of
the work on the reservoirs and an annual appropriation of
$26,800.[19]

The Congresses of 1884 and 1885 gave the matter no
attention. On April 1, 1886, the commissioner of Indian
affairs reminded the secretary of the interior of the unpaid
award and advised that $144,038.18 be paid the Indians
for damages for the years from 1883 to 1887, inclusive. The
laches of Congress may be attributed in part to a disposition
to let the matter run and pay what damages should actually
be done. So the matter stood until the appointment of the
Northwest Indian Commission. In the council at Leech
Lake the demand for damages done by the reservoirs then
in operation was renewed and harped upon until the commissioners saw that some allowance must be made or no

[19] *Damages to Chippewa Indians*, 1–4, 20–37. Marshall was absent from
the meeting on November 10.

agreement could be reached. Their proposition of $150,000 as payment in full was satisfactory and it was written into the agreement.[20]

At many points in the palaver the Indian orators pleaded that the negotiation be postponed and that a delegation of chiefs and braves be called to Washington to confer directly with the Great Father. The commissioners assured them that the agreement must be made there and then if at all, but that a delegation of not less than twelve chiefs and head-men should be called to Washington at the expense of the government to consult with the Great Father about matters relating to the welfare of their people. An appropriate article was added to the agreement. The council had then been going on for a week and little remained but to satisfy some curious souls about details. One Indian wanted to know what kind of a cookstove he would get. Another did not want maimed oxen, but " something that will go fast." Another desired to know whether they could take their preacher along to White Earth. Bishop Whipple said, " The shepherd goes with the sheep, always." The agree-ment was signed on September 7 by thirteen chiefs and many headmen, representing almost two-thirds of the Leech Lake Pillagers.[21]

Having gained the consent of the two principal Indian communities to the agreement, the commissioners turned their attention to the smaller bodies on Cass Lake, Lake Winnibigoshish, Mille Lacs, and Gull Lake, and at White Oak Point. At Raven's Point, on the north shore of Lake Winnibigoshish, they met the chiefs and headmen of the Winnibigoshish and Cass Lake bands, some four hundred in number. They rehearsed the arguments and appeals now familiar to the reader and listened to objections, serious and frivolous. One orator raised a question that the commis-

---

[20] 49 Congress, 1 session, *Senate Executive Documents*, no. 117 (serial 2340) ; *Northwest Indian Commission Report*, 45, 98.

[21] *Northwest Indian Commission Report*, 16, 45–47, 101–112.

sioners wisely avoided. He wanted to know " what guarantee
have we got that we will remain there [*at White Earth*];
that the Great Father will not remove us again." After three
days in council a unanimous vote for the agreement was
obtained on September 16.[22]

The commissioners made their next endeavor with the
bands of Chippewa of the Mississippi that, for reasons difficult to fathom, had been removed from Sandy Lake and
Rabbit Lake to White Oak Point in 1867. Of these Indians
the commissioners said: " There are a few praiseworthy
exceptions, but as a whole they are the most degraded band
in the State. They eke out a scanty living by hunting,
fishing, and picking berries during the warm weather, and
in the winter sell their women in the lumber camps." The
braves they met were insolent and were opposed to removal.
Bishop Whipple reminded them that they had no physician
and that hundreds had died from pestilence at the dam.
They had no schools. That year a hundred thousand dollars'
worth of pine had been destroyed by fire. Consolidation, he
told them, was " just as certain . . . as that the sun will go
down to-night or rise to-morrow morning." Colonel Sheehan
appeared on the second day with a letter from Father
Aloysius. The good priest begged the chiefs and Indians at
White Oak Point to consider the proposals made by the honest and good men sent directly by the president. " This is
the best treaty," he wrote, " that was ever offered to the
Indians in the United States since one hundred years. . . .
I consulted also the Catholic bishop in Saint Cloud, and he
told me to tell the Indians also of your place to sign the
treaty and move to White Earth. . . . Do not listen to any
foolish talk of Indians or white men who only deceive you.
I believe it is the will of God that all of our red brethren shall
go to White Earth and be forever a strong, united, and prosperous people." The admirable counsel was mostly lost

[22] *Northwest Indian Commission Report*, 16, 112–120.

upon those barbarians. The head chief, "Little Frenchman," who had been favorable from the first, signed the agreement. Seventeen other signatures were obtained on September 21 and these represented ninety-six souls, which the commissioners thought to be a majority of all of the bands actually resident on the reservation.[23]

Opposition was expected from the bands at Mille Lacs, "for the most part an idle, shiftless, vagabond set," living in absolute barbarism. Except for three or four old log shanties, there was not a house on the reservation. These Indians were under the influence of "a few superstitious, beggarly old chiefs and medicine men, who may or may not be in the power of the whisky men and lumber thieves." In a council that opened on October 9 the commissioners explained the articles of the agreement and enlarged upon the attractions of White Earth, only to meet with immediate and absolute refusal. When the rebuff was made known at Washington it brought from the secretary of the interior a letter expressing the surprise and disappointment of the Great Father, President Cleveland, and his desire that the Northwest Indian Commission should make another effort to induce the Mille Lacs Chippewa to move to White Earth, "where all the Chippewas will be united in one happy and prosperous family." The commissioners made another appointment for a council at Mille Lacs on November 3. They found present only a minority of chiefs and braves, to whom they rehearsed the old story and offered twenty-five thousand dollars in cash for the slender right of occupancy that the bands had retained under the treaty of 1863. But twelve, representing some fifty souls, were found willing to sign. On their first journey to Mille Lacs the commissioners stopped at Gull Lake and obtained without difficulty a unanimous vote for the agreement from the 155 people left there.[24]

[23] *Northwest Indian Commission Report*, 17, 121–132; Indian Office, *Reports*, 1871, p. 590; 1872, p. 209. See also *ante*, n. 6.

[24] *Northwest Indian Commission Report*, 17–19, 27–37.

There remained only the Chippewa of Lake Superior to be brought, if possible, into the happy family. After the long delay for the second council at Mille Lacs, it was too late in the season to think of reaching the distant Bois Fort and Grand Portage bands. By the courtesy of the agent at La Pointe, Wisconsin, who had the Fond du Lac band under his care, the commissioners were able to meet with representatives of that band near Cloquet on November 16. They found those Indians, some four hundred in number — not more than fifty full-bloods — well advanced in civilization, well dressed and polite, and generally speaking English. They had built comfortable houses without material aid from the government. The commissioners laid before them the advantages and attractions of White Earth but did not advise them to move.[25]

The reader is asked to note and to approve a departure from the strict order of time in this story. There was a negotiation with the Red Lake Indians between the councils at White Earth, from August 5 to 11, and those at Leech Lake, from August 30 to September 7. There can be no question that when, in October, 1885, Bishop Whipple laid his plan for the Chippewa of Minnesota before the authorities in Washington he hoped that all the bands would be consolidated on the White Earth Reservation. It is clear that the commissioner of Indian affairs, the secretary of the interior, and President Cleveland so understood it. When, in the summer of 1886, it came to framing instructions for the Northwest Indian Commission it was found that the Red Lake Indians were in a distinct situation. They were occupying over three million acres, to which they had never ceded their Indian title. It was therefore thought best not then to raise the question of removal, but to induce them to agree to a reduction of their territory, the land relinquished by them to be sold by the government. The proceeds from the sale of the

[25] *Northwest Indian Commission Report*, 19, 38.

land were to be deposited in the treasury to draw interest indefinitely and the interest was to be expended for the good of the Red Lake Indians.

The commission met the Indians on Red Lake on August 17, 1886. Complaints by the Indians that the boundary line of their country had been run wrong and that a large piece of their territory had been taken from them occupied the sessions of two days. After the Indians were made to understand that the commissioners had no authority to take up that matter, they were willing to consider the proposed agreement. It was found that they were ready to entertain the idea of giving up a large part of their country because of threatened incursions by white men and thefts of pine timber, especially along the international boundary line. In the agreement, which was signed on August 23, the Red Lake Indians ceded outright to the United States over two million acres. This land the government agreed to survey, appraise, and classify into timbered and untimbered portions. It embraced, according to the commission, " a vast timber zone, said to be of almost incalculable value." The details of sale and investment were identical with those of the White Earth agreement. In order to carry out a policy of making allotments in severalty, it was agreed that the Indians should cede the retained million acres, incorrectly called the " diminished reservation," to the United States in trust for the purpose. The agreement as signed pledged the United States to provide schools for all children, to employ the necessary farmers, artisans, and physicians, and to expend immediately one hundred thousand dollars for a sawmill and a gristmill and for building a house and supplying a cookstove, a yoke of oxen, and an outfit of farming tools for every head of a family, every male over eighteen, and every widow without a family, who should be found industrious and in actual need. The government was to be reimbursed out of the proceeds of the sale of the lands. No reference was made in the agree-

ment to removal to White Earth, but Bishop Whipple in a
session of the council could not refrain from hinting at a
great consolidated Ojibway nation living together and drawing a large annual income from a common fund.   " But the
Great Father does not demand this of you," he said.[26]

The commissioners had come short of their ideal of a complete voluntary consolidation of the Chippewa of Minnesota,
but they had gained the consent of a considerable numerical
majority to move to White Earth and begin the white man's
way of living.   The agreements made with the Indians were
not treaties, for in 1871 Congress had by law declared that
" no Indian nation or tribe within the territory of the United
States shall be acknowledged or recognized as an independent
nation, tribe, or power with whom the United States may
contract by treaty."   The Indians who had agreed to move
to White Earth gave up all their " right, title, and interest "
in their old reservations, to receive in exchange individual
allotments of " agricultural (and not pine) land " at White
Earth, but not until after all the residents of White Earth had
taken up like allotments.   When located, the allotments were
to be patented to the several allottees, but were to be held for
them in trust by the United States for fifty years, or longer
if so ordered by the president.   At the end of the term the
lands were to be released to the respective owners or their
heirs as they should appear, according to the laws of Minnesota.   When all allotments, both to White Earth residents
and to the immigrants, should have been patented, the residue
of lands on the reservation — mostly timbered lands, of
course — were to belong to the consolidated bands in common, to be held, however, by the United States in trust for
fifty years, or longer if the president should so direct.   It was
stipulated that allottees who should run short of timber for
their own use might cut what they needed, under the supervision of the agent, from the unallotted lands held by the

[26] *Northwest Indian Commission Report*, 12, 14, 22–25, 82–95.

tribe in common. As to the lands ceded by the Indians at Leech Lake and elsewhere, it was agreed that they should be surveyed, appraised, and sold under the direction of the secretary of the interior, at not less than the appraised value, for cash to the highest bidder. Timbered lands were to be sold in tracts of not more than forty acres, on sealed bids after public advertisement. Untimbered lands might be sold in quarter-section lots, one-fourth of the price to be paid in cash and the remainder in three equal annual payments, with interest at five per cent.

The Northwest Indian Commission, having completed its work in the field, made up and signed its report, which was addressed to the commissioner of Indian affairs, on December 1, 1886, at St. Paul. Agreement to consolidation had been secured from large majorities of all the Mississippi bands and of the Pillager and allied bands residing on reservations except the small one of some two hundred souls on the Mille Lacs Reservation. The refusal of those Indians, said the commission, ought not to defeat the purposes of the government in respect to consolidation; the agreements were just and fair and, if ratified and faithfully carried out, would prove a blessing to all the Chippewa of Minnesota. The members informed the commissioner that they had met hatred and opposition at every step from the whisky-sellers, from the men living in adultery with Indian women, and from the men looking with greedy eyes upon the Indian lands — all anxious to use the Indians as a key to the United States treasury.

The commissioner of Indian affairs deliberated long upon the report and the two agreements, which were submitted with it. It is not known that he had any prejudices. On February 11, 1887, he forwarded the papers to his superior, the secretary of the interior, with a careful analysis of the agreements and his recommendation that the White Earth agreement be ratified. He was not so well satisfied with the

Red Lake agreement. The Red Lake Indians, he wrote, having a right of occupancy only, had no right to sell the timber or to have it sold for them, and they would receive from the proposed sales an amount out of proportion to their needs. He therefore withheld his recommendation. Secretary Lamar submitted the papers to the president on February 17, recommending the ratification of the two agreements, although they were not entirely satisfactory. On February 28 President Cleveland laid the matter before both houses of Congress without comment. But three days remained of the life of the Forty-ninth Congress. All that the houses could do, or perhaps all that they cared to do, was to order the papers printed and referred to their respective committees on Indian affairs.[27]

THE NELSON ACT OF 1889

On January 4, 1888, Knute Nelson, representative in Congress from the fifth Minnesota district, introduced a bill for the relief and civilization of the Red Lake Chippewa Indians. It was read and referred to the House committee on Indian affairs, of which Nelson was a member.[28] On March 1 following, that committee reported a substitute bill

[27] *Northwest Indian Commission Report*, 12-22.
[28] 50 Congress, 1 session, *House Journal*, 204 (serial 2529). This was not the first bill proposed relating to the Red Lake Indians and their reservation. One was introduced in the House in 1884 and another in 1886. See the reports of the House committee on Indian affairs, 48 Congress, 1 session, *House Reports*, no. 183 (serial 2253), and 49 Congress, 1 session, *House Reports*, no. 176 (serial 2435), recommending the passage of these bills. The two reports are similar in content. The opening paragraphs of both assert that the great reservation of three million acres is of little use to the twelve hundred Red Lake Indians and that their thrifty and energetic white neighbors in the vast Red River Valley need timber. The reports agree in recommending the survey of the whole Red Lake Reservation and the separation of pine from agricultural lands; the allotment in severalty of agricultural lands to the Indians and the opening of the remainder to settlement after the allotments have been completed; the appraisal and sale of pine lands at auction at not less than two dollars an acre; the deposit of the proceeds of all sales in the United States treasury, to be held there as a fund for thirty years, bearing interest at three per cent annually; and the expenditure of the interest and of the principal, if desirable, by the secretary of the

for the relief and civilization of all the Chippewa of Minnesota. This bill was accompanied by a report devoted principally to laying the ghost of the agreements negotiated by the Northwest Indian Commission of 1886. The main objection to those agreements was that the " novel, vicious, and dangerous " method of disposing of the surplus Indian lands by sale at auction on sealed bids was unusual and allowed "land speculators and land sharks," rather than actual settlers, to get possession of them. Those lands, said the committee, ought to be classified into pine and agricultural lands and the agricultural lands should be disposed of under the homestead law. It would be monstrous to allow 2,700,000 acres of the people's land to be put up and struck off at auction like goods at a sheriff's or bankrupt sale, in view of the pressing tide of landless poor in the crowded cities. Objection was made to the Red Lake agreement because it gave eleven hundred Red Lake Indians an enormous advantage over other Chippewa — the proceeds of over a million acres. The committee filed exhibits showing protests of over four hundred and fifty individual Chippewa from five reservations against ratification of the agreements. The substitute bill was submitted as " a just and practical measure." [29]

The essential features of the new bill were these: (1) The Chippewa of Minnesota were to cede to the United States all the Indian reservations in the state except the White Earth and Red Lake reservations. (2) All the Chippewa of Minnesota except the Red Lake bands were to be concentrated on the White Earth Reservation and given allotments in severalty, as proposed in the aborted agreements of 1886. The Red Lake Indians were to take up their allotments on their own reserve. The lands remaining on the White Earth and Red

interior for the welfare of the Red Lake Indians. The report of 1886 suggests that the proceeds of all the sales might amount to two and a half or three million dollars.

[29] 50 Congress, 1 session, *House Journal*, 999 (serial 2529) ; *Red Lake Chippewa Indians of Minnesota* (50 Congress, 1 session, *House Reports*, no. 789 — serial 2600).

Lake reservations after allotments had been made were to be ceded. (3) No cessions of land or relinquishments should take place on any reservation until after the consent of two-thirds of all the male adults of that reservation had been obtained and the president had approved the agreement. To make possible a fair count of the Indians' votes on the question, the bill provided for a census of all the bands. (4) To obtain the cessions of land from the Indians, to take the census and the vote, to make the allotments and payments, and to supervise the removal of the Indians, the secretary of the interior was directed to appoint three commissioners, one of them to be a citizen of Minnesota. (5) The lands ceded by the Indians were to be surveyed as public lands were surveyed and classified as pine and agricultural lands. The agricultural lands were to be disposed of at a dollar an acre under the homestead law. The pine lands were to be appraised by three competent men appointed by the secretary of the interior, but at not less than three dollars an acre. The House committee on Indian affairs appears not to have foreseen that in hawking pine lands at auction opportunity would be offered for the intrusion of pine sharks or speculators. It therefore provided for the sale of all the acquired pine lands in forty-acre lots at public auction to the highest bidder for cash; but not more than one-tenth of the pine lands should be offered for sale in any year. (6) All moneys received from the sales of lands of both kinds, after deductions were made for the costs of the census, of the cessions, of the removals and allotments, and of the surveys and appraisals, were to be deposited to the credit of the Chippewa of Minnesota in the treasury of the United States, to remain there as a permanent inviolable fund for fifty years and to draw interest at three per cent annually. One-half of the interest was to be paid in equal shares in cash to heads of families and orphan minors; one-fourth was to be paid in equal shares to all other classes of Indians; and the remaining fourth was

to be used for establishing and maintaining Indian schools.
At the end of the term the principal sum was to be divided
equally among " all of said Chippewa Indians and their issue
then living."

The bill came up for consideration on the floor on March
8, 1888. In the colloquy — there was no debate proper —
some amendments were proposed, most of them of little consequence, with one exception of transcendent importance:
that providing that individual Indians need not move to White
Earth, but might remain on their old reservations and take
up their allotments thereon. This proviso was agreed to
without debate. Its logical effect, to nullify concentration,
was apparently not perceived; its actual historical effect will
be touched upon in later pages. Nelson conducted the colloquy with such good humor and address that a colleague who
objected to certain features of the bill said that the gentleman
from Minnesota had " such a persuasive, clever manner about
him " that he could hardly find it in his heart to criticize his
bill. The bill was passed without roll call.[30]

The Senate committee on Indian affairs, to which the bill
was referred in ordinary course, was in no haste. There is
reason to assume, as it will soon appear, that members of the
committee desired to study the matter on the ground at first
hand. On October 3, 1888, they brought in a complete
substitute for the Nelson substitute bill. Senator Edmunds
asked Senator Dawes of Massachusetts, as " head mugwump "
of Indian affairs, to explain it. Dawes referred to the agreements negotiated by the Northwest Indian Commission and
said they were good agreements as far as they went, but
they " did not cope with the main trouble, the disposition of
the pine lands." A bill drawn by a member of the House
committee on Indian affairs had passed the House but it did

[30] *Congressional Record*, 50 Congress, 1 session, pp. 1886–1889. The bill
is printed in the *Record*. James E. Cobb of Alabama made the motion to allow
those Chippewa who so desired to take their allotments on their old reservations. Nelson said, " I have no objection to it."

not embody the views of the Senate committee, which had
therefore brought in a substitute bill having for its purpose
to " capitalize " the pine lands for the benefit of the Indians.
He and two colleagues had been " out there " and had found
the reservations in a very demoralized state. The bill was
the result of consultations with lumbermen of the West who
had no interest in the matter, to whom the committee had
appealed on account of their experience, and part of the bill
had been "mapped out" by them. The Senate passed the
substitute bill, with slight amendment, without division. The
Fiftieth Congress closed its first session on October 20 and
the bill went over to the second session and to conference.[31]

On December 17, 1888, the Senate concurred in the report
of the conferees and on the following day the managers on
the part of the House recommended concurrence. In an accompanying statement they said that the substitute was " in
substance and form really the House bill." There were
several noteworthy departures, however: one, a provision
that any residue of pine lands remaining after the single
public sale might be sold at private sale, but not for less than
the appraised value; another, a provision that pine lands
must be sold, not at three dollars an acre or more, but at a
price that would yield at least three dollars per thousand feet
of lumber, board measure, for all the pine found in a given
tract; and a third, that agricultural lands should be opened to
homestead entry at a dollar and a quarter, instead of a dollar,
an acre.

Three days later a lively debate took place in the House
upon the pine land features of the bill, Nelson taking the
leading part in defense of the bill. Sixty thousand people of

[31] *Congressional Record,* 50 Congress, 1 session, 1971, 9129–9131, 9353, 9616.
The Dawes substitute is printed in full in the *Record.* In some byplay Dawes
referred to Sabin of Minnesota as having the bill in charge. Sabin said that
the senator from Massachusetts was the author of the bill, as he had " disem-
boweled the original bill and substituted one of his own." Dawes said, " I
drew the bill." Still the measure has always been called the "Nelson bill "
or the " Nelson Act."

his district, he said, desired him to obtain the opening of the Chippewa reservations and the colonization of the Indians where they could become good and useful citizens. He had two reasons for favoring the rapid disposition of the pine lands. One of them was that it would put a stop to frauds committed by lumbermen abusing the homestead and preemption laws. "They," he said, meaning, of course, only a class of lawless lumbermen, "have sent their mill-hands and choppers to go and settle on them, some for a week, some for a month, and then to go to the local land office and prove up or commute, as the case may be, and then get a transfer of the title." Another reason was that certain lumbermen of Minnesota, who were opposing the bill, had for years been getting Indians to set fires to the pine woods and then to apply to the interior department for leave to sell dead and fallen timber. Granted this leave, the enterprising lumbermen would get the timber for a trifle — "just about what it costs the Indians to cut and bank it." Objection was made to private sales of pine not disposed of at the proposed public sale. "Everybody . . . knows," said one member, "that wherever great bodies of these lands are thus offered at public sale at a fixed minimum price not one acre in a thousand is ever sold at public sale if thereafter the lands are to be subject to private entry. . . . Gentlemen living in public-land States know what this means." Nelson's reply was that it was a good plan to allow the residue from the public sale to be sold at private sale, for settlers might then come in and acquire small pieces of forty, eighty, or one hundred and sixty acres. The conference report was agreed to by a vote of 131 to 33. On January 14, 1889, the "Nelson bill" was approved by the president and became a law.[32]

There was much to justify congressional legislation for the relief and civilization of those unfortunate people, who, with the exception of the residents of the White Earth Reser-

[32]*Congressional Record*, 50 Congress, 2 session, 273, 336, 396–400, 829; *Statutes at Large*, 25: 642–646.

vation, were in no better condition than that described by Bishop Whipple in his letter of October 14, 1885, to the secretary of the interior; they were even more degraded. It was absurd that seven or eight thousand barbarians — perhaps two thousand families — should be occupying four and a half million acres of land of great value both for agriculture and for its standing pine timber. White men had built up to the borders of the reserves and some had trespassed on them. It was believed that Indians were capable of civilization; other Indians had become orderly citizens and some of the Chippewa had made a good beginning; the White Earth experiment was full of promise. Segregation of Indians on limited but sufficient areas, where barbaric life would be given up for the practice of husbandry, was essential to their civilization. Congress did not intend to strip the Chippewa of their right of occupancy without remuneration, but proposed a payment liberal beyond precedent. They were not to be put off with thirty cents an acre for arable land as the Sioux had been in 1858, but were to have a dollar and a quarter an acre. The proceeds, added to the great sum for which their pine lands would be sold, would make a very large fund, to be preserved and administered for the benefit of the Indians and, after fifty years, to be equally divided among them. In the case of the Sioux in 1851 the principal sum was not to be saved for distribution.[33]

While the bill was pending pine was the outstanding subject of consideration. In that day the practice, long established in Europe, of cutting only the ripe trees and leaving the younger ones to mature, thus maintaining a perpetual forest yielding revenue, had not been thought of in a country where trees were things to be cut down. Government pine and Indian pine, it was thought, ought to be harvested as soon as possible to save it from destruction by tornadoes, fires, and lawless lumbermen. It should be remembered that

[33] *Ante*, 1: 281; 2: 218.

the act as passed was in fact only a proposal toward agreements to be made with different tribes or bands of the Chippewa of Minnesota, which must ultimately be approved by the president of the United States.

While the Northwest Indian Commission was laboring with the Chippewa of Minnesota in 1886 to induce them to concentrate into one happy family on the White Earth Reservation, the so-called "Dawes bill" was under consideration in Congress. This bill had the wide scope of civilizing Indians generally throughout the United States. It authorized the president to establish any reservation Indians on allotted lands to be patented to individual Indians, but to be held in trust for them by the United States for a term of twenty-five years, and it provided for the sale of the surplus of lands after the completion of allotments, and the accumulation of a fund in the treasury to be expended for the welfare of the Indians. An outstanding feature was that modifying the naturalization laws by conferring citizenship upon Indians who should establish permanent homes on their allotments and adopt the habits of civilization. The Dawes bill became a law on February 8, 1887, and had notable effects upon the Chippewa of Minnesota.[34]

THE UNITED STATES CHIPPEWA COMMISSION

The inauguration of the scheme set forth in the Nelson Act for the relief and civilization of the Chippewa of Minnesota, mapped out, so Senator Dawes said, by experienced lumbermen who had no selfish interest in it, was the duty of a commission provided for in the law. On February 26, 1889, President Harrison appointed as chairman Henry M. Rice, well known to the readers of this history. He was much experienced in Indian affairs and especially intimate with Chippewa interests. As colleagues Rice had the Right Reverend Martin Marty, Roman Catholic bishop of Dakota,

[34] *Statutes at Large*, 24: 388–391.

and Joseph B. Whiting of Wisconsin, who had much to learn about the aborigines. The commissioners met in St. Paul on June 11. To apprise the Indians of their coming and to prepare them for the important matters to be laid before them, they had several hundred copies of the Nelson and Dawes acts printed and sent out to missionaries, teachers, traders, and others. They invited Bishop Whipple and Archbishop Ireland each to name a delegate to attend the councils and aid in conciliating the Indians. Bishop Whipple sent the Reverend E. Steele Peake, Breck's successor at the Gull Lake mission; Archbishop Ireland sent Father Aloysius. A force of "messengers" was employed to take, or to begin taking, the census required by the law.[35]

On June 29 the commission began a series of councils with the various bands of the Chippewa of Minnesota, which took them from the Red Lake agency to Grand Portage at the tip of the "triangle" and did not end until November 21. The proceedings of the councils were similar. Rice presided with great tact, grace, and patience, and laid open the proposed agreement, which was interpreted phrase by phrase into Chippewa. Bishop Marty enlarged upon the advantages and blessings offered by the Great Father and his Great Council at Washington. Whiting appealed to the natives to accept the generous propositions and indulged in impassioned valedictory addresses.[36]

[35] *Chippewa Indians in Minnesota*, 1, 9, 13, 27 (51 Congress, 1 session, *House Executive Documents*, no. 247 — serial 2747). This document, which includes the report of the commissioners, dated December 26, 1889, will be cited hereafter as the *Rice Report*. When tardily completed the result of the census was as follows:

	Total Souls	Adult Males	Acres of Land
Red Lake and Pembina bands	1,386	386	3,200,000
Mississippi bands	3,002	734	857,686
Pillager and Lake Winnibigoshish bands	2,208	600	423,440
Lake Superior bands	1,708	458	275,815
Total	8,304	2,178	4,756,941

[36] *Rice Report*, 13, 23, 67, 92, 115, 147, 171, 175. Some examples of Whiting's eloquence will illustrate the situation. To the Indians at White Earth he said: "The Government, like you, wearies of these long delays. . . . When it was finally about to give up in despair about making a treaty, it sent for him [*Chairman Rice*]. . . . You may know that he lives in a beautiful

The same general line of argument was employed at all the councils. The Indians were reminded that game was becoming so scarce that they could not live much longer by the chase. They must turn to cultivating the land. As farmers they would need but a small part of the land they had been holding. At one of the councils Whiting said that his home county of twenty-four townships in Wisconsin had forty thousand inhabitants and could accommodate as

home, in the most beautiful portion of St. Paul, surrounded by a loving family and every comfort. It was a great sacrifice for him to leave it for your sake. In sorrow his family parted from him, and he now believes that this is the last opportunity these Indians will have to make a treaty with the Government which will be satisfactory to them, saying, 'As their friend for forty years and more I must go to them.' I beg you not to throw aside his counsel lightly, for no other friend like him can come to you."

At the close of the council at White Earth, Whiting said: "Chiefs and men of White Earth, after many long, weary, and anxious days our work is done; and I reverently implore the blessing of the Great Spirit upon it and you. . . . During all this time your deportment has been such as to challenge our high admiration for you as men of honor, integrity, and sound judgment. . . . We believe that a bright prospect is before you, but you must not expect that your pathway will be all flowers. . . . We believe that if you follow the advice of this venerable and wise chief [White Cloud] you will . . . move onward in the path of progress and upward into the better way of civilization, upward into the warm sunlight of Christianity, and upward into the haven of rest at last."

On August 20 he spoke the final words at the councils at Leech Lake. "Pillagers, I have only words of kindness and good will to speak to you. . . . I had heard that you were a people of dash and courage, with full convictions of what you should do. You are a band which has a history as wide as the country. . . . I come to you a stranger, but it is my highest honor to follow the way that he [Rice] leads in your behalf." In the absence of Flatmouth, head chief of the Pillagers, his sister, Ruth Flatmouth, acknowledged queen of the Pillagers, who had "adopted religion," was the first to sign the agreement. Whiting, referring to her, said: "And now one word to your queen. . . . I charge you to see that no harm shall come to her. . . . Ruth Flatmouth, noble daughter of a noble chieftain! I ask the Great Spirit that her bark may be gently borne to the farther shore. Pillagers, I bid you a kindly farewell."

At the last council at Mille Lacs, Whiting gave the Indians his counsel in regard to intemperance, said to be too common with that band. "You have seen drunken men; men who have taken so much of this burning liquid that they were men no longer. It makes the brave man, the kind-hearted brother, the loving father, it makes him as hideous as the horrid serpent that bites you. It makes him as filthy as the wolverine, that wallows in his filth. It makes men fierce as the tiger, that springs upon a man to destroy him. And above all, it destroys . . . that part of the man which hereafter goes to dwell with the Great Master of Life. . . . So now, my last words: Live soberly, industriously, honestly, and you will succeed. We shall not all meet again. . . . And now, as I leave you, I shake hands with your chief and I shake hands with you all."

many more. The Indians were told that, if they would agree
to it, the government would take the lands for which they
would have no use, sell them to white men for a large sum,
and keep the money safe in the treasury of the Great Father.
Said Rice, "Here is a store-house of money to be drawn
upon for your wants." The government would pay a liberal
interest from year to year, which would be helpful, and
at the end of the fifty years would divide the principal
equally among the Chippewa. As a sweetener, the commissioners promised that the government would begin to pay
that interest in advance, so that the Indians would not have
to wait for surveys, appraisals, and sales. No promise was
made of any definite sum to be obtained from the land sales,
but the Indians were allowed to believe that it would be
great, if the pine should be sold immediately, before being
destroyed by fires or devastated by thieving lumbermen. The
illogical provision of the law that individual Indians might
take their allotments on their several old reservations disposed them to entertain the propositions of the draft agreements. Compulsory removal to White Earth would have
shut the door to any negotiations. Farewell to Nelson's hope
of an early colonization of the Chippewa and the transfor-
mation of those barbarians into good and useful citizens,
so much desired by his sixty thousand constituents.[37]

Much of the time spent in the councils was used by the
Indian spokesmen in airing complaints of the failure of
the Great Father to keep his promises and protect them from

[37] *Rice Report, passim,* especially pp. 5, 68–71, 76, 84, 86, 87, 92, 106, 135,
169. In regard to the dangers to pine, Whiting said at Red Lake, "Unless
something is done for you now, five years hence this vast body of timber will
be destroyed." Bishop Marty, at the same place, said: "The rest of the
land which is now being used up, stolen from you, or burnt off will be taken
hold of by the Great Father for his children. He will sell your pine." Rice
said to the Indians at White Earth, "The pines [*at Red Lake*] are burning
rapidly"; and later he said to the same Indians, "You all know that your
pines are burning. . . . Your trees are being stolen and burned." A spokesman of the Red Lake Indians said: "We are never the cause of the destruction of any pine on this reservation. We are surrounded by whites; they
keep thieving from us and setting fires."

injuries. The Red Lake Chippewa complained that their east boundary line had been run wrong, by mistake or otherwise. The Pillager and Mississippi bands renewed their long-standing claim for damages caused by the reservoir dams on Lake Winnibigoshish, Leech Lake, and Pine River, including pay for 46,920 acres of land ruined by overflows. The Pillagers also renewed a much older claim. In 1847 they had sold to the government nearly seven hundred thousand acres west of and adjoining the Long Prairie Reservation for the Winnebago, upon which to transplant the Menominee from Wisconsin. The Pillagers had been paid about fifteen thousand dollars. The Menominee had refused to occupy the reservation and in 1884 the government had taken the land back and paid the Menominee $242,686 for it. The Pillagers claimed that a wrong had been done them and the commissioners admitted it. At Mille Lacs the Indians complained of errors in their boundaries, of white men squatting on their land, and of the cutting of their pine. The bands at Fond du Lac presented a claim for the value of land of which they had been deprived by a wrong survey. Several bands united in demanding the recovery of $177,600 justly due them as principal and interest under the treaty negotiated at La Pointe on September 30, 1854. The commission admitted that a " palpable error " had been committed to the damage of the Indians and promised their influence toward remedies.[38]

The members of the " United States Chippewa Commission " signed their report at St. Paul on December 26, 1889. The greater part of it was devoted to a history of their transactions, in the course of which they stated the engagements they had made to have the claims of the Indians for damages and arrearages investigated and adjusted. They suggested that under the operation of the agreements the Chippewa

[38] *Rice Report*, 3–5, 14–24, 75, 120, 121, 126, 167, 186. On the transactions of the government with the Pillagers and the Menominee in regard to the proposed Menominee reservation, see *ante*, 1: 320. The Menominee were to have served as a buffer between the mutually hostile Sioux and Chippewa.

must no longer be regarded as tribal Indians, but as citizens, at present poor and helpless, living wretchedly in single-room wigwams or huts. They should be supplied with saw-mills, cattle, and implements of husbandry. Ten acres of maple timber should be set apart for every family and a sufficient tract of pine should be held on every reservation area for common use. A suitable tract should be kept for government buildings for the use of physicians, blacksmiths, carpenters, and missionaries. Unconsciously the commissioners were recommending the reservation system without reservations. Emigration to White Earth they thought desirable, and they recommended an appropriation to pay the expenses of Indians desiring to visit the reservation with a view to settlement. The commission ventured no opinion of its own as to the value of the pine ceded, but gave the estimate of various persons at from twenty-five to fifty million dollars.[39]

The act directed the commissioners to negotiate for the complete cession of all lands of the different bands or tribes except those of Red Lake and White Earth. With the latter bands they were authorized to obtain the cession " of all and so much of " their respective reserves as would not be required to make and fill allotments. The Red Lake bands, after some concessions had been made by the commission in regard to the boundary of the lands to be retained by the Indians, readily consented to a reduction of more than two million acres.

At White Earth there was opposition to any reduction. On the fourth day of the council Gustav Beaulieu, a prominent mixed-blood, asked whether the commission would promise not to open any part of the reservation to white settlement. Rice replied that under the Dawes Act, after all allotments had been taken and everybody had been satisfied, the Indians could apply to the president for leave to

[39] *Rice Report*, 13–27. See especially pages 13, 24, 25.

dispose of any lands left over. Four days later, on July 24, Beaulieu demanded more directly to know whether the reservation was to remain intact. To this Rice replied that the commission was "distinctly of the opinion that for your own safety and protection you should part with a small portion of this reservation" and asked Beaulieu to put his question in writing, with his reasons for opposing reduction, to be answered the next morning. Beaulieu accordingly renewed his question and expressed himself strongly against any diminution of the reserve. He opposed the sale of "a single solitary foot." At the close of a long and wandering debate, in which the matter of reduction was but slightly touched upon, Rice suggested that the eastern tier of townships contained a great deal of pine and, since it had already been surveyed, could be put upon the market in a short time, where it would bring in a large sum of money. In the afternoon of the next day, July 26, White Cloud wanted to know "how much would be taken off our reservation . . . and why it should be done." Rice promptly replied that the commission had thought of taking off six townships, but after making inquiries and "ascertaining how the pine lies, your improvements, and the facilities for getting down your rivers," had concluded that four townships could be spared. There were two reasons why the Indians should give up this land. The pine was being stolen or burned; eventually the Indians would get nothing for it. "Wherever there is a pine forest belonging to the Indians," he said, "it is now, and always has been, and always will be a source of endless trouble." The second reason was that the arrangement would relieve them of trouble and would provide a fund to assist them in their farming. Bishop Marty took up the parable about getting means to improve farms and added that pine sold was not lost. "The sooner it [the pine] is sold," he said, "the sooner you will escape the miserable condition in which some of you now are. You will not then be dependent upon the snake root." White Cloud was satisfied with the arrangement. That this extraordinary mutilation of the White Earth Reservation was desired by persons interested in pine as well as by Indians need not be argued. In its report the commission mentioned the cession as an accomplished fact,

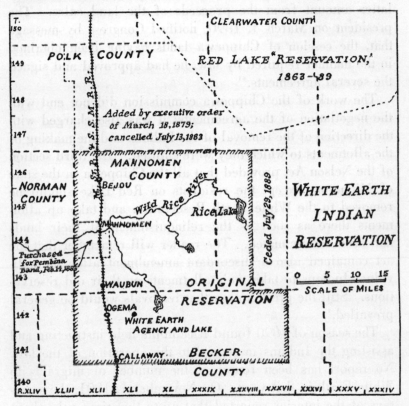

without explanation except to say that as the timber was liable to be stolen or burned the Indians desired an early sale. Those four townships will come again into view.[40]

On January 30, 1890, the secretary of the interior transmitted to the president the report of the Chippewa commission in a letter in which he analyzed and carefully

[40] *Rice Report*, 2, 3, 14, 15, 25, 95–102, 105, 106, 110. Townships 143, 144, 145, and 146 were those eliminated. In answer to another question, Rice

reviewed it. With the report he submitted a draft of a bill for the appropriation of $573,630 for the payment of arrearages — damages by dams and reservoirs — and $250,000 for costs of surveys, appraisals, allotments, and "relief" of Indians; but the government was to be reimbursed for the latter amount from the proceeds of the land sales. The president on March 4, 1890, notified Congress by message that, the cession of Chippewa lands having been obtained in the manner required by law, he had approved and signed the several agreements.[41]

The work of the Chippewa commission did not end with the negotiation of the agreements; it was also charged with the direction of the removal of the Indians and the making of the allotments to which they were entitled. The third section of the Nelson Act provided that all the Chippewa in the state of Minnesota except the residents on Red Lake should be removed to the White Earth Reservation and take up allotments there as soon as the relinquishment of their lands had been consummated. The reader will remember that the act contained also a discordant amendment allowing individual Indians to take their allotments on their old reservations. Still the presumption that removals would be general prevailed.[42]

The season of 1890 found Rice in the field instructing and assisting the Indians in regard to the operation of the law. No report has been found of the number of migrants to White Earth in that year. On November 1, 1891, the secretary of the interior reported that up to that time only about 400 Indians had been removed. By September 1, 1893,

said, "There are quarter-sections among your pine worth $20,000." If half of the 576 quarter sections in the four townships were pine and the value was placed as low as $10,000 a quarter section, a sum of $2,880,000 was concerned. The proceeds from the sale of the pine were to be added to the general Chippewa fund, but this fact was not clearly brought out at the White Earth council; and many of the Indians probably were under the impression that the money was to be paid to them directly.

[41] Rice Report, 1–12.

[42] Statutes at Large, 25: 642–644; Rice Report, 2; Secretary of the Interior, Reports, 1892, pp. 1, li.

that number was increased to 643, not counting 85 who went back to their old homes. In 1894 the chairman who succeeded Rice upon the latter's resignation reported that up to June 7 of that year, out of 4,000 subject to removal, but 775 Indians had moved from the old reservations to White Earth to stay. The secretary therefore instructed the commission to notify the Indians concerned that their option of moving to White Earth would cease on October 1, 1894. Removals thereafter were negligible.[43]

The commission began making allotments on White Earth on December 9, 1891, but the Indians refused to accept them. Congress, on February 28, 1891, had amended the Dawes Act by reducing the size of new Indian allotments generally from one hundred and sixty to eighty acres. The White Earth Chippewa refused to accept the moiety and on March 15, 1892, lodged a formal protest in Washington. Later many individuals, probably advised by the commissioners, consented to take up eighty-acre allotments so located that when Congress should award them the full amount promised by the Chippewa commission and guaranteed by treaty additional eighties adjoining could conveniently be patented to them. By September 1, 1893, 2,209 eighty-acre allotments had been selected at White Earth. The secretary of the interior earnestly recommended that Congress grant the full amount and a bill was introduced for the purpose. It was not the pleasure of Congress, however, to make good the promise of quarter-section allotments to the Chippewa until April 28, 1904, and then under circumstances of an extraordinary character.[44]

THE APPRAISAL AND SALE OF CEDED PINE LANDS

The required survey of the ceded Chippewa lands was promptly undertaken under the direction of the United States

[43] Secretary of the Interior, *Reports*, 1890, p. xxvi; 1891, pp. viii, xlii; 1893, p. xxii; 1894, p. x; Indian Office, *Reports*, 1894, p. 29; 1900, p. 52.

[44] 52 Congress, 1 session, *Senate Executive Documents*, no. 99 (serial 2901); *Allotments to Indians on White Earth Reservation, Minnesota* (58 Congress,

general land commissioner and was prosecuted from year to year with sufficient dispatch. The examination and appraisal of the timbered lands were placed by law in the hands of the secretary of the interior. The work of examination was begun on the ceded lands of the White Earth Reservation in the fall of 1891 by a corps of examiners appointed by John W. Noble, secretary under the Harrison administration. In March, 1893, Hoke Smith became secretary of the interior under Cleveland. From information that reached him he found that the work performed by the examiners appointed by his predecessor was not to be relied upon; they had underestimated timber near logging streams and had overestimated that distant from water. In May, 1893, he dismissed the whole crew and appointed a new corps of twenty-seven men, thirteen from Minnesota and fourteen from other states, the latter not familiar with pine. This crew remained in service until October 31, 1896, but because of the exhaustion of appropriations it was unemployed for nearly six weeks in 1894 and from November 14, 1895, until June 30, 1896, seven and a half months. A part of its work had been the reëxamination of tracts examined by the former party on the Red Lake and White Earth reservations.[45]

2 session, *House Reports*, no. 2460 — serial 4583) ; *Statutes at Large*, 24: 388; 26: 794; Secretary of the Interior, *Reports*, 1892, pp. 1, li; 1893, p. xxii. The act of 1904 is discussed *post*, p. 266. The personnel of the Chippewa commission was frequently changed. It was reduced to one member, Darwin S. Hall, in 1896 and was discontinued in 1900. It was the opinion of Secretary Hoke Smith in 1894 that the results of the commissioners' work in obtaining removals and allotments were not commensurate with the expenses. The commissioner of Indian affairs was of the same opinion. Secretary of the Interior, *Reports*, 1894, pp. x, lvi; Indian Office, *Reports*, 1890, p. xli; 1892, p. 81; 1893, p. 34; 1894, p. 29.

[45] Secretary of the Interior, *Reports*, 1891, p. xliii; 1895, p. xi; 1896, p. xx; 1898, p. xxxiii; *Statutes at Large*, 25: 643; *Crookston Daily Times*, April 27, 1893, p. 3. In the *Mississippi Valley Lumberman* (Minneapolis), April 28, 1893, p. 6, is a statement by the land commissioner, Silas W. Lamoreux, that a report from his inspector, William Bull, had led him to dismiss the chief of the crew and to stop the entire appraisement. Bull had told him that appraisers had reported minimum estimates to the government and had furnished a syndicate with the correct figures. Mention of the organization of the new corps and lists of its members appear in the *Lumberman*, May 19, p. 4; the *Pioneer Press* (St. Paul), May 18, p. 2; and the *Crookston Times*,

Neither the framers of the Nelson Act of 1889 nor their advisers, the disinterested lumbermen, nor the sturdy settlers in the Red River Valley could have expected any needlessly long delay in seeing the act in beneficent operation. Under its terms, however, no sales could take place until the surveys, estimates, and appraisals of all the ceded land had been completed. While the work of the second corps of examiners was going on it occurred to some friend of the Indians that it was not necessary to defer all sales of their pine until all the estimates should be completed. Indeed, it would be better to make early sales, as much timber was being destroyed by fires and winds, and lumbermen would not care to buy on estimates more than two years old. Accordingly a bill was brought up in Congress in the session of 1894 to authorize the sale of Chippewa pine from any of the ceded lands whenever one hundred thousand acres should have been examined. Amended upon the advice of the department of the interior to restrict its operation to the White Earth and Red Lake cessions, the bill was passed by the House so late in the session that it could not be taken up in the Senate. The Indians and their friends were left to wait until the winter of 1896, when the same bill, with but slight changes, was introduced. It met with no opposition and became a law on February 26. The act, according to its title, was an amendment to the Nelson Act of 1889 and provided that whenever an area of one hundred thousand acres — or less in the discretion of the secretary of the interior — of the pine lands ceded and relinquished from the White Earth and Red Lake reservations should have been surveyed, examined, and appraised, the secretary of the interior should proclaim

May 19, p. 1. In the *Times* for May 22, p. 3, is a statement by Bull that the " pine ring " attempted to bribe him. The *Anoka County Union* (Anoka), September 27, 1893, p. 1, asserts that Republican examiners were discharged and their places filled with men who did not know a pine from a basswood. The *Minneapolis Journal*, October 6, 1893, p. 9, criticizes the removal of Republican examiners and the manner in which Secretary Hoke Smith and Commissioner Lamoreux made up the new crew.

them in the market and advertise them in ten specified cities in Minnesota and five cities in other states for sale at the local land offices of the districts within which the lands were situated. They were to be sold in tracts of forty acres at public auction to the highest bidders for cash, but never for less than the appraised value. Any residues unsold were to be held for private entry at the estimated value.[46]

On April 24, 1896, the commissioner of the general land office instructed the registers and receivers of the Minnesota land offices at Duluth and Crookston to offer for sale on July 1 and 15, respectively, 115,342.78 acres, containing 225,977,000 feet of pine, on the Red Lake cession. The sales took place accordingly and 65,038.33 acres were sold, all but 2,400 at Crookston. What amount of timber was harvested from those acres will probably never be known; the estimates made by the second crew of examiners, as will shortly appear, were "absolutely worthless." There remained 50,304.45 acres unsold and subject to private entry.[47]

---

[46] *Chippewa Indians in Minnesota* (53 Congress, 2 session, *House Reports*, no. 459 — serial 3269) ; *Congressional Record*, 613, 6534, 6552; 54 Congress, 1 session, *House Reports*, no. 119 (serial 3457) ; *Congressional Record*, 158, 997, 1693, 2266; *Statutes at Large*, 29: 17; Secretary of the Interior, *Reports*, 1895, pp. xi, xii.

[47] Secretary of the Interior, *Reports*, 1896, p. xxi; Land Office, *Reports*, 1896, pp. 101–103; 1897, p. 259. In his *Report* for 1898, p. xxxiii, the secretary of the interior said that the pine on the sixty-five thousand acres had been estimated by the second board of examiners at 118,224,000 feet. The sales amounted to $369,282.34 — about $3.13 to the thousand, a value not extravagant when $5.00 had been paid for "dead and down." The *Mississippi Valley Lumberman*, July 24, 1896, p. 14, states that, in the afternoon of the day of the sale at Crookston, prominent lumbermen selected, without contests, the tracts they desired. Among the buyers were the Weyerhaeusers, Shevlin-Carpenter and Company, and Wright and Davis of Saginaw, Michigan. The *Crookston Times*, 1896: July 15, p. 4; 17, p. 4, tells of light sales at auction and heavier purchases at private sale. Whole townships were taken at private sale. The *Graham Report*, 1648, contains the following testimony as to the manner in which the sale was conducted. "The auctioneer read the descriptions. . . . He calls it and there was no bidders at all, only two men. Meehan . . . and Tom Shevlin was there. On one side of the lake [*Red Lake*] Meehan was bidding and on the other side Shevlin was bidding. On one side Shevlin would say 'I will take it' and on the other side Meehan would say 'I will take it' and that was all there was to it. . . . I was there for two days." For a description of this report, see *post*, n. 50.

On August 24, 1896, David R. Francis was appointed secretary of the interior in place of Hoke Smith, who had resigned. Upon taking office Francis found such an accumulation of complaints and charges against the pine land examiners in Minnesota, doubtless accompanied by satisfactory evidence, that he summarily discharged the whole gang. As if to justify this drastic action, on October 20, 1896, he dispatched an inspector to the Chippewa country to study the situation there. The report of the inspector, dated December 31, 1896, made some surprising revelations. Eighty-five quarter sections reported as containing 9,635,000 board feet of lumber were found by actual measure by calipers to contain 17,271,000 feet. One section reported as containing 65,000 feet was found to have 902,000; another was raised from 11,000 to 295,000; a third, from 135,000 to 421,000. It was found that the tracts underestimated had generally already been sold to purchasers who evidently had had their own cruisers in the field. The cost of the examinations to date had been $151,290, whereas they should have cost not more than $52,000. In transmitting the report of the inspector on January 26, 1897, the Democratic commissioner of Indian affairs stated his conviction that the estimates previously made were " absolutely worthless," unjust in the extreme to the Indians, and against the interests of the United States. As a result of the inspector's discoveries all the unsold pine lands were temporarily withdrawn from sale.[48]

Secretary Francis appears to have been content to let his successor, whom McKinley would appoint in the following March, wrestle with the problem of the examination and appraisal of the Chippewa pine. Cornelius N. Bliss, the

[48] Secretary of the Interior, *Reports,* 1896, pp. iii, xxi, cxxxi; 1898, p. xxxiii. The report of J. George Wright, Indian inspector, followed by 130 pages of statistics and testimony, is published as *Pine Lands and Pine Timber on Red Lake Reservation, Minn.* (55 Congress, 1 session, *Senate Documents,* no. 85 — serial 3562) and as *Correspondence Relating to Timber on the Chippewa Indian Reservations,* 101–242 (55 Congress, 3 session, *Senate Documents,* no. 70 —

new secretary, selected a new board that began work on September 1, 1897. Seventeen members were from Minnesota, acquainted with the country and experienced in examining timber; six were from other states and were also supposed to be expert in woodcraft. In his report for 1898 Secretary Bliss took occasion to express his satisfaction with the work being done by this board and to point out that by reason of their superior experience the examiners had discovered a greater proportion of timbered land than had been reported by their predecessors. A public sale of pine lands held in August of that year resulted in the disposal of some twenty-one thousand acres, at a purchase price of approximately $173,000.[49]

Criticisms of the handling of Chippewa affairs in Minnesota continued to be addressed to the department of the interior, however; and when Ethan Allen Hitchcock took office as secretary, on February 20, 1899, he felt that the whole matter demanded immediate consideration. His first move was to gain time and light. In pursuance of authority obtained by him from Congress he issued, on March 30, 1899, an order suspending all appraising, examining, and cutting of timber and all land sales and shortly thereafter

serial 3731). A few examples of the comparative estimates of the number of thousands of board feet in the same tracts, made by the two examining corps, throw doubt on the accuracy of both estimates:

| First Corps | 130 | 175 | 50 | 95 | 200 | 320 | 150 | 53 | 13 |
| Second Corps | 12 | 0 | 100 | 475 | 400 | 65 | 25 | 182 | 98 |

Comments on the Red Lake " pine muddle " appear in the *Mississippi Valley Lumberman*, 1897: January 15, p. 9; 29, p. 8; and the issue of February 5, p. 18, contains an account of an interview of Secretary David R. Francis with Thomas H. Shevlin, Senator Cushman K. Davis, Commissioner Lamoreux, and Representative Loren Fletcher. The secretary decided not to reinstate any of the former estimators. In the *Pioneer Press*, January 1, 1897, p. 1, Andrew Douglas, chief estimator, defends his work.

[49] Secretary of the Interior, *Reports*, 1898, pp. xxxiv, xxxv; Land Office, *Reports*, 1898, pp. 68, 104–106; 1904, p. 340 (serial 4797). The commissioner's instructions to examiners, dated August 3, 1897, are in Land Office, *Reports*, 1898, pp. 125–127. Each tract was to be examined by three men at different times and each man was to record his estimate made in the field. In the *Mississippi Valley Lumberman*, 1897: July 30, p. 12; August 13, p. 12, may be found notices of appointments of the third corps of estimators.

instituted an investigation of alleged illegal cutting of timber
and of the methods being employed by the examiners. The
results of this inquiry, he reported, " demonstrated the wisdom of the course pursued by the department."

Thus matters stood in the summer of 1900, when the
senators and representatives from Minnesota made known to
the secretary of the interior that it would be for the good
of the Indians if the pine lands from the four ceded townships of the White Earth Reservation — a reëxamination of
which had been completed by the third corps of examiners
during the winter of 1899 — could be sold and the agricultural lands opened to settlement. Secretary Hitchcock took
counsel with his commissioners of the general land office
and of Indian affairs and on October 6, 1900, ordered
39,922.48 acres, containing 76,384,000 feet of lumber, to
be sold on November 27, 1900. The sale accordingly took
place at Crookston and 26,264.43 acres, appraised at
$173,758.40, were sold for $198,108. Not many days
thereafter information reached the secretary that there had
been collusion among bidders and a conspiracy to limit
competition. He therefore refused to approve the sales and
ordered that patents thereon be withheld until his further
orders. In a few instances, when purchasers had satisfied
him that they had bought in good faith, had paid fair prices,
and had not been parties to any conspiracy to hold down
prices, the secretary presently approved the bids; in the
larger number of instances he let it be known that his order
of suspension would stand until after a reliable official of
the department should have found on investigation that no
irregularities had occurred.[50]

[50] Secretary of the Interior, *Reports*, 1899, p. xvii; 1900, p. lvi; 1901, p.
lxxiii; 1902, p. 29; *Report in the Matter of the Investigation of the White
Earth Reservation*, 282 (62 Congress, 3 session, *House Reports*, no. 1336 —
serial 6336). This report, which will be cited as the *Graham Report*, was
that of a House committee on expenditures in the department of the interior,
ordered by a resolution of 1911 to take action along with similar committees
for other departments. What influences directed this committee to examine
into the transactions past as well as present have not been revealed. The

Why the poor Indians were left without an addition to
their fund in the treasury and the lumbermen, with their
capital and logging outfits idle for two years, has not been
reported. It was not until November 18, 1902, that the
secretary was pleased to direct the commissioner of the
general land office to make a thorough investigation of the
Crookston sale with a view to cancellation of the entries if
it should be found that the bidders were not rightfully
entitled to them. But the commissioner was not given time
for an investigation. The secretary suddenly changed his
mind and adopted a different procedure. On November 21
the officials at the Crookston land office were instructed to
give notice to the several entrymen that they were allowed
thirty days from the time of the notice to show cause why
their entries should not be canceled. The notice was duly
given and all the entrymen, seventeen in number, filed their
affidavits declaring that they had bid in good faith, that the
lands had brought as much as they were worth, that there

full committee of seven members held six meetings in Washington in July
and August, 1911, and devolved further investigation upon a subcommittee
of three, James M. Graham of Illinois, Henry George, Jr., of New York, and
Frank W. Mondell of Wyoming. Mondell was unable to take part in the
subcommittee investigations. The other two members held hearings in Minneapolis beginning on January 23, 1912, and at Detroit, Minnesota, from February
5 to February 21. The report was signed by four members; two others presented minority views. The minority had not examined the voluminous record,
they said, but had found on its face evidence of extreme exaggeration and
reckless charges. It is not necessary to pass judgment on the controversy.
The report is valuable for the numerous authenticated documents inserted and
for a great mass of *ex parte* testimony from which some facts may be established. It was the conclusion of the majority of the committee, from " undisputed testimony," that the Crookston sale had been fraudulent, that false
estimates had been used, and that there had been gross collusions among
the real purchasers, most of whom had stood by mute while dummies (paid
agents) did the bidding. The committee found in abstracts of titles, proof
of conspiracy. Deeds filed many years after the sale practically divided great
areas between two lumber companies, the Nichols-Chisholm and the Wild
Rice lumber companies. This conclusion is on page v of the *Report*. Abstracts of titles are on pages 316–363, and following page 440 is an insert
showing the timber holdings acquired by the two companies at the sale. A
history of the Nelson Act and operations under it is given in Secretary of the
Interior, *Reports*, 1898, pp. xxxi–xxxvi. The *Mississippi Valley Lumberman*,
December 14, 1900, p. 17, criticized the suspension of the transactions; the
timber, it was claimed, had been well estimated and had brought more than
the appraised value; the government had no right to back out of its bargain.

had been no agreements to hold down prices, and that in some cases there had been strong competition.

On February 4, 1903, the commissioner of the general land office furnished the secretary with abstracts of the depositions and, as instructed, added his advice in the case. The commissioner acquitted all the buyers of any connection with underestimates made by examining corps. Six of them, whose purchases amounted to a total of less than two thousand acres, he exonerated. In regard to the others, it was his judgment that there was not sufficient evidence available to prove that there had been fraudulent combination. He thought it not worth while to hold a hearing. The government's case had been much weakened by the delays. A fortnight later, on February 18, the secretary instructed the commissioner to pass all the entries for patents except those of two buyers, one of whom had bought nearly one-fourth of all the lands. The cases of those two were later settled to the satisfaction of the department and the Crookston sale became a closed incident. Neither the secretary of the interior nor the commissioner of Indian affairs made any reference to it in succeeding annual reports; but eight years later much information was divulged in an investigation conducted by a congressional committee.[51]

THE LOGGING OF DEAD AND DOWN TIMBER

The forest regions of Minnesota, like other portions of its area, from time to time had been visited by destructive tornadoes, which in various quarters had leveled lanes of timber of considerable area. Fires, originated by lightning, by the carelessness of white hunters, and by other agents, had burned over large areas. In many cases they had killed the timber without consuming it and, if cut without much delay, the lumber was as good as that from living trees. For some years before the Nelson Act was passed the Indians

[51] *Graham Report*, 276–285, 294–313.

had been allowed by departmental authority to cut and sell dead timber, standing or fallen. It was deemed a wise policy to encourage the Indians to labor; and many of them did labor with commendable efficiency. There was little thought of their getting more than wages out of dead and down timber.[52] Shortly after the passage of the Nelson bill this policy was expressly authorized by Congress. On February 16, 1889, a brief act was passed authorizing the president to grant permits from year to year, under proper regulations, to Indians residing on reservations to cut and sell dead timber, standing or fallen, the proceeds to be retained by the Indians. In the season of 1889–90 eleven million feet of such timber were cut on the reserves by some three hundred Indians, aided by eight whites. Over fifteen million feet were cut in the season of 1890–91 and nearly eighteen million in that of 1891–92. The amount dropped to four million feet in 1894–95, but rose to nearly eleven million in the following season.[53]

The plan worked so well for the reservations that interested persons recommended that it be extended to the lands ceded by the Chippewa under the Nelson Act. To effect this purpose, in 1897 the convenient and much too familiar procedure of putting a " rider " on the Indian appropriation bill was adopted. The paragraph provided that Chippewa of Minnesota who had any interest or rights in the proceeds from the sale of ceded Indian lands or of the timber growing

[52] The Minnesota Indian agent reported that 4,102,900 feet of dead and down pine were cut and sold on the White Earth Reservation during the season of 1884–85; that about 300,000,000 feet of pine were destroyed on the Red Lake and White Earth reservations by two " cyclones " and fires of mysterious origin in October, 1886, and in May and June, 1887; and that 3,883,410 feet of dead and down timber, worth $20,157.07, had been banked and marketed by Indians on the White Earth Reservation between December, 1887, and August, 1888. Indian Office, Reports, 1885, p. 116; 1887, p. 129; 1888, p. 149.

[53] Statutes at Large, 25: 673; Indian Office, Reports, 1890, p. 112; 1892, p. 277; 1894, p. 152; 1895, p. 176; 1896, p. 170. The Chippewa agent was of the opinion that all dead and down timber on the White Earth Reservation could be disposed of during the winter of 1896–97. The Mississippi Valley Lumberman, February 15, 1889, p. 9, quotes the opinion of the Milwaukee Sentinel that the Indians were being robbed of the value of their pine.

thereon might cut and sell dead timber, standing or fallen, on such ceded lands. This was notice to lumber companies and logging contractors that they now had access not merely to the dead and down timber on the diminished reservations, but also to that on all lands ceded under the Nelson Act. As these lands belonged to the public domain, the control of the operations on them was in the hands of the commissioner of public lands, while the Indian office retained control on the reservations. There was no loss of time in rescuing dead and down timber. Fifty permits were issued for the logging season of 1897–98 for cutting seventy million feet on ceded lands. Because the winter was an open one but fifty-five million feet were banked and sold. For the next season, that of 1898–99, permits were granted for cutting one hundred and eighteen million feet on ceded lands, but only about seventy-five million feet were actually cut and banked.[54]

The method of operation was ingenious in conforming to law, if not to department regulations. Cruisers of lumber companies would discover areas of dead and down timber and some agent or other person, on behalf of the companies, would discover Indians to apply for permits to cut and sell. Half-breeds and half-breed wives of white men got practically all the logging permits. When they could not read and write, English-speaking attorneys in fact were duly appointed to act for them and were paid for it. The permits were at once virtually turned over to logging contractors, white or of mixed blood.[55]

Before the logging season of 1897–98 was fairly over, complaints began to pour in to Washington of the slaughter

[54] *Statutes at Large,* 30: 90; Secretary of the Interior, *Reports,* 1898, p. xxxv; Indian Office, *Reports,* 1898, p. 181; 1899, part 1, p. 214; Land Office, *Reports,* 1899, p. 78.

[55] *Correspondence Relating to Timber on the Chippewa Indian Reservations,* 25, 33, 35, 40–43, 47 (55 Congress, 3 session, *Senate Documents,* no. 70 — serial 3731). This document was furnished by the secretary of the interior in response to a resolution of the Senate, passed on January 6, 1899. It includes a long extract from the report of the secretary for 1898 (pp. 2–8) and a special report of the commissioner of the general land office, dated January 10, 1899,

of live timber adjacent to dead and down, of the employment of white woodmen instead of Indians as required by the regulations, and of frauds upon the Indians in the repurchase of logging outfits and in excessive exactions for goods supplied them by contractors. A letter dated September 20, 1898, of which a copy reached the commissioner of public lands through Loren Fletcher, a Minnesota congressman, may serve as an example, perhaps exaggerated, of these complaints. The writer alleged that a very careful estimate by competent cruisers showed that not over five per cent of the pine timber filed on could honestly be classed as dead and down; that filings had been made on all the valuable tracts of white pine on the reservations for the purpose of cutting the dead and down timber and that contracts containing these lands would be sent to Washington for confirmation. " It is a fraud and a steal from beginning to end." The commissioner, Binger Hermann, assured Fletcher in a reply a fortnight later that he had given the matter careful attention and had found no evidence of fraud, injustice, or carelessness in the business.[56]

Continued attacks upon the general land office in Minnesota newspapers induced the commissioner on October 13, 1898, to dispatch two special agents to investigate the logging

regarding the Chippewa ceded lands (pp. 8–14). On page 92 are logging statistics for the diminished reservations for the season of 1897–98.

[56] *Timber on the Chippewa Reservations*, 14–22, 41 (serial 3731). Fletcher, in a letter to Hermann accompanying the copy of the letter referred to, said that he hoped that the commissioner of Indian affairs would put a stop to the cutting of dead and down timber; that the previous winter's cut had cleared up all that was going to waste; and that such cutting, by leaving limbs and brush, invited forest fires. Fletcher was a very good judge of pine. It is unfortunate that the signature of the letter forwarded by him was omitted in printing. The writer was very well informed on the subject. A graphic account of the dead and down " swindle " is given by the Reverend Joseph A. Gilfillan in a letter of December 9, 1910, to Warren K. Moorehead. " The glory of the State of Minnesota," he wrote, " was gone when in the nineties her magnificent pine forests that covered so large an area of her northern part were fired to get the Indians' pine for 75 cents a thousand." The letter is in the *Graham Report*, 2059. See also Gilfillan's statement in *Hearing of the Chippewa Indians of Minnesota before the Committee on Indian Affairs, House of Representatives, February 2, 1899*, 5–11 (Washington, 1899).

of dead and down timber on the ceded lands of the Chippewa
reservations. Both agents were lawyers of considerable
experience and capacity. Their report, made on December
8, satisfied the commissioner that there " was no foundation
for the charges made, and that the work had been most carefully performed, and in strict compliance with the law."
A letter written to the commissioner on the same day, December 8, by one of the special agents was somewhat more
critical.[57] Complaints of mismanagement and fraud in the
logging operations on the White Earth Reservation reached
the Indian office also and led to the detail of an inspector
to make an investigation. In a report, dated December 12,
1898, that agent informed the office that a personal examination of many tracts had convinced him that the complaints of
the Indians were well founded. More than one-half of the
timber cut was of the best green and young pine. His observations warranted the statement that there was practically
no dead and down merchantable timber left on the reservations and that dead and down lumbering was a farce.[58]

As already related, Ethan Allen Hitchcock took office as
secretary of the interior on February 20, 1899, and gave
his immediate attention to the problems connected with the
Chippewa of Minnesota. With the authority of Congress he
suspended all operations on the ceded lands and appointed
an inspector and a special agent to investigate the alleged
cutting of green timber under dead and down contracts and
to report on the existing plan of estimating and selling Chippewa pine lands. The investigators not only discovered that

[57] The report of the special agents, F. J. Parke and H. H. Schwartz, is in
Timber on the Chippewa Reservations, 33–51. Schwartz's letter of December
8, which is worth careful reading, is on pages 30–33. Commissioner Hermann's judgment may be found on page 13.
[58] Timber on the Chippewa Reservations, 67–100. The report of the special agent, James E. Jenkins, is on pages 84–88. He found that, on an
average, only from fifteen to twenty per cent of the laborers employed were
Indians. On several tracts he found that of the logs cut, hardly forty per
cent were dry; on one pile eighty-six out of ninety-nine were green. The
Crookston Times, December 12, 1898, p. 8, gives a report of Jenkins' investigation.

twelve million feet of green timber had been unlawfully cut, but they also collected from unfortunate principals whose employees had mistakenly cut over bounds the sum of fifty-five thousand dollars without resort to prosecution. One firm, after many efforts to secure a compromise, was at length obliged to settle a judgment of over ninety-three thousand dollars. The secretary of the interior was doubtless justified in remarking that the sale of dead and down timber was " the most convenient vehicle for fraud that had yet been furnished those who were seeking to despoil the Indians." He felt himself obliged, however, the day after his order for suspension, to abate the vigor of his action by permitting the execution of existing contracts. With that exception, nearly two years passed without operations for the rescue of dead and down timber.[59]

On November 1, 1900, the commissioner of Indian affairs represented to the secretary of the interior that there still remained on the diminished reservations a large amount of dead and down timber, which should be cut and disposed of. The secretary therefore directed that logging of such timber be resumed under the personal supervision of the acting agent at Leech Lake, Captain W. A. Mercer. On the nineteenth of the same month the commissioner of Indian affairs recommended the resumption of dead and down logging on the ceded Chippewa lands also. The secretary a month later ordered such resumption, under the supervision of Captain Mercer. That agent's report of August 20, 1901, shows that an aftermath of nearly fifty million feet of dead and down timber was gleaned, besides twelve million feet of growing timber cut by loggers, through inadvertence or otherwise.[60]

[59] *Statutes at Large*, 30: 924, 929; Secretary of the Interior, *Reports*, 1899, pp. xvii, xxix; 1900, p. lv; 1902, p. 28; Land Office, *Reports*, 1899, p. 76; Indian Office, *Reports*, 1899, part 1, pp. 135, 209.

[60] Indian Office, *Reports*, 1901, part 1, pp. 68, 247. The *Minneapolis Journal* for April 20, 1901, part 2, p. 1, contains an elaborate account of the operations of the preceding winter of cutting dead and down timber. Secretary Hitchcock put a stop to it on April 24, 1901. See the *Minneapolis Journal*,

It was believed that more green timber had been cut on the White Earth Reservation than had been reported to the agent. A rescale, made in the summer of 1901, of a quantity of logs that were still banked at the landing places showed that "trespass" cutting of green timber valued at twenty-nine thousand dollars had been done by one concern; and the government called upon the contracting purchasers to make payment for it. After a litigation concluded in May, 1904, a jury found for the government in the amount of $18,138.01. Had it been found that the cutting had been willful, a penalty of thirty-six thousand dollars would have been exacted. The interior department was quite content to put an end to further lumbering of dead and down Chippewa pine.[61]

THE MORRIS ACT

Secretary Hitchcock acted wisely in suspending the sales of Chippewa pine in 1899, if not in temporarily permitting some operations in dead and down lumbering. But the Nelson Act was still in force. The Indians had the right to have their tribal fund in Washington built up from sales of land and timber useless to them after allotments were made, and Minnesota lumbermen had the right to buy them at reasonable prices. There was pressure for reopening sales, and the Minnesota delegation in Congress knew their politics too well to be indifferent. In his annual report for 1900, dated November 28, the secretary of the interior expressed his dissatisfaction with the operation of the Nelson Act of 1889 and gave notice that he would at an early day suggest to Congress a remedy for the better protection of the Indians. In January, 1901, the secretary met in conference Senator Nelson, Representatives Frank M. Eddy, James T.

April 24, 1901, p. 1. The secretary in his report for the year makes no reference to the transactions. Captain Mercer was relieved of his duties at the close of 1901. Indian Office, *Reports*, 1902, part 1, p. 221.

[61] The judgment roll in the case — The United States v. The Commonwealth Lumber Company — is in the office of the clerk of the United States district court in Fergus Falls.

McCleary, and Page Morris of Minnesota, and the commissioners of the general land office and of Indian affairs. The Chippewa pine situation was thoroughly discussed. It was decided that Eddy and Morris should consult with Senator Nelson and draw up a bill that would provide for the sale of pine, not according to estimates made in the woods on the stump, but on "bank scale" — that is, on actual measurements log by log made at the landing points before shipment — and that would also provide for sales, not at public auction, but on sealed bids. A bill was drawn, but in the session of 1901 there was no action.[62]

In 1902 a measure introduced by Representative Morris was passed by Congress after some delay caused by lumber interests that strove unsuccessfully to have the bill amended so as to authorize sales of pine at public auction, instead of on sealed bids. The reader knows how a sale at public auction was operated at Crookston. Representatives Eddy, Fletcher, and Tawney labored for sales at public auction until the last. In reporting the bill to the House, the committee on Indian affairs said that no act had been more troublesome to the government than the act of 1889; the department of the interior had found the suspension of its operation to be the only remedy for its evils. The original plan was unsatisfactory and great frauds had been practiced in estimating timber; and the committee might have added that there had been collusions between buyers. Nearly three million acres of land had been ceded by the Chippewa of Minnesota; one hundred and sixty thousand acres of timber had been sold and five hundred thousand acres of arable land had been homesteaded; the receipts into the treasury to date had been $1,040,440.49 and the government had paid out

[62] Secretary of the Interior, *Reports*, 1900, p. lvii, 1901, pp. liii, lxxiii; *Conference between the Secretary of the Interior and the Members of the Minnesota Delegation in Congress, to Ascertain a Better Method for the Sale and Disposal of the Pine Timber on Indian Reservations in That State, January 19 and 23, 1901* (Washington, 1901). The interior department has a copy of this pamphlet and the Minnesota Historical Society has a photostatic reproduction of this copy.

or advanced $2,800,000. In his brief explanation of the bill, Morris informed the House that lumbermen had been getting ten dollars' worth of pine when perhaps they had paid three, and he believed that the remaining pine would bring between seven and ten million dollars. He did not know whether the proposed act would absolutely prevent fraud, but he believed that, if there was any method under heaven that would prevent fraud, that proposed in the bill would do it.[63]

The Morris Act as passed was in form an amendment to the Nelson Act " for the relief and civilization of the Chippewa Indians in the State of Minnesota," replacing sections 4 and 5 of that act. The essential features of the Morris Act were these: Bodies of timber, without the land, were to be sold from time to time, after extensive advertisement in the state and elsewhere in great markets, on sealed bids. No bids were to be considered for less than five dollars a thousand feet for white pine and four dollars for Norway and the secretary was authorized to reject any and all bids. To determine the amount of timber to be paid for, loggers were required to stamp and bark-mark every log where cut and every log was to be numbered and scaled by competent scalers, appointed by the secretary, who were to act under

[63] Congressional Record, 57 Congress, 1 session, pp. 1313, 3812. Action on amending the Nelson bill was deliberate. On February 4, 1901, House bill 14019 was introduced and referred to the committee on Indian affairs. On December 3, 1901, House bill 2006 was introduced and referred. On January 13, 1902, House bill 8757 was introduced and referred. None of these bills was reported. On February 4, 1902, Morris introduced House bill 10789. This bill was seriously studied in committee but, being unsatisfactory, was replaced by House bill 13328, introduced by Morris on April 3, 1902. It was reported and underwent consideration. On March 3 Nelson, at the request of Clapp, introduced Senate bill 4284. It provided for sales of timber at auction, but was amended by the Senate to require sales on sealed bids and was passed. The House struck out the whole bill except the enacting clause and inserted its own bill, number 13328. After some skirmishing, the Senate concurred on June 25, 1902, and its bill, number 4284, thus amended, became the " Morris Act." The history of these bills may be traced through the indexes to the Congressional Record, 56 Congress, 1 and 2 session, and 57 Congress, 1 session. 57 Congress, 1 session, House Reports, nos. 1473, 1655 (serial 4404), relate to House bill 13328 and Senate bill 4284 respectively.

a superintendent appointed by him. The land thus cleared of merchantable pine was to be classed as agricultural land and opened to homestead entry at a dollar and a quarter an acre. The act had the additional merit that it repealed the act of 1897 relating to dead and down timber.[64]

In December, 1902, shortly after the passage of the Morris Act, the examination and classification of the ceded Chippewa lands was resumed, and the work was completed in March, 1904. The first sales of timber under the Morris Act were in 1903 and the three sales made in that year were so satisfactory to the secretary of the interior that in his report for the year, made in advance of the complete returns, he estimated that the Indians would get three million dollars, whereas under the old law they would have received not more than five hundred thousand dollars. In fact, the amount realized from the sales was over four million dollars. There was a million-dollar sale in 1904, but in succeeding years there were smaller sales or none at all. The largest sale was made in 1910, when bids amounting to more than two and a half million dollars were accepted by the government. The aggregate from all sales up to that time amounted to nearly seven million dollars. In 1917 it had reached nearly nine million dollars. After that there were annual driblets, which in 1925 had increased the grand total to nearly ten millions, thus fulfilling Judge Morris' expectation. The whole amount of pine that had been logged under the Morris Act was 1,321,093,198 feet, board measure. The amount cut was generally in excess of the government estimates. In 1917 the excess amounted to 350,000,000 feet.[65]

It happened with the Morris Act, as with others, that a provision ostensibly intended for the advantage of farmers and small loggers inured to that of the great lumber interests;

[64] *Statutes at Large*, 32: 400–404. For the provisions of the act relating to a forest reserve, see *post*, p. 259.

[65] Secretary of the Interior, *Reports*, 1903, p. 28; Interior Department, *Administrative Reports*, 1911, vol. 1, p. 121; 1912, vol. 1, p. 139; 1914, vol. 1, p. 149; 1917, vol. 1, p. 183; Land Office, *Reports*, 1925, p. 26.

namely, that which separated the pine timber from the land
and provided for its separate sale. The lumber companies
had no use for "cut-over lands" and no desire to hold them
subject to taxation until advancing settlements might so
enhance their value that the temporarily sunken capital
could be recovered. If they could have had that clause of
the Morris bill drawn by their own attorneys, they could
not have been better served. There was a further advantage
to them in this "joker," as it has been called in the literature
on the subject. The author of the bill was not aware that
there had been standing in the statute books of Minnesota
since 1899 an act forbidding any corporation not organized
for the construction or operation of railways, canals, or
turnpikes to acquire, hold, or own over five thousand acres
of land, except such lands as may have been granted to it
by the legislature or by Congress. It was exceedingly convenient for a great lumber company to be free to buy the timber
on ten thousand acres or more and not be burdened with a
similar area of taxable land.[66]

THE CHIPPEWA NATIONAL FOREST

An important provision of the Morris Act was that which
set apart a large area of cut-over pine land as a forest reserve
to be held and administered under the forest reserve act of
1891. In 1898 General Christopher C. Andrews, chief fire
warden of Minnesota and, later, commissioner of forestry,
in the course of a journey into central northern counties,
was much impressed with a view of a beautiful forest of
white pine on the south shore of Cass Lake, with trees a
hundred years old growing so close together that a horse
and buggy could not be driven between them. The lake, ten
miles long by eight wide, contained two handsomely wooded
islands, the larger of them having a small lake bordered by

[66] Minnesota, *Laws*, 1899, p. 131; *Graham Report*, 242. On pages 750–759
of this *Report* Judge Morris explains at length how he worked up the Morris
bill and assumed all responsibility for it.

a pine forest. The place seemed to him ideal as a health and pleasure resort. Upon a suggestion from Andrews, a special committee of the state medical societies visited Cass and Leech lakes and in a report made in December, 1898, unanimously recommended that the legislature be urged to take action toward the establishment of a state sanitary resort in the pine region.[67]

Andrews mentioned his idea of a health and pleasure resort to members of the Minnesota Federation of Women's Clubs. It was not only taken up ardently, but was enlarged into a scheme for a great park similar to some already established, such as the New York state park in the Adirondacks and those of the United States in the Yellowstone region and about Mount Ranier. A committee of the federation focused enough influence on the legislature of 1899 to secure the adoption of a memorial to Congress to hold up sales of land about Cass, Leech, and Winnibigoshish lakes for two years so that the state might, if it should be deemed expedient, buy the land for a park.[68]

In July, 1899, Andrews made a second visit to Cass Lake and saw, to his profound disgust, that many acres of the beautiful forest had been "lumbered" in the previous winter by a squaw man under the dead and down fraud. The result of this visit and further thought on the subject was his conversion to the greater scheme of the federated women. In his report for 1899 he arrayed a battery of arguments for a national park and he added a draft of a bill, for presentation to Congress, for a commission to negotiate with the Chippewa Indians for the extinguishment of their interest in the whole of the four reservations around Cass, Leech, and Winnibigoshish lakes, in order that the area might be converted into a national park. The boundaries of the proposed

[67] United States, *Statutes at Large*, 32: 402, 403; Minnesota Chief Fire Warden, *Reports*, 1898, pp. 54–57.

[68] Christopher C. Andrews, *Recollections, 1829–1922*, 293 (Cleveland, 1928); Chief Fire Warden, *Reports*, 1899, pp. 30, 32; *Laws*, 1899, pp. 507–509.

park would include 611,692 acres of land and 218,470 of water. Indian allotments already covered 121,802 acres of land. The remaining 489,790 acres of land, of which 100,000, more or less, were merchantable pine lands, on a near estimate would cost the government three million dollars. The timbered parts of the park would be administered according to forestry principles: mature timber would be harvested, with the exception of some groves of the handsomest and oldest pine, young growth would be protected, and some bare areas would be planted.[69]

Colonel John S. Cooper of Chicago, who at some time had reached the Chippewa country, formed or absorbed the idea of a great national park at the head of the Mississippi Valley. In July, 1899, he got together " a couple of dozen men " of St. Paul and Chicago, who organized the Minnesota National Park and Forestry Association. It was decided to arouse the attention of Congress and for this purpose to conduct a great excursion including as many of its members as could be induced to go to the region. Invitations were extended to the president and his cabinet, to senators and congressmen, and to many other official people. James J. Hill, on behalf of the Great Northern Railway, offered a special train from St. Paul. The Chicago, Burlington, and Quincy brought the Chicago party. On the evening of September 29, 1899, a great banquet was spread in the Merchant's Hotel in St. Paul. Judge Charles E. Flandrau, Governor John Lind, Archbishop Ireland, and Representative Joseph G. Cannon of Illinois were in places of honor. The speeches were all in favor of the park as a general proposition. Archbishop Ireland said that Congress ought to make a gift of the park and prove that a democracy loves the beautiful and esthetic. Colonel Cooper said, " This whole business was started by the good ladies of Minnesota." A night train took the party of a hundred, more or less, to Walker, Minnesota. The citizens

69 Chief Fire Warden, *Reports*, 1899, pp. 30–41.

of that town, then about two years old, entertained them with a boat ride on Leech Lake, a luncheon on board, and a sumptuous banquet in the evening in the big dining hall of the Hotel Pameda. A short night ride took the excursionists to Cass Lake. Sunday was spent in a camp prepared on an island in Cass Lake. On Monday some of the party went fishing, but the greater number were taken to the beautiful lake on the island. There they assisted in the ceremonious christening of "Lake Helen," named for a daughter of Representative Cannon. A night train took the party to Minneapolis, where they were entertained by Thomas H. Shevlin at the Minneapolis Club on the evening of October 3. Some of the best speeches were made there. The company then dispersed and the society dissolved.[70]

The national park project caught the attention and presently the favor of a large public and many leading newspapers gave it wide publicity and approval. The State Federation of Women's Clubs opened a campaign that was to last nearly two years. A committee of the federation went to Washington to arouse the interest and support of officials and members of Congress in the scheme. In 1901 Mrs. William E. Bramhall of St. Paul, chairman of the legislative

[70] This account is derived mainly from a booklet of twenty-two pages entitled *The Rescue of Helen*, printed "by the Roycrofters" at East Aurora, New York. The style betrays the authorship of Elbert Hubbard, who was a member of the expedition. See also the *Pioneer Press*, 1899: September 14, p. 12; 28, p. 1; 29, p. 1; 30, pp. 1, 4; October 1, p. 10; 2, p. 8; 3, p. 3; the *St. Paul Globe*, 1899: September 24, p. 23; 30, pp. 1, 2; and the *Minneapolis Journal*, 1899: October 3, p. 1. The *Duluth News Tribune*, 1899: October 4, p. 4, in an editorial approved the project as an abstract proposition and suggested that a reserve of moderate size be established under the control of the government forester. The *Cass Lake Times*, September 28, pp. 1, 4, accused timber interests of being back of the plan and of trying to prevent more lumber from coming on the market; Congress had no right to appropriate money for the park. Ninety per cent of the people of the region, said the *Times*, were opposed to it. The issue of October 5, pp. 1, 4, ridiculed the excursion, traveling in "magnificent palace cars, with colored attendants and liveried lackeys," and quoted the *Brainerd Tribune* of September 30: "These lordlings propose to fence in . . . a 'game preserve' for the exclusive use of the wealthy and aristocratic classes." The *Times* of October 12, p. 4, quoted words of condemnation regarding the congressional junket from several neighboring newspapers.

committee, was accorded a hearing on the floors of the state
Senate and House. Persons far outside of Minnesota joined
these advocates of the park, hoping to save a great unbroken
wilderness in which the noble recreations of hunting and
fishing might be enjoyed. During the whole year of 1901
the agitation for the park was kept up. Opposition broke out
in Duluth, at Cass Lake, and at points on the northwestern

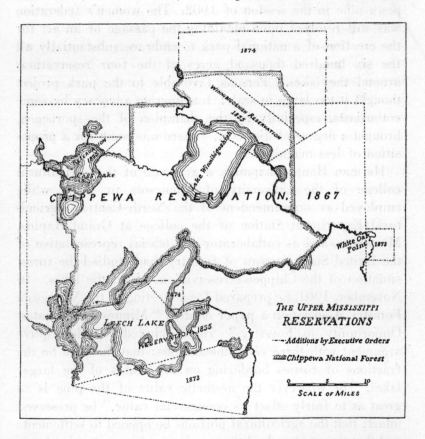

THE UPPER MISSISSIPPI
RESERVATIONS

- - - Additions by Executive Orders

▨▨▨ Chippewa National Forest

SCALE OF MILES

branch of the Great Northern Railway. The stoppage of
lumbering, it was urged, would be ruinous to the business of
those places. The lumber interests in general, however, were
content to let the park project run on, expecting that the wild,

impracticable scheme would direct attention from the quiet adoption of their favorite measure for allowing sales of pine at public auction. In the rapidly growing towns springing up around the railroad stations inside the reservations land speculators had appeared and they opposed a project that would leave no arena for their activities. It was the general expectation that Congress would take some action on Chippewa pine in the session of 1902. The women's federation was still resolved upon obtaining the passage of an act for the creation of a national park to embrace substantially all the six hundred thousand acres of the four reservations around the lakes. Persons favorable to the park project thought it too large in scale. Intemperate advocacy by some enthusiasts, especially by the champion of the sportsmen, brought a degree of discredit. There was room for a proposition of less magnitude.[71]

Herman Haupt Chapman, a graduate of the agricultural college of the University of Minnesota in 1899, while employed as superintendent of the North Central Agricultural Experiment Station of the college at Grand Rapids, Minnesota, and as collaborator and official representative of the United States bureau of forestry, had studied the forest situation of the Chippewa reservations about the lakes. In November, 1901, he prepared for a meeting of the Minnesota Forestry Association a paper entitled " Minnesota's Greatest Opportunity in Forestry." He concluded his descriptive argument with three recommendations: that the pine on the fractions of forties bordering on the shores of the larger lakes, " or wherever the aesthetic value of the pine is so great as to fairly offset its commercial value," be preserved intact; that the agricultural portions be opened to settlement; and that the one hundred thousand acres known as pine lands

[71] *Pioneer Press*, 1900: December 12, p. 4; 24, p. 5; 26, p. 4; 1901: January 6, p. 4; 8, p. 1; *St. Paul Globe*, 1901: April 3, p. 2; 5, p. 3; *Duluth Evening Herald*, 1901: February 23, p. 8; *Duluth News Tribune*, 1901: August 20, p. 4; September 12, p. 4; December 31, p. 2; Andrews, *Recollections*, 293.

be excluded from settlement and placed under control of the government.[72]

Chapman sent copies of the article to the members of the Minnesota delegation in Congress, and on December 3, 1901, he described his plan in detail in a personal interview with Morris. The representative was pleased with the practical suggestion, but was not ready to embody it in the bill that he was about to introduce. At Morris' request, Chapman presented his views in person to the other members of the Minnesota delegation and it found much favor with them. The Minnesota women were soon reconciled to it, but it met with opposition from some of the Cass Lake and Duluth interests.[73] On January 23, 1902, the Minnesota delegation met to consider the Morris bill and proposed amendments. Gifford Pinchot, United States forester, outlined the Chapman plan and was reported by newspapers as the author of it. The result was an understanding that a bill containing the principle of a forest reserve would have the support of all. Pinchot helped prepare the measure introduced by Morris.[74]

The Morris Act made no mention of a national park, but it provided that on two hundred thousand acres of pine lands on the four reservations, to be selected by the forester of the department of agriculture, each purchaser was to leave standing, for the purpose of reforestation, five per cent of

[72] Chapman to the author, March 3, September 15, 26, 1928, Folwell Papers. The paper is in the *Mississippi Valley Lumberman*, January 17, 1902, p. 90. Chapman has been professor of forest management in Yale University since 1911.

[73] Chapman to the author, March 3, 1928, Folwell Papers; Chapman, " Minnesota National Forest," 10, a typewritten copy of an unpublished paper " written about 1910 "; Chapman Scrapbook, 96. This scrapbook, which is in the possession of the Minnesota Historical Society, contains newspaper clippings, letters, and statements by Chapman regarding the national forest project, including clippings from the *Pioneer Press*, 1902: January 16, p. 6; the *Evening Tribune* (Minneapolis), 1902: January 17, p. 4; and the *Duluth News Tribune*, 1902: January 3, pp. 1, 4; 9, p. 4; 12, p. 4.

[74] *Minneapolis Daily Times*, 1902: January 24, p. 2; 25, p. 6; *Minneapolis Tribune*, 1902: January 24, p. 1; Chapman, " Minnesota National Forest," 12; Chapman Scrapbook, 129; Pinchot to Chapman, February 3, 1902, in Chapman Scrapbook, 138; Pinchot to the author, September 19, 1928; copy of a letter from Chapman to Pinchot, September 15, 1928, Folwell Papers.

the pine, which was to be selected and reserved under rules
to be prescribed by the forester and approved by the secretary of the interior. The lands thus cleared were to remain
as a forest reserve, to be protected and managed by the forester. The land and timber on the islands in Cass and Leech
lakes, not less than one hundred and sixty acres on Sugar
Point and all of Pine Point on Leech Lake, and ten sections
to be selected by the forester with the approval of the secretary of the interior were to be reserved from sale or settlement. The islands in Cass and Leech lakes and the lands
reserved on the peninsulas on Leech Lake were to remain
as Indian lands under the control of the interior department,
and any Indian allotments on those lands were not to be
affected by the act; but no such restricting clause was applied
to the ten sections to be reserved, and, when selected, they
were opened virtually as a park.[75]

The interests that had opposed these provisions of the
Morris bill before it was passed did not become reconciled
to them and planned to secure their repeal. They obtained
from the legislature of 1905 the passage of a memorial to
Congress asking for the opening of the national forest reserve
to settlement. In anticipation of the session of Congress in
1906 the commercial clubs of St. Paul and Minneapolis
adopted and gave wide publication to a memorial and appeal
for the preservation of the forest reserve. Protest voiced
in many quarters was so loud and strong that the Minnesota
delegation refused to support any bill that would destroy
the forest reserve.[76]

By an act of May 23, 1908, Congress created " in the
State of Minnesota a national forest " and minutely described

[75] *Statutes at Large*, 32: 402, 403. The ten sections selected, which, according to the notices posted on them, were "reserved for the benefit of the
people" and were "open to all lawful use and enjoyment," are described in
the *Minneapolis Journal*, 1903: August 26, p. 6; 27, p. 3. The views of the
secretary of agriculture, James Wilson, on the forestry paragraph of the bill
are in 57 Congress, 1 session, *Senate Reports*, no. 864, p. 2 (serial 4260).

[76] Chapman to the author, September 15, 26, 1928, Folwell Papers; *Memorial
and Appeal in the Matter of Minnesota Forestry and Park Reservations* (De-

its boundaries. The forest included the pine lands that had been selected under the Morris Act, with some sixty-nine thousand acres eliminated, and the islands, the peninsulas, and the ten park sections. The act provided that Indian allotments within the boundaries of the forest might be sold to the government or exchanged for allotments outside the forest, and that the lands so relinquished should become part of the forest reserve. It also increased the amount of pine to be left standing for reforestation from five to ten per cent. The legislature of Minnesota in 1927 withdrew from sale and settlement all the state lands within the boundaries of this national forest reserve and added them to the permanent state forest reserves. The area so classified was 72,525.69 acres. By an order of the department of agriculture of July 5, 1928, the Minnesota National Forest, as the reserve had been known, was renamed the "Chippewa National Forest." The higher lands are already well covered with a thrifty young growth of pine.[77]

THE TRAGEDY OF WHITE EARTH

It was the expectation of the government, from the time of the establishment of the White Earth Reservation in 1867, that eventually all the Chippewa of Minnesota would be consolidated there in a rich and beautiful country, where, safe from the white man's whisky jug, they would become pros-

cember 1, 1905). The *Memorial* was drafted by Chapman and signed by the commercial clubs of St. Paul and Minneapolis. A resolution adopted by the Minnesota State Federation of Women's Clubs on October 19, 1905, asking Congress to uphold the reserve, is appended. There were seven thousand interested women. The memorial of the Minnesota legislature does not appear in the *Laws* of 1905, but it was presented to the United States Senate on January 11, 1906, by Senator Clapp. See *Congressional Record*, 59 Congress, 1 session, 942. Bills relating to the national forest reserve in the session of 1906 may be traced in the index to the *Congressional Record*, 59 Congress, 1 session, under Senate bills 2397 and 6452, and House bills 13661, 17723, and 20046.

[77] *Statutes at Large*, 35: 268–272; Minnesota, *Laws*, 1927, p. 355; *Pioneer Press*, July 6, 1928, p. 7; Chapman, "Minnesota National Forest," 16; Pinchot to Clapp, April 22, 1908, in Minnesota Forestry Commissioner, *Reports*, 1907, p. 56; Chapman to the author, September 15, 28, 1928; Howard Hopkins to

perous and orderly citizens. Their allotted lands were to be free from taxation and inalienable except to members of the Chippewa tribe. The task, far from pleasant, of relating the failure of this beneficent program is now before us. The virtual destruction of the White Earth Reservation has been effected by means of a series of legislative and administrative acts that have the appearance of a systematic, premeditated scheme. This may well be discredited, but it remains a fact that there was a logical sequence to them, which has been thought by many to justify such a conjecture. The underlying motive was simply the immemorial greed of the white man for land and for the exploitation of natural resources.

In 1885, as already related, Bishop Whipple warned Congress and the president that the White Earth Reservation could be saved only by the consolidation of the Chippewa and by their adoption of civilized life. The hoped-for settlement of all the Chippewa on the reservation did not materialize. The Rice commission in 1889 had been instructed not to remove the Red Lake Indians and it was obliged to concede to the other bands the privilege of taking up allotments on their old lands. Still it was hoped that many would be lured to White Earth by the liberal promises of stock, tools, and seed for those who would like to farm. A few dribbled in from year to year, but at no time was there an emigration of any whole band. Even the announcement that all Chippewa entitled to move to White Earth must do so by October 1, 1894, or be considered as having decided to take their allotments on the old reservations had little effect. In that year the residents on the White Earth Reservation numbered only 1,287, and but 9,125 acres of land were under cultivation.[78]

the author, October 23, 1928, Folwell Papers. The act of 1908 provided also that $1.25 an acre for all the lands covered by the act, as well as the value of the pine left standing, be paid into the permanent fund of "all of the Chippewa Indians in the State of Minnesota." In a letter to the author, October 6, 1928, in the Folwell Papers, J. A. Fitzwater of the United States forest service discusses sales of pine under the act of May 23, 1908.

[78] Ante, pp. 200, 220, 222, 229, 234; Indian Office, Reports, 1894, pp. 29, 149–151.

While the government was conducting its futile experiments in the nineties, white population was filling the Red
River Valley and spreading along the east and north bounds
of the reservation, in which some hundreds of thousands of
acres of the finest land on the continent lay unbroken and
uninhabited. It was human nature, and American nature, to
desire the opening of this land to the uses of civilization
and incidentally to the profit of the first occupants. The
first inroad on the land allotted to settlers on the White
Earth Reservation was made feasible by an act of Congress
of May 27, 1902, providing that heirs of deceased Indian
allottees might, with the approval of the secretary of the
interior, sell and convey lands that had descended to them.
When so approved, the conveyance transferred a full and
unrestricted title. In the cases of minor heirs, guardians
duly appointed by the proper court might act for them.[79]

The act was put into effect by rules approved by the secretary of the interior on June 26, 1902. Their operation was
at once so injurious that the secretary refused to confirm the
first sales and, on October 4, 1902, approved a body of
amended rules from which better results were expected. One
of them required that a list of the lands to be offered for
sale should be posted in the office of the Indian agent, or
officer in charge, for ninety days before the time of sale, and
another provided for the submission of sealed bids before
the time of sale. An additional rule, issued on September
18, 1903, required the advertisement of sales, with lists of
the lands to be offered, in the " weekly edition of the newspaper of widest circulation in the county " in which the lands
were situated. In his report for 1904 the commissioner of
Indian affairs stated that the sales of inherited lands to a very
great extent had been made to the same group of persons,
with results detrimental to the Indians and demoralizing to
communities. Reports of special agents disclosed the existence of cliques and combinations of schemers, who " fleece

[79] United States, *Statutes at Large*, 32: 275.

the Indian of the last penny within a few hours after the agent has turned over to him the proceeds of a sale." In one case "all the Indian finally received was a broken-down horse and carriage and a few chips and stones." The secretary of the interior emphasized the statements of the commissioner and on September 19, 1904, added to his rules for the sale of inherited Indian lands a paragraph providing that the proceeds of all such sales should be deposited in the nearest United States depository subject to check by heirs or guardians of minor heirs, in amounts not exceeding ten dollars a month. The act for the sale of inherited Indian lands applied generally to all reservations where allotments had been taken up. The number of such sales on the White Earth Reservation and the amount of the proceeds were not very large, but the effects of the law under a change of circumstances were of no little moment as the beginning of a series of spoliations.[80]

In 1904 the Minneapolis, St. Paul, and Sault Sainte Marie Railway Company, having previously acquired a right of way according to law, built a line through the western tier of townships of the White Earth Reservation. Five railroad stations were located at convenient intervals and town sites were laid out about them on land acquired under the law for the sale of inherited allotments — "dead Indian land." These nuclei of settlements at once became centers of agitation for the release of neighboring Indian lands to white settlement. The further development of movements toward

[80] Secretary of the Interior, Reports, 1903, pp. 34, 202–206; 1904, p. 36; Indian Office, Reports, 1904, part 1, pp. 62, 66; 1905, part 1, pp. 30, 61; 1906, p. 94. During the year ending on June 30, 1905, sixty-three tracts, amounting to 4,970.19 acres, on the White Earth Reservation were sold for $57,760.35; the average price per acre was $11.62. The commissioner of Indian affairs in his report for 1905 remarks upon the well-known evils checked by the order of the department requiring the deposit of the proceeds of the sales of inherited lands. In his report for the following year the commissioner speaks of opposition to the rules adopted for the protection of the Indians, of attempts to collect absurd claims, and of corrupt transactions on the part of the whites. The Detroit Record (Minnesota), April 8, 1904, p. 4, contains a list of tracts to be offered for sale on various dates.

this end, however, was postponed and overshadowed for a
time by a more modest operation, having for its object the
harvesting of the stand of pine timber still remaining on the
reservation.[81]

The department of the interior had steadily held to the
policy — the only reasonable one — of refusing to approve
allotments on timbered lands. Such allotments would have
been a spoliation of all the Minnesota Chippewa. By ways
not known about, some allotments had been made " uninten-
tionally " on such lands. In December, 1899, Representative Frank M. Eddy from Minnesota introduced in the House
a bill to authorize the sale of pine on such allotments and
the deposit of the proceeds in the United States treasury to
the credit of the Chippewa fund. The bill was reported back
from the committee on Indian affairs and was referred to
the House calendar, but made no further progress.

In the Indian appropriation bill of 1904 there was inserted
in a long catena of miscellaneous items a paragraph, introduced as an amendment by Senator Moses E. Clapp and
later called " the Clapp rider of 1904," authorizing the
Chippewa of Minnesota, with the consent of the secretary of
the interior and under such rules as he might establish, to
sell the timber on their allotments, notwithstanding any
restrictions, present or future. The timber on the allotments
of minors might be sold by their fathers, mothers, Indian
agents, or officers in charge. A further provision made it
the duty of the secretary to establish such regulations for the
disposition of the proceeds of the sales as might be necessary
to protect the Indians.[82]

The Clapp rider of 1904 was calculated to operate on a
greater scale than the previous casual locations of a few

[81] *Graham Report,* 245, map facing 1112; Railroad and Warehouse Commission, *Reports,* 1905, p. 15. The stations were Callaway, Ogema, Waubun,
Mahnomen, and Bejou. See the map on page 233, *ante.*

[82] *Sale of Pine Timber on White Earth and Red Lake (Diminished) Reservations* (56 Congress, 1 session, *House Reports,* no. 492 — serial 4023) ; *Congressional Record,* 56 Congress, 1 session, 56, 2566; 58 Congress, 2 session,
700; *Statutes at Large,* 33: 209. The *Graham Report,* 2533, 2536–2540, con-

allotments on pine lands, and it did become so operative by means of a measure introduced into the Senate on March 25, 1904, entitled " A bill to provide allotments to Indians on White Earth Reservation, in Minnesota." This measure needs explanation. The Rice commission of 1889, acting under its instructions and the Dawes Act as it then stood, promised in good faith to all the Minnesota Chippewa allotments of one hundred and sixty acres of land upon their compliance with certain conditions as to cultivation. The change of 1891 in the Dawes Act reducing allotments to eighty acres seemed to the Indians another example of the white man's perfidy. The action of the commission in setting aside additional allotments awaited the ratification of Congress so long that it was despaired of. The Indians found no champion sufficiently influential to secure the attention of Congress until the session of 1899–1900, when Representative Eddy introduced a bill to grant the White Earth Indians the full allotments promised them. The report of the house committee gave a full account of the claim, with exhibits of corroborating documents and letters of approval from the commissioner of Indian affairs and the secretary of the interior. No action was taken and the matter rested four years longer.

Four days after the Clapp rider became a law Senator Clapp introduced the bill mentioned, which had for its ostensible object to make good the promise of the government of full quarter-section allotments to the Chippewa of White Earth. It passed the Senate without debate or division. When it came to the House, Halvor Steenerson, representative from the ninth Minnesota district, took it in charge and obtained unanimous consent to its consideration and immediate passage. On this account, or because he had previously introduced an identical bill, the title " Steenerson bill " came into use. It became law on April 28, 1904.[83]

tains testimony that the Clapp rider of 1904 was drafted in the Indian office and transmitted to the chairmen of the Indian affairs committees.

[83] *Ante,* 2: 208; *Congressional Record,* 56 Congress, 1 session, 56, 2566; 58 Congress, 2 session, 3660, 4413, 5546, 5825; *Statutes at Large,* 33: 539;

The two measures so contemporaneous fitted into each other as if they had been matched for a purpose. The Clapp rider of 1904 provided for the sale of allotment pine and the Steenerson Act furnished the pine. No one concerned could have been ignorant of the fact that to supply to each allottee on White Earth his additional eighty acres and to supply allotments to any who had neglected to select them would exhaust the whole area of the reservation. The interior department was accordingly constrained to depart from its established usage and authorize allotments on timbered lands. This was, of course, a rank and scandalous injustice to all who had taken their allotments on the less valuable agricultural lands, especially to those who had, by cultivating successive lots of ten acres, become entitled to tracts of one hundred and sixty acres.

The Indian agent at White Earth was informed by a communication of June 7, 1904, that he had been designated to make the allotments. In the year that elapsed between the passage of the two bills and the beginning of allotment on April 24, 1905, there was ample opportunity for all Indians entitled to new allotments to examine the available tracts, if they were so disposed, and to make notes of their relative values. Cruisers of lumber companies also made their examinations and notes. As there were still standing on the White Earth Reservation some three hundred million feet of pine, as roughly estimated, it was worth their while. The full-blood Indians, ignorant of the hieroglyphics on the surveyors' corner stakes, were at a disadvantage as compared

Allotments to Indians on White Earth Reservation in Minnesota (56 Congress, 1 session, House Reports, no. 493 — serial 4023) ; Detroit Record, 1904: April 29, p. 6; Tomahawk (White Earth), 1904: April 14, p. 4; 21, p. 1; 28, p. 1; The Land Allotment Question of the Chippewas of the Mississippi on the White Earth Reservation, Minn. (Detroit, Minnesota, 1900), a letter from Theodore H. Beaulieu to Frank M. Eddy, dated January 29, 1900, and printed as a four-page pamphlet. For Steenerson's earlier introduction of the same bill, providing for additional allotments, see Congressional Record, 58 Congress, 2 session, 685. On Steenerson's adoption by the Indians and their desire to have him take up a quarter section of land, see the Graham Report, 822–827, and the Tomahawk, June 23, 1904, p. 1.

with the mixed-bloods, many of whom were men of some education and experience in woodcraft. On the day before the allotment was to begin, a large number of mixed-bloods formed a line leading to the agent's office, in expectation of being admitted in order. When the full-bloods arrived in the morning and saw themselves thus excluded, they held a stormy consultation and made such demonstration of their indignation that the agent, Simon Michelet, was glad to make the suggestion that they form another line, so that one full-blood and one mixed-blood applicant might be admitted together. Had this proposition not been made and agreed to, it is probable that blood would have been spilled that day. Agent Michelet went on with his allotments as duly authorized. He assumed that there would be land enough to furnish additional allotments to all Indians entitled to them and therefore did not make the allotments on a pro rata basis as the law required. In consequence a number, estimated at five hundred, got no additional land.[84]

In the course of a congressional investigation made some years after these additional allotments, evidence was taken and recorded to the effect that they were permeated with fraud. It was deposed that mixed-bloods with survey notes in hand had easily picked out the choice tracts of pine, while the full-bloods generally had been obliged to take such as the accommodating agent was pleased to suggest. It was further charged that the agent, or some one with his permission, had before the appointed day marked in pencil on the tract books the names of persons, mostly mixed-bloods, who were to get the better lands. The books themselves appeared to show where such names, written in pencil, had been written over in ink. It was further alleged that many

[84] *Graham Report,* vi, vii, x, 524, 527–541, 558, 570–572, 586, 609, 649; Warren K. Moorehead, *The American Indian in the United States,* 70–73 (Andover, Massachusetts, 1914). In the *Detroit Record,* April 28, 1905, p. 4, is a long illustrated article on the allotments of April 24. See page 1522 of the *Graham Report* for testimony that there were many mixed-bloods present from Duluth, Minneapolis, St. Paul, St. Louis, and Chicago, and page 2056 for instructions sent to Michelet for making allotments.

CHIPPEWA INDIANS RECEIVING LAND ALLOTMENTS
[From photographs taken at the White Earth agency, in the museum of the
Minnesota Historical Society.]

of the choice tracts of pine had gone into the hands of persons likely to fall under the influence of the emissaries of lumber companies expecting to operate on the reservation. Cases were brought to notice of favored allottees having had unfortunate selections "switched" to better ones, from which others had been evicted.[85]

Complaints covering all these points were lodged in the Indian office in behalf of the full-bloods and the commissioner of Indian affairs sent an experienced special inspector, Thomas Downs, to investigate them. In his report, dated June 13, 1905, Downs exonerated the Chippewa agent from blame, but he thought that the mixed-bloods, with their knowledge of the situation, had taken an unfair advantage of the full-bloods and had got the best of the lands, especially in the timber district. He therefore recommended that all the additional allotments be annulled. In view of the complaints that had come direct to his office and of the disclosures in the report of the special agent, the commissioner on July 6, 1905, annulled all the allotments so far made and instructed Agent Michelet, with the aid of Downs, to take up anew the work of making allotments under the Steenerson Act "in a fair and impartial manner to all the Indians, treating all classes alike." The allotments, the commissioner said, should be made in a manner satisfactory to the Indians, especially to the full-bloods and to those mixed-bloods least able to look after their affairs.[86]

There were many Indians, however, the greater number mixed-bloods, who had no fault to find with the allotments that had been made by Agent Michelet. Vigorous protests against annulment were made through Senator Clapp to the Indian office. The commissioner, Francis E. Leupp, took up the study of these protests, of the petitions with which the office was "bombarded," and of the Downs report, and

---

[85] *Graham Report*, 543, 547–550, 587–589, 619–621, 624. On page 699 is a list of erasures, pencil notations, and changes made on tract books, presumably prior to the allotments.

[86] *Graham Report*, 555, 557–559.

stated his conclusions in a letter to the secretary of the interior on September 6. Omitting reference to the charges of partiality and unfair play, he considered it to be a case of a squabble between opposing factions on the reservation. His counsel was that another inspector be sent out to ascertain the wishes of a majority in regard to the additional allotments, whether they preferred that the Michelet allotments should stand or that a " drawing " be made for them similar to the system used by whites when new lands were opened to settlement.[87]

After a day's deliberation, the secretary on September 7 directed Inspector James McLaughlin "to ascertain the wishes of the Indians " in a council with as large an attendance as possible. The inspector reached White Earth on September 17 and the next day he mailed to the chiefs and leading men notice of a council to be held on the twenty-fifth at one o'clock in the afternoon, requesting the attendance of all Indians interested in additional allotments of land under the Steenerson Act. The notice was posted in the post office where the Indians generally received their mail. The whole number of persons entitled to additional allotments was 2,811, according to the annuity rolls at the agency. What number attended the council was not stated in the inspector's report of October 6, 1905, but it was, he said, "the largest representative gathering " that had been held for many years; the leading men were present and the subject was fully discussed and understood. When the question was put as to how many favored standing by the Michelet allotments, one hundred and thirty voted in the affirmative and five in the negative; nineteen, having withdrawn, did not vote. The majority included fifty-four full-bloods, thirteen of whom were chiefs representing more than three-fourths of the Mississippi and Otter Tail Chippewa. It is in evidence that the inspector refused to postpone the vote for four days

[87] *Graham Report,* 560–567.

to give time for further notice and insisted upon an immediate decision. His conclusion was that Michelet had allotted
the lands as impartially and as equitably as possible and that
a new allotment would give greater dissatisfaction.[88]

In his report the inspector stated that from interviews with
many full-bloods through a capable and disinterested interpreter he had learned that the opposition to the Michelet
allotments was due to the attitude of the Reverend Charles
Wright, a Protestant Episcopal clergyman, the oldest son of
White Cloud, whose claim to the hereditary chieftainship of
the Mississippi Chippewa had not been fully recognized.
The Indian cleric thus characterized was not disposed to see
the April allotments confirmed without protest. On November 25 he appeared in the office of the commissioner of
Indian affairs in Washington with two letters of introduction
to the president and a petition signed by 376 Indians, pro-
testing against the Michelet allotments. Four grounds of
complaint were set out: three hundred allotments had been
made to persons not entitled to reside on the reservation;
the same family had been allotted more than one valuable
tract of pine, in some cases every member of a family having
received one; many full-bloods had received cut-over land;
and practically all the good pine lands had been given to the
mixed-bloods. The petitioners asked that allotments be made
first to full-bloods and second to mixed-bloods entitled to
them, and only to such. They elected Charles Wright, their
head chief, to present their petition and speak for them.
Said Wright in his testimony before the Graham committee:
" I went to see Commissioner Leupp and handed him that
petition. He said, ' no.' There is no show. He shook his
head. He said the allotment to be stand." Wright then
called at the White House with letters of introduction from
Senator Knute Nelson and Governor Johnson, to be informed
that President Roosevelt could not see him unless he

[88] *Graham Report*, 568–574, 800.

(Wright) obtained permission from the commissioner. He departed for his home to pay out of his salary of thirty dollars a month the fifty dollars he had been obliged to borrow for the journey.[89]

On December 2, 1905, Commissioner Leupp, in a long letter to Wright, replied to the allegations of the petition. The kernel of his answers to the four complaints was that if any Indian would come forward with specific charges of injuries received and would submit proofs, he would make a special inquiry to find out the truth. The commissioner added some remarks in defense of his ruling. Under the law mixed-bloods were on an even footing with full-bloods. When Agent Michelet had allowed the full-bloods to form a separate line on April 24 he had performed an act of grace. When complaint had been made of the allotments so far made they had been suspended and Inspector McLaughlin had been sent to " talk over the situation " and find out what the Indians wanted. He had called a council and when the talk was over had taken a vote. " Where were your 376 petitioners when that vote was taken? " Leupp asked. That they did not know the vote would be taken was a lame excuse. " It is foolishness to plead that they did not have a chance. They did have a chance, and they deliberately threw it away," he said. Observing that Wright had added to his name the title " Chief White Cloud of the Chippewa Indians," the commissioner administered a virtual reprimand and said that the assumption of the title weakened the force of his signature.[90]

The bald assertion of the Graham committee that the McLaughlin council was " a council of the lumber companies, by the lumber companies, for the lumber companies " may be regarded as a theory derived from subsequent observation and inference. That certain lumber companies were

[89] *Graham Report,* ix, 799, 801, 815–818; *Pioneer Press,* November 24, 1905, p. 2. On the Graham committee, see *ante,* n. 50.

[90] *Graham Report,* 803–806. See page 794 for Wright's claim to the chieftainship.

interested in the Clapp rider of 1904 and the contemporaneous Steenerson Act is well known. The rider was so drawn as to allow lumbermen to dicker with individual Indians for their pine and it was the expectation of the lumbermen that they would be able to do so. The Indian office, however, with a commendable desire to protect the Indians, decided to offer all the merchantable pine of the reservation at a single sale; that is, the government, acting as trustee, would obtain by means of sealed bids maximum prices for the different kinds of timber that allottees desired to sell. Anybody knowing Indians would know that all they had would be put up for sale. Early in August notice was given by advertisement of a so-called " sale " to take place on September 5, 1905. It was doubtless assumed that all the individuals or companies likely to be interested would have ascertained through their expert cruisers the amount, quality, and value of the several kinds of timber; but it was on the protest of interested lumbermen that the time was too short that the sale was postponed to November 15. The published regulations required the successful bidder to establish a sawmill on the reservation for the manufacture of lumber and to employ Indians as far as practicable. The value of the timber, less one-half of the cost of scaling, was to be paid to the Indian agent and to be deposited by him in a national bank subject to check by the owner of the timber bought, " unless otherwise stipulated in contracts with particular Indians."

In anticipation of the sale the Indian office procured an estimate of the merchantable timber on the reservation, not from an expert in the business but from the supervisor of the Indian schools. It was a " superficial, hurry-up estimate " and was not complete at the time when the sale was advertised. The commissioner seems to have had misgivings about the schoolmaster's figures. From the forestry service he borrowed an inspector, who was also a timber expert, and sent him to White Earth to make an examination — not an estimate — of the timber on the reservation. His conclusions were embodied in certain "memoranda," which one would think should have justified the commissioner in suspending, if not canceling, the sale. It would be unjust, said the inspector, to sell all the timber in one immense block, making no distinction between timber situated on good logging waters and that distant therefrom. The timber should be sold by townships, with separate bidding for sections. The pine timber should be sold separately from the hard wood. His principal criticism was that in the pedagogue's estimate the amount of pine had been greatly underestimated and that of hard wood, greatly overestimated. His valuation of white pine on the stump was twelve dollars a thousand feet and of red (Norway) pine, ten dollars.[91]

On the appointed day, November 15, 1905, nine bids were opened at the White Earth agency. The highest bid technically was a "trick bid" put in by Thomas Shevlin of Minneapolis, in the name of the Lyman-Irwin Lumber Company, a Minneapolis firm. The trick consisted in offering ridiculously high figures on hard-wood timber on overestimated amounts and low prices on the pine on ridiculously underestimated amounts. A second bid by Shevlin in behalf of the Nichols-Chisholm Lumber Company, of which he owned a controlling interest, employed the same trick in a less exaggerated form. The best bid in fact was that of a Wisconsin lumberman, Fred Herrick, who offered two dollars a thousand feet more for the pine than the Nichols-Chisholm Company. As there were probably some three hundred million feet of pine, at a conservative estimate, Herrick's bid would have given the Indians about six hundred thousand dollars more than the Nichols-Chisholm bid. Shevlin's attorney made a demand through the White Earth agent that the department of the interior determine the best bidder according to the published estimates. The Lyman-Irwin

91 *Graham Report*, ix, 646–651, 1962, 1965, 2033–2036, 2213, 2260.

Lumber Company claimed to be the highest bidder. If the department should rule otherwise, said the attorney, the company would take measures to protect its rights.

Shevlin, however, occupied himself in engineering a protest against the confirmation of the sale. Minnesota lumbermen were already thinking about a better way to obtain the White Earth pine than at public sale in block. They did not intend to suffer any Wisconsin lumberman to encroach on their Minnesota forests and they did intend to buy timber of individual Indians. On November 20 Senator Clapp forwarded to Washington by telegraph a protest from five Indian chiefs and added for the information of the commissioner that the sending of the protest "would seem an act of supererogation in view of the character of the bids." The senator was in Washington on the day when the award was to be decided upon and proposed to enjoin the commissioner because "the law did not authorize this kind of a sale at all." The commissioner stayed in his office after hours to give opportunity for service of process. There was a conference on the subject at the White House, attended by the president, the secretary of the interior, the commissioner, and the senator.[92]

On November 27 Commissioner Leupp, in a letter to the secretary, offered his advice in regard to the disposition of the bids. As to the bids on hard wood, he could not ignore their "uncertainty — to put no harsher name upon it." He thought the Wisconsin bid worthy of consideration. But none

[92] *Graham Report*, x, 650, 660, 1964, 1965, 1983, 1992, 2205, 2212–2218, 2255, 2258, 2278–2280; *Minneapolis Journal*, December 1, 1905, p. 2. On the basis of the estimates the Lyman-Irwin bid amounted to $2,695,000; the Nichols-Chisholm, to $2,560,200; and the Herrick, to $2,385,000. Protests against the sale and against acceptance of any of the bids appeared in the *Duluth News Tribune*, 1905: November 14, p. 1; 16, p. 1; the *Minneapolis Journal*, 1912: January 28, p. 1; the *Mississippi Valley Lumberman*, 1905: September 22, p. 21; October 27, p. 21; the *Evening Tribune* (Minneapolis), 1905: November 14, p. 3; the *Detroit Record*, 1905: November 17, p. 4; the *Duluth Evening Herald*, 1905: November 16, p. 8; the *Crookston Times*, 1905: November 15, p. 1; 20, p. 8.

of the proposals reached the valuations set by his secret emissary. Senator Clapp, who had been of counsel for some of the great lumber companies, had advised him that all the bids were too low. The commissioner therefore recommended that all should be rejected. On the next day Secretary Hitchcock, concurring in the commissioner's views, ordered the bids rejected.[93]

When the well-meant effort of the department of the interior to obtain for the White Earth Chippewa allottees owning timber a fair price at a single so-called " sale " came to naught, the Indians might, with the consent of the Indian agent, dispose of the timber on their allotments by logging it themselves or by contracting with others to do it for them, but all contracts had to have the approval of the commissioner of Indian affairs. This procedure was not satisfactory to the interested parties, and it was not difficult to devise another plan for " the relief and civilization of the Chippewa " of White Earth — one that would permit the disposal of land as well as timber and would relieve the transactions from the supervision of the Indian office. Why should allottees having timber to sell get rich, while those who had obtained agricultural tracts stayed poor? Most of them had not moved to their allotments; many had never seen them.[94] What Congress had done for the Indians owning timber Congress could do for those who had only bare land. Various propositions were made for their " relief." A plan was worked out for which Representative Steenerson was willing to father the necessary legislation. He was not confident of carrying a separate bill through the House against the opposition of the interior department and the House committee on Indian affairs. It was therefore arranged that Senator Clapp, who favored the plan, should see to it that when the Indian

[93] *Graham Report,* 660, 661, 1983.

[94] Secretary of the interior to the president, December 30, 1903, with regulations enclosed; acting secretary of the interior to the commissioner of Indian affairs, October 14, 1904, with enclosures, photostats in the possession of the Minnesota Historical Society; *Graham Report,* 1843, 1847.

appropriation bill should come in regular course to him as chairman of the Senate committee on Indian affairs, a suitable paragraph would be inserted as an amendment. The House had a rule forbidding the introduction of new legislation into appropriation bills; hence the amendment would have to originate in the Senate. The scheme worked as planned and the " Clapp rider of 1906 " became law on June 21, 1906. It provided that "all restrictions as to sale, incumbrance, or taxation for allotments within the White Earth Reservation in the State of Minnesota, now or hereafter held by adult mixed-blood Indians, are hereby removed . . . and as to full bloods, said restriction shall be removed when the Secretary of the Interior is satisfied that such adult full-blood Indians are competent to handle their own affairs." The Indian appropriation act of 1907 reënacted the paragraph, changing the word " now " to " heretofore," thus enlarging the scope of its application.[95]

There is no proof of a conspiracy for taking advantage of the Clapp rider of 1906, but there is abundant evidence that some persons had been watching the progress of the legislation and getting ready to do business under it. In fact, enterprising mixed-bloods and whites residing on or near the reservation had actually begun operations before the passage of the rider. They started in by obtaining from Indians, both mixed-blood and full-blood, mortgages running for ten years, with interest at ten per cent collected in advance, in consideration of a small advance of cash, ordinarily twenty-five dollars, and a promise to pay two hundred and seventy-five dollars when the Clapp rider should become law. These mortgages were multiplied rapidly after the Clapp rider actually took effect. In the course of three weeks, from June

[95] *Graham Report*, 666, 668; *Congressional Record*, 59 Congress, 1 session, 5784, 6463, 7424, 8264, 8348, 9157; *Statutes at Large*, 34: 353, 1034. The paragraph was disagreed to by the House, but was agreed to, with an unimportant amendment, in conference. The *Record* does not show any opposition to the measure by other representatives from Minnesota. The senior senator from Minnesota offered no objections.

21 to July 16, some two hundred and fifty mortgages were recorded in Becker County alone. The first use of the money received by many of the Indians was to buy whisky and beer at Detroit and get drunk on it. The next was to buy all sorts of useless trash, broken-down horses, worn-out buggies, and even aged pianos. Many Indian families encamped near Detroit, weltering in a frenzy of debauch.[96]

The main purpose of the Clapp rider of 1906 was not to enable certain persons to lend money to Indians at high interest; these persons were out for the Indians' land. Their next proceeding was to convert the mortgages taken into deeds, thus acquiring the lands at prices ridiculously low, averaging five dollars an acre, according to the superintendent of the White Earth Indian agency, for land worth twenty-five. Purchases from adult mixed-bloods might be strictly legal, even though they were not equitable; but full-bloods and minors were not legally competent to sell. In utter violation of law, land sharks from near and far bought allotments of full-bloods and took their deeds and had them recorded. Such deeds were accompanied by affidavits that the allottee was an adult mixed-blood Indian. Some operators did not scruple to obtain conveyances from minors, also reënforced by affidavits that the grantors were of full age. Ignorant Indians were fleeced, not merely in the amounts of

[96] Graham Report, xi, 246, 722–724, 731, 767, 2660, 2667; Moorehead, American Indian, 77–88; Minneapolis Journal, 1906: July 17, p. 1; 18, p. 1. On July 18 the Journal telegraphed to its Washington correspondent: "Staff man finds disgraceful conditions at Detroit where land speculators ply Indians with liquor and secure mortgages on their 80-acre allotments for not exceeding $300 each. Town filled with drunken Indians since June 21. . . . Will department do anything to save for Indians their second allotment still to be made under Steenerson Act?" On the same day the Indian office telegraphed Agent Michelet for a report on the situation. He replied by telegraph on the nineteenth. Many mixed-bloods were taking advantage of the Clapp rider, he said. A certain spendthrift element was spending its money for liquor, but this was a small part. He had not learned of any case where Indians had been made drunk to sell or mortgage. Conditions in towns adjoining the reservation were improving. Indians who had not encumbered their allotments would now be prudent. If any full-bloods were holding themselves out as mixed-bloods he would interfere and refer the cases to the United States attorney. He had begun investigations and would report. Graham Report, 2752; Minneapolis Journal, July 21, 1906, p. 2.

money paid or promised them, but also in the kinds of money. Buyers of land gave them tokens of tin redeemable only in merchandise at certain stores. Lumber companies paid in duebills, which storekeepers and saloon-keepers cashed at a discount, the heavier because they were marked on their face "non-negotiable." The greater number of Indian allottees presently got rid of their money in Indian ways, but some intelligent mixed-bloods used theirs as well as white people would have used it under like circumstances. The "saturnalia" was over in a few months, but land speculation continued long afterwards, as first purchasers were obliged or pleased to sell. One investor from Iowa, president of a bank at Ogema, acquired some eighteen thousand acres.[97]

In the cases of allotments with timber on them, as might have been expected and was expected, the large lumber companies operating in the region had an advantage. They had sawmills and piling grounds, logging railroads, dams and sluices, experienced officials and agents, and organized crews

---

[97] *Graham Report*, xi, xiv, 113, 246, 2239, 2646–2648, 2652. Newspaper accounts of the time report the immediate effects of the Clapp rider of 1906. The *Minneapolis Journal*, July 20, 1906, p. 1, says that many full-bloods, by swearing that they were mixed-bloods, were thus "doing" the whites. The *Detroit Record*, June 22, p. 4, and July 13, p. 2, says that information of the passage of the Clapp amendment "is good news for the reservation people and the entire surrounding country" and "has created new interest in that section." The issue of July 20 speaks of the account in the *Minneapolis Journal* as "grossly exaggerated." The *Fergus Falls Weekly Journal*, July 26, p. 2, substantiates the *Journal* account and says that the Indians are in the hands of land sharks, horse-traders, and dealers in trinkets. An article in the *Detroit Record*, August 3, p. 1, says that the Clapp amendment is a good law but that it does not go far enough. The *Cass Lake Voice*, July 28, p. 1, calls the article in the *Minneapolis Journal* "yellow" and says that the Indians will sell the lands and pay off the mortgages, which are low; they have committed some extravagances, but it will teach them a good lesson; it will be better to let the Indians do as they please. The *Crookston Times*, July 10, p. 7, quotes the *Red River Review* (Hendrum) as saying that the affair is doing no damage to the Indians, but that the land should have been opened to homesteaders. The *Times*, July 18, p. 8, says that a disgraceful carnival of land-grabbing on one side and of drunkenness on the other is in progress. The *Pioneer Press*, July 21, p. 6, cites Michelet's telegram stating that the frauds had been grossly exaggerated. A map in the *Graham Report* following page 1818 shows in color the land sold or mortgaged and the land on which suits had been filed by the government.

of workmen. The Indians had no use for timber and were
ready and eager to sell. The Nichols-Chisholm Lumber
Company, the Park Rapids Lumber Company, and the Wild
Rice Lumber Company at once began purchasing and in the
course of three years were in possession of most of the
merchantable pine on the White Earth Reservation. The
purchases were made in part from competent mixed-bloods
who had the right to sell, but in larger part from land
sharks who had bought of full-bloods and minors who had
no right to sell. That the active stockholders of the companies were ignorant of the character of the latter purchases
is not probable. Certain prominent mixed-bloods were employed in the transactions of both sorts. The purchases were
separated by watersheds and were drained by streams leading to or toward the respective places of manufacture. This
segregation so moderated competition that the companies
were able to fix the prices of pine much below those bid
at the abortive sale of 1905, but under the circumstances
not outrageously unfair. The Nichols-Chisholm company,
which bought about one-half of the pine, paid approximately
eight dollars and a half a thousand feet for white pine.[98]

Agent Michelet remained in office until May 1, 1908. So
far as known, in his reports to the Indian office he made no
mention of any serious mischief resulting from the operation of the Clapp rider of 1906. His successor, John R.
Howard, testified that in the fall of 1910 he found that some
seventy-five per cent of the allotments had been sold and that
there were numerous banks, land-dealers, and other concerns
who made it their business to handle Indian lands. Agent
Howard may have adequately reported the state of things;

98 *Graham Report*, xv, 246, 248, 2224, 2227, 2236, 2272. Facing page 1112
is a map showing the area purchased by the three big companies. As shown
by the map, the Nichols-Chisholm Company had bought about one hundred
and fifty million feet, the Park Rapids Company about thirty-eight million,
and the Wild Rice Company about twenty million, all in eight townships in
the southeastern part of the reserve. The places of manufacture of the companies respectively were Frazee in Becker County, Park Rapids in Hubbard
County, and Ada in Norman County, all at long distances from the timber.

if so, his representations awoke no inquiry at Washington. The serene complacence of the Indian office and the department of the interior was not disturbed by reports that all was not well at White Earth until the midsummer of 1909.[99] In that year there was residing in Andover, Massachusetts, a scientist named Warren King Moorehead, who was much interested in Indian ethnology and was engaged in teaching, lecturing, and writing books. He was also curator of the department of archeology of Phillips Academy at that place. As a young man he had been employed as an assistant in the Indian section of the Smithsonian Institution and later had explored cliff houses in the Navaho country in New Mexico for Professor Frederick W. Putnam of Harvard University. These employments naturally led to studies of Indian history and customs and to an interest in living Indians. He attended some of the conferences of the " Friends of the Indian and Other Dependent People " at Lake Mohonk and, at the instance of Senator Lodge, President Roosevelt appointed him a member of the United States Board of Indian Commissioners on December 19, 1908.[1]

A few weeks after his appointment Moorehead became informed in a casual manner that there was suffering among the Chippewa Indians on the White Earth Reservation in Minnesota. The information must have been of an alarming character, for he immediately applied to the commissioner of Indian affairs to be appointed to the regular Indian service. Leupp appointed him a special agent on March 3, 1909, and gave him leave to investigate at White Earth. Moorehead reached Pine Point, in the southeast portion of the reservation, about the middle of March. Within fifteen minutes after his arrival he realized that conditions were bad. His first move was to have all the Indian cabins within five or six miles examined by two physicians. He sent to St. Paul for a stenographer, employed two interpreters, and

[99] *Graham Report*, 102–104, 123.
[1] *Graham Report*, 2039–2041; *Who's Who in America*, 1908–09.

set about taking statements and affidavits. He soon became convinced that "the Indians had been swindled out of the major portion of their property" and that nearly all of them were sick or diseased. By the end of April he had taken 117 affidavits involving over a million dollars' worth of property wrongfully taken from Indians. He then heard that the lumber and land interests intended, if possible, to prevent him from taking those documents to Washington; and threats accumulated to such an extent that he felt obliged to escape by a night train from Ogema on the "Soo" railroad, having given out that he would leave by the Great Northern at Park Rapids.[2]

The Indian office was at first not disposed to credit Moorehead's revelations as to swindling, poverty, and disease, and did not evince great interest in his affidavits and recommendations. The commissioner was short of funds and permitted the scientist to resign his special agency. Moorehead, however, was not content to have his revelations ignored. What means of persuasion were used does not appear, but the Indian office presently concluded that the special inspector's findings called for further inquiry, at least, and for corroboration by some one of wider experience in Indian affairs than the Andover ethnologist. The commissioner, therefore, on June 30, 1909, reappointed Moorehead temporarily for three months and associated him with Edward B. Linnen, an experienced and trusted Indian inspector.[3]

The two men began their investigation at White Earth early in July. It closed with their joint report, dated September 30, 1909, and addressed to the secretary of the interior. If the secretary and the commissioner had imagined that the volunteer observer had been led astray and fed up with fictitious yarns and documents they were

[2] *Graham Report*, 1945–1951, 2041, 2045–2047, 2062–2064; Moorehead, *American Indian*, 69. In the Folwell Papers is a memorandum of an interview on May 12, 1913, of the author with John R. Howard, superintendent of the White Earth Indian agency in 1909, to the effect that Moorehead was offered a bribe of twenty-five thousand dollars, which he refused, of course.

[3] *Graham Report*, 1817, 2048.

to be disappointed. The joint report showed a state of things at White Earth much worse than Moorehead had reported. It disclosed that, according to the estimates of the inspectors, fully ninety per cent of the allotments to full-bloods had been sold or mortgaged and that eighty per cent of the whole acreage of the reservation had passed into private hands. Full-bloods had received not more than ten per cent of the value of their land and timber. Mortgages had been placed to run as long as ten years, interest had been paid in advance out of the loans, and foreclosures had been prompt. In scarcely any case did the Indian know what he was doing. In a separate section of the report it was stated that, although the sale of liquor on the reservation was expressly forbidden by treaty, saloons were in full swing in the railroad villages on the reservation as well as in many places just outside the boundaries, and that, according to interpreters, " nearly all of the Indians who sold were under the influence of liquor " and " frequently the interpreters and land buyers persuaded them to drink." Another section gave the names of bankers and others who had been acquiring farming lands of full-bloods and minors by " every scheme that human ingenuity could devise."

The physical conditions of the Indians at White Earth the inspectors found to be " very bad." Fully sixty per cent of the people were afflicted with tuberculosis, from thirty to thirty-five per cent with trachoma, and from fifteen to twenty per cent with syphilis; and the diseases were on the increase. Their report was accompanied by a roll of the full-blood band, over five hundred in number, and by more than five hundred affidavits and statements.[4]

THE WHITE EARTH LITIGATION

The report of Linnen and Moorehead on conditions at White Earth woke up the Indian office. On October 8, 1909,

[4] This account is based upon Moorehead, *American Indian*, 73, 89, and upon extracts from the joint report and the testimony of Moorehead in the *Graham*

Commissioner Valentine wrote out a memorandum intended to give everybody in his department notice of the seriousness of the White Earth situation. He wanted "to go to the bottom of the thieving" in the White Earth country regardless of who might be hit and he wanted all the assistance he could get. "We have a big fight," he said. "We will have all kinds of opposition. I want to stake my own reputation in getting justice in this thing and in getting these people punished." [5]

The report of the inspectors also produced a prompt response in the office of the secretary of the interior. On October 16 the first assistant secretary wrote to the attorney-general stating the situation as revealed and asking him to designate a special attorney to take such legal action as should be found necessary. Within a few weeks Marsden C. Burch, a capable and zealous special assistant to the attorney-general, was in Minnesota on a visit of observation. Before the end of the year a force of men under Burch's direction, furnished by the Indian office and the department of justice, went to White Earth, where they spent the winter and spring in obtaining data for the preparation of suits to recover the lands for the full-bloods and minors and to prosecute the guilty persons. In the following summer Burch began filing complaints in equity, in the office of the clerk of the United States district court at Fergus Falls, against persons charged with having obtained allotted lands and timber from White Earth Indians, full-bloods and minors, who had no right to sell or convey. In the course of a year nearly a thousand suits were filed. The progress of these suits and others filed later, involving 142,000 acres

Report, 730–737, 2048. The full report of the investigators is not available. Moorehead's employment was extended but he resigned on October 31, 1909. Some paragraphs in his sworn statement to the Graham committee suggest that he was not *persona grata* at the Indian office at that time and later; he may have caused too much trouble. *Graham Report*, 2045, 2047, 2050.

[5] *Graham Report*, 1817, 2045–2051, 2164. See pages 2179–2186 for a fruitless attempt to discredit the commissioner's memorandum because it had not been filed until two years after it was written.

of land worth $2,000,000 and timber worth $1,755,000, can only be summarized here. As Burch was obliged to give a large part of his time in 1911 and the following year to conducting the investigations of the Graham committee, he was the less active in prosecuting the cases; and it needs to be said that he and his successors were embarrassed, not to say blocked, by an unexpected obstacle.[6]

The Clapp rider of 1906 in simple terms authorized the adult mixed-bloods of the White Earth Reservation to sell their allotments, apparently assuming that everybody would understand what "mixed-blood" meant and who the "mixed-bloods" were. To aid him in selecting the proper persons to be prosecuted, the government attorney devised a plan for readily ascertaining the blood status of the Indians. From office files he had a card index prepared showing the name, age, sex, and so forth of each individual and his allotment. A special Indian agent, John H. Hinton, sent to Burch's assistance, attended the annuity payment at White Earth in the fall of 1910 and, as each Indian was counted, noted his "blood" on his card. From the cards was made up the so-called "Hinton roll." This roll, dated December 31, 1910, contained the names of 927 Indians designated as full-bloods on the White Earth Reservation, with their sex and the numbers of their several allotments, both original and additional, indicated. A certificate at the end of the roll stated that the "accurate, authentic and complete" roll had been made up from information furnished by the allottees themselves, their parents, and older Indians acquainted with their family history. The Hinton roll no

---

[6] *Graham Report*, 20, 30, 48, 71, 1317, 2164, 2361–2365; Indian Office, *Reports*, 1911, p. 42. On December 10, 1909, the commissioner of Indian affairs wrote to the secretary of the interior that the White Earth matter was the most important of any in connection with the Indian side of his administration. It is in evidence that, on his first visit to Minnesota, Burch held a conference with representatives of the Nichols-Chisholm, the Park Rapids, and the Wild Rice lumber companies. They were "very tractable" and "very decent in every way," he said, and consented to satisfactory stipulations in regard to the removal of timber.

doubt served the purpose of the government attorney for the time being, but it was soon challenged and later, as will appear, was altogether discredited.[7]

On November 23, 1912, there was a meeting at Detroit, Minnesota, of a hundred or more persons interested in the operation of the Clapp rider of 1906. Senators Nelson and Clapp and Representative Steenerson were there. When the question of identifying and separating the full-bloods and mixed-bloods came up, a prominent mixed-blood denounced the Hinton roll, stating that in several instances brothers and sisters had been placed on different lists. The need of an authentic and official census to replace the Hinton roll was obvious. The idea was not new. In the session of 1911 Senator Clapp had offered an amendment to the Indian appropriation bill to provide for a complete census of the White Earth allottees. A commission of three persons was proposed, to consist of the Chippewa agent, a member to be appointed by the secretary of the interior, and a third to be chosen by a general council of the White Earth band. The amendment was agreed to by the Senate but was lost in conference. It may be doubted whether the proposition was made seriously or with any expectation that it would be adopted.[8]

It is probable that the senators and the representative present at the Detroit meeting came to an understanding in regard to what action would be taken at the session of Congress about to open. This is what happened. On January 24, 1913, Steenerson introduced into the House a bill to provide for a White Earth roll commission of two persons, one to be designated by the department of

[7] *Graham Report*, 56, 1301, 1319. The Indian office published the Hinton roll in pamphlet form with the title, *Lists Showing the Degree of Indian Blood of Certain Persons Holding Land upon the White Earth Reservation in Minnesota and a List Showing the Date of Death of Certain Persons Who Held Land upon Such Reservation* (Washington, 1911). Persons of "4/4 Indian blood" are listed on pages 39 to 51.

[8] *Detroit Record*, November 29, 1912, p. 1; *Congressional Record*, 61 Congress, 3 session, 1411, 2657–2660.

justice and the other by the senior judge of the United States district court for Minnesota. The bill had the usual reference to the committee on Indian affairs and reappeared on February 7 with an accompanying House report, which included letters from the departments of justice and the interior, dated January 30, 1913, approving of the measure. The bill was referred to the House calendar, but it never appeared there. It did appear, however, for reasons not revealed, as an amendment to the pending Indian appropriation bill offered by Senator Clapp on February 25. No serious objection was made to it and it would have become law had not the whole Indian appropriation bill been talked to death in the last days of the short and last session of the Sixty-second Congress.[9] The Sixty-third Congress met in its first regular session on April 7, and the defunct appropriation bill came to life with a new file number. It was approved on June 30, 1913. The commissioners were promptly appointed and five thousand dollars were placed at their disposal, but the prosecution of their duty was delayed by an unexpected incident.[10]

The government attorneys had assumed from the first that a "mixed-blood" meant a person having one-half or more white blood, and had multiplied their prosecutions accordingly. This theory was traversed by the attorney for

[9] 62 Congress, 3 session, *House Reports*, no. 1459 (serial 6334); *Congressional Record*, 2014, 2762, index under House bill 26874.

[10] *Congressional Record*, 63 Congress, 1 session, index under House bill 1917; *Statutes at Large*, 38: 88; interview with Ransom J. Powell, April 14, 1925. The department of justice selected Gordon Cain as one commissioner, and Judge Page Morris appointed Powell, counsel for the defendants, as the other. Ransom J. Powell was graduated from the law school of the University of Minnesota in 1898. In 1904 he became junior partner of an attorney having a large number of lumber suits on hand and in 1905 he was of counsel for the Minnesota lumber companies opposed to the confirmation of the so-called "Herrick sale" of the White Earth timber. Upon the death of the senior member of his firm, he became counsel of record for the Nichols-Chisholm Lumber Company and later chief solicitor for all the defendants in the government's numerous White Earth equity suits. For eleven years he was occupied almost exclusively with this litigation. He spent much time on the reservation and studied the Chippewa language so as to understand the substance of their conversation. His appointment on the roll commission

the defendants. The lawyers arranged to submit three selected test cases to the United States district court on an agreed stipulation of facts, leaving the only question to be considered that of defining the term "mixed-blood" and incidentally that of "full-blood." After hearing and argument, Judge Page Morris sustained the contention of the government in two of the cases and dismissed the third case. His decision was that an Indian having one-eighth part or more of white blood was a mixed-blood and all others were full-bloods. All three cases were appealed to the United States circuit court of appeals, which overruled the court below in the two cases that had been decided favorably to the government and held that an Indian having any identifiable amount of blood other than Indian was a mixed-blood. The government then appealed to the Supreme Court of the United States. This tribunal, on June 8, 1914, affirmed the decision of the circuit court of appeals. Under the Clapp rider of 1906 all adult mixed-bloods had the right to sell their allotments; consequently the number of possible prosecutions was greatly diminished.[11]

The zealous lawyer who had hoped to see justice done at White Earth would now have been free to go on with his prosecutions but for the fact that the exigencies of national politics had required his retirement late in 1913 to make room for a brother of the secretary of the navy under the Wilson administration. The new appointee was unfamiliar with Indian matters in general and had everything to learn

shows the estimation in which he was held by Judge Morris. The author is much indebted to Powell for the use of documents and for information given in interviews. Interview with Powell, recorded in Folwell Papers, June 4, 1926.

An amendment to the Indian appropriation bill of 1913 required one of the roll commissioners to be chosen from the assistants to the attorney-general and to act under his direction, instead of being selected by the department of justice. The obvious object was to have the government attorney on the ground serve also as roll commissioner, the attorney for the defendants being his colleague. *Statutes at Large*, 39: 136.

[11] *Transcript of Record*, cases 873, 874, 875, a printed "paper book" prepared for the submission of the cases on appeal from the circuit court of appeals to the United States Supreme Court; 234 *United States*, 245–262;

about White Earth affairs. While waiting for the decision
of the Supreme Court on the blood question, he decided
to go on with the trials of a number of cases in which the
proportion of blood was of minor, if of any, importance.
They were put on the calendar of the United States district
court at Fergus Falls in November, 1914. The spring and
summer of that year were occupied by the attorneys in
gathering testimony and preparing for the trials. Judge
Morris, called out of the state on judicial duties, could not
hold the usual November term. In December it was agreed
to submit the cases to a special master in chancery as a
referee. A St. Paul attorney acceptable to counsel was
appointed on January 18, 1915, and hearings in the cases
went on during the spring and summer of that year. By
September thirty-five of them had been tried, all but three
of which the government lost. One result was a change
of tactics in the contest.[12]

By this time all parties had become weary of the law's
delays. Those who had bought farming lands on the reservation wanted their titles cleared. The lumber companies,
who had already cut and marketed some or all of the
merchantable pine on the reservation, wanted their accounts

Attorney-General, *Reports*, 1913, p. 44; *Minneapolis Journal*, April 5, 1914,
section 1, p. 6. A copy of the *Transcript of Record* is in the Minnesota State
Library. The three cases were: The United States *v.* the First National Bank
of Detroit, Minnesota; The United States *v.* the Nichols-Chisholm Lumber Company, the Minneapolis Trust Company, and Hiram R. Lyon; and The United
States *v.* the Nichols-Chisholm Lumber Company, the Minneapolis Trust Company, and Hovey C. Clark. It should be noted that none of the prosecutions
sounded in fraud, a thing hard to prove. Judge Burch's reason for not alleging fraud is given in the *Graham Report*, 1308. "I framed a bill as mild
as a May morning," he said. The bill of complaint in the leading case, ver-
bose in form, but simple in substance, is in *Transcript of Record*, 3–8. The
United States was the owner of the fee simple of a certain allotment, the
defendant's mortgage was therefore void, and the United States asked its
annulment.

[12] Powell to his clients, January 28, 1915, copy; Powell to Folwell, May
24, 1926, Folwell Papers; *Minneapolis Journal*, June 19, 1914, p. 13. The
new government attorney was the Honorable Charles C. Daniels of North
Carolina. The attorney of record for the Nichols-Chisholm Company soon became and remained chief counsel for all the defendants, who contributed to a
common fund for expenses.

with the government closed, although they were not at all eager to have the cases in which they were defendants hurried through the courts. Before any suits had been brought and even afterwards they had professed a desire to make just and amicable settlements. Their able counsel knew how to interpose the motions and continuances appropriate for procrastinating litigation, frequently renewing suggestions of settlements. It was natural that an opinion should be entertained that the government counsel who had been so unsuccessful in the late trials should give place to one more energetic. Some influential Democratic politicians thought that a good Democratic lawyer of Minnesota might be more successful than a Bryan Democrat from North Carolina. The department of justice decided to send out a new man to study the situation and to expedite action to secure the restitution of lands to Indians who had no right to sell and to compel persons who had bought at prices notoriously low of those who were competent to sell to pay enough more to make prices fair.[13]

An investigation soon convinced the new attorney, Francis J. Kearful, that the government could win but few of the suits, and those only at great expense. Witnesses had died or moved away and of those whom a subpœna would reach some could not be depended upon where the government was prosecutor. Criminal prosecution had long been outlawed. Persuaded that settlements out of court were much to be desired, he communicated his conclusion to the defendants' counsel, who had long been of that opinion. The two lawyers worked out and agreed upon a plan, which in substance was as follows: genuine full-bloods should have

---

[13] *Minneapolis Journal,* 1915: November 9, p. 1; 10, p. 9; December 19, section 6, p. 6; 24, p. 1; *Minneapolis Tribune,* 1915: November 22, p. 1; 23, p. 4; *Detroit Record,* 1915: December 17, p. 1; interviews with Daniels and others, recorded in the author's notebooks, 7: 126, 132, 134, 144. A faction of mixed-bloods called the "Beaulieu gang" opened fire on Daniels. The attorney-general gave notice of his intention to send a new representative to look after White Earth matters. Powell to Gregory, September 8, 1915, and Gregory's reply, September 21, 1915, in the possession of Powell.

their lands restored to them by decree of court; mixed-bloods competent to sell should have their cases dismissed; and in all other cases, which constituted the greater number, defendants should pay into the Indian office the difference between the actual value of their original payments and the fair value of the property at the time of sale, as it should be agreed upon, with interest at six per cent up to the date of settlement. Parties not content with the arrangement were left to litigate.[14]

The compromise, approved and sanctioned at Washington, was a step toward the final disposition of the controversies, but it involved a still unsettled problem — that of segregating the full-bloods and the mixed-bloods. The plan called for the exact identification of full-bloods. The roll commission was now waked up to resume its function. The Minnesota member, Ransom J. Powell, was still in office. The department of justice sent on a new special attorney, Robert C. Bell, to have charge of the settlements and to serve on the roll commission. He was selected evidently on account of his qualifications for the duties and not to pay anybody's political debt. The commissioners could not presume personally to pick out from the hundreds of White Earth Chippewa those who in fact had no dilution of white blood in their veins. A bulky manuscript containing the results of an *ex parte* investigation, carried on at great expense by the defense to ascertain, if possible, by the genealogical tabulation of a large number of families what Indians were in fact full-bloods, was so inconclusive as to be of little use. But a way was found to solve the insoluble.[15]

In some of the cases that had already been tried the question of blood had come up and both parties had called

[14] Robert C. Bell to the author, June 10, 1926, Folwell Papers; interview with Powell, recorded in Folwell Papers, April 23, 1926; *Minneapolis Journal*, 1918: May 1, p. 1; 5, section 1, p. 12.
[15] Interviews with Robert C. Bell, May 7, 21, 1918, recorded in the author's notebooks, 8: 66; interviews with Powell, recorded in Folwell Papers, April 23, June 4, 1926. The genealogical manuscript, the compilation of which cost more than twenty thousand dollars, is in the possession of Powell.

in experts to testify. The government obtained a deposition of Dr. Aleš Hrdlička, an anthropologist connected with the United States National Museum; the defense put on the stand Dr. Albert E. Jenks, professor of anthropology in the University of Minnesota. Both declared that it was possible for persons having sufficient knowledge and experience to identify the full-bloods of any tribe of American Indians. The department of justice decided to call Dr. Hrdlička to its aid. For many years he had been making examinations of individual Indians of various tribes of North and South America, his special object being to develop a method by which to identify full-bloods. He had formed a " definite scientific standard " by which full-bloods could be distinguished from mixed-bloods. The criteria he found, among other characteristics, in the shape of heads, the color of eyes, the color of skin and its reaction to pressure, the color, thickness, and character of hair, and the structure of teeth. Dr. Hrdlička and one of the commissioners, Bell, spent two months in 1916 on the reservation and examined and gave detailed reports on 696 out of some 800 allottees claiming to be, or believed to be, full-bloods.[16]

A new cause of delay in making the roll now appeared. The " compromise " required only a designation of the full-bloods, the remainder to be considered mixed-bloods. It was now discovered that the act of June 30, 1913, creating the commission provided that the roll should show the " quantum of Chippewa Indian blood " of each allottee enrolled. This had already been found impossible. A second amendment to the act mentioned was needed. Inserted in the Indian appropriation bill of 1917, it required that the roll should show

[16] Hrdlička, " Anthropology of the Chippewa," in *Holmes Anniversary Volume: Anthropological Essays*, 198–227 (Washington, 1916); Jenks to the author, May 21, 1926, Folwell Papers; Jenks, *Indian-White Amalgamation; An Anthropometric Study* (University of Minnesota, *Studies in the Social Sciences*, no. 6 — Minneapolis, 1916); interview with Bell, May 7, 1918, recorded in the author's notebooks, 8: 66; United States National Museum, *Reports*, 1916, p. 30. Dr. Jenks spent seven months in visiting all the Mississippi bands of the Chippewa. His judgment was that pure full-bloods were scarce.

simply whether the individual was of full or of mixed blood.
Dr. Hrdlička's scientific examinations having decided that,
the proper entries were made.[17]

It had not been necessary for the two attorneys to postpone
settlements of cases in which defendants had bought land or
timber of obviously incompetent allottees — chiefly minors
either of full or mixed blood. Progress was slow at first,
but settlements multiplied as defendants found from examples that they would be dealt with fairly. There were
instances in which it was found very difficult to ascertain the
actual value of what an Indian had in fact received for
his allotment, but after patient inquiry fair and acceptable
conclusions were reached. In ascertaining the value of land
the commissioners were assisted by appraisers or examiners,
one appointed by the attorney-general, one by the secretary
of the interior, and a third by the defendant if he desired
to name one. In general they were content with the government appraisals. The values fixed for lands at the time the
Clapp rider went into effect ranged from two and one-half
to five dollars an acre for cut-over pine land and from seven
and one-half to twenty-five dollars for agricultural land.

The main body of the suits in equity were thus settled by
the close of the year 1918; but some, requiring correspondence and travel, dragged along. The law creating the
roll commission stipulated that the White Earth roll should
not be approved by the court and filed until the settlements
had been completed. On November 12, 1920, Judge Page
Morris, sitting in the United States district court at Fergus
Falls, confirmed the roll, which was then filed, and the docket
was cleared of the White Earth controversy, which had been
going on for ten years. The whole number of allottees enrolled was 5,173. Dr. Hrdlička had found 126 full-bloods,
of whom 104 were living at the time the roll was filed. The

---

[17] *Statutes at Large*, 38: 88; 39: 379; *Minneapolis Tribune*, November 1,
13, 1920.

commissioners included on the roll the names of 282 deceased allottees whom they agreed to consider full-bloods.[18]

It had not been generally understood that the number of full-bloods would be found to be so small, but it was easily explainable. French traders had been taking Chippewa wives and raising large families from near the beginning of the seventeenth century until long after the surrender by the French of all North America east of the Mississippi to the British in 1763. British traders followed French example until they evacuated the Northwest in 1815. French and British, especially Scotch, names abound in all Chippewa rolls. After 1816 the American Fur Company scattered its traders far and wide in Chippewa country, to intermarry and raise children. One of the most prominent of the mixed-blood families on the White Earth Reservation was descended from an ancestor who had come over in the " Mayflower." Army officers, soldiers, lumbermen, travelers, and occasionally missionaries had added to the dilution and squaw men who had taken to wife Indian women having shares in annuity goods or cash or in distributions of land or scrip were numerous.[19]

The whole number of suits actually filed in court up to September 1, 1915, was 1,609; but there were many additional cases listed in the attorney-general's office. Altogether the number of controversies must have reached twenty-five hundred and it may have amounted to three thousand. The additional cases were settled on the same basis as those that were filed. Of the cost of this long litigation and its incidents no accounting has been attempted. In the judgment of one best situated for forming a probable estimate, the cost to the government was not less than half a million dollars and that to the defendants could not have been much, if any, less.

[18] *Detroit Record*, 1918: May 10, p. 1; 31, p. 2; 1919: May 2, p. 1; *Fergus Falls Daily Journal*, 1920: November 12, p. 1; 13, p. 1; typewritten statement of Powell, June 4, 1926, Folwell Papers. Numerous copies of the roll were made and one is in the possession of the Minnesota Historical Society.

[19] Jenks, *Indian-White Amalgamation*, 2–5.

The whole amount paid by the lumber companies in settlement of 132 suits was something over seventy thousand
dollars.[20]

The effects of the compromise, long waited for, were
immediately beneficial and were gratefully welcomed.
Thousands of acres of land whose titles had lain under cloud
became marketable, burdens were lifted from many
consciences, warring factions ceased their contentions, and
peace fell on White Earth. Commissioner Valentine's im-
petuous resolve to have "those people" punished had not
been fulfilled. The historian may deem it proper to avoid
recording the names of only the few men fully ascertained
out of the many who participated in the White Earth iniquity,
but he may free his mind on their behavior. For this purpose
the words of the disinterested anthropologist, Dr. Hrdlička,
may serve him: "They [the White Earth Chippewa] became
a rapid and easy prey of lumber companies and a multitude
of land sharks, as a result of which, within a few years,
hundreds of individuals, including full-bloods and minors,
were pauperized, and the White Earth affair has become
one of the most shameful pages in the history of the white
man's dealings with the Indian." [21] A member of the board
of Indian commissioners who was present at the final scene in
November, 1920, wrote that "the records of White Earth
Indian exploitation by unscrupulous white men, some of
them prominent citizens and business men, aided by their
hired mixed-blood agents, constitute some of the blackest
pages in the history of the American Indian." It is painful
to add that no member of the Minnesota delegation in Congress in all those years entered protest or recorded a vote
against the vicious legislation and, so far as is known, no

[20] Interviews with Powell, recorded in the Folwell Papers, May 15, June
4, 1926; Powell to the author, May 24, June 5, 1926, and accompanying statements, Folwell Papers. The Nichols-Chisholm Company settled seventy-two
suits for $48,497.14; the Park Rapids Company, fifty-four suits for $23,015.00;
and the Wild Rice Company, six suits for a negligible amount.

[21] Hrdlička, in Holmes Anniversary Volume, 200.

Minnesota public man raised his voice in behalf of the plundered Indian. Bishop Whipple had died in 1901.[22]

The Red Lake Chippewa

In an earlier volume of this work a brief account was made of the migration of the Chippewa Indians from an eastern habitat and of the movement of a large body along the south shore of Lake Superior on to the area of Minnesota. William W. Warren relates that about 1730 the fires of many Chippewa wigwams were lighted on Sandy Lake in Aitkin County and a village was established there. Provided with guns and gunpowder, they spread south and west, driving the brave but ill-armed Dakota before them. To put a stop to this drive and to incessant warfare, the United States in 1825 persuaded the Chippewa and the Dakota to sign a treaty of peace at Prairie du Chien and to draw between their respective countries a line not to be crossed by a road of war. This treaty left the Chippewa in undisputed possession of more than half of the area of Minnesota.[23]

The Chippewa bands represented at the council at Prairie du Chien had their homes and hunting grounds in Michigan, Wisconsin, and Minnesota, all the way from the Sault de Ste. Marie to the Red River. They formed no confederacy of tribes, but held their right of possession in common. In later times this tenure in common was disregarded, notably in the treaties of 1837, 1854, 1855, 1863, and 1866, and the United States dealt with separate bands of tribes as if they were high contracting powers competent to alienate without

[22] Malcolm McDowell, in Board of Indian Commissioners, *Reports*, 1921, pp. 110–115. McDowell found but 80,700 acres out of the 700,000 acres originally held in trust by the government now held by 693 Indians. White Earth had the appearance of an abandoned reservation. Most of the adult Indians had been obliged to leave and look for work in white communities. Those who remained were in fact squatters on land owned and held for sale by white men. The best Indian farm seen was one of thirty acres planted mainly to corn.

[23] *Ante*, 1: 80, 146; William W. Warren, "History of the Ojibways, Based upon Traditions and Oral Statements," in *Minnesota Historical Collections*,

the consent of other groups — a mistaken policy, in the opinion of the Rice commissioners. The Nelson Act of 1889 conformed to this policy, with a noteworthy departure: that the Red Lake cession was to be confirmed by a two-thirds vote of all the male adult Chippewa in Minnesota. According to the text of the bill, the Red Lake Chippewa were to cede the whole of their great reservation, 3,569,694.29 acres, with the exception of such areas as should be needed for making allotments to the 1,168 souls then residing on the reservation.[24]

When the Rice commission came to negotiate with the Red Lake Indians it found them indisposed to the proposition in general and to the allotment plan in particular. In the council held on July 3, 1889, one of the oldest and most influential chiefs said: "I will never consent to the allotment plan. I wish to lay out a reservation here, where we can remain with our bands forever." In the remaining three days of the councils no reference was made to allotments, except for a statement by Rice that the selection of allotments would not be made until the president ordered it. It became clear that the Red Lake Indians would have nothing but a definite tract of land to be held in common; commissioners had to agree to that or get no agreement. The chiefs described the tract they would prefer to retain. It included the whole of Red Lake, "plenty of . . . pine," in accordance with Bishop Marty's advice, and a great area of swamp, valueless to the white man, from which the Indian "got a great deal of game and other means of subsistence." After a discussion in open council the lines of the proposed reservation, adjusted so as to leave open the mouths of streams running into Red Lake through pine lands, were agreed to.[25]

5: 177, 188 (St. Paul, 1885). The line of 1885 is shown on the map on page 191, ante.

[24] Rice Report, 9, 14; Statutes at Large, 25: 642; Board of Indian Commissioners, Reports, 1921, p. 104.

[25] Rice Report, 71, 79–83.

Roughly described, the " diminished reservation " was a rectangular body including the greater part of Upper Red Lake, the whole of Lower Red Lake with narrow marginal belts, and a large triangular extension ending in an acute angle on Thief River some six miles above Thief River Falls.

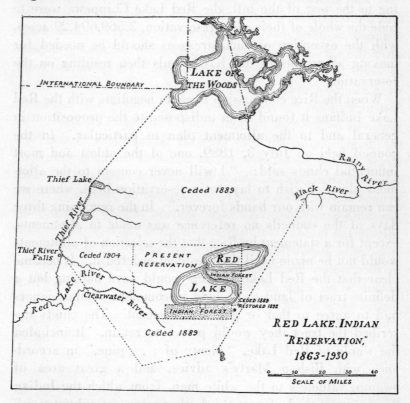

INTERNATIONAL BOUNDARY

LAKE OF THE WOODS

Rainy River

Thief Lake

Ceded 1889

Black River

Thief River

Thief River Falls

Ceded 1904

PRESENT RESERVATION

RED

INDIAN FOREST

LAKE

CEDED 1889 RESTORED 1892

Ceded 1889

Lake

River

Clearwater River

Red

INDIAN FOREST

RED LAKE INDIAN "RESERVATION," 1863-1930

0   10   20   30   40

SCALE OF MILES

The brief agreement, signed by 247 out of 303 male adults, was considered by them simply as a relinquishment for value of all their lands except the tract within the definite bounding lines agreed upon in council. Without doubt the Red Lake Indians believed that they were retaining a real reservation, to belong to them in common forever. It is true that the agreement concluded with the statement that the lands described were reserved for the purpose of filling allotments;

but to this the Indians gave no heed because they did not intend that there should be any allotments. The tract, commonly spoken of as of 700,000 acres, was afterwards ascertained to contain 663,452 acres.[26]

It was understood and suggested by the Rice commission that the tract reserved for allotments would at some time be reduced in area, but that that would not take place until after the surveys and estimates called for by the agreement of 1889 had been completed, as large portions of the tract were swampy and untillable. But that reduction was not in fact to wait for the completion of the surveys and estimates required by the Nelson Act, which took effect in 1890. In the decade following that year all the counties of the Red River Valley received a great access of rural population. All desirable farming lands went into private hands. The people of Red Lake County, who numbered 12,195 in 1900, became weary of seeing a large portion of their county lying idle in the hands of Chippewa Indians. It is probable that it became known that through a paragraph quietly inserted in the Indian appropriation bill of 1901 a way might be found to get some of that Indian land into market without conforming to the dilatory conditions of the Nelson Act. That paragraph provided that the secretary of the interior might negotiate through any Indian inspector with Indian tribes for the cession of portions of reservations and make agreements subject to ratification by Congress. The result of much agitation was an understanding to make trial of the act. On January 30, 1902, the mayor of Thief River Falls, then a city of some two thousand inhabitants, appeared in Washington. On that date he addressed a letter to the secretary of the interior stating that he had been sent by his city council to present its petition that the secretary appoint an Indian inspector to negotiate with the Red Lake Indians for the cession of some eleven townships on the western end of

26 *Rice Report*, 9, 15, 28: Board of Indian Commissioners, *Reports*, 1921, p. 104.

their reservation, which were occupied only by a few wandering families. The lands, he wrote, were all arable or meadow lands, without any pine to cause such trouble as had arisen on other reservations, and their occupation by thrifty settlers would be beneficial to both Indians and whites. The letter was accompanied by a statement, signed by Senators Nelson and Clapp and the seven representatives from Minnesota, most heartily indorsing the petition and recommending it to the favorable consideration of the secretary.[27]

The secretary seems to have been quite willing to oblige the Minnesota delegation and the people of Red Lake County. On February 10 he designated James McLaughlin, one of the oldest, most capable, and most trusted of his corps of Indian inspectors, to undertake the desired negotiation and two days later furnished him with a letter of instructions drawn by the commissioner of Indian affairs. The inspector promptly made the journey to Minnesota and on March 4 opened a council with the adult males of the Red Lake bands at the Red Lake agency. The sessions, as usual, dragged along while the Indian spokesmen rehearsed their tales of grievances — loss of land by bad surveying, false classification of lands, and false estimates of timber on the lands they had ceded in 1889, the capital instance of which, they alleged, was a cut of three million feet of pine on a contract for seventy million. They complained also that white men fished in Red Lake. The inspector tactfully listened to the

<hr>

[27] *Statutes at Large,* 31: 1077; *Thief River Falls News,* 1901: December 5, p. 1; 26, p. 1; 1902: January 16, p. 1; *Rice Report,* 15; *Chippewas of Minnesota: Hearings before the Committee on Indian Affairs, House of Representatives, from January 21 to March 22, 1920,* 147 (Washington, 1920). This will be cited hereafter as *Chippewa Hearings* (1920). The *News,* September 26, 1901, p. 1, reported the arrival in the city of W. A. Jones, commissioner of Indian affairs, on his way to Red Lake, and his statement that he favored the opening of the lands and would do all in his power to effect it. The state of Minnesota brought suit in the United States Supreme Court to enjoin the secretary of the interior from selling sections 16 and 36 of townships on the reservation, claiming that all sections so numbered had been given to the state. The court refused to sustain the claim. *Minnesota v. Hitchcock,* 185 *United States,* 373, 395; *Thief River Falls News,* October 17, 1901, p. 1.

harangues, explained that he had no authority to treat with them on such matters, and promised to make a special report of their complaints at Washington. He admitted that many of them were well founded.

The speeches of McLaughlin are very good reading. He told the Indians that they were land poor. They could sell 250,000 acres and have 550,000 left, which was more than they could use. White settlers were surrounding them; the Great Father himself could not stop the flood of immigrants. It would be the part of wisdom to dispose of their surplus land, provide comforts for their older men and women, and give the younger men a start in business. He then assured the Indians that he would make them the best offer for their land that he had ever made, and he had made many offers. He would give them three times what the government got for its lands. They could take that, or they could take the chance of getting $1.25 an acre under the law of 1889. The Indians, however, were in no haste to accept even so liberal an offer, and dickering went on for five days before they yielded to the inspector's eloquence. To break down their reluctance he brought forward two considerations not included in his written instructions. One of them was his assurance, repeated many times in his speeches, that, after a portion of the lands had been sold, the remaining great body of their reservation would belong to them independent of all other Chippewa people. The other consideration related to allotments. He said to the Indians that in a short talk with the commissioner of Indian affairs a few minutes before he left Washington he was told that he might be very liberal in regard to the price of the land and that he might promise that they would receive allotments double the size allowed by the law as it stood, one hundred and sixty acres instead of eighty acres; and more than that, that they would be allowed to select their allotments on either agricultural or pine lands, as they should please. Why such a proposition was made to Indians who had not taken allotments and who did not intend to take them remains a matter for speculation. It may not be said that the interior department then intended to establish a new allotment policy, but the Red Lake instance served as a precedent for the doubling of allotments on the White Earth Reservation two years later, engineered by the same statesmen.

After repeated mention of generous feasting and of the large amount of ready cash with which the old men would be comforted, the large majority of the adults were won over and on March 12 signed the agreement drawn up by the inspector. The Red Lake Chippewa ceded to the United States that part of their reservation lying west of the line between ranges 38 and 39 west of the fifth principal meridian, some 256,152 acres, for the sum of $1,000,000. Within ninety days after the ratification of the agreement by Congress, $250,000 were to be distributed in equal shares to the Indian men, women, and children. The remaining sum, $750,000, was to be paid in fifteen annual installments, each amounting to about thirty-seven dollars per capita. In separate sections it was expressly provided that the Red Lake Indians should possess their diminished reservation independent of all other Chippewa bands and should be entitled to allotments of one hundred and sixty acres of either agricultural or pine lands. It was further agreed that the sum of five thousand dollars should be employed to pay the forty-two families living on the ceded lands for moving to the main reserve and for removing their dead. McLaughlin had traveled the length of the tract and had seen most of their houses. He estimated the average value of their personal effects at one hundred dollars.[28]

The business at the Red Lake agency was concluded on March 17. On the next day the inspector mailed to the secretary of the interior his agreement, with a letter of advice

[28] *Chippewa Hearings* (1920), 148, 201–231.

containing a list of the eleven townships and fractions of townships ceded and another of the heads of the forty-two Indian families, comprising 129 persons, to be moved. It was his opinion that if every adult Indian could have been reached the vote for the agreement would have been unanimous. The secretary referred the papers to the commissioner of Indian affairs, who on March 28 returned a report with a draft of a bill, recommending its passage by Congress. On April 3 the commissioner of the general land office gave his approval to the agreement, and on the same date the secretary transmitted the documents to the speaker of the House of Representatives, asking the favorable action of Congress. On the next day the junior senator from Minnesota, Moses E. Clapp, introduced the bill in the Senate. It consisted of a long preamble repeating the McLaughlin agreement, a section ratifying it, and another appropriating $250,000 for meeting the first installment of the payment. The bill, with a few minor amendments, was passed on April 18 and went to the House. On May 8 the House committee on Indian affairs reported it without amendment. The matter, which had sped along so gayly with the ardent approval of the secretary and the commissioner, the unanimous support of the Minnesota delegation, and the sanction of the Indian committees of both houses, slackened its gait. On June 18, when it came up in ordinary course, it was withdrawn by unanimous consent. It is in evidence that Speaker Cannon was opposed to the large appropriation in the bill " because of the condition of the treasury." [29]

This defeat probably suggested the experiment of a procedure that would not require an appropriation. In the congressional session of 1903 a measure was passed, without

[29] *Chippewa Hearings* (1920), 196, 200, 231, 244; *Congressional Record,* 57 Congress, 1 session, 3646, 4030, 4368, 5199, 7045; *Agreement with the Red Lake and Pembina Bands of Chippewa Indians of Minnesota* (57 Congress, 1 session, *House Documents*, no. 532 — serial 4361). This document appears also as an appendix to *Senate Reports*, no. 1087 (serial 4261), and *House Reports*, no. 1936 (serial 4405), of the same session. It contains McLaughlin's report and department papers relating to the matter.

debate or objection, as a section of the Indian appropriation
bill of the year. The new plan, instead of having the government buy the land for a definite purchase price, made the
United States a trustee to take over certain Indian lands to
be relinquished, to dispose of them, and to pay the proceeds
to the Red Lake Indians. The act required the consent of
those Indians, and McLaughlin was again appointed to negotiate with them. In councils held in the spring of 1903 his
eloquence was without effect. The Indians did not like the
idea of payments conditioned on sales, much preferring
the cash deal that they had made the year before. " Give
us the treaty we made with you; that is what we want," said
the chiefs. They utterly rejected a proposition contained in
the act that they should donate to the state of Minnesota for
schools twenty-two sections of land worth fifty-seven thousand dollars.[30]

But the "relief" so much desired by Minnesota citizens,
by the Minnesota delegation, and by government officials was
not to be disregarded. There was a special session of Congress in the fall of 1903. On November 19 Senator Clapp
introduced a bill to provide for extinguishing the Indian title
to a part of the Red Lake Reservation. It was, as usual,
referred to the committee on Indian affairs. On December
11, in the regular session, Clapp reported the bill without
amendment. It came up in ordinary course and was passed
without debate or division. What there was in that bill that
was unsatisfactory to the House committee on Indian affairs
is not known, but on February 5, 1904, the committee
reported a complete substitute, which was printed in the
Congressional Record. It was drawn in such a way as to
render further negotiation with the Indians unnecessary.
Representative Steenerson briefly explained the bill and said

[30] *Chippewa Hearings* (1920), 194; *Statutes at Large,* 32: 1009. The insertion in the Indian appropriation bill of the section authorizing the sale of
the Red Lake Reservation is recorded in the *Congressional Record,* 57 Congress, 2 session, 2183. The progress of the bill thereafter may be traced in
the index, under House bill 15804.

that the Indians would get more for their land by the trustee method than the million dollars offered them in 1902. The new bill recited the McLaughlin agreement of 1902 in full and added as an amendment the abortive proposition of 1903, freed from the objectionable items. It contained the liberal provision that the sum of twenty thousand dollars be allowed the forty-two families for their improvements and for the cost of moving themselves and their dead. As no attorney or friend of the Indians appeared with objections, it may be assumed that it had been informally ascertained that the new bill would be satisfactory to the Indians. The framers of the bill had not forgotten to have it guarantee to the Red Lake Indians the independent possession of their reservation thus diminished and the privilege of taking allotments of one hundred and sixty acres of either agricultural or pine lands. The secretary of the interior was given power to make rules and regulations for the sale of the land which should remain in force until all of it should be sold. The act provided that the land should be sold in parcels of one hundred and sixty acres, not more than one parcel to an individual and for not less than four dollars an acre. There was to be little opportunity for gobbling large amounts for speculation.[31]

The first sale at public auction took place on June 20, 1904, at Thief River Falls. On July 14 it was adjourned to be resumed at Crookston, Polk County, on October 3. The aggregate amount realized from the sales was $679,676.85 for 114,135.87 acres, about $5.95 per acre. Later sales

[31] *Red Lake Indian Reservation* (58 Congress, 2 session, *Senate Reports,* no. 36 — serial 4570) ; *Indians of Red Lake Reservation, Minn.* (58 Congress, 2 session, *House Reports,* no. 735 — serial 4578) ; *Congressional Record,* 58 Congress, 1 session, 358; 2 session, 110, 1113, 1692, 1898; *Statutes at Large,* 33: 46–50; *Thief River Falls News,* 1904: February 11, p. 1; 18, p. 1; 25, p. 1; E. B. Meritt, assistant commissioner of Indian affairs, to the author, August 16, 1927, Folwell Papers. The *Thief River Falls News,* December 24, 1903, p. 1, contains a statement by Commissioner Jones that he favored a change of policy in dealing with Indians; he believed that their consent to the sale of reservation lands should not be required.

brought the amount up to $1,265,000, all of which was paid in cash to the Red Lake Indians.[32]

The fiat of Congress of 1904 established the Red Lake Chippewa in indisputable possession of their reduced reserve; but the act, it is claimed, was illegal, wrongful, and even dishonorable. The reservation established by the Nelson Act was, it is asserted, merely a temporary one, to last until the Red Lake Indians should have taken their allotments; then the whole tract of seven hundred thousand acres, in round numbers, was to be administered under the Nelson Act for the benefit of all the Chippewa of Minnesota. Under the jurisdictional act of 1926 suit was brought the following year in the United States court of claims to recover from the United States, because of its wrongful act, the sum of $5,469,698.20, with interest at five per cent from February 20, 1904, as indemnity for the land and the sum of $800,000, also with interest at five per cent, as reimbursement for money expended by the government from the Chippewa trust fund for the maintenance and improvement of the Red Lake Reservation. The case is still (1929) pending.[33]

The secretary of the interior did not expedite the selection of allotments on Red Lake as he had done on the White Earth Reservation. He evidently thought it neither just nor wise to compel the Red Lake Indians by force to take their allotments or to abandon their claim to independence. The Red Lake Chippewa, preferring their tribal life and not encouraged by what they have seen going on at White Earth to abandon it, have not yet selected allotments. The interior department has had good reason for letting them have their

[32] Interior Department, *Reports*, 1904, p. 342; *Chippewa Hearings* (1920), 245; *Thief River Falls News*, 1904: June 23, p. 1; 30, p. 1; July 7, p. 1; 14, p. 1; October 13, p. 1; *Crookston Times*, 1904: October 1, p. 8; 3, p. 8; 8, p. 8.

[33] *Statutes at Large*, vol. 33, pp. 48–50; vol. 44, part 2, pp. 555–557; *Chippewa Hearings* (1920), 350; The Chippewa Indians of Minnesota *v.* the United States, *Petition* (United States Court of Claims, no. H76); Steenerson to Buck, November 4, 1926, copy, Folwell Papers. The petition was filed on February 26, 1927.

way; it would be impossible to make fair and equal allotments. One Indian might pick out a quarter section of pine worth a hundred thousand dollars, while another might be compelled to take a tract worth a thousand dollars or less, or to go without.[34]

The resulting situation of the Red Lake Indians differs from that of the other Chippewa bands. As they have had no allotments to sell, white men have not entered their reservation and spread themselves generally over it. It is still Indian country. In receipt of large annual payments and with expectations of more, the Red Lake Indians have not taken to farming on any considerable scale. A large number still dwell in small cabins of one or two rooms and get a living by hunting, fishing, and gathering berries and wild rice.[35]

After the White Earth Reservation had been stripped of its pine by enterprising lumbermen according to law, there remained at Red Lake " the finest stand of white pine that has ever grown on God's footstool." The same enterprising lumbermen who had operated on other reservations, or their younger assigns, were naturally looking for the lawful opening of that timber to market. A convenient precedent was found in the acts of Congress of 1902 and 1908, creating the Minnesota National Forest out of portions of reservations about Leech Lake. The latter act provided for the sale of all the merchantable pine timber in the described territory except ten per cent to be selected by the forester of the United States. The proceeds of the sale were to be placed to the credit of all the Chippewa Indians of Minnesota. On January 7, 1915, Senator Knute Nelson introduced a bill for the creation of a national forest to embrace about a hundred

---

[34] *Chippewa Hearings* (1920), 112, 160, 353. As the act of 1889 fixed the term of the permanent Chippewa fund at fifty years, to run from the completion of all allotments, that term has technically not yet begun. Charles H. Burke, commissioner of Indian affairs, to the author, October 4, 1927, Folwell Papers.

[35] *Chippewa Hearings* (1920), 345; Board of Indian Commissioners, *Reports*, 1921, p. 107.

thousand acres in the southeast part of the Red Lake Reservation. It was the short session of Congress and the bill was not reached.[36]

The measure reappeared in the session of 1915–16 and was passed as an amendment to the Indian appropriation bill. In substance, the amendment provided that the Red Lake Indian Forest should be administered by the secretary of the interior " in accordance with the principles of scientific forestry, with a view to the production of successive timber crops " and that the secretary be authorized to manufacture and sell such standing pine and oak timber as had ceased to grow, as well as other marketable timber from time to time, as he might deem advisable. It was provided in the bill that after all expenses of management were paid, the proceeds were to be deposited in the treasury to the credit of the Red Lake Indians, to draw four per cent interest. No promise was made that the fund would ultimately be distributed to the Indians, nor was any term of years fixed for the payment of the interest. Under the ruling of the United States Supreme Court that Congress has absolute control of tribal Indians and their property for their benefit, it may be understood that the final disposition of the fund was left to Congress. The accruing interest the secretary was authorized to expend according to his discretion for the benefit of those Indians.[37]

It was not expected that the secretary of the interior would build sawmills and logging railroads and undertake to cut, manufacture, and market the Red Lake timber by employed agents and laborers. To secure efficient lumbering and keep down costs of administration, he adopted what he thought the wiser course, that of engaging a single experienced and responsible agency to execute the large enterprise. On November 5, 1917, bids from four responsible and reputable

[36] Chippewa Hearings (1920), 247; Statutes at Large, 32: 402; 35: 268–271; Congressional Record, 63 Congress, 3 session, 1095, 3773.

[37] Statutes at Large, 39: 137; Congressional Record, 64 Congress, 1 session, 1752, 2310, 4759, 7846, 7865, 8275, appendix, 1100–1102; Board of Indian

Minnesota firms were opened and on November 19, 1917, under the secretary's authority, the superintendent of the Red Lake Indian School entered into contract with the International Lumber Company, which at the time had its principal place of business at Minneapolis, for the sale to it of all merchantable dead timber and of all live timber of every kind marked for cutting by an officer of the Indian service on a certain described portion of the Red Lake Indian Forest, estimated at some fifty thousand acres. It was understood and agreed, however, that approximately eighty per cent of the timber on the area could be properly classified as fallen, dead, or mature and must be cut under the contract. It is obvious that this liberal construction of the law was gratifying to the contracting company, and also that the first of the succeeding crops of timber could not be harvested in the present generation. The tract was a parallelogram eighteen and a quarter miles long in the southern part of the Red Lake Indian Forest, its eastern portion extending to the south shore of Lower Red Lake with a frontage of three miles and a quarter.

The department of the interior must have been well advised as to the proper terms of such a contract. It contained every safeguard suggested by experience calculated to secure efficient lumbering and just accounting. Every log was to be measured by government scalers and not a tree was to be cut until it was paid for. The price to be paid for

Commissioners, *Reports*, 1921, p. 104; Lone Wolf *v.* Hitchcock, 187 *United States*, 553. There was no debate in either house on the Red Lake paragraphs, but a member from Illinois who had lived in Minnesota and had visited the Chippewa had leave to " extend his remarks " in the appendix of the *Record*. His principal objections to the measure were that it would virtually reduce the Red Lake Reservation by ninety thousand acres against the wishes of the Indians, that it reposed too large powers in the secretary of the interior, especially in the disbursement of the interest on the resulting fund, and that it contemplated the immediate sale of all the timber to the advantage of interested lumber companies. The act restricted allotments of agricultural lands fronting on a lake to eighty acres. The Red Lake Indian Forest as described in the act included lands in ranges 32 to 36, inclusive, in townships 150 and 151, and in ranges 32 to 34, inclusive, in townships 152 and 153 — approximately 107,000 acres. See the map on page 298, ante.

white pine was $14.10 a thousand feet; for Norway, $10.25; and for spruce, $10.00. These were war-time prices. The document contained the singular provision that no member or delegate in Congress should have any share, part, or interest in the contract, and it cited a section of the penal laws of the United States fixing a maximum penalty of three thousand dollars for assuming such an interest and declaring void a contract made under such circumstances. It was no compliment to the members of the Minnesota delegation or others in Congress that the secretary of the interior thought it proper to warn them not to disobey a law as well known to them as to himself. The principal provision for the maintenance of a permanent forest was that forbidding the cutting of trees with a diameter of less than twelve inches at four and a half feet from the ground. The number of such trees in an ancient forest could not have been great. The contractors were forbidden to do needless damage to young growths and seed trees and were required to burn slashings in such a manner as to prevent the spread of fires and to do all in their power to suppress forest fires. The amount of timber taken off was 105,042,800 feet, for which the International Lumber Company paid the sum of $1,395,585.46.[38]

The ostensible purpose of securing the passage by Congress of the act of May 18, 1916, establishing the Red Lake Indian Forest, was the enrichment of the Red Lake Indians; the actual purpose, it is no slander to say, was to enrich some lumber concern. The creation of a forest reserve was a convenient and popular expedient to effect the leading purpose. Without consulting experts the interior department at one stroke decreed the immediate harvest of a great part

---

[38] *Chippewa Hearings* (1920), 161–165; Indian Office, *Reports*, 1920, p. 52; *Statutes at Large*, 35: 1109; letters to the author from E. B. Meritt, assistant commissioner of Indian Affairs, August 22, 1927, and from Charles H. Burke, commissioner of Indian affairs, October 4, 1927, Folwell Papers; "Record of Incorporations, State of Minnesota," K3: 484, in the office of the secretary of state. The commissioner of Indian affairs, in his *Reports*, 1920, p. 52, mentions the sale of white and Norway pine lumber at Redby for $38.50 a thousand feet, mill run, number 5 or better.

of the merchantable timber on the reservation. The principles of scientific forestry would have dictated, first, the cutting only of dead timber, standing or fallen, and thereafter the removal of dead, diseased, and dying trees year by year; second, the complete clearing of limited areas from decade to decade for replanting by seed trees or others. On such a plan successive crops of timber could have been provided for and the cost of administering the forest could have been derived from the sales. It may be admitted that no great profit would have accrued to any lumber concern. As a result of the policy adopted more than fifty thousand acres were cleared at one swoop, to lie idle for a lifetime while a new crop grows up to merchantable size. The new growth is already reported as showing satisfactory promise, but the next harvest is far away.[39]

After the sale of the timber on the fifty thousand acres of the forest reserve, there were left on its remaining acres sixty-five million feet of pine timber. In regard to that the interior department found reason for a change of policy. Instead of selling to timber contractors, it was decided to cut and manufacture the timber under the direction of a superintendent and to put the product on the market. In 1925 a sawmill at Redby costing, with logging outfits, $244,475.76 was put into operation. The plan is to cut and sell some five million feet during a season. The lumber readily sells at prices ranging from nineteen to a hundred dollars a thousand feet. In conformity with the principles of forestry, selective cutting is practiced wherever practicable, and where not, seed trees are left. Indian labor is employed except for skilled positions.[40]

[39] Chippewa Hearings (1920), 80, 350, 351; Minnesota Chief Fire Warden, Reports, 1900, p. 37; letters to the author from Webster Ballinger, September 21, 1927; from William T. Cox, former state forester, August 30, October 5, 1927; and from Charles H. Burke, commissioner of Indian affairs, October 4, 1927; and the author to Mark L. Burns, superintendent of the Red Lake Indian agency, July 22, 1927, with replies interlined, Folwell Papers.

[40] Letters from the author to Burns, with replies interlined, July 22, November 4, 1927; Burns to the author, September 16, 1927, Folwell Papers; Bemidji Sentinel, February 27, 1925, p. 1.

The part of the Red Lake Reservation outside the boundaries of the forest reserve — some three hundred thousand acres — consists largely of swamps. The act of 1916 authorized the secretary of the interior to sell all the timber on this land and to administer the proceeds under the act of March 3, 1883, which provided that the proceeds of sales of timber and other products of Indian reservations not the result of the labor of a member of the tribe should be turned into the treasury for the benefit of the tribe, and under the act of March 2, 1887, which authorized the secretary of the interior to use the money carried on the books of the department under the caption " Indian moneys, proceeds of labor " for the benefit of the tribes according to his discretion.[41]

THE BATTLE OF SUGAR POINT

Although many thousands of Chippewa Indians were living in the northern parts of Minnesota before the white men came and have ever since continuously dwelt there, but one hostile outbreak worthy of mention has taken place; and in that but a handful of a single band was concerned. In 1898 some two hundred Pillagers had their homes on Bear Island in Leech Lake and on the adjacent mainland. The island, which is about four miles long, north and south, and nowhere more than two miles wide, lies parallel with and three miles distant from the eastern shore of the lake. It was heavily timbered, except where small clearings had been made. The Bear Island band recognized one Bugonaygeshig as its leader. He bore the same Indian name, differently spelled, as that of the notorious Hole-in-the-Day. The war correspondents of the Twin City newspapers, abbreviating the name as it sounded to them, called him " Old Bug " and used that disrespectful epithet throughout their elaborate and conflicting narratives. The Pillagers, in general, had the

[41] *Statutes at Large*, 22: 590; 24: 463; 39: 137; Board of Indian Commissioners, *Reports*, 1921, p. 104.

reputation at the time of being an " unregencrate and turbulent " people, but there is good evidence that this particular band was composed of well-disposed and uncommonly industrious Indians. They still hunted, fished, and gathered berries and wild rice, but they derived a good part of their subsistence from their gardens. They wore the white man's dress, decorated with some of their traditional beadwork patterns.[42]

The operations of the Nelson Act of 1889 had been disappointing to the Pillagers at Leech Lake and, after eight years, they were in an ugly mood generally. But the trouble to be described grew out of local and comparatively trivial events and involved but a small and isolated band. In April, 1895, the Bear Island leader was arrested for furnishing an Indian with whisky. The witness disappeared and Bugonaygeshig was discharged. In June of the same year he was served with a subpœna as a witness, to which he gave no attention. When he was arrested under an attachment for contempt of court, a party of tribesmen rescued him. In the following October warrants were issued for the arrest of Bugonaygeshig and twelve others. There must have been reasons for taking time in the matter, for it was not until May, 1897, that the Chippewa agent got nine of the thirteen into court. All pleaded guilty to the charge of resisting officers and were sentenced to thirty days in jail. In October, 1897, another Indian was given the same punishment. Bugonaygeshig and two others remained at large and no haste was made to get them into custody. The fifteenth of September, 1898, the time of the annuity payment at the

[42] Frank R. Holmes, in Minnesota in Three Centuries, 4: 245 (New York, 1908). Characterizations of the Pillagers appear in the Pioneer Press, 1898: September 29, p. 1; October 7, p. 1; and October 12, p. 1. The issue of October 7, p. 1, reports that Joseph Woodbury, the son of Hole-in-the-Day, in an interview said, " The old rascal has stolen my father's name." " Bugonaygeshig " is the spelling used generally in the newspaper and other accounts of the disturbance. In Frederick W. Hodge, ed., Handbook of American Indians, part 1, p. 557 (Bureau of American Ethnology, Bulletins, no. 30 — Washington, 1910), Hole-in-the-Day's Indian name is given as " Bagwunagijik."

Chippewa agency near the southwest angle of Leech Lake, was selected as a convenient time to make the arrests and to demonstrate the power of the Great Father.

Bugonaygeshig attended the payment and while there was arrested by a deputy United States marshal, either on a charge of selling liquor or as a witness in the case of another under a similar accusation. A party of braves, fifty or more in number, excited by illicit whisky, rescued him from custody and departed to their island. The United States marshal at St. Paul procured warrants for the arrest of twenty-two participants and deemed it prudent to ask for a detail of soldiers to support his deputies in making the arrests. The war department at Washington authorized by telegraph a detail of twenty men. A detachment of that number from Fort Snelling, commanded by Lieutenant Chauncey B. Humphreys of the Third Infantry, arrived at Walker late on September 30 and two days later went into camp at the agency, some five or six miles distant from Walker across an arm of the lake. Humphreys found the Indians about the agency in a state of excitement and heard rumors that a large body of them were arriving to fight. He accordingly telegraphed for a reënforcement of a hundred men and a Gatling gun. Marshal R. T. O'Connor, who had also come up on September 30, was dissuaded from making any immediate attempts to serve his warrants and he permitted a call to be made for a council of Pillagers.[43]

The council met at the agency on the third. The attendance of Indians was not large and none of the Bear Island band came. The Chippewa orators rehearsed at length the wrongs and insults, real and imaginary, that their people

[43] Indian Office, Reports, 1899, part 1, p. 133; Secretary of War, Reports, 1899, part 1, p. 23; Pioneer Press, 1898: September 29, p. 2; October 2, p. 1; 4, p. 1; 16, part 1, p. 4; Minneapolis Tribune, October 2, part 1, p. 1. The Pioneer Press, the Minneapolis Tribune, the Minneapolis Journal, and the Duluth News Tribune from September 29 to October 30 contain daily reports of the trouble at Leech Lake. A good account of the disturbance is that by Louis H. Roddis, "The Last Indian Uprising in the United States," in the Minnesota History Bulletin, 3: 273–290 (February, 1920).

had suffered from the white men. The agent and the local
Indian inspector strove adroitly to appease their indignation
and advised submission to the authorities of the Great Father.
They got no satisfactory replies and the futile council dispersed.

The Bear Island Indians, instead of attending the council,
were engaged in transporting themselves and their families
to the mainland and in making a bivouac near Bugonaygeshig's home on Sugar Point, of which Bear Island would
be the extension if the lake were sufficiently lowered. Late
on October 4 Brigadier General John M. Bacon, department
commander, arrived at Walker and with him, Captain and
Brevet Major Melville C. Wilkinson, Lieutenant Tenny Ross,
and eighty men of Company E of the Third Infantry. On
the same day Marshal O'Connor and the inspector paid a
visit to " Old Bug " on Sugar Point. A council was held
with some forty or fifty Indians, and the marshal, of course,
demanded the surrender of the men he had come to arrest.
This the braves absolutely refused.[44]

The result of a consultation at Walker that night was the
plan to send Major Wilkinson's command to Sugar Point on
the following morning to enable the deputy marshals to serve
the warrants. At daybreak on October 5 two small steamers
with the officials on board left the dock at Walker, one of
them towing a barge carrying the soldiers. It was nine
o'clock when the flotilla completed its thirty-mile run and
landed in front of Bugonaygeshig's cabin on Sugar Point.
This rude cabin of logs was situated near the center of a
small cultivated patch surrounded by a large area from
which the timber had been cut and in which weeds and
bushes had grown up. Outside of this was heavy timber.
In and around Bugonaygeshig's house some half a dozen
Indians were seen. One of them was recognized by Deputy
Marshal Timothy J. Sheehan, who arrested him and after

[44] Secretary of War, *Reports*, 1899, part 1, pp. 21, 24. Accounts of the
futile council are in the newspapers of October 4 and 5.

a struggle placed him in irons in one of the boats. While this was going on four or five Indians left the cabin armed with rifles. A skirmish line thrown out to the edge of the woods found no Indians. Leaving a guard at the landing place, General Bacon with the main body of the company made a march of two miles or more around the shore of the point by way of reconnaissance. He saw some old men but no warriors. Some squaws laughed contemptuously.

It was about midday when the party returned and the order was given to let the men eat and rest. The company was lined up and ordered to stack arms. A recruit bungled in such a way that his piece was discharged. Instantly two signal shots came from the woods, followed by a volley of bullets, apparently from all quarters. One soldier fell dead and two others were wounded. Although nearly three-fourths of the command were very raw recruits, they were but momentarily disconcerted. Their officers, exposing themselves with gallantry, soon got them into a firing line, covered by such surface inequalities as there chanced to be. For half an hour volley firing was repeated by the Indians and thereafter desultory shots continued until about four in the afternoon. About three o'clock Major Wilkinson received a wound in the left leg. He had it dressed by the surgeon and returned to the firing line. A few minutes later he was shot through the abdomen and he died in an hour and a half. Sergeant William Butler, crossing the field to inform General Bacon of the major's death, was instantly killed by a bullet through the brain.

In the evening trenches were dug, sentries were posted for the night, and preparations were made against a probable attack in the morning. Occasional shots were fired into the place, but there was no concerted attack. In the evening William Russell, an Indian policeman, who probably feared death should he fall into the hands of the hostiles, undertook to leave the ground in a canoe. One of the guards, thinking it might be an enemy that he saw in the dark, ordered him to halt and, when disobeyed, fired with fatal effect. About nine o'clock on the morning of the sixth a soldier who left cover to gather some potatoes was instantly killed. In addition to those named, three private soldiers were killed in the affair and a dozen or more persons were wounded. Colonel Sheehan was one of the wounded, as was also Indian Inspector A. M. Tinker.[45]

General Bacon with his detachment returned to Walker on the seventh and, in response to rumors that a general uprising of the Pillagers was imminent, began making dispositions for a campaign. Lieutenant Colonel Abram A. Harbach, who had come up from Fort Snelling with two hundred and nine men and five officers, was stationed at the Leech Lake agency. Lieutenant James T. Moore brought up ninety-five men, whom he divided into two parties to guard the Leech Lake and Winnibigoshish dams. Governor Clough ordered Battery A of the Minnesota National Guard to Cass Lake and Battery B to Deer River. Several companies of the Fourteenth Minnesota Infantry were sent to occupy the principal stations of the Great Northern Railway north of the Leech Lake Reservation. The Pillagers were thus surrounded by a cordon of troops that it would have been madness to oppose. There was little need, however, for this

[45] The Twin City and Duluth newspapers of October 6, 7, and 8, 1898, contain accounts of the battle. See especially the *Pioneer Press* of October 7, p. 1, for Colonel Sheehan's "graphic description" of the battle, and October 8, p. 1, for the "Story of Carnage," by Will H. Brill, staff correspondent. See also "The Battle of Sugar Point," in *De Lestry's Western Magazine*, 3: 1–7 (November, 1898), by the same author. Three newspaper correspondents accompanied the soldiers to the point and witnessed the fight from behind trees and stumps. In the *Pioneer Press* of October 6, p. 1, and October 8, p. 1, are maps of Leech Lake and the scene of the battle. These maps are reproduced by Roddis in the *Minnesota History Bulletin*, 3: 282 (February, 1920). Major Wilkinson, who was near the retiring age, had a proud record of service both in the volunteer and in the regular army and had been brevetted for meritorious conduct. He had made many warm friends in Minnesota and a vast crowd gathered at his funeral at Fort Snelling. Brief accounts of his career may be found in Indian Office, *Reports*, 1898, p. 1091, and the *Minneapolis Tribune*, October 16, 1898, section 3, p. 3.

display of force. With the exception of the Bear Island band, the Pillagers, although indignant because the Great Father had not kept his faith and had not protected them against fraud and robbery, had no idea of making war. Of the Bear Island band but thirty-five men had taken up arms and of those but nineteen, who formed the party that had fired on the soldiers, owned Winchester rifles. It has been regarded as highly probable that those men would not have fired had they not been maddened by what seemed to them an attack when the gun of the recruit was accidentally discharged. Had they seriously so desired, from ambush they could easily have annihilated General Bacon and his escort on his reconnaissance in the forenoon. It was thought by some at the time that the original expectation of the Bear Island group was merely to overawe Lieutenant Humphreys and his party when they should come up with the marshal.[46]

Safely reëstablished at his base of operations, General Bacon awaited the arrival of the commissoner of Indian affairs, W. A. Jones. When the commissioner came, on October 10, the control of affairs was very readily turned over to him. He willingly sacrificed the national dignity and proceeded to treat with the Bear Island Indians as if they were a high belligerent power, entitled to make war and conclude peace. He employed as his intermediary, Father Aloysius, the veteran head of St. Benedict's Mission at White Earth, who was well known and justly esteemed by all the Chippewa. Near midnight on the eleventh the reverend father met forty Bear Island chiefs and warriors in council on Black Duck Point. At first they were in no happy frame of mind and began to rehearse their wrongs and insults. A canoe load of hardtack, pork, coffee, tea, sugar, flour, and tobacco at length

[46] Secretary of War, *Reports*, 1899, part 1, p. 21; Minnesota Adjutant General, *Reports*, 1900, pp. 31, 211–213; Holmes, in *Minnesota in Three Centuries*, 4: 247. Governor Clough's correspondence with the United States attorney-general, Henry C. Corbin, with regard to dispatching troops to guard citizens in the vicinity of Leech Lake, is in the *Pioneer Press*, October 9, 1898, part 1, p. 1.

had a mollifying effect and Father Aloysius was able to carry back word that they were disposed to discuss matters with the commissioner.[47]

On October 12 the commissioner personally met the hostiles. He was firm in insisting upon the surrender of the men named in the warrants. The Indians were equally firm in declining to surrender them, at least without some promise of immunity for the war party and of redress of general grievances. On successive days there were councils at the agency, with representatives present from the Pillager bands in general. On the fifteenth twenty-five chiefs and braves, doubtless moved by the advice and entreaties of Father Aloysius, published an address to the state and the country. They regretted the death of brave men in an attack as unexpected as it was unavoidable. The Pillagers had risen against injury and oppression just as white men would have done. They knew that fighting could result only in their ruin. They would take the advice of the commissioner and the reverend father and would refrain from further hostility. They trusted that the Great Father would do them justice and would be lenient with their tribesmen, who had erred under great provocation. At a final council with the hostiles at Black Duck Point on the seventeenth, two of the men wanted surrendered, and it was understood that others would do likewise. They were not precipitate about it, however, and it was not until the twentieth of October that eleven more were in custody at the agency. Bugonaygeshig was not of the number. The Bear Island leader preferred his freedom under the tall pines and no deputy marshal volunteered to take him prisoner. The captives were taken by train to Duluth, accompanied by Father Aloysius. As none of them could put up bail in the sum of five hundred dollars, all lay in jail until the next day, when they were arraigned for trial before Judge

[47] *Minneapolis Tribune, Pioneer Press*, October 11, 12, 13, 1898; *Graham Report*, 1241. Father Aloysius' story of the midnight conference is in the *Graham Report*, 1254–1256.

William Lochren, sitting in the United States district court. A *nolle prosequi* was entered in the case of one of the Indians. A " jury of their peers," after deliberating thirty-five minutes, found the rest of them guilty, as indicted, of resistance to arrest and of conspiring to resist. Four were sentenced to confinement in jail for ten months and to pay a fine of one hundred dollars each; six got eight months' imprisonment and a hundred-dollar fine; two boys, one a son of " Old Bug," were let off with fines of twenty-five dollars and sixty days in jail.[48]

Commissioner Jones felt that the punishment of the men who had given themselves up while many others, equally guilty, remained at liberty, ought not to be so severe and on December 13 he proposed that the attorney-general be requested to secure the remission of the fines and the reduction of the jail sentences to two months, if the culprits would promise to be good Indians. The attorney-general advised the president that, the law having been vindicated, further punishment was not necessary and that a show of clemency would be beneficial. On January 3, 1899, President McKinley issued full pardons for all the culprits.[49]

From a military point of view the little Pillager army had come off victorious. It had withstood a greatly superior force, which it had forced back on its base without, so far as is definitely known, the loss of a single Indian. One of the braves said of the affair: " Heap fight up there, Indians kill heap soldiers, whip 'em lots; no Indian shot, Indians dodge." When all was over Bugonaygeshig and eight of the men wanted by the marshals were at large in their native wilderness and no further effort was made to find and arrest them. Before the end of October all the troops, regular and volunteer, had been withdrawn, except a single company of

[48] The progress of the councils may be followed in the Twin City and Duluth newspapers from October 12 to 22. The *Duluth News Tribune*, October 22, p. 1; 23, p. 1, contains full accounts of the trials.

[49] Indian Office, *Reports*, 1899, part 1, p. 134; United States Attorney-General, *Reports*, 1899, pp. 246, 269; *Minneapolis Journal*, January 4, 1899, p. 1.

the Third United States Infantry, which was held at Walker for some months.[50]

By this time the reader will have wondered whether the first and only serious outbreak of the Chippewa against white man's authority had its origin simply in the liberation, by a crowd of half-drunken Indians, of a local chief from the custody of a United States marshal. The arrest of Bugonaygeshig was merely the last of a series. For a long time United States marshals, some of them mixed-blood Chippewa, had, for the sake of the fees, arrested Indians and carried them before the United States court at St. Paul or Duluth. Other Indians were subpœnaed as witnesses and were virtually held in custody pending and during trials. These arrests and detentions were mostly for the clandestine sale of liquor and there were cases in which the persons making or securing the arrests had themselves furnished, or had connived at furnishing, the liquor. Sometime previously Bugonaygeshig had been taken to Duluth as a witness in a liquor case. For some reason he had failed to receive his witness fees and mileage and had been obliged to walk to his home, over a hundred miles away, suffering considerable hardship on the journey. It has been claimed that he was purposely deprived of his fees. At any rate, he swore a white man's oath that he would never again obey a process from court. In this resolution he had abundant sympathy, which was a reason for his rescue at Walker on September 15.

The arrest and the rescue, however, were but surface phenomena. Below them lay fundamental sources of dissatisfaction and irritation. Under them all lay the immemorial loathing and lodged race hatred of the red man for the white. Upon this rested strata of particular grievances, over which the Indians, in their innumerable councils, nursed their wrath and poured out eloquent maledictions upon the faithless white man and, at times, upon mixed-blood traitors. Of least ac-

[50] Secretary of War, *Reports*, 1899, part 1, p. 24.

count was the complaint of delays and irregularities in the payment of annuities. It was claimed that the Indian office had allowed Chippewa from Wisconsin and Michigan to intrude upon the Minnesota reservations and to obtain allotments of land to which they had no right. The dams built by the government in the eighties to create the reservoir system about the headwaters of the Mississippi had overflowed some forty thousand acres of their rice fields, for which they had received very inadequate remuneration. The promises of large receipts for the sale of a great part of their old reservation had not been realized; the proceeds had been swallowed up by charges for estimating pine timber and the expenses of a superfluous Chippewa commission. The Indians also believed, and rightly, that the estimates of pine were fraudulent, to their great damage. Logging contractors, under permits to cut and remove only dead timber, standing or fallen, had shamelessly stolen and carried off great amounts of live timber, and the government agents apparently had connived at it. These complaints were common to most, if not to all, of the Chippewa of the time. There was one ground of complaint, however, particular to the Pillagers, of long standing and much mulled over among them. In 1847 the Pillager band ceded to the United States an area of nearly seven hundred thousand acres lying west and north of the Long Prairie Reservation of the Winnebago, between the Long Prairie River and Otter Tail Lake, in consideration of a small compensation and the establishment of the friendly Menominee of Wisconsin between the Pillagers and the hated and dreaded Sioux. Because the Menominee were unwilling to move to the proposed new home, the government left them where they were and in 1854 paid them $242,686 for the Minnesota tract. The Leech Lake Pillagers ever afterward contended that they had been swindled. They had sold the land, not for the money, but for protection against the Sioux.[51]

[51] Indian Office, *Reports*, 1898, p. 1091; 1899, part 1, p. 135; Holmes, in *Minnesota in Three Centuries*, 4: 246; *Pioneer Press*, October 10, 1898,

The comment of Governor David M. Clough in his retiring message to the legislature of 1899 is perhaps not too severe: " A series of acts and neglects most wrongful to the Indians of Minnesota, by a blunder more criminal in its results than the neglects and acts which preceded it, took a small party of troops to Leech Lake in this state. . . . The climax to a long course of folly and wrong in dealing with the Pillagers, precipitated bloodshed and led to the death of a number of brave and noble-hearted men. This in turn came very near causing an outbreak of all the Minnesota Chippewas." [52]

THE PRESENT SITUATION

The Chippewa Indians are a dying race. Of the 12,990 consolidated Chippewa residing in Minnesota on June 30, 1928, but 1,077, or about eight per cent, are classed as full-bloods; of the 1,766 remote Red Lake Chippewa, 438, or about twenty-five per cent, are full-bloods. The scarcity of full-bloods is very marked among certain bands: of the White Earth Mississippi Chippewa, for example, but 6 persons out of 3,433 were reported as full-bloods in 1926; of the Gull Lake band, numbering 552, there were but 4; out of 697 of the Pembina band but 6 were full-bloods. An educated and very intelligent mixed-blood gentleman said in conversation with the author that he doubted whether there was in fact a single full-blood living in the state. The white settlements have so penetrated and spread that Indian communities are few and small; the bark wigwam long ago disappeared, except for the amusement of summer tourists, and Indian dress is rarely seen except at pageants. Three-fourths of the Minnesota Chippewa are off the reservations, so-called, and only

p. 2. On the treaty of 1847, the Nelson Act of 1889, and the reservoir system constructed during the eighties, see *ante*, 1: 321; 4: 209, 219. The Indian side of the trouble is presented by Gus H. Beaulieu in the *Pioneer Press*, October 1, pp. 1, 4. The *Pioneer Press* for October 12, p. 2, contains a letter from Ely Wright of Cass County to the secretary of the interior, stating the causes of the outbreak.

[52] Clough, *Message*, 1899, p. 6.

about five per cent of them are residing on their original allotments.[53]

The agency that is doing most to advance the civilization of the Chippewa and to assimilate them into the general society is school education. In the year ending on June 30, 1926, there were 2,277 Chippewa enrolled in public schools and 825 in nonsectarian government day and boarding schools. A remainder of 425 were in two Roman Catholic mission schools.[54] The older of them, at White Earth, is especially worthy of the reader's notice. He is already aware that when the White Earth Reservation was set apart by the treaty of 1867, it was expected that all Minnesota Chippewa would move from their old reservations to that promised land where, secure from the white man's temptations, they would dwell in a consecrated Indian country. That hope, he knows, was not fulfilled; but the natural attractions of the region and the inducements offered to immigrants by the government allured considerable numbers from the various bands to move and settle there. In the course of a decade some fifteen hundred had made their homes on White Earth. Missionaries, both Protestant and Catholic, had come with the first parties of immigrants. In 1874 the Reverend Ignatius Tomazin established a Catholic mission and a day school at White Earth; but his missionary labors carried him over most of the northern part of Minnesota, and the work was found too difficult for one priest to handle. In November, 1878, the abbot of St. John's Abbey in Stearns County appointed the Reverend Aloysius Hermanutz, better known as Father Aloysius, as missionary to the Indians at White Earth. The young man had come from Wurttemberg in

[53] Indian Office, *Reports*, 1926, p. 34; Secretary of the Interior, *Reports*, 1928, p. 267; 234 *United States*, 245–262; interview with Edward L. Rogers, recorded in the author's notebooks, 10: 14–17. The principle followed in determining the blood status of the Chippewa is discussed in letters to the author from Edgar B. Meritt, assistant commissioner of Indian Affairs, June 21, July 5, 1927, and from Edgar A. Allen, superintendent of the consolidated Chippewa, June 20, July 14, 1927, in the Folwell Papers.

[54] Indian Office, *Reports*, 1926, p. 40.

southern Germany at the age of seventeen and had joined
the Benedictine community at St. John's Abbey. After six
years of study and discipline he was ordained priest in 1876.
On November 5, 1878, he arrived at White Earth, accompanied by two sisters of the Benedictine order, Sisters Lioba
Braun and Philomena Koetten, who at once opened a school
in a converted stable building. As later endowed and expanded, it took the name of St. Benedict's Orphan Industrial
School. For such situations the traditional devotion of Bene-
dictines to labor and education is well adapted. It may be
believed that no other three persons have done as much for
the enlightenment of the White Earth Chippewa.[55]

Progress has also been made toward improving health conditions among the Indians. Public health work, which was
begun about thirty years ago with the establishment of a
nursing service on a modest scale, has been gradually expanded to include the maintenance of four general hospitals,
a tuberculosis sanatorium, four institutional and four field
physicians, six institutional nurses, and several field nurses.
Most of these activities are carried on under the direction
of the Indian office, but in recent years the state has assumed
a share of the responsibility and is at present contributing
toward the support of three of the field nurses. Great effort
is being made — through home and school visits, class work,
and clinics — to inculcate in the Indian the fundamental principles of healthful living and to teach him to improve his
condition by his own efforts. The task presents many difficulties, because the habits and customs of many years must
be replaced by new ones, but real progress is being made.[56]

Although the Chippewa will assuredly lose their existence
as a distinct race and will be absorbed in the enveloping

[55] Indian Office, *Reports,* 1877, p. 129; Aloysius Hermanutz, "St. Benedict's Mission and School," in the *Indian Sentinel,* 1911, p. 26; *Tomahawk,*
1926: May 13, p. 1; 27, p. 1; the Reverend Cuthbert Goeb to the author,
July 17, 1926, Folwell Papers. Father Aloysius died on September 4, 1929.
[56] Adelia Eggestine, "The Minnesota Indian Health Service," and Elizabeth Sherer, "The Work of the Indian Nurses in Minnesota," in Minnesota

white population, no early date can be fixed for the consummation of that absorption. Until the end of the fifty-year trust period provided for in the Nelson Act of 1889, which technically has not yet begun, the Minnesota Chippewa will all be Indians according to law, unless Congress can be induced to shorten the period by authorizing the earlier distribution of the tribal fund in the treasury, which amounted to over six million dollars in 1920. Such a disposition of the fund has long been desired by intelligent Indians and by white friends and has often been discussed in the meetings of the General Council of the Chippewa Indians of Minnesota, organized in 1913. Numerous bills to accomplish this have been introduced in Congress, but all of them have failed of passage. The bill of 1925 as perfected by its friends is the best example. The title, "A bill authorizing the classification of the Chippewa Indians of Minnesota as competents and incompetents," was a misnomer suggested by the opening section, which provided for a commission of three members, one to be appointed by the president, another by the secretary of the interior, and the third by the Chippewa Indians of Minnesota, to divide the Indians into two classes. The first class was to be composed of all adults competent to manage and control their property; the other class was to include adult incompetents and minors. This classification was ancillary to the main purpose of the bill, which provided that as soon as the rolls of the two classes should be completed the secretary of the interior should divide equally among all the persons named on the two rolls all but a half million dollars of the Chippewa fund in the treasury. Thereupon he was to pay each competent Indian his share in cash. The aggregate shares of the incompetents and minors were to be held in the treasury and to draw interest at the rate of five per cent, the principal and interest to

Department of Health, Division of Child Hygiene, *News Letter*, August, 1928; Eggestine, *Public Health Nursing among the Minnesota Indians*, a reprint from the *Trained Nurse and Hospital Review*, November, 1929.

be expended under the direction of the secretary of the interior for their support, education, and maintenance. The obvious intent of the bill was to terminate the guardianship of the United States over all the competent Indians and leave them to live and act simply as citizens of their state.[57]

It will be recalled that Congress, if it sees fit, may make appropriations for cash per capita payments from the tribal fund before the final distribution of the principal. In December, 1920, a group of the Minnesota Chippewa presented resolutions to Congress alleging that hundreds of their children were being deprived of school privileges because of the lack of sufficient food and warm clothing and that trachoma, tuberculosis, and other diseases were raging in their country. They demanded emergency relief, and Congress responded by authorizing the payment of one hundred dollars to each and every Indian on the rolls of the Minnesota Chippewa. Having once yielded, Congress has been importuned again and again, and five emergency payments, totaling $325 per capita, have been made to 1929. Fortunately for the Indians, the depletion of the fund by these payments, which have amounted to about four million dollars, has been partly offset by large additions to compensate for the surrender of Indian rights in the Chippewa National Forest and for lands disposed of under the Homestead Act.[58]

In the meantime a measure has been passed and put into operation with the approval of the general council that may result in a large increase of the fund. Intelligent Chippewa, whatever their blood status might be, knew as well as white

[57] *Congressional Record*, 69 Congress, 1 session, 405. A copy of the classification bill of December 7, 1925, H.R. 438, is in the Folwell Papers. Three classification bills were introduced in the session of 1928. See *Chippewa Hearings* (1920), 169, 263. A wide range of Chippewa affairs was covered by the inquiry. Bills providing for the distribution of the trust funds may be traced through the indexes to the *Congressional Record*, under "Indians, Chippewa."

[58] *Tomahawk*, 1920: December 9, p. 1; 1922: June 1, p. 4; *Statutes at Large*, 42: 221; 43: 1, 798, 816, 1052; 44: 7, 173; 45: 314.

men, or at least well enough, the iniquities, unintended iniquities, that had resulted from the act of January 14, 1889, as
interpreted by Congress and as administered by the department of the interior through the general land office and the
Indian office, such as false classifications of land, underestimates of timber, and bungling with allotments. The capable
attorney employed by the White Earth Indians soon after the
organization of the general council made up a long list of
grievances that were mulled over in the councils. It was believed and asserted that the Chippewa had been robbed of
many millions of dollars, which Congress had never been
willing to pay and never would pay. The outcome was a resolution to resort to the United States court of claims for a hearing and a judicial determination of stated claims, a proceeding
that required the consent of Congress. A "jurisdictional
bill" was passed by Congress in February, 1925, but failed
to become law because of a pocket veto. On May 14, 1926,
however, the president approved a bill, passed by both houses
without opposition, which authorized the court of claims "to
hear, examine, and adjudicate and render judgment in claims
of the Chippewa of Minnesota and of any bands thereof aris-
ing out of the Nelson Act of 1889 or acts subsequent thereto."
No individual claims were to be heard by the court. It was
provided that the Indians should be represented by two attorneys or firms of attorneys, one to be appointed by a committee
of five to be selected by the White Earth Indians from among
their number, and the other by a similar committee selected
by all the other Chippewa of Minnesota. Each of the two
attorneys or firms was to be paid a salary of six thousand
dollars a year for not more than five years, and upon the final
determination of the litigation each was to be allowed such
additional compensation as the court should deem just and
proper, but not more than five per cent of the amount recovered, nor in any event more than forty thousand dollars. The
attorneys' fees and all their actual and necessary expenses in

the prosecution of the suit were to be paid out of the trust funds of the Minnesota Chippewa in the treasury.[59]

The two firms of attorneys were promptly appointed and entered upon their term of service. At the present writing five petitions have been filed in the court of claims praying judgment against the United States for an aggregate sum of $42,254,393.99, with interest, and for costs and disbursements.[60]

[59] *Statutes at Large*, vol. 44, part 2, pp. 555–557; *Chippewa Hearings* (1920), 105; *Congressional Record*, 68 Congress, 2 session, 4008, 4441, 4595; 69 Congress, 1 session, 8511, 8643, 10230.

[60] The Chippewa Indians of Minnesota *v.* the United States, *Petitions* (United States Court of Claims, nos. I176, I1155, I1163, H192, H279); interview with Edward L. Rogers, March 23, 1927, recorded in the author's notebooks, 10:16.   The petitions were filed, respectively, on February 26, April 13, April 21, May 5, and July 5, 1927.

V. THE WILL OF THE PEOPLE

THE ELECTIVE FRANCHISE

THE phrase "government by the people," if all the people are included, has no literal sense unless it stands for government by opinion, which Bryce describes as the real government of American commonwealths. When government implies the enactment and enforcement of law with an ultimate sanction of armed power, it is obvious that such rule must be intrusted to some fraction of the whole body capable of framing laws and, when combined in sufficient numbers, of compelling obedience. The deposit of the elective franchise is therefore the prime concern in constituting free states, whether by documentary constitutions struck out in bulk in special conventions or by those edited out of ancient customs and statutes of organic character enacted in emergencies. The electorate is, or should be, the sovereign power.

What purely constructive rights of suffrage, if any, existed in the area of Minnesota under French, British, and Spanish jurisdictions it is not worth while to inquire. Equally futile would be an investigation as to what rights of suffrage might have been enjoyed had there been inhabitants while parts of Minnesota were included in the areas of various territories of the United States.[1]

The earliest instance of serious account of the exercise of the elective franchise in the area of Minnesota was the election of Joseph R. Brown in 1840 as a delegate from St. Croix County to the legislature of Wisconsin Territory. In that year the right to vote belonged to free white male citizens twenty-one years of age or over who had resided in the terri-

[1] James Bryce, *The American Commonwealth*, 2: 267–273 (New York, 1910). A graphic account of the successive jurisdictions in Minnesota is given in West, *Sibley*, 118. The Ordinance of 1787 gave the suffrage to "free male inhabitants of full age."

tory for six months. It may be assumed that no material change in the qualifications for voting had taken place when the citizens of the abandoned rump of Wisconsin Territory on October 30, 1848, elected Henry Hastings Sibley as their delegate in Congress.[2]

The organic act of Minnesota Territory, approved on March 3, 1849, granted to every free white male inhabitant above the age of twenty-one years who resided in the territory at the time of the passage of the act the right to vote and to be eligible to office at the first election. For subsequent elections the qualifications for voting and holding office were to be prescribed by the legislative assembly of the territory, except that those privileges could be granted only to citizens of the United States and to declarants for naturalization who should make oath to support the Constitution of the United States and to obey the provisions of the organic act. The first territorial legislature — that of 1849 — granted the right of suffrage to three classes of adult males who had resided in the territory for six months: white citizens; declarants for naturalization who had lived in the United States for two years; and civilized Indian mixed-bloods.[3]

The enabling act of February 26, 1857, simply authorized the " legal voters " to elect delegates to the appointed constitutional convention. The constitution to be formed was to be subject to the approval and ratification of the people of the proposed state, and apparently it was assumed that the same " legal voters " would be competent to ratify or reject it. The Republican wing of the convention did not take this simple view. In the schedule reported by Dr. Thomas Foster on August 17 it was proposed that all " persons who have resided in the proposed State three months, and are otherwise duly qualified to vote " as prescribed in the article on the

<hr/>

[2] *Ante*, 1: 233, 239–241; Wisconsin Territory, *Laws*, 1836–38, p. 408. Voting may have taken place in the area of Minnesota before 1840, when St. Croix County was part of Crawford County, Wisconsin.

[3] Minnesota Territory, *Laws*, 1849, p. 6; Minnesota, *Legislative Manual*, 1929, pp. 3–7.

elective franchise of the constitution, then in the making, should be entitled to vote for or against the ratification of the constitution and for the officers to be elected under it. The schedule reported to the Democratic convention proposed that " every free white male inhabitant over the age of twenty-one years, who shall have resided within the limits of the State for ten days previous to the day of said election, may vote for all the officers to be elected . . . and also for or against the adoption of the Constitution." The joint committee of conference reported this section without change and it was adopted by both conventions and became part of the constitution.[4]

When it came to establishing the permanent deposit of the elective franchise, both convention bodies were disposed to act conservatively and to conform to the practice of the new northwestern states. As ratified, the constitution bestowed the privilege of voting upon an electorate of male persons twenty-one years of age or over, resident in the United States one year, in the state four months, and in their several election districts ten days before any election. This electorate was to be derived from four classes of persons: white citizens of the United States; foreign-born persons who should have declared their intention to become citizens under the naturalization laws; civilized mixed-bloods; and Indians found competent to vote after being examined in a district court.[5] The

[4] Minnesota Constitutional Convention (Republican), *Debates and Proceedings*, 505; (Democratic), 564, 674; *Legislative Manual*, 1929, p. 9.

[5] Minnesota, Constitution, article 7, section 1. The proceedings of the Democratic convention show that the Democratic draft of the article on the elective franchise, as amended on the floor, was adopted by the compromise committee with trifling changes. The draft was a close copy of the corresponding article of the Wisconsin constitution of 1848. The debate in the Democratic wing of the convention discloses some interesting and diverging views. The paragraph extending the suffrage to full-blood Indians found capable of exercising it was proposed by Joseph R. Brown, whose judgment in Indian matters carried much weight. Judge Flandrau warmly supported him and read to the convention a manuscript petition, signed by Paul Mazakutemani and eleven other members of the Hazelwood Republic, praying that all civilized and educated Indians, whether mixed-bloods or full-bloods, be made citizens of Minnesota and granted all the privileges of citizens. Sibley offered an amendment, which

composition of the electorate remained unchanged until 1868, when a constitutional amendment changed the reading of the phrase " white citizens of the United States " to " citizens of the United States," thereby extending the suffrage to negro citizens.[6]

Of the male immigrants who swarmed into Minnesota in the last quarter of the nineteenth century the greater number of those who were of age sought naturalization, complied with the lawful conditions, and took out their first and second papers in due course. Some of them, however, discovered that as mere declarants they had advantages over full citizens. In particular, they could not be drawn for jury duty and they had the right to sue in the United States courts. Yet in respect to the franchise they had the same privileges as citizens. The legislature of 1895 submitted a constitutional amendment to remedy the situation. It took the now usual form of a restatement of section 1 of article 7 and omitted the second item in the list of persons theretofore entitled to vote, namely, declarants for naturalization. The amendment was duly ratified at the general election of 1896. Since then no person born an alien has been allowed to vote in Minnesota until three months after his full naturalization and to secure that he must have resided in the United States five years and in the state one year.[7]

A proposition offered in the Democratic wing of the constitutional convention of 1857 to extend the electoral privilege to married women was ignored as too frivolous for

he afterwards withdrew, to strike out the word " white " before " citizens of the United States." His reason was that, under the then recent Dred Scott decision, there were no other than white citizens of the United States. *Debates and Proceedings* (Democratic), 422–437, 580, 597, 599, 663.

[6] Anderson, *History of the Constitution*, 178, 278; *Laws*, 1868, pp. 149–151. The history of the amendment to admit negroes to the electorate is given *ante*, 3: 7. Had the electors rejected the amendment, the negro would have had to wait only until March 30, 1870, when the fifteenth amendment to the national Constitution took effect and made him a citizen elector. United States, *Statutes at Large*, 16: 1131.

[7] *General Laws*, 1895, p. 7; 1897, p. iv; Anderson, *History of the Constitution*, 180, 230. Anderson omits this amendment from his table on page 282. There were 97,980 votes for the amendment and 52,454 against it.

notice. But the agitation for that "reform" was soon heard in Minnesota, and, as in other states, it became more vigorous in the last years of the Civil War, when woman's efficiency in nursing sick and wounded soldiers was proved not only in the remote general hospitals, but also in the field hospitals and on transports. Thousands upon thousands of women did the work of the sanitary and the Christian commissions. The admission of negroes to the electorate, partly on the ground of the heroic behavior of negro soldiery, added volume to the swelling clamor of "votes for women."

Nothing was achieved, however, until 1875, when a slight concession was obtained. The legislature of that year was induced to submit for ratification an amendment to the constitution empowering the legislature to provide by law that women might vote for school officers and measures and might hold school offices. To secure the necessary majority of votes a policy was contrived that indicated that whenever women should get into politics they would know how to play the game. It was decided to make a "gumshoe" campaign so as not to arouse malignant opposition. Then the state committees of the two great political parties were persuaded to have their tickets printed so as to read, "For the amendment of Article VII relating to electors — Yes." Opposers were thus obliged to unbutton their coats, get out their glasses, fumble for a pencil, and cross out "yes" and write "no." There were 19,468 patriots who took the trouble to scratch their tickets, but as 24,340 left them undefaced, the amendment was ratified. The legislature of 1876 passed the desired law and thereafter women braved the mobs at the polling places, had their names taken down, and saw their little tickets tucked into separate ballot boxes. There was rejoicing. But the concession was consoling rather than gratifying; it was an "entering wedge," as Richard Chute, an advocate of the bill, remarked later.[8]

[8] *Debates and Proceedings* (Democratic), 586; *General Laws*, 1875, p. 18; 1876, p. 29; Anderson, *History of the Constitution*, 179, 279; interview of the

Twenty years ran by. Few women cared for school suffrage alone and fewer still cared for the offices. Moreover, the privilege was a grant that might be revoked by any legislature. To get this fortuitous concession converted into a constitutional right was the next and modest goal of the reformers. They obtained from the legislature of 1897 the submission to the electors of a constitutional amendment that, if ratified, would confer upon women possessing the qualifications required of male electors the right to vote for school and library officers and upon measures relating to schools and libraries and make them eligible to any school and library offices. Nearly two-thirds of the votes cast on the proposal were in favor of it. At the same election, that of 1898, was ratified the amendment requiring a majority of all votes cast at the election to ratify an amendment to the constitution. It is noteworthy that both amendments would have failed had such a majority vote been required at the time.[0]

The advocates of full suffrage for women, increasing in numbers and confident of ultimate success, carried forward their cause from the platform and through the press. Their bills for full suffrage or for further extension of suffrage were introduced into every legislature. Some died in committee, some passed one house, but none passed both houses. The Minnesota electorate, restrained by immemorial tradition and by the surviving conviction that Sacred Scripture excluded women from independent public activities, was slow to welcome the innovation. The ancient prejudice slowly

author with Richard Chute. According to Elizabeth C. Stanton, Susan B. Anthony, and Matilda J. Gage, eds., *History of Woman Suffrage*, 3: 652 (New York, 1881), the ratification of the amendment was due largely to the way in which the ballots were printed. An amendment to authorize women to vote in local option elections was submitted to the electors in 1877 but was defeated. *General Laws*, 1877, p. 22; Anderson, *History of the Constitution*, 179, 280.

[9] *Ante*, 3: 227; *General Laws*, 1897, pp. 331, 345; Anderson, *History of the Constitution*, 179, 282. Unsuccessful efforts to secure woman suffrage legislation in the nineties are discussed in Stanton, Anthony, and Gage, *Woman Suffrage*, 4: 775–777.

gave way, however, against the untiring assaults of the propagandists, who were encouraged by the progress made in other states. The legislature of 1919 in its regular session passed a concurrent resolution asking the United States Senate to join with the House of Representatives in its action in proposing a suffrage amendment to the national Constitution; and the same legislature, in anticipation of the ratification of the nineteenth amendment, passed an act extending to women the right to vote at presidential elections.[10]

When Congress at length, in June, 1919, submitted to the states the nineteenth amendment, forbidding denial of the franchise on account of sex, the popular mind in Minnesota was favorable to its ratification. The governor had called a special session of the legislature of that year to consider certain propositions in regard to the election laws, and on the first day of the session, September 8, he appeared before the houses in joint convention with a message and an announcement that action upon the proposed amendment would be their first business. They took him at his word. The moment the members of the House had taken their seats in their chamber, a joint resolution was introduced, which, after reciting the act of Congress submitting the amendment, briefly added, " the said . . . amendment . . . is hereby ratified by the legislature of the State of Minnesota." The rules were suspended and the resolution was given the three readings required by the constitution and was passed by a vote of 120 to 6. It was sent at once to the Senate in the usual way, where it was taken up and passed, also under suspension of the rules, by a vote of 60 to 5. In expectation that the matter would come up, the galleries were filled with women, among them many of the most prominent leaders of the woman suffrage movement in Minnesota. After the voting the ordinary decorum of the houses was abandoned for long-continued demonstrations of flag-waving, cheering, and the singing of the " Battle

---

[10] *Senate Journal*, 1919, p. 122; *House Journal*, 140, 191; *Laws*, 89, 757; Stanton, Anthony, and Gage, *Woman Suffrage*, 6: 324.

Hymn of the Republic." The proceedings culminated in
" an old-fashioned chicken dinner " served, during a recess,
in the Capitol restaurant by ladies of the Twin Cities to the
members who had so gallantly helped to grant suffrage to
women.[11]

The passage of the joint resolution committed the state to
ratification, but the legislature went further and passed an act
giving women with the same personal qualifications as male
electors the right to vote whenever the legislatures of three-
fourths of the states should have ratified the nineteenth
amendment. No act of the legislature could or can amend
the state constitution; no amendment having been proposed,
the word " male " still stands, empty and superfluous, in the
constitution. The nineteenth amendment became effective on
August 26, 1920, and Minnesota women accordingly voted
for the first time for all purposes at the general election of
that year.[12]

Voting for school and library officers and upon school and
library measures had accustomed many women to visiting
the polls and casting ballots. The " entering wedge " of
1876 had done its work. The increase in the total number
of votes cast and counted, from 425,202 in 1918 to 797,945
in 1920, shows that the women of Minnesota responded to
the duty laid upon them.[13]

With the adoption of the nineteenth amendment the American people have gone to the limit in extending what was once
the privilege of the vote. Every person of age is presumed
to be capable of intelligent action on any question of politics

[11] United States, *Statutes at Large*, 41: 362, 1832; Joseph A. A. Burnquist,
Message, 1919, special session, 1; Minnesota, *House Journal*, 1919, special session, 10; *Senate Journal*, 12; *Laws*, 105. Accounts of the demonstrations
following the passage of the resolution by the legislature are given in the
Minneapolis Morning Tribune, September 9, 1919, p. 1, and the *St. Paul
Pioneer Press*, September 8, 1919, p. 10. Discrepancies in the *Minneapolis
Journal*, September 8, p. 18, may be attributed to the preparation of its report
of the proceedings before they took place.
[12] *House Journal*, 1919, special session, 138, 141–143; *Senate Journal*, 118,
142, 211–213; *Laws*, 98.
[13] *Legislative Manual*, 1919, insert after p. 670; 1921, insert after p. 526.

or government and to be willing to act. The experiment will go on indefinitely. Only in some far-off time, some future century, will it be possible as part of a counter-revolution to restrict the privilege on the basis of considerations such as property, permanence of residence, education, and moral character.

THE DEVELOPMENT OF THE ELECTION CODE

In a republic the problem second in importance to that of defining the franchise is the enactment of laws necessary and proper for the conduct of elections, especially in countries like the United States, where the legislature directs and regulates administration in its minutest details. The second legislature of the Territory of Minnesota, in framing the chapter on elections for the Code of 1851, had abundant examples for guidance in the laws of the various states and territories, in particular those of Wisconsin Territory, which had been in force for two years in the area of Minnesota. This chapter, which became the pattern for much of the later legislation, was not materially changed during the territorial period and it was, to use a printer's phrase, "lifted" bodily into the compilation of laws issued early in 1859.[14]

The legislature of 1860, the first to be controlled by the Republican party, saw the need of law improvement and was very willing to undertake it. Defects revealed in the operation of the election law and changed circumstances called for modifications of it. Instead of passing separate amendments to the territorial code, the legislature adopted the wiser policy of enacting a new general law retaining the good and approved portions of the old one and inserting desired amendments. For the most part this policy has been continued ever since and consequently election officers have not been obliged to ransack many session laws to learn their duties.[15]

[14] Revised Statutes, 1851, pp. 44–55; Public Statutes, 1849–58, pp. 138–151 (St. Paul, 1859).
[15] General Laws, 1860, pp. 146–165. The work of the legislature of 1860 is discussed ante, 2: 63.

In spite of all the pains taken to perfect the election law of 1860, the trial of it at the election of the same year disclosed so many defects that the legislature of 1861 found it desirable to repeal it bodily and to reënact it with proper amendments. The provisions of this new code apparently served so well toward getting honest votes into the ballot box and toward securing a fair count and canvass that they remained for many years without material changes. They were embodied in the compilations of the statutes issued in 1866 and 1878. Complaints were being made in some of the larger cities, however, of violations of the election laws and there were demands for remedial legislation. The legislature of 1878 responded by passing a stringent amendatory act for the conduct of elections in cities with populations exceeding twelve thousand, a principal object of which was the prevention of voting by persons not qualified electors, as is apparent from certain provisions to be described in another connection.[16]

The legislature of 1887 enacted a general election law repealing the chapter on elections in the *General Statutes* of 1878 and acts amendatory to it. The main features of course remained unchanged in the new act, the principal innovations being modifications in election procedure. The code was destined to a short life, however. For many years voices of complaint had been heard, ever swelling louder, of the mischievous activities of the machine in politics, of the employment of money in political campaigns, and of the habitual herding of workingmen to the polls according to the suggestion of employers, individual and corporate. To enable voters to approach the polls, to deliver their ballots according to their judgments and consciences, and to see them dropped into the ballot box without fear of consequences was a desideratum more easily thought of than achieved.

---

[16] *Post*, p. 357; *General Laws*, 1861, pp. 95–125; 1878, pp. 133–142; *General Statutes*, 1866, pp. 53–69; 1878, pp. 37–61 (third edition). The law of 1878 applied only to St. Paul, which had a population of 33,178, and Minneapolis, which had 32,721 inhabitants. Secretary of State, *Reports*, 1875, p. 98.

All the plans that had been tried had failed, and the situation was propitious for the adoption of a new one — the so-called Australian ballot system, which was inaugurated in 1889 and with modifications and extensions has been in use ever since.[17]

By this time it had become the custom for each legislature to amend the election law. As custom and law had required the distribution of copies of the existing law to every precinct in the state at every general election, it was deemed most convenient to continue the policy of repealing existing law and reënacting the main body with desired amendments. The legislatures of 1891 and 1893 followed this procedure and enacted general laws, the principal innovations in which were modifications of the Australian system, of registration requirements, and of election procedure. The *Revised Laws* of 1905 embraced the provisions of the *General Statutes* of 1894 and subsequent new legislation, relating chiefly to corruption in elections, the primary system, and details of election procedure.[18]

The next two decades witnessed important developments in election legislation. The primary system was modified and greatly extended; the election of judges and certain other public servants was taken out of the field of politics and placed on a nonpartisan basis; the political party was legally defined and officially recognized; more stringent precautions were introduced to prevent the corruption of electors, election officials, and candidates; and numerous

[17] *General Laws*, 1887, pp. 7–40. Accounts of election evils appear in Bryce, *American Commonwealth*, 2: 146–155; M. Ostrogorski, *Democracy and the Organization of Political Parties*, 2: 367–400 (translated by Frederick Clark — New York and London, 1902); "The Money Power in Politics Again," in the *Nation*, 44: 204 (March 10, 1887); Joseph B. Bishop, "Insufficient Restriction of Campaign Expenditures," in the *Forum*, 15: 148–153 (April, 1893); Jeremiah W. Jenks, "Money in Practical Politics," in the *Century Illustrated Monthly Magazine*, 44: 940–952 (October, 1892 — new series, vol. 22). A full discussion of the Australian ballot system in Minnesota is given *post*, pp. 353–356.

[18] *General Laws*, 1891, pp. 23–66; 1893, pp. 16–78; *Revised Laws*, 1905, pp. 27–68.

measures having for their purpose the perfection of the election machinery were passed and put into operation.

The legislature of 1923 provided by law for the compilation and publication of the general statutes of the state, including all general laws in operation up to the close of that session. The election laws in the published volume include 349 sections and cover 47 large double-column pages in fine type. It might have been assumed that years would pass before additional legislation would be needed; but at the election in November, 1924, it was found that some provisions of the law were not particularly adaptable to first class cities operating under home rule charters. The defects were remedied by an act of 1925, which reprinted forty-four sections of the code of 1923 with insertions, additions, or omissions, most of which either excepted cities of the first class operating under home rule charters from certain provisions of the law or made special provisions for them.[19]

ELECTION PROCEDURE

In the election code of 1851 the elementary duty of dividing the counties into election districts was devolved upon county commissioners, who were required to appoint three electors, " capable and discreet persons," as judges of election in each district. Forty days before a general election the clerk of the board of county commissioners of each county made out and furnished to the sheriff three written notices of the election for each precinct. These the sheriff posted in suitable public places in the several districts. The judges appointed two clerks of election and designated a constable to exercise his office in case of disorder.

When election day came the judges and clerks took an oath to perform their duties to the best of their abilities and, in particular, " studiously " to " endeavor to prevent fraud,

[19] *Laws*, 1923, pp. 89–91; 1925, pp. 688–706; *General Statutes*, 1923, pp. 39–85.

deceit and abuse " in conducting the election. It may be charitably assumed that the compilers inserted the words quoted because they were found in the laws of some older states and not because of any expectation that in the youthful territory persons would be found who would need to be " studiously " watched for attempts at such depravity. Poll books and stationery were supplied by the clerks of the election, and a ballot box with a lock and key and a slit in the top to admit the passage of a single folded ticket and no more was provided by the judges of election at the expense of the county. Before the polls were opened the ballot box was examined and, if necessary, emptied; it was then locked and the key was put into the keeping of one of the judges. At some convenient moment between nine o'clock in the morning and twelve noon, one of the clerks made proclamation of the opening of the polls. All was ready for the solemn sovereign act. Each elector handed to one of the judges, in the presence of them all, his folded written or printed ticket containing the names of all the persons for whom he intended to vote. The judge made sure that the ballot was single and, if no challenge was offered, dropped it into the consecrated ballot box. As the vote was cast, each clerk recorded the name of the elector in his separate poll book. The polls closed at four o'clock in the afternoon.

Immediately after the closing of the polls the canvass began and continued without adjournment. The first proceeding was a comparison of the poll books, which, agreeing or made to agree, showed how many electors had voted. The number was written out in the poll books. The ballot box was then unlocked and opened and the ballots were taken out and counted to ascertain if the number was exactly that of the number of electors who had voted. If more ballots were found than voters, they were put back into the box and the excess number were drawn out by a judge and destroyed. This was called " purging " the ballot box. Next the judges counted the votes cast for each candidate. As they were ascertained the totals were written out in the poll books. A certificate was entered in the poll books and signed by the judges and the clerks. This closed the election. One of the poll books was then wrapped up, securely sealed, and taken by one of the judges or clerks, selected by agreement or lot, or by some other person agreed upon by the judges, to the office of the clerk of the county commissioners. The other poll book, with the ballot box, was deposited with one of the judges, to be subject to the inspection of any voter.

On the twentieth day after the election, or sooner if all the returns were in, the county canvassing board, consisting of the clerk of the county commissioners and two justices of the peace summoned by him, met to break the seals of the poll books, compare the votes cast in the county for the several candidates, and ascertain which one had received the highest number of votes for each office. The clerk thereupon made out certificates of election for members of the legislative assembly and for county and precinct officers and forwarded abstracts of the votes to the secretary of the territory. The votes for delegate to Congress were canvassed by the secretary and the marshal of the territory, in the presence of the governor. As soon as the result was ascertained the governor issued a certificate of election to the successful candidate.[20]

In 1861 the policy of having the county commissioners establish the election districts was abandoned and each organized township and city ward was made an election district. Township supervisors were designated judges of election and the town clerk was one of the clerks of election; the other election clerk was appointed by the judges. City councils appointed the judges for each ward and the judges appointed the two clerks of election.

[20] *Revised Statutes*, 1851, pp. 44–53. The oath required of the judges and clerks of election has ever since been exacted of them.

An important departure was made in the substitution of "election returns" for the poll books theretofore delivered to the county canvassing board. The law required that each ticket be distinctly read as it was counted and, as soon as read and canvassed, "strung by one of the judges upon a string." The canvass completed, the clerk set down on a paper known as "the returns of the election" the names of all persons voted for and the number of votes received by each. The returns were then signed by the judges and clerks, inclosed in a sealed cover, marked as election returns from such and such a district, addressed to the county auditor, and intrusted to one of the judges selected by agreement or lot, who was to deliver them to the county auditor within five days. One of the poll lists with which the clerks were provided went with the returns and the other went to the office of the town or city clerk, where also the strung ballots were deposited.

On or before the tenth day after the election the county canvassing board — the county auditor and two justices of the peace — opened the precinct returns and proceeded to make consolidated statements of them, called "abstracts." On one sheet were shown the votes for state officers, judges and clerk of the supreme court, and judges of the district court; on another, those for county officers; and on a third, those for presidential electors and representatives in Congress. All of them, when certified and signed by the board, were deposited in the auditor's office; a copy of each was mailed to the secretary of state; and a second copy of the abstract of votes for state officials was directed to the speaker of the House of Representatives. At the close of the canvass the board declared the persons who had received the highest number of votes for the several county offices duly elected and the county auditor delivered to each a certificate of election; but their commissions were issued by the governor upon receipt of the abstract from the secretary of state.

The returns for presidential electors and representatives in Congress were canvassed by the governor and the secretary of state in the presence of the state auditor, the attorney-general, and one or more judges of the supreme court; and the persons elected were given certificates signed by the governor, sealed with the great seal of the state, and counter-signed by the secretary of state. In conformity with section 2 of article 5 of the state constitution, the duplicate returns for state offices, judges of the supreme and district courts, and the clerk of the supreme court, sent to the speaker of the House of Representatives, were opened and canvassed before both houses of the legislature within three days after their organization. This practice continued until after the adoption of an amendment to the state constitution in 1877 creating a state board of canvassers to consist of the secretary of state assisted by two or more of the judges of the supreme court and two disinterested judges of the district court.[21]

An amendatory act of 1878 relating to cities of over twelve thousand inhabitants contained some innovations in preliminary arrangements and election procedure. The appointed constables were required to keep open a space six feet square about the ballot box, so that electors might approach it without molestation. Ballots were to be printed in plain type on white paper, without cuts or devices by which a voter's " politics " might be disclosed. As each elector advanced to vote, a judge received his ballot and laid it on top of the ballot box, at the same time announcing the name of the voter. Then if the person was known, or was found to be

[21] General Laws, 1861, pp. 97–100, 102–108; 1878, p. 15. In the election laws the title " election district " has been given to the elementary geographical election unit, though the popular term " precinct " is occasionally used. The amendment of 1877 creating a state board of canvassers was adopted on a second submission. It was rejected in 1873, when the negative vote was 25,694 and the affirmative, 12,116, the total vote for governor being 77,057. The vote for adoption in 1877, when the total vote for governor was 98,614, was 36,072; for rejection, 21,814. Anderson, History of the Constitution, 174, 279, 280.

entitled to vote then and there, the clerks entered his name on their poll lists and added a serial number. This number was marked by the judge on the back of the ballot, which was then dropped into the ballot box. The judge was required to purge the box " with his face averted," obviously to prevent peeking. How the plan of marking ballots with the serial number entered on the poll lists was found and declared by the state supreme court to be in violation of the constitutional guaranty of a secret ballot the reader who recalls the Donnelly-Washburn election contest that followed the election of 1878 will understand. A rigorous process was prescribed for the canvass. The judges were required to read each ballot separately and to " proclaim to the clerks " the names of candidates voted for. Each clerk was to " mark down upon the tally list " the votes for each candidate in columns properly headed and it was made the duty of the judges, after the completion of the canvass, to draw a red line across the name of every person on the registers who had not voted.[22]

The law of 1887 added the chairman of the board of county commissioners to the county canvassing board; but any three members were to constitute a quorum. The consolidated reports of the board to be forwarded to the secretary of state, formerly called " abstracts," were denominated " statements." In cities of twelve thousand or over elections were to be conducted in the same manner as that provided for elections in general, with certain exceptions; in particular one of the judges was to be charged with receiving the ballots and numbering them, and the other two severally were to handle the two registers; as soon as a person had voted, the judges having charge of the registers were to write " Voted " or " V " after the elector's name. The most conspicuous change

[22] *General Laws,* 1878, pp. 133–135, 141. The decision of the Minnesota supreme court declaring that the serial numbering of voters and ballots was unconstitutional is given in the case of John B. Brisbin v. James Cleary and others, 26 *Minnesota,* 107–109. The Donnelly-Washburn election contest is discussed *ante,* 3: 388–400.

was in the number of ballots and ballot boxes to be used
in cities of over five thousand inhabitants. There were to be
at least six kinds of ballots, which were to be indorsed, in
" Great Primer Roman Condensed Capitals," respectively:
State, Judiciary, County, Legislature, Congress, and Town or
City. When presidential electors were to be chosen, a seventh
ballot, indorsed Electors, was to be used. A separate ballot
box was to be provided for each kind of ballot, and additional
boxes were to be used when constitutional amendments, the
removal of county seats, or officers and measures not specifically provided for by the law were to be voted upon. When
the judges came to canvassing, they were required to open
the boxes and count the ballots therein in the following order:
(1) Electors, (2) State, (3) Congress, (4) Legislature, (5)
Judiciary, (6) Town or City, (7) County; and other boxes,
if any were used, might be opened and the votes counted in
such order as the judges might prefer. The Australian ballot system, adopted in 1889 and discussed at length in a
succeeding section of this chapter, reduced the number of
ballot boxes to three — according as candidates and measures were voted upon by the electorate of the entire state,
an individual county, or an individual city. In 1891 a fourth
ballot box was ordered for the ballots of women, who voted
on school and library matters.[23]

In cities and villages local committees of political parties
were authorized by the law of 1891 to furnish lists of names
of proper persons to be appointed judges of election in the
several precincts, and city and village authorities were required to appoint from the lists judges from the various
parties in turn. The forenoon of election day was made a
compulsory half holiday for employees of every kind to
give them the opportunity of voting, and the general election
day was added to the list of legal holidays. Newspapers were

[23] *Post,* pp. 353–356; *General Laws,* 1887, pp. 9, 13–15, 18–21, 35; 1891, p.
43. The cities of over five thousand were Brainerd, Duluth, Faribault, Mankato,
Minneapolis, Red Wing, Rochester, St. Paul, Stillwater, and Winona. Secretary
of State, *Reports,* 1886, appendix B, p. 96.

authorized to print sample ballots in their columns as news. Bystanders were forbidden to congregate within one hundred feet of the polling places. No policeman was to remain in the place unless stationed there by the judges; and when so stationed he was not to seek to influence voters.[24]

The association of surviving soldiers and sailors of the Civil War, under the title " Grand Army of the Republic," was ever, as it still is, a highly patriotic body. It is not known when or where the proposition was first voiced for the display of the national flag over polling places on election days. At the Minnesota state encampment of the association in 1897 a resolution was adopted asking the legislature then in session to take action. In response to this appeal, on March 25, 1897, a bill was introduced into the House. The members were so well disposed to the measure that they suspended their rules and passed it as soon as the roll was called, by a vote nearly unanimous. The Senate, not so precipitate, allowed the House bill to take the usual course. When it came to passage on April 17 there was but one negative vote. It may be assumed that the bill, which was passed as introduced and not changed in a syllable, had been drafted by some member of the G.A.R. with legal and perhaps legislative experience. It was not a mere pious exhortation. It directed city and village councils and township boards of supervisors to display the national flag on a suitable staff over every voting place on general election and registration days and to keep it flying every hour of such days. The cost of the equipment and display was to be included in election expenses. It was made the duty of judges of election to have the law carried out and to include in their returns a statement of the days upon which the flag had been displayed. To encourage them in this patriotic duty the law provided that for any willful failure judges should lose their whole per diem. The good custom has ever since been observed and the dormant patriotism of many a

[24] General Laws, 1891, pp. 25, 26, 37, 44, 46, 65, 197.

voter has been awakened as he has approached the polls and
has seen the stars and stripes "full high advanced." No
objections have been heard from manufacturers of and dealers in bunting.[25]

A more accurate and less laborious canvass of the vote
was the object of an act of 1905 establishing a voting machine commission. The essential things in election procedure — the deposit of the ballot, the tally, and the count
— all demand not only honesty, but also some dexterity of
hand and eye and the utmost pains to avoid errors. It is
a matter of common knowledge that errors in the count are
frequent. In many of the contests in Minnesota and elsewhere it has been found that errors have been made, often
impartially divided among the candidates. After the introduction of the Australian ballot in 1889 the count became
increasingly laborious, lasting through long and late hours.
It is probable that experience with this system suggested the
adaptation of the old and well-known numbering machine
to the counting of votes. Such machines consist essentially
of a series of parallel disks so geared together that pressure
on the unit disk actuates successive disks counting tens, hundreds, and so on to capacity. They had long been in use for
numbering tickets, bank notes, stocks, bonds, and so forth.
It needed but little ingenuity for inventors to contrive machines that required the voter merely to press a button to have
his vote numbered; it took a great deal of ingenuity to add
the checks, releases, and other devices to prevent duplication
and to tally along with the number of votes the number of
voters. A considerable number of voting machines were
soon manufactured and put into partial use in New York,
New Jersey, and a few other states. They were legalized

[25] Grand Army of the Republic, Department of Minnesota, *Proceedings*,
1897, pp. 129, 170; *House Journal*, 1897, p. 681; *Senate Journal*, 576, 671,
679, 697, 864; *General Laws*, 343. The same legislature passed an act
imposing a fine of not over one hundred dollars or not more than three
months' imprisonment upon anyone who should use the flag for advertising
purposes. *General Laws*, 1897, p. 600.

in seventeen states by 1906. As early as 1897 a Minnesota
law had authorized county commissioners, city councils, and
village boards to provide for their use in general elections.[26]

In response to continued agitation the Minnesota legislature of 1905 created a voting machine commission, consisting of the attorney-general and two other members who
should be either master mechanics or graduates of a school
of mechanical engineering. The commission was authorized
to examine sample machines submitted to it, after receiving an examination fee of one hundred and fifty dollars,
and to report to the secretary of state the names of all
machines that filled the specifications of the law. The principal requirements with which a machine must comply in
order to receive the approval of the commission were: that
it insure absolute secrecy of the vote; that it permit the elector
to vote once and but once for all the candidates and upon
all propositions for whom and upon which he should be entitled to vote; that it permit the elector to change his vote at
any time up to the moment that his vote should be finally
registered; and that it insure a mechanically correct count.
The governing board of any city, village, or town was authorized to buy and use any machine approved by the commission.
In the course of that year, 1905, and the two years following,
the Minnesota commission approved several voting machines
and filed certificates for them in the office of the secretary
of state.[27]

There was little enthusiasm, however, for voting by
machinery. The machines would not prevent the " fixing "
of the voter or assure correct returns of the election or honest
canvassing by the county boards. The experiment might
have been long and indefinitely put off but for the circum-

[26] *Knight's Cyclopædia of the Industry of All Nations*, 303, 490, 1419, 1751
(London, 1851) ; *General Laws*, 1897, pp. 556–558. A supplementary act extending the permission to town boards and authorizing the use of voting machines in all elections was passed in 1899. *Laws*, 1899, pp. 401–403.

[27] *General Laws*, 1905, pp. 400–404; notes on voting machines, including
memorandum on machines examined by the state board and reports to the
secretary of state on the examinations, Folwell Papers.

stance that one of the machines approved by the commission had been invented by a citizen of St. Paul and was, or would be, manufactured in Minneapolis. The great interest aroused, especially in Minneapolis, encouraged the council of that city to make a trial of the home-made machine. On June 26, 1908, the purchase of one hundred and sixty-six machines was ordered at seven hundred dollars apiece, to be ready for the general election of 1908. The operation of the machines in that year was satisfactory enough to induce the city council, in February, 1910, to order sixty more of them at the same price. They were used at both elections of 1910.[28]

The mechanical operation of the apparatus was excellent, but there was disappointment in regard to speed. It was expected that six hundred voters might be accommodated at each precinct. In practice, however, it was found that not more than two hundred and fifty could vote, even when the polls were open until nine o'clock in the evening. Voters neglected to prepare themselves and they hesitated before voting, fearing to touch the wrong "plungers." This was no fault of the machine and practice would probably have remedied it. There was also much dissatisfaction because of the failure of the machine to allow the "rotating" of the names of candidates. A scheme of second-choice voting at primaries adopted by the legislature in 1912 put it entirely out of use at such elections, but it was used at the general election of that year. The council in 1913 decided to buy no more voting machines. For the general election of 1914 it was determined to use those on hand and in repair and to supplement them with paper ballots of the old kind as authorized by an act of the legislature of 1913. The combination was altogether unsatisfactory. The second-choice

---

[28] Minneapolis City Council, *Proceedings*, 1908, p. 438; 1910, p. 161; letters to the author from Emelia C. Pearson, of the city clerk's office, October 6, 1925, and from Henry N. Knott, former city clerk, October 1, 1925, Folwell Papers. Miss Pearson's letter is accompanied by a list of citations of dates on which voting machines were up before the city council, covering a period from January 13, 1905, to May 9, 1924.

voting at primaries was repealed in 1915 and the machines might have been used thereafter, but the council in the following year decided not to use them for either of the elections of that year. Repeated efforts to sell some or all of them have failed. The 226 voting machines bought by the city of Minneapolis at a cost of $158,000 repose in a subbasement of the city hall.[29]

A law passed in 1911 provided that the judges of election, instead of delivering the ballots cast and counted at a general election to the town or city clerk in the locked and sealed ballot boxes, should inclose them in suitable envelopes, to be furnished by the county auditor, in colors corresponding to those of the ballots — white, blue, red, and pink — with the signatures of the judges over the sealed parts, and send them to the county auditor. Stringent provisions in the election law of 1912 for the preservation of ballots after the canvass suggest that this plan had been found unsatisfactory, at least in the large cities and counties, after a single trial. For counties of two hundred thousand and over and cities of fifty thousand and over the act revived the old plan of having the used ballots strung and tied in bundles, sealed with wax over the knots of the "substantial twine," and put back in the ballot boxes. Each box was then to be locked and sealed by a piece of firm paper placed across the opening between the lid and the body and each judge was required to write his name on the paper. The boxes were to be "returned" to the office of the county auditor or the city clerk, who was directed to store them in such a manner as to admit of actual inspection of their exteriors. Any candidate was authorized to maintain a "visual watch" of the boxes, day and night, until the expiration of the time for filing contests. In case of a contest either party might maintain such a watch, in which case the auditor or city

[29] Interview with Henry N. Knott, former city clerk of Minneapolis, recorded in the Folwell Papers, September 18, 1925; Minneapolis City Council, *Proceedings*, 1913, p. 1179; 1914, pp. 1078–1080; 1916, p. 263; *Laws*, 1913, p. 667.

clerk was authorized to appoint a watchman of his own, so that the boxes in question might not be left in the custody of the watchmen of either party. One cannot help wondering whether there had been such actual tinkering with the used ballots as to require these rigorous regulations.[30]

THE AUSTRALIAN BALLOT

In 1857 the legislative body of South Australia, at the instance of Francis S. Dutton, passed a bill to insure the secrecy of the ballot. Similar laws were soon passed in other Australian provinces. The English Parliament, after long debates and bitter opposition, embodied the principle in its Ballot Act of 1872. American states also took time to consider the plan. Henry George, the author of *Progress and Poverty*, in an article in the *North American Review* in 1883, described in graphic paragraphs the iniquities of political machines and recommended the adoption of the Australian system. But there was no haste. The state of Kentucky was the first to adopt it, but not until February 24, 1888. Massachusetts was a close second on May 30 of the same year. The next year many legislatures had it under consideration. Minnesota was one of the few that then, in 1889, adopted it, but only for cities of ten thousand or more; two years later, however, the system was extended to all election districts of the state.[31]

The well-known features of the Australian ballot system are printed ballots furnished at public expense, containing the names of candidates and the titles of measures to be voted for; and small compartments, closed by a door or cur-

[30] *General Laws*, 1911, p. 355; 1912, p. 21. An act of 1925 provided for the use of the tally sheets, with certain indorsements, as official returns of primary elections in cities of the first class under home rule charters. *Laws*, 1925, p. 694.

[31] John H. Wigmore, *The Australian Ballot System as Embodied in the Legislation of Various Countries*, 3–8, 15, 22–28, 37–151 (Boston, 1889); Henry George, " Money in Elections," in the *North American Review*, 136: 201–211 (March, 1883); Andrew C. McLaughlin and Albert B. Hart, eds., *Cyclopedia of American Government*, 1: 101 (New York and London, 1914); *General Laws*, 1889, pp. 12–40; 1891, pp. 37–45.

tain, into which the voter retires to put his X mark opposite the names of the candidates and measures of his choice, with no one to molest or to intimidate him. The act of 1889, however, provided that by putting his mark into a certain square near the head of the ballot he voted a whole party ticket and did not need to mark individual names. The ballots supplied at public expense were to be of three colors: white, for all candidates to be voted upon throughout the entire state and amendments to the state constitution, to be furnished by the state auditor; blue, for all other candidates voted upon by an entire county, to be supplied by county auditors; and red, for candidates voted upon throughout a whole city, ward, or precinct, to be furnished by city clerks. The ballots of each color were to be assembled and bound in blocks of one hundred. The names of candidates were to be those nominated in party conventions, duly certified. Each party nominee was to pay a fee of fifty dollars to have his name entered on a white ticket, ten dollars to have it on a blue ticket, and five dollars to have it on a red one. Other persons could be nominated by petition signed by qualified electors of the district or political division equal in numbers to one per cent of the total vote cast at the last election in the same district or political division. When, after the polls were duly open, a citizen should come forward to offer his vote, one of the judges, after ascertaining whether he was entitled to vote, was to tear off for him one white, one blue, and one red ballot, on the backs of which he should write his, the judge's, initials. The elector was then to enter one of the booths, where he would find an indelible pencil or pen and ink. After making his X marks according to his judgment and conscience, he was to fold his ballots so as to show the judge's initials. Upon leaving the booth he was to hand his ballots to one of the judges, who was to pronounce audibly the elector's name so that it might be checked on the list of registered voters. If the name appeared on the list, the judge should slip the ballots into the several colored boxes. The elector should then retire from the room.[32]

From the exceedingly minute regulations introduced in the general election law of 1893 in regard to the preparation of ballots, it would appear that the Australian system as it had been operated had not fully secured the promised secrecy of the ballot. It was provided that all ballots must be printed with black ink on paper thick enough to prevent the printing from showing through and all ballots of the same color were to be absolutely uniform in style, size, thickness, shade of color, and types. On the backs of all should be printed the words, "Official Ballot," with the date of the election and a facsimile of the signature of the official supplying them. No sample ballots were to be printed on red, white, or blue paper. Polling places in cities with populations of over twelve thousand must be selected on the ground floors of buildings, and each polling place must have a door opening into a street at least forty feet wide. A judge might go out and receive the votes of persons physically unable to enter the room, with an elector as a witness, if so desired by the voter. Very precise regulations were made in regard to the printing and the use of tally sheets. When it came to canvassing, the clerks were to enter the votes on tally sheets, as the judges counted the ballots one by one, numbering them consecutively in the order counted and stringing them. In election districts in cities of over twelve thousand the appointment of an extra election judge, to be known as a "ballot judge," and of two additional clerks was authorized to facilitate balloting, counting, and canvassing.[33]

The Australian ballot system had not been long in operation before it was discovered that when there were several

[32] *General Laws*, 1889, pp. 12–40. The law authorized the use of a separate white ballot for presidential electors to prevent too long a state ballot; and it was stipulated that whenever the district of a congressman or a state legislator extended further than the limits of a single city, the blue ballot should be used.

[33] *General Laws*, 1893, pp. 20–28, 41, 48, 51, 57–61.

aspirants to an office the one whose name appeared first on the ballot had a considerable advantage. Because of indifference or ignorance some voters would take the easy way and make their marks against the name first seen. To remedy the mischief, the primary election law of 1899 provided that the positions of the names for each office should be changed in such a way that the name of each aspirant should appear at the top, at the bottom, and at intermediate positions on the ballots an equal number of times. The legislature of 1901 provided for the "rotation" of candidates' names in much the same way for general elections, in cases where more than one candidate was to be elected to the same office. It is not known what actual or reputed abuses of this process had called for a remedy, but the legislature of 1915 added to existing law a paragraph requiring the officials charged with the preparation of the primary election ballots to be governed by their legal advisors in making up instructions for the printer for "rotating, laying and tabbing such ballots" and to exact of the printer a bond of from one thousand to five thousand dollars, conditioned upon his observance of the law and of their instructions. Another paragraph of the same act made these requirements applicable to general election ballots in cases where two or more persons were to be elected to the same office. Acts of the legislature of 1919 required that a pink ballot be used for state-wide propositions and questions and that on the general election ballots the words "nominated without party designation" should appear after the names of all candidates so nominated.[34]

THE REGISTRATION OF ELECTORS

The election law of 1861 was the first to embrace a registration scheme. Fifteen days before the election the judges,

[34] *General Laws*, 1899, p. 451; 1901, pp. 88–90; 1915, pp. 224, 227, 230; 1919, pp. 72, 226.

using the poll lists of the last preceding election, made up an alphabetical list of all persons in the district known to them to be lawful voters. Three copies of the list were posted in public places with notices of the days and hours when the judges would be in session to make corrections in the list. For two hours before the opening of the polls on election day corrections might also be entertained. Each clerk was provided with a copy of the corrected poll list and as each elector dropped his ballot into the ballot box his name was checked on both lists.[35]

An act of 1878 provided for a more elaborate registration scheme, obviously to prevent voting by persons not qualified electors. The judges and clerks of election of each district were made a " board of registry " and were required to meet on Tuesday, two weeks before election, and make up an alphabetical list of qualified voters, using the poll list of the last election and adding the names of others known or given in as competent. A copy of the list was posted where the last election had been held and another was retained by one of the judges. On Tuesday, one week before election, the board of registry met again to revise and correct the retained list. One copy of the corrected list was held by one of the judges and constituted the " register " for the election. Severe penalties were prescribed for infraction of these provisions. The law of 1887 provided that in cities of over twelve thousand, at the end of each day's registry the judges of election were required to sign their names at the end of every page of the register, so that no new names could be added without discovery; on the day before the election, the registers were to be delivered to two judges representing the two leading political parties, one register to be given to each judge. A principal innovation of the general election law of 1891 was a requirement that in cities of forty thousand or more no elector should have his name

35 *General Laws*, 1861, pp. 98–102.

placed upon the registers unless he should first appear personally before a board of registry, or register by affidavit of absent person, and make oath to answer truly questions in regard to his qualifications for voting; in 1905 this provision was restricted to cities of more than fifty thousand inhabitants.[36]

The registration of voters in cities before every general election, especially in those where personal attendance was required, was found to be costly to the public, a burden to the voter, and one of the reasons for the notorious failure of many to vote. In response to frequent suggestions, the legislature of 1923 instituted an experiment in permanent registration of voters, but only in cities having a population of more than fifty thousand inhabitants governed by a home rule charter — Minneapolis, St. Paul, and Duluth. It made the city clerk a commissioner of registration and gave him authority to appoint deputies and clerks, subject to civil service law, and to procure all necessary equipment. He was required to make, as soon as possible, a list of all the qualified voters in his city, to be known as the " original registration list " and to be preserved in his office and not to be taken out unless by order of court, and also a duplicate registration list to be open for public inspection. Both of the lists were to be made on cards of suitable size and were to contain entries of the voter's name, residence, ward, election district, age, term of residence, nativity, citizenship, the date of his registration, and his signature. For each election the commissioner was required to prepare alphabetical lists of the voters in each precinct, to be known as " election registers," and to deliver them to the judges of election. After the election the words " voted " or " not voted," as the case

---

[36] *General Laws,* 1878, pp. 138–142; 1887, pp. 32, 34; 1891, p. 33; 1897, p. 12; *Revised Laws,* 1905, p. 44. Other modifications of the registration process were enacted into law in 1893, 1895, and 1897. *Laws,* 1893, pp. 31–40; 1895, pp. 288–291; 1897, p. 12.

might be, were to be entered in proper spaces on each voter's cards in the original and duplicate registration lists. From year to year new registrants might have their names added up to fifteen days before any general election, upon making application and an oath as to qualifications. At the end of each calendar year the clerks of registration were required to revise the lists and to eliminate any "excess names," and if it were found that any voter had not voted at least once in two calendar years his cards were to be taken out of the lists and he could not vote again until after a new registration. Violations of the law by officers and employees and fraudulent tampering with the registration cards were declared felonies.[37]

An act of 1925 excepted cities of the first class operating under home rule charters from certain requirements that did not fit in with the new permanent registration system and another act made some changes in the permanent registration law for these cities. One of these amendments provided that after any change of name due to marriage or divorce a new registration must be made; another required the commissioner of registration to remove from his registration lists every fifteen days the cards of all electors whose deaths had been reported to him by the city health officer; and a third required judges of election to enter on the election registers the words "voted" or "not voted" immediately after the voter's ballot had been accepted and deposited in the ballot box. This would seem to indicate that judges in some cases had made such entries from memory, with resulting errors. It was, of course, impossible to make the entry "not voted" until the close of the polls. Another act of the same year permitted absent voters making proper application in writing, accompanied by an affidavit as to their qualifications, to be permanently registered; and still another required all cities having over ten thousand and under fifty thousand

[37] *Laws,* 1923, pp. 416–422.

inhabitants to provide for permanent registration of voters by January 1, 1926.[38]

ABSENTEE VOTING

In 1862 an extraordinary departure was made from the ancient principle that electors could vote only in the districts in which they were domiciled. At an extra session of the legislature there was passed an act to enable soldiers and sailors absent from their homes in the service of the United States to vote at general elections during the continuance of the war. The governor was authorized to appoint six commissioners, each to travel to an assigned part of the country, taking with him the ballots of the two opposing parties for free distribution. Each soldier offering to vote was sworn as to his competency by the commissioner, who received the voter's ballot in a sealed envelope, directed to the judges of election of his district and indorsed with his name and his company or regiment. The sealed envelope, after being indorsed with the commissioner's certificate, was delivered by the commissioner in person or by mail to one of the judges of election of the voter's district. On election day the envelope was opened and the ballot was counted. The empty envelopes were deposited with town or city clerks. Twelve hundred dollars were appropriated to carry out the act and the commissioners were allowed three dollars a day and their necessary expenses. It is apparent that not all the lawful provisions for insuring honest voting could operate under such circumstances.[39]

An act of 1911, a daring innovation, provided for voting at general elections by electors absent from their home precincts. Judges of election were authorized to issue to absentees certificates of registry. Upon presentation of his

[38] *Laws*, 1925, pp. 347–349, 477, 526–530, 693, 696–700. The cities with populations between ten and fifty thousand were Austin, Faribault, Hibbing, Mankato, Rochester, St. Cloud, Virginia, and Winona.

[39] *General Laws*, 1862, extra session, 13–18.

certificate to the judges of election in any district on election day and identification by two resident voters, the absentee might have his vote for presidential electors, constitutional amendments, and state officers received and counted. A copy of the certificate was to be mailed to the judges of election who issued the original, with an indorsement showing that the elector had voted. In 1913 the law was changed to require the judges who received the vote of an absentee to withhold it from the ballot box and send it, securely enveloped, by registered mail, along with the certificate brought by the voter, to the auditor of the county of his residence. At the meeting of the county canvassing board the envelope was to be opened and the vote was to be credited to the proper precinct.[40]

Why the discovery was made so tardily that a large number of qualified voters in the national guard regiments called out by the president for service on the Mexican border in 1916 would be kept from home until after the November election and would thus lose their votes, and why anyone was seriously concerned about this privation are questions that had better not be guessed at. It was not until October 26 that Governor Burnquist issued his proclamation for a special session of the legislature to convene on the twenty-eighth, only ten days before the election. In his proclamation the governor said that the absent soldiers ought not to be disfranchised, that the attorney-general had advised him that a valid law could be passed to give them their votes, that other states had taken such action, that a one-day session would be enough, and that the cost would be only the mileage of members.

The houses assembled, accordingly, and at twelve o'clock listened to Governor Burnquist's brief and pithy address. " I hope, " he said, " that you will unanimously pass the bill drawn by the attorney general and then adjourn." In a brief

[40] *General Laws*, 1911, p. 419; 1913, p. 365.

afternoon session both houses passed, without a dissenting vote, a bill to enable members of the Minnesota National Guard to vote when they should be outside the state in the service of the United States on the day of a general election. The title of the act was in general terms; the text clearly applied it only to the then pending election of November 7. The procedure to be followed was similar to that employed in the Civil War for enabling Minnesota soldiers out of the state to vote. The governor was authorized to appoint commissioners, one or more for each regiment, to visit the troops, collect the ballots of those entitled to vote, and deliver them in sealed envelopes to the secretary of state. The secretary was to forward them to county auditors, who were to open and canvass the ballots, credit them to the proper precincts, and report the results of the canvass to the county canvassing boards. To get the ballots into the hands of the soldiers, the law required county auditors to " exercise all possible diligence " in making lists of all members of the guard in their counties, with the precincts to which each member belonged. These lists, with a sufficient supply of blank county and municipal ballots, were to be sent to the secretary of state. From these auditors' lists the secretary of state was required to cull out and make a list of the legal voters in each regiment and to deliver to the voting commissioners a set of ballots for each soldier, together with two envelopes, one larger than the other, and a blank affidavit of his right to vote. On election day each soldier was to mark his ballots as he would if he were at home and seal them up in his small envelope. This, with the completed affidavit, he was to place in the large envelope, which he was to seal and deliver to the commissioner. On both envelopes the obviously necessary indorsements were to be made. In most of the counties the auditors conformed to the law and added to the vote of each precinct the votes of the soldiers in Texas. In other counties the soldier votes were kept separate, and in some cases, owing to irregularities, the state canvassing board threw such votes out.[41]

In 1917 an act was passed "authorizing voters absent from the election district of which they are residents on the day when any general election is held to vote therein by having their marked ballots delivered to the judges of election therein through the agency of the United States Post Office Department." The obvious purpose was to enable electors of the state to vote from any place in the United States other than Alaska and the island possessions. For the purposes of the act the term "general election" included any city election, except primary elections, and any county option election. Under the act an elector intending to be absent might obtain, upon application to the county auditor, blank ballots and a "ballot envelope." Wherever he might be, he could mark the ballots and seal them in the "ballot envelope." This envelope he was to place inside a "return envelope," previously addressed by the auditor to the judges of election of the voter's precinct and indorsed, "Return Envelope. Postmaster deliver on Election Day." If the judges were satisfied, by comparison of signatures on accompanying certificates, that the proceeding was regular and if no challenge was offered, they were to break open the envelopes, take out the ballots, put them into the proper colored boxes, and count them as if they had been cast in person.[42]

The framers of the constitution, following long precedent, were diligent in regulating the procedure, since they

[41] *Minneapolis Journal*, 1916: October 26, p. 1; 27, p. 11; 28, p. 1; 29, city section, p. 1; *St. Paul Pioneer Press*, October 27, p. 10; 29, section 2, p. 1; *Martin County Sentinel* (Fairmont), November 7, p. 6; *House Journal*, 1916, pp. 1, 8; *Senate Journal*, 1, 7, 9, 11, 14; *Laws*, 3–9; indorsement by Burnquist on a letter to him from the author, September 7, 1925, Folwell Papers; *Legislative Manual*, 1917, p. 351. The Senate and House journals and the laws for the special session of 1916 are bound with those for 1917. The *Minneapolis Journal*, October 29, city section, p. 1, estimates that the act affected three thousand voters. The *Pioneer Press*, October 29, section 2, p. 1, gives the names of the six commissioners appointed — one for each of the four regiments on the border and two additional.

[42] *Laws*, 1917, pp. 82–93.

could not limit the powers, of the state legislature. Section 20 of article 4 as adopted and never modified requires that every bill shall be read on three different days in each separate house and that no bill shall be passed until it shall have been read twice at length; that no bill shall become a law unless it is voted for by a majority of all the members elected to each branch and the vote is recorded in the journals; and that every bill after its passage shall be carefully enrolled, signed by the president of the Senate and the speaker of the House, and finally approved by the governor. These constitutional requirements were not deemed obligatory upon the Minnesota Commission of Public Safety, empowered by the law creating it to do all acts and things necessary and proper for the public safety " non-inconsistent with the constitution or laws of Minnesota." No such dilatory routine to guard against error and precipitance for that patriotic body! To change the law of the state it had only to pass at any meeting a resolution by a majority of the members present and publish it. In a session on April 30, 1918, the commission, aware that the Minnesota soldiers and sailors who had been called out of the state for service in the World War must lose their votes at the primary election on June 17, according to the law as it then stood, at once sought to relieve this disability and found as reasons for an example of extraconstitutional legislation the public safety, military expedience, and comfort to " our men . . . while they are away." The commission therefore issued its Order number 31 authorizing Minnesota soldiers and sailors to vote at the 1918 primary election. The procedure of the commissioners was brief and simple. They had only to modify chapter 68 of the laws of 1917 authorizing absent electors to vote at any general election by mail, chiefly by striking out the words " general election " and inserting " primary election," and limit the application of the act to absent soldiers and sailors in the service of the United States within the territorial limits of the United States.[43]

Without additional modification of the law the great body of Minnesota soldiers and sailors who had been transported abroad were doomed to lose their votes at the general election in November, 1918. The commission was ready for the emergency; the same reasons existed for its interference now as before. On September 10, 1918, it issued an order " Providing a Method Whereby Minnesota Soldiers and Sailors May Vote at the 1918 General Election." The method was as simple as that for the primary. It was necessary only to provide that chapter 68 of the laws of 1917 should be applicable to all soldiers and sailors in the service of the United States, whether within the territorial limits of the United States or elsewhere.[44]

THE GROWTH OF THE PRIMARY SYSTEM

The election act of 1887 contained certain provisions for regulating the political caucus or volunteer primary election. For the purposes of the act the term " primary election " was defined as an election " held by any political party, convention, organization or association, or delegates therefrom, for the purpose of choosing candidates for office, or the election of delegates to other conventions, or for the purpose of electing officers of any political party, organization, convention or association." Presiding officers and " inspectors " at such elections were required to sign and swear to an oath such as that required by inspectors at general elections and were authorized to administer oaths in certain cases. Only qualified electors might vote.[45]

[43] Laws, 1917, pp. 373–377; Commission of Public Safety, Report, 1, 109–115; Minutes of Proceedings, 2: 382–394. It was not until 1923 that absentees in general were privileged to vote at primary elections. Certain minor changes in the act were made in 1925. Laws, 1923, p. 100; 1925, pp. 342–347.

[44] Commission of Public Safety, Report, 126–132; Minutes, 2: 509–520.

[45] General Laws, 1887, pp. 38–40.

By a legislative act passed in 1895 this political caucus, in so far as its choice of delegates to party conventions was concerned, was converted into a quasi-official primary election. Due notice of the time and place of holding the primary election in the several precincts was required. It was to be called to order by the chairman or secretary of the local party committee; a chairman, a clerk of election, and two judges, who were put under oath, were to be elected viva voce. The vote for delegates, which was to be cast only by qualified electors, was to be by ballot. After the judges had counted the votes and the chairman had announced the result, the chairman and the clerk were to furnish certificates to the delegates elected.[46]

The year 1899 was marked by the passage of an act for the nomination of candidates for certain offices at official primary elections under most of the conditions and penalties of the general election law. It applied to candidates for city and county offices, judges, and elective members of school, library, and park boards within counties having a population of two hundred thousand or more. Hennepin County was the only one in which the experiment could be tried. The procedure of the general law of 1893 was adopted with appropriate modifications. The outstanding novelty of the act was the privilege of original proposal of himself for public office by any qualified elector. Any such elector who submitted an affidavit stating that it was his bona fide intention to run for a certain office, presented a petition signed by five per cent of the electors who had voted at the last election for the candidate of his party for the office aspired to, and paid a filing fee of ten dollars, was entitled to have his name printed on the official ballot prepared for his party by the county auditor for the coming primary election. Nomination by petition as provided for in the act of 1889 and subsequent acts, however, remained lawful. Separate

[46] *General Laws*, 1895, pp. 661–664.

ballots for each political party were to be printed, but the ballots of all parties were to be given out to qualified registered voters as they presented themselves at the polls and were identified and found competent. A judge was to "instruct" them to vote only their respective party tickets, but to return all the ballots folded and pinned together. The clerk of the district court in each county was added to the county canvassing board. That board was required merely to "file" a statement of results in the office of the county auditor, without the usual safeguards against delay, loss, change, or mutilation. As if it was anticipated that errors might occur accidentally or otherwise in making up the party ballots, it was provided that, upon complaint by any candidate or elector, the supreme or district court should order the person complained of to correct alleged errors or show why corrections were unnecessary. Disobedience was a contempt of court.[47]

An act passed in 1901 gave to Minnesota the distinction of being the first state in the Union to enact a compulsory primary election law applicable to the entire state. The operation of the official primary election system in Hennepin County had been so satisfactory that the legislature of 1901 extended it to the other counties and to candidates at all elections, except town, village, or special elections and those for general state officers and for members of school, library, and park boards in cities of fifty thousand or less. There were only two marked departures from the act of 1899. One was that voters were to receive only the ballots of their respective parties at the polls; each must declare his party affiliation, the fact of his having supported his party at the last election, and his intention to support the same at the coming election. The other enabled an elector to become a candidate for an office in the primary election upon filing an affidavit stating that it was his bona fide intention to run

47 *General Laws*, 1899, pp. 447–461.

for a certain office and paying a filing fee of ten dollars for a county office or twenty dollars for a state office. It was no longer necessary for a candidate to present a petition signed by five per cent of the electors who had voted at the last election for that office. A separate brief act of the same year guaranteed to each political party the right to the exclusive use of the name it had adopted and forbade a candidate to have his name on more than one ballot.[48]

On May 18, 1912, Governor Eberhart issued a proclamation summoning the two houses of the Minnesota legislature in extra session on June 4, for the purpose of enacting a state-wide direct primary law applicable to all state officers, a corrupt practices act, and a reapportionment law. It is known that there was at the time a general sentiment in favor of these propositions, but there had been no clamor for immediate action. Most people would have been willing to wait for a new legislature to meet six months later. It has been intimated that Governor Eberhart's enthusiasm for them was enkindled by suggestions of interested friends that a new election law with novel elements might insure his and their reëlections in the coming November. He found both houses, upon their assemblage, responsive to his wishes, except that they had no desire to attempt a reapportionment of the legislature. The state-wide primary bill, passed on June 17 without a single negative vote, contained a scheme to require a majority and not a mere plurality vote to nominate. Instead of being restricted to voting for one of the aspirants to an office, the elector was allowed to cast a second vote for any one of his party aspirants left in the field. Another innovation very generally favored was one intended to take the judges, county superintendents of schools, and municipal officers out of politics. This was to be effected by the use of a separate ballot, to be known as a "non-partisan primary ballot" for judges — supreme, district, probate,

[48] General Laws, 1901, pp. 297–305, 524; McLaughlin and Hart, Cyclopedia of American Government, 2: 448.

and municipal — county superintendents of schools, and officers of cities of the first class, that is, those of over fifty thousand. No second-choice votes were allowed on these separate ballots, but the two aspirants who received the highest number of votes were to be nominees, entitled to have their names placed on the general election ballot; if but one or two should file, he or they were to become nominees automatically. It is noteworthy that this act restricted the operation of the primary system, in so far as the nomination of municipal officers was concerned, to cities of the first and second class.

A rule was obviously needed for the canvass of first-choice and second-choice votes. If the count should show that any aspirant had received a majority of all the first-choice votes cast for an office, he was to become the nominee. If, not, then the one who had the smallest number of first-choice votes was to be dropped and the second-choice votes cast by his supporters were to be added to the first-choice votes of those for whom they had been cast. If the result should be a majority for any aspirant, he was to become the candidate; if not, the process was to go on until some one should have a majority. The scheme was not in operation for long, however. In 1915 the second-choice privilege was abolished and the earlier and simpler plan of voting for only one of the candidates in the field was reëstablished.[49]

As a corollary of the state-wide primary system, the election act of 1912 provided for a more extensive regulation of the political machines. It defined a political party as one that had presented candidates for office at three or more

---

[49] *Minneapolis Journal*, 1912: May 16, p. 2; 17, p. 1; 18, p. 1; June 4, p. 1; *Minneapolis Tribune*, May 18, p. 4; 20, p. 4; June 4, p. 1; 5, p. 7; *St. Paul Pioneer Press*, May 17, p. 1; June 4, p. 1; *Martin County Sentinel*, May 24, pp. 2, 6; June 7, pp. 5, 6; *Senate Journal*, 1912, pp. 1, 29, 35–37, 40–45, 49, 55–66, 70, 99, 104–108, 110–112, 126; *House Journal*, 53, 68–72, 85–97, 109, 145, 154; *General Laws*, 1912, pp. 4–22; 1915, p. 228. Governor Eberhart's address to the legislature strongly urging nominations of "all elective public officials, national and state" by direct primary is published in the *Minneapolis Journal*, June 4, 1912, p. 1.

biennial elections within the preceding ten years, or that
should file a petition signed by a number of its members
equal to at least ten per cent of the whole number of votes
cast at the last general election. Each party was required
to have its party committees, as follows: first, a state central
committee to be appointed at a meeting of the party nominees
for state officers, for the state legislature, and for senators
and representatives in Congress and hold-over United States
and state senators, the meeting to be held at the State Capitol
the second Thursday after a primary; second, a congressional
committee for each congressional district, to be elected at
the same time; third, a county committee for each county,
to be elected at a meeting of the nominees for the legislature
and for county offices and of hold-over state senators and
county officers one week after the primary at the county
courthouse; and fourth, a city committee for each city to be
chosen at a meeting of all city nominees at the city hall.
The numbers of the committeemen were left to the discretion
of the several meetings. Each committee and its officers were
to exercise customary powers so far as they were consistent
with the act.[50]

In his message to the legislature of 1913 Governor Eberhart said: "There is no valid reason why this system of
direct nominations should not be extended to the office of
President of the United States. The people are competent
to elect their officials and it follows that they are also equally
competent to nominate." The executive proposition was
easily entertained. The primary system was in the air.
Political parties could not be annihilated, but their machines
might be controlled. The statute unanimously passed by
the legislature of that year provided for a "presidential
preference primary election" to be held throughout the
state on the second Tuesday in March of the appropriate
years. Three objects were embraced: a popular expression

[50] *General Laws*, 1912, pp. 4, 20. The provision for the election of county
party committees was repealed in 1913. *Laws*, 1913, p. 549.

of the party preferences for president and vice president; the nomination of presidential electors for each political party; and the election of delegates to the national convention of each party. The procedure of the existing primary election law was to be followed, except that no registration of voters was required. Qualified voters had only to declare their party affiliations and receive the party ballot. Any eligible person might file for elector or delegate on declaring his full membership in a party and might have his name placed on the party ballot. The person receiving the highest number of votes for delegate was elected as such and the person who obtained the next highest number became his alternate.

The names of aspirants for the presidency and vice presidency could be placed on the ballots only on petition of two per cent of the total number of voters who had voted at the last presidential election for the party candidate. The act required delegates to carry out the wishes of the voters to the best of their judgment and ability, but it attached no penalty for neglect or refusal. Provision was made for paying the necessary expenses of delegates to national conventions, to an amount not exceeding one hundred and fifty dollars to each delegate, after proper vouchers had been filed with the state auditor. Neither the presidential preference primary nor the popular election of delegates to national conventions proved satisfactory, however, and the entire act was repealed in 1917. Two years later, at a special session of the legislature in September, 1919, an act was passed providing for the nomination of presidential electors by delegate conventions called and held under the supervision of the state central committees of the several political parties.[51]

[51] Adolph O. Eberhart, *Message*, 1913, p. 7; *House Journal*, 1913, p. 1803; *Senate Journal*, 1565; *General Laws*, 1913, pp. 654–657; 1917, p. 183; 1919, extra session, 48. The legislature of 1915 amended the act of 1913 by requiring that candidates for delegate specify in their affidavits their choice for president. Delegates were required to appoint their alternates, who were also to declare

The seventeenth amendment to the Constitution of the United States for the popular election of senators in Congress, ratified by the legislature of Minnesota on June 12, 1912, was to take effect on May 31, 1913. In anticipation of that assured fact, the legislature of 1913 provided by law for the appropriate changes in the election laws. Any person eligible to the Senate might aspire to be nominated as a candidate at the primary election by filing his sworn affidavit in the office of the secretary of state and paying a filing fee of one hundred dollars. He was obliged to declare his party affiliation and his intention to vote the party ticket at the coming election. The procedure was then the same as that for state officers through the primary and general elections. The names of the candidates for senator in Congress were ordered placed at the top of the state ballot.[52]

Another act passed in 1913 amended the primary law of the previous year by enlarging the list of officers to be placed upon nonpartisan ballots for primary elections to include, along with the judges and the municipal officers of cities of the first class, all members of the state legislature, all elective county officers, and municipal officers of cities of the second class; and it was also provided that when only two persons should file for a nonpartisan office, or one person of any political party for a state office, thereby becoming nominees automatically, their names were to be omitted from the primary ballot but were to be placed upon the general election ballot. In 1921 cities of the third class with home rule charters were authorized to hold primary elections for municipal officers, nominations to be by nonpartisan ballot.[53]

The political machine had been hobbled and political party activities had been regulated, but they had survived.

their choice for president. The ballots were to be printed in such a way as to allow the voter to express his choice for vice president. The section providing for the reimbursement of delegates for their expenses was repealed. *Laws*, 1915, pp. 507–509.

[52] *General Laws*, 1912, p. 56; 1913, pp. 756–758.
[53] *General Laws*, 1913, pp. 542–550; 1921, p. 15.

State laws could not abolish national parties. The Minnesota legislature of 1921 essayed an experiment by giving to political party conventions a legal, almost an official, character. The act passed provided for a party primary election to be held in every election district on the second Tuesday in March in each even-numbered year, for the purpose of electing delegates to county conventions to be held within ten days thereafter. The county conventions were to elect delegates to the state convention and to congressional district conventions of the party to be held on dates to be fixed by the state central committees. Any person, if a qualified elector, might file as a candidate for delegate to a county convention upon stating his residence and his party affiliation. The general election laws were to apply so far as practicable. The judges and clerks were to be those who would officiate at the next general election. The number of delegates to which an election district was entitled was to be based upon the vote cast in the district for the party's candidate for governor at the last general election. County conventions had no powers except the adoption of a platform, the election of delegates to the state and congressional district conventions, and the election of a county committee. Congressional district conventions were empowered to indorse candidates for Congress and to elect a congressional district committee. The state conventions were authorized to adopt a platform, to indorse candidates for all officers to be voted for by voters of the entire state, including United States senators, to nominate presidential electors in the proper years, and to elect delegates at large to the national party conventions. On the primary election ballots after the name of each candidate so indorsed was to be printed the statement that he was indorsed by one or more party conventions as the case might be. State central committees were to be composed of two members from each congressional district, selected at the state conventions by the delegates representing such districts, one member selected by each candidate indorsed for office by the state conventions, and one member selected by each candidate for Congress indorsed by a congressional district convention.[54]

The system of party delegate conventions set up by the legislature of 1921 was not satisfactory to any party. It was repealed in 1923 by an act providing for a return to the system established by the act of 1895 and subsequent amendments to it. Candidates whose nominations were not required to be made by a primary election might be nominated by delegate conventions called for the purpose. The act specifically required that nominations for presidential electors be made in delegate conventions called by the state central committee of the several parties, as provided for in 1919. State central committees and congressional district committees were to be elected at a meeting of the nominees for state officers and senators and representatives in Congress of each party to be held on the second Thursday after the primary election.[55]

" CORRUPT PRACTICES " LEGISLATION

It is evident that from the beginning the legislature of Minnesota was desirous of providing for unimpeachable elections — to encourage election officials to be careful and diligent in the exercise of their solemn duties, to keep all fraudulent ballots out of the ballot box, and to secure a fair count of all that went in, correct and prompt canvasses of the returns, and an immediate record of results. It is not pleasant to record that in the Christian republic of Minnesota it was deemed necessary to secure these ends by denouncing severe penalties. The act of 1851 attached a penalty of from fifty to five hundred dollars for violations of the law in general by any election official and, in particular, a penalty

[54] *Laws*, 1921, pp. 401–406.
[55] *Laws*, 1923, pp. 124–127, 128–130.

of five hundred dollars for the failure of a judge to deliver
the sealed poll book to the clerk of the county commissioners
within the time prescribed by law. Disorderly conduct on
the part of any voter was punishable by a fine not to exceed
fifty dollars.[56]

A more elaborate code of penalties was included in the
election law of 1861. The failure of a judge to deliver election returns intrusted to him to the county auditor within five
days after an election, with seals unbroken, was punishable
by a fine of five hundred dollars or imprisonment in jail
for from six to twelve months. A judge, clerk, or other
person who should willfully fail to perform any duty required by the election law incurred hard labor in the state
prison for from six to twelve months.

The law made some discrimination in assigning penalties
for violations of the law by persons other than election
officials, but all were sufficiently rigorous. Any person willfully voting in the wrong precinct and any person not a
qualified elector who should vote became liable to a term of
imprisonment in jail. Hard labor in the state prison for
from six months to a year awaited: anyone convicted of
voting more than once, called " repeating "; any resident of
another state who should vote in Minnesota; anyone advis-
ing or aiding another to go or come into another county or
election district to vote, knowing that the person was not
qualified to vote therein; anyone convicted of furnishing a
ballot to an elector who could not read and informing him
that it contained names not thereon or of fraudulently changing his ballot; and any person fraudulently putting a ballot
into the box — " stuffing the ballot box." A fine of from
one hundred to five hundred dollars and imprisonment in
the county jail for from one to six months were allotted to
offenders who should attempt by threats or bribery to influence an elector not to vote or to vote contrary to his

[56] *Revised Statutes*, 1851, pp. 49, 50, 52.

pleasure and to those who should advise or aid a person not a qualified elector to vote. Any person whose vote was challenged and who made a false oath was deemed to have committed perjury and was liable to the statutory penalty for that crime. Further to encourage virtue and honest voting and canvassing of votes, the act of 1861 declared that every person sentenced to the state prison for violation of the act should be deemed to be forever incompetent to be an elector or to hold any office of honor, trust, or profit within the state until pardoned by the governor.[57]

The act of 1878 providing for elections in cities of over twelve thousand inhabitants also embodied penalties of drastic character for violations of the law. In one section judges of election were threatened with a fine not to exceed a thousand dollars or imprisonment for not more than a year, or both, for seven specified violations and, in a separate paragraph, with a like penalty for any willful neglect of duty. The same penalty was provided for any person who should remove poll books, tally lists, or ballots from the place of deposit, or should deface, mutilate, or change them; for any person who should willfully or corruptly ascertain and publish how any elector had voted; and, as if it was considered probable that improper use might be made of the serial numbers entered on the ballots and poll books, for any judge who should wrongfully ascertain by comparisons of the poll book with the ballots, or who should allow any other person to ascertain, how any elector had voted. A clerk of election found guilty of neglect of any duty or of fraud, corruption, or misbehavior was to be fined not more than five hundred dollars or imprisoned for not over six months, or both; and any judge, clerk, or messenger deputed to carry poll books, tally lists, and ballots to their proper depository who should fail to deliver them within the time prescribed by law, with seals unbroken, incurred the same

[57] *General Laws*, 1861, pp. 114, 120–122, 124.

penalty. Any official who should be found guilty of fraud
in canvassing the votes, in making abstracts, or in issuing
certificates of election was to suffer a fine not to exceed
five hundred dollars or imprisonment for not more than a
year, or both. A judge or clerk who willfully failed to
count or record the votes as provided by law was subject
to a fine of a thousand dollars or imprisonment for a year,
or both. Any city clerk or county auditor who willfully
neglected or refused to perform any duty required of him
by the act incurred a fine of not more than five hundred
dollars and was also liable to the person injured by his
neglect to a like amount, which might be recovered in an
action. Imprisonment for not less than a year was to be
visited upon anyone who registered in the wrong district or in
more than one district and also upon any member of the
board of registration who willfully violated any provision
of the act or who was guilty of fraud in the execution of
his duties. Any false statement made before a board of
registration was to be deemed perjury and punished as such.

The act also embodied provisions regulating the distribution of intoxicating liquors on election day, intended to
insure more orderly and honest voting on the part of a
certain element of the electorate. The sale of intoxicating
liquors under license had always been a lawful branch of
merchandising in Minnesota on all secular days. Experience
had shown that in the larger cities patrons of saloons had
at times purchased liquor for immediate consumption in
inordinate quantities. Excessive indulgence had had its
notorious effects in increasing intoxication to a degree that
caused disorder, exposed citizens to temptation, and, in some
instances, disqualified them for the intelligent exercise of
the cherished elective franchise. To remedy the evil the
legislature inserted a section forbidding the sale or gift of
liquor at large on election day and ordering all saloons
closed from five o'clock in the morning until six in the

afternoon. As if there was doubt as to whether saloon-keepers would be patriotic and generous enough to forego their profits without encouragement, the law provided for a penalty of a fine of from twenty-five to one hundred dollars for each offense. It was also made the especial duty of every mayor, sheriff, and constable and of other officers and magistrates to enforce the statute. Finally, it was made the duty of the mayor of every city to which the law applied to make proclamation the day before election warning saloon-keepers that the provisions of the law would be strictly enforced. To keep him from forgetting that duty, he was made subject to a fine of one thousand dollars or imprisonment in jail for sixty days, or both, for failure to perform it. The election law of 1889 for cities of ten thousand and over stipulated that no election should be held in a saloon or barroom or in any contiguous or adjoining place and made it a misdemeanor for any person to introduce liquor in any way into a polling place or for any judge or clerk to drink or to be intoxicated there.[58]

The general election law of 1893 made the defamation of candidates for office by writing, printing, posting, or distributing anonymous posters or circulars a crime punishable by a fine of one hundred dollars or by imprisonment for six months in jail, or both. If the statements made were untrue, the offender was deemed guilty of libel and was subject to civil or criminal prosecution.[59]

The leading section of the so-called "Corrupt Practices Act" passed by the legislature of 1895 declared that the giving or receiving of any money, thing of value, or employment for inducing a person to vote a particular ticket

[58] General Laws, 1878, pp. 136–138, 139, 141, 142; 1889, p. 23. Two other sections of the act of 1878 carried small penalties. An elector who made a false statement concerning his residence to the clerk at the polls was to be fined fifty dollars or imprisoned ten days, or both; and a fine of fifty dollars or imprisonment for sixty days, or both, was the penalty for tearing down or defacing a posted registration list.

[59] General Laws, 1893, p. 77.

or to refrain from voting should constitute the crime of bribery, punishable with imprisonment in the state prison for not more than five years and a forfeit of five hundred dollars with costs of prosecution. The act further declared any person who, before or after election, should receive any kind of remuneration for voting or for neglecting to vote guilty of bribery; but the milder penalty of three months in jail was attached. The act provided that the payment of "legal expenses bona fide" incurred at or concerning any election should not be deemed bribery and added a list of ten specifications of expenses that might be considered legal. It further placed limits on the aggregate amounts that a candidate or his agent might disburse. Where the vote was five thousand or less the limit was two hundred and fifty dollars. For every hundred votes up to twenty-five thousand two dollars were added; for every hundred votes up to fifty thousand one dollar was added; for every hundred votes over fifty thousand fifty cents were added. The act took effect upon its passage, on April 26, 1895.[60] It is known that it had its expected effect in lessening bribery and in promoting the more careful handling of campaign funds. It gave candidates good reasons for refusing to contribute to many legal expenses in excessive amounts. That the aggregate amount of campaign expenses was materially reduced may be doubted. If claims of disappointed candidates may be trusted, an unprecedented amount of money was spent in the campaign of 1896 in Minnesota.

The legislature of 1897 passed an act making it a misdemeanor for any person other than the judges of election to handle ballots during the canvass or for a judge to permit others to handle them, and also for any person other than the clerks to make any entry or mark on a tally sheet or for any judge or clerk to permit the same to be done. Another required judges in districts with fewer than twelve

[60] *General Laws*, 1895, pp. 664–674.

thousand inhabitants to file, along with their regular returns, a summary statement of the votes cast for each candidate, which was to be immediately open to the public.[61]

The enactment of a new corrupt practices act at the special session of 1912 would indicate that the act of 1895 had not sufficiently diminished the excessive and immoral use of money in politics. The legislature again undertook to limit and regulate such employment of money. The purposes for which candidates might in person or by agents pay or promise to pay remained substantially unchanged; but the amounts to be expended were scheduled as follows: for a governor, seven thousand dollars; for other state officers, thirty-five hundred dollars; for a state senator, six hundred dollars; and for a member of the House of Representatives, four hundred dollars. Candidates were required to make all disbursements for legitimate election expenses under their personal direction or through party or personal campaign committees and no person or firm could spend more than fifty dollars for political purposes except through a political committee. The state central committee was authorized to make further disbursements for legal purposes, which should not exceed ten thousand dollars. Any candidate was authorized to appoint a separate personal campaign committee of one or more persons, by writing duly filed, whose acts were to be presumed to be his own. The act did not in · terms allow any compensation for the committee's services. The term "campaign manager" soon came into use and has continued in use. Rigorous requirements were made for an official audit of all campaign expenses. Every candidate and every secretary of a committee was required to submit to the proper filing officer, every fortnight during a campaign and on the Saturday before a primary or a general election, a verified statement in minute detail of his transactions, on blanks furnished by the secretary of state. If

[61] General Laws, 1897, pp. 454, 615.

such statements were not duly filed, the candidate's name could not be placed on the official ballot for primary or general election.

The word " bribery " did not appear in the statute, but the law abounded in prohibitions of acts to which the term might well apply. It forbade any person to pay or to promise any reward for inducing another to be or to refrain from being a candidate for office or to solicit any compensation for such purpose. It forbade any person to induce or prevail upon an elector to give or to refrain from giving his vote at any primary or general election and forbade any elector to accept money or anything of value for his vote or his abstinence from voting. That such interdicts should not be interpreted to apply only to money or property considerations, the law went further and specifically made it unlawful for any candidate in person or otherwise to give " any meat or drink or other entertainment or provision, clothing, liquors, cigars or tobacco," with intent to influence votes and for any elector to accept such gifts. It was made unlawful for any person to pay electors for loss of time or expenses in going to register or to vote; for any person to pay for personal services at any caucus, primary, convention, or election for any purposes connected therewith; and for any person, committee, or organization to convey electors, except members of their own households, to the polls.

The law did not affirmatively forbid contributions to church fairs and suppers, Sunday school picnics, or school entertainments to make friends and gain prestige generally, but it did forbid any person to solicit contributions on behalf of any religious or charitable organization from any candidate or to invite him to buy tickets to any entertainment or ball or to pay for space in any book, program, periodical, or other publication. The ordinary contributions of candidates to their churches and the regular payments to other organizations of which they were members were excepted.

There was at the time a widespread belief that some corporations, especially some among those owning or controlling public utilities, desirous of favorable legislation, state or municipal, of administrative rulings, and even of lenient judicial holdings, were spending large sums of money, not so much in the direct purchase of votes as in packing caucuses and steering conventions. It may be assumed that a legislature framing a corrupt practices act would not have set up such a sweeping and absolute prohibition of corporation activities in politics without reason. In terms impossible to mistake, the law, expanding somewhat chapter 291 of the laws of 1905, forbade any kind of payment or promise of payment of money or anything of value by a corporation doing business in the state for any political purpose whatsoever. A penalty of ten thousand dollars was denounced for any violation of any of the provisions of the law by a corporation. If the corporation convicted was domestic, it might be dissolved; if foreign it might forfeit its right to do business in the state. To put teeth into the prohibition, a fine of from one hundred to five thousand dollars or imprisonment in the state prison for from one to five years, or both, was to be the lot of any officer, employee, agent, attorney, or representative acting for the corporation that should violate the law.

The restriction of the unbridled and often unconscionable use of the press in politics was one of the prime objects of the new legislation. It required that any campaign literature tending to influence votes must bear on its face the names and addresses of the author, of the candidates favored, and of the person, firm, corporation, or committee causing its publication. Newspapers, magazines, and periodicals intending to publish "any matter whatsoever of a political nature" were required to file in the office of the secretary of state, six months before any primary or general election, a sworn statement giving the names of the owners of the paper and, if a corporation, the names and addresses of the owners of the shares. The paper was thus to be qualified and made in fact responsible for its utterances, if its owners were in fact responsible. All persons were forbidden to pay or promise to pay a newspaper, directly or indirectly, for the publication of matter intended to influence votes unless such matter should appear under the special heading, " Paid Advertisement," with a statement of the amount of money paid for its insertion and the names and addresses of the author and of the candidate in whose behalf it should be published. Newspapers were forbidden to ask or to accept any other remuneration for such publication. The papers, of course, retained their constitutional right to print political news and to discuss the merits of public men and public measures. One result much appreciated by candidates was an end to exactions by publishers of small newspapers for supposed favorable influence.

To abate a recognized nuisance the law forbade any candidate or person to circulate or to cause to be circulated in any place campaign literature of any kind on the day of any primary or general election. The same section forbade attempts within one hundred feet of the polling place to persuade electors to vote or to neglect to vote for any candidate or measure. This put an end to hangers-on who time out of mind had infested polling places. Intimidation of electors was forbidden in general and employers of labor were strictly forbidden to issue any threat or prediction of injury to employees if a particular ticket should be elected. Betting on the result of an election or a primary was absolutely forbidden and was made a ground of challenge against the right of an elector to vote.

In but three instances were penalties specified in the body of the act, but a section near the end provided for the punishment of violations by imprisonment in jail for from one to twelve months or in the state prison for from one to three years, or by fines ranging from twenty-five to one thousand dollars, or by both imprisonment and fines. After the passage of this act politics were cleaner and probably less expensive, for minor positions at least.[62]

The reader who has patiently toiled through this chapter will probably be pleased to take a rest. At any rate, he will appreciate the difficulty to be met and, if possible, overcome in the conduct of elections, especially where great masses of voters of all degrees of intelligence and morality are concerned. He may thank the author, however, for not loading him with additional accounts of legislation with reference to challenges at the polls and election contests and with a mass of details of comparative unimportance, such as changes of days and dates. In regard to the graver matters he may entertain himself with a perusal of chapter 1 of the *General Statutes of Minnesota*, 1923. There, spread out on forty-seven large, double-column pages, in fine types, he may find the election law of Minnesota before three legislatures had operated upon it. Legislatures pass laws, but the supreme court passes upon their constitutionality. In many instances Minnesota election laws have been annulled by decisions of the supreme court. As the activities of election officials are purely ministerial, they are all subject to judicial scrutiny. Any elector fancying himself to have a cause of action against an official or a fellow elector for violation of election law may bring suit for damages. How many such prosecutions have been begun and dropped without trial, or have been decided by district courts without appeal cannot be guessed, but more than four hundred election cases have been decided by the supreme court on appeal.[63]

The difficulties and evils attending elections in a democracy

[62] *General Laws*, 1912, pp. 23–40. The author paid Cyrus Northrop fifty cents for transporting him to the polls and back on November 5, 1912, and took his receipt.

[63] Mark B. Dunnell, *Minnesota Digest: A Digest of the Decisions of the Supreme Court of the State of Minnesota*, 2: 778–811 (second edition — Owatonna, 1927).

might probably be mitigated by a restriction of the suffrage —
to freeholders or householders or to owners of a certain
amount of personal wealth, all with at least a common school
education.   The modern drift toward the widest possible
extension of the elective franchise does not promise any
such solution.   But this wide extension of the suffrage has
so cheapened it that great numbers of qualified electors
do not care to vote, especially upon constitutional amendments and charters.   In times of unusual political excitement
party leaders put forth every effort to " get out the vote."
Of late years a simplification of election procedure by what
its advocates call the " short ballot " system has been much
agitated.   The proposition is to elect but few, say half a
dozen, state officers and to leave all other positions to be
filled by appointment.   In view of the present state of the
public mind, the plan does not need serious consideration.[64]

[64] McLaughlin and Hart, *Cyclopedia of American Government*, 1: 104;
Richard S. Childs, " Ballot Reform: Need of Simplification," and Arthur
Ludington, " Proposed Methods of Ballot Simplification," in American Political
Science Association, *Proceedings*, 6: 65–92 (Baltimore, 1910).

VI. THE ACTS OF THE APOSTLES

CHRISTOPHER C. ANDREWS, APOSTLE OF FORESTRY

In earlier volumes of this history mention has been made of Christopher C. Andrews as captain and colonel in the Third Minnesota Infantry and brigadier general of volunteers in the war of the slaveholders' rebellion, and of his candidacy for representative in Congress in 1868, in which he suffered defeat by Donnelly's insurrection in the Republican party. General Andrews was to add to his creditable military career many years of valuable public service. In June, 1869, President Grant appointed him minister to Sweden and Norway, with residence in Stockholm, and he held that position for eight and a half years. He literally magnified the office, making it more than a round of social affairs and court functions. Before the Civil War he had varied his law practice with extensive travel, mostly in the West, and by recording his observations for newspapers he had become a ready writer. At Stockholm he entered upon a study of Sweden, and in the course of his ministry the United States government published more than thirty of his reports, on such subjects as agriculture, commerce, labor, education, finance, and taxation.[1]

In his first year in Sweden Andrews made a journey into the west central part of that country to inform himself in regard to the iron mines there and the production of the widely known "Swedish iron," reduced by the use of charcoal. In the course of his travels he was impressed by the

[1] *Ante,* 2: 94, 303; 3: 16; *Appletons' Cyclopædia of American Biography,* 1: 73 (New York, 1887–1900); *Short Sketch of General C. C. Andrews* (n. p., n. d.), a four-page folder. A list of Andrews' reports from Sweden is given in a letter from Alice E. Andrews to the author, October 9, 1927, in the Folwell Papers.

numerous checkerboard patches of forest, with their trees in various stages of growth. This was Andrews' first lesson in forestry and it led him to study the Swedish forestry system and to prepare a report upon it. Hamilton Fish, secretary of state, had the report included in the foreign relations documents of 1872–73.[2]

Upon his return from abroad General Andrews changed his residence from St. Cloud to St. Paul and at once took an active part in the affairs of the latter city, without losing his interest in forestry. In February, 1880, he read before the St. Paul Chamber of Commerce a report from a committee, of which he was chairman, appointed to consider the propriety of memorializing Congress for a grant of lands to endow a school of forestry at St. Paul. The memorial and bill that accompanied the report were presented in Congress by Senator McMillan of Minnesota on March 2, 1880, and referred to the committee on public lands. Nothing further was heard of them.[3] In 1882 Andrews read a paper on his hobby at a forestry congress in Cincinnati. So far his studies, writings, and addresses had made little impression upon the public. Minnesota people could not believe that there would ever be a shortage of timber for all their uses. Twelve years were to run by before he revived his efforts in behalf of a forestry system. During three of them, from 1882 to 1885, he was out of the country

[2] Andrews, "To Prevent Forest Fires," in *Northwestern Agriculturist,* 9: 273 (September 15, 1894). Andrews' "Report on the Forests and Forest Culture of Sweden" is in 42 Congress, 3 session, *House Executive Documents,* no. 1, part 1, pp. 602–646 (serial 1552). A revised edition — a pamphlet of thirty-five pages with the title, *Report on Forestry in Sweden* (Washington, 1900) — was printed in accordance with a resolution introduced by Senator Knute Nelson and adopted on January 24, 1900.

[3] *Daily Pioneer Press* (St. Paul and Minneapolis), February 17, 1880, p. 7; *Saint Paul Daily Dispatch,* February 16, 1880, p. 4; Andrews, *Recollections,* 251; *Congressional Record,* 46 Congress, 2 session, 1248, 3506. The report to the St. Paul Chamber of Commerce, with the memorial, the bill, and other documents, was printed and referred to the committee on agriculture. 46 Congress, 2 session, *Senate Miscellaneous Documents,* no. 91 (serial 1891).

as consul general of the United States at Rio de Janeiro. From his observations there he wrote a very interesting book on Brazil.[4]

On September 1, 1894, forest fires broke out in Pine County and completely destroyed the village of Hinckley. A careful count placed the number of dead at 413. On the fifteenth of that month the *Northwestern Agriculturist* of Minneapolis published an article entitled " To Prevent Forest Fires," by Andrews. The forest fires so lately quenched furnished a text for an appeal for the public control of forests and the perpetuation of forest growth.

The legislature of 1895, the first after the Hinckley fire, was very willing to entertain propositions for the prevention of forest fires and it passed a bill, which was approved on April 18, " for the preservation of forests of this state and for the prevention and suppression of forest and prairie fires." The bill as introduced was the work of General Andrews and was modeled upon the New York law, which provided for the creation of a forest commission to enforce the law; the legislature, however, was pleased to be economical and made the state auditor forest commissioner without increase of salary and authorized him to appoint a competent deputy, with the title chief fire warden, a salary of twelve hundred dollars, and authority to enforce the law. The leading provision of the act made the supervisors of towns, the mayors of cities, and the presidents of village councils fire wardens, with authority to act upon their own motion for the prevention or suppression of fires in their respective jurisdictions and to report to the chief fire warden at St. Paul. Details of the act are not important here, but it may be remarked that the trifling compensation allowed to local fire wardens and persons employed by them was probably

---

[4] *Sketch of Andrews,* 3. The title of the book is *Brazil, Its Condition and Prospects* (New York, 1887).

intended to prevent them from running up unconscionable bills against their counties and the state. For forest fire prevention during dry and dangerous seasons the law allowed an additional expenditure of five thousand dollars.[5]

It was General Andrews, of course, whom the auditor appointed as chief fire warden. His primary duties were to have general charge of the local fire wardens, to instruct them in regard to their duties under the forest preservation law, and to receive their reports. As town supervisors were changing from year to year, these were continuing duties. In 1895 the whole number of fire wardens who performed services and received instructions was 1,282. The force thus organized for fighting fires was none too efficient, but it was better than none. The pay of local wardens was too low to secure a steady watch. In a few counties commissioners refused to approve wardens' accounts. In the first year of the operation of the fire prevention act fires were numerous enough in both forest and prairie, but there was no loss of life and that of property was small. The whole expense of administration for the fiscal year ending on July 31, 1896, including the chief warden's salary, was $2,020.

Forest preservation was no simple matter in regions where every year there were hundreds of logging camps, thousands of settlers clearing land, swarms of land and timber seekers, prospectors for minerals, and pothunters and timber thieves hostile to the law. There were many miles of railroads in the timbered regions, some of them logging roads that were tardy or negligent in keeping their rights of way

[5] William Wilkinson, *Memorials of the Minnesota Forest Fires in the Year 1894*, 48, 103–125 (Minneapolis, 1895); Chief Fire Warden, *Reports*, 1895, pp. 3–13, 55; *Senate Journal*, 1895, p. 436; *House Journal*, 744; *General Laws*, 472–477, 784; Andrews, *Recollections*, 286; the author to Alice E. Andrews, September 22, 1927, and Miss Andrews' reply on the same sheet, Folwell Papers. The sixteen annual reports of General Andrews, first as chief fire warden and later as forestry commissioner, cover the period from 1895 to 1910, inclusive. The half-tone illustrations are instructive and beautiful.

clear of combustible material and in installing spark
arresters. As the law did not require lumbermen to burn
the tops and branches of trees cut, commonly called "slashings," these were left to lie where they fell, to be fuel for
spreading fires. Still there was doubt among the people as
to whether the state need have any concern about fires in
the pineries in the remote northern wilderness, or about
prairie fires that the farmers could suppress by neighborhood coöperation. A proposition in the legislature of 1897
to repeal the act of 1895, however, did not prevail.[6]

The operation of the law from year to year nevertheless
was to the good and the system gained in repute. The legislature of 1905 dignified General Andrews' office by changing
his title to forestry commissioner and raising his salary to
fifteen hundred dollars! The change of title did not materially alter his duties in kind, but the burden of them was
continually increased by the spread of settlements and the
extension of lumbering. The natural interest of the people
living in the forested regions moved them generally to obey
the fire prevention law; but there were some who, either from
sheer recklessness or from deviltry, did not obey. Local fire
wardens were reluctant to prosecute neighbors and few convictions were obtained. There was need of an intermediate
agency.[7]

On September 4, 1908, the mining village of Chisholm
in St. Louis County, having a population of about three

[6] General Laws, 1895, p. 472; Chief Fire Warden, Reports, 1895, pp. 13,
22–54, 65, 98, 103, 114, 132, 170–175; 1897, p. 15; 1902, p. 30. The Report
for 1898, pp. 7–9, quotes remonstrances from the commissioner of the general
land office and the chief of the division of forestry against the threatened
repeal of the law of 1895, and a compliment to General Andrews. The bill to
repeal the act of 1895, House file 849, was passed by both houses near the
end of the session and enrolled, but it was not approved by the governor.
See House Journal, 1897, pp. 1151, 1203; Senate Journal, 925. The author
remembers suggestions that the fire warden's office was a sinecure for the
brave old general.

[7] General Laws, 1905, p. 494; Revised Laws, 1905, p. 358; Chief Fire
Warden, Reports, 1899, p. 4; 1903, p. 5; 1904, p. 4; Forestry Commissioner,
Reports. 1905, p. 25; 1909, p. 27.

thousand, was almost wholly destroyed by a forest fire. A strong wind had brought it down from a fisherman's camp about ten miles to the northwest, where it had started, and it set fire to twenty acres of slashings partly within the village limits. No lives were lost but the property loss was great. It included, it was estimated, two million dollars' worth of standing timber. Upon the heels of this disaster Commissioner Andrews urged the legislature of 1909 to provide a more effective means for enforcing the fire prevention law. An amending act passed in that year authorized the forestry commissioner, in case of "a dry and dangerous season," to appoint a corps of forest rangers to " inspect, assist or compel the activity of local wardens." The pay of rangers was not to exceed five dollars a day, with necessary expenses. The commissioner asked for an annual appropriation of twenty-eight thousand dollars as an emergency fund. The legislature gave him half of it, with an additional two thousand dollars to be used for prosecutions. The service performed by twenty-four rangers during the summer of 1909 and by twenty-six between June 1 and September 1, 1910, met expectations. Local wardens were stimulated, many fires were checked, and some violators of the law were convicted. More might have been accomplished had it not been necessary to lay off the rangers on September 1, 1910, because of lack of money to pay them.[8]

The year 1910 was the driest of any year in Minnesota on record, according to a report of the United States weather bureau. There were more than nine hundred forest fires in 395 townships in 29 counties. The most destructive was that which on October 7 swept over the villages of Baudette and Spooner on Rainy River in Lake of the Woods County.

[8] Forestry Commissioner, *Reports*, 1908, pp. 6, 9–12, 32, 36–40, illustration facing p. 20; 1909, p. 35; 1910, pp. 6, 13; *Revised Laws*, 1905, pp. 358–360; *General Laws*, 1909, pp. 198–205; *Duluth Evening Herald*, September 8, 1908, p. 1.

Twenty-nine persons perished and damage to the amount of a million dollars was wrought. The commissioner, in a special report made to the legislature on January 18, 1911, asked for an appropriation to pay 8,944 persons for fighting the fires of 1910. The houses voted $94,700, which was not enough, and accounts had to be settled by pro rata payments.[9]

It was the expectation of the forestry commissioner that the legislature of 1911, in view of the immense devastations of the foregoing season, would provide money enough to pay local fire wardens and their helpers liberally, to extend the ranger service, and to prosecute offenders vigorously. He therefore prepared a bill containing the provisions that he thought necessary and appropriate under the circumstances for the protection of timber worth one hundred million dollars, of which fifteen million dollars' worth belonged to the state. The bill called for the appropriation of two hundred thousand dollars, or so much thereof as might be necessary, for ranger and patrol service in dry and dangerous weather; of thirty-five thousand dollars for the pay and disbursements of the forestry commissioner's office and of local fire wardens; and of thirty thousand dollars for the prosecution of offenders. Railroad companies were to be required to maintain continuous patrols along their lines in timbered or prairie regions from April 1 to November 15; lumbermen were to burn slashings cut between November 1 and April 1 at the time of cutting and those cut between April 1 and November 1, before the following January; persons desiring to camp for a day or more on lands near forests or prairies were to notify town clerks of the sites of proposed camps and the probable length of time they would be occupied, and were to file a promise in writing

---

[9] Forestry Commissioner, *Reports*, 1910, pp. 3, 6, 19–37, 41, map facing p. 6. The special report covers pages 3 to 40.

to obey the law regarding camp fires. It was also proposed that the forestry commissioner, whose title should be changed to " forester," should be appointed by the governor, and that the governor might also appoint as assistant forester an honor graduate of a forestry school. The House committee on forestry could not think of any such liberality for forest preservation and considered a different bill.[10]

Minnesota people had not all been reckless of the devastation of their splendid forests. In 1876 the Minnesota State Forestry Association had been formed and had done useful, if not conspicuous, service. In 1899 the legislature passed a bill drawn by Judson N. Cross, a Minneapolis lawyer who appreciated trees. It established a state forestry board, to be composed of two ex officio members — the chief fire warden and the professor of horticulture in the agricultural college of the University of Minnesota — and seven other members to be appointed by the governor, three to be recommended by the regents of the university and the other four, by four different organizations, to keep the board out of politics, it may be assumed. Its function was to manage the " forest reserves " of the state, tracts of land acquired by gift or set aside by law for forestry purposes.[11] Shortly after the passage of this act, John S. Pillsbury made the state a gift of a thousand acres of cut-over pine land in Cass County and the legislature turned over to the state forestry board some two thousand acres of land that had been forfeited because of delinquent taxes. In 1903 a committee of the forestry board established a small nursery of pine and spruce on the Pillsbury tract. Two years later, in 1905, the state received a gift from Congress of twenty thousand acres of low-grade land for " forestry purposes." The lands

10 Forestry Commissioner, *Reports*, 1908, p. 12; 1910, pp. 41–49.

11 Chief Fire Warden, *Reports*, 1897, p. 77; 1898, pp. 46–52; *General Laws*, 1899, pp. 229–234. A similar bill was passed by the House in 1897, but it failed in the Senate. *House Journal*, 1897, p. 637; *Senate Journal*, 836; Chief Fire Warden, *Reports*, 1896, p. 102.

selected, which were in St. Louis County, came under the management of the forestry board.[12]

The forestry board, already more than an ornament, was willing to have its powers enlarged. A bill drawn by it was passed by the legislature of 1911, with reductions, however, in salaries and appropriations. The act turned over to the board the management of all state forest reserves, the supervision of forest protection and reforestation, and the handling of all moneys accruing for those purposes. It authorized the board to appoint as state forester a trained forester, who should have power to appoint an assistant forester and other necessary employees, subject to approval by the board, and power to dismiss subordinates; and it provided for the appointment of a secretary for the board at a salary of not more than eighteen hundred dollars. General Andrews was eighty-two years old in 1911. Although he showed no signs of aging and felt himself as competent as ever, it was the opinion of the board that a younger man, especially qualified for the duties in the field, should take the office of state forester and that the less exacting duties of secretary should be devolved upon General Andrews. He accepted the position gracefully and discharged its duties with great fidelity until his death on September 21, 1922. He had been in the forest service of the state, conducting an extensive administration and handling large sums of money, for twenty-six years. His average salary had been $1,650, about that of a bank clerk or a college tutor! The activities of the competent and efficient state forester, William T. Cox, under a law less stringent than that proposed by General Andrews and with only seventy-five thousand dollars for all the purposes of the new act, cannot be followed here.[13]

[12] Chief Fire Warden, *Reports*, 1900, p. 136; 1901, p. 37; 1904, pp. 28–30, 32; *General Laws*, 1901, pp. 551–554.

[13] Forestry Commissioner, *Reports*, 1910, p. 50; *Sketch of Andrews*, 4; *General Laws*, 1911, pp. 151–160.

At no time while he was in office did General Andrews consider himself a mere police officer, charged only with supervising the prevention and suppression of forest and prairie fires. He saw to it that into section 3 of the act of 1895 creating the office of chief fire warden and prescribing its duties there was inserted a paragraph reading: " He shall investigate the extent of the forests in the state, together with the amounts and varieties of the wood and timber growing therein . . . the method used, if any, to promote the regrowth of timber, and any other important facts relating to forest interests." He fought fires faithfully, but his heart was not in that part of his work. In his first annual report he roughly bounded the coniferous and hardwood regions of the state and gave an estimate, derived from various sources, of the amounts and kinds of standing timber. The final footings showed an area of 11,890,000 acres of forest lands and 24,790,575,000 board feet of timber, of which 18,476,475,000 feet were pine — about three-fourths white pine. The figures were not, of course, exact, but they showed the great extent and value of the Minnesota forests.[14]

At the time when Andrews made his first report the average annual cut of pine for the preceding three years had been a billion and a half board feet. In 1898 he moderately estimated that in twenty years the Minnesota pine would be practically exhausted. He did not propose to limit or reduce the cut. Private persons who had lawfully bought and paid for timber, he said, including sagacious buyers of land left over at auction sales for private entry, had good right to cut it as the market demanded. If any had come into possession of timbered property by fraudulent use of scrip or of homestead or stone and timber rights — and such " a system of

14 *General Laws*, 1895, p. 473; Chief Fire Warden, *Reports*, 1895, pp. 115, 131, and frontispiece. A revised estimate of the amount of white pine in three counties, increasing the total number of feet for the state by 2,600,000,000, is given in *Reports*, 1896, p. 66.

plunder," he stated, had been in operation — having acquired title, they also had the right to act at pleasure.[15]

With the vanishing point of the Minnesota forests so near at hand, Andrews faced the problem of reforestation. He became a teacher of scientific and practical forestry. His lessons in forestry, in successive reports, were not arranged in a formal series, schoolmaster fashion, but he made points in a way to challenge attention and interest, as a lawyer argues before a jury. His " principles of forestry " he frequently put in a nutshell. First, forests should occupy only land unfit for agriculture — sandy, hilly, or rocky land; second, a forest should be perennial, its annual cuttings equal to its annual growth; third, forests should be harvested in strips or blocks, so as to promote natural reseeding from neighboring trees; fourth, a new forest should be planted thick and should be thinned out judiciously as it grows.[16] He repeatedly dwelt upon the advantages of forestry. A forest, he would say, was an inviolable capital constantly rejuvenated by nature, drawing but one-twelfth as heavily upon the mineral substances in the soil as did farm crops. Regarded as a business, a properly administered forest would, at fiscal maturity, which was about eighty years for pine, yield annually a return of three per cent compound interest on the investment. He urged also considerations other than pecuniary. Forests traversed by roads would clothe waste lands with beauty and, like the Black Forest of southwestern Germany, would become resorts for health and recreation. Like that famous forest, they might include farms and manufacturing villages. The efficacy of the forest floor in checking the run-off of rain and melting snow and the washing away of the soil he duly represented.[17]

[15] Chief Fire Warden, *Reports*, 1895, p. 118; 1897, p. 25; 1902, p. 36.
[16] Chief Fire Warden, *Reports*, 1897, pp. 26–28; 1898, p. 68; 1899, p. 19; 1900, p. 42; 1902, p. 36.
[17] Chief Fire Warden, *Reports*, 1896, p. 110; 1897, pp. 31–33; 1900, p. 41; 1901, pp. 27, 30, 38; 1903, pp. 52, 56; 1905, p. 33; 1906, p. 24.

Andrews' reports included lessons on the methods of forestry: the preparation of the soil, the selection of species, the collection of seed — difficult in the case of conifers — the planting by seed or by seedlings from nurseries, and successive thinnings. In the fourth year of his office the chief fire warden procured from a competent practicing forest expert a plan and estimate for a two-million-acre forest of pine in Minnesota.[18]

General Andrews inserted in all his reports, excepting the first, descriptive and statistical accounts of the perpetual forests of European countries, in charge of special branches of administration under scientific supervision and employing large bodies of workmen. Growing on waste lands, they are highly profitable. The opinion that in the United States perpetual forests must be owned by states was either explicit or implicit in many of his reports. Trusting that his exhortations might have had their hoped-for effect upon the public mind, he prepared a draft of a bill for the submission of an amendment to the state constitution for a tax levy of three-tenths of a mill, the proceeds to be expended by the state forestry board for the production and maintenance of forests and for the purchase of lands suitable for foresting. The legislature of 1909 passed the bill, after reducing the tax rate to one-fifteenth of a mill. At the general election of 1910 the number of affirmative votes was a majority of all the votes cast on the question, but not of the whole number of ballots cast at the election. Had the amendment been ratified, the tax yield would have been some seventy-two thousand dollars a year; though a beggarly sum, it might

18 Chief Fire Warden, *Reports*, 1898, pp. 60–66; 1903, p. 57; 1904, pp. 40–48; Forestry Commissioner, *Reports*, 1906, pp. 27–46; 1908, pp. 57–62. In 1897 Andrews sent to every public school teacher in the state, through city and county school superintendents, a copy of a paper prepared by Professor Samuel B. Green, entitled "Outlines of a Few Lessons in Forestry." The paper, which is good reading, is printed in Chief Fire Warden, *Reports*, 1897, pp. 35–44.

have made possible the beginning of a magnificent system of state forests.[19] The forest commissioner was not without hope that some private owners of timbered lands might be disposed to manage them on forestry principles if they were relieved of the annual property tax. A companion bill, doubtless drawn by him, for a constitutional amendment to authorize the legislature to exempt lands devoted to forestry from the annual tax burden was passed by the legislature of 1909, only to be rejected by the people in 1910.[20]

From year to year Andrews made trips of observation into the northern pine counties of the state. In the summer of 1899 he was on Cass Lake, on the south shore of which, to his " surprise and indignation," he found many acres of beautiful virgin pine despoiled by a squaw man under a dead-and-down-timber contract. When he visited the large island in Cass Lake and saw the most beautiful piece of woodland in Minnesota in danger of like desolation, he resolved to do what he could to prevent it. At the moment he thought that Congress, following a few precedents, might set aside that island and a strip of the lake shore as a national park. As he saw what was happening to the pine of the region in general, his views expanded into a conception of

[19] Chief Fire Warden, *Reports*, 1896, pp. 88–99; 1901, p. 30; 1902, pp. 43–45; Forestry Commissioner, *Reports*, 1907, pp. 21–25; 1908, pp. 47, 52; 1910, p. 66; *General Laws*, 1909, p. 704; Anderson, *History of the Constitution*, 283. The vote was 100,168 for the amendment and 63,962 against it. The total vote at the election was 310,165.

[20] Forestry Commissioner, *Reports*, 1908, p. 53; *General Laws*, 1909, p. 705; Anderson, *History of the Constitution*, 283. The vote on the amendment was: yes, 87,943; no, 73,697. The total vote at the election was 310,165. Sixteen years passed before a legislature was again willing to authorize tax exemption on private forests. That of 1925 submitted an amendment to the constitution to that end, which was ratified in 1926 by a vote of yes, 383,003 and no, 127,592, the whole number of votes cast being 722,781. To give effect to the amendment, the legislature of 1927 passed " an act providing a comprehensive plan for afforestation and reforestation of lands." The act exempted the land of " auxiliary forests " privately owned from annual taxes, with the exception of eight cents on the dollar of assessed value. It imposed a tax of ten per cent of the value of the timber when harvested. *Laws*, 1925, p. 773; 1927, pp. 356–368; *Legislative Manual*, 1927, insert facing p. 184.

a park of some eight hundred thousand acres, land and water, including the Chippewa reservations about Cass and Leech lakes and Lake Winnibigoshish. He drafted a bill for the creation of a commission to negotiate with the Indians for a cession of those reservations " as a whole, in lieu of the manner of disposing of the lands " as prescribed by the Nelson Act of 1889. Any lands acquired were to be and remain a national park. His hope was that the magnificent forests thus redeemed would be administered according to established principles of forestry and yield a perpetual revenue. This beginning resulted in the creation, under the Morris Act of 1902, of a forest reserve of two hundred thousand acres, which was included in the national forest created by an act of 1908. The act of 1902 authorized the sale at auction of all the pine timber on the tract, without the land, to be cut clean except for five per cent of the pine, which should be left standing for seed trees and should be selected by the forester of the department of agriculture. General Andrews was comforted with the recognition of the principles of scientific forestry. It may be questioned whether the application of them has been scientific.[21]

It appears that, after launching the project that resulted in the creation of the Chippewa National Forest, Andrews was concerned about rescuing more forested land from early devastation. On May 10, 1902, he addressed a letter, which was written, he says, after a year's reflection, to the commissioner of the general land office, recommending that some five hundred thousand acres of land in Cook and Lake counties be set apart by the president as a forest reserve. He described the tract as hilly and rocky, with third- or fourth-rate soil — land which settlers would not take up;

[21] Chief Fire Warden, *Reports,* 1899, pp. 30–41; 1900, p. 44; 1901, p. 44; United States, *Statutes at Large,* 32: 400–404; 35: 268–272. For a fuller account of the origin of the Chippewa National Forest, see *ante,* p. 253.

it was, he said, natural timber land. On June 30, 1902, the commissioner replied that, upon his favorable report, the secretary of the interior had ordered that the lands described be temporarily withdrawn from market. Such was the first step of a long pursuit that ended on February 13, 1909, with President Roosevelt's proclamation setting apart as a public reservation the lands forming the Superior National Forest, about five hundred thousand acres.[22]

Mention has been made of a gift of twenty thousand acres of low-grade lands for experimental purposes made to Minnesota by Congress in 1904. The beginning of the movement resulting in this benefaction was made by General Andrews. At a meeting of the state forestry board held on May 27, 1903, a resolution drawn by him declaring that all vacant public lands of third or fourth grade should be declared better adapted to forestry than to agriculture was adopted. On September 2 of the same year the executive committee of the board, of which Andrews was a member and secretary, was instructed to prepare and have introduced in Congress a bill for an act to grant to the state for forestry purposes all such vacant public lands as the surveyor-general might from time to time certify to be of third or fourth grade. Senator Knute Nelson introduced the bill, which met with immediate opposition on the grounds that it was too far-reaching and that it set a dangerous precedent. Nelson suggested a more modest appeal and introduced a bill to grant to the state for experimental forestry purposes not more than twenty thousand acres of vacant public lands described as of third or fourth grade in the field notes of the government surveyors. The Senate could not refuse Nelson's request for less than a township of useless land for

[22] Chief Fire Warden, *Reports*, 1902, pp. 37–40; Forestry Commissioner, *Reports*, 1908, pp. 68–72; United States, *Statutes at Large*, 35: 2223, and insert. The act giving the president power to set apart lands for forests is in *Statutes at Large*, 26: 1103.

so worthy a purpose. The report of the House committee
on public lands, of which Volstead and Lind of Minnesota
were members, informed the House that Minnesota had a
well-organized bureau of forestry engaged in reforestation
and could make good use of the land. The bill became a
law on April 28, 1904, and the grant was accepted by the
state legislature on March 30, 1905.

General Andrews was on the committee of the state forestry
board charged with selecting the lands granted. The committee found in St. Louis County land that no settler would
take up and no lumberman would look at, utterly worthless
for agriculture but of value for forestry purposes. A forester could plant in the crevices of the rocks, among the
bowlders, and in the sands and swamps seedlings that would
grow up into a magnificent forest. The lands selected are
parts of townships 63 and 64, range 13, in St. Louis County,
north and west of Burntside Lake, one of the most beautiful
of Minnesota's "ten thousand" lakes. The Burntside
Forest contains, within itself and bordering it, forty-three
lakes connected by canoe routes.[23]

Judging from his reports, General Andrews took much
pride in his part in securing the creation of Minnesota's
forest parks. To the end of his long life of nearly ninety-
three years he was honored and respected in and beyond
Minnesota, but his services in the cause of forestry were
appreciated by but few of a generation that looked upon
forests as superfluous timber to be cut down and used up.

[23] Chief Fire Warden, *Reports*, 1904, pp. 28–30; Alice E. Andrews to the
author, October 18, 1927, Folwell Papers; *Congressional Record*, 58 Congress,
2 session, 2013, 3972, 4284, 4405, 5053, 5694, 5781, 5825. The original bill,
Senate bill 2684, is on page 276. See also Andrews, *Recollections*, 295. A
minute description of the Burntside Forest as explored in 1904 is in Forestry
Commissioner, *Reports*, 1905, pp. 34–49. A bill, drawn by General Andrews
and introduced by Senator Nelson, to grant Minnesota eighty acres to round
out the Pillsbury tract passed the Senate, but the House refused to consider
it. *Congressional Record*, 58 Congress, 1 session, 398; 58 Congress, 2 session,
486, 862, 945, 1294, 1896, 4201.

By the time of his death in 1922 the magnificent virgin pine forests of Minnesota had disappeared, as he had predicted, and the people were importing lumber from the Pacific states and paying high charges for freight. The beginnings of reforesting were inconsiderable. Upon his record, without challenge, General Christopher C. Andrews stands as Minnesota's apostle of forestry.

THEOPHILUS L. HAECKER, APOSTLE OF AGRICULTURAL COÖPERATION

Agricultural coöperation of the consumer type made its first appearance in the United States on a considerable scale in the eighteen seventies, but in the fields of production and marketing it was unimportant until the last decade of the nineteenth century, when three inventions had made it economically profitable in the dairy industry. These were the silo, introduced from abroad about 1875; the centrifugal cream separator, also of foreign invention, which came into use in America about 1890; and the Babcock test for ascertaining the amount of butter fat in milks, an American invention of 1890.[24] The man who gave to this type of coöperation its direction and impetus was Theophilus L. Haecker.

Haecker was born in Liverpool, Ohio, on May 4, 1846, of parents of German origin. When he was seven years old the family moved to a farm at Cottage Grove, Wisconsin, where Theophilus attended the local district school in winter and helped on the farm in summer. In the fall of 1863, at the age of seventeen, he entered the University of Wisconsin, but he was unable to complete the year's work because of ill health. On March 11, 1864, he enlisted in the Thirty-seventh Wisconsin Infantry and because of his fine penmanship was

[24] Norman S. B. Gras, *A History of Agriculture in Europe and America*, 309, 329 (New York, 1925).

CHRISTOPHER C. ANDREWS
[From a photograph taken in 1889, in the museum of the Minnesota Historical Society.]

THEOPHILUS L. HAECKER
[From a photograph taken in 1906, in the possession of Mr. Haecker.]

soon detailed as clerk at regimental headquarters. Later he was detached and placed in charge of the hospital supplies of the Ninth Army Corps. He served also as regimental bugler, and at the grand review of the Army of the Potomac in Washington at the close of the war he had charge of the drum corps of his regiment.

After obtaining his discharge, on July 27, 1865, he spent two years on a farm at Hampton, in Franklin County, Iowa, to which his parents had removed while he was in the army. In the spring of 1867 he reëntered the University of Wisconsin, registering for the classical course, but ill health again forced him to discontinue his college work and return home. In 1870, after a couple of years spent in teaching, he moved to Hardin County, Iowa, and there established the *Ackley Independent,* which became during the three years of Haecker's ownership, one of the leading country papers of northern Iowa. In February, 1874, he returned to Cottage Grove and settled on a stock and dairy farm ten miles from Madison; but he had barely become established when he was offered the position of executive clerk in the office of the governor of Wisconsin. This he accepted and held for seventeen years, from 1874 to 1891, during sixteen of which he continued to reside on his farm and manage it. During his long years of service at the Capitol he acquired great influence, as is revealed by the fact that for twelve years he reviewed the cases that came before the governor for pardon. In January, 1891, he joined a class in the dairy school of the University of Wisconsin, in which he was almost at once made an assistant to the instructor.[25]

Such was the career that preceded Haecker's removal to Minnesota at the age of forty-five. He had worked on farms, had served as a soldier in the army, had taught school, had

[25] Johnson, *University of Minnesota,* 339–341; Marion D. Shutter and John S. McLain, eds., *Progressive Men of Minnesota,* 160 (Minneapolis, 1897); *Who's Who in America,* 1928–29.

published a successful newspaper, had operated a stock and dairy farm of his own for many years, and had given long service in a governor's office, where he had become accustomed to the consideration of matters of state-wide scope. Although he had no college diploma to exhibit, who shall say that he was not well educated?

When the regents of the University of Minnesota had under consideration the matter of adding a dairy school to the department of agriculture, John S. Pillsbury and Knute Nelson, of the committee on agriculture, visited Madison and there became acquainted with Haecker and his work. On their recommendation Haecker was appointed, on September 15, 1891, as instructor in the new dairy school for six months at a salary of seventy-five dollars a month, and eight months later he was reëlected at a salary of twelve hundred dollars a year. In 1893 he was made professor of dairy husbandry and he served in that capacity until his retirement in 1918.[26]

One of his first undertakings in Minnesota was a survey of creameries, which revealed the fact that many of them were not operating and others were badly managed. The most successful were a group of coöperative creameries in Freeborn County, particularly one in the Danish community of Clark's Grove, which was organized under certificates of agreement and by-laws drawn up in the Danish language. Believing that coöperation would be advantageous to other farmers, Haecker published a pamphlet containing suggestions for the establishment of coöperative creameries, in which he included model articles of organization based on the Clark's Grove system. He laid particular stress on the feature that allowed each member but one vote in the management. From now on Haecker seized every opportunity to

[26] University of Minnesota, Catalogues, 1893–94, p. 27; president's report, in Board of Regents, Reports, 1893–94, p. 41; Board of Regents, Minutes, B 1: 379, 385; Haecker, " Twenty-two Years' Study in Milk Production," in Hoard's Dairyman, 48: 632, 648 (December 25, 1914); Berry H. Akers, " Minnesota Honors Prof. Haecker," in the Farmer, January 10, 1925, p. 3.

preach coöperation to the dairymen of the state. The results of his labors were apparent in the growth of the dairy industry and particularly in the rapid spread of the coöperative system of creameries, except near the Twin Cities, where stock companies predominated. The coöperative plan was soon adopted also for farmers' elevators and with the lapse of years it had a wide expansion.[27]

As the coöperative movement progressed the agricultural experiment station at the university gave it countenance and assistance. Beginning in 1913 it issued a series of bulletins on coöperation in a number of different fields, including one published in January, 1923, that contains a list and an analytical summary of coöperative associations in Minnesota. The total number in 1922 was approximately forty-five hundred, which did a business of one hundred and forty-four million dollars in the preceding year. Of these, 2,060 were selling organizations; 210, buying organizations; 501, producing organizations; and 178, insurance organizations; farmers' telephone companies numbered 1,648. By 1927 the business of coöperative concerns in Minnesota had increased to two hundred million dollars.[28]

On April 15, 1929, a bill for farm relief was introduced into the lower house of Congress that granted federal aid to

[27] Haecker, "The Dairy in Minnesota," in *Farm, Stock and Home*, 8: 379 (October 1, 1892); *Farm Students' Review*, 1: 24 (February, 1896); Arthur J. McGuire, "The Minnesota Dairy School," in *Farm Students' Review*, 7: 195 (November, 1902); H. Bruce Price, *Farmers' Co-operation in Minnesota, 1917–1922*, 28–33 (University of Minnesota, Agricultural Experiment Station, *Bulletins*, no. 202 — St. Paul, 1923); record of an interview with Haecker, April 1, 1929, and Arnold F. Hinrichs to the author, April 16, 1929, Folwell Papers. An appreciation of Haecker's services in the development of coöperative creameries in Minnesota is given in Lionel Smith-Gordon, "Co-operation in the New World: Minnesota and Her Neighbours," in *Better Business*, 2: 54–73 (November, 1916). This is a quarterly journal of agricultural and industrial coöperation published in Dublin, Ireland.

[28] Price, *Farmers' Co-operation*, 4–7; Hinrichs to the author, April 16, 1929, Folwell Papers. The writer of this letter comments on the recent establishment of two successful federations of coöperative associations. One of them, the Land O'Lakes Creameries, has a membership of 460 local creameries representing one hundred thousand farmers. On page 42 of a pamphlet entitled *Agriculture in Minnesota*, published by the agricultural experiment station in 1929, is a map showing the distribution of coöperative creameries.

the coöperative movement. It provided that the sum of five hundred million dollars be set aside as a revolving fund to be administered by a federal board, among other purposes for encouraging the organization of producers into coöperative associations and "promoting the establishment and financing of a farm marketing system of producer-owned and producer-controlled coöperative associations." The bill was passed without material change and was approved by the president on June 15.[29]

After Professor Haecker had seen the principles of true rural coöperation launched and fair voyages made by other captains and crews, he relaxed his attention to that subject and devoted his energies to the study of another phase of the dairy industry. He engaged in a series of laboratory investigations into the behavior of Minnesota cows, the cost of maintaining them, and the cost and value of their milk. The results were published in bulletins of the agricultural experiment station and hundreds of thousands of copies were distributed. This laboratory work Haecker continued until his retirement on August 1, 1918.[30]

Various other contributions to the improvement of the dairy industry were made by Haecker. He added to the curriculum of the dairy school a short course, given during the winter months, in improved methods of making butter and cheese. He traveled widely throughout the state, addressing audiences at dairy institutes, immigrant conventions, buttermakers' associations, and county fairs. For a time he was editor of the dairy department of *Farm, Stock and Home*, and in 1892 and 1893 he edited a similar department of the *Annual* published by the Minnesota farmers' institutes. For

[29] *Congressional Record*, 71 Congress, 1 session, 27, 49, 2886–2894, 2978.

[30] *Hoard's Dairyman*, 48: 632, 648 (December 25, 1914); United States Department of Agriculture, *List of Bulletins of the Agricultural Stations in the United States from Their Establishment to the End of 1920*, 76–80 (*Bulletins*, no. 1199 — Washington, 1928); University of Minnesota, Agricultural Experiment Station, *Reports*, 1918–19, p. 16. The bulletin of Haecker's that had the widest popularity was one entitled *Feeding Dairy Cows*, which was reprinted many times. Record of an interview with Haecker, April 1, 1929,

several years he served as secretary of the Minnesota Dairy-man's Association, during which he attended all its sessions, answered queries, and compiled its annual proceedings for publication. He contributed many articles to farmers' pub-lications in Minnesota and other states, in which he constantly advised farmers to select the dairy type of cattle, to adopt accepted feeding standards, and to establish community creameries.[31]

Haecker's services have been given wide recognition. More than twenty years ago the Minnesota Dairyman's Association passed a resolution expressing appreciation of his leadership in the dairy industry and acknowledging the indebtedness of the state to him. In 1923 the University of Wisconsin pre-sented him with a testimonial honoring him as a national leader in the fields of cattle-feeding and coöperative dairy-ing, and two years later the University of Minnesota gave him similar recognition and named its new dairy building Haecker Hall in his honor. A poll conducted in 1929 by a dairy magazine of national circulation placed Haecker and Dr. Clarence H. Eckles, the present chief of the division of dairy husbandry, on a list of ten scientists of world renown who have made outstanding contributions to the dairy in-dustry. Haecker may be hailed as an apostle of agricultural coöperation, not only in Minnesota, but in all America.[32]

HASTINGS H. HART, APOSTLE OF PUBLIC CHARITIES

The restraint and the punishment of criminals have been an immemorial function of the state. The relief of the sick,

Folwell Papers; Agricultural Experiment Station, *Agriculture in Minne-sota*, 43.

[31] Agricultural Experiment Station, *Reports*, 1892, p. 6; 1895, p. ix; 1896, p. xi; *Farm Students' Review*, 1: 40, 57, 184 (March, May, December, 1896); *Hoard's Dairyman*, 28: 283 (May 28, 1897); Thomas Shaw, "Minnesota State Dairy Institute," in Minnesota Farmers' Institutes, *Annuals*, no. 8, pp. 43–48 (Minneapolis, 1895); Hinrichs to the author, April 16, 1929, Folwell Papers.

[32] Minnesota Dairyman's Association, *Proceedings*, 1897, p. 270; *Who's Who in America*, 1928–29; Akers, in the *Farmer*, January 10, 1925, p. 3; *Minneapolis Morning Tribune*, April 15, 1929, p. 6.

of the poor, and of defectives has in all times been the duty and the privilege of the family group, supplemented in Christian countries by the ministrations of the church. In the United States, probably more than in any other Christian land, the excessive divisions of the church have so weakened or dissipated its energies and reduced its efficiency that the state, in one or another of its political units, has been compelled to enter the field of charity. The spread of disease, especially when epidemic, the growing needs of the destitute, the multiplication of persons defective in body or in mind — all magnified by a rapid increase of population, native and immigrant, and a civilization ever more complex — have compelled the states to organize agencies and institutions for the relief and care of dependents and defectives.

Minnesota, following the example of the older states, early established state institutions and agencies for corrections and charities as conditions demanded. The state prison was opened at Stillwater in 1851; up to that year convicts sentenced to imprisonment were confined in county jails. The state reform school for delinquent boys and girls was provided for in 1866. The school for the deaf and dumb at Faribault was opened in 1863 and that for the blind, three years later. To the latter a school for imbeciles was attached in 1879. In the territorial years the care of insane persons who could not be kept in homes seems to have been left to county authorities acting under the poor laws. Insane persons from Minnesota were boarded in hospitals in Iowa and Missouri during the years from 1862 to 1869. In the latter year a state hospital for the insane was opened at St. Peter, replacing the temporary one established there three years earlier, and in 1879 a second one was opened at Rochester.[33] The legislature of 1883, disposed toward liber-

[33] *Laws*, 1851, p. 6; 1866, p. 22; 1879, p. 39; Minnesota Institution for the Deaf and Dumb, *Reports*, 1863, p. 4; Institution for the Deaf, Dumb, and Blind, *Reports*, 1866, p. 9; Minnesota Hospital for Insane, *Reports*, 1867, p. 3; 1868, p. 16; 1869, pp. 5, 22; Board of Control, *Reports*, 1927–28, p. 144.

ality, passed a bill to create a state board of corrections and charities, whose duty it was to " investigate the whole system of public charities and correctional institutions of the state, examine into the condition and management thereof, especially of prisons, jails, infirmaries, public hospitals, and asylums," make biennial reports showing their condition, and offer suggestions for their improvement.[34]

It was obviously intended that the investigations and the collation of the results should be the work of a secretary, whom the board was authorized to appoint. For that position Hastings Hornell Hart, a graduate of Oberlin College, who for the preceding three years had been pastor of a Congregational church in Worthington, Minnesota, was selected. He had made no application for the appointment and it was not until after long consideration that he accepted it. His acceptance was received by the board on July 10, 1883, and he began work soon afterwards. In by-laws adopted by the board on August 7 the secretary was required to study the whole subject of corrections and charities, to devise a system of statistics for institutions, to conduct the correspondence of the board, to record its proceedings, and to make out the biennial report. In his experience as a village pastor Hart had acquired little information in regard to large-scale charities and corrections. He therefore at once set about the investigations imposed upon him. Members of the board were associated with him in many of the visitations.[35]

The results of the survey were given in the first biennial report of the board, that for 1883–84. In the various state institutions much was found to commend. The hospitals for the insane, however, were overcrowded and there was immediate need for a third hospital. The employment of untrained attendants, on duty day and night, sleeping in the

---

[34] *Ante*, 3: 152–159; *General Laws*, 1883, p. 171.
[35] Board of Corrections and Charities, *Reports*, 1883–84, pp. 10, 13; 1897–98, p. 57; Upham and Dunlap, *Minnesota Biographies*, 305.

wards, and receiving the pay of servant girls and farm hands, was sharply condemned. It was recommended that the school for imbeciles, no longer an experiment, be separately housed. The management of the state prison was complimented, but the policy of confining first offenders, many of them between sixteen and twenty-one years of age, with hardened convicts was disapproved of and the introduction of a reformatory policy of some kind was suggested.[36]

When it came to county and municipal institutions and agencies, there was little to be said in commendation. Of twenty-six city and village lockups, but seven were fit for use. Very few of fifty-four jails were in tolerable condition. In general they were foul-smelling prisons, built like the cages of wild beasts, too dark for reading with comfort, and without chairs, tables, bed linen, or provisions for bathing. As a rule the cells were six and a half by eight feet and seven feet high, often containing six prisoners. In not more than twenty were there separate rooms for women. In these jails were confined persons in arrest who were not allowed bail or were unable to obtain it, convicts undergoing punishment, among them boys taking compulsory education in crime, and persons alleged to be insane awaiting action by the probate court. The survey found but one county poorhouse, that of Hennepin County, worthy of full approval. Most of the poorhouses were old farmhouses taken over by the county; the overseer of many of them was the lowest bidder for the place. The chief abuse was the failure to separate the sexes. There was a general lack of sewerage, ventilation, and bath-

[36] *Reports,* 1883–84, pp. 14–16, 19–23, 25. On page 255 is the secretary's description of the reformatory at Elmira, New York. A remarkable address was given by Gordon E. Cole at a meeting in the Capitol on December 22, 1886, called by the board of corrections and charities to consider the question of establishing a reformatory for young delinquents. See *Reports,* 1885–86, pp. 288, 290–310. The author was a member of the state board of corrections and charities from July 2, 1895, to April 2, 1901. On the latter date the duties of that board were transferred to the state board of control, created by the legislature in 1901. *Reports,* 1895–96, p. 58; *General Laws,* 1901, pp. 128–147.

ing facilities. Dirty floors and windows, rusty stoves, and foul and infested bedding were common. On the whole, however, the county poorhouses were better than the county jails. Many years were to pass before there was much improvement in either.[37]

In none of the institutions was an annual inventory of property made and preserved. This fact and another discovered in the survey, that each institution had its own way of classifying accounts, made it impossible to establish an effective comparison of the expenses of the institutions or to trace them from year to year. On February 16, 1886, the secretary laid before the board an outline of a system of uniform accounting for the institutions under its charge. The board approved it and proposed a conference with the state auditor, the public examiner, and the superintendents and stewards of the state institutions. Such a conference was held on March 26 and a committee was appointed to prepare a uniform classification of accounts to be submitted to the trustees of the various state institutions for their approval. On June 22, at a general meeting of the board of corrections and charities, the auditor, the public examiner, and the governing boards of the institutions, called by Governor Hubbard, the plan of classification and accounting that had been matured was submitted and agreed upon. The legislature of 1889, adopting and expanding the principle of this system of accounting, provided for the establishment of a uniform system for all the charitable, correctional, and educational

---

[37] *Reports*, 1883–84, pp. 28, 30, 72, 77–79, 183, 184, 187. The numbers in Minnesota jails in 1885 are given in *Reports*, 1885–86, pp. 93, 97–99. The whole number in jails was 4,291; of these 1,802 were imprisoned in default of paying fines, 13 were detained as witnesses, 76 were vagrants, 164 were insane, 55 were under sixteen years of age, and 224 were between sixteen and twenty-one. The law establishing the board stated that plans for county jail buildings must be submitted to it for approval; this requirement was extended in 1887 to include municipal lockups as well; and in 1895 a law forbade villages and cities to take steps for the purchase or erection of lockups until plans for such buildings were approved by the board. *General Laws*, 1883, p. 171; 1887, p. 144; 1895, p. 645; *Reports*, 1895–96, p. 73.

institutions of the state, including the university and the normal schools.[38]

It is not possible here even to enumerate the activities of the state board of corrections and charities, of which Hart was the guiding spirit for fifteen years. Of the seventy-three recommendations of the board during that time, fifteen were withdrawn; of the remaining fifty-eight, thirty-eight were adopted by the legislatures, three were partially adopted, twelve were pending at the end of the fifteen-year period, and but five were rejected. It was at the instance of the board that the reformatory at St. Cloud was established; that industrial training was introduced into the reform school; that the parole system was introduced into the state prison and a school was established there; and that laws were passed for the regulation of the construction of jails and lockups, for municipal and county outdoor relief, and for the deportation from the state of nonresident insane and paupers. The influence of the board was felt in the codification of the prison laws and in the establishment of the state public school at Owatonna.[39]

For his position Hart was fitted by natural endowment, character, and temperament. His extensive knowledge of the field and his readiness for service in any emergency commanded the confidence of his board and the respect of legislative committees and governors. It was his modest custom to await the unanimous approval of the board before drafting bills and resolutions or issuing instructions to heads of institutions and county commissioners. Numerous addresses and

[38] Reports, 1883–84, p. 27, 45; 1885–86, pp. 17, 39–42; General Laws, 1889, p. 463. An account of the success of the new system of accounts and a classified statement of expenditures by the state correctional and charitable institutions for the biennium ending on July 31, 1888, is given in Reports, 1887–88, pp. 14, 88.

[39] Reports, 1897–98, pp. 7, 41, 56–60. Among the recommendations made by the board was that for the introduction of the so-called "Wisconsin plan" for the care and treatment of the chronic insane, which is described in Reports, 1897–98, pp. 46–51; 1899–1900, p. 12. See also ante, 3: 247, for

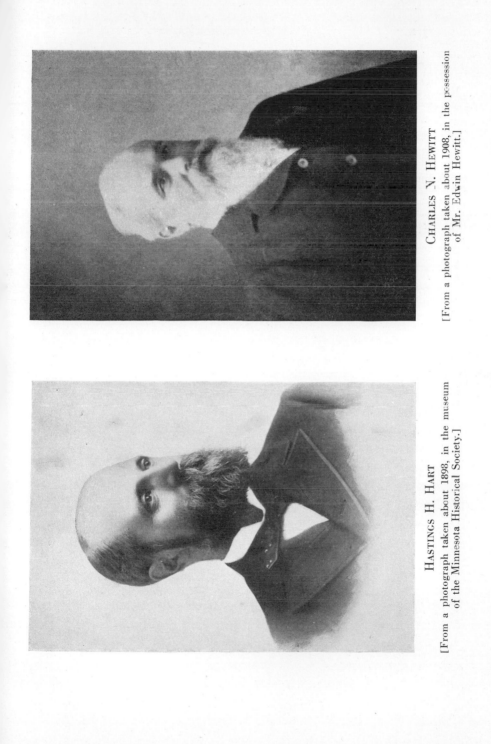

CHARLES N. HEWITT

[From a photograph taken about 1908, in the possession
of Mr. Edwin Hewitt.]

HASTINGS H. HART

[From a photograph taken about 1898, in the museum
of the Minnesota Historical Society.]

newspaper articles, always in excellent taste, gained the confidence and the sympathy of the public. If the correctional and charitable institutions and agencies of Minnesota were advanced into the front rank of those among the states, that was due to Hart's leadership. His resignation, which became effective on March 31, 1898, was accepted by the board with sincere regrets and cordial commendation to his new field. Attached to the Russell Sage Foundation of New York City, he is still employed in the work of social beneficence to which his life has been devoted. Hastings Hornell Hart may be enrolled by unanimous consent as Minnesota's apostle of public charities.[40]

CHARLES N. HEWITT, APOSTLE OF PUBLIC HEALTH

The employment of the supreme power of the state and nation for contending with the greatest of all human enemies, disease of body and mind, is a very modern practice. The care of the sick was formerly wholly the duty of the family and the neighborhood, under the counsel of physicians, who looked upon their patients — the word originally meant " sufferers " — as private clients. The earliest example of extra-home care was, no doubt, the relief and maintenance of the sick poor, always by local agents. The abating of nuisances injurious to health and comfort easily followed, and then quarantine against smallpox and other contagious diseases. The Minnesota Code of 1851 authorized justices of the peace, village trustees, and city councils to exercise these functions. The *General Statutes* of 1866 made town supervisors local boards of health. The recognition of health as a matter of public concern, and of the authority of the state to prevent disease and promote general health was made

Governor Lind's advocacy of the plan and a suggestion of the reason for rejecting it.

[40] *Reports*, 1897–98, pp. 41, 57.

by the legislature of 1872 upon the initiation of Charles Nathaniel Hewitt, M.D.[41]

Dr. Hewitt had come to Minnesota and settled in Red Wing in 1866, with an experience out of the ordinary. After his completion of a college course and graduation at a medical school, he spent four years in general practice in Geneva, New York. During the four years of the Civil War he served an surgeon of a regiment of volunteer engineers that had been raised in his section of the state. Hooker's medical director said of him, " He is the best regimental surgeon in the Army of the Potomac." He was brevetted lieutenant colonel for meritorious services. A happy circumstance enabled him, soon after the close of the war, to take over an extensive professional practice in Red Wing and its vicinity. The standing and income soon acquired would have contented the ordinary practitioner, satisfied with the worthy career of village and country doctor. Dr. Hewitt was not of the ordinary type. He was a student, a thinker, and a dreamer of a larger scope for medical service. His army experience had taught him that there were remedies not carried in his medicine chest and that the prevention of disease by the physician ought to be as important as the cure. On one occasion he stamped out a threatened decimation of the command by requiring the camp to be broken up, the terrain thoroughly cleaned, new drains and sinks dug, and a safe water supply found. Typhoid disappeared as quickly as it had come. Sanitation of the camps became his hobby.[42]

Massachusetts in 1869 took the lead in the creation of state boards of health, and California followed two years later. Minnesota was entering the third decade of its existence, with its population of nearly 450,000 mainly rural,

[41] *Revised Statutes*, 1851, pp. 124–126; *General Statutes*, 1866, p. 145; *General Laws*, 1872, pp. 64–66.
[42] Memorial sketch of Dr. Hewitt by the author, in *Minnesota Historical Collections*, 15: 669–686. The present account was written after a study of original material. The author was graduated at the same college, served in

but Dr. Hewitt thought it none too soon to make a beginning of state ministration to the general health. He prepared for the legislature of 1872 a bill modeled upon the Massachusetts law. The annual appropriation provided was only five hundred dollars and the bill passed with slight opposition. The act created a state board of health of seven physicians and gave it a very large order for so small an allowance. It prescribed these duties for the board: to establish communication with local boards of health and with public institutions; to take cognizance of the health and life of the people generally; to make sanitary investigations as to causes of disease, especially during epidemics; to study the source of mortality and the effects of localities, employments, and circumstances upon public health; to devise a plan of vital statistics; to serve as an advisory board to the state in hygienic and medical matters; to have charge of quarantines; and to establish and enforce measures necessary to the public health. The act authorized the board to elect one of its number executive secretary and fixed his annual salary at two hundred dollars. As was expected, Dr. Hewitt was given the office.[43]

Governor Austin promptly appointed the first board, naming highly reputable physicians selected, it may be assumed, by the leading spirit. The first meeting was held in St. Paul on March 26, 1872. At that time the state assumed the most important welfare duty of preserving and promoting the health of the people, with its supreme power made available for the purpose. In the year mentioned there were a thousand cases of smallpox in Minnesota, with about two hundred and fifty deaths; diphtheria and scarlet fever were also prevalent, especially among children, with fatal results in many communities; and typhoid fever, generally endemic, was often

the same regiment for three and a half years, and was intimate with Hewitt to the end of the doctor's life.

[43] State Board of Health, *Reports*, 1889–90, p. 4; *Senate Journal*, 1872, p. 327; *House Journal*, 649; *General Laws*, 64–66.

epidemic. The obvious duty was to attack these terrible scourges and give counsel in regard to treatment and, above all, prevention. The first need was a means of communication with physicians and local authorities. Until that time town supervisors had been local boards of health, but in 1873 the legislature, as advised, required town boards to elect a town board of health of not less than three members, one of whom was to be a physician.[44]

For the first decade of its activities the state board of health prudently maintained a campaign of education. To have enforced laws and regulations by the usual sanctions of fine and imprisonment would have been resented by people accustomed to believe that nobody could be deprived of liberty and property except by due process of law. To arouse the people at large to a realization of the needless losses they were suffering from premature deaths and of the enormous damage wrought by both curable and preventable sicknesses, and to inform them how these evils might be mitigated, if not banished, was obviously of primary importance. "Circulars of instruction" and tracts on smallpox, typhoid fever, and diphtheria were issued and distributed. Articles on those diseases by members of the board were printed in the annual reports. The versatile secretary not only wrote continually, but he also on many occasions exercised his native gift of ready speech. He talked to children and youths in school, spoke before teachers' institutes, and lectured in colleges, seminaries, and church conferences. "Sanitary councils," so called, held in the larger cities and widely advertised and well attended, did much to arouse public interest and break down prejudice against what some people considered officious meddling with private matters.[45]

[44] Board of Health, *Reports*, 1872, p. 7; 1873, pp. 5–7, 9–11, 63; 1876, pp. 50–53; 1878, pp. 32–46; *General Laws*, 1873, p. 117.
[45] Board of Health, *Reports*, 1874, p. 5; 1875, p. 13; 1876, pp. 7, 69; 1879–80, pp. 51, 100; 1881–82, p. 312. Selections from tracts issued for popular distribution may be found in *Reports*, 1893–94, appendix 4. The

After ten years of exhortation, the state of the public mind seemed to warrant the use of the public authority in curbing contagious diseases and promoting general health. It was the opinion of the state board of health that efficient local boards of health not only prevent the occurrence and the spread of epidemics but that they also reduce the average sick rate by one-fourth and that of deaths by one-fifth. The legislature of 1883 passed an act, prepared for it, " relating to infectious and epidemic diseases." In case of actual or threatened outbreaks of such diseases, the state board was authorized to make " regulations " in regard to house-to-house visitations, medical aid and nursing, quarantine, disinfection, and burial of the dead. It was made the duty not only of physicians but also of every person knowing of a case of contagious disease to report it to the local board of health. All parents and guardians were required to have their children frequently and effectively vaccinated against smallpox. This drastic provision was later construed by law to be in force only in cases of actual epidemic outbreak. The teeth of the act were in the section that made violations of the law and of the " regulations " of the state or local boards of health misdemeanors punishable by fine or imprisonment, or both.[46]

Regulations were issued in the following year for the isolation or quarantine of diphtheria and smallpox patients and, later, of scarlatina and typhoid fever cases, and for the isolation of animals suspected of having rabies. The effect upon diphtheria was the most striking because it was not expected by medical men. In 1882 there were 1,602 reported deaths from that disease in Minnesota; five years later, in 1887,

proceedings and important papers and addresses given at the sanitary council held in St. Paul on February 16 and 17, 1881, are in Reports, 1879-80, pp. 35-63. References to later sanitary conferences appear in Reports, 1881-82, p. 16.

[46] Board of Health, Reports, 1873, p. 9; 1893-94, appendix 4, tract 15; General Laws, 1883, pp. 178-186.

there were 788, a reduction of over one-half; in 1895 the number was 466, a little more than one-fourth the number of deaths reported thirteen years before. In that period the population of Minnesota had doubled. The struggle against smallpox was kept up with vigor. As the law provided for the vaccination of all minor children, it was of supreme importance that the supply of vaccine virus should be of unquestionable purity. To that end Dr. Hewitt established an original vaccine station on a farm near his home at Red Wing. The product was sent free to local boards of health and health officers; sales to others, largely without the state, made the station self-sustaining. In 1890 the doctor spent six weeks of his vacation in London studying the best English practice of vaccination and methods for the prevention of diphtheria.[47]

The protection of communities against the actual ravages of infectious and contagious diseases was but a part, and at length the smaller part, of the activities of the Minnesota state board of health, led by its enthusiastic executive secretary. It was toward the prevention of such diseases and others that the greatest efforts of the board were directed. This task was the harder because of the survival of the ancient pious belief that sicknesses were divine visitations as penalties for sinful conduct or warnings against transgression. It took a long crusade to persuade legislatures to enact laws demanding penalties for and making regulations against food adulteration, pollution of streams, offensive trades, foul slaughterhouses, and underground bakeries.[48]

[47] Board of Health, *Reports*, 1883–84, pp. 183, 234; 1891–92, pp. 41–43, and accompanying tracts on scarlatina, diphtheria, rabies, and typhoid fever; 1893–94, p. 19; 1895–96, p. 10; *St. Paul Pioneer Press*, May 17, 1891, p. 8; *Hastings Gazette*, May 30, 1891, p. 1; *Public Health in Minnesota*, 8: 39 (May and June, 1892). A history of diphtheria in Minnesota by Dr. Franklin Staples, a member of the board, is in *Reports*, 1878, pp. 28–46.
[48] Board of Health, *Reports*, 1872, p. 45; 1884–86, p. 20; Hewitt, "Notes upon Certain Adulterations and Sophistications of Foods," in *Reports*, 1875, pp. 129–137; *General Laws*, 1885, pp. 292, 296; 1889, p. 51; 1895, pp. 484–490. In the order for the visitation of the sick, in the Book of Common Prayer of the Protestant Episcopal Church, sickness is represented as "our heavenly Father's correction," "fatherly visitation," and "God's visitation."

Numerous reports of cases of rabies, the terribly infectious
— never contagious — disease resulting from bites of mad
dogs, aroused the anxiety of Dr. Hewitt to have the state
board of health equipped for the treatment of that disease by
inoculation, already made known to the world by Louis
Pasteur. To be sure of the method, the doctor spent another
six weeks of his European vacation in 1890 in the Pasteur
Institute in Paris, where he met the great man and received
instruction from his assistants. His recommendation that a
Pasteur institute for the observation of cases of suspected
rabies be established in Minnesota was not fulfilled for many
years.[49]

The legislature of 1885 laid upon local boards of health
the duty of isolating and, when necessary, killing domestic
animals attacked by infectious or contagious diseases, and
gave the state board large powers of supervision and the
authority to establish quarantines and to have animals killed
in case the local boards should neglect or refuse their duty.
Later, in 1903, when diseases of domestic animals had increased in number, a state live stock sanitary board was
created and the state board of health was relieved of a heavy
and, at times, disagreeable duty.[50]

The endeavors of the state board of health were not confined to measures to be enforced by law. The board, and in
particular its indefatigable secretary, proposed to enlighten
the whole community by means of circulars, tracts, contributions to the press, and frequent addresses. In these Dr. Hewitt

[49] Board of Health, *Reports*, 1891–92, p. 23, and accompanying tract on
rabies; *Public Health in Minnesota*, 6:18–21, 48–50. From a series of eleven
letters written by Hewitt in Europe between November 23, 1889, and May 7,
1890, and published in *Public Health in Minnesota*, 5: 99–104, 106, 115–
120 (December, 1889–February, 1890); 6: 5–8, 13–16, 18–24 (March–May,
1890), it appears that Hewitt spent the greater part of his leave in public
health investigations. Pasteur's triumph over rabies is discussed in René
Vallery-Radot, *The Life of Pasteur*, 414–417 (New York, 1923). In the
Folwell Papers is a typewritten extract from the diary of Mrs. Charles N.
Hewitt, dated April 13, 1890, which gives an interesting account of her
visit to the Pasteur Institute.

[50] *General Laws*, 1885, pp. 267–270; 1903, pp. 636–643.

was fond of quoting Franklin's motto, "Public health is public wealth." In March, 1885, he began the editing and publishing of a monthly periodical, in octavo form, entitled *Public Health in Minnesota*, which was continued until 1893. Copies were sent free to local boards of health and township clerks. The circulation reached thirty-seven hundred in 1890. Through these means he dwelt incessantly upon the importance of the ventilation of dwellings and schoolhouses and the use of sanitary closets, such as dry earth closets, for human excrements and of pure water for cooking and drinking. Hundreds of analyses of well waters from different parts of the state made by Dr. Hewitt personally disclosed numerous waters to be unfit for use. Many cities and villages were constrained to erect waterworks.[51]

Following the enactment of the law of 1869 creating a bureau of statistics in the office of the secretary of state, town and county clerks reported annually to the commissioner of statistics the births and deaths registered by them. Although liberal fees were provided, the service was carelessly performed and the consolidated returns published by the commissioner were of little concern to any except the curious people who feast on statistics. It was obvious that a registration faithfully kept and intelligently interpreted would form a health history of the people and would add to the knowledge of means for preventing sickness and premature death. It was not until 1887 that the legislature was pleased to trans-

[51] Board of Health, *Reports*, 1889–90, p. 11; Hewitt, "Water: Its Composition, Sources, Impurities, and the Methods of Collecting, Preserving, and Purifying It for Drinking and Domestic Use," and D. W. Hand, "Ventilation: Its Principles and Practice as Applied to Domestic Use," in *Reports*, 1875, pp. 25–39, 41–54; Hewitt, "The Principles Involved in the Heating and Ventilation of Existing Common School Houses and Suggestions for Their Practical Application," in *Reports*, 1876, pp. 31–43. On earth closets see *Reports*, 1883–84, p. 401, and *Public Health in Minnesota*, 1: 55–57; 4: 40–42. Sanitary water surveys and analyses of waters of the state appear in many of the *Reports* and in numerous issues of *Public Health*. There was some irregularity in the issues of *Public Health*, of which there were ninety-four in all. The successive numbers were appended to the *Reports* from 1884 to 1893.

fer the duty of collecting registration returns, which were to be furnished month by month, to the secretary of the state board of health. The first report was made by him on September 1, 1888, and the series thus begun and improved upon from time to time has given Minnesota a high place in the registration area of the country.[52]

The devoted secretary entertained still other ideas in regard to public health that he was obliged to leave as projects to be carried out, if at all, after his time. After many years a Pasteur institute for treatment for rabies and a hospital for inebriates were established. His schemes for township nurses and for systematic physical examination of school children have not yet been realized.[53]

In 1874 Dr. Hewitt was elected non-resident professor of public health at the University of Minnesota, probably the first appointment of the kind in the country. During that year and for twenty-seven years thereafter, he gave a course of lectures on public health. They varied in scope from year to year, but the program for 1877, under the title, " Some of the Problems of Our Civilization in the View of Hygiene," may serve as an example. The lectures were given under the following titles: " Health and Hygiene, Public and Private "; " Disease; Causes and Prevention "; " Poverty and Pauperism "; " To Young Men "; Hygiene and Education ";

[52] *Ante*, 3: 18–20; General Laws, 1869, p. 110; 1887, pp. 197–199; Board of Health, *Reports*, 1872, pp. 8, 46; 1873, pp. 11–14; report on vital statistics, 1886–88, accompanying *Reports*, 1886–88.

[53] Board of Health, *Reports*, 1873, p. 16; 1891–92, p. 10. In *Reports*, 1873, pp. 19–48, is a report on inebriate asylums in Massachusetts, New York, and Illinois, made by Dr. Hewitt in accordance with an order from Governor Austin, and on pages 49–62 is a report by Dr. Hewitt on statistics of drunkenness in Minnesota for 1873, with wise counsel for the use of moderation in dealing with the immemorial evil. Under the title, "The Relations of Scholastic Methods to the Health of Pupils in the Public Schools," in *Reports*, 1877, pp. 69–108, is a summary by Dr. Hewitt of the results of an extensive inquiry by questionnaire. Varying opinions about coeducation are given. Under the same title, in *Reports*, 1878, pp. 115–119, a plan is given for taking physical measurements of school children and youths. The Pasteur institute, which was established in 1907, was discontinued in 1921. The hospital farm for inebriates was also established in 1907. Board of Health, *Reports*, 1907–08; *General Laws*, 1907, pp. 387–392.

" Crime and Criminals "; " The Family and the Home "; and "Success in Life." Early in his service he conceived the idea of obtaining a physical history of all the students of the university. Upon his suggestion the regents in 1877 ordered that a physical examination of every student be made upon his matriculation and that reëxaminations be made from year to year during his attendance. He made a brave beginning in the fall of 1877 and continued making tests and measurements in person for four years, until multiplying engagements obliged him to give them up. It was the doctor's hope, or dream, that a department or school of public health might at length be developed in the university for the training of health officers and instructors in hygiene. He therefore declined a professorship of hygiene and sanitation in the department of medicine when it was organized for instruction in 1888.[54]

Dr. Hewitt rendered another, and an exceptional, service to the university and to the medical profession. The first president of the university was committed to a policy of delaying the opening of professional schools until they could be established as something more than low-grade institutions demanding no other scholastic preparation than that of the common schools. Sympathizing with this policy, Dr. Hewitt drew up a plan for the organization of a college of medicine and surgery, the faculty to act, not as a teaching body, but as an examining board. It was laid before the regents on June 29, 1882, and was favorably entertained and referred to a committee. The president of the university, as a member of the committee, reduced the scheme to statutory form. It was adopted on January 5, 1883, and a faculty of five professors was elected. As was expected, the legislature of 1883 passed an act requiring all practitioners of medicine

[54] Board of Health, *Reports*, 1874, p. 5; 1877, pp. 9, 71; 1878, pp. 116–125; 1879–80, pp. 157–163; Board of Regents, Minutes, B 1: 311, 316, 322. The program of instruction in public health in a later year is given in Board of Health, *Reports*, 1893–94, p. 19.

and surgery to be licensed by the faculty of the college, graduates in medicine upon presentation of their diplomas and others when found satisfactory after examination by the faculty. The physicians and surgeons of the state willingly conformed to a rule intended to suppress quacks and pretenders. A series of examinations to test the qualifications of any who might be in practice without diplomas was planned; but few of these, however, and only those who had studied seriously under preceptors, were examined and licensed. As a member of the faculty for five years Dr. Hewitt took his full share of the duties. The organization was superseded in 1888 when three medical colleges of St. Paul and Minneapolis disbanded and their faculties merged into the department of medicine of the University of Minnesota, which, because of the foundation laid, was able to base its curricula on a higher plane than had generally existed.[55]

During his long years of service, contending with general ignorance, professional indifference, and legislative parsimony, the doctor's labors were not without appreciation. His handling of epidemics compelled professional admiration and public approval. His writings made him widely known at home and, at length, abroad. He aided in organizing the American Public Health Association and became its president. He was made a foreign associate of the Society of Medical Officers of Health of England and of the Société d'Hygiène of France. His college conferred upon him the degree of doctor of laws. After conducting for twenty-five years the public health service of the state, which he had created, Dr. Hewitt began a new year expecting to be continued in office as usual. On January 11, 1897, he learned that his term of service had expired and that he had not been reappointed.

[55] Board of Regents, Minutes, B 1: 243–254; Johnson, *University of Minnesota*, 153–158; *General Laws*, 1883, pp. 167–169; Richard O. Beard, "A History of the Medical School," in the *Minnesota Alumni Weekly*, May 5, 1921, p. 4; Beard to the author, September 13, 1927, Folwell Papers.

The reasons for this sudden decapitation without warning, as if for some misbehavior or notorious incompetency, remain unknown. A physician of high standing and a professor in the university college of medicine became executive secretary and maintained for many years the established efficiency and repute of the service. Dr. Hewitt resumed his private practice in Red Wing and for several years continued it for old clients. He died on July 7, 1910. Had he been content to remain in private practice and use his natural and acquired gifts for surgery, he would in the ordinary course of things have enjoyed an ample income and have laid by a considerable fortune. For many years he was content to accept an honorarium ridiculously small so that he might carry on the great work he had at heart. Charles Nathaniel Hewitt is hereby written down as Minnesota's apostle of public health.[56]

In his message to the legislature of 1899 Governor David M. Clough was pleased to record his appreciation of the labors of the Minnesota state board of health. After stating that great progress had been made during the previous twenty-five years in the prevention of disease, he added: " In that work the Minnesota Board of Health has been a most important agent, the labor of but one other similar board in the nation — that of Massachusetts — taking precedence in the respect which it has won in the medical world in the United States and in Europe. . . . The broad scientific work of the Minnesota board and its wise administration in the past are

[56] *Reports*, 1895–96, p. 14. He wrote: " The best of my life and effort have gone into this work. I have spared neither time, labor, nor thought to make it what it ought to be. Such as it is, the record is made and closed." His first year's salary was two hundred dollars, and for the following eight years he was content with five hundred dollars. For the next two years he received a thousand dollars a year, and for one year, fifteen hundred dollars. Beginning with the fiscal year ending on July 31, 1886, he received twenty-five hundred dollars a year, and in 1893 his salary was raised to thirty-five hundred dollars. See the financial statements accompanying the *Reports*. A probable explanation for the discontinuance of Dr. Hewitt in office is given in a letter from Mrs. Charles N. Hewitt to the author, September 19, 1927, in the Folwell Papers. In his unpublished report for 1921, a typewritten copy of which is in the Folwell Papers, Dr. Albert J. Chesley makes complimentary references to Dr. Hewitt and his work.

ground for belief that a continuance of such administration will keep Minnesota where it now is, at the front in this most beneficent work for human well-being." [57]

CHARLES M. LORING, APOSTLE OF PARKS AND PLAYGROUNDS

The day on which Charles Morgridge Loring arrived in Minneapolis to take up his residence was a fortunate one for that city. He was born in Portland, Maine, on November 13, 1833, the son of a shipmaster trading in the West Indies. After he had finished school he made some voyages in his father's vessels; but he did not like the life and resolved to try his fortune in the then remote West. For four years he was employed in a wholesale house in Chicago. Advised that the climate of Minnesota might improve his health, which was none too robust, in 1860 he went on to Minneapolis, then a town of 2,564 inhabitants and an annex to the city of St. Anthony, which boasted a population of 3,258. He entered at once upon a career of merchandising, followed by milling and operations in real estate. Many prosperous years ensued, during which Loring and his associates built up fortunes considerable for the day. [58]

In those days, from 1860 to 1880, the people of Minneapolis were inflamed with an ambition to have their town at the falls, with its great water power, become the equal, if not the superior, in numbers and wealth of the capital city at the head of navigation of the great river. There was a group of citizens who consulted together over plans for attracting population, diversifying the industries, and expanding the trade of the town. In this group Loring was eminent. He was by nature public-spirited; none was more willing to give

[57] Clough, *Message*, 1899, p. 32.
[58] Upham and Dunlap, *Minnesota Biographies*, 450; Shutter and McLain, *Progressive Men of Minnesota*, 46; *United States Census*, 1860, *Population*, 257.

of his time and means for the good of Minneapolis. Such were his manners, gracious but not condescending, so modest was he in proposing measures, and so level-headed in counsel, that no other citizen was more frequently called upon for unpaid, nonpolitical service. It was not his nature to be wholly absorbed in private affairs. He might have said of himself, in the words of Walt Whitman, " I am one of the citizens; whatever interests the rest interests me." At some time or other, with some overlapping, he was a member of the board of trade, of the city council, of a civic improvement association, of the courthouse commission, and of a free dispensary board, and a trustee of Lakewood Cemetery, of the Washburn Home for orphans, and of the Universalist church. He was a member of the Minnesota State Forestry Association and a life member of the Minnesota State Horticultural Society and of the Minnesota Historical Society. These activities must be passed without further remark to give room for another series that gave him and his city a wider repute than all the rest.[59]

In the fourth year of his residence in Minneapolis, 1864, Loring persuaded the owner of a small triangular duck pond a fraction of an acre in area, now included in the Gateway park, to give it to the town and he persuaded the town trustees to build a fence around it. Then began a campaign of much-needed education. The Minneapolis people believed that the picturesque forest and prairie just outside the town limits was all the park they would ever need. In 1864 the town supervisors, who had been instructed to buy a twenty-acre tract for $6,000 for a park, neglected to make the purchase. In 1865 a committee appointed at a special town meeting refused to buy a tract of forty acres for $8,500. In 1866 a majority of citizens at a special election voted down a proposi-

[59] Horace B. Hudson, ed., A Half Century of Minneapolis, 185, 346 (Minneapolis, 1908) ; Minneapolis Sunday Tribune, March 19, 1922, section 1, p. 3.

tion to buy Nicollet Island, some forty acres in area, which was offered at $47,500. In 1869 an offer of forty acres for $25,000 was declined. In 1872 William S. King made an offer of two hundred and fifty acres around Lake Harriet for $50,000, which was refused. It was suggested that he wanted to unload his farm property on the city. These properties have since become worth many millions.[60]

Indifference and opposition were not, however, to continue indefinitely. In 1880 the population of the city, which in 1875 had been 32,721, was 46,887, and by 1885 it had increased to 129,200. With this increase in numbers there was an access of pride and hope. A new Minneapolis spirit appeared. In 1880 a small appropriation was made for the improvement of a block of land in south Minneapolis that had been given to the town in 1857 and had remained a common cow pasture. Loring personally attended to laying out some walks and planting trees on it. Still there was opposition to taxation for city ornamentation, when the burden for indispensable improvements was heavy. It was not until January 29, 1883, that the board of trade was tardily induced to entertain the subject of parks. On that date a resolution was adopted in favor of obtaining legislation authorizing the creation of a board of park commissioners. In spite of opposition by the city council, the Hennepin County delegation in the state legislature secured the passage of a bill drafted by the Minneapolis Board of Trade with a rider that, as it required a referendum to the electors, was probably expected to defeat the bill. There was lively opposition, especially by the Knights of Labor, who protested against the extravagance; but the act was ratified by a vote of 5,327 to 3,922. The board of commissioners thus created was given liberal powers by the act, and a later amendment

[60] Minnesota State Horticultural Society, *Trees, Fruits, and Flowers of Minnesota*, 1902, p. 2; Charles M. Loring, "History of the Parks and Public Grounds of Minneapolis," in *Minnesota Historical Collections*, 15: 600; *Minneapolis Journal*, December 9, 1906, section 1, p. 5.

authorized it to acquire lands by purchase or condemnation, to borrow money on its bonds for payments, and to assess the property benefited for the cost of the several tracts. The board was also given the control of the planting and care of shade trees on streets.[61]

When the commissioners named in the act met for organization on March 14, 1883, they made Loring their president, which office he held until the close of 1890. It is no disparagement of Loring's excellent associates to say that they willingly allowed him to take the lead and hold it. For years he might have been seen any day during the working season in the field in consultation with the landscape artist or directing the superintendent. During that period the wise policy was adopted of acquiring by purchase or gift, of which there were admirable examples, lands suitable for park purposes and little else. The result was a splendid outline plan, to be developed later, which included features that have won the Minneapolis park system wide fame and praise. There was a scheme for neighborhood parks that would be accessible from the homes of many; one of these, called Central Park, reclaimed from a duck pond and a marsh, was later named Loring Park. The Ole Bull statue by Jacob Fjelde is one of its ornaments. Among the greater projects were the preservation of the shores of Lakes Harriet and Calhoun and of the Lake of the Isles and Cedar Lake from desecration by the building of encircling parkways; the building of Kenwood Parkway from Loring Park to the Lake of the Isles over commanding heights; the construction of Minnehaha Parkway following the creek of that name for five miles to Minnehaha Falls; and the acquisition of more than

[61] Secretary of State, *Reports*, 1875, p. 71; 1885, appendix A, p. 26; *United States Census*, 1880, *Population*, 226; Loring, in *Minnesota Historical Collections*, 15: 599, 601, 602; *Special Laws*, 1883, pp. 404–413; 1889, pp. 560–574; *Daily Minnesota Tribune* (St. Paul and Minneapolis), 1883: March 31, p. 6; April 1, p. 4; 4, p. 4. The *Tribune* for February 8, 1883, p. 6, reports the unanimous adoption by the Minneapolis city council of a resolution denouncing the park project, with the reasons given by the council.

a hundred acres about those falls and of the wooded banks of the Mississippi for many miles.[62]

If a poll could have been taken in 1890 on the question as to what citizen of Minneapolis was best qualified in all respects for the duties of a park commissioner, the tally would have shown few or no votes in opposition to Loring. He was nominated for reëlection, but a local Democratic landslide deprived the city of his official services for two years. He was returned to the board in 1892 and was immediately elected its president. At the close of that year he was constrained to resign both his presidency and his membership because he was interested in certain property proposed to be taken for park purposes. By this time the park system had been substantially blocked out, large portions of desirable property had been acquired, and improvements had been advanced. A settled public sentiment gave the park policy its approval and a considerable number of citizens had learned how to employ talent for design and business ability for superintendence. His willing services in all these years had earned for Loring the title he had been accorded, " father of the park system of Minneapolis." [63]

[62] Minneapolis Board of Park Commissioners, Record, A: 2 (March 14, 1883). The manuscript record of the board is in a series of bound volumes in its office. Loring was elected president by unanimous vote, on motion of John S. Pillsbury. The selection, virtually by Loring, of Horace W. S. Cleveland, landscape architect, and of William M. Berry as superintendent of parks was a valuable service. Both understood the importance of establishing a new system, which would make the most of natural features — terrain, contours, waters, groves of trees, and even swamps. See Board of Park Commissioners, Reports, 1884, p. 5; 1886, p. 10; and Horace W. S. Cleveland, Suggestions for a System of Parks and Parkways for the City of Minneapolis (Minneapolis, 1883). Central Park was renamed Loring Park on motion of the author, who was a member of the board of park commissioners from 1889 to 1906, inclusive. Record, B: 140 (December 20, 1890).

[63] Board of Park Commissioners, Proceedings, 1893, pp. 1, 5, 89, 91; 1894, pp. 6, 12, 96; Sunday Tribune (Minneapolis), November 9, 1890, p. 2. Expressions of regret over Loring's failure of reëlection in 1890 appear in the Tribune, November 11, 1890, p. 5; the Minneapolis Journal, December 26, 1890, p. 4; and the Minneapolis Times, November 9, 1890, p. 4. The Tribune, January 31, 1891, p. 5, said: " The travesty of an election held on November 2 last lost to the city of Minneapolis one of its best public servants. Though Mr. Loring ran about 3,000 votes ahead of his ticket, the landslide of the Democracy carried him down with the remainder of the candidates nominated

Those labors, however, were but the beginning of a life-long crusade. In the years following his retirement from office, Loring renewed a previous effort to arouse public sentiment in other cities and villages of the state in favor of parks and civic improvement. Provided with apparatus for illustration, he gave lectures in St. Paul, Duluth, Rochester, Little Falls, Glencoe, Windom, Fergus Falls, Red Wing, Northfield, and other places, which were everywhere appreciated and praised. The talks were not merely entertaining gossip about city glorification, but were full of practical suggestions in regard to the selection and acquisition of lands; he often recommended for park purposes such lands as were unfit for cultivation and advised that only necessary improvements be made at first, and embellishments be left until later. Instruction, based upon long experience, was given in the selection of trees and shrubs and in their planting and care. For these lectures Loring neither asked nor accepted compensation. If the cities named and others in the state are now provided with attractive parks and playgrounds, as many of them certainly are, they have to thank Loring for having given them their start.[64]

Throughout his adult life Loring was a frequent contributor to newspapers. Aside from letters of travel, his contributions related chiefly to civic affairs, to parks and playgrounds, to street construction, to building lines, and to tree-planting. He often denounced the billboard nuisance and the nailing of posters on street trees.[65]

Loring's influence was not confined to Minneapolis nor to Minnesota. Visitors from other states who had heard of

on the Republican ticket." The origin of the park system and its development to 1892 are described in Albert J. Boardman, "Minneapolis Parks," in Board of Park Commissioners, *Reports*, 1892, pp. 33–47. An appreciation of the services of the early officials of the board is given in *Reports*, 1912, pp. 30–32.

[64] Scrapbooks kept by Loring, which are now in the possession of his grandson, Harold R. Ward of Minneapolis, abound in accounts of the lectures.

[65] In his scrapbooks are many clippings of Loring's newspaper contributions, which unfortunately are without dates and proper citations of papers.

the Minneapolis park system sought his counsel, which was always gladly given. For several years he was a member of the American Park and Outdoor Art Association and in 1899 and 1900 he was its president. His reports and addresses and his interviews with delegates from many parts of the country contributed greatly to the objects of that body.[66]

A separate chapter would be needed to relate Loring's activities in another state. In the early eighties a threatening infirmity sent him for a winter to Riverside, California, which was then a small town in the orange district, and continuing ill health caused him to spend his winters there until the last three years of his life. He bought some property in Riverside and at once took a leading part in a movement for village improvement, especially in the planting of shrubs and trees. He undertook the planting of pepper trees along the entire length of Walnut Street, and on a piece of land on Little Rubidoux Mountain he planted rare shrubs from many parts of the world. In 1906 Loring entered heartily into the enterprise of converting the larger Mount Rubidoux into a scenic park. He had the mountain made a bird sanctuary, one of the first in the country, and had erected, perhaps at his own expense, the St. Francis Shrine, a fountain for birds and animals. He planted, or caused to be planted, some seventy-five thousand trees around the base of the mountain. During the World War Loring supplied funds for planting trees along the road from Riverside to the government aviation field ten miles out in the country. On April 18, 1923, a tablet set in one of the great granite rocks of Mount Rubidoux was unveiled, showing the inscription, " In Honor of Charles M. Loring, Tree Lover and Civic Enthusiast." April 18 is recognized in Riverside as Loring Day, and memorial exercises are held at Loring Rock on Mount Rubidoux.[67]

[66] *Minneapolis Tribune,* 1898: June 24, p. 2; 25, p. 11; 1899: July 7, p. 7; *Minneapolis Journal,* 1898: June 24, p. 6.

[67] This summary of Loring's work in California is founded chiefly on a sketch accompanying a letter from DeWitt V. Hutchings to the author,

Loring's service as park commissioner in Minneapolis did not end with his resignation in 1893. After the lapse of a decade he was elected by the board to fill a vacancy in its membership. For three years ending with 1906 he took his full share of committee drudgery. In the last year he erected at his own expense the warming house for skaters in Loring Park. Years passed and the infirmities of age crept gradually on, but Loring's interest in the parks never abated. With the permission of the board he erected in 1917, at the expense of many thousands of dollars, the well-known artificial cascade in Glenwood Park, forty feet in height, one of the most notable and attractive embellishments of the park system.[68]

The idea of a monument to those Minnesotans who had laid down their lives in the World War was shared by many. It was characteristic of Loring to think of a scheme of planting on public grounds memorial trees that should be perpetually cared for and replaced. It was his idea that the trees should be planted at suitable places along the " Grand Rounds " of the park system. On February 5, 1919, he notified the park board that, if it would designate the Grand Rounds as a memorial drive, he would place in trust a sum of money sufficient to yield an interest of twenty-five hundred dollars a

January 24, 1929, in the Folwell Papers. A biographical sketch of Loring in the *Minneapolis Sunday Tribune*, March 19, 1922, section 1, p. 3, also contains some information concerning his benefactions to Riverside. Frank A. Miller, proprietor of the Glenwood Mission Inn, of world-wide reputation, and Henry E. Huntington joined in securing the property and building the scenic road on Mount Rubidoux and expanding the park. For the erection of the St. Francis Shrine, Loring secured the services of Francois Scotti, whom he afterwards employed to design and construct the cascade in Glenwood Park in Minneapolis. See the *Minneapolis Morning Tribune*, August 3, 1918, p. 10. Riverside is indebted also to Mrs. Loring for generous gifts to various institutions in the city.

[68] Board of Park Commissioners, *Proceedings*, 1904, p. 6; *Reports*, 1917, p. 18; 1918, p. 36; *Minneapolis Morning Tribune*, August 3, 1918, p. 10. See *Proceedings*, 1906, p. 97, for the adoption of a resolution of appreciation of Loring's services moved by the author, and the *Minneapolis Tribune*, 1906: December 4, p. 5; December 6, p. 4; the *Minneapolis Journal*, 1906: December 9, section 1, p. 5; and the *Daily Pioneer Press*, 1906: December 4, p. 4, for notices of his retirement and recognition of his work on the park board.

year for the perpetual care of trees planted by the roadside. It was suggested by Theodore Wirth, superintendent of the board of park commissioners, that a portion of the Grand Rounds treated in a formal manner and on a large scale would be a more suitable and imposing monument than a longer drive bordered by scattered trees or groups of trees. Loring willingly fell in with this proposal, which was agreed to by the park commissioners, and a portion of the Grand Rounds eight and a half miles in length in the northwest quarter of the city, where settlement was still sparse, was designated by the board as a memorial drive and the northernmost three and a half miles were selected for elaborate and formal treatment.[69]

In its northern course the drive is 330 feet wide and in its eastern, 200 feet. There are roadways and promenades along the entire length. On the margins of the planting spaces are American elms planted one hundred feet apart, all the gift of Loring. Close by each of 568 trees is a marker in bronze bearing the name and notation of service of a soldier, sailor, marine, or nurse from Hennepin County who died in the World War. At the square turn at Forty-fifth Street stands a replica of the Saint-Gaudens statue of Abraham Lincoln without the chair. On June 11, 1921, the Victory Memorial Drive was dedicated. There was a procession of soldiers of the World War, a few survivors of the Civil War, the mayor and aldermen, the park commissioners, and delegations from many societies and orders. A veteran officer

[69] Board of Park Commissioners, *Proceedings*, 1919, pp. 10, 30, 42, 281; *Reports*, 1919, pp. 23, 79, map. The name " Grand Rounds " for a proposed encircling parkway connecting the larger and principal parks was suggested in a report of a committee on park development, of which the author was chairman, submitted to the board on March 14, 1891. Various portions of the Grand Rounds without formal designation have been constructed, in all some forty-five miles, until at the present time but a short stretch in the southeast quarter of the city remains to be added. See Board of Park Commissioners, *Reports*, 1890, pp. 22–28; 1921, pp. 12, 71. The title "Victory Memorial Drive" has been restricted to the portion of the Grand Rounds that is formally planted. Wirth to the author, December 17, 1928, Folwell Papers.

of the Civil War gave the stirring and appropriate dedicatory address.[70]

Loring paid to a reliable trust company the sum of fifty thousand dollars in fulfillment of his promise and as a last token of devotion to the welfare and embellishment of his beloved city. He died on March 18, 1922.[71] Honors then to Charles Morgridge Loring as Minnesota's apostle of parks and playgrounds for health and beauty.

EDWARD D. NEILL, APOSTLE OF EDUCATION

On April 23, 1849, a young Presbyterian minister, the Reverend Edward Duffield Neill, who was to become one of the most enterprising citizens of St. Paul and a prominent figure in the territory and the state, arrived in the capital city. He had had a college and theological education, had married, and for a year or more had been a missionary near Galena, Illinois. His primary duty of gathering together a congregation and erecting a building for it did not prevent him from participating in community affairs, especially in those pertaining to education. Toward the end of the year he was appointed a school trustee, before the town was subdivided

[70] Descriptions of the Victory Memorial Drive and accounts of its dedication are in the *Minneapolis Sunday Tribune*, 1921: March 6, section 1, p. 8; June 12, section 2, p. 1; the *Minneapolis Journal*, 1921: June 11, p. 1; June 12, section 1, p. 1; and Board of Park Commissioners, *Reports*, 1919, p. 23. A list of the names on the bronze markers is in the Folwell Papers. The Honorable Ell Torrance gave the dedicatory address. Loring said of the memorial, "These trees will be fresh memorials as each year new life and buds and leaves appear — a living monument and true type of immortality." He was not well enough to participate in the dedication. Early in the day, however, he rode over the drive with the author. On November 26, 1921, Marshal Ferdinand Foch of France, after passing over the drive, wrote, "I am very happy to visit this memorial which, in its conception and its execution, I consider magnificent." *Reports*, 1921, p. 95.

[71] Board of Park Commissioners, *Reports*, 1919, p. 12. Obituary notices reciting Loring's numerous services to his city, state, and country, were published in the *Minneapolis Sunday Tribune*, March 19, 1922, section 1, pp. 1, 3; and the *Minneapolis Journal*, March 19, 1922, section 1, pp. 1, 13. The *Northwestern Miller*, 129: 1258 (March 22, 1922), said: "In the instance of Charles M. Loring . . . is afforded the very exceptional case of a miller who turned away from the pursuit of wealth and the exactions of business, while yet in the very prime of life . . . to follow the ideals which inspired his soul."

EDWARD D. NEILL

[From a photograph taken about 1890, in the museum of the Minnesota Historical Society.]

CHARLES M. LORING

[From a photograph taken about 1903, in the museum of the Minnesota Historical Society.]

into districts. At an election on September 2, 1850, he was made a trustee of school district number 2, with Joseph R. Brown for a colleague. When the board of education of St. Paul was organized in 1856, Neill became its secretary and superintendent of schools ex officio. In a chapter on territorial officers in the Code of 1851 provision was made for a territorial superintendent of schools. Governor Ramsey appointed Neill, who held the office for nearly two years and then turned to another quarter of the educational field.[72]

It was the general belief of the times that the public had no concern about schooling above that of the common primary school. Boys to be " educated " were sent to church academies and colleges and girls to " female seminaries," also under church nurture. Neill had no difficulty in obtaining from the legislature of 1853 a charter of incorporation for the Baldwin School and in persuading Governor Ramsey, William R. Marshall, and half a dozen other enterprising citizens to become its board of trustees. The name was given in compliment to Matthias W. Baldwin of Philadelphia, head of the already large locomotive works of that city, who had given some money for the school and was expected to give more. It was opened in 1853 with Neill as president. The beginning was promising, but it was too early in the history of St. Paul for a school supported by tuition receipts to prosper. After a precarious existence of some years it was closed.[73]

It was the expectation of its founder that the Baldwin School would be preparatory to a college, and in the boom

[72]Autobiography of Neill, in his *Historical Notes of the Ancestry and Descendants of Henry Neill, M.D.*, 15–17 (n. p., 1886); J. Fletcher Williams, *A History of the City of Saint Paul and of the County of Ramsey, Minnesota*, 212, 245, 278, 362, 463, 465 (*Minnesota Historical Collections*, vol. 4 — St. Paul, 1876); obituary sketch in *Minnesota Historical Collections*, 8: 497–501; *Revised Statutes*, 1851, p. 42.

[73] Minnesota Territory, *Laws*, 1853, pp. 44–46; Neill, *Descendants of Henry Neill*, 16; Williams, *Saint Paul*, 347; Neill, *Thoughts on the American College; Also Brief History of Macalester College*, 12 (St. Paul, 1885). This pamphlet will be cited hereafter as Neill, *Macalester College*. There is a sketch of Baldwin in *Dictionary of American Biography*, 1: 541 (New York, 1928).

year of 1855 the College of St. Paul was created under the general territorial incorporation law. The trustees of the school were also among the trustees of the college. Neill, of course, became president of the college. The people of St. Paul, who numbered but 4,716 in 1855, had other things nearer at heart than endowing colleges. Presbyterians were not numerous and those of the old school did not warm to the enterprise of a new-school minister. The small sum subscribed was spent on a college building. The College of St. Paul dropped out of sight in the ruin wrought by the panic of 1857.[74]

Neill was not to wait long for another engagement in the educational field. The University of Minnesota had been chartered by the legislature of 1851 and had been promised by Congress an endowment of two townships of public land, 46,080 acres. The first board of regents elected by the legislature had fathered a private preparatory school in a small wooden building built by subscription. If it had been kept up, it might have become the basement story of the institution. In the general speculative frenzy of 1855 the regents abandoned the school and resolved to have a college on another site. They got leave from the legislature of 1856 to borrow fifteen thousand dollars at interest not to exceed twelve per cent. For security, they mortgaged a " campus " that they had bought mostly on credit. The amount was sufficient to erect all the buildings that would be needed for many years. The infatuated regents, probably expecting to raise money by sales of stumpage on lands that had not actually been donated but only reserved, let a contract for the erection of a wing of a great stone building to cost $49,600. Contractors and builders were content to take the

[74] Williams, *Saint Paul*, 212, n.; *Laws*, 1856, p. 94; Neill, *Descendants of Henry Neill*, 16; Neill, *Early Days of the Presbyterian Church in Minnesota; the Substance of a Discourse Delivered before the Synod of Minnesota, September 26, 1873*, xxii, n. (n. p., n. d.); Henry D. Funk, *A History of Macalester College; Its Origin, Struggle and Growth*, 31–35 (n. p., 1910); *Weekly Minnesotian* (St. Paul), August 8, 1855; *Daily Minnesota Pioneer* (St. Paul), August 10, 1855.

regents' notes, doubtless in expectation of legislative relief.
With no money for such a purpose in the treasury, the in-
dulgent legislature of 1858 authorized the regents to sell
their bonds to the amount of forty thousand dollars on such
terms as they could obtain. The scandalous history of the
university debt cannot be followed here. But the regents
had a building, ample and imposing for the time, and they
desired very much to have it put into use. Where could they
find a man better qualified to advise and manage than the
capable, versatile, and popular educator, Neill, commended
to them by Senator Henry M. Rice? They elected him
chancellor of the university, a title to his taste.[75]

After his experience in starting schools, the chancellor was
in no haste about opening a preparatory department, and to
undertake college work was, of course, impossible. His
office became a sinecure. He prepared a bill, however, for
the reorganization of the university, which was passed by
the legislature of 1860. Its object was to provide for the
government and regulation of the institution, which had been
converted into a state university to be the beneficiary of the
doubled land grant ingeniously inserted in the enabling act.
The act provided for a board of regents to consist of the
governor, the lieutenant governor, the chancellor, and five
electors of the state to be appointed by the governor, with the
advice and consent of the Senate. The chancellor was to be
elected by the board of regents for the same term as that of
a judge of the district court, which was then seven years,
and his compensation was to be designated by the legislature.

[75] Johnson, *University of Minnesota*, 17–25; Neill, *Descendants of Henry
Neill*, 17; *Laws*, 1851, pp. 9–12; 1856, p. 173; 1858, p. 287; reports of the
board of regents, in *Council Journal*, 1855, appendix, 16–19; 1856, appendix,
16; Board of Regents, *Reports*, 1861, p. 18; Superintendent of Public Instruction, *Reports*, 1860, p. 15. See *Laws*, 1851, p. 41, for a memorial to
Congress for a grant of land and *House Journal*, 1851, pp. 69–71, for a House
report recommending the passage of the incorporation bill. It may be
surmised that Neill wrote both the report and the bill. In a letter of
November 12, 1858, Isaac Atwater urged Neill to accept the chancellorship
of the university and emphasized the necessity of arousing the public to a
realization of the need for a university. Neill Papers.

The last provision indicates an expectation that the chancellor's salary might come from the state treasury.[76]

The new state board of regents at its first meeting, held on April 5, 1860, elected Neill chancellor of the university. The legislature of that year provided by law that the chancellor of the university should be ex officio state superintendent of public instruction. Moved by a passage in the message of Governor Ramsey, the third state legislature, that of 1861, undertook a revision of the school code. A Senate committee reported a bill prescribing the salary of the chancellor-superintendent. A lively opposition sprang up against the combination. The incumbent apparently regarded the chancellorship of minor importance and on February 25, 1861, he resigned it. On March 7 the school code was enacted and it carried a provision for a state superintendent of public instruction to be elected by the legislature. On the same day in joint convention of the houses Neill was elected to the office by a vote of 55 to 6. The board of regents at its next meeting requested him to withdraw his resignation of the chancellorship. This he did and he held the two offices for a brief period. In July, 1861, however, following his appointment as chaplain of the First Minnesota Infantry, he resigned the superintendency. The chancellorship seems not to have been vacated by law until 1864, and then incidentally, but it was virtually void after the summer of 1861.[77]

A decade was to pass during which Neill's activity in education was to remain in suspense, with a notable exception that may be conveniently mentioned here. After some years of waiting, there seems to have been reason in 1864 to believe

[76] *General Laws,* 1860, pp. 264–267; Anderson, *History of the Constitution,* 227.

[77] *Ante,* 2: 84, n.; Board of Regents, *Reports,* 1860, p. 2; 1861, pp. 17–19; *General Laws,* 1860, p. 211; 1861, p. 72; 1864, pp. 63, 64; *Senate Journal,* 1861, p. 154; *House Journal,* 416; Ramsey, *Message,* 1861, p. 9; Neill, *History of Minnesota: from the Earliest French Explorations to the Present Time,* 640–643 (fourth edition, Minneapolis, 1882). In his *Report* for 1860 as superintendent of public instruction, Neill urged that the school laws be revised.

that Matthias W. Baldwin would be disposed to resume contributions to higher education in Minnesota. On March 3 of that year the legislature, at Neill's instance, amended the act of 1853 incorporating the Baldwin School by changing the title to Baldwin University. Baldwin died in 1866 without leaving any bequest to that university.[78]

After a year's service as regimental chaplain of the First Minnesota, Neill resigned and was appointed hospital chaplain, U.S.A., and assigned to a large army hospital in Philadelphia. This duty occupied him until January, 1864, and the following month he was appointed an assistant secretary to the president. He held that position until the close of Johnson's administration. In 1869 President Grant sent him abroad as United States consul at Dublin, but the duties did not interest him and before the close of his second year in the consulate he was back in Minnesota, resolved to resume educational work on a plan he probably had already conceived. Many months were spent in a study of the situation.[79]

The large Winslow House, built in St. Anthony for southern tourist patronage, had been vacant since the early days of the war. A lease was obtained for a hundred dollars a month and on September 10, 1872, Neill opened "Jesus College," with himself as provost, in the old hotel. Two departments were announced: the Baldwin Grammar School, a classical and English school preparatory to the University of Minnesota; and the School of Christian Literature, "supplemental to the State University." The name was chosen for the college to show that, while wholly Christian, it would not interpret Christianity according to the schools of Luther, Calvin, or Laud. "It is a name above every other name," said Neill, ". . . and far more appropriate than the name . . . of any

[78] Neill, *Macalester College*, 13; Funk, *Macalester College*, 36; *Special Laws*, 1864, p. 354.

[79] *Ante*, 2: 84, n.; Neill, *Descendants of Henry Neill*, 20; Neill, *Minnesota*, 650, n. (fourth edition); *Pioneer and Democrat* (St. Paul), June 23, 1861, p. 1; Neill to Ramsey, May 7, 29, July 22, 1862, Ramsey Papers.

rich man . . . who may have given some wealth to education " after his death. In the School of Christian Literature a three-year course of studies was arranged, including the life of Jesus, the geography and history of Palestine, biblical and Christian antiquities, evidences of Christianity, Butler's *Analogy*, the history of the Christian church to the time of Constantine, and the history and doctrines of the Nicene Creed. Without some knowledge of Jesus and of the history of the Bible and the church, said Neill, no man could be thoroughly educated. The charge for tuition and board and room for the year of thirty-eight weeks was two hundred and eighty dollars, with an extra charge for washing. The program of lectures and recitations was arranged so as not to interfere with those of the university. Thus the students might enjoy all the advantages of that institution without additional cost. It was the hope of the founder that Christian parents would send sons to Jesus College for " gentle home culture " under Christian influences. As the university was at that time, 1872, a preparatory school with a nucleus of a score of students of college rank, giving free instruction, and only a mile away, a private preparatory school collecting tuition fees, however well manned and conducted, could not be expected to survive. After a short struggle, Jesus College expired. The provost's idea of a residential college or hall like those of Oxford and Cambridge was fifty years in advance of the time. The dream faded away.[80]

[80] Frank C. Coolbaugh, " Reminiscences of the Early Days of Minnesota, 1851 to 1861," in *Minnesota Historical Collections*, 15:484; *Jesus College, near the University of Minnesota, at the Falls of Saint Anthony: Announcement for 1872*, a four-page folder with an illuminated initial and a woodcut of the Winslow House; Neill, *Jesus College, Its Aim and Name, Stated in a Letter to the Mayor of Minneapolis*, a four-page folder, dated at the Falls of St. Anthony, November 1, 1872, with a seal blazoning a group of books, a cross, the American flag, and the motto, " Christo et Patriæ"; Funk, *Macalester College*, 37–42; Neill, *Macalester College*, 14. A galvanized iron angel twenty-two feet long revolved on a mast above the cupola of the building. It was Neill's hope that the divinity schools of the Protestant churches would be clustered about the university. In the Neill Papers is a letter from the author to Neill, April 29, 1872, wishing the college success.

While the experiment was going on, without much promise of success, the versatile provost thought out a new educational project, or possibly revived an old one: that of establishing an American college, Christian but not sectarian, with the old hotel building as a first home. The building was then owned by Charles Macalester of Philadelphia, a patriot and philanthropist, into whose hands it had come by a mortgage foreclosure. A correspondence with him resulted in his promise to give the building to such a college, provided the sum of twenty-five thousand dollars were raised toward its endowment. On December 9, 1873, Macalester died, but in his will provision was made for the gift. Within a few months the required endowment fund was subscribed and on March 5, 1874, the legislature changed the name of Baldwin University to Macalester College. Neill became president.[81]

It was known that Macalester desired the establishment of a college on a broad Christian basis, not exclusively sectarian. Such was President Neill's preference. He would have been pleased with Presbyterian support without Presbyterian control. After his return to the state at the end of his long absence, Neill was not the great figure in Presbyterian circles that he had been in the territorial period and the early days of statehood. The Presbyterian members of his board, although personally attached to him, did nothing to advance an enterprise not distinctly denominational. They had an additional reason for apathy — Neill's desertion from Presbyterian ranks in 1874 to ally himself with the Reformed Episcopal church, an offshoot from the Protestant Episcopal church. His excursion lasted sixteen years.[82] There was a sentiment among Minnesota Presbyterians that Macalester College, with two-thirds of its board of trustees of the Presby-

[81] Macalester to Neill, June 4, July 26, August 23, October 16, 28, 1873, Neill Papers; Neill, *Macalester College*, 14; Funk, *Macalester College*, 37, 42–47; *Special Laws*, 1874, p. 331.

[82] Neill, *Macalester College*, 15; Funk, *Macalester College*, 150; Neill, *Descendants of Henry Neill*, 22.

terian faith, ought to do something for the church. On October 12, 1878, the Minnesota synod appointed a committee to confer with the Macalester trustees. The outcome of negotiations was the transfer of the college and its property to synodical control in 1880. The next year, 1881, a gift of forty acres of land in what was then a suburb of St. Paul was made to the college. In February, 1883, the old Winslow House property was sold for forty thousand dollars, and in the year following a building was erected on the new campus. President Neill resigned in 1884 and accepted the professorship of history, English literature, and political economy, a combination not extraordinary in those days. When the time came for the beginning of instruction, the branch of history, which he was better fitted to teach than any other subject, was taken from him, much to his displeasure.

Macalester College was ceremoniously opened on September 16, 1885. When the first catalogue appeared, the name of the founder and senior professor was placed at the bottom of the faculty roll, which was not consolatory to a man of his taste and temper. He held his chair until his death on September 26, 1893. He acted as librarian for some years and secured for the college a gift of a thousand volumes, as well as several substantial donations of money for the purchase of books.[83] Edward Duffield Neill, D.D., first superintendent of public instruction of territory and state, titular chancellor of the University of Minnesota, and founder of Macalester College, may well be named Minnesota's apostle of education.

WILLIAM S. PATTEE, APOSTLE OF JURISPRUDENCE

The retarded development of the University of Minnesota through ill-advised financing has been elsewhere related.

[83] Funk, *Macalester College*, 55, 60–63, 82, 100, 135, 142, 155; Neill, *Descendants of Henry Neill*, 21; Neill, *Macalester College*, 16; Macalester College, *Catalogues*, 1885, p. 5; *Daily Pioneer Press*, September 17, 1885, p. 8; September 27, 1893, p. 1.

Although the university was chartered on February 25, 1851, it was not until 1869 that a freshman class was formed in the academic department, called the college of science, literature, and the arts. The board of regents was so much occupied with experiments toward the opening and expansion of the college of agriculture, as prescribed by the act of February 18, 1868, which merged the Morrill land grant with the original land grant by Congress for a university, that for some years no consideration could be given to organizing the colleges of law and medicine provided for by the charter of 1868. A general plan of university organization, adopted in 1870, contained the novel proposition of requiring for admission to the professional schools two years of college work. This policy was adhered to until after the change in the presidency of the university in 1884.[84]

Overtures toward the opening of the two professional schools were being made, however, by lawyers and physicians of Minneapolis and St. Paul who were desirous of holding professorships and willing to give of their time for little or no compensation. As time went on, such proposals were renewed with much persistence, and finally the regents, believing that the academic and agricultural departments had been firmly established, were disposed to entertain them. At a meeting of the board on January 28, 1888, it was resolved to establish a department of law, and William Sullivan Pattee was elected to be its head with the title of dean. The choice was a happy one.[85]

Pattee had passed his boyhood on a farm in the state of Maine. After his graduation from Bowdoin College in 1871, he spent three years teaching, two of them in the Greek department at Lake Forest University, Illinois. For four years he was superintendent of schools at Northfield, Minnesota, during which he continued the law studies he

[84] *Ante*, pp. 61, 65, 73, 83–85, 99; Johnson, *University of Minnesota*, 23, 26, 35.
[85] Board of Regents, Minutes, B 1: 302, 304, 317–321.

had begun in undergraduate days. After his admission to the bar in 1878, he practiced law for ten years. In 1885 he was a representative in the state legislature. The following year he was appointed a member of the state normal school board of Minnesota and was elected its president. He held the two offices for twelve years.[86]

The university catalogue of 1887–88 announced that a department of law would be opened in September, 1888, and that any person eighteen years of age or over who was of good moral character and could satisfy the faculty as to his general education might be matriculated. The course of study was to cover two years.[87] On September 11, 1888, Dean Pattee delivered his inaugural address on " The Science of Jurisprudence " in the chapel of the old main university building. While the primary business of a law school, he said, was the better education of young men for the practice of the law as it actually was rather than as it might be, yet the study of the law as a science, and a progressive science, was an additional function; law as a science had its place in a school supported by the people. At two o'clock on the same day the dean met thirty-two applicants in a basement room of the old building. An experienced teacher, he knew how to keep school the first day. The dean's private law books, on shelves back of his desk, formed the library of the college. The faculty consisted of one professor — the dean himself — and sixteen lecturers, all practicing lawyers, many of them already eminent at the bar. With the tuition fee fixed at

[86] *Ante*, 3: 180; *Minneapolis Star*, August 22, 1907, p. 8; Cornelius W. G. Hyde and William Stoddard, eds., *History of the Great Northwest and Its Men of Progress*, 254–256 (Minneapolis, 1901); Hiram F. Stevens, ed., *History of the Bench and Bar of Minnesota*, 1: 238–241 (Minneapolis and St. Paul, 1904); Hudson, *Half Century of Minneapolis*, 162.

[87] University of Minnesota, *Catalogues*, 1887-88, p. 88. The title " Department of Law " was used in the act of 1851 and in university catalogues and announcements until 1894, when the title " College of Law " was adopted. On February 14, 1912, it was changed by resolution of the board of regents to " The Law School," to conform to traditional usage. Board of Regents, *Minutes*, February 14, 1912; interview with Professor James Paige, November 8, 1928, recorded in Folwell Papers.

forty dollars a year, the financial situation was discouraging. To increase the receipts and to provide for students whose employments did not permit them to attend day classes, evening sessions were begun toward the end of October. The first year's enrollment was thus increased to sixty-seven, of whom three were graduated at the end of the year. A circumstance that gave the school public recognition and attracted students was an act of the legislature of 1889 providing that upon presentation of their diplomas to the state supreme court or to any district court of the state graduates of the college might be admitted to practice in all the courts of the state without further examination.[88]

From the day of this modest beginning to that of his death on April 4, 1911, Dean Pattee had no other material interest than that of building up the law school in numbers and efficiency. He was sensible to the infamy of the great number of existing law schools in the country that had been engaged in taking boys from the common schools and, in the course of two winter sessions, turning them out to practice law. Eager though he was to raise the standards of admission and graduation, he found it necessary under the circumstances to advance by gradual steps. Tuition could not be free as it was in the agricultural and academic departments. Except in regard to buildings, the law school must be self-supporting. A first step in advance was taken in September, 1892, when the course for night students was extended to three years. In 1894 a third year was added to the day students' course.[89]

[88] Johnson, *University of Minnesota*, 142–144; University of Minnesota, *Catalogues*, 1888–89, p. 99; *Minneapolis Tribune*, September 12, 1888, p. 4; *General Laws*, 1889, p. 202. A law of 1891 made it mandatory on the state supreme court or any district court of the state to order its clerk to issue certificates without fees. In 1917 a law was passed requiring all candidates for admission to the bar to be examined under rules prescribed by the supreme court. *General Laws*, 1891, p. 118; 1917, p. 419.

[89] *Minneapolis Tribune*, April 5, 1911, p. 3; University of Minnesota, *Catalogues*, 1888–89, p. 41; 1892–93, p. 170; 1894–95, p. 164; Board of Regents, *Reports*, 1887–88, p. 8; Johnson, *University of Minnesota*, 145; interview with Professor Paige, November 8, 1928, recorded in Folwell Papers.

In the fall of 1891 a policy previously announced, which had been planned to invite students into wider fields of legal study and, incidentally, to increase the enrollment somewhat, went into effect. A graduate course of one year, leading to the degree of master of law, was given. The subjects offered included general jurisprudence, political science, constitutional law and history, and Minnesota practice. In 1897 an additional year of graduate studies was added, leading to the degree of doctor of civil law. These courses, which were taken by almost three hundred men, were offered until the close of Dean Pattee's service. A succeeding administration deemed it wise to suspend them.[90]

A policy of gradual advances in the requirements for admission was also adopted. Beginning with the year 1892–93, applicants who were not graduates of universities or colleges, state normal schools, or state high schools were subjected to examinations in the common school branches. Two years later, in 1894, matriculants were required to have the same qualifications for admission as academic freshmen, with the exception of the foreign language requirement. This rule, with modifications of detail, was in force until 1909, when one year of freshman academic work was exacted. There remained another advance, long hoped for and deferred. In June, 1910, the last year of Dean Pattee's service, announcement was made that in order to enter the college of law candidates for the degree of bachelor of law must have completed two years of work in the academic department of the University of Minnesota or in some other university or college of equal rank. In the dialect of the present time, law students in Minnesota were required to have had a junior college education. The ideal of a plan advanced prematurely forty years before was now realized in the University of Minnesota.[91]

[90] University of Minnesota, *Catalogues*, 1891–92, p. 141; 1892–93, p. 171; Johnson, *University of Minnesota*, 145.

[91] *Ante*, p. 67; University of Minnesota, *Catalogues*, 1892–93, p. 169; 1894–95, p. 163; *Bulletins*, vol. 12, no. 12, p. 14 (June 30, 1909); vol. 13, no. 7, p. 13 (June, 1910).

In the twenty-two years from 1888 to 1910, Dean Pattee had seen the law department of the university grow from the modest beginnings described to an institution with a high standing among American law schools. During those years the enrollment had increased from 32 to 614, but it fell to 376 in the next year, 1911, when junior college preparation was required. Pattee's service had been a most laborious one, since he had really conducted three law schools — a day school, a night school, and a graduate school. His studies were necessarily confined mainly to the subjects that he himself taught, but he found time, or took it, to prepare valuable "case books" on contracts, equity, and real and personal property. A favorite subject was the philosophy of jurisprudence, upon which he began lecturing in 1896. In fragments of time left from daily instruction and administrative duties he wrote out the chapters of his work on *The Essential Nature of Law,* which was published in 1909. The hundred or more authorities commended to students in an appendix indicate extensive and profound study. The keynote of the treatise is expressed in the subtitle, *The Ethical Basis of Jurisprudence.* An orthodox, theistic, intuitional philosophy is frankly assumed. Content to accept the popular vague and elastic use of the word "law," the author liberally defines the word as "truth regulative of power." In the physical world there are such truths known by conception; in the mind of man there are laws of thought known by intuition. As man lives in a physical and rational system, so he lives in a moral system of society. Service to his fellows is the highest good to them and to himself. The supreme law of human action is summed up in the two great commandments of the Master. On the basis of the moral law jurisprudence has grown up as a branch of applied ethics with enforceable sanctions to outward obedience to that law. Recognition of jurisprudence as a branch of applied ethics has many advantages, which the author sums up in glowing terms:

It gives to jurisprudence itself the highest possible dignity; it raises the administration of justice from a selfish scramble by litigants and counsel for unrighteous ends, to a dignified effort on the part of judge, counsel and advocate, to discover where the golden thread of moral principle runs in the complicated affairs of human life, and to settle the rights of the parties interested according to the demands of that principle; it dignifies the office of the judge, by making him a priest at the altar of moral law, and it raises the office of counsel to the exalted life work of one devoted to the advocacy of unselfish love in the complicated details of human life.[92]

Upon this brief record William Sullivan Pattee may be enrolled, without fear of dissent, as Minnesota's apostle of jurisprudence.

Le Grand Powers, Apostle of Labor

It is well within the memory of the author when, in his rural neighborhood, the carpenter, the mason, lather, and plasterer — they were one then — the blacksmith, the wheelwright, the tanner, the chair-maker, the cabinetmaker, the tailor, and the shoemaker were substantial independent citizens and artisans. They lived in their own houses, with orchards, gardens, pigsties, and flocks of poultry. Some of them were school and church trustees, constables and justices of the peace. How this socio-economic status was soon dislocated and at length superseded by the factory system is a matter of common knowledge.

The year 1850 was pivotal in American industry. In the previous half century associations of craftsmen, mostly with benevolent objects, had existed in larger cities. From the year mentioned, these associations took on a new form and a new name, that of "trade-unions." As a rule, the unions preserved the benevolent features of the associations, but they made their leading purposes the securing of better wages and continuous employment for artisans and skilled laborers

---

[92] Johnson, *University of Minnesota*, 142, 145; *Minnesota Alumni Weekly*, January 10, 1910, pp. 1, 3; April 10, 1911, pp. 4, 7; William S. Pattee, *The Essential Nature of Law, or the Ethical Basis of Jurisprudence* (Chicago, 1909), especially pp. 159, 174, 243.

WILLIAM S. PATTEE

[From a portrait painted about 1905 by Miss Grace
McKinstry, in the Law School building of the University of Minnesota.]

LE GRAND POWERS

[From a photograph taken in 1892, in the museum of the
Minnesota Historical Society.]

and the suppression of competition by unskilled operatives, through collective bargaining.[93]

The decade beginning in 1880 was an epoch in the American labor movement. Trade-unions multiplied and merged into a grand national union, the American Federation of Labor. This organization had a rival whose allurements drew great numbers of workers into its fold — the Knights of Labor, which had its beginning in a single assembly in Philadelphia in 1869 as a secret society with a password and a ritual. Local assemblies were formed thereafter and were grouped into district assemblies. In 1878 a national assembly was organized, which the next year elected Terence Vincent Powderly as grand master workman. Under his leadership the order, abandoning much of its secrecy, increased rapidly and enormously in numbers, which mounted to over fifty thousand in 1883 and to seven hundred thousand in 1886.[94]

The number of members of the Knights of Labor in Minnesota is not known, but they formed a large and enthusiastic body, ready, according to their principles, to go into politics and secure their objects by legislation, if possible. An opportunity came to them in 1886 to unite with the Farmers' Alliance. The platform adopted in a joint convention of the two bodies at St. Paul on September 1 and the long catena of " demands " of the Knights separately embodied in it have been fully stated elsewhere in this work. A leading demand was the establishment by law of a bureau of labor statistics. As the substance of the platform was absorbed into that of the Republican party, the Republican majority in the legislature of 1887 promptly passed the desired bill. It provided for a commissioner of labor statistics to be appointed by the governor, with the consent of the Senate, at a salary of

[93] John R. Commons and associates, *History of Labour in the United States*, 1: 108–111, 350–353, 575–607 (New York, 1918).

[94] Commons, *History of Labour*, 2: 197–202, 245, 310–314, 334, 338, 344, 396, 409.

fifteen hundred dollars. It was made the duty of the bureau to " collect, assort, systematize and present in annual reports to the legislature . . . statistical details relating to all departments of labor in the state, especially in its relations to the commercial, industrial, social, educational and sanitary condition of the laboring classes "; to visit establishments employing labor and to make a record of the methods of protection used; and to " see to it that all laws regulating the employment of children, minors and women, and all laws established for the protection of the health and the lives of operatives in workshops and factories " were enforced, to prosecute in court offenders against such laws, and to record in reports to the legislature all violations of such laws and the proceedings in each case. The commissioner was authorized to subpœna witnesses and take testimony in matters relating to the duties of the bureau. Any employer who should refuse to permit the commissioner to enter his factory or workshop or who should fail to make any reports requested within the time prescribed by the commissioner was to be fined ten dollars for each day of delay.[95]

Governor McGill appointed as commissioner John Lamb, commended to him by the Knights of Labor. A civil engineer by profession, Lamb had some of the qualifications desirable for the position and, during the three years and more that he held it made as good a beginning as could be expected under a law without effective sanctions and with the aid of but one clerk. With the exception of an investigation into child labor and the condition of women in factories, his reports for 1887–88 and 1889–90 covered chiefly such subjects as school attendance and manual training in schools. When it became known that Governor Merriam had decided to make a new appointment, leading men in labor affairs placed before him the name of a citizen who was not a laboring man nor a member of any labor organization, Le Grand

[95] *Ante*, 3: 169–171; *General Laws*, 1887, pp. 199–201.

Powers, a Universalist minister of Minneapolis. He was known to labor leaders as a sympathizer with the grievances and aspirations of working people. He had invited a Knight of Labor to speak in his church and had addressed some street railway strikers at a street meeting. The author knew him as a serious student in the field of political economy. He understood that the betterment of the laboring classes was a part of a general social amelioration to come, not from a war of classes, but from friendly coöperation. The governor, however, appointed a former clerk in the bureau, who was among those who had petitioned for the appointment of Powers. He accepted after securing Powers as his deputy. After holding the office for three months, he resigned to accept another position, and Powers became commissioner.[96]

Powers had no experience as a wage earner, but he had talent. He at once planned " a study of all national organizations and detailed statistics of all local unions " in the state, but, finding that too extensive, he confined his investigation to twenty of the leading unions having national or international organization, beginning with the Cigar Makers' International Union of America and ending with the Brotherhood of Locomotive Firemen. The study of the selected unions revealed them as little republics, deciding all important matters by vote. The officers in some of them were little more than clerks. In general the unions were managing their finances more economically than the business corporations with which they could be fairly compared. The accounting systems of some of the older unions were not excelled by those of any mercantile or manufacturing concerns. The primary objects of the unions were, of course, to obtain for their members ample wages, limits on the hours of labor, and safe and sanitary conditions for work. There were secondary advantages that may have brought more recruits to their ranks, such as

[96] Powers to the author, October 12, 30, November 18, 1927, Folwell Papers.

mutual insurance, under various names, for accident, sickness, death, and unemployment, and " benefits " for members forced to travel in search of work and for men out on authorized strikes. The Brotherhood of Locomotive Firemen, for example, disbursed in the years 1890 and 1891 benefits amounting to $359,000, out of total receipts of $417,498.

For all such solidly established beneficent associations, the commissioner demanded friendly recognition, justice, and protection by law. Modern employers, he maintained, should not assume the position of the old nobility and claim absolute control of workers as if they were serfs. They should recognize the unions, consult with them, and respond to their demands for arbitration in case of disagreements. No " iron clad contracts " to bind men to refrain from membership in unions should be tolerated; it should be a penal offense to exact such a contract. The law, said the commissioner, " should seek to compel all others [employers] to do what even now the well meaning do without law." [97]

With a scholar's training and taste, Commissioner Powers set about the study of apprenticeship in industries, a subject of vast importance in a country where so large a percentage of the population was employed in industries, working under many diverse conditions and circumstances. Resorting to reputable authority, he traced the apprentice system back to the Middle Ages, when craft guilds strove with the burgess aristocracy for the right to regulate the admission of boys to their trades. That struggle went on, moderated more or less efficiently by legislation, until near the close of the eighteenth century. By that time the double-acting steam engine, the spinning jenny, and the power loom had set the fashion of the factory system that was soon to be extended

[97] Bureau of Labor Statistics, *Reports*, 1891–92, pp. 245–253, 255–354. Powers knew what work was. As a boy and youth he had worked on a farm, in a sawmill, and in a woodworking shop, with numerous special machines, all of which belonged to his father. Powers to the author, December 11, 1927, Folwell Papers.

to all industries, with trifling exceptions. Then the ancient apprentice system broke down. The factory system called, not for skilled artisans trained as apprentices, but for mere machine-tenders. Women and children could tend machines. Using their advantage, employers assumed the right to decide arbitrarily what kinds and numbers of persons they would employ and what their wages and hours of labor should be.[98]

Against the resultant degradation of skilled operatives there was revolt, which tardily took organized form. A few local unions were formed in eastern cities in the early years of the nineteenth century, but it was not until near the middle of the century that the number of trade unions became considerable and national organizations were established. Just after the close of the Civil War there was a great increase, and in the quarter century following all industries of importance were unionized and confederated. Armed with the actual or threatened strike, the unions now demanded concessions, among them the right to determine the number and kind of apprentices to be admitted to shops, mills, and factories. Employers, on the defensive, protested against having their businesses run by other people. The old struggle of centuries was on again. Masters fought with lockouts, men with strikes. Neither party alone, as a class, held the commissioner, could be trusted to determine a controversy in which the public was so greatly concerned. The state, therefore, by just law duly enforced, must decide at what ages and under what conditions youth should be employed in industries, leaving it to associated employers and their organized operatives to agree, by friendly conferences, as to the number of apprentices to be employed. Such was his conclusion from an historical survey and an intensive study of the professions, principles, and practices of sixty great unions.[99]

[98] *Reports,* 1893–94, pp. 126–382, especially pp. 126–134, 139, 371–382.
[99] *Reports,* 1893–94, pp. 144–146, 371–382; Commons, *History of Labour,* 1: 109–112; 2: 45–48.

The act of 1887 creating the bureau of labor statistics gave it permission to visit and inspect factories, but no authority to require improvements in conditions; and, with but one clerk or " deputy," the well-intended efforts of the bureau yielded results of little importance during the first two years of its existence. Commissioner Powers was able to make a considerable extension of factory inspection. In the biennium 1891–92 his inspector visited 445 establishments. He found but 121 of them in satisfactory condition; 107 complied with his recommendations in full and 97, in part; 23 promised compliance; and 97 others would do nothing to make their shops safe and healthful.[1]

In the course of these inspections record was made of 172 establishments in which 276 accidents had occurred. Of these accidents, 26 had resulted in death, 79 in amputations, 17 in broken bones, and the remainder in sundry lacerations. This record started the commissioner on a new line of study. He estimated roughly that the financial loss from accidents in the United States was one hundred and fifty million dollars a year, a sum larger than the loss from fires. Minnesota had her proportional share. This enormous loss to state and nation was falling " almost exclusively upon the wage earners," except in cases in which benevolent employers were pleased to contribute. Injured employees had no recourse except lawsuits, to the comfort of ambulance chasers; and this was rarely effective because of the manipulation of liability laws by employers and the operation of the common-law principles that workmen in dangerous occupations, in consideration of appropriate wages, assume all ordinary risks of accident and that contributory negligence on the part of employees relieves employers of responsibility. The question of a remedy for this hardship, one that would make employers careful to provide safety appliances and methods and would

[1] *Reports*, 1887–88, pp. 5–9; 1891–92, pp. 87–104. Governor McGill, in his *Message*, 1889, gives credit to J. P. McGaughey, " deputy, or clerk," for gathering valuable statistics.

cause employees to be careful to use them and to coöperate for their own safety and for the prevention of damage to property, was discussed at length.

The German system of compulsory accident insurance through associations of employers, under imperial supervision, was sympathetically described by Powers. The system required all the employers in an industry to contribute to an insurance fund, from which employees injured by accident at any time or place were indemnified according to a schedule fixed by law. It went into effect in 1885, and at the end of the year 1890 the number of workmen insured was 13,619,750. The effect of throwing the responsibility for accidents upon employers was to lessen the number of injuries. The commissioner proposed that Minnesota adopt the German plan, which should be put into operation by voluntary associations of employers. It was not until the year 1913 that the legislature of Minnesota was pleased to enact an efficient "workmen's compensation act." [2]

To illustrate the effect of machinery in cheapening the price of bread and improving its quality, Powers included in his report for 1891–92 an illustrated article describing the evolution of the flour mill from the primitive " knocking stane " used in the island of Shetland to the latest roller mill in Minneapolis, where the labor of one man makes the flour of hundreds. He described the new milling process, which made a market for the spring wheat of Minnesota and in 1891 added twenty-seven million dollars to the income of Minnesota farmers. [3]

His experience during a biennium convinced the commissioner that further legislation was needed to give his bureau desirable efficiency. Upon his suggestion the act of 1887 was replaced in 1893 by one that changed the title of the

[2] *Reports*, 1891–92, pp. 104, 117–126, 129–139, 148–155; *General Laws*, 1913, pp. 675–694.
[3] *Reports*, 1891–92, pp. 156–222. Pages 223 to 244 contain an historical sketch of the toll taken by grist mills.

bureau to "bureau of labor." The new act increased the number of officers and employees of the bureau and enlarged its powers and the scope of its investigations. The commissioner of labor was authorized to appoint an assistant commissioner, a factory inspector, two deputies, and two assistant deputies, one of whom was to act as railway inspector. It was made the duty of the bureau to enforce not only all laws regulating the employment of children, minors, and women and those for the protection of the health, lives, and limbs of operatives, but also all laws enacted for the protection of the working classes. The bureau was instructed "to collect, assort, arrange and present" in its reports statistics relating to coöperation, strikes or other labor troubles, and trade-unions and their effect upon labor and capital, in addition to the statistical details required by the act of 1887. Any person called upon to testify who refused or neglected to do so was liable to a fine of fifty dollars or imprisonment for thirty days. Any owner or occupant of a factory, mill, or workshop who should refuse to admit the commissioner or any officer or employee of the bureau in discharging his duties might be fined one hundred dollars or imprisoned for ninety days. All information supplied by owners, operators, or managers of establishments employing labor was to be regarded by the bureau as confidential. The salary of the commissioner was raised to twenty-five hundred dollars.[4]

Upon the recommendation of the commissioner, the legislature of 1893 enacted a law " for the protection of Employes." The act required, among other things, that all dangerous machinery and dangerous places in or about factories and workshops and all " hoistways, hatchways, elevator wells and wheelholes " should be protected by proper guards; that all factories, mills, and workshops should be kept clean, sanitary, and properly ventilated; and that all buildings where labor was employed should be provided with proper and sufficient

[4] *Laws,* 1893, pp. 96–99.

means of escape in case of fire. The legislature of 1895 passed acts for the regulation of child labor, an act forbidding blacklisting and coercing employees, and one providing for the sanitary regulation of bakeries.[5]

In his report for 1893–94 the commissioner of labor included the results of an investigation into chattel mortgages and pawnbrokers' loans in Minneapolis in 1893. The selling price of the goods purchased under chattel mortgages in that year was $772,536.36. More than two thousand (2,211) chattel mortgages for borrowed money on file in the city clerk's office were found to be exacting usurious interest. In ninety-five typical cases specially investigated, interest varied from 41 to 480 per cent per annum. In 1893 pawnbrokers made 23,090 loans amounting to $142,248.12; small loans were made at an interest rate of ten per cent a month and larger loans, at lower rates, ranging from three to eight per cent a month. The commissioner did not look to law to prevent such extortions, but rather to a system of lending to small borrowers by reputable money owners at rates of interest corresponding to the risks and losses of the business; he suggested fourteen per cent per annum as a fair rate.[6]

The year 1893 was one of general financial depression, as is well known. The price of wheat had greatly fallen off and loud complaint was heard that Minnesota farmers were taking heavy losses, many of them losing their farms by mortgage foreclosures. To ascertain the weight of these

[5] *Reports*, 1891–92, p. 86; *Laws*, 1893, pp. 99–106; 1895, pp. 165, 386–389, 391, 484–486; Powers to the author, November 14, 1927; the author to Powers, November 19, 1927, with replies interlined, Folwell Papers. The act regulating bakeries required bakeshops to be well lighted and drained and free from rat holes; their floors were to be impermeable and not more than four feet below ground level; bakers were not to sleep in the shops; ample closets and dressing rooms were to be provided apart from the shops; bakers were to wear caps, slippers, and linen suits, which were to be kept clean and used only in the bakeshops; and no person in whose house existed an infectious disease was to be employed in a bakery or other establishment for the manufacture of food. The commissioner was obliged to persuade a senator and a representative to visit some St. Paul bakeshops in order to obtain serious consideration of his bill.

[6] *Reports*, 1893–94, pp. 17–59, especially pp. 21, 30–35, 41.

assertions, the commissioner sent agents into eleven representative counties. They visited every farm in two townships in each of the eleven counties selected and some farms in a single township in a twelfth county, 1,798 in number, including 243 held by tenants. The tabulated figures indicated that Minnesota farmers were generally holding their own and that those who had diversified their crops and had taken on live stock were prospering. Tenants were on the way to independence.[7] This investigation led to a wider one into the amount of real estate mortgage indebtedness in the state over a long term of years, from 1859 to 1893, and the number and amounts of foreclosures and redemptions. An analysis of tables compiled by the bureau showed that the burden of mortgage debt on farms was becoming lighter and that a large proportion of farms lost by foreclosures were being redeemed. The commissioner's far-reaching and laborious survey led to the conclusion " that the volume of mortgage debt bore no relation to misfortune. They were a sign of progress rather than of misfortune." [8] A later inquiry into the subject of taxation led the commissioner to the inference that unimproved lands were taxed at a higher rate than improved land, especially in the newer counties. To remedy this and other inequalities, it was recommended that the state resign to cities and counties all taxes on property, real and personal, and derive its revenue from imposed taxes on corporations, incomes, and inheritances and from license fees. There would then be no need of equalizing the assessments among the several communities.[9]

These statistical exercises within the state attracted the attention and approval of eminent and expert economists elsewhere. Upon the recommendation of a body of them

[7] *Reports*, 1893–94, pp. 60–125, especially pp. 60, 62, 64, 66, 70–74.

[8] *Reports*, 1893–94, pp. 383–546, especially pp. 383, 411–412, 491–494, 537–542; Powers to the author, November 14, 1927, Folwell Papers.

[9] The report for 1895–96 was not printed and the manuscript has not been found. An abstract dated December 15, 1898, is on file in the governor's office. See Powers to the author, November 14, 1927, in the Folwell Papers.

Powers was appointed statistician of agriculture in the United States bureau of the census. His work in this department led to his assignment to the division of wealth, debt, and taxation, and, later, to the division of financial and other statistics of cities. In the course of the latter duty he worked out the uniform system of accounting for counties and cities that is still in use in many states. After two decades of efficient and satisfactory service, he retired in 1918, at the age of seventy-one, to begin the rest he had earned. There will be none to challenge the title of Le Grand Powers as Minnesota's apostle of labor.[10]

MARIA SANFORD, APOSTLE OF CULTURE AND PATRIOTISM

In the summer of 1880 the regents of the University of Minnesota made a number of changes in the faculty of the academic department. One of the resulting vacancies was to be filled by a woman, who was to teach and also to perform such duties as those discharged by deans of women at the present time. The author, as a member of a committee of the regents, interviewed a number of capable aspirants for the position. At Chautauqua, New York, he met one who opened the conversation by saying, "I am forty-three years of age and I have taught twenty-four years." After her graduation from a Connecticut normal school — there had been no college for women accessible to her and had there been one, home engagements would have kept her from attending — she had taught in a rural common school for ten dollars a month, in a graded school, in a high school, and in an academy. In the meantime she had broadened her education by pursuing faithfully a course of reading in history and science that John Fiske, the eminent historian, had outlined for her at her request. For ten years, beginning in 1869,

[10] Powers to the author, November 14, 1927, Folwell Papers. Le Grand Powers is living in Washington, D.C. There is a sketch of his life with a summary of his work as commissioner of labor in the *Daily Pioneer Press*, December 25, 1898, p. 7.

she had been professor of history in Swarthmore College, Pennsylvania, the first woman, it is claimed, to have held that rank in America.[11]

On August 6, 1880, Maria Louise Sanford was elected to an assistant professorship of rhetoric in the University of Minnesota. A year later she was promoted to a full professorship, which she held until the summer of 1909, when, having passed her seventy-second birthday, she was granted one of the Carnegie "retiring allowances," which have given peace and comfort to so many college teachers during their last years. The teaching of rhetoric was a laborious task. Tradition had made it the duty of colleges to train all students for writing and public speaking throughout their whole college lives. Although the burden of class instruction was not unduly heavy, the reading and criticism of a great mass of "compositions" and the training of students who were to speak on the chapel stage entailed continuous and exhausting labor, not to be slighted by one with a New England Puritan conscience. Even after rhetoric was made an elective subject for upper classmen, in the nineties, the registration was so large that the rhetoric department exacted more time and strength from its teachers than any other department. Maria Sanford was not one to be content with the old-fashioned catechetical drill upon measured portions of a textbook, but devoted herself to her students and to studies by which she might give better instruction. With her larger knowledge, her experience, and her ideals of education, she related the subject to life and illumined it with passages from a richly-stored memory. Said one of her students many years afterwards, "She was the best teacher I ever had."[12]

Miss Sanford made her first public address in 1868, while attending a teachers' institute at Allentown, Pennsylvania. In

[11] Helen Whitney, *Maria Sanford*, 50–54, 62, 64, 69, 80, 83, 110 (Minneapolis, 1922).

[12] Board of Regents, Minutes, B 1: 208; Whitney, *Maria Sanford*, 90, 111–116, 199.

the absence of a regular speaker she was asked to explain
her method of teaching a certain subject. The impression
she made with her excellent sentiments and remarkable delivery led to invitations to speak at other institutes at a time
when public speaking by women was under the ban in most
communities. In a lecture entitled " Lessons in Manners and
Morals," which she gave frequently, she developed a favorite
subject—moral training in the school as a supplement to that
in the home.[13]

During all her forty years of college teaching, from 1869
to 1909, Professor Sanford lectured to teachers' institutes
and farmers' institutes more frequently than her colleagues
thought proper. Addresses to farmers' wives, which gave
much satisfaction and delight, gained many friends for the
university at a time when the tardy development of the agricultural department had aroused hostility among farmers.
She spoke to mixed audiences on authors and subjects in
literature, and after her trip in 1899 to London, Paris, Venice,
Florence, and Rome, she entertained audiences with lectures
on art illustrated with lantern slides, then still a novelty.[14]

The end of Miss Sanford's college labors in 1909 was
signalized in an extraordinary manner. Upon a petition of
the graduates of that year, she was selected to deliver the
commencement address, a distinction probably never before
accorded a woman. In it she discussed the opportunity of the
university to train students for service in society and to in-
spire them " to make the state a shining example of justice,
happiness and peace" and pointed out the duty of every
graduate, however moderately endowed with natural gifts,
to go out with a firm resolve to make the most of himself in
order to be of greatest service to his community. She spoke
also of the high privilege that fell to the university of maintaining an "atmosphere of learning" in which scholarship

13 Whitney, *Maria Sanford*, 73–77.
14 Whitney, *Maria Sanford*, 97, 116–119, 176–179.

should be stimulated. Such an atmosphere was the greatest need in the university of the day.[15]

The regents accorded to Miss Sanford upon her retirement the title of professor emeritus, but it was said of her that she did not know she had "retired." Although nearly seventy-three years old, she was to enter upon a period of service of wider scope and influence than any previous one. Invitations to give lectures and addresses began to come in at once, and the satisfaction she gave made her increasingly popular; she had no need to employ a manager or to attach herself to a lecture bureau. She spoke to school and college audiences, to teachers' institutes and "extension" students, to church congregations and societies, white and colored, to Jewish and Catholic associations, to various women's clubs, to a congress of mothers, and to Indian children. Her discourses were in greater part on scholastic and literary subjects, but she spoke also on temperance, sex hygiene, cremation, and woman's suffrage, to which she was a late convert. Her engagements carried her east to New York and the District of Columbia; south to Virginia, North Carolina, Georgia, Florida, and Tennessee; and west to Montana, California, Oregon, and Washington.[16]

At the convention of the National Federation of Women's Clubs at San Francisco in 1912, which she attended as the guest of the Minnesota delegation, she made an address that gave her a national reputation. Her subject was the one with which she had begun her career of public speaking fifty-four years before — "The Value of Moral Power in the School Room." Reporters said of the address that it made the most profound impression of any given at the convention and that it moved the immense audience to enthusiastic admiration.

[15] Whitney, *Maria Sanford*, 201–214.
[16] Whitney, *Maria Sanford*, 215–257, 272. A poem written by Oscar W. Firkins in honor of Professor Sanford at the time of her retirement is given on page 202.

In 1915, at the instance of a Minneapolis newspaper, Miss Sanford made a study of the experiment in school housing and instruction then in progress at Gary, Indiana, which was being widely discussed in the press. Of one of five addresses that she made in Gary, a child wrote — and her words may serve as a general description of Miss Sanford's platform appearance in the last days — "The little old-fashioned lady appeared quite suddenly in the big new-fashioned school. Her quick light step was that of a girl. Her snow white hair, combed straight back from her forehead and coiled in a knot at the nape of her neck, was just the way our grandmothers do. Her black silk was just the kind we would want her to wear, and just the kind our grandmothers wear today. As she stepped on the platform a breathless hush fell on the audience. Every one wanted to hear the message that the little old-fashioned lady had to bring to us. When she spoke a look of surprise came into the faces of the audience. Her voice was as clear as a bell. It rang through the room strong and clear. Every one was quiet from the fourth grade to the twelfth. . . . She told us — O, so many things." [17]

In 1918 the governor of Minnesota sent Maria Sanford, lately decorated with an honorary doctorate by Carleton College, to New York City as his representative at the national conference on unemployment. Her speech at a full session was a " telling " one. In July of the same year an historic pageant entitled " The Torch-Bearers " was presented on the broad steps of the splendid facade of the Minneapolis Institute of Fine Arts for the benefit of the Jewish war relief fund. At the proper moment Maria Sanford appeared amid spectacular surroundings to voice the mind and will of the nine thousand persons present. " Go forth; " she said, " you are the torch bearers of a higher civilization. . . . Go forth, bear light and freedom and joy! Your courage shall defeat

[17] Whitney, *Maria Sanford*, 234–239, 249.

the oppressor! Your strength shall trample his ranks in the dust! Your self-sacrifice and devotion shall bind up the broken hearted and bring to those who sit in darkness and the shadow of death light and life, victory and peace."

From many addresses given in Minneapolis in the next year, 1919, two may be singled out as exceptionally impressive — one in St. Mark's Church, at a memorial service for British war heroes, and another at an open-air Easter service in Farview Park, when she exhorted her audience not to be content with the political freedom secured by the boys returning from European battlefields, but to seek the nobler freedom typified by Christ, the risen Lord. During this year, also, as on a previous occasion, she preached, during an illness of the minister, in the Congregational church of which she was a trustee. In the course of her lecturing journeys she had often given religious discourses on Sundays.[18]

Miss Sanford's last appearance on the platform was the most dramatic of all. At the opening session of the national convention of the Daughters of the American Revolution held in the beautiful Memorial Continental Hall in Washington on April 19, 1920, two figures appeared on the stage — one, a young girl, " a dark southern beauty," holding a great silken American flag; the other, a frail old lady for whom the audience for a moment was filled with compassion. Her opening words, " Hail thou flag of our fathers, flag of the free," banished apprehension; a hushed attention fell on the audience, which continued to the closing words of the address: " Most beautiful and most glorious shalt thou be as the messenger of such a nation, bearing to the ends of the earth the glad tidings of the joy and the glory and the happiness of a people where freedom is linked with justice, where liberty is restrained by law, and where 'peace on earth, good will to men' is the living creed." [19]

[18] Whitney, *Maria Sanford*, 271, 289–291, 297, 301.
[19] Whitney, *Maria Sanford*, 305–307, 320–322. The apostrophe to the flag delivered on this occasion was an elaboration of one originally given impromptu.

MARIA SANFORD

[From a photograph taken in 1916, in the Lee Brothers collection in the museum of the Minnesota Historical Society.]

THOMAS B. WALKER

[From a photograph taken in 1916, in the Lee Brothers collection in the museum of the Minnesota Historical Society.]

On the morning of April 21, two days after this appearance, she was found dead in her bed, with a smile of peace on her face.[20] No one is better qualified to bear the title of Minnesota's apostle of culture and patriotism than Maria Louise Sanford.

THOMAS B. WALKER, APOSTLE OF ART

In the summer of 1862 Thomas B. Walker, then a young man of twenty-two, was making a journey in the West to find a market for grindstones manufactured from the sandstone from the quarries at his home in Berea, Ohio. At McGregor, across the Mississippi from Prairie du Chien, he learned by accident of a promising town, previously unknown to him, somewhere upstream. He took passage on the first upward-bound steamer and found Minneapolis. No grindstones were wanted there, but he sold two carloads in St. Paul. When they came up for delivery they were checked off by James J. Hill, then a clerk on the levee. Soon thereafter Walker established a residence in Minneapolis that was to last during the rest of his life. For some years he was engaged in railroad and government surveying. His preparation for that work was a desultory and uncompleted course in Baldwin University at Berea. The government surveying was in part in the pine-timbered region along the upper Mississippi above Crow Wing. He saw the vast wealth in that pine waiting for development and noted the richest and most accessible locations for lumbering. That knowledge was capital for him. By unremitting industry, regularity of conduct, and absolute integrity he won the confidence of men who had money to invest in pine. It was easy to form a partnership with one of them, which lasted for many years.

For more than half a century the organizations of which Walker was a member and a leader bought and sold pine lands, carried on lumbering, and operated sawmills at Minne-

[20] Whitney, *Maria Sanford*, 309.

apolis and elsewhere. In later years large tracts of pine lands were acquired in the northeastern counties of California and a sawmill of immense capacity was put into operation. This enterprise, however, passed into the hands of the incorporated Red River Lumber Company, of which Walker retained the presidency after retiring from active management. In all these enterprises he followed a policy that has of late been advertised as a new departure, that of promptly paying high wages for labor. No strike ever took place in his organizations.[21]

The ordinary man of affairs would have needed all his time and strength to carry on a business so extensive, which required constant financing. Walker found time to hold a bank presidency for many years, to build and maintain a central market house for the city, to erect buildings for wholesale firms, to lay out a town site, which was later absorbed by Minneapolis, and to organize the Minneapolis Business Men's Union, which is still in existence under another name.[22] These multifarious business engagements did not deter him from social and public activities. He served as one of the managers of the state reform school for many years. He was consistently Republican in politics and threw effective influence toward the selection of nominees for major positions, though he sought none for himself. In 1895 he prepared and published a pamphlet on *Low Tariffs and Hard Times*, which was published and distributed by the National Republican League.[23] In 1896 he gave an address defending the single gold standard of money. Speaking on the subject of trusts,

[21] Thomas B. Walker, " Memories of the Early Life and Development of Minnesota," in *Minnesota Historical Collections*, 15: 455–478; interview with Walker's son, Archie D. Walker, September 25, 1928, recorded in Folwell Papers.
[22] " Sketch of the Life of the Honorable Thomas B. Walker," in the *Daily Minneapolis Times*, July 30, 1903, p. 12; Shutter and McLain, *Progressive Men of Minnesota*, 59.
[23] *Minneapolis Tribune*, December 24, 1895, p. 6; *Minneapolis Journal*, July 28, 1928, p. 2; Walker, *Low Tariffs and Hard Times: A Review of Our Tariff Rates, from 1821 to 1895* (Minneapolis, 1895); Eugene V. Smalley, ed., *History of the Republican Party*, 418 (St. Paul, 1896).

he expressed his disapproval of the formation of great industrial units.[24] The operation of communism as he had observed it among the Chippewa Indians aroused in him a deep repugnance against socialism in any of its forms, which he frequently expressed in public.[25]

An eminent example of Walker's social services was his leadership in the creation of the Minneapolis Public Library, which absorbed, without obliterating, the Minneapolis Athenæum. Upon the organization of the public library board in 1885 he was elected a trustee by popular vote, and by vote of the board was chosen its president. By successive elections he held the two offices to the end of his life, on July 28, 1928, a period of more than forty years. He subscribed a large sum to the fund raised by citizens for the erection of the handsome and capacious library building. The Minnesota Academy of Sciences was an organization in which Walker took much interest, holding the presidency for a term and participating in the discussions.[26]

To the affairs of his church, Methodist Episcopal, and of the Young Men's Christian Association Walker gave unstinted time and effort, and for them he prepared a number of papers and addresses. Especially for the benefit of members of the Young Men's Christian Association he compiled and published at his own expense a booklet entitled " *Whom Do Men Say That I the Son of Man Am?* " The work consists mainly of excerpts from the writings of distinguished personages testifying to the divinity of Christ and contains

[24] *Minneapolis Tribune*, 1896: May 12, p. 5; 13, p. 4; *Minneapolis Journal*, 1903: May 11, p. 6; 12, p. 4. In a letter to the author, October 15, 1928, in the Folwell Papers, Archie D. Walker gives a list of pamphlets written by his father.

[25] *Minneapolis Journal*, May 14, 1902, p. 4; April 27, 1903, p. 6; *Daily Pioneer Press*, May 18, 1903, p. 4; Walker, in *Minnesota Historical Collections*, 15: 467–470.

[26] Horace B. Hudson, *Dictionary of Minneapolis and Vicinity*, 1915, pp. 1, 88; Return I. Holcombe and William H. Bingham, eds., *Compendium of History and Biography of Minneapolis and Hennepin County, Minnesota*, 205 (Chicago, 1914); *Minneapolis Journal*, July 28, 1928, p. 1. In Minnesota Academy of Sciences, *Bulletins*, 5: 2–18, is an article by Walker on " Ancient Glass and Pottery."

eulogies, by a number of eminent Jewish rabbis and scholars, of Jesus, the great teacher of mankind, as the successor of the Hebrew prophets.[27]

In addition to all these enterprises and engagements, Walker reserved time, labor, and a great deal of money for an interest that was at first a mere recreation, but which became a serious and absorbing avocation: the collection and study of works of art. He came to look upon the fine arts, not as merely decorative, but, through improvement of taste, as stimulating to right conduct and noble living. They were for him a great and beneficent agency for culture.

Affairs went so well with Walker that six years after he entered upon his pine enterprises he was able to move his family into a home of his own, substantial and commodious because it was to shelter a large group of sons and daughters. Not long afterwards he learned that a neighbor who had brought to Minneapolis a copy of one of the portraits of Washington by Rembrandt Peale was pleased or obliged to part with the picture. Walker bought it as an ornament for his library. It was probably the first example of a fine work that he had ever seen. He was greatly pleased with it and decided to indulge in the purchase of more pictures as opportunity should occur. Some desultory purchases followed, and it was not long before he resolved to make a considerable collection of meritorious works of art, especially paintings, which would be an ornament not only to his home but to the city as well. To inform himself for this purpose he bought and read a number of the standard histories of art. In 1880 he added a room to his house to hold his increasing acquisitions. His purchases went on steadily from year to year, increasing somewhat in the early nineties, when

[27] The first edition of this work was published in 1903 with the cover title, "*The Son of Man*," and the second in 1911, with the cover title, *The Testimony of the Ages*. Brief accounts of Walker's religious articles and addresses are in the *Minneapolis Tribune*, April 22, 1901, p. 5; the *Daily Minneapolis Times*, February 8, 1904, p. 8; and the *Midland Christian Advocate*, 15: 413 (May 22, 1901).

he spent some months in Paris and London. In 1894 a large extension to his house was built; the collections, many of which were taken from storage, were displayed; a curator was employed; and the Walker Art Gallery was opened to the public without charge. Up to that time visitors had been welcome, but it had been necessary for them to ring for admittance. Much larger extensions to the home gallery were made in 1909 and 1912, and nearly a hundred paintings and more than three thousand objects of art were accommodated in the Minneapolis Public Library and its branches.[28]

The Minneapolis Society of Fine Arts was incorporated on January 31, 1883, and Walker held the presidency from 1888 to 1893. As his heart was set upon building up a great private collection, he could not become greatly interested in the society. He gave the use of land for a building for the art school and contributed liberally to guaranty funds. The society, with a numerous membership and a board of directors elected for short terms, was not adapted for the custodianship of a great gallery of art. Walker wisely followed his independent course.[29]

In later years Walker found pleasure in extending his purchases into other fields. He bought three hundred miniature painted portraits of distinguished personages, mostly Americans, which formed a little gallery of themselves. He also added in large numbers cut and uncut gems, pieces of old jewelry, and objects of jade, pottery, bronze, carved ivory, and ancient glass. A unique acquisition of historic, if not of artistic, interest was a group of over a hundred portraits

[28] *Minneapolis Journal*, July 29, 1928, section 1, pp. 1, 4, 5; Archie D. Walker to the author, October 15, 1928, Folwell Papers; interviews with Mrs. Ernest F. Smith, Walker's daughter, September 14, 1928, with Archie D. Walker, September 25, 1928, and with R. H. Adams, October 18, 1928, accompanied by a rough sketch of the Walker house, all recorded in Folwell Papers; Eugen Neuhaus and Seymour de Ricci, *Report on the Paintings of the T. B. Walker Art Collections* (Minneapolis, 1919).

[29] A typewritten "Historical Sketch of the Minneapolis Society of Fine Arts, 1883 to 1911" by the author is in the Folwell Papers. See page 1 and note 9.

of notable Indians, painted from the life by Henry H. Cross. Among them may be found portraits of Hole-in-the-Day, Little Crow, Little Six (Shakopee), Medicine Bottle, and John Other Day, mentioned elsewhere in this history.[30]

The expansion of the collections at length required more spacious rooms for their display, and their removal from a neighborhood that had become surrounded by hotels and commercial buildings was desirable. Upon a happily chosen site, worth some $150,000, Walker erected the well-known and conspicuous building fronting on Loring Park. The cost, including that of installation, was $317,996.05. The building, which is 160 by 200 feet in its outside dimensions, is of the style called Venetian Byzantine. The upper story is skylighted and is partitioned into eighteen galleries, all occupied by paintings. There are single rooms for works of the old masters, American landscapes, paintings of the Barbizon school, and those of Cazin and Turner. Portraits of men occupy two rooms and portraits of women, two other rooms. The paintings in the main rooms are unclassified. In the lower story are displayed the Indian pictures and an overflow of paintings, and in 115 cabinets and wall cases are the vast collections of jades, potteries, ivories, bronzes, ancient glass, gems, and jewelry and the three hundred miniature painted portraits of persons of eminence. No exact inventory of the collections has been made. The number of paintings catalogued is 339, in addition to the Indian collection, which numbers 132. The whole number of individual objects is estimated by Mr. R. H. Adams, the devoted curator for many years, at about six thousand.[31]

Walker was not unmindful at the age of eighty-five that his personal proprietorship and management could not con-

---

[30] Walker Art Galleries, *Alphabetical List of Artists with Biographical Sketches; Title, Size, and Brief Description of Paintings* (n. p., 1927); *Illustrated Catalogue of Indian Portraits* (n. p., 1927).

[31] Archie D. Walker to the author, October 3, 15, 1928, Folwell Papers; interview with R. H. Adams, October 18, 1928, recorded in Folwell Papers; Walker Art Galleries, *List of Artists; Description of Paintings*, p. 4.

tinue indefinitely, and he planned for the creation of a corporation that should have perpetual succession. On April 1, 1925, the Walker Foundation was duly organized under the laws of Minnesota. The articles of incorporation declared the purpose of the foundation to be " to foster and to promote educational artistic and scientific interests," and its plan to be to establish, own or control, maintain, and exhibit museums and galleries of art and science, to acquire books, manuscripts, scientific collections, and objects of fine and industrial arts, to provide lectures and entertainments, and to receive property and use it for any of the above purposes. The original members of the foundation were members of Walker's family, but other persons may become members by contributing sums ranging from five thousand to twenty-five thousand dollars. To this corporation Walker, on December 31, 1926, alienated by deed of gift the galleries building, its site, and all its contents, to be held and administered for the purposes and plans of the foundation. On May 9, 1927, Walker transferred to the foundation two hundred shares of his stock holdings, worth $222,000, as a permanent endowment fund. In his will he expressed his desire that the collections be expanded and the galleries be enlarged. The new proprietary, the Walker Foundation, reopened the galleries to the public on May 21, 1927.[32]

The money value of this great benefaction is necessarily a matter of conjecture. Art galleries are not bought and sold *en bloc* in a market. The investment in Walker's darling recreation cannot be guessed. He kept no memoranda, much less any ledger account of his purchases, travel expenses, building, and maintenance. That in a community that had

[32] Archie D. Walker to the author, October 15, 1928, Folwell Papers; interview with him, September 25, 1928, recorded in Folwell Papers. For estimates of the value of the art collection, see the *Minneapolis Journal*, August 28, 1928, p. 1; the *Minneapolis Morning Tribune*, August 29, 1928, p. 3; and Josiah E. Brill to the author, October 4, 1928, in the Folwell Papers. There are appreciations of the merits of the Walker collections, many of them highly eulogistic, in Walker Art Galleries, *List of Artists; Description of Paintings*, and in Neuhaus and de Ricci, *Walker Art Collections*.

been organized as a territory less than thirty years and as a state less than twenty years and in a city chartered less than ten years a man of business should have entertained the idea of an art gallery was certainly out of the ordinary; that he should have followed up a studied plan for its development for fifty years, should have expended a large fortune on it, should have given his acquisitions a splendid housing, and, finally, should have bequeathed them with a noble endowment for the perpetual delight of his townsmen and the glory of his city and state, is a record that beyond question justifies the enrollment of Thomas Barlow Walker as Minnesota's apostle of art.[33]

Henry B. Whipple, Apostle to the Indians

On October 13, 1859, at the age of thirty-seven, Henry Benjamin Whipple, who had been pastor of a missionary parish in Chicago, was consecrated in Richmond, Virginia, bishop of the Protestant Episcopal church. Forty days later he was at Gull Lake in the southern part of Cass County, Minnesota, to visit a mission to a Chippewa band resident there, then in charge of John Johnson (Enmegahbowh). James Lloyd Breck, the founder of the mission, had been driven out of the country by drunken Indians and his successor, the Reverend E. Steele Peake, had taken refuge at Crow Wing, on the east bank of the Mississippi a few miles below Gull Lake.[34]

[33] It may safely be said that no private citizen of Minnesota has been so frequently written up for the public as has Thomas B. Walker. Upham and Dunlap, in *Minnesota Biographies*, 819, give twenty citations of biographical sketches. See also Platt B. Walker, ed., *Sketches of the Life of Honorable T. B. Walker; a Compilation of Biographical Sketches by Many Authors* (Minneapolis, 1907).

[34] *Ante*, 1: 181; 2: 207; Whipple, *Lights and Shadows*, 27, 29–31; Tanner, *Diocese of Minnesota*, 295–300; Stephen H. Riggs, "Protestant Missions in the Northwest," in *Minnesota Historical Collections*, 6: 162–166; Whipple Diary, November 23, 1859. The diary, which covers the years from the time of his consecration as bishop to February 9, 1874, with the exception of the period from June 9, 1862, to June 13, 1863, is in the possession of the Minnesota Historical Society.

Bishop Whipple had much to learn about Indians and the Chippewa situation, but he learned fast. It was a sad time for the Chippewa. Under the treaties of 1854 and 1855 the disastrous consequences of the annuity system were working the same demoralization and havoc that they had wrought on the Dakota under the treaty of 1837. Many of the Chippewa had abandoned their ancient and normal way of living by hunting and fishing and were living in idleness, gambling and drinking. The distribution of money and goods at the annual payments to individuals and heads of families had broken down respect for chiefs and for their traditional authority. Most of the missions of the American Board of Commissioners for Foreign Missions and the American Missionary Association had been abandoned. Enmegahbowh, however, still remained with the Chippewa.[35]

In a letter of April 9, 1860, to President Buchanan, Bishop Whipple embodied the conclusions of his primary studies. Fire water was the curse of the Indians, he said. "Although every treaty pledges" to the Indians "protection against its sale and use . . . thus far all efforts have proved ineffectual." The Indian agents had no police to enforce the law of Congress. It was useless, said the bishop, to resort to white man's courts with judges elected by a border population. He denounced the policy of making treaties with Indians as equal powers, the annuity system, and the sending of the Chippewa to widely separated reservations. The degradation and helplessness of these American pagans, he said, ought to appeal to every Christian heart. The letter was no doubt duly jacketed and placed on file. The bishop apparently went to Washington in the fall of 1860 to plead for justice for the red men, but no account of his visit has been found.[36]

The interested reader of this history will easily recall the concentration of the Dakota, more commonly called the

[35] *Ante*, 1: 160, 306–308; Riggs, in *Minnesota Historical Collections*, 6: 165.
[36] *Ante*, 1: 165, 307; Whipple, *Lights and Shadows*, 50–53, 66.

"Sioux," under the operation of the treaties of 1851 on a reservation astride the upper reaches of the Minnesota River. It was not until the fall of 1853 that the lower Sioux bands were moved from their old villages to make new homes on the reservation. As has been related, none of the missionaries who had labored among them for so many years felt obliged to care for their souls under the new circumstances. For seven years the lower Sioux enjoyed no regular gospel privileges, but, under the beneficent guardianship of Agent Joseph R. Brown, they made gratifying beginnings in civilization. According to Brown's philosophy, religion could not be "got" by savages. He could have brought in missionaries if he had so desired.[37]

The salvation of the Dakota was as dear to Bishop Whipple as was the salvation of the Chippewa. In June, 1860, at the time of the annual payment, he was at the Redwood agency. Wabasha, Good Thunder, and Taopi came to him with the complaint that the Great Father had not paid the Dakota for the lands on the left bank of the Minnesota nor given them a school. That was one of the grievances that roused the Indians to a state of mind that led to the outbreak of 1862. In October Samuel D. Hinman, whom Bishop Whipple had selected for the duty, began the Mission of St. John at the lower agency. The bishop was deeply interested in this venture. He visited it in December of the same year, at the time of the payment in June, 1861, and in December of that year, when the chiefs assembled by Little Crow acceded to demands of the traders. His last visit was made early in July, 1862. The labors of the missionary were blessed, but "there was a dark cloud lowering on the border." The blanket Indians were turbulent and bold, and their noisy dances disturbed the mission services; a secret society called

---

[37] The treaties of 1851 and the removal of the Sioux to the reservation are discussed *ante*, 1: 281, 284, 353; and accounts of Brown's work and the decline in missionary work among the lower Sioux appear *ante*, 2: 207, n., 219, 221.

the " Soldiers' Lodge " was being formed; the payment had
been delayed two months; the traders had stopped credits;
and the Indians had been told that the traders would get all
the money due from the sale of their lands and half of the
annuities for the year. Still, alarming as the situation was,
there was no fear or expectation of any such Indian war as
that which broke out on August 18, 1862.[38]

The reader has already been told of the outcry from all
over the state, " Death to the murderous Sioux." General
Pope expressed his intention " utterly to exterminate the
Sioux " if he had the power, and even Sibley said that he
would " sweep them with the besom of death." While the
popular mind was in this hysterical state, Bishop Whipple
was the only man of influence who had any word of extenua-
tion for the Sioux. In communications printed in the *Saint
Paul Pioneer* in December, 1862, he set forth the deep-lying
grounds for the Indian animosity and the particular grievances that caused the outbreak. The savages who had done
the murders, he said, must meet their doom as fixed by law,
but no innocent Indians should suffer; mob violence was
" subversive to all law." It may be presumed that Bishop
Whipple's account of the Sioux Outbreak and its causes given
to the president in the fall of 1862 led Lincoln to make his
careful study of the record of the military commission and
to reduce the number of Indians to be executed from about
three hundred to thirty-nine. There was little left for Bishop
Whipple to do in behalf of the Sioux and after their removal
to Dakota Territory in 1863 they passed out of his care.[39]

After the exodus of the Dakota, the Chippewa of Minnesota were the objects of Bishop Whipple's ministrations

[38] *Ante*, 2: 218, 399; Whipple, *Lights and Shadows*, 60, 62, 106, 138; Tanner,
Diocese of Minnesota, 386, 387, 389–392.
[39] *Ante*, 2: 190, 203, 208, 258; *Minnesota in the Civil and Indian Wars*,
2: 198, 233, 257, 289 (St Paul, 1891–99); John B. Sanborn, " Bishop Whipple
as a Mediator for the Rights of Indians in Treaties," in *Minnesota Historical
Collections*, 10: 714 (part 2); *Saint Paul Pioneer*, 1862: December 3, p. 1; 17,
p. 1. Whipple, in his *Lights and Shadows*, 123, gives the erroneous date of
September, 1862, for the publication of his letters.

until 1895, when a division of the diocese turned them over to the bishop of Duluth. No adequate account of Bishop Whipple's labors with and for those Indians can be attempted here, if indeed any such account could be made from the limited material now available. In the three years following his first visit to Gull Lake he made six journeys to Chippewa reservations. Twice, on visits to Leech Lake and Red Lake, he journeyed five hundred miles.[40] At Red Lake he learned that in the previous year, 1861, an attempt had been made to obtain the consent of the Red Lake Chippewa to a treaty allowing one hundred and fifty thousand dollars for traders' claims. The head chief, Madwaganonint, defeated the attempt. The chief told the bishop that the white men would come again and ask for a treaty. " Will you tell me what to say to them?" he asked. The bishop told him to ask for houses, cattle, farming tools, and schools. On October 2, 1863, a treaty was made by a government commission at the Old Crossing of the Red Lake River. It provided for the cession of Indian rights over some three million acres in the extreme northwest corner of Minnesota and of a large adjacent area in the northeast corner of North Dakota. There was no mention of houses or cattle or farming implements and nothing explicit about schools, but it was stipulated that five thousand dollars a year might be expended for " agriculture, education, the purchase of goods, powder, lead," and such other purposes as might be prescribed by the president. One hundred thousand dollars were allowed for traders' claims and for damages to steamboats.[41]

In the winter following, the Red Lake chief, who had refused to sign the treaty because there was no provision for

[40] Whipple Diary, March 11, July 19, 1860; February 2, July 31, 1861; January 13, 1862; Tanner, Diocese of Minnesota, 481, 511, 515. The bishop's papers have not been accessible to the author.

[41] Whipple, Lights and Shadows, 74, 143; Statutes at Large, 13: 667–671. On March 15, 1864, Whipple recorded in his diary that he left for Washington to inform the government that the Red Lake Indians did not know the character of the treaty they had made and that it was " from beginning to end a fraud and must sooner or later bring another Indian war."

houses, cattle, or schools, walked a hundred and fifty miles
to lay his troubles before Bishop Whipple. A few weeks
later a delegation of Red Lake chiefs and braves appeared
in Washington. Bishop Whipple was there to act as their
unpaid counsel. For two weeks he pleaded their cause, but,
as he says, he might as well have whistled against the north
wind. He then informed the commissioner of Indian affairs
that he would continue his argument in the public press. A
new treaty was made on April 12, 1864. It provided for the
cession of the same area included in the treaty of the previous
October. There was no allowance for traders' claims, nor
for annual bonuses to the chiefs to hold them subservient.
For clothing, farming tools, and so forth, twelve thousand
dollars a year was guaranteed; for iron, steel, and blacksmith
tools, fifteen hundred dollars; and for carpentering, one
thousand dollars. A sawmill with a run of millstones was
to be built. The bishop and his clients, however, were
obliged to make some concessions. For the payment of
damage claims against the Indians, seventy-five thousand
dollars were allowed; to chiefs for provisions, clothing, and
presents to their people, twenty thousand dollars; and to the
head chief, five thousand dollars. The mixed-bloods got
their grants of one hundred and sixty acres of land apiece,
which were to have been patented after five years of residence
and cultivation, commuted into an immediate benefaction of
scrip, to be located within the area ceded. The attentive
reader knows to what uses scrip might be put by those with
the proper knowledge. The bishop wrote that this struggle
for a better treaty for the Red Lake Chippewa was " one of
the severest personal conflicts " of his life.[42]

[42] Whipple, *Lights and Shadows*, 143–145; *Statutes at Large*, 13: 689–692.
In a letter to Joel Bassett, November 14, 1866, in the Bassett Papers, Whipple
expressed his deep interest in the reform of " this abominable Indian system."
Bassett was appointed Chippewa agent upon the urgent request of the bishop.
Whipple was one of the commissioners representing the United States at the
negotiation of the treaty of March 19, 1867, establishing the White Earth
Reservation. *Statutes at Large*, 16: 719.

The reader has already been informed of other activities of Bishop Whipple in behalf of the Chippewa, among them his protest in 1885 against the opening of the White Earth Reservation to white settlement, his appeal to President Cleveland, and his services on the Northwest Indian Commission. His ministrations to the White Earth mission, over which he placed the Reverend Joseph A. Gilfillan, can only be referred to here as part of the burden he bore for the Chippewa.[43] On his record Henry Benjamin Whipple will be acknowledged by all as Minnesota's apostle to the Indians.

NEWTON H. WINCHELL, APOSTLE OF SCIENCE

In an inaugural address presented on December 22, 1869, before the regents, faculty, and student body of the newly-formed University of Minnesota, the author of this history suggested as a proper duty of a state university the conduct of a geological and natural history survey of the state. The proposition was renewed in his annual report for 1870. The board took no formal action, but the president of the university, presuming upon its approval, prepared for the legislature of 1872 a bill providing for such a survey. With influential members of the board in the state Senate to father it, the bill passed with little opposition. It has been said that this was the first instance of charging a state university with such an enterprise.[44]

Correspondence undertaken at once resulted in the calling of Newton Horace Winchell, then an assistant geologist on the Ohio survey, to begin the work. It had been the original intention that the several branches of the survey should be prosecuted by members of the faculty of the university under the general direction of the executive. Winchell had not so

[43] *Ante,* pp. 200, 202, 204, 207, 215, 217; Tanner, *Diocese of Minnesota,* 480. For further biographical information on Whipple, see Upham and Dunlap, *Minnesota Biographies,* 846, and references.

[44] Folwell, *University Addresses,* 1, 53; Board of Regents, *Reports,* 1870, p. 50; *General Laws,* 1872, pp. 86–88; *Senate Journal,* 377; *House Journal,* 584.

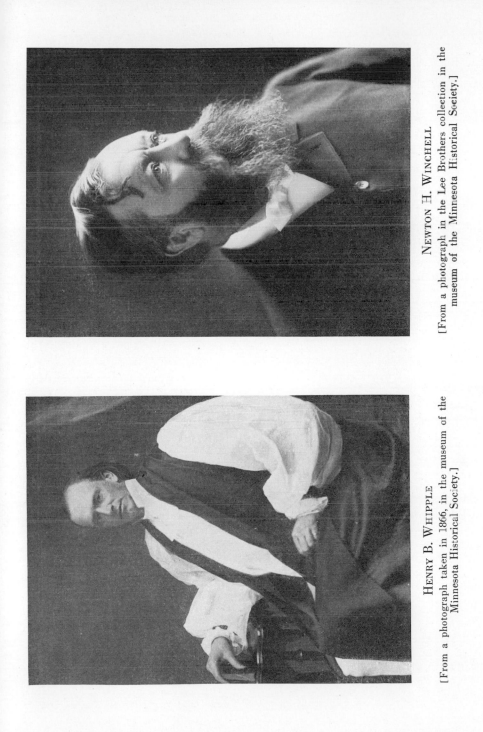

HENRY B. WHIPPLE
[From a photograph taken in 1866, in the museum of the
Minnesota Historical Society.]

NEWTON H. WINCHELL
[From a photograph in the Lee Brothers collection in the
museum of the Minnesota Historical Society.]

understood from the correspondence but desired the position
of state geologist in charge of all branches. Without controversy he was so designated. He was also elected to the
chair of geology and mineralogy and for some years he gave
all the instruction needed in those fields.[45]

The first work undertaken was a general reconnoissance of
the visible — the " surface " — geology of the state and the
tentative location of the rocks in the geological series as accepted at the time by American geologists. Igneous and
metamorphic rocks were found to occupy a large portion of
the state. The results were recorded in a very interesting
manner in the first annual report, that of 1872. Successive
annual reports, twenty-four in number, contain the results
of careful studies of the several counties and of investigations
of special topics. In obedience to an act of the legislature
of 1873, an investigation was made into the peat beds of the
inhabited parts of the state. The conclusion was that the
amount of high-grade peat was much less than had been expected and that most of it would require manufacture to make
of it a desirable fuel. The negative result served to prevent
needless, or at least premature, investment of capital.
Another waste of expenditure was prevented by the report for
1873, which showed that, since all the rocks of the state lay
below those of the carboniferous epoch, it would be useless to
bore or dig for coal in Minnesota. Excellent building stones,
clays, and sands that could be adapted to various uses were
found in abundance, especially in the valley of the Minnesota.[46]

The original appropriation of one thousand dollars a year
was inadequate for the work of the geological survey, and in
his first report Winchell suggested that "the state lands
known as *salt lands* be so sold or appropriated . . . as to be
available for that purpose." The enabling act of 1857 had

[45] Board of Regents, Minutes, B 1: 58, 60–64, 74, 76, 80, 81, 83.
[46] Geological and Natural History Survey, *Reports*, 1873, pp. 88–127;
General Laws, 1873, pp. 202, 255.

granted to the state all the salt springs, not exceeding twelve in number, to be found within its borders, " with six sections of land adjoining or as contiguous as may be to each " — 46,080 acres in all — " to be used or disposed of " as the legislature should direct. In 1858 Governor Sibley sent out Pierre Bottineau and James D. Skinner, an engineer living in St. Paul, to select the lands, and on November 27 of that year they filed their report, which described six sections adjacent to each of twelve springs, which they had personally examined; all but eighteen sections, unsurveyed land in unceded Indian territory, lay in townships 131 to 136, ranges 42 to 46, within the present limits of Otter Tail and Wilkin counties. On November 30 the governor furnished the land office at Otter Tail City with a list and a map of the lands being claimed by the state and requested that they be reserved from preëmption and sale. Soon thereafter he retired from office and apparently no further action was taken until about ten years later. In the meantime the eighteen sections of unsurveyed lands — about eleven thousand acres — had been included within the limits of the White Earth Reservation, established in 1865; and local land officers had allowed adverse claims to be entered against some of the lands in other sections. In 1871, 26,444 acres free from adverse claims were certified to the state. Twelve sections of these lands —7,643 acres — were granted by the legislatures of 1870 and 1872 to the Belle Plaine Salt Company, which was interested in the development of what was believed to be a salt spring at Belle Plaine in Scott County. The company sank an exploratory well but no water of commercial value was found. The legislature of 1873 then placed the remainder of the state's salt spring lands at the disposal of the university board of regents for financing the geological and natural history survey. The balance available at that time was only 18,771 acres, but this amount was subsequently more than doubled by the certification of additional salt spring lands

to the state; and the work of the survey was paid for principally from the proceeds of these lands.[47]

With meager appropriations and tardy sales of the lands,
the progress of the survey was slow during the first decade.
For seven years the state geologist, filling the chair of geology
and mineralogy in the university, could give only the summer
season to field work.[48] At length sufficient material had been
collected and interpreted to warrant the compilation of a final
record. The first volume of the *Geology of Minnesota*, constituting the *Final Report* of the survey, was published in
1884 as a quarto of 697 pages. More than a hundred pages
were devoted to an historical sketch of explorations and surveys in Minnesota; a chapter was given to the physical
features of the state — its geographical position, elevations,
surface character, soils, forests, and so forth; sixty-one pages
were given to an interesting account of its known building
stones — the granites, the limestones, and the sandstones
of various qualities and values; and the remainder of the
volume was devoted to individual surveys of twenty-nine
counties in southern and southwestern Minnesota, under the
uniform headings: surface features, geological structure,
and material resources. Maps in color and illustrations
were inserted to ornament and explain the text.

The second volume was submitted for publication in 1885,
but the printing was delayed until 1888. It was wholly

[47] Geological and Natural History Survey, *Reports*, 1872, p. 119; 1873,
pp. 75, 77, 79–87; 1895–98, pp. xvii–xix; Minnesota, *Legislative Manual*, 1929,
p. 10; *Special Laws*, 1870, pp. 421–424; 1872, p. 428; *General Laws*, 1873, p.
255; 1875, p. 124; 1885, p. 285; Governor's Archives, A: 53, 65–68; United
States, *Statutes at Large*, 20: 352; *Salt Spring Lands in Minnesota* (45 Congress, 2 session, *Senate Reports*, no. 258 — serial 1790) ; Pillsbury, *Message*,
January 6, 1881, p. 24; " Approved Lists, Salt Spring Lands," a bound volume
containing the lists of selections made and copies of the letters of certification,
in the office of the auditor of state. The management of the salt spring lands
by the board of regents may be traced by consulting the heading " Salt Spring
Lands," in the index to the minutes of the board, and the file of correspondence
relating thereto, in the office of the university comptroller.

[48] Board of Regents, *Minutes*, B 1: 151, 164, 168, 174. On June 6, 1878,
Winchell was relieved from teaching and was instructed to prosecute the geological survey with all possible dispatch.

devoted to the surveys of thirty-nine central counties, five of which were treated by the state geologist and the remainder by an assistant geologist, Warren Upham, a distinguished name among American geologists. The chapter on Hennepin County contains Winchell's very notable account of the recession of the Falls of St. Anthony from Fort Snelling, a distance of some eight miles. His estimate of the time occupied by this recession was 7,803 years.

The third volume appeared in two parts, issued in 1895 and 1897, respectively. The subtitle of each was *Paleontology*, a word compounded of three Greek words and Greek to the ordinary citizen; so also is the text of the volume. The author of the present work recalls the time when the belief was general that the world " and all that therein is " were created in six ordinary days some six thousand years ago. Since then studies of rocks and soils by men of science have led to the interpretation of the " days of creation " as immense periods of time of millions of years each. Rocks have been found to exist in an ascending series from a common base of igneous origin containing no traces of life. On this common bed have been built successive layers, distinguishable partly by structure and chemical composition but more completely by traces, impressions, casts, and remains of plants and animals, called fossils, in a rising scale from mollusks to mammals. The third volume of the *Final Report* contains lists, descriptions, and illustrations of the fossils found in the rocks of Minnesota. The lay reader will find little he can understand in the text, but if he will glance over the numerous engraved plates he will be astonished and delighted with the representations of the wonderful and beautiful forms of vegetable and animal life that once existed in the state.

The fourth volume, which is in large part the work of assistant geologists, came out in 1899. Its 629 pages include the reports of geological investigations in fifteen counties

covering roughly the northern one-third of the state. The
areal geology of the state had now been covered, though not
completed. More was left to be done than had been done,
according to the preface.

A year later, in 1900, the fifth volume was in print. It
opens with an essay on structural geology. The body of the
volume is given to a treatise on the petrographic geology and
a description of the crystalline rocks of Minnesota, based
upon the examination of three thousand microscopic thin
sections of rock. In preparation for this treatise and at his
own expense, Winchell spent the year from May, 1895, to
May, 1896, and the first half of 1898 in laboratory work at
the Museum of Natural History in Paris. This was his only
vacation in twenty-three years.[49] Near the close of the volume
Winchell announces his abandonment of the theory that the
iron ores of the Mesabi Range are of organic origin and
presents his hypothesis of chemical origin brought about by
volcanic eruptions.[50]

By this time the regents of the university had decided that
the work of the geological survey must soon be brought to
a close in order that some progress might be made on the
natural history survey with the balance of the funds available. The *Final Report* was concluded with the issue of a
sixth volume in 1901, consisting of maps printed in the previous volumes, with brief synoptical descriptions that were,
in some instances, corrective. This atlas is very convenient
and serviceable and the colored map following the preface,
showing the geological systems of the state below the drift,
is instructive.[51]

[49] Geological and Natural History Survey, *Reports*, 1895–98, p. vii.
[50] Winchell, *Geology of Minnesota*, 5: 76, 990–999.
[51] Board of Regents, Minutes, B 1: 507, 524, 541. In Geological and
Natural History Survey, *Reports*, 1895–98, pp. xxi–xxvii, Winchell outlines
some of the phases of the geology of the state that still remained to be investigated. The investigations thus far conducted, as presented in the *Final
Report*, he said, constituted only "a kind of connoissance" and should serve
as a foundation for a more minute survey.

The act of 1872 creating the survey provided also for a museum of extensive scope. Although the collections were confined mainly to samples from the rocks and deposits examined in the course of the survey, they became considerable in amount and value. The state geologist was curator, and when he was not occupied in field work or otherwise engaged, he gave much time to the arrangement and classification of the specimens.[52]

On January 1, 1888, Winchell, in collaboration with other western geologists, issued the first number of the *American Geologist*, the first journal in the country devoted wholly to geology and the related sciences. It was issued monthly in octavo form. After some years Winchell became the sole editor and proprietor and it may safely be assumed that no pecuniary profit resulted from the enterprise. He tired of the labor of love, however, and with the issue of volume 36 in 1905 he brought it to a close.

Winchell had not been in Minnesota six months when he brought together a company of citizens interested in science and proposed an organization for coöperation. In the winter of 1873 the Minnesota Academy of Natural Sciences was founded. He took no office at that time but in later years he served three terms as president. He was at all times its most productive member.

Winchell had no sooner disposed of the *American Geologist* than he ventured into the divergent field of anthropology. On May 1, 1906, he began work on the last of his major publications, *The Aborigines of Minnesota*, published by the Minnesota Historical Society in 1911 as a sumptuous quarto volume of 759 pages, with abundant illustrations. This work, which is one of great interest and permanent value, is a veritable cyclopedia of information about the aboriginal dwellers in Minnesota — the possible Eskimo dwelling on the edge

[52] *General Laws,* 1872, p. 87; Geological and Natural History Survey, *Reports,* 1895–98, p. xii.

of the receding continental glacier six or seven thousand years ago, the mound builders, and the two great Indian nations of recent times. On April 24, 1914, Winchell delivered an address before the Iowa Academy of Science on "The Antiquity of Man in America Compared with Europe." Eight days thereafter, on May 2, after a brief illness and a surgical operation, he died at the age of seventy-five years. A meeting of the Minnesota Academy of Sciences on June 2, 1914, was devoted to memorial addresses, which were eulogistic without extravagance. The labors and achievements thus briefed are good warrant for the statement of one of his colleagues: "For upwards of forty years Professor Winchell stood as the pioneer, as the leader and director of scientific knowledge in the state of Minnesota in its broadest and truest sense." [53] He is therefore here accorded the title of Minnesota's apostle of science.

[53] *Minneapolis Journal*, May 3, 1914, pp. 1, 2; *St. Paul Pioneer Press*, May 3, 1914, p. 7; *Minnesota Historical Collections*, 15: 824–830; Minnesota Academy of Sciences, *Bulletins*, 5: 74, 92, 121–151 (July, 1914; May, 1917). The name of the Minnesota Academy of Natural Sciences was changed to Minnesota Academy of Sciences in 1902.

CONSOLIDATED INDEX

CONSOLIDATED INDEX

CONSOLIDATED INDEX

Each work referred to in the footnotes is indexed under author, editor, or, if anonymous, title, with reference to a citation containing bibliographical information. The names of authors and editors are distinguished by the use of small capitals; titles of printed works are indicated by italics and those of works in manuscript and of articles in printed works, by quotation marks. Boldface numerals refer to volumes and are to be understood as applying to all page references that follow until the next volume number appears.

Abbe, Mrs. S. B., **2**: 381n
ABBE, Mrs. S. B., "Hole-in-the-Day and the Sioux Outbreak," **2**: 374n
Abert, J. J., **1**: 122n, 127n, 460, 461
ABERT, J. J., "Plan of the Military Reserve at Fort Snelling," **1**: 427n
Abolitionists, attitude of Democrats and Republicans toward, **2**: 69
Academy of Sciences, *see* Minnesota Academy of Sciences
Accault, Michael, explorer, **1**: 27, 31n, 32
Acker, W. H., **2**: 28n, 77n, 78
Act Proposing a Loan of State Credit, **2**: 48n
Acton Township, Meeker County, warfare with Sioux, **2**: 158–160, 174; murders, 239, 283, 392, 415–417, 432
Ada, **4**: 280n
ADAMS, ANN, "Early Days at Red River Settlement," **1**: 149n
ADAMS, C. F., JR., Recollections, **2**: 67n
ADAMS, C. F., SR., Diary, **2**: 67n
Adams, Gen. C. P., **2**: 165n, 312n, 314n; commands Hatch's Battalion, 293; wounded, 311
Adams, Cuyler, **4**: 22, 24n
Adams, E. E., **3**: 493n, 494n, 499n
ADAMS, E. E., "Nelson-Kindred Campaign," **3**: 148n
ADAMS, HENRY, *United States,* **1**: 78n
ADAMS, J. Q., *Memoirs,* **1**: 70n
ADAMS, JOHN, *Works,* **1**: 498n
Adams, R. H., **4**: 470
Adams, S. E., **1**: 512n, **2**: 28n
Adams Papers, **2**: 165n
Address at the Inauguration of William W. Folwell, **4**: 67n
Address to the Holders of the Minnesota State Bonds, **3**: 426n

Administration and finance, commission of, **3**: 321; powers, **4**: 126; contest for control of university, 127–133
Agate Bay, **4**: 15, 16
Agreement with Red Lake and Pembina Bands, **4**: 303n
Agricultural college, *see* Agricultural College of Minnesota; University of Minnesota
Agricultural College Board, **4**: 83
Agricultural College of Minnesota, Glencoe, **4**: 80–85
Agricultural experiment station, *see* University of Minnesota
Agricultural Society, *see* Minnesota State Agricultural Society; State Agricultural Society
Agriculture, beginnings, **1**: 105, 230, 230n, 232; societies, 360, 361, 430; statistics relating to: *1860–70*, **2**: 65n, **3**: 3, 58, 60, 62, *1870–80*, 62, 110, 111, 140, 141, *1890*, 192, 193, *1900*, 251, 252, 252n, *1920*, 322; improvements, **2**: 344, **3**: 140; growth, *1860–70*, 1, 3; attempt to obtain crop and acreage census, *1866*, 20n; extended to prairie lands, 62–64; farmhouses described, 64; crops raised, 63, 64, 66, 193; bonanza farming, 65, 193, 208, 541; affected by grasshopper plague, 97–112; affected by chinch bug, 111; beginnings of diversification, 140; evil effects of specialization, 140, 157; farmers' institutes, 179; legislation for farmers demanded, 199; taxation of farmers, 247, **4**: 458; farm-crop and stock census, *1918*, **3**: 563; economic status of farmers, **4**: 148; farm loans, 149; taught in schools, 187; on Indian

489

reservations, 196, 197, 262, 296n, 307; in Red River Valley, 199; agricultural coöperation, 402, 404–406; conditions during nineties, 458; school, *see* University of Minnesota. *See also* Dairy industry; Farmer-Labor party; Farmers' Alliance of Minnesota; Fruit-raising; Grain; Granger movement; Grasshopper plague; Homestead Act; Minnesota State Agricultural Society; People's party; Transportation; Wheat

Aisne-Marne offensive, **3**: 534

Aitkin, W. A., **1**: 84n, 151n, 156, 157n, 174, 178, 269n

Aitkin County, **3**: 147n, **4**: 33, 296

Aiton, G. B., **4**: 185

Aiton, Rev. J. F., **1**: 204

Aiton, Mrs. Mary B., **2**: 64

Akeley, H. C., **3**: 208n

Akepa, Sioux chief, **2**: 122

AKERS, B. H., " Minnesota Honors Prof. Haecker," **4**: 404n

Albert Lea, **3**: 490, 492, 495, 496, 497

Aldrich, Cyrus, **1**: 417n, **2**: 68n, 107, 334; congressman, 28n; aspires to senatorship, 107; approves execution of condemned Sioux, 203n; introduces bill for relief of victims of Sioux Outbreak, 246; introduces homestead bill, 331; vote on Morrill bill, **4**: 79n

Alexandria, **2**: 243, **4**: 190; home of Nelson, **3**: 146, 498; railway station, 443, 458n, 459, 460

Alexandria Post News, **3**: 492

Algonkin Indians, **1**: 2

Algonquian Indians, **1**: 6, 16, 32, **4**: 190

Aliens, demand for restriction of property rights, **3**: 188, 199, 202; denied franchise, 224, **4**: 333; registration, *1918*, **3**: 561. *See also* Foreigners; individual nationalities

Allan, W. C., **2**: 161n

Allanson, G. G., **2**: 122n

Allanson, Mrs. G. G., **2**: 122n

Allatoona, battle, **2**: 322

Allen, Capt. C. J., **4**: 209

Allen, Lieut. James, on Schoolcraft expedition, **1**: 115, 115n, 117, 124; report, 116n, 204

ALLEN, PAUL, ed., *Expedition of Lewis and Clark*, **1**: 89n

Allis, Lorenzo, **3**: 411, 413, 417n

Allotments to Indians on White Earth Reservation (serial 4023), **4**: 267n

Allotments to Indians on White Earth Reservation (serial 4583), **4**: 235n

Allouez, Father Claude, **1**: 18, 80; establishes mission, 16, 43; at Indian council, 17

Aloysius, Father, *see* Hermanutz, Rev. Aloysius

Alteration of House Bill 342, **1**: 330n

ALVORD, C. W., *Illinois Country*, **1**: 26n; *Mississippi Valley in British Politics*, 52n; " Travels of Carver," 59n; " Genesis of the Proclamation of 1763," 65n; *Cahokia Records*, 70n

America First, **3**: 554n

American Board of Commissioners for Foreign Missions, **1**: 115, 173, 174, 183, 189, 200, 201, **4**: 473. *See also* Missionaries; Missions

American Expeditionary Forces, **3**: 530

American Federation of Labor, **4**: 449

American Fur Co., **1**: 126, 172, 173, 240, 312n, 371, **4**: 294; organized, **1**: 132; reorganized, 132; headquarters, 133; growth, 133; attempts to recover lost credits, 159, 169n; loses monopoly of fur trade, 163; taken over by Chouteau and Co., 163, 240n; absorbs Columbia Fur Co., 190; posts: 215, Mackinac (Michilimackinac), 103, 133, 162, 172, 443, Fond du Lac, 104, 174, Sandy Lake, 104, 151n, 174, Mendota (New Hope), 161, 164n, 216, 219, 422, 440, Madeline Island, 173, Lac qui Parle, 257; interest in treaty negotiations, 277n, 287, 323; political factor in Rice-Sibley campaign, 371; interest in Faribault claim, 440–444; opposition to Sweetser, 462. *See also* Fur trade

American Geologist, **4**: 484

American House, **2**: 4n

American Missionary Association, **4**: 473

American Park and Outdoor Art Association, **4**: 431

American Public Health Association, **4**: 423

American Railway Union, **3**: 200

American Society of Equity, **3**: 541

Americanization work, **3**: 560

Ames, Dr. A. A., **3**: 517; candidate for governor, 172, 173, 221; sketch, 172

Ames, A. E., **2**: 28n

Ames, Rev. C. G., **1**: 376n, 401

Ames, C. W., **3**: 570n; statue commissioner, 283, 284n, 285n; member commission of public safety, 557, 558n, 566

Amos, A., *Trials Relative to the Destruction of Selkirk's Settlement*, **1**: 215n

Anawangmani, Simon, Sioux Indian, **2**: 391, 428

Anderson, C. L., *Report on Geology*, **4**: 3n

Anderson, Capt. Joseph, **2**: 105n, 192n; at battle of Birch Coulee, 152, 153, 175, 387, 389; sent to New Ulm, 168

Anderson, T. L., **2**: 15

Anderson, William, *Constitution of Minnesota*, **2**: 1n; *City Charter Making in Minnesota*, **3**: 521n

Andersonville, Georgia, **2**: 306

André, Father, **2**: 269

Andrews, Gen. C. C., in the Civil War, **2**: 94, 304; candidate for congressman, **3**: 16; promotion of forestry, **4**: 253, 254, 387–402; minister to Sweden and Norway, 386; consul general at Rio de Janeiro, 388; death, 402

Andrews, C. C., " Narrative of the Third Regiment," **2**: 92n, 94n; " Surrender of the Third Regiment," 94n; *Recollections*, **4**: 254n; " To Prevent Forest Fires," 387n; " Forests and Forest Culture of Sweden," 387n; *Forestry in Sweden*, 387n

Andrist, C. M., " An Appreciation of Governor Hammond," **3**: 294n

Annuities of Certain Sioux Indians, **2**: 423n

Anoka, **2**: 378; designated railway station, 42; garrisoned, 243; insane asylum, **3**: 248

Anonymous Letter to Springer, **3**: 397n

" Anson Northup," steamboat, **3**: 351n

Antietam, battle, **2**: 86

Anti-Monopolist, **3**: 86n

Anti-Monopolists, hold state conventions, **3**: 48, 49, 82, 116; in legislature of *1874*, 49; hold joint caucus with Democrats, 86; party organ, 86n; organize Independent party, 116; support Donnelly, 117. *See also* Donnelly, Ignatius; Granger movement; Greenback party

Appleby, W. R., *Cuyuna Ores*, **4**: 23n

Arctander, J. W., **3**: 411, 413, 414, 414n, 417n

Arkansas River, explorers, **1**: 20, 100; Jolliet's map, 21

Armstrong, G. W., **1**: 415, 420n

Armstrong, J. W., **1**: 57n

Army, increased for World War, **3**: 314. *See also* National Guard; individual military units

Army of Occupation, **3**: 537

Army of the Cumberland, **2**: 320, 321

Army of the Potomac, **2**: 9, 101, 102, **4**: 66, 104

Artillery, troops organized, **2**: 98; number in Civil and Indian wars, 339. *See also* individual artillery units

Ashby, N. B., *Riddle of the Sphinx*, **3**: 188n

Assawa Lake, **1**: 124

Assiniboia, **1**: 213

Assiniboine River, **2**: 294, 444, **3**: 374

Astor, J. J., **1**: 132n, 133n; sketch, 131

Atkins, J. D. C., **4**: 201

Atwater, Judge Isaac, **2**: 366n, **4**: 437n

Atwater, Isaac, *Minneapolis and Hennepin County*, **1**: 423n; biographical sketch of Flandrau, **2**: 136n

Auguelle, Antoine, explorer, **1**: 27

Austin, Horace, **2**: 105, **3**: 72, 76, 83, 171, 360, 409; criticizes Sibley, **2**: 176n; deals with mob at Mankato, 205; on Sibley expedition of *1863*, 271; account of first battle of New Ulm, 368; sketch, **3**: 17; elected governor, 17, 18; position in railroad difficulties, 32, 34, 35, 39, 44, 46, 49, 52; reëlected, 36; endeavors to secure release of prisoners at Fort Garry, 78, 380–383; checks riots in Brainerd, 79; aspires to senatorship, 85; criticizes county treasurers, 120; characterizes J. R. Brown, 349; advocates payment of state railroad bonds, 426; urges adjustment of Dutch loans to railroads, 448; on university board of regents, 4: 72n; appoints members of board of health, 415

AUSTIN, HORACE, "The Frontier of Southwestern Minnesota in 1857," 2: 225n

Austin, 3: 400, 401; election law applicable to, 4: 360n

Austin Register, 3: 401, 403

Australian ballot, 3: 189, 202, 4: 340, 347, 349, 353–356

Austrians, number: 1875, 3: 73; 1910, 558. See also Aliens

Averill, Gen. J. T., 2: 343n, 3: 17, 18n

AYER, MRS. ELIZABETH T., "Frederick Ayer," 1: 174n

Ayer, Rev. Frederick, 1: 178n, 182n, 2: 378; sketch, 1: 173; compiles Chippewa spelling book, 174; compiles Chippewa grammar, 176

Baasen, Francis, 2: 4n, 25, 26n, 28n

Babbitt, 4: 25n

Babcock, L. A., 1: 263, 2: 17

Baccarat sector, 3: 532

BACKES, W. J., "General Zebulon M. Pike," 1: 91n

Backus, Mrs. G. J., 2: 314

BACON, J. D., Warning against Townleyism, 3: 543n

Bacon, Brig. Gen. J. M., at Leech Lake Indian uprising, 4: 315–318

Bad Boy, Chippewa chief, 2: 375, 381n

Bad Hail, Sioux chief, 1: 259

Bailey, Capt. H. S., 2: 192n

Bailly, Alexis, 1: 133, 165, 166n, 216, 279, 283n, 438, 484n, 2: 28n

Bain, J. F., 3: 386

Baker, B. F., 1: 137n, 197n, 216, 249n

Baker, Howard, 2: 415, 416, 417

Baker, Mrs. Howard, 2: 417

Baker, Gen. J. H., 2: 70n, 272n, 3: 244; commands post at St. Louis, 2: 305, 307n; brevetted brigadier general, 307n; account of first battle of New Ulm, 373; eulogizes Hubbard, 3: 164; candidate for congressman, 242; eulogizes Ramsey, 268

BAKER, J. H., "Sources of the Mississippi," 1: 128n; "Alexander Ramsey," 248n; Governors of Minnesota, 249n; "Transportation in Minnesota," 2: 267n; "Address in

Celebration of the Anniversary of the Treaty of Pike with the Sioux," 3: 349n; "Lake Superior," 4: 1n

Bakeries, act regulating, 4: 457, 457n

Balcombe, St. A. D., 1: 384, 400n, 408, 2: 146n, 257n

Bald Island, 1: 12, 39

Baldwin, M. W., 4: 435, 439

Baldwin Grammar School, 4: 439

Baldwin School, 4: 435, 439

Baldwin University, 4: 439; name changed to Macalester College, 441

Ball's Bluff, battle, 2: 86, 87

Bank of Minnesota, proposed, 1: 330; building, 3: 485

Banks, failure, 1: 364, 2: 57; laws governing: referred to by Sibley 1: 23, passed, 57, revision, 62, 3: 226, discussed in constitutional convention, 1: 413; national, established, 2: 58; examination, 3: 121–124; demand for new forms of banking, 199, 201, 543, 550n; growth in Twin Cities, 253; department of banking, 287. See also Bank of Minnesota; Financial conditions; Panics

Bannatyne, A. G. B., 2: 444

Baptists, 3: 427n

BARBÉ-MARBOIS, FRANÇOIS DE, Louisiane, 1: 76n

Barnard, Dr. Alonzo, 2: 384

Barnard, J. F., 2: 383n

Barnesville, 3: 445, 458, 458n, 467

Barnum, E. P., 3: 149

Barr, G. T., 3: 218

Barton, Ara, 2: 28n

BARTON, WINIFRED W., John P. Williamson, 2: 233n

Bassett, Joel, 4: 477n

Bassett Creek, 3: 333

Baudette, damaged by fire, 4: 391

Baxter, G. N., 3: 487, 489

BAXTER, J. P., Cartier, 1: 1n

Baxter, Judge L. L., 3: 504

Bazille, Charles, 3: 271

Bean, A. M., 2: 370, 373

Bean, Maj. J. L., 1: 147n

Bear Island, 4: 312

Bear Island Indians, uprising, 4: 312–323

Beard, H. B., 4: 100, 102

BEARD, DR. R. O., "Medical School," 4: 423n

Beauharnois, marquis de, 1: 45n, 46

Beaulieu, Clement, 2: 28n

Beaulieu, Gustav, **4**: 231, 232, 323n

BEAULIEU, T. H., *Land Allotment Question of the Chippewas*, **4**: 267n

Beauregard, Gen. P. G. T., **2**: 85

Beaver, Lieut. F. J., **2**: 275n

Beaver Bay, **4**: 10

Beaver Creek, **2**: 152, 155

Becker, G. L., **1**: 410, **2**: 18, 28n, 53, 62n; candidate for governor, **3**: 197, 203; railroad president, 450

Becker County, **3**: 147n, 148, **4**: 280n; ravaged by grasshoppers, **3**: 103; Lord Gordon in, 362, 363, 364; mortgages of Chippewa allotments, **4**: 278

Bee, Capt. B. E., **2**: 404, 406n

Bejou, **4**: 265n

BELCOURT, G. A., "Department of Hudson's Bay," **1**: 216n

Belden, H. C., **4**: 47

Belden, William, **3**: 371n

Belgium, **4**: 57

BELL, C. N., *Selkirk Settlement*, **1**: 214n; *Original Letters Relating to the Selkirk Settlement*, 215n

BELL, EDWIN, "Early Steamboating on the Minnesota and Red Rivers." **2**: 148n

Bell, R. C., **4**: 291, 292

Belland, Henry, Sr., **2**: 109, 272n, 286n

Belle Plaine, **2**: 148, 148n

Belle Plaine Salt Co., **4**: 480

Belm, Capt. John, **2**: 142

Belmont, attacked by Sioux, **2**: 123

Beltrami, G. C., **1**: 216; accompanies Long expedition, 109; searches for sources of Mississippi, 109–111

BELTRAMI, G. C., *Pilgrimage*, **1**: 57n; "Capt. Jonathan Carver," 57n; *La découverte des sources du Mississippi*, 111

Benjamin, Dr. John, **2**: 284n

Benson, J. R., **3**: 374, 375, 377

Benson, William, **4**: 155

Bentley, L. R., **3**: 374, 376, 377, 383

Benton County, **3**: 103, 147n; population in *1850*, **1**: 352n

Berdan, Col. Hiram, **2**: 99

Berghold, Rev. Alexander, **2**: 365

BERGHOLD, ALEXANDER, *The Indians' Revenge*, **2**: 109n; *Prairie-Rosen*, **3**: 72n

BERGLUND, ABRAHAM, *Steel Corporation*, **4**: 33n

Berkey, Peter, **2**: 244

Berry, C. H., **1**: 512n, **2**: 28n, 31

Berry, W. M., **4**: 429n

Betourney, Judge, **3**: 376, 378, 383

Better Business, **4**: 405n

BIBAUD, MICHEL, *La Bibliothéque Canadienne*, **1**: 46n

BIENVILLE, CÉLORON DE, "Journal de la campagne," **1**: 50n

Bierbauer, Capt. William, **2**: 373

Biermann, Adolph, elected state auditor, **3**: 189; investigation of timber sales, 206, 206n, 504, 511

"Big Burning," **1**: 124

Big Eagle, Sioux subchief, cited, **2**: 131n, 133, 178n, 179n, 239, 241n; pardoned, 262; explains Acton murders, 415

Big Fork River, **4**: 192

Big Mound, battle, **2**: 270–272, 275, 275n, 429, 434

Big Sioux River, **2**: 223, 404; railroad to: provided for, 38, chartered, 42; Indian settlement, 261

Big Stone County, **3**: 102, 147n

Big Stone Lake, **2**: 222, 267, 427; Sioux murders, 123, 434

Big Thunder (Little Crow IV), **1**: 153, 156, 179, 185, 202, 205, 206, 447n

Big Woods, **2**: 158, 239, 243, 285n, 286, 415, **4**: 79, 81

BIGGAR, H. P., *Trading Companies of New France*, **1**: 15n

Billings, H. A., **4**: 98

Biloxi, **1**: 40, 73

Biography of Red River Regions, **3**: 264

Birch Coulee, **2**: 120, 385; battle: 152–155, 158, 176, command of troops disputed, 156, 387–390, monument commemorating, 386, 388, 389, 390, casualties, 392, 393n

Birch Lake, **4**: 19

BISHOP, HARRIET E., *Floral Home*, **1**: 64n

BISHOP, J. F., "The Yellow Medicine Massacre," **2**: 114n

BISHOP, J. W., **2**: 321; "Narrative of the Second Regiment," 91n; *Story of a Regiment*, 318; *Van Derveer's Brigade*, 318n; "St. Paul and Sioux City Railroad," **3**: 110n

Bismarck, North Dakota, socialist center, **3**: 542

Biwabik, **4**: 21

Biwabik Mine, **4**: 19

Black, Mahlon, **1**: 264, **2**: 28n
Black Dog, Sioux chief, **1**: 156, 447n
Black Duck Point, **4**: 318, 319
Black Eagle, Sioux subchief, **2**: 400, 401
Blackfeet Indians, **2**: 290
BLACKSTONE, WILLIAM, *Commentaries,* **3**: 227n
BLAINE, J. G., *Twenty Years of Congress,* **3**: 6n
BLAIR, E. H., *Indian Tribes,* **1**: 18n
Blair, F. P., Jr., **2**: 60
Blake, J. D., and Co., sues railroad, **3**: 42, 50, 56
Blakeley, Russell, **4**: 210
BLAKELEY, RUSSELL, " Discovery of the Mississippi," **1**: 13n; "Opening of the Red River," **2**: 164n
Blakely, David, **4**: 105
Bland-Allison Act, **3**: 127, 243
Bliss, Maj. John, **1**: 147n
Blizzard of *1873,* **3**: 71
Blooming Prairie, **3**: 563, 569
Blue Earth County, **2**: 203, **3**: 98, 101; fortified against attack, 169; Indian attacks, 170, 345, 346; efforts to capture Indian bandits, 349
Blue Earth Indian Reservation, **2**: 243, **4**: 193; established, **1**: 319, 482; progress, 320; relinquished, 320
Blue Earth River, **2**: 200, **3**: 61; fortifications against Sioux, **2**: 169, 188; fort on, *see* Fort L'Huillier
" Blueberry War," **3**: 79–81
Boal, J. M., **1**: 460, **2**: 26
Board of control, advocated, **3**: 248; established, 262, **4**: 410n; curtailment of duties, **3**: 287
Board of corrections and charities, **3**: 152, 248, 248n, 261; work, *1883–98,* **4**: 409–413
Board of health, state, **3**: 154, **4**: 415–421, 424
Board of pardons, **3**: 224, 226
BOARD OF REGENTS, Minutes, **4**: 61n
Board of visitors, **3**: 263
BOARDMAN, A. J., "Minneapolis Parks," **4**: 430n
Boardman, L. M., *see* Boardman Cavalry
Boardman Cavalry, goes to relief of New Ulm, **2**: 134, 136; variant accounts of services at New Ulm, 363–374

Boards, regulating arts, trades, and professions, **3**: 156–158
Bobleter, Col. Joseph, **3**: 243
Boeckmann, Dr. Egil, **4**: 134
BOGGESS, A. C., *Settlement of Illinois,* **1**: 70n
Boiler inspection, **3**: 156
Bois Brulé River, **1**: 24, 39, 114
Bois brûlés, **1**: 110, 129n, 214, 214n, 226, 229
Bois des Sioux, **3**: 355
Bois Fort Indians, **4**: 215; cede land, 191; acquire reservations, 192. *See also* Chippewa of Lake Superior; Deer Creek Indian Reservation; Nett Lake Indian Reservation; Vermilion Lake Indian Reservation
Bonanza farming, *see* Agriculture
BOND, FRANK, " *Louisiana* " *and the Louisiana Purchase,* **1**: 497n
BOND, J. W., *Minnesota and Its Resources,* **1**: 250n
Borup, Dr. C. W. W., **1**: 174, 312n
Borup family, **1**: 471, 472
Boswell, F. J., **3**: 377
BOTSFORD, ISAAC, " Brackett's Battalion," **2**: 99n
Bottineau, Pierre, **1**: 223; selects salt spring lands for state, **4**: 480
Boucher, Réné, **1**: 45
Boucherville, sieur de, **1**: 46n
BOUGAINVILLE, L. A., " Mémoire," **1**: 48n
Boundaries, **1**: 37, 390; prescribed by organic act, 247; prescribed by enabling act, 393; discussed in constitutional convention, 405–412; southern, determined, 486–489; eastern, determined, 489–495; northern: proposed by Continental Congress, 496, negotiations concerning, *1782,* 497–499, *1814,* 500, *1822–27,* 500–502, *1842,* 502, surveys, 500, 501, location, **3**: 382n
Boundaries of Wisconsin, **1**: 495n
BOURNE, E. G., " Travels of Jonathan Carver," **1**: 54n
Bousquet, Charles, **1**: 68n
Boutwell, Rev. W. T., accompanies Schoolcraft expedition, **1**: 113, 115n, 175; journal, 115n, 176n; sketch, 175; missionary activities, 175–177, 178, 184
BOWE, JOHN, *With the 13th Minnesota in the Philippines,* **3**: 233n

Bowen, A. C., **3**: 543n
Bowman, G. D., **1**: 430
Boyd, Lieut. George, **2**: 451n
Brackett, G. A., **2**: 276n; directs operations to save falls, **3**: 336; character, 372; activities in connection with arrest of Lord Gordon, 372, 376, 377, 380, 381, 385; mayor of Minneapolis, 373, 376
Brackett Scrapbooks, **3**: 371
Brackett's Battalion of Minnesota Cavalry, organized, **2**: 99, **4**: 18; Civil War service, **2**: 99; on Sully expedition of *1864*, 296, 298; on frontier duty, *1865*, 299; number in Civil and Indian wars, 339; detachment pursues Indian raiders, *1864*, 346
Brackett's Hall, Minneapolis, **3**: 384
Braden, W. W., **4**: 18, 45, 46, 48
Bradley, Maj. George, **2**: 192n
Brady, Judge J. R., **3**: 370
Bragg, Gen. Braxton, **2**: 91, 92, 99, 316, 319, 320, 321n, 323
Brainerd, railway station, **3**: 79, 442, 443, 444, 455; riots, 79; land agency, 147; election law applicable to, **4**: 347n
Bramhall, Mrs. W. E., **4**: 256
Brandt, C. C., **4**: 157
Brandt, Ernst, **2**: 363
Brass, Mrs. Maggie, *see* Snana
Braun, Sister Lioba, **4**: 325
BRECK, CHARLES, *James Lloyd Breck*, **1**: 182n
Breck, Rev. J. L., **4**: 227, 472; founds mission, **1**: 181, **2**: 207, 380
Breckenridge, **3**: 102, 373; railroad terminus, **2**: 42, **3**: 61, 441, 442, 447n, 458, 458n, 467; Sioux murders, **2**: 124
Breckinridge, J. C., **2**: 66
Brewer, Judge D. J., **3**: 472, 473
Brewer, W. H., **4**: 69, 91
Brice's Cross Roads, battle, **2**: 305
Brill, Judge H. R., **3**: 392, 464
BRILL, W. H., "Battle of Sugar Point," **4**: 317n; "Story of Carnage," 317n
Brisbin, J. B., **1**: 385, 390, **2**: 102n, **3**: 392; defends Cox, 411, 413, 414, 417n; sketch, 414
Brissett, Edmund, **1**: 352
British, **3**: 13; rivalry with French, **1**: 16, 50–53; territorial gains, 44,

51, 73, 74, 495; relations with Indians, 50, 50n, 53, 69, 100, 100n, 101n, 103; retention of lake posts after *1703*, 70–72; nature of settlements, 74; operations of traders after *1783*, 106, 108, 131, 145, *see also* Hudson's Bay Co., Northwest Co.; trade in U. S. restricted, 132; number in *1870*, **3**: 59; evacuation of Northwest, **4**: 1; explorations for ore, 1; mining colony of Cornishmen, 16; intermarry with Chippewa, 294; territorial gains, 294; negotiations with, concerning boundaries, *see* Boundaries. *See also* Canada; Fur trade; Ghent, treaty; Hudson's Bay Co.; Northwest Co.; War of *1812*
BRODERICK, T. M., *Titaniferous Magnetite Deposits of Northeastern Minnesota*, **4**: 42n
BROMLEY, E. A., "Old Government Mills at the Falls of St. Anthony," **1**: 140n; account of the defense of Hutchinson, **2**: 163n
BRONAUGH, W. C., *Youngers' Fight for Freedom*, **3**: 114n
Brooks, Jabez, **1**: 181n, **4**: 71
Brookston, **4**: 20
Brotherhood of Locomotive Firemen, **4**: 452
Brower, J. V., Mille Lacs survey, **1**: 80; Itasca basin survey, 127–129; Itasca State Park commissioner, 128
BROWER, J. V., *Minnesota*, **1**: 12n; *Memoirs of Explorations*, 12n; *Mississippi River*, 39n; *Kathio*, 80n; *Itasca State Park*, 114n, 129n
Brown, A. G., **2**: 11, 13
BROWN, A. L., "Narrative of the Fourth Regiment," **2**: 95n; *Fourth Regiment*, 95n
Brown, Angus, **2**: 428
Brown, Judge C. L., **3**: 289n
Brown, Ellen, **2**: 122n
Brown, H. F., **3**: 497
BROWN, J. A., ed., *Cottonwood and Watonwan Counties*, **3**: 72n
Brown, J. R., **1**: 167, 222, 235, 238, 443, 458, 466, 481, **2**: 28n, 280, 294, 399n, 400n, 414, 426, 427, **3**: 354; fur-trader, **1**: 164n, 232, 293; sketch, 231, **3**: 349–351; farmer, **1**: 232, 423; lumberman, 233; justice

of the peace, 233; legislator: of Wisconsin Territory, 233, **4**: 330, of Minnesota Territory, **1**: 256, 329, 379, 380, 383n, 395n, 480, of state, **2**: 40n, 406; lays out town site of Dakotah, **1**: 234, 491; favors organization of Minnesota Territory, 237, 491; public printer, 263, 379; at treaty negotiations, *1851*, 283, 293, *1867*, **2**: 418, 419; in constitutional convention: **1**: 400, 402n, 404, 411, 412n, 413, 414, 415n, 418, 420, 420n, **3**: 516, 517, **4**: 99n, 332n, author of election schedule, **2**: 2, member of committee on state seal, 358; election commissioner, 2, 3, 4, 390n; aspires to senatorship, 7, 8; urges ratification of Five Million Loan amendment, 48; flight of household from Sioux, 121; on Sibley expedition of *1862*: commands burial squad, 151, reconnoiters, 152, 157, at battle of Birch Coulee, 153, 156, 387–390, wounded, 153; services in connection with execution of condemned Sioux, 210; Indian agent: takes Indian delegation to Washington, 218, 394, services to Sioux, 219–221, **3**: 354, **4**: 474, evaluates lands ceded by Sioux, **2**: 397, 398; on Sibley expedition of *1863*, 267n, **3**: 354; at Fort Ridgely, **2**: 383; receives major's commission, 390; estimate of Cullen, 409; agitates restoration of annuities, 421; Indian colonization scheme, **3**: 28; newspaper editor, 348n; builds motor vehicles, 351–354, 356; transportation projects, 354–357; death, **2**: 421, **3**: 76, 347, 357; obituary articles, 347–349

Brown, Mrs. J. R., **2**: 122, **3**: 350n, 354

Brown, Maj. Gen. Jacob, **1**: 135

Brown, Orlando, **1**: 271, 313–318

Brown, S. J., **1**: 457, **2**: 387, 399n, 441n; criticizes Sully expedition of *1863*, 280; testifies in Sisseton and Wahpeton claim case, 426

BROWN, S. J., "Reminiscences," **2**: 122n; *In Captivity*, 122n

Brown County, **1**: 231, **2**: 242; Indian attacks, 115, 121, 282, 445, 447; number killed during Sioux

Outbreak, 392; ravaged by grasshoppers, **3**: 97, 101, 102; disloyalty, 565. *See also* Milford; New Ulm

Brown Papers, **1**: 232n

Brownell, G. W., **1**: 493, 495

BROWNING, WILLIAM, "Early History of Jonathan Carver," **1**: 53n

Brown's Falls, *see* Minnehaha Falls

Browns Valley, **2**: 267, 426, **3**: 541

Brownsdale, **3**: 47

Brownsville, **3**: 529

BRUCE, A. A., *Non-Partisan League*, **3**: 543n

Brûlé, Etienne, **1**: 3n, 4, 6, 6n

Brûlé River, *see* Bois Brûlé River

Brunet, Francis, **1**: 123

Brunson, Rev. Alfred, **1**: 137n, 160n, 204–206, 207

BRUNSON, ALFRED, "Sketch of Hole-in-the-Day," **2**: 377n; "Murder of Hole-in-the-Day," 377n

Brunson, B. W., **2**: 328n

Bryan, W. J., presidential candidate, **3**: 219, 221, 223, 257, 281, 282; secretary of state, 312

BRYANT, C. S., "Sioux Massacre," **2**: 109n; *Great Massacre*, 113n

BRYCE, GEORGE, *Hudson's Bay Company*, **1**: 8n; *Original Letter Relating to the Selkirk Settlement*, 215n

BRYCE, JAMES, *American Commonwealth*, **3**: 291n

Buade, Lake, *see* Mille Lacs

BUCHAN, JOHN, *The Great War*, **3**: 313n

Buck, C. F., **3**: 7n

BUCK, S. J., *Illinois in 1818*, **1**: 91n; *Agrarian Crusade*, **3**: 37n; *Granger Movement*, 39n

Buckman, C. B., **3**: 185n

Buell, Maj. S. A., **2**: 92, 99, 138, account of first battle of New Ulm, 367

BUELL, S. A., "Judge Flandrau in the Defense of New Ulm," **2**: 137n

Buerger, Capt. E. A., **2**: 167

Buffington, L. S., **4**: 105

Bugonaygeshig, Chippewa Indian, **4**: 312–321

Building stones, **4**: 479, 481

Bull, William, **4**: 236n, 237n

Bull Run, first battle, **2**: 80, 82, 85, 87, 102, 335; second battle, 100

Bunker, A. E., **3**: 114

Bunker, Capt. C. S., **3**: 80

Bunn, C. W., **4**: 133n
Burbank Stage Co., **3**: 452
Burch, M. C., **4**: 284–288, 289n
Bureau of labor, **3**: 287; name changed to bureau of labor, industries, and commerce, 287. *See also* Bureau of labor statistics
Bureau of labor statistics, work, **4**: 449–456; name changed to bureau of labor, **4**: 456
Bureau of statistics, **3**: 20, 58
Burnquist, J. A. A., **3**: 547, 560; sketch, 294; succeeds to governorship, 294, 295; vetoes mine-tax bill, 307; favors highway construction, 310; denounces Nonpartisan League, 547; elected governor, 548; chairman commission of public safety, 557; orders home guard to forest fire region, 565; suspends officials for disloyalty, 565; prohibits convention of People's Peace Council, 566; urges provision for soldier vote, **4**: 361
Burnside, Gen. A. E., **2**: 319
Burntside Forest, **4**: 401
Burntside Lake, **4**: 401
Burpee, L. J., *Pathfinders of the Great Plains*, **1**: 47n
Burrace, H. S., ed., *Early English and French Voyages*, **1**: 1n
Burt, David, **4**: 75, 76, 155
Burt, David, *Concerning Those Books*, **3**: 120n, **4**: 157n
Business, *see* Economic conditions; Financial conditions; Labor; Manufacturing; Panics; Trade; various industries
Butler, Dr. Levi, **2**: 304
Butler, Nathan, **3**: 362, 363
Butler, Nathan, "Boundaries and Public Land Surveys," **1**: 226n
Butler, William, **4**: 316
Butter manufacture, *see* Dairy industry
Butterfield, C. W., *Brûlé's Discoveries*, **1**: 3n; *Discovery of the Northwest*, 5n
Butternut Creek, **2**: 170

Cadillac, sieur de, **1**: 43n
Cadotte, J. B., **1**: 68
Cady, Capt. J. S., **2**: 283, 286
Cahill, Patrick, **3**: 523, 524
Cain, Gordon, **4**: 287n

Calderwood, W. G., **3**: 498n
Calhoun, J. C., **1**: 102, 134, 135, 169, **4**: 1
Calhoun, Lake, **3**: 92, **4**: 428
Callaway, **4**: 265n
Camp Atchison, **2**: 268, 276, 276n, 277, 284
Camp Hamilton, **3**: 233
Camp Kearny, **2**: 293n
Camp Lincoln, **2**: 202
Camp Llano Grande, **3**: 529
Camp McClellan, **2**: 285n, 450
Camp Mackenzie, **3**: 235, 237, 521
Camp Meade, **3**: 235, 235n, 521
Camp Mills, **3**: 317, 531
Camp Poland, **3**: 233
Camp Pope, **2**: 266, 282
Camp Ramsey, **3**: 231, 234
Camp Release, **2**: 168n, 192, 430, **3**: 354; monument on site of, **2**: 185n; location, 192n; arrest of Indians at, 194, 195, 196n
Camp Thomas, **3**: 232, 233, 244, 245
Campbell, A. J., interpreter, **2**: 163n; testifies before military commission, 285n; on expeditions in pursuit of Inkpaduta, 408, 412, 413; testifies in Sisseton and Wahpeton claim case, 433
Campbell, Baptiste, **2**: 351n
Campbell, Duncan, **1**: 144, 441
Campbell, Prof. Gabriel, **4**: 67n
Campbell, H. C., "Radisson's Journal," **1**: 9n; *Radisson and Groseilliers*, 9n; ed., *Wisconsin in Three Centuries*, 22n
Campbell, J. L., **2**: 347–349, 350, 351, 351n
Campbell, Peggy, **1**: 144
Campbell, Scott, **1**: 186, 442, **2**: 351n
Canada, **1**: 2, 44; controlled by trading companies, 14; government, 15; cessions to British, 44, 52, 73; under British, 64–66, 496; negotiations for establishment of southern boundary, *see* Boundaries. *See also* British; French
Canadian Pacific Railroad, **3**: 451, 459, 460
Cannon, J. G., **3**: 280, **4**: 255, 256, 303
Cannon Ball River, **2**: 297
Cannon Falls, **2**: 315
Cantwell, Matthew, **2**: 182n

Capital, established at St. Paul, **1**: 244, 260, 382, **3**: 8; scheme to remove, **1**: 381–387, 405, **3**: 8–10

Capitol, state, memorials to troops, **2**: 87n, 314, 315, 321, 322n, 372n; erection of new building, **3**: 10n, 206, 269, **4**: 104; history, **3**: 138; burned, 138, **4**: 104; temporary use of market house, **3**: 138; description and cost, 269–271; use of old building, 271; memorial statues, 283

CAREY, J. R., "History of Duluth," **1**: 178n

Carleton College, **3**: 294, **4**: 463

Carlton County, **3**: 147n, 564, **4**: 3

Carnegie Steel Co., **4**: 31, 32

Carp, Johann, **3**: 447n, 450, 451, 454, 456

CARR, LUCIEN, *Missouri*, **1**: 76n

Cartier, Jacques, **1**: 1

Carver, Jonathan, **3**: 96; sketch, **1**: 53; exploring expedition, 54–58; plans western expedition, 59; death, 60; alleged land grant from Sioux, 60–64

CARVER, JONATHAN, *Travels*, **1**: 58, 58n

Carver (village), **1**: 437, **2**: 174

Carver Centenary, **1**: 57n

Carver Papers, **1**: 57n

Carver's Cave, **1**: 57

Cashman, T. E., **3**: 558n

Cass, Lewis, **1**: 160n, 231, 269n; sketch, 101; expedition, 102–106; negotiates Indian treaties, 105, 145, 146, 306, **4**: 1; commissions Schoolcraft, **1**: 112

Cass County, **2**: 374, **4**: 7, 103n, 323n; pine nursery in, 393

Cass Lake, **3**: 208n, **4**: 196n; explorers, **1**: 98, 104, 111, 114, 116; name, 98, 104; supposed source of Mississippi, 98, 104, 105; project for park, **4**: 253, 257, 259; pine near, 398. *See also* Chippewa National Forest

Cass Lake (village), **4**: 317

Cass Lake Indian Reservation, **1**: 307, **4**: 193, 195, 196n; established, 192; unsuitable for permanent reservation, 201; Indians agree to consolidation, 212, 218; partly included in forest reserve, 254, 258–260, 307, 399. *See also* Chippewa Indians

CASTLE, H. A., *St. Paul*, **1**: 250n; "General James Shields," **2**: 7n; address in honor of Hall, **3**: 83n; "Reminiscences of Minnesota Politics," 84n

"Catholic Church and the Modern Mind," **4**: 182

Catholic Total Abstinence Union, **3**: 176

Catholics, *see* Roman Catholics

Catlin, George, **1**: 119

CATLIN, GEORGE, *Letters and Notes*, **1**: 119n

Catlin, John, **1**: 238, 239n

Catlinite, *see* Pipestone quarry

Cavalry, organized, **2**: 99. *See also* Brackett's Battalion of Minnesota Cavalry; Second Regiment of Cavalry

Cavanaugh, J. M., **2**: 18, 19

CAVELIER, JEAN, *Relation du voyage*, **1**: 35n

Cavelier, Robert, *see* La Salle

Cedar Lake, Minneapolis, **4**: 428

Cedar Mills, **2**: 162

Cemetery Ridge, **2**: 308, 313

Census, *1840*, **1**: 351; *1849*, 244, 316, 351; *1855*, 380, 388; *1857*, 359, 389, 418; *1860*, **3**: 1, 58, 59, 480n; *1865*, 1, 2, 480n; *1870*, 58; *1875*, 62, 73, 480, 480n; *1880*, 139, 480n; *1885*, 480n; *1890*: 192, 480, 487, controversy of Minneapolis and St. Paul, 479–489; *1895*, 226; *1900*, 194, 251–255; *1910*, 558; *1920*, 322; bureau, 194. *See also* Agriculture; Population

Centennial Exposition of *1876*, **3**: 136

Central Park, Minneapolis, **4**: 428

Centreville, **2**: 85

Chain of Lakes, **2**: 170

Chamberlain, Selah, holds state railroad bonds, **3**: 423, 426, 438, 438n; sues railroad companies, 428–430; makes proposition for settlement of bonds, 432, 433, 434; secures settlement, 440

Chambers, John, **1**: 271

Champlain, Samuel de, **1**: 5, 6n, 13; explorations and discoveries, 2, 3, 4, **4**: 1; founds Quebec, **1**: 2; joins alliance against Iroquois, 2; studies Indians, 4; manager of the Hundred Associates, 14; governor of New France, 14; death, 6

CHAMPLAIN, SAMUEL DE, *Œuvres*, 1: 2n; *Voyages*, 2n
Champlain, Lake, 1: 2
Champlain Tercentenary, 1: 2n
Champlin, Capt. E. T., 2: 181n, 182n
Chandler Mine, 4: 17
CHANEY, J. B., biography of Brower, 1: 129n; "Narrative of the Second Company of Sharpshooters," 2: 87n
Chapman, H. H., 4: 258, 259n, 261n
CHAPMAN, H. H., "Minnesota's Opportunity in Forestry," 4: 258; "Minnesota National Forest," 259n; scrapbook, 259n
Charitable institutions, 3: 119, 121; legislation relating to, 152, 153; administration, 261, 4: 410–412; establishment of board of control, 3: 262; establishment of board of visitors, 263; early history, 4: 408. *See also* Board of control; Board of corrections and charities; Board of visitors; Insane asylums
Charleston Convention, 2: 66n
Charlevoix, P. F. X. de, 1: 59; cited, 42, 43, 45
CHARLEVOIX, P. F. X. DE, *Nouvelle France*, 1: 1n, 45n; *Journal d'un voyage*, 45n
Chase, C. L., 1: 399, 2: 21
Chase, Capt. Jonathan, 2: 267n
Chase, R. P., 4: 130
CHASE, R. P., *Statement to the Legislature (1923)*, 2: 387n
Chaska mission, *see* Missions
Chaskay, R. H., 2: 250, 251, 252
Chatfield, A. G., 1: 378
Chattanooga, 2: 316, 322; battle at, 91, 319–321, 327n; monument to Minnesota troops, 319
Chattel mortgages, 4: 457
Chequamegon Bay, explorers, 1: 9, 16; fort, 39; missions, *see* Missions: La Pointe; trading post, *see* La Pointe
Chester, A. H., 4: 9, 10, 13
CHESTER, A. H., "Iron Region of Minnesota," 4: 8n
CHETLAIN, A. L., *Red River Colony*, 1: 215n
Cheyenne River, 2: 268, 294, 428
Chicago, 3: 45, 48, 60; railroad connection with St. Paul, 2; banking center, 253; *1912* political conventions, 539, 540

Chicago and Rock Island Railroad, 1: 358
Chicago, Burlington, and Quincy Railroad, 4: 255
Chicago Great Western Railroad, 3: 34n
Chicago Land Verein, 2: 133n
Chicago, Milwaukee, and St. Paul Railway Co., 3: 179, 4: 88
Chicago Symphony Orchestra, 4: 105, 106
Chickahominy, 2: 101
Chickamauga, battle, 2: 91, 307, 316–318; monument commemorating, 316, 319n
Chicken-raising, *1880–90*, 3: 193
Child labor, 3: 170, 201, 226; act regulating, 4: 457
Childs, H. W., 3: 206, 4: 47
Chippewa Half-Breeds of Lake Superior, 1: 471n
Chippewa Hearings, 4: 300n
Chippewa Indian Reservation, established, 4: 193, 194, 195; enlarged, 196n; partly included in forest reserve, 254, 258–260, 307, 399
Chippewa Indians, 1: 53, 68, 107, 141, 240, 2: 277, 291, 3: 79; relations with Iroquois, 1: 80; habitat, 80, 88, 307, 4: 190, 296; Pike holds council with, 1: 98; land cessions: *1820*, 103, *1837*, 159, 160, 4: 190, 192, *1847*, 1: 310, 321, 4: 322, *1851*, 1: 288, *1854*, 306, 3: 162, 4: 191, *1855*, 1: 306, 4: 191, 192, *1863*, 1: 307n, 3: 22, 23, 4: 191, 193, 197, 476, *1864*, 1: 307n, 3: 26, 4: 194, 477, *1866*, 1: 307n, 4: 191, 192, *1867*, 3: 30, 4: 195, *1889*, 220, 231–233, 250, 297; Cass holds council with, 1: 104; spelling book, 174; grammar, 176; council at Fort Snelling, *1850*, 257–259; "Cornstalk War," 325; alliance with Sioux rumored, 2: 124, 188, 380; loyalty to whites commemorated, 133n, 382; disturbance of *1862*, 146, 374–381; attack by, feared, 243, 287; plan for exiling, 258; agency, 374, 3: 24; treaty with Red Lake and Pembina bands postponed, 2: 376; attitude toward whites, 378; offer services against Sioux, 380; efforts to concentrate, 3: 22–24, 26, 29, 4: 192, 235, 261, 262, 324; civilizing of,

3: 23, 26, 4: 196, 198, 201, 225, 231, 323, 325, 473; Leech Lake uprising, 3: 233, 240, 528, 4: 312–323; divisions, 190n; board of visitors, 193; location of pine timber, 195, 199, 200, 216, 225, 232, 255, 307; education, 196, 197, 201, 222, 324; exploitation of lands and pine by whites, 199, 203, 207, 262–283, 295, 299; destruction and theft of pine, 200, 213, 216, 224, 229n, 230, 232, 243, 322; appraisal and sale of lands and timber, 204, 208, 215–225, 229–243, 249–253, 299–306, 308–312; allotments: unsuccessful attempts to provide for, 205–207, 216, provided for, 196, 206, 220–222, 226, 229, 231, 234, 235, 260–262, 266, 297–299, 302, 306, made, 235, 265, 267–272, 306; tribal fund: proposed, 205, 208, 219n, negotiations of 1889 relating to, 221, 225, 229, 234n, 249, 307n, proceeds from sales added to, 250, 252, act of 1908 relating to, 261n, 307, suit brought to recover money expended from, 306, bills for distribution, 326, per capita payments from, 327, additions to, 327, litigation expenses, 329; claim damages for destruction of property by reservoir project, 210–212; census: 221, 227, commission to compile, 286, 287n, 291–294; logging of dead and down timber, 224, 238n, 243–249, 252, 254, 322; affected by Dawes Act, 226; bill for payment of damages to, 234; litigation over White Earth spoliation, 283–296; attempts to determine blood status, 285–288, 291–293, 324n; number of full-bloods, 292, 293, 294, 323; intermarriage with whites, 294; battle of Sugar Point, 312–323; sale of liquor to, 313, 314, 321; population statistics, 323; absorption of race prophesied, 325; bring claims into court, 328, 329. See also "Blueberry War"; Chippewa reservations; Fur trade; Indian treaties; Indians; individual bands; individual reservations; Missions; Mixed-bloods; Nelson Act; Northwest Indian Commission; Scrip; Sioux-Chippewa warfare; U. S. Chippewa Commission

Chippewa Indians in Minnesota (serial 2747), see Rice Report
Chippewa Indians in Minnesota (serial 3269), 4: 238n
Chippewa National Forest, 4: 307, 327; project for establishment: 254–259, 398, newspaper comments, 256n, opposition, 257; provision for forest reserve: 259, 399, movement for repeal, 260, 261n; Minnesota National Forest: created, 261, 307, 399, renamed "Chippewa National Forest," 261
Chippewa of Lake Superior, habitat, 4: 190n; cede land, 191; acquire reservations, 192; Indian commission holds council with, 215; census of, 227. See also Bois Fort Indians; Chippewa Indians; Chippewa reservations; Deer Creek Reservation; Fond du Lac Reservation; Grand Portage Reservation; Indian treaties; Nett Lake Reservation; Vermilion Lake Reservation
Chippewa of the Mississippi, 4: 197; habitat, 190n; cede land, 191; acquire reservations, 192–195; number in 1867, 196; sell land, 198n; agree to consolidation, 213, 214, 218; census, 227n; claim damages for destruction of property, 230; represented at council, 270; chieftainship claimed by Wright, 271; scarcity of full-bloods, 293n; population statistics, 323. See also Chippewa Indians; Chippewa reservations; Gull Lake Reservation; Mille Lacs Indians; Mille Lacs Reservation; Rabbit Lake Indians; Rabbit Lake Reservation; Rice Lake Reservation; Sandy Lake Indians; Sandy Lake Reservation; White Oak Point Reservation; White Earth Reservation
Chippewa reservations, 1: 307, 2: 374, 4: 192–196; ceded for Leech Lake Reservation, 3: 22, 23; ceded, 1889, 4: 220; cutting of dead and down timber, 244; included in forest reserve, 254, 258–260, 307, 399. See also individual reservations
Chippewa River, 2: 173; lumbering, 1: 159
Chisholm, 4: 49; population statistics, 51; schools, 52; partially destroyed by fire, 390

Chittenden, R. H., **2**: 385
Chouart, Médard, *see* Groseilliers
Chouteau, Pierre, Jr., and Co., **1**: 126, 269n; takes over American Fur Co., 163. *See also* American Fur Co.
Christian, G. H., **3**: 69, 70, 71n
CHRISTIAN, G. H., " Early Roller Mills," **3**: 70n; autobiographical sketch, 71n
Christian, J. A., and Co., **3**: 131
Christianson, Gov. Theodore, **3**: 295, 321
Churches, established, **2**: 64n; statistics relating to, **3**: 58, 254, 255n; exempt from taxation, 289n. *See also* individual denominations; Missionaries; Missions; Y.M.C.A.
Chute, Col. Richard, **2**: 28n, 38n, 242, **3**: 345, **4**: 5n, 334
Chute, S. H., **3**: 335n, **4**: 5n
Chute Papers, **1**: 371n
" Circular Address of the Territorial Republican Convention," **1**: 376n
Cities, incorporated, **2**: 21; constitutional provision relating to, **3**: 224, 517, 519, 520n; home rule, 224, 519–521; legislation relating to, 226, 287, 516, 517
Civil War, **2**: 234, **3**: 1; public opinion prior to, **2**: 68–74; southern confederacy established, 76; Fort Sumter occupied by Confederates, 76; first tender of troops, 77; recruiting and organization of troops, 77–81, 88, 89–92, 95, 96, 98–106, 234, 236, 337–339; military operations, 80, 82, 85, 86, 87, 91, 92–95, 96, 98–102, 302, 303–327, 335, 336, 339, 451, *see also* individual battles; departure of First Minnesota, 84; Minnesota troops in: number, 101, 103, 339, losses, 340n, 392, 451–453, Indians and half-breeds, 421; draft planned, 102, 103; return of troops, 340; history of Minnesota's participation in, published, **3**: 163. *See also* individual batteries, companies, and regiments; Slavery
Claiborne, W. C. C., **1**: 78
Claim of Hon. H. M. Rice, **1**: 317n
Claims for Depredations by Sioux Indians, **2**: 111n
Clapp, Senator M. E., **2**: 435, **3**: 214, **4**: 261n, 269; sketch, **3**: 264; elected, 264; reëlected, 265; senatorial career, 265; convention chair-

man, 274; interest in legislation relating to Chippewa Indians, **4**: 251n, 265, 266, 275, 276, 286, 287, 300, 303, 304
Clapp rider, *1904,* **4**: 265, 266n, 267, 273; *1906*: enacted, 276, 277n, operations under, 277–280, use of term " mixed-blood," 285, 286, 288
Clark, Charlotte O., **1**: 232
CLARK, D. E., " Early Forts on the Upper Mississippi," **1**: 37n
Clark, Maj. Edwin, **2**: 374n, 381n, 382n
Clark, Gen. G. R., **1**: 69, 70, 89
Clark, Judge Greenleaf, **3**: 88, 268, 360
CLARK, GREENLEAF, "Judge Flandrau," **2**: 136n; " Bishop Whipple," 208n
CLARK, J. T., " Reminiscences of Hole-in-the-Day," **2**: 377n
Clark, Thomas, **4**: 3
Clark, Lieut. W. A., **2**: 160
Clark, Gen. William, **1**: 141n, 143, 146, 158
Clarke, J. H., **3**: 375, 377, 379, 379n, 383, 385, 387
Clark's Grove, coöperative creamery, **4**: 404
Clausen, A. C., **3**: 209
Clay County, railroad building in, **3**: 444; liquor sales in, 563
Clearwater, refuge from Indians, **2**: 124
CLERCQ, A. J. DE, ed., *Recueil des traités,* **1**: 77n
Cleveland, President Grover, **3**: 197, **4**: 200, 202, 214, 215, 219; suggests Johnson for presidency, **3**: 286n
Cleveland, H. W. S., **4**: 429n
CLEVELAND, H. W. S., *System of Parks,* **4**: 429n
Climate, false notions of, **4**: 135
Cloquet, **4**: 215; forestry station, 108
Cloud, The, Sioux Indian, **2**: 413
Cloudman, Sioux chief, **1**: 155, 185
Clough, D. M., **2**: 314, **3**: 243, 512, 513n, **4**: 47; succeeds to governorship, **3**: 205, 217, 218; sketch, 216; elected lieutenant governor, 217; reëlected, 217, 491; elected governor, 219, 221, 241, 244, 494, 497; attitude toward Washburn, 222, 244, 495, 497; urges economy, 226; mobilizes troops for Spanish-Ameri-

can War, 231; sends troops to quell Leech Lake Indian uprising, 233, 240, **4**: 317, 318n; supports Lind for governor, **3**: 245, 246; denounces treatment of Chippewa Indians, **4**: 323; praises board of health, 424

Clough, Senator G. W., **3**: 405, 407

Clough, W. P., **3**: 405

Cloutier, Andrew, **1**: 264

Coates, Capt. H. C., **2**: 451

Cobb, Daniel, **3**: 18n

Cobb, J. E., **4**: 222n

Cochran, A. E., **2**: 442

Cochrane, W. F., **3**: 71n

Code of *1851*, **1**: 262–265, 381, **3**: 228, **4**: 338; provisions for public health, 413; provisions for education, 435

Coe, Rev. Alvin, **1**: 174n

Coe, W. T., **3**: 523

COE, W. T., *Diary*, **3**: 524n

Coffin, Samuel, **2**: 366, 367, 370

Coffman, L. D., **4**: 134

Coggswell, Senator Amos, **2**: 70n, **3**: 56; in constitutional convention, **1**: 403, 404, 407, 409, 420

COLBY, C. W., "Jesuit Relations," **1**: 5n

Cold Harbor, battle, **2**: 302

Coldwater, Camp, **1**: 137, 138

Cole, A. L., **3**: 279n

Cole, G. E., **2**: 360, **3**: 180, 360, 419, 437n, **4**: 141n, 410n

Cole, T. F., **4**: 38n, 40n

Coleraine, **4**: 25n

Coliseum, **4**: 103–108

College of St. Paul, **4**: 436

Coller, J. A., **4**: 134

Collins, A. C., **2**: 182n

Collins, L. L., **3**: 528n, 552

COLLINS, L. L., *151st Field Artillery*, **3**: 317n

Collins, Judge L. W., **2**: 178n, 181n, 182n; sketch, **3**: 272; aspirant for governorship, 272–275; legislator, 411n, 414; in Cox trial, 414

COLLINS, L. W., "Expedition against the Sioux," **2**: 274n

Collis, Gen. C. H. T., **3**: 371

Colonization Society of North America, **2**: 133n

Columbia Fur Co. (Tilton and Co.), post on Lake Traverse, **1**: 107; organized, 161, 190; merged with American Fur Co., 190

Colvill, Gen. William, leads charge at Gettysburg, **2**: 310, 339; wounded, 311; address by, 314; commands artillery regiment, 339; burial, 315; statues, 314, 315

Colvill Monument Association, **2**: 314

COMAN, KATHARINE, *Economic Beginnings of the Far West*, **1**: 13n

Commission of Public Safety, *see* Minnesota Commission of Public Safety

COMMISSIONER OF CORPORATIONS, *Report on the Steel Industry*, **4**: 30n

COMMITTEE ON ORGANIZATION, *Report*, **4**: 61n

Common Schools, *see* Education

COMMONS, J. R., *History of Labour*, **4**: 449n

Company of New France, *see* Hundred Associates

Comstock, S. G., **3**: 492, 497

Conference to Ascertain a Better Method for the Sale of Pine Timber, **4**: 250n

Congregation of our Lady of Lourdes, **4**: 110

Congregational Conference of Minnesota, **3**: 427n

Congressional elections, *see* Elections

Conry, Rev. J. J., **4**: 174, 179

Conscription, for World War, **3**: 315, **4**: 187

Conservation of natural resources, **3**: 200, 550n

Consolidated Middlings Purifier Co., **3**: 71n

Consolidated schools, *see* Education

Constitution (Minnesota), Congress authorizes, **1**: 389–392; sources consulted in making, 404; provisions debated in constitutional convention, 405–414, 418; ratified, 421, **2**: 1, 2; schedule, 1, 3, 4, 5, 12, 357; amendments relating to: loans, 22, 45–49, 56, terms of state executive officers, 22, legislative sessions, 63, **3**: 119, 145, suffrage, 8, 119, 224, 227, 307n, **4**: 333, 334, 335, issuance of railroad bonds, **3**: 44, handling of state funds, 77, governor's veto power, 119, terms of state officials and members of legislature, 119, elections, 119, 145, land sales, 119, special legislation, 124, 517, 518, jury trials, 192, crea-

CONSOLIDATED INDEX

503

tion of board of pardons, 224, 226,
government of cities, 224, 519, 520n,
condemnation of property, 224, in
vestment of school fund, 224, 224n,
4: 147, 148, 149, taxation, 3: 224,
226, 258, 286, 289n, 307, 308, 4:
55, disposition of internal improvement land fund, 3: 224n, 420, ratification of constitutional amendments, 227, 4: 335, highways, 3:
309, 310, state railway bonds, 423,
435, 440, swamp-land fund, 4: 146n,
administration of school lands, 146,
religion in schools, 171, 173, 174,
canvass of votes, 345; manner of
amendment: criticized by Sibley,
2: 23, described, 356; provisions
concerning: loans, 44, state seal,
358, location of capital, 3: 9, succession in lieutenant governor's office, 217, private property, 263, school
lands, 4: 45, university, 108, 129,
130, suffrage, 332; analyzed, 2:
355–357; rejection of proposed
amendments, 3: 7, 259, 286, 289n,
4: 148, 335n, 345n, 397, 398; popular vote on revision, 3: 225; number of amendments after 1898, 227,
227n; legislative procedure, 4:
364
Constitution (U. S.), 4: 72; ratification of amendments, 3: 3, 4, 296–
306, 4: 333n, 336, 372; demand for
simpler method of amending, 3:
540
Constitutional convention, 4: 98;
proposed, 1: 389; act providing
for, 395; appropriations for, 396,
420; election of delegates, 396; dis-
pute between Democrats and Republicans, 396–400, 403; formation
of two assemblies, 400, 403; seating
of delegates, 400–403; personnel,
403; agreement on single constitution, 414–420, 4: 331–333; action
on state seal, 2: 357; action concerning corporations, 3: 516, 517;
action on school matters, 4: 137.
See also Constitution (Minnesota)
Consumers' United Stores Co., 3:
555
Contested Election of Donnelly vs.
Washburn, 3: 390n
Cook, Franklin, 3: 334, 340, 342, 343,
344
Cook County, state lands, 4: 12

Cooke, Jay, and Co., 3: 72, 444, 445,
4: 9n
Coolbaugh, F. C., "Early Days of
Minnesota," 4: 440n
Cooley, C. R., 3: 518n
Cooley, D. N., 2: 300, 435
Coon Rapids, 3: 340
Cooper, Judge David, 1: 316, 2: 4n;
represents Ramsey in investigation,
1: 466; opposes Five Million Loan,
2: 48; on commission negotiating
with Chippewa, 378
Cooper, Col. J. S. 4: 255
Copper, 4: 1, 2, 3, 191. See also
Mining
Copway, George, Chippewa Indian, 1:
205
Corcoran, Rev., 4: 176
Corinth, battle, 2: 95, 95n, 96, 98,
102; painting, 327n
Cornell, F. R. E., 3: 382
"Cornstalk War," 1: 325
Corporations, laws governing, re-
vised, 2: 63; creation in America,
3: 515; mining, regulations con-
cerning, 4: 35; law relating to
ownership of land, 253. See also
Cities; Railroads; Trusts
Correctional institutions, 3: 121, 152,
179; established, 4: 408, 412; ad-
ministration, 411. See also Board
of corrections and charities
Corrupt Practices Act, 4: 378. See
also Elections
Corse, Gen. J. M., 2: 322, 449
Coteau des Prairies, 1: 117, 121, 268,
2: 256, 3: 111n, 355
Cottonwood County, ravaged by grasshoppers, 3: 97, 101, 102
Cottonwood River, 2: 121, 144, 362
Coues, Elliott, ed., New Light, 1:
24n; "Memoir of Pike," 91n
Counties, organized, 2: 21; govern-
ment revised, 63; constitutional
provisions, 357; terms and salaries of officers, 3: 106n, 145; criti-
cism of treasurers, 120; examina-
tion of accounts, 121, 122, 123; tax
system, 249
County option, 3: 551. See also
Liquor; Prohibition
Courcelles, sieur de, 1: 19, 25
Coureurs de bois, 1: 6, 43, 66, 67
Courier-News (Fargo), Nonpartisan
paper, 3: 554
Courtland, Sioux murders, 2: 115

Courts, Judicial districts established, 1: 252; constitutional provision for, 2: 356; U. S. district courts: 3: 88, 116n, 4: 284, 287, 289, 293, 320, cases tried, 308, 487–489; judges' terms shortened, 3: 145; supreme court clerk's term lengthened, 145; demand for reform of legal procedure, 170; constitutional amendment relating to juries, 192; struck juries, 228–230; separate election of judges recommended, 288; tenth judicial district created, 400; district courts of Minnesota, 4: 49; judges elected on nonpartisan basis, 4: 340, 368. See also Elections; individual counties; Supreme Court of Minnesota; Supreme Court of the U. S.

Cowan, Thomas, 2: 28n

Cox, Capt. E. St. J., 2: 28n, 105n, 145n; sent with reënforcements to New Ulm, 138, 139n; on Sibley expedition of 1862, 168, 170; impeached and convicted, 3: 130, 272, 410–417; expungement of impeachment proceedings, 130, 418; sketch, 409; judicial career, 410; death, 418

Cox, W. T., 4: 394

Crary, Rev. B. F., 2: 84n, 4: 184

Crawford, Charles, 2: 172n, 252; testifies in Sisseton and Wahpeton claim case, 426, 427

Crawford, Winona, 3: 350n

Crawford County, Wisconsin, 4: 331n; established, 1: 231; reduced, 233

Cray, Judge Lorin, 2: 205n

CRESWELL, R. J., Among the Sioux, 2: 142n

Cretin, Rt. Rev. Joseph, 1: 224, 3: 176

Croffut, W. A., 3: 366

CROFFUT, W. A., "A Bogus Peer," 3: 365

Crooks, Hester, 1: 176

Crooks, Mary, 2: 391

Crooks, Ramsay, 1: 103, 169, 172, 440, 441, 442, 443, 2: 51n, 177n, 3: 351

Crooks, Col. William, 2: 28n, 149n, 177n, 387, 430, 441; commands Sixth Minnesota in Indian campaigns, 150, 177, 267n, 275n; member of military commission, 192n; details detachment for service at Birch Coulee, 388, 389

CROOKS, WILLIAM, "First Railroad in Minnesota," 3: 422n

Crookston, grasshopper plague, 3: 102; railway station, 443, 447, 459, 460; school of agriculture, 4: 108; land and timber sales, 238, 241–243, 250, 305

Cross, J. N., 4: 393

Cross Lake, battle, 1: 81

Crow Creek Indian Reservation, 2: 288, 301; removal of lower Sioux to, 259, 437, 439; Moscow Expedition, 260, 261n, 439–441; Santee removed, 261; agency, 280

Crow Wing, 3: 79, 443, 4: 465; battle, 1: 81–84; trading post, 351, 372; designated railroad station, 2: 42; negotiations with Hole-in-the-Day, 376, 378; treaty with Chippewa, 379; Indian attack planned, 381n

Crow Wing County, 3: 79, 4: 22, 23

Crow Wing River, 4: 190, 191, 195; explorers on, 1: 117, 123, 129n; Chippewa agency on, 2: 374

CROWELL, Iron Ores of Lake Superior, 4: 26n

CRUIKSHANK, E. A., "Robert Dickson," 1: 100n

Crystal Lake, 2: 187

Cullen, Maj. W. J., Indian agent, 1: 326; superintendent of Indian affairs, 2: 28n, 102n, 149n, 220, 409; suggests reduction of Sioux reservations, 394; approves traders' claims, 399; warns Sioux to deliver Inkpaduta, 410, 412; trouble with Sioux, 411

Cullen Frontier Guards, 2: 149n, 192n, 389

Culver, Lieut. N. K., 2: 129

CURTIS, FRANCIS, Republican Party, 1: 375n

Curtis, Gen. S. P., 2: 350

CURTISS-WEDGE, FRANKLYN, ed., Rice and Steele Counties, 1: 437n; Wright County, 2: 30n; Renville County, 154n; Mower County, 3: 401n

Cut Nose, Sioux Indian, 2: 122

Cuyuna Iron Range, 4: 21–24, 54. See also Iron mining; Mining

Dablon, Father Claude, 1: 20n, 21n

Dairy industry, transportation of products, 3: 62; growth, 157, 193,

252, 252n; university dairy school, 4: 96, 404; coöperation, 404; Haecker's services, 404-407

Dairyman's Association, see Minnesota Dairyman's Association

"Dakota," steamboat, 3: 384

Dakota (Dakotah) County, population, 1850, 1: 352n; senatorial elections, 3: 11; county fair, 46n

Dakota Friend, 1: 209n

Dakota Territory, 2: 392, 3: 97, 103, 116n

Dakota Indians, see Sioux Indians

Dakotah, county seat of St. Croix County, 1: 234

DALE, O. G., ed., Chippewa and Lac qui Parle Counties, 3: 296n

Damages to Chippewa Indians, 4: 210n

DANA, C. A., Recollections of the Civil War, 2: 318n

Dana, Rev. M. M., 3: 152

Danes, at Clark's Grove, 4: 404

Daniels, Dr. A. W., 2: 143n

DANIELS, A. W., "Reminiscences of Little Crow," 2: 225n

Daniels, C. C., 4: 288-290

Daniels, Dr. J. W., 2: 412; services on Indian expeditions, 155, 275n; physician at Sioux agency, 411n

DANIELS, J. W., "Indian Outbreak, 1862," 2: 151n; "General Sibley's Campaign," 269n; diary, 389n; narrative of Spirit Lake massacre, 411n; "Sisseton Agency," 420n

Daniels Papers, 2: 269n

Daumont, see St. Lusson

Davenport, Iowa, imprisonment of Sioux convicts, 2: 262, 285n, 293, 301, 437

"Davenport," steamer, 2: 259

DAVIDSON, G. C., North West Company, 1: 67n

Davidson, Col. J. H., 3: 361

DAVIDSON, J. N., In Unnamed Wisconsin, 1: 63n

Davis, C. H., 4: 33, 34, 40, 238n

Davis, C. K., 2: 314, 3: 52, 100, 116, 171, 293, 328n, 484, 495, 501, 4: 240n; urges restoration of Sioux annuities, 2: 424, 435; attorney for Medicine Bottle, 446; attitude toward railroads, 3: 50, 56; sketch, 81; elected governor, 83-85; candidate for U. S. senator: 1875, 85 87, 1887, 87, 174, 1893, 203, 1899, 250;

advises suit against state auditor, 88; declines renomination for governorship, 112, 182; activities in connection with grasshopper plague, 98, 100, 101; counsel for Page, 129, 174, 404, 406; supports Kindred, 148n; eulogizes Sibley, 162; career, 1875-86, 174; senatorial career, 175, 203; opposition to Merriam, 204; speaks on monetary issues of 1896, 220, 221n; treaty commissioner, 237, 238n, 250; summary of public services, 250; addresses, orations, and published works, 250; election of successor in Senate, 264; address at unveiling of Pillsbury statue, 267n; address at laying of corner stone of Capitol, 269; enters law partnership with Kellogg, 298; counsel for Seeger, 360; counsel for Cox, 412n; urges settlement of state railroad bonds, 430, 431; urges settlement of Dutch loans to railroads, 449; death, 175, 250, 264

Davis, C. R., 3: 277n

Davis, E. P., 1: 408

DAVIS, E. W., Future of the Lake Superior District, 4: 26n; Magnetic Concentration of Iron Ore, 4: 26n

Dawes, H. L., 4: 222, 223n, 226

Dawes Act, 2: 419, 422, 4: 266; provisions, 226, 231; copies distributed, 227; amended, 235

Dawson, 3: 295, 296

Dawson Sentinel, 3: 296

Day, F. A., contest over seat in Senate, 3: 217-219, 219n; secretary to Johnson, 277, 278n; in senatorial election of 1895, 491, 493; lieutenant governor, 494

DAY, F. A., Johnson, 3: 277n

Day, H. G., 3: 285n, 491

Dayton, L. C., 1: 336, 4: 84n

Dead Buffalo Lake, battle, 2: 273

DEAN, W. B., "Capitol Buildings of Minnesota," 3: 270n

Dean, W. J., 3: 197

Debates and Proceedings, 1: 394n, 396n

DE COSTA, B. F., "Jacques Cartier," 1: 1n

Dedication of the Wood Lake Monument, 2: 182n

Deer Creek Indian Reservation, 4: 192. See also Bois Fort Indians

Deer River, 4: 317
De la Barre, William, 3: 71, 136, 137
DE LAND, C. E., "Verendrye Explorations and Discoveries," 1: 47n
Delano, Col. F. R., 2: 375, 3: 425, 445, 449
Demarais, Joseph, 2: 285n
Democrats, 1: 245, 365, 374, 394, 421, 458, 2: 106, 3: 486; organized in Minnesota, 1: 369; candidates for territorial delegacy, see Olmsted, Rice; state convention, 376; in elections: 1856, 394, 1857, 2: 2–4, 6–8, 12, 1858, 59, 61, 1860, 66, 1861, 100, 100n, 1862, 333, 1868, 3: 10, 16, 1869, 18, 1870, 17, 1872, 75, 76, 1873, 49, 80, 1875, 86, 1877, 410, 1878, 117, 1880, 118, 1881, 144, 1882, 149, 1883, 144, 150, 1886, 171, 172, 173, 1888, 182, 277, 1890, 187, 189, 4: 429, 429n, 1892, 3: 196, 197, 1894, 197, 198, 277, 1896, 219, 220, 221, 223n, 1898, 241, 277, 1900, 256, 257, 1902, 277, 1904, 275, 277, 278, 1906, 279, 1908, 281, 1912, 540, 1914, 293, 1918, 547, 1922, 549, 551, 1924, 552n; strength in Minnesota: 1: 411, 1860–65, 3: 10, 1876–81, 115; decline of power, 2: 34; oppose Mrs. Swisshelm, 34–36; attitude on railroads, 2: 48, 3: 33, 36; in legislature of 1861, 2: 68; attitude on abolitionists, 69; attack Pope and Ramsey, 242; nominate Welles for governor, 337; nominate Rice for governor, 343; given federal offices by Cleveland, 3: 197; denounced by Prohibitionists, 202; attitude on silver question, 1896, 219, 220; Nicollet County organ, 276; propose Johnson for presidential nomination, 281; in constitutional convention, 516. See also Constitutional convention; Elections; Liberal Democrats; Social Democrats
Denonville, Marquis, 1: 22n
DENONVILLE, MARQUIS, "Memoir," 1: 37n
Dentan, Rev. Samuel, 1: 203, 204
Department of the Northwest, 2: 170, 187, 189, 266. See also Pope, Gen. John
Des Moines River, 2: 123n, 401, 402, 405

Detroit (Michigan), 1: 101, 105, 135
Detroit (Detroit Lakes, Minnesota), 3: 147, 362; Chippewa investigation, 4: 242n; Indian debauch at, 278
Detroit Lake, 3: 363
Detroit Lakes, see Detroit
Devil's Lake, North Dakota, 2: 163, 266, 268, 276, 285, 294, 295, 300, 418; reservation: suggested, 256, established, 419, allotments to Indians, 422, sale of unallotted land, 422, agency, 428; Sioux camp, 265
DEWEY, D. R., Financial History, 3: 127n
Diamond Mill, 3: 131, 135
Dickson, Col. Robert, 1: 100n, 190
Diggles, Maj. A. M., 3: 232
DILLON, H. N., Sioux dictionary, 1: 452n
Dillon, Judge J. F., 3: 429, 446, 448, 464n
DILLON, J. F., Municipal Corporations, 3: 516n
DIONNE, N. E., "Chouart et Radisson," 1: 7n
Disloyalty, see World War
District courts, see Courts
District of Minnesota, 2: 189, 202, 295, 336, 350, 449
District school tax, 4: 136, 139, 142–145, 147, 149
Dodd, Capt. W. B., 2: 28n; spreads news of Sioux Outbreak, 135; services against Sioux, 136, 138, 139, 370n, 373; founds St. Peter, 143; killed, 143; character, 143
Dodge, Henry, treaty commissioner, 1: 159; U. S. senator, 238n
Dodge, O. E., 4: 4, 5n
Dole, W. P., 2: 186n, 257n, 376, 378, 3: 22, 26
Dollier de Casson, François, 1: 25n
Donahower, Capt. J. C., 2: 225
DONALDSON, THOMAS, "Catlin Indian Gallery," 1: 119n; Public Domain, 328n
Donnelly, Frank, 1: 326
Donnelly, Ignatius, 1: 394, 2: 77, 171, 335, 360, 371, 3: 39n, 74, 105, 185n, 197, 491; sketch, 2: 60, 3: 11; candidate for state senator, 2: 61; campaigns for Ramsey, 61; lieutenant governor: elected, 61, 63, 3: 11, appeals for recruits, 2: 102, reports

on first battle of New Ulm, 366, 371; aspires to colonelcy of Second Minnesota, 91n; candidate for congressman: *1862*, 107, 333, 334, 335, 336, **3**: 11, *1864*, 11, 25, *1866*, 11, *1868*, 15, 16n, *1870*, 17, *1876*, 117, contest with Washburn, *1878*, 117, 388–399, *1884*, 166; career as congressman, 11–15, 24, **4**: 154; controversy with Washburn, **3**: 14, 325–332, **4**: 346; candidate for U. S. senator: *1869*, **3**: 16, *1875*, 86, 117, *1889*, 186, *1895*, 494, *1898*, 241; candidate for governor: *1869*, 17, *1888*, 183n, *1890*, 188, *1892*, 196; interest in Indian affairs, 24, 25, 27; lectures before granges, 47; supports Liberal Republican movement, 75; interest in *St. Paul Dispatch*, 82; publishes *Anti-Monopolist*, 86n; political leader, *1865–75*, 90; dominates third party movement in Minnesota, 116, 196; favors remonetization of silver, 127; eulogizes Windom, 151; literary achievements, 165, 167, 168n, 187, 474–479; lectures and debates, 168; connection with Farmers' Alliance, 169, 170, 188; state legislator, 173, 174, 207, 223; favors control of corporations, 180; furthers pine timber and ore land investigations, 207, 223, 505, 506, 512, **4**: 46, 47; at national Populist convention, *1896*, **3**: 222; drops middle name, 329n; interest in land grant for railroad, **4**: 8n; furthers school legislation, 154, 156, 160; death, **3**: 265

DONNELLY, IGNATIUS, " To the Foreign-Born Citizens of Minnesota," **2**: 60n; *Facts for the Granges*, **3**: 47n; *Atlantis*, 165n; *Ragnarok*, 166n; " Delia Bacon's Unhappy Story," 168n; *The Cipher in the Plays*, 168n; *The Great Cryptogram*, 168n; " The Shakespeare Myth," 168n; *Cæsar's Column*, 187n; *Doctor Huguet*, 187n; *The American People's Money*, 187n; *The Golden Battle*, 187n

Donnelly Papers, **2**: 61n

Dooley, Maj. W. J., **2**: 267n

Doty, J. D., **1**: 222; negotiates Sioux treaties, *1841*, *see* Indian treaties, Sioux

DOTY, J. D., journal of the Cass expedition, **1**: 102n

Douglas, Andrew, **4**: 240n

Douglas, S. A., **1**: 328, 338, 374, 376, 425, 427, 409, **2**: 66; aids in establishment of Minnesota Territory, **1**: 235, 236, 243, 246, 365; favors admission of Minnesota to Union, 391; chairman of U. S. Senate committee on territories, **2**: 9, 13, 15

Douglas County, **3**: 102, 146, 362, **4**: 7

Douglass, Capt. D. B., **1**: 98, 102, 104

Dousman, H. L., **1**: 240, 283n, 441, 459, 463n, 465, 466, 494, **2**: 4n, **3**: 335

Dousman Papers, **1**: 235n

Dowanneyay, Sioux Indian, **2**: 122

Dowling, M. J., **3**: 264

Dowling School, **4**: 124

Downie, Maj. M. W., **2**: 311

Downs, Thomas, **4**: 269

Draft, *see* Conscription

Drake, E. F., **3**: 34, 421, 423

DRAPER, L. C., " Early French Forts," **1**: 37n

Draper, Simeon, **1**: 329

Drew, W. S., **2**: 28n

Driscoll, Fred, **3**: 328n

Drummond's Island, **1**: 103

Du Gay, Picard, *see* Auguelle

Du Luth, sieur, **1**: 30, 37; character, 22; exploring and trading expeditions, 22–24, 24n, 30, 31, 79; various spellings of name, 22n; death, 30

DU LUTH, SIEUR, " Mémoire," **1**: 30n

Duluth, **3**: 60, 189, 250, 363, **4**: 5, 10, 14, 15, 18, 25, 33, 42, 319, 321; railroad station, **3**: 45, 48, 60, 61, 70; beginnings, 61; grain elevators, 68, 161, 196, 208, 211; secondary metropolitan center, 253; home guard station, 318; proposed railroad terminal, **4**: 11; timber land sales, 15, 238; mining speculations, 20; smelting and steel plants, 27; Morgan Park laid out, 28; land office, 45; population statistics, 51; opposition to park project, 257, 259; election law applicable to, 347n; permanent registration of voters, 358

Duluth and Iron Range Railroad Co., **3**: 299, **4**: 11, 12, 20, 32; railroad built, 15

Duluth and Winnipeg Railroad, 4: 20, 33

Duluth, Missabe, and Northern Railway Co., 4: 20, 29, 30

Duluth, Mississippi River, and Northern Railroad Co., 4: 33

Dunn, Senator H. H., 3: 218, 219n

Dunn, R. C., sponsors investigation of timber sales, 3: 206, 207, 272, 504, 505; state auditor, 223, 514n, 4: 46, 47; sketch, 3: 273; candidate for governor, 273–275; in Cox impeachment, 411n, 415

Dunnell, M. H., 3: 150, 4: 61n; superintendent of public instruction, 152, 184

Dunning, W. A., Reconstruction, 3: 3n

Durant, E. W., 2: 28n

Durant, E. W., "Lumbering on the St. Croix," 1: 224n

Durrie, D. S., "Carver and ' Carver's Grant,' " 1: 59n

Dustin family, 2: 283, 286, 442, 443

Dutton, F. S., 4: 353

Duvall, Col. W. P., 3: 526

Dyke, W. H., 2: 28n

Eames, H. H., 4: 3, 4, 5–7

Eames, H. H., Metalliferous Region, 4: 4n; Geological Reconnoissance, 6n

Eames, R. M., 4: 3, 4, 7, 8

Eastern Railway of Minnesota, 4: 33, 34

Eastman, C. A., 2: 438n

Eastman, John, 2: 432, 438n, 3: 347n

Eastman, Maj. Seth, 1: 460, 507; surveys Fort Snelling Reservation, 506, 515n; commissioner for sale of Fort Snelling Reservation, 506, 509

Eastman, Seth, map of Fort Snelling Reservation, 1: 515n

Eastman, W. W., 3: 335, 347n

Eatonville, 1: 75n, 185, 187

Eberhart, A. O., 3: 283; lieutenant governor, 2: 314; succeeds to governorship, 3: 293; sketch, 293; gives appointments to Preus, 295; advocates election legislation, 4: 368, 369n, 370

Eckles, C. H., 4: 407

Economic conditions, 1860, 2: 65; during Civil War, 3: 1; after 1865, 2; occupations engaged in, 1870, 58; effects of railroad building, 60;

in the eighties, 143; influenced by World War, 322; rise of monopolies, 538–541. See also Banks; Financial conditions; Five Million Loan; Labor; Manufacturing; Panics; Taxation; Trade

Eddy, F. M., 3: 274, 4: 249, 250, 265, 266

Edgerton, A. J., army officer, 2: 168; railroad commissioner, 3: 42, 50, 52, 442; appointed senator, 115; declines to run for senator, 116; later career, 116n; favors remonetization of silver, 127

Edmunds, G. F., 3: 465, 473, 4: 222

Education, schools: land grants, 1: 244, 393, 4: 73, 77–79, 135, act establishing, 1: 256, 4: 136, 138, building, 1: 360, 430, 2: 64n, 4: 52, 141, 170, 185, remarks of Sibley on, 2: 23, local taxation in mining districts, 4: 51, 52, state aid, 77n, 149–151, 169, 170, 186, 188, taxes, 136, 142–145, 149, 151, 184; literary and library associations, 1: 360; school lands: conservation, 2: 23, 33, 62, 68, 3: 268, 273, depletion, 223, 500–503, 504, 506, 510, 515, laws concerning, 500, 501n, 502, administration, 4: 137, 139, 140, 141, 143, 183; constitutional provisions, 2: 357, 4: 137; state superintendents mentioned, 2: 360, 4: 152, 153, 155, 164, 165, 183, 184; national bureau, 3: 12; of negroes, 13; statistics relating to: 1870, 58, 1876–81, 119, 120n, 1900, 253, 254n; legislation relating to election of school officials, 120, 306n, 520, 4: 334, 335, 337, 347, 366, 367, 368, 369; demand for free text-books, 3: 170, 226, 248; parochial schools, 196, 4: 165, 168, 174, 174n; school fund, 3: 223, 224, 503, 504, 506, 510, 515, 4: 55, 56n, 59, 138, 145–149, 184, 188; junior college movement, 66–72, 73n; denominational schools, 73; high schools, 74–77, 141; high school board, 76, 77n, 185, 188; state department created, 77n; agricultural college, 79–85, see also University of Minnesota; of crippled children, 124, 125, see also Dowling School; special legislation for St. Paul, 136; school districts, 136, 137,

139, 141, 142, 168; textbook legislation, 151–162; state board, 151n, 166, 188; normal school board, 152, 172, 188; compulsory education, 162–168; use of foreign languages curtailed, 166; compilation of laws relating to, 167; development of consolidated schools, 168–170; religion in schools, 170–174; teaching of moral principles required, 172; coöperation of parochial and public schools at Faribault, 174–183; state supervision, 183–189; office of state superintendent reviewed, 183–185; inspection of schools, 185; expansion of curricula, 186; study of school situation, 187; night schools, junior colleges, and schools for the handicapped established, 187; commission of education provided for, 187; among Chippewa Indians, 196, 197, 198, 201, 309, 324; physical examination of children urged, 421, 421n; in St. Paul, 434; superintendents of public instruction, 438; revision of school code, 438. *See also* Indians; individual institutions; Libraries; Missionaries; Normal schools; University of Minnesota

Educational Association, *see* Minnesota Educational Association

Egan, Judge J. J., **2**: 387

Eighth Regiment Minnesota Volunteers, organized, **2**: 103, 104; detailed for frontier defense, 243, 282; detachment pursues Indian marauders, 283; on Sully expedition of *1864*, 296, 298, 299; Civil War service, 302, 302n; number engaged in Civil and Indian wars, 339

Elections, schedule governing, **2**: 1, 3; of state officers: *1857*, 1–4, 136, *1858*, 59, *1859*, 59–62, 335, *1860*, 68, 390n, *1861*, 100, *1862*, 333, *1863*, 336, 337, *1865*, 343, **3**: 21n, *1867*, 10, 21, 21n, *1869*, 17, *1873*, 49, 80, 82–85, *1877*, *1879*, 115, *1881*, *1883*, 144, *1886*, 171–173, 175, *1888*, 182, *1890*, 187, 188, 486, *1892*, 195–197, *1894*, 197–203, 273, 277, 491, 505, *1896*, 220–222, 244, *1898*, 241–246, 273, 505, *1900*, 256, 257, *1902*, 257, *1904*, 272–275, 277, *1906*, 279, 293, *1908*, 279, 282, 293, *1910*, 293,

1912, 293, 294, *1914*, 293, 295, *1916*, 295, 320, *1918*, 295, 320, 547, *1920*, 295, 320, 548, 549, *1922*, 295, 320, 551, *1924*, 295; of U. S. representatives: *1857*, **2**: 1, 2, 12, 18, *1862*, 333, 334, 336, **3**: 11, *1864*, 11, 25, *1866*, 11, *1868*, 10, 16, *1870*, 17, *1874*, 91, 410, *1876*, 117, *1878*, 117, 388–400, *1880*, 118, *1882*, 145, 146–149, *1884*, 166, *1886*, *1888*, 242, *1890*, 189, 240, *1902*, 257n, *1906–12*, 293, *1918*, 548, *1922*, 549; of U. S. senators, by state legislature: *1857*, **2**: 2, 6–8, 13, *1859*, 62, *1863*, 106–108, 333, *1865*, 340–342, *1869*, **3**: 16, *1870*, 16, *1871*, 73, *1875*, 85–87, 117, *1877*, 115, *1881*, 116, *1883*, 149, 150, *1887*, 87, 174, *1889*, 184–186, *1893*, 203, *1895*, 204, 489–497, *1899*, 250, *1901*, 205n, 264, *1905*, 265, *1907*, 205n, 498, *1911*, 265, *1913*, 205n, 498; on constitutional amendments, **2**: 22, 47–49, 56, *see also* Constitution; laws regulating, 59, 63, 64n, **3**: 21; presidential: *1860*, **2**: 66–68, *1864*, **3**: 21n, *1868*, 10, 21n, *1872*, 75, 76, 115, 115n, *1876*, 115, 115n, *1892*, 198, *1896*, 219, 221, 222, *1900*, 256, *1912*, 539–541, *1916*, 313; of state senators: *1873*, 117, 410, *1875*, 117, *1894*, 277, *1898*, 277, *1902*, *1904*, 293; held biennially after *1884*, 145; of state representatives: *1886*, 173, *1888*, 277, *1894*, 491, *1896*, 223, *1898*, 246, *1908*, *1910*, 294, *1922*, *1924*, 321; of U. S. senators, by popular election: 188, 198, 199, 201, **4**: 372, *1916*, **3**: 297, 299, *1918*, 205n, 498, 498n, *1922*, 299, 320, 549, *1923*, 321, 552, *1924*, 321, 552; Australian ballot, 189, 202, **4**: 353–356; of judges: *1872*, **3**: 400, *1877*, 410, *1879*, 408; influenced by corporations, 538; in North Dakota, *1916*, 544; regulated by commission of public safety, 560; absentee voting, 562, **4**: 360–365; referendums on school legislation, 158, 159; development of election code, 338–341; election procedure, 340, 341–353; primary system, 340, 351, 352, 365–374; measures to prevent corruption in, 340, 341, 352, 356, 357, 374–385; registration of electors, 356–360; of presidential electors, 371, 373. *See also* Suffrage

Eleventh Regiment Minnesota Volunteers, recruited, **2**: 103, 105; colonelcy, 106; organized, 339; number engaged in Civil War, 339

Elk Lake, **1**: 115

Elk River, **3**: 36; battle, **1**: 81

ELLET, E. F., *Pioneer Women*, **1**: 140n

Elliott, Judge C. B., **3**: 289n

ELLIOTT, C. B., *The Philippines*, **3**: 238n

Elliott Memorial Hospital, **4**: 125n

ELLIS, A. G., "J. D. Doty," **1**: 458n

Ely, E. F., **1**: 177

Ely, **4**: 17

Ely Journal, **1**: 178n

Embalming, state regulation of, **3**: 157

Emerson, C. L., **2**: 28n

Emmett, Lafayette, territorial attorney-general, **1**: 382; in constitutional convention, 403, 410, 412, **4**: 99n; in Ramsey investigation, **1**: 466

Enabling act, **1**: 392, 395, **3**: 8, 9n, **4**: 44, 98–102, 331, 479

Engagés, **1**: 67, 113, 133, 167, 351

English, *see* British

Enmegahbowh, J. J., missionary to Chippewa, **1**: 182, 205, **2**: 380, **3**: 26, **4**: 197, 472; testimony relative to Sioux-Chippewa alliance, **2**: 380, 381n

ENMEGAHBOWH, J. J., "Extracts from letters to Hon. Nathan Richardson," **2**: 375n; *Enmegahbowh's Story*, **2**: 380n

Episcopal Church, first Minnesota bishop, **2**: 206. *See also* Breck, Rev. J. L.; Enmegahbowh, J. J.; Gilfillan, Rev. J. A.; Hinman, Rev. S. D.; Peake, Rev. E. S.; Whipple, Bishop H. B.; Wright, Rev. Charles; Missions

Erie, Lake, **4**: 24, 25, 26

Espionage Act, **3**: 569

Esprit, Pierre d', *see* Radisson

Estimates for Chippewa Treaty, **3**: 24n

Euclid Iron Mining Co., **4**: 49

Eustis, W. H., **3**: 489; candidate for governor, 244, 256; sketch, 244, **4**: 122–124; endows hospital and home for crippled children, 108, 124, 128n; donates site for school for crippled children, 124; death, 126

Evans, D. H., **3**: 548

Evans, R. G., **3**: 264

Evarts, W. M., **3**: 465

Eveleth, **4**: 19; population statistics, 51

Excelsior, **1**: 360

Execution of Treaty with the Winnebagoes, **1**: 164n

Facts about the War, **3**: 570n

Facts for the Farmer, **3**: 546n

Facts Kept from the Farmer, **3**: 546n

Fair Oaks, battle, **2**: 86, 336

FAIRCHILD, H. S., "Real Estate in St. Paul," **1**: 233n

Fairhaven, **2**: 283, 286

Fairmont, garrisoned, **2**: 243

Falstrom, Jacob, **1**: 207

Faribault, Alexander, **1**: 164n, 278, 297, 459, 467, **2**: 149n, 150; assists Sioux settlers, 263

Faribault, David, Sr., **2**: 250, 251n, 285n

Faribault, J. B., **1**: 133, 144, 164n, 283n, 459; sketch, 437. *See also* Faribault claim

Faribault, Oliver, **1**: 197

Faribault, Pelagie, *see* Faribault claim

Faribault family, **2**: 252

Faribault, **4**: 200; designated railway station, **2**: 38, 42, **3**: 45; Sioux settlement, **2**: 263, 264; site of Sioux habitat, 400, 401n; home guard station, **3**: 318; election laws applicable to, **4**: 347n, 360n; charitable institutions, 408

Faribault County, ravaged by grasshoppers, **3**: 98

Faribault claim, Pelagie Faribault granted Pike's Island, **1**: 144, 437; J. B. Faribault ousted, 438; attempt to establish claim, 438–445

Farley, J. P., receiver for St. Paul and Pacific Railroad Co., **3**: 446, 450, 462; raises loan, 447; constructs trackage, 447; manager of First Division Co., 450, 457, 459, 460, 463; sues for share of railroad properties, 462

Farm and Labor party, **3**: 183n

Farm, Stock and Home, **3**: 189, **4**: 94

Farmer-Labor party, in Minnesota politics, *1922–24*, **3**: 299, 320, 549,

553; organization, 548; platform, 550n; in state legislature, 553n. *See also* Nonpartisan League

Farmers' Alliance of Minnesota, **3**: 174, 486, 553, **4**: 93; growth, **3**: 169; platform, 169, **4**: 449; in elections: *1886*, **3**: 169–171, 173, *1890*, 187–189; becomes third party, 187; merged in People's party, 196; coöperates with Knights of Labor, **4**: 449. *See also* National Farmers' Alliance

Farmers' and Laborers' Union of America, **3**: 188

Farmers' institutes, **4**: 91

Farmers' Lecture Course, **4**: 89–91

Farmers' Nonpartisan League, *see* Nonpartisan League

Farming, *see* Agriculture

Farmington, battle, **2**: 96

FARNHAM, D. R., "Wright County," **2**: 30n

Farquhar, Maj. F. U., **3**: 338n, 343, 344

Farrell, J. J., **3**: 552n

Farrell, Capt. W. B., **2**: 312

Father Mathew Temperance Society, **3**: 176

Featherstonhaugh, G. W., **1**: 42n, 117, 457

FEATHERSTONHAUGH, G. W., *Canoe Voyage*, **1**: 42n; *Geological Reconnoissance*, 118n

FEATHERSTONHAUGH, J. D., "G. W. Featherstonhaugh," **1**: 117n

Federal Highway Act, **3**: 311

Federal Steel Co., **4**: 32

Federation of Labor, *see* Minnesota State Federation of Labor

Federation of Women's Clubs, *see* Minnesota Federation of Women's Clubs

Fergus Falls, **4**: 190, 284, 289, 293; Lord Gordon in, **3**: 362, 364; proposed railway station, 443

Ferries, **1**: 429, 433

FIELDHOUSE, W. R., "The Flour Milling Industry of Minneapolis," **3**: 70n

Fifteenth Regiment of Infantry, Minnesota Volunteers, organized, **3**: 234; Spanish-American War service, 234–236, 521–526; mutiny in, 235, 522–528

Fifth Iowa Cavalry, Minnesota troops in, **2**: 99

Fifth Regiment Minnesota Volunteer Infantry, **3**: 15, 144, 175; organized, **2**: 95; Company B: 96, 130, casualties at Fort Ridgely, 133n; Company C: reënforces garrison at Fort Ridgely, 96, 128, 230, rejoins regiment, 96, casualties at Fort Ridgely, 133n, detachment garrisons Fort Ripley, 374; Company D: garrisons Fort Abercrombie, 96, 164, rejoins regiment, 96; in Civil War battles: Farmington, 96, Corinth, 96, 98, 102, Nashville, 326, 327; chaplaincy, 97; aids settlers at Sioux agency, 112; in battle of Redwood Ferry, 113, 392; aids in quieting Indians at Yellow Medicine, 229, 230, 231n; memorial, 327n; number in Civil and Indian wars, 339; history published, **3**: 163

Fillmore County, **3**: 403

Financial conditions: demand for monetary reforms, **3**: 116, 170, 188, 194, 198, 199, 201, 243; national monetary legislation, 126–128, 220, 243; in the nineties, 226, **4**: 457; in the Twin Cities, **3**: 253. *See also* Banks; Economic conditions; Panics; Silver; Taxation; Trust companies

Finley, H. H., **3**: 394, 396, 397, 398

First Battalion Minnesota Infantry Volunteers, **2**: 302, 339

First Battalion of Artillery, **3**: 528

First Battery Minnesota Light Artillery, mustered, **2**: 98; Civil War service, 98, 302, 307. *See also* Artillery

First Battery of Light Artillery, **3**: 528

First Company of Minnesota Sharpshooters, Civil War service, **2**: 99; becomes Co. A., Second Regiment United States Sharpshooters, 99

First Division, St. Paul and Pacific Railroad Co., organized, **3**: 441; building operations, 441; leases properties of St. Paul and Pacific, 443, 445; fails to finish proposed lines, 443–445, 446, 448; in financial straits, 444, 446, 448–451; controlled by Northern Pacific, 445, 448; bill to disfranchise, 449; Hill and others obtain control, 453–462; merged in St. Paul, Minneapolis,

and Manitoba Railway Co., 462.
See also St. Paul and Pacific Railroad Co.
First Minnesota (One Hundred and Fifty-first) Field Artillery, **3**: 317. *See also* One Hundred and Fifty-first Field Artillery
First Minnesota (One Hundred and Thirty-fifth) Infantry, **3**: 316
First National Bank, St. Paul, **3**: 121, 183, 468n
First National Guard, **3**: 80
First Regiment Heavy Artillery, Minnesota Volunteers, **2**: 339
First Regiment Minnesota Mounted Rangers, **2**: 243, 339, **3**: 409; organized, **2**: 105; on Sibley expedition of *1863*, 267n, 276n; detachment stationed at New Ulm, 281; pursues Indian marauders, 281; detachments garrison frontier, 282; number in Indian wars, 399
First Regiment Minnesota Volunteer Infantry, **2**: 293, 303, 308, 312, 313n, 335, 336, 386, **4**: 81; mobilization, **2**: 78–81, 88; service on Minnesota frontier, 81, 88; mustered, 82; chaplaincy, 84, 84n, **4**: 184, 438, 439; Civil War service: **2**: 84, 86, 87, 89, 302, 307, 315, at battle of Bull Run, 80, 82, 85, 102, 335, Second Co. of Minnesota Sharpshooters attached to, 86, 100, artillery attachment, 87, at battle of Gettysburg, 308–313, 451; casualties, 85, 86, 311, 451; history published, 85; memorials, 87, 313–315, 327n; mustered out, 302, 316; number in Civil War, 339
Fish, E. W., *Donnelliana*, **2**: 60n
Fisher, S. J., "Jane Grey Swisshelm," **2**: 36n
Fisher, W. H., **3**: 466, 467, 468
Fisher's Landing, **3**: 447, 458n
Fishing, *1860*, **2**: 64n
Fitzhugh's Woods, battle of, **2**: 303
Five Million Loan, **2**: 22, **3**: 9; bill providing for: passed, **2**: 45, provisions, 46, 50, arguments for and against, 47, submitted to electors, 47–49; failure to secure priority of lien for bonds, 49–51; depreciation of bonds, 52; repudiation of bonds opposed by Sibley, 52; Ramsey's plan for cancellation of bonds, 53; attitude of public, 55; bonds discussed by legislature, 56;

bank failures, 57; foreclosures, 328; bonds issued, **3**: 139, 418, 423; demands and proposals for redemption of bonds, 113, 115, 163, 422–434; bonds redeemed, 139, 143, 434–441. *See also* Railroads
Five Million Loan Pamphlets, **2**: 44n
Fjelde, J. H. G., **2**: 314n
Flandrau, Judge C. E., **2**: 28n, 50, 50n, 139n, 223, 224, 387, 394, 406, 407, 411, **3**: 350, **4**: 255; in constitutional convention, **1**: 402n, 409, 410, 411, 419, **2**: 409, **4**: 332n; sketch, **2**: 135; notified of Sioux Outbreak, 135, 366, 367; organizes volunteers against Sioux, 136, 371; elected captain of volunteer forces, 136, 138, 365, 371; at battle of New Ulm, 139, 141, 142, 143, 366, 367, 370n, 371, 372, 374, **3**: 409; services in Indian campaign of *1862*, **2**: 168–170; commissioned colonel, 169; supreme court judge, 219, 409; account of first battle of New Ulm, 366; address at dedication of Birch Coulee monument, 388; Sioux agent: pursuit of Inkpaduta, 404, 408, arranges for rescue of captives held by Inkpaduta, 407, 408; candidate for governor, **3**: 10, 21n; eulogizes Sibley, 163
FLANDRAU, C. E., "Bishop Whipple," **1**: 172n; "Territorial Lawyers and Courts," 234n; *Minnesota*, 402n; "The Indian War of *1862–1864*," **2**: 114n; "The Ink-pa-du-ta Massacre," 401n; "The Late Indian Difficulties," 401n; "State-Building in the West," 407n; *Encyclopedia of Biography*, **4**: 84n
Flandreau, South Dakota, **2**: 261, 431
Flatmouth, Pillager chief, **1**: 115n, 149n, **4**: 228n
Flatmouth, Ruth, **4**: 228n
Fletcher, Hezekiah, **1**: 480, 481
Fletcher, J. E., **1**: 314, 315, 317n, 319, 479, 482n
Fletcher, Loren, **4**: 240n; assists in arresting Lord Gordon, **3**: 78, 373; detained as witness, 375; arrested, examined, and indicted, 376, 377, 380, 381, 382, 383; newspaper owner, 506n; interest in Chippewa pine situation, **4**: 246, 246n, 250
Flour-milling, beginnings, **3**: 30, 480; cost of transporting products, 46; statistics: *1870*, 60, *1878*, 131,

1880, 69, 141, *1891*, **4**: 455, *1900*,
3: 252, 253; improved equipment,
66, 68–70, 71n, 136–138, 140, **4**:
455; use of spring wheat, **3**: 68,
4: 455; explosion at Falls of St.
Anthony, **3**: 131–136. *See also*
Grain; Wheat

Flower, M. D., **3**: 80

Floyd, J. B., and sale of Fort Snelling Reservation, **1**: 505–515

Foch, Marshal Ferdinand, visits Minneapolis, **4**: 434n

FOLEY, M. O., *Mayo Clinic*, **4**: 122n

Foley, Peter, **3**: 522, 523, 524, 527

Folsom, W. H. C., **2**: 31, 358

FOLSOM, W. H. C., *Fifty Years*, **1**:
178n; "Lumbering in the St. Croix
Valley," 227n

Folwell, Dr. W. W., sketch, **1**: vii,
4: 66; plan for organization of university, 66–72; interest in high
schools as preparatory schools, 74;
plans lecture course for farmers,
89; urges construction of university buildings, 103, 104; university
president, 105, 422; recommends
removal of university, 109n; on
board of corrections and charities,
410n; on Minneapolis board of
park commissioners, 429n; urges
geological and natural history survey, 478

FOLWELL, W. W., "The Five Million
Loan," **2**: 37n; *University Addresses*, **4**: 67n; "Memorial of Hewitt,"
414n; "Minneapolis Society of
Fine Arts," 469n

Fond du Lac, trading post of: North-
west Co., **1**: 68, 88, 97, American
Fur Co., 104, 174; mission, *see*
Missions; treaty, *see* Indian treaties

Fond du Lac Indian Reservation, **4**:
192

Fond du Lac Indians, acquire reservation, **4**: 192; council with, 215;
claim compensation for land, 230

Food, legislation governing sale, **1**:
158

Forbes, W. H., **2**: 28n, 150, 446, **3**:
350

Foreigners, statistics: *1860*, **2**: 64n,
1870, **3**: 59, **4**: 171, *1875*, **3**: 73,
1880, 140, *1895*, 226, *1900*, 251,
251n, 254, *1910*, 558; naturalization, **4**: 332, 333; rights, 333. *See
also* Aliens; individual nationalities

Forest City, **2**: 174; preparations
against Sioux attacks, 158, 159, 161,
174n; plundered by Sioux, 162;
number killed during Sioux Outbreak, 392; sends party to scene of
Acton murders, 417

Forest fires, **3**: 212, 319, 564, **4**: 388,
390, 391

Forest reserves, provided for, **4**: 253,
259, 307, 399, 400, 401; management, 393, 394. *See also* Chippewa
National Forest; Red Lake Indian
Forest

Forestry, principles, **4**: 311

Forestry Association, *see* Minnesota
State Forestry Association

Forests, preservation, **4**: 387–402;
statistics on extent, 395

Forney, Col. J. W., **1**: 337, 339

Forrest, Gen. N. B., **2**: 92, 93, 306

Forsyth, Maj. Thomas, **1**: 136, 446

FORSYTH, THOMAS, "Journal of a
Voyage," **1**: 64n

Fort Abercrombie, **1**: 503, **2**: 268,
376, 445, **3**: 355; regular troops
relieved by detachment of First
Minnesota, **2**: 81; garrisoned by
volunteers, 81, 164, 243, 282, 293;
established, 164; attacked by
Sioux, 165–168, 428, 430, 431, 434;
defense planned by Pope, 187; detachment sent to Fort Ripley, 277;
reenforcements planned by Sibley,
1864, 294; number killed during
Sioux Outbreak, 392

Fort Armstrong, **1**: 135

Fort Atkinson, **1**: 240, 309, 311

Fort Beauharnois, **1**: 46, 47n; mission, *see* Missions

Fort Blakely, **2**: 305

Fort Crawford, **1**: 104, 105, 135. *See
also* Prairie du Chien; Fort Shelby

Fort Crèvecoeur, **1**: 28, 33

Fort de Chartres, **1**: 73

Fort Detroit, established, **1**: 43n;
British occupation, 51, 70; attacked
by Pontiac, 53; surrendered, 72n

Fort Donelson, battle of, **2**: 99

Fort Douglas, **1**: 214, 215

Fort Duquesne, **1**: 51

Fort Frontenac, established, **1**: 26;
captured by British, 51; mission
at, *see* Missions

Fort Gaines, **1**: 229, 301, 372, 429

Fort Garry, **2**: 287n, 443, 444, **3**: 77,
375, 376, 376n, 379, 380; transportation to, 351, 355, 356, 357, 447,

452; Lord Gordon at, 372; prelates at, 378, 378n. *See also* Winnipeg
Fort Gratiot, **1**: 43n
Fort Harrison, treaty, *1816*, **1**: 103n
Fort Howard, **1**: 135
Fort Kaministiquia, *see* Fort William
Fort L'Huillier, **1**: 41, 42n
Fort Mackinac, **1**: 44, 51, 53, 55, 71, 100n
Fort Miami, **1**: 32, 33
Fort Niagara, **1**: 70
Fort Oswego, **1**: 70
Fort Pierre, **1**: 48, **2**: 278, 287n
Fort Pontchartrain, *see* Fort Detroit
Fort Randall, **2**: 258, 259, 260, 266
Fort Rice, **2**: 265; established, 299; council with Sioux, 418
Fort Ridgely, **1**: 503, **2**: 155, 187, 193, 201, 222, 234, 236, 266, 267n, 277, 282, 299, 346, 366, 404, 405, 408, 409, 411, **3**: 352; Indian agency, **1**: 353; garrisoned, **2**: 81, 128, 148n, 171, 176, 243, 282, 345; refuge during Sioux Outbreak, 109, 112, 120, 121, 122, 150, 150n; first battle, 120; objective of Sioux, 126, 137; history and description, 127; second battle: 129–133, 229, 285n, 427, 428, 431, 432, trial of participants, 196n, casualties, 392, 393n; erection of monuments, 129n, 133n, 382; relieved by McPhail, 150, 383, 384; relief ascribed to others, 383–386; aid sent to Birch Coulee, 153; training of Sibley's troops, 173; decrease in forces, 175; force sent in pursuit of Spirit Lake murderers, 223; arrival of annuities, *1862*, 238; reënforcement planned by Sibley, 294
Fort Ripley, **1**: 503, 505, **2**: 206, 277, 379, **3**: 80, 355; sale of reservation proposed, **1**: 507; garrisoned, **2**: 81, 128, 230, 243, 374, 375, 376, 378; defense planned, 187; reënforcements planned, 294; description and location, 374; reënforcements sent to Crow Wing agency, 374; warned of Chippewa attack, 375; refuge from Chippewa, 375
Fort St. Anthony, *see* Fort Snelling
Fort St. Antoine, **1**: 37
Fort St. Charles, **1**: 48
Fort St. Croix, **1**: 24n
Fort St. Joseph, **1**: 43, 43n

Fort St. Louis (at Fond du Lac), **1**: 68, 69n
Fort St. Louis (on Illinois River), **1**: 34, 34n, 35
Fort St. Pierre, **1**: 48
Fort Shelby, **1**: 100n. *See also* Fort Crawford; Prairie du Chien
Fort Snelling, **1**: 62, 92n, 105, 107, 109, 111, 117, 119, 123, 125, 129n, 130, 140, 183, 301, 311, 351, **2**: 95, 98, 128, 149n, 194, 224, 277, 383, 406, **3**: 334n, **4**: 314, 317; Pike purchases site for, **1**: 93, 446; established, 101, 135–140; reservation repurchased, 136, 446; Indian agency, 140, 146, 148, 149n, 154, 322, 422, *see also* Taliaferro; first church and Sunday school in Minnesota, 192, 232; surveys delimiting reservation, 218, 221, 422, 447n, 514; reservation enlarged, 220–222; Indian councils, 257, 258, 289, 296; reduction of reservation and sale of excluded area, 424–428, 430–432, 434, 515, **3**: 30; sale of reservation: legislation and negotiations, **1**: 432, 503–509, congressional investigation, 509–512; commandeered by military authorities in *1861*, 433, 514; portion of reservation regained by U. S., 434, 515; troops transferred to Fort Ridgely, 503; rendezvous for militia, **2**: 78, 82; departure of First Minnesota, 84; objective of Sioux, 126; Indian camp, 200, 203, 249, 251, 252–255, 263; headquarters of Sixth Minnesota, 243; Sioux prisoners, 265, 293; departure of Hatch's Battalion, 292; trial of Sioux chiefs, 445; mobilization point for Spanish-American War troops, **3**: 234, 239; Third U. S. Infantry, 240; First Minnesota Field Artillery, 317, 529, 530, 531; arrival of first troops in *1819*, 349; treaties negotiated, *see* Indian treaties; whisky traffic, *see* Liquor. *See also* individual commandants; Squatters
Fort Snelling as a Military Depot, **1**: 512n
Fort Snelling Investigation, **1**: 428n
Fort Sumter, occupied by Confederates, **2**: 76
Fort Totten, **3**: 355

Fort Wadsworth, **3**: 28, 355
Fort William (Kaministiquia), **1**: 23, 24n, 44, 67n
Fortifications, built as protection against Indians, **2**: 161, 169, 188, 243. *See also* Forts Abercrombie, Ridgely, Ripley; New Ulm
Forty-fifth Regiment, U. S. Volunteer Infantry, **3**: 239
Forty-second Division, in World War, **3**: 317, 531–538. *See also* One Hundred and Fifty-first Field Artillery
Foster, M. B., **3**: 64n
Foster, Dr. Thomas, **1**: 303n, 405, **2**: 48, 107, **4**: 331; secretary to treaty commission, **1**: 287, 288
FOSTER, THOMAS, "Rough Notes for an Introduction to a History of Minnesota," **1**: 24n
Fountain Cave, settlement near, **1**: 220, 221
Fourteenth Regiment of Infantry, Minnesota Volunteers, **3**: 231, 233, 240; at Leech Lake, **4**: 317
Fourth Regiment Minnesota Volunteers, organized, **2**: 92, 95; frontier service, 95; Civil War service: 95, on Sherman's march, 302, at siege of Vicksburg, 322; on Indian campaign, 174; memorial to, 322n; number in Civil and Indian wars, 339
Fowler, Col. S. K., **2**: 150
Fox, W. F., *Regimental Losses in the Civil War*, **2**: 311n
Fox Indians, **1**: 39, 43, 45, 46, 46n, 457
Fox-Wisconsin route, **1**: 19n, 30, 36, 105, 146; controlled by Fox Indians, 39, 43, 135
FRANCHÈRE, GADRIEL, "Narrative of a Voyage," **1**: 68n
Franchise, *see* Suffrage
FRANKLIN, BENJAMIN, *Writings*, **1**: 52n; *Interest of Great Britain Considered*, 52n
Franklin (village), **4**: 31, 59; battle, **2**: 323
Frazee, **4**: 280n
Frazer, J. J., **1**: 298, **2**: 148, 252
Fredericksburg, battle, **2**: 86
Freeborn, William, **1**: 390, **2**: 28n
Freeborn County, **3**: 403, **4**: 83n, 404
Freeborn County Standard, **3**: 490
Freeman, Lieut. Ambrose, **2**: 276n

Free-soil party, **1**: 373, 374
Freitag, Irving, **3**: 572
Fremont, Lieut. J. C., **1**: 126
French, D. C., **3**: 267, 269
French, Lafayette, **3**: 402
French, nature of settlements, **1**: 15, 49, 74, **4**: 1; proclamations of sovereignty, **1**: 16, 17, 23, 33, 34n, 37, 42, 50; imperial policy, 16, 17, 36, 50, 76; rivalry with British, 16, 50–52, 53; relations with Indians, 26, 32, 37, 39, 43, 44, 45, 46, 46n, 50n, **4**: 294; trade policy, **1**: 39, 44; territorial cessions, 44, 51, 73, 74, 78, 495, **4**: 294; attempts to reach Pacific, **1**: 47, 48, 49; regain Louisiana from Spain, 76–78; mixed-bloods on White Earth Reservation, **4**: 197; Indian trade, *see* Fur trade
French and Indian War, **1**: 51
Frenière, Antoine, **2**: 253n, 255n; at Sioux trials, 199n; accompanies McPhail to Fort Ridgely, 384, 385
Frenière, Narcisse, **3**: 350n
Frenière family, **2**: 252
Fridley, A. M., **1**: 317n, 478, **2**: 28n
Friends of the Indian and Other Dependent People, **4**: 281
Frink, C. E., **2**: 182n
FRITSCHE, L. A., ed., *Brown County*, **2**: 115n
Fronchet, Desiré, **2**: 124
Frontenac, comte de, governor-general of New France, **1**: 23, 36, 39; interest in explorations, 19, 21, 22; imperial policy, 36; death, 42; Charlevoix's estimate of, 42
Frontier Avengers, **2**: 138, **3**: 409
Fruit-raising, **3**: 64
Fuel administration, during World War, **3**: 563n
Fuller, A. G., **2**: 20
Fuller, Jerome, **1**: 378n, **2**: 399n
FUNK, H. D., *Macalester College*, **4**: 436n
Fur trade, French, **1**: 22, 26, 50, 66; British, 43n, 66–68, 106, 108, 131, 145, 496; British-French competition, 53; liquor traffic in connection with, 86, *see also* Indians: gifts and sale of liquor to; protected and regulated by U. S. government, 132, 140; independent traders, 163, *see also* Coureurs de bois; profits, 163, 164, 164n, **2**: 214; traders'

expenses, **1**: 163, 165, 265, 268, 269n; decline, 163, 268; size of operations, 163; prices charged by traders, 163n, 164, 165; character of traders, 164, 169; articles of exchange, 164n; evils, 168; factory system, 168; government monopoly proposed, 169; of Red River settlements, 226; posts, 268, 351; value of exports, *1860*, **2**: 65n; at St. Paul, **3**: 479. *See also Coureurs de bois;* Indians; individual traders and trading companies

Furber, J. W., **2**: 41

Gaines's Mill, **2**: 234

Galaxy mill, **3**: 131

Galbraith, T. J., in constitutional convention, **1**: 403, 405; election commissioner, **2**: 2; family saved from Indians, 118; organizes Renville Rangers and reënforces Fort Ridgely, 128; Indian agent, 147, 151, 194, 208, 217, 219, 236, 240, 248; held responsible for Sioux Outbreak, 172; states cause of outbreak, 212, 213n; Indian policy, 221; character and ability, 222n; difficulties with Sioux in spring of *1862*, 228–236; testifies before Sioux commission, 247; plan for removal of Sioux, 256; acknowledges Other Day as rescuer of family, 264; estimates number killed in outbreak, 391

"Galena," steamboat, **2**: 396n

Galinée, R. de B. de, **1**: 25n

GALINÉE, R. DE B. DE, " Le voyage de MM. Dollier et Gallinée," **1**: 26n

Galtier, Rev. Lucian, **1**: 223

Galusha, R. B., **3**: 457, 461

GANNETT, HENRY, *Boundaries of the United States*, **1**: 393n

Garden City, **1**: 360; fortifies against Sioux, **2**: 170; Indian murders near, 346; sends force to search for Indian bandits, 349; sends reënforcements to New Ulm, 373; decline, **3**: 67

Gardner, Abbie, **2**: 407, 408, 408n

Gardner, Rowland, and family, **2**: 402

Garvie, S. B., **2**: 28n

Gary, E. H., **4**: 38n, 40

GASTON, H. E., *Nonpartisan League*, **3**: 542n

GATES, F. T., *Rockefeller and the Merritts*, **4**: 30n

GAUTHIER, JULIE C., *Minnesota Capitol*, **3**: 270n

Gavin, Rev. Daniel, **1**: 200, 203, 204, 451

Gay, Picard du, **1**: 27

GAYARRÉ, CHARLES, *Louisiana*, **1**: 74n

Gaygwedosay, *see* Kegwedzissag

Gemmell, W. H., **4**: 134

General Council of the Chippewa Indians of Minnesota, **4**: 326

GEOLOGICAL AND NATURAL HISTORY SURVEY, *Final Report*, **4**: 6n, 481–483

Geological surveys, plan for, **4**: 2; in mineral region, 3, 5–8, 9–11; in St. Croix Valley, 3; of state, 478–481

George, Henry, Jr., **4**: 242n

George, Col. James, **2**: 318

Georgetown, **2**: 292

Gere, Lieut. T. P., **2**: 113n, 114, 132, 147

Gere, W. B., **2**: 28n

German Land Association of Minnesota, **2**: 133n

Germans, number in state: *1860*, **2**: 64n, *1870*, **3**: 59, *1875*, 73, *1880*, 140, *1910*, 558; attacked by Sioux, **2**: 110, 115; found New Ulm, 133n; attitude during World War, **3**: 553, 558, 567, 571; join Nonpartisan League, 553. *See also* Aliens; Foreigners

Gervais, Benjamin, **1**: 223

Gervais, Pierre, **1**: 223

Gettysburg, battle, **2**: 308–313, 315, 339, 451; memorials, 313–315, 327n

Ghent, treaty, *1814*, 101, 131, 145, 500

Gibbs, J. L., **3**: 218

Gibson, Paris, **4**: 72n

Gideon, P. M., **3**: 64n

Giguere, Onisime, **2**: 444, 445

Gilbert, Cass, designs Capitol, **3**: 269, 270, 284; disapproves choice of statue site, 284, 284n

Gilbert, H. C., **1**: 470, 471, 475

Gilbert, Joseph, **3**: 571, 572, 573, 574

Gilbert, Rt. Rev. M. N., **3**: 213

Gilfillan, C. D., **2**: 343, 390

GILFILLAN, C. D., "Early Political History of Minnesota," **1**: 239n

Gilfillan, Rev. J. A., **4**: 197, 200, 210, 246n, 478

GILFILLAN, J. A., *The Ojibway*, **1**: 170n

Gilfillan, J. B., **3**: 265, 437n, 438n

GILFILLAN, J. B., "Who Named Minneapolis?" **1**: 430n; "University of Minnesota," **4**: 98n

Gilfillan, Judge James, **2**: 106, 339, **3**: 404, 409, 435, 464, **4**: 5n

Gillespie, J. I., **3**: 344

GILLETTE, J. M., "The North Dakota Harvest of the Nonpartisan League," **3**: 542n

Gilman, C. A., **3**: 405, 438n

Gilman, J. M., **2**: 102n, **3**: 438n; candidate for Congress, 25; counsel for Seeger, 360

Glazier, Capt. Willard, **1**: 127

Glencoe, **2**: 148n, 159, 159n, 163, 174, **4**: 84, 85; defense against Sioux, **2**: 161, 174n, 243; agricultural college, **4**: 79–85

Glendale, **2**: 102

Glenwood, **3**: 548

Glenwood Park, Minneapolis, **4**: 432, 432n

Glimpses of the Nation's Struggle, **1**: 326n

Glyndon, **3**: 444, 447

Godfrey (Otakle), **2**: 199, 209

Gold, search for, **4**: 2, 6–8; gold rush to Vermilion Lake, 4–6

Gold standard, **3**: 126, 194, **4**: 466

Gonnor, Father Nicolas de, **1**: 45, 46n

Good Hail, Enos, Sioux Indian, **2**: 413

Good Road, Sioux chief, **1**: 153, 156

Good Thunder, Sioux chief, **2**: 173, **4**: 474

Goodhue, J. M., **1**: 251, 260, 361, 370, 372

GOODHUE, J. M., "The First Days of Saint Paul," **1**: 251n; account of treaty of Traverse des Sioux, 279n

Goodhue County, **3**: 99, 571

Goodrich, Judge Aaron, **1**: 252n, 378n, 381n, **2**: 66

GOODRICH, AARON, "Early Courts in Minnesota," **1**: 252n

Goodrich, E. S., **1**: 343, **2**: 4n, **3**: 347, 348n

Goose Nest Lake, **2**: 431

Goose River, **2**: 419

Gordon, Lord Gordon, activities in Minnesota, **3**: 77, 362–366, 371n; activities in New York, 77, 366–370; escapes to Canada, 78, 371,

371n; illegal arrest, 78, 372–375; arrest and trial of captors, 78, 375–384; personal appearance, 365; career, 387; commits suicide, 385

Gordon, H. L., **2**: 315, **3**: 149

GORDON, H. L., "Gettysburg: Charge of the First Minnesota," **2**: 315n; *Address to the Voters of the Fifth Congressional District*, **3**: 149n

Gorman, Capt. James, **2**: 237

Gorman, W. A., **1**: 358, 396, 399, 406n, 413, 417, **2**: 20n; treaty commissioner, **1**: 318, 319, 479–482; messages, 329, 343, 346, 348, 379; attitude toward railroad legislation, 329, 330, 336, 340, 341, 343, 346, 348, 388, 410, **2**: 39, 48; appointed governor, **1**: 377; sketch, 377; connection with capital removal scheme, 383, 386, 408; attitude toward statehood, 388, 390, 394; in constitutional convention, 398, 399, 403, 409, 412, 417, **4**: 137; commissioner in Ramsey investigation, **1**: 466; opposes establishment of Blue Earth Reservation, 482; aspires to senatorship, **2**: 7, 8; calls extra session of *1857* legislature, 40; colonel First Minnesota, 79–81, 82; attorney for Medicine Bottle, 446

Gotzian, Col. P. H., **3**: 523

Gould, O. B., **3**: 411n, 415

Government of Minnesota, constitutional provisions for, **2**: 355–357; salaries and terms of officers, **3**: 77, 145, 357, 361; economy urged, 226; reorganization, 321, **4**: 126. *See also* Cities; Constitution; Counties; Courts; Elections; Laws; Legislature; Suffrage; Taxation; Townships

Governor's Archives, **2**: 26n

Grace, Rt. Rev. T. L., **2**: 449, **4**: 110, 193

Graham, Dr. Archibald, and purchase of Fort Snelling Reservation, **1**: 505–514

GRAHAM, HUGH, "Secondary Education in Minnesota," **4**: 142n

Graham, J. M., **4**: 242n

Graham committee, **4**: 241n, 242n, 268, 271, 272, 284n, 285

Graham Report, **4**: 241n

Grain, transportation, **3**: 60, 62; introduction of grain elevator, 66–68; inspection and grading, 67, 161,

170, 208, 210, 211, 543; demand for elevators and warehouses, 196, 198, 202, 319, 543; law providing for state elevator declared unconstitutional, 211. *See also* Flourmilling; Wheat

Grammar and Dictionary of the Dakota Language, **1**: 203, 448–452

Grand Army of the Republic, **3**: 257, 272, 273, 494, **4**: 107, 348

Grand Portage, **1**: 23n; trading post, 58, 67, 111n

Grand Portage Indian Reservation, **4**: 192

Grand Portage Indians, **4**: 192, 215. *See also* Chippewa of Lake Superior

Grand Rapids, **4**: 19; school of agriculture, 108

"Grand Rounds," Minneapolis park system, **4**: 432, 433n

Grange, *see* Minnesota State Grange

Granger, Gen. Gordon, **2**: 318

Granger acts, *see* Railroads

Granger movement, growth, **3**: 37–39, 47, 54, 55, **4**: 93; in Minnesota politics, **3**: 47, 49, 82; decline, 55, 168; fails to achieve economic reform, 541. *See also* Anti-Monopolists; Independent party; Minnesota State Grange; Patrons of Husbandry; Railroads

Granite Falls, **2**: 286n

Grant, Charles, **2**: 269, **4**: 11

Grant, Capt. H. P., **2**: 151n; on Sibley expedition of *1862,* 148n, 149n, 152, 153, 155; controversy over command at Birch Coulee, 156, 387–390; member of military commission, 192n

Grant, U. S., **2**: 319, 320, 322, 323, 324, **3**: 82, **4**: 107, 199; Minnesota vote for, **3**: 10, 76, 115, 115n; reconstruction policies, 75; grants hearing on behalf of arrested Minnesotans, 381

Grant County, **3**: 102

Grasshopper plague: appearance and habits of Rocky Mountain locust, **3**: 93–97; areas infested, 97–112; relief measures for victims, 97, 99, 103, 107, 111n; investigations, 101, 105; measures to combat, 103, 105–107, 108, 109, 111; conference at Omaha, 104, 106, 108; ceases, 110

Great Britain, *see* British

Great Lakes, **1**: 6, **4**: 25; claimed by French, **1**: 50. *See also* Huron; Superior

Great Northern Iron Ore Properties, **4**: 36–40; leased to U. S. Steel Corporation, 58

GREAT NORTHERN IRON ORE PROPERTIES, *Reports,* **4**: 35n; circular to holders of certificates, 36n

Great Northern Railway Co., **1**: 226, **2**: 149n, **3**: 61, 272, 273, 462, 494, **4**: 33–37, 40, 255, 282, 317. *See also* St. Paul and Pacific Railroad Co.

Great Western Mining Co., **4**: 37

Great Western Railway Co., **1**: 327, 328

Greeley, Horace, warns Ramsey of opposition, **2**: 106; presidential candidate, **3**: 75, 76, 115, 115n; relations with Lord Gordon, 365, 367, 368, 371n

Green, Corp. C. H., **2**: 93

Green Bay, **1**: 105; explorers, 5, 12, 19, 20, 30, 37, 45, 55; trading post, 67

Greenback party, **3**: 552; organized, 117; supports Donnelly, 117; agitates for monetary reforms, 126. *See also* Silver

Greenville, treaty, *1795,* **1**: 103n, 131

Greenwood, A. B., **2**: 220, 394, 395, 396

GREER, J. N., *Education in Minnesota,* **4**: 73n

Gregg, O. C., **4**: 91

GREGORY, J. G., *Jonathan Carver,* **1**: 59n

GREGORY, WINIFRED, *Bibliography of Minnesota Mining and Geology,* **4**: 24n

GRESHAM, W. G., ed., *Nicollet and Le Sueur Counties,* **2**: 135n

Grey Iron, *see* Medicine Bottle

Greysolon, Daniel, *see* Du Luth

Groseilliers, sieur de, alleged discovery of Mississippi River, **4**n, 11–13; sketch, 7; explorations, 7–13, 79; connection with formation of Hudson's Bay Co., 8

GROUT, F. F., *Magnetite Deposits of the Eastern Mesabi Range,* **4**: 44n

Grover, M. D., **3**: 469

Grow, G. A., **2**: 60

GRUNER, J. W., *Geology of the Mesabi Range*, **4**: 45n

Guignas, Father Michel, **1**: 45, 46n

GUIGNAS, MICHEL, "Voyage up the Mississippi," **1**: 45n

Gull Lake, **4**: 197

Gull Lake Indian Reservation, **2**: 374, **4**: 192, 193; disturbance of *1862*, **2**: 374–382; cession, **3**: 23. *See also* Missions

Gull Lake Indians, acquire reservations, **4**: 192–195; visited by Bishop Whipple, 200; council with Indian commission, 212, 214; agree to consolidation, 214; population statistics, 323. *See also* Chippewa Indians; Chippewa of the Mississippi; Chippewa Reservation; White Earth Reservation

GUNN, H. G., "Selkirk Settlement," **1**: 214n

Guntown, battle, **2**: 305

Currell, John, **3**: 79

Gustavus Adolphus College, **3**: 293

Hadley, C. B., **3**: 522, 528

Haecker, T. L., sketch, **4**: 402–404; contributes to improvement of dairy industry, 404–407

HAECKER, T. L., "Twenty-two Years' Study in Milk Production," **4**: 404n; "The Dairy in Minnesota," 405n; *Feeding Dairy Cows*, 406n

Haecker Hall, **4**: 407

Hahn, W. J., **3**: 435

Hale, J. P., **2**: 60

Hale, Maj. W. D., **2**: 315n, **3**: 495n

Half-breeds, *see* Mixed-bloods

HALKETT, JOHN, *Statement Respecting Selkirk's Settlement*, **1**: 214n

Hall, D. S., **4**: 236n

HALL, D. S., *Minnesota State Agricultural Society*, **1**: 361n

Hall, H. P., **3**: 82, 348

HALL, H. P., *Observations*, **1**: 385n

Hall, Liberty, **4**: 85n, 157

Hall, Col. N. J., **2**: 313n

Hall, Rev. Sherman, **1**: 173, 175–177

Hall, W. S., **2**: 31

Halleck, Gen. H. W., **2**: 95, 99, 187, 188, 208, 242, 251, 266

HALLOCK, CHARLES, "Red River Trail," **1**: 116n

Hamblin, E. O., **2**: 100

Hamlin, Condé, **3**: 273

Hammond, W. S., supports Johnson, **3**: 282, 284; delivers address at unveiling of Johnson statue, 284; elected governor, 298; sketch, 293; death, 294

Hanchett, Dr. A. H., **4**: 3

HANCHETT, A. H., *Report of the State Geologist*, **4**: 3n

Hancock, Rev. J. W., **1**: 204, 452n

Hancock, Gen. W. S., **2**: 309, 310, 311, 450

Hand, Maj. D. W., **3**: 522, 523, **4**: 420n

HANEY, L. H., *Congressional History of Railways*, **2**: 37n

HANSEN, M. L., *Old Fort Snelling*, **1**: 133n

Harbach, Lieut. Col. A. A., **4**: 317

Harriet, Lake, **4**: 427, 428; mission, *see* Missions

Harrison, Hugh, **3**: 183n

Harrison, Samuel, **1**: 61, 62

HARRISSE, HENRY, *Nouvelle-France*, **1**: 21n

Hart, Rev. H. H., **3**: 152, **4**: 409–413

HARTSOUGH, M. L., *The Twin Cities as a Metropolitan Market*, **2**: 253n

Harwood, A. A., **4**: 61n, 72n

Haskell, Joseph, **1**: 230n

Hastings, **3**: 11, 103, 165; refuge from Indians, **2**: 124; railroad station, **3**: 61; insane asylum, 248

Hatch, Maj. E. A. C., organizes battalion for campaign against Indians, **2**: 290; sketch, 290; obtains surrender of Sioux Indians, 293; member of commission negotiating with Chippewa, 378; capture of Little Six and Medicine Bottle, 443–445

Hatch Act, **4**: 89

Hatch's Independent Battalion of Cavalry, organized, **2**: 290; march to Pembina, 291; battle with Sioux, 292; garrisons Fort Abercrombie, 293; number in Indian war, 339

Hauenstein, John, **2**: 363

Haupt, Gen. Herman, **2**: 308

Hawk Creek, **2**: 119

Hay, E. G., **3**: 487

Hayden, W. G., at first battle of New Ulm, **2**: 366, 367, 371, 372, 373; account of battle, 371

HAYDEN, W. G., *Recollections*, **2**: 372n

Hayes, President R. B., appoints Ramsey secretary of war, **3**: 87; Minnesota vote for, 115, 115n
Hayner, H. Z., **1**: 378n
HAYNES, F. E., *Third Party Movements*, **3**: 117n; *Social Politics*, 543n
Haywood, W. D., **3**: 568, 569
Hazelwood, **2**: 427, 428, 430, 434; mission, *see* Missions
Hazelwood Republic, **2**: 220, 222, **4**: 332n
Health, *see* Public health
Heard, I. V. D., **2**: 179, 188, 198, 199, 387; acting judge advocate of military commission, 192n; credits Boardman Cavalry with saving New Ulm, 365
HEARD, I. V. D., *Sioux War*, **1**: 301n
Hearing of the Chippewa before the Committee on Indian Affairs, February 2, 1899, **4**: 246n
Hearley, John, **4**: 182n
Heart River, Sully expedition, **2**: 297, 298
Heffron, Rt. Rev. P. R., **4**: 110n
Heintzelman, Gen. S. P., **2**: 85
Heiskell, W. K., **1**: 506–508
Helen, Lake, **4**: 256
Henderson, **2**: 120, 149n, 159, 200, **3**: 352; incorporated, **1**: 379; objective of Sioux, **2**: 126; refuge from Sioux, 224; garrisoned, 243; burial place of J. R. Brown, **3**: 76; founded, 350
HENING, W. W., ed., *Statutes at Large*, **1**: 69n
Hennepin, Father Louis, **1**: 31n; sketch, 27; exploring expeditions, 27–30, 79, 457; discovers Falls of St. Anthony, 29
HENNEPIN, LOUIS, *Louisiana*, **1**: 23n, 31; *Nouvelle découverte*, 31
Hennepin County, **3**: 99; established, **1**: 429; ravaged by grasshoppers, **3**: 103; probate practice, 191n; district court, 229, 335, 336n, 440, 518n; in elections of *1904*, 274, 275, 275n; sale of timber on school lands, 503; primary election system, **4**: 366, 367; poorhouse, 410
Hennepin Island, **3**: 336, 338, 340, 342, 344
Hennepin Bi-Centenary, **1**: 32n
Henry, Alexander, **1**: 67n, **4**: 1
"Heresy of the Parochial School," **4**: 183n

Hermann, Binger, **4**: 246, 247n
HERMANN, BINGER, *Louisiana Purchase*, **1**: 78n
Hermanutz, Rev. Aloysius, missionary at White Earth, **4**: 208, 213; services to Indians, 227, 318, 319; sketch, 324; death, 325n
HERMANUTZ, ALOYSIUS, "St. Benedict's Mission and School," **4**: 325n
Hernando de Soto, Lake, **1**: 128
Heron Lake, **2**: 223, 402, 405
Herrick, Fred, **4**: 274, 275n, 287n
Hewitt, Dr. C. N., services in promotion of public health, **3**: 154, 155, **4**: 414–424; sketch, 414, 424
Hewitt, **3**: 541
Heywood, J. L., **3**: 114
Hibbing, **4**: 19, 33; population, 51; schools, 52; election law applicable to, 360n
Hicks, Judge H. G., **3**: 411n, 438n
HICKS, J. D., "Political Career of Donnelly," **2**: 60n; "Organization of the Volunteer Army in 1861," 79n
Highway commission, **3**: 309, 310. *See also* Roads
Hill, A. P., **2**: 310
Hill, Charles, **2**: 438n
Hill, J. J., **3**: 348, **4**: 39, 255, 465; delivers address, **2**: 314; statue commissioner, **3**: 268n; accused of dominating Republicans, 273n; acquires control of St. Paul and Pacific Railroad, 451–462; sketch, 452; sued for railroad properties, 463–474; attitude in Nelson-Washburn campaign, 494; acquires railroads in iron district, **4**: 33; ore land transactions, 34–36, 38n; and Lake Superior Co., 35; testifies before investigating commission, 40
HILL, J. J., "Agriculture in Minnesota," **1**: 363n
Hill, J. N., **4**: 33, 36
Hill, L. W., **4**: 36
Hill, W. J., **4**: 36
Hill, Griggs, and Co., **3**: 452
Hill Papers, **1**: 116n
Hilton, C. L., **3**: 308, 558n
Hinckley, destroyed by fire, **3**: 212, **4**: 388
Hinds, Henry, **3**: 405
Hinman, Rev. S. D., **2**: 113n; in charge of Sioux mission, 207, **4**: 474; baptizes Sioux converts, **2**: 254; accompanies Sioux exiles, 259;

recommends removal of homeless Sioux to reservation, 263

HINSDALE, B. A., *Old Northwest*, 1: 69n

Hinton, J. H., 4: 285, 286

Hinton roll, 4: 285, 286n

Historical Society, *see* Minnesota Historical Society

Hitchcock, E. A., 4: 240, 241, 247, 248n, 249, 276

Hiuka, Sioux Indian, 2: 285

Hoag, Charles, 4: 81n

HOBART, CHAUNCEY, *Methodism in Minnesota*, 1: 181n

HODGE, F. W., ed., *Handbook of American Indians*, 1: 80n

HOLBROOK, F. F., "Early Political Career of Donnelly," 1: 394n; *Minnesota in the Spanish-American War*, 3: 232n

Holcombe, R. I., 2: 151n, 390

HOLCOMBE, R. I., *State Agricultural Society*, 1: 361n; *First Regiment*, 2: 86n; " Big Eagle's Story," 113n; ed., *Minneapolis and Hennepin County*, 3: 70n

Holcombe, William, 1: 238, 263, 491, 495, 2: 25, 62, 78n

Hole-in-the-Day (the elder), Chippewa chief, 1: 149n, 150, 151, 152, 154, 155, 155n, 157, 191

Hole-in-the-Day (the younger), Chippewa chief, 1: 258, 259, 3: 26, 29, 4: 194, 312, 313n, 470; heads insurrection, 2: 375, 376, 377, 378, 381, 382; alliance with Little Crow rumored, 380

Holl, Mathias, 2: 182n

HOLLAND, BJORN, "Nelson's Boyhood Days," 3: 147n

Holler, J. A., 3: 203

Holmberg Act, 4: 170n

Holmes Anniversary Volume, 4: 292n

Holt, Gen. Joseph, 2: 448, 449

Home Guard of Minnesota, organized, 3: 318, 559; ordered to zone of forest fires, 565

Home rule, *see* Cities

Homestead Act, 2: 331–333, 344, 4: 327

Homesteading, 3: 62

Hood, Gen. J. B., 2: 322, 323, 324, 325

Hooker, Gen. Joseph, 2: 319, 320

Hopkins, Robert, *see* Chaskay, R. H.

Horn, H. J., 2: 28n

Horseshoe Ridge, 2: 316, 317, 318

Horticultural Society, *see* Minnesota State Horticultural Society

Hospital and Home for Crippled Children, *see* Minnesota Hospital and Home for Crippled Children

Hotchkiss, Capt. W. A., 2: 99, 307

House of Representatives, *see* Legislature

Houston County, aids victims of grasshopper plague, 3: 99; damage to wheat crop, 111n; district court, 403

HOWARD, ASHER, ed., *Leaders of the Nonpartisan League*, 3: 554n

Howard, J. R., 4: 280, 282n

Howard Lake, 2: 283, 442

Hoy, Michael, assists in arrest of Lord Gordon, 3: 373–375, 377, 378; arrested and examined, 375, 376, 383; assaults Clarke, 387

Hrdlička, Dr. Aleš, aids in identifying full-blood Chippewa, 4: 292, 293; quoted, 295

HRDLIČKA, ALEŠ, "Anthropology of the Chippewa," 4: 292n

HUBBARD, ELBERT, *Rescue of Helen*, 4: 256n

Hubbard, Gen. L. F., 3: 168, 172; regimental colonel, 2: 96; brevetted brigadier general, 96; at battle of Nashville, 326, 327; declines nomination for Congress, 3: 15; supports Davis for governor, 83; twice elected governor, 144; legislation enacted during term, 145, 152–162, 261, 4: 411; proposes biennial elections, 3: 145; returns to private life, 162, 164; service in Spanish-American War, 163; character and achievements, 164; delivers address, 268; criticizes impeachment procedure, 417n; railroad bond commissioner, 423; death, 164

HUBBARD, L. F., "Fifth Regiment," 2: 96n; "Minnesota in the Battles of Corinth," 97n; *Minnesota in the Battles of Nashville*, 327n

Hubbard County, 4: 280n; named, 3: 164; lumbering, 4: 199

HUDSON, E. E., "Farmers' Alliance and Nonpartisan League," 3: 555n

HUDSON, H. B., ed., *Minneapolis*, 1: 453n

Hudson's Bay Co., 1: 67, 3: 351, 378, 451; chartered, 1: 8; surrenders political authority, 87; liquor traffic, 87; Northwest Co. merges with, 87; operations after *1783,* 113, 499; posts, 190, 215; land grant to Selkirk, 213; transportation of goods, **2**: 164, **3**: 351, 452; owns transportation companies, 452. *See also* British; Fur trade; Indians

Huey, William, **2**: 138, 139n, 143

Huggan, Nancy M., **1**: 280

HUGGAN, NANCY M., "Story of Nancy McClure," **1**: 280n

Huggins, A. G., **1**: 189

Huggins, A. W., **2**: 121, 432

Huggins, Mrs. A. W., **2**: 250

Hughes, Thomas, **2**: 128n, 367

HUGHES, THOMAS, "Site of Fort L'Huillier," **1**: 42n; "Treaty of Traverse des Sioux," 279n; "Steamboating on the Minnesota," 361n; *Welsh in Minnesota,* **2**: 137n; Blue Earth County, 170n; "Inkpaduta Massacre," 225n

Humboldt mill, **3**: 131, 135

Humphrey, Dr. P. P., **2**: 109

Humphreys, Gen. A. A., **3**: 341

Humphreys, Lieut. C. B., **4**: 314, 318

Hundred Associates, organized, **1**: 14; causes for failure, 14; surrender franchise, 15

Hunter, Andrew, **2**: 119

HUNTINGTON, GEORGE, *Robber and Hero,* **3**: 114n

Huron, Lake, discovery, **1**: 3, 3n; French proclamation of sovereignty over, 17

Huron Indians, **1**: 2, 4, 4n, 5, 7, 10, 43, **4**: 1

HURTER, H. S., "Narrative of the First Battery of Light Artillery," **2**: 99n

Hutchinson, **2**: 118, 120, 160, 174, 284, 286; preparations against Sioux attacks, 158, 174n; plundered by Sioux, 163; garrisoned, 243; soldiers killed during Sioux Outbreak, 392

HYDE, C. W. G., ed., *Great Northwest,* **3**: 242n

Iberville, sieur d', **1**: 40

Illinois, constitution, **3**: 40; railroad litigation, 57; natives of, in Minnesota, 73; represented at conference on grasshopper plague, 103; adjusts railroad debt, 424; land grants, **4**: 82n, 135

Illinois Central Railroad, **1**: 329, 331, 332, 346

Illinois Indians, **1**: 20

Illinois River, explorers on, **1**: 20, 27, 33, 34, 35; Jolliet's map of, 21

Illiteracy, **3**: 58, 254, 254n, **4**: 187

Immigration, **1**: 359, **2**: 64n, 344, **4**: 333; occupations of immigrants, **1**: 360; effect on business, 362; encouragement of, **3**: 1, 19, 64, 226; federal bureau proposed, 12; extent, *1860–75,* 62; distribution of immigrants, 62, 140; demand for restriction, 198, 201; of socialists, 539. *See also* Foreigners; Population; individual nationalities

Income tax, *see* Taxation

Independent party, **3**: 116, 117. *See also* Greenback party

Independent school districts, *see* Education

Indian Barbarities in Minnesota, **2**: 197n

Indian reservations, *see* individual reservations

Indian trade, *see* Fur trade

Indian treaties:
Chippewa, Saulteur at Sault de Ste. Marie, *1820,* **1**: 103; at Fond du Lac, *1826,* 306, **4**: 1; Mississippi bands at Fort Snelling, *1837,* **1**: 159, 163, 177, 213, 227, 233, 266, 351, **4**: 190, 192, 296; Mississippi and Lake Superior bands: *1847,* **1**: 305, 310, *1854,* **4**: 473; Pillagers, *1847,* **1**: 321, **4**: 230, 322, 323n; at Pembina, *1851,* **1**: 288, 291, 305; Lake Superior bands at La Pointe, *1854*: 306, 307, 358, 470, **4**: 2, 191, 192, 230, 296, issue of scrip to half-breeds in execution of, *see* Scrip; Mississippi, Pillager, and Winnibigoshish bands at Washington: *1855,* **1**: 182n, 306–308, 358, **4**: 191, 192, 193, 296, 473, *1863,* **1**: 307n, **3**: 22–26, 29, **4**: 193, 194, 214, 296, *1864,* **1**: 307n, **3**: 26, 29, **4**: 194, *1867,* **3**: 30, **4**: 195, 206, 324, 477n; Red Lake and Pembina bands: *1863,* 191, 192, 296, 476, *1864,* 192n, 477; Bois Fort band, *1866,* **1**: 307n, **4**: 191, 192, 296

Menominee, *1848,* **1**: 321; *1854,* 321

Northwestern tribes at Prairie du

Chien, *1825*, **1**: 146, **4**: 190, 296; *1830*, **1**: 158, 208, 274, 308, 322, 482

Sioux, at mouth of Minnesota River, *1805*, **1**: 92–94, 134, 136, 159, 213, 217n, 439, 440, 446; at Portage des Sioux, *1815*, 133; at Fort Snelling, *1820*, 144, 446, 447n, *see also* Faribault claim; at Washington, *1837*, 160, 163, 208, 210, 213, 217, 227, 233, 266, 205, 297, 351, 438, 439, 446, **2**: 216, 438, **4**: 473; Sisseton, Wahpeton, and Wahpekute at Traverse des Sioux, *1841*, **1**: 196, 266n, 457–459; Mdewakanton, *1841*, 266n, 450; attempt to negotiate at Mendota, *1849*, 271–274; Sisseton and Wahpeton at Traverse des Sioux, *1851*: 305, 426, **2**: 216, 424, 438, **4**: 193; appropriations for, **1**: 275, appointment of commissioners, 275–277, negotiations, 278–281, painting, 279n, terms, 281, 287, 289, "traders' paper," 282–284, 289, 295, 296, 297, 299, 301, 464, 467, 468, ratified, 290–292, 304, 465, amendments, 291, 293–295, **2**: 393, execution, **1**: 292–296, 299–303, 353, charges against Ramsey, *see* Ramsey; Wahpekute and Mdewakanton at Mendota, *1851*: 211, 426, appropriations for, 275, appointment of commissioners, 275–277, terms, 284, 286, 287, 324, "traders' paper," 284, 297, negotiations, 285–287, ratification, 290–292, amendments, 291, 293–295, 354n, execution, 292–294, 295–299, 303, 353; Wahpekute and Mdewakanton at Washington, *1858*: negotiations, **2**: 218, 394–396, terms, 218, 219, 227, 395, 396, ratification, 396, execution, 218, 227, 396–399, 400; Sisseton and Wahpeton at Washington, *1858*: negotiations, 218, 394, 396, ratification, 396, execution, 218, 227, 396–398, 400; Sisseton and Wahpeton at Washington, *1867*, 418–420; various bands at Laramie, Wyoming, *1868*, 439

Sioux-Chippewa, at Fort Snelling, *1820*, **1**: 105, 145; *1838*, 155n;

1843, 259; provision concerning, in treaty of northwestern tribes, *1825*, 141n, 147, 207

Winnebago, *1829*, *1832*, *1837*, **1**: 308, 309; at Washington, *1846*, 310, 478; on Watab River, *1853*, 318, 479–482; at Washington, *1855*, 319, 482, **4**: 193; provision concerning, in treaty of northwestern tribes, *1825*, **1**: 308

Indian Tribes in the Northwest, **2**: 111n

Indiana, land grants to, **4**: 82n, 135

Indians, **1**: 2, 12, 20, 43, 53, 113, 177, 367; councils with, 10, 17, 146, 158, 273; methods of warfare, 82, 83, 84, 85, 150, 157, **2**: 125; sale and gifts of liquor to: **1**: 83, 86, 92, 94, 98, 147, 165, 203, 209, 211, 219, 220, 254, 280, 287, 309, 458n, **2**: 207, 222, 228, 395, 415, acts forbidding, **1**: 165, 166, 256, **2**: 256; influence of whites, **1**: 85–87, 168, 208, 366; culture, 85, 170; law, 148, 153, 157; debts to traders: 159, 269n, 289, 296, 309, 464, **3**: 23, recognized in treaties, **1**: 160, 160n, 268, 282, 307, 458n, 459, **4**: 476, *see also* "Traders' papers"; agencies, **1**: 165n, *see also* individual agents and agencies; influence of traders, 166, 167, 210, 268, 269, 275, 279n, 281, 310, 467; treaty-making, 169n, 208, 268–270, 275, 277, 279n, 366, **4**: 217, 473, *see also* Indian treaties; religion, **1**: 170; attitude toward Christianity, 171; taught agriculture by whites, 178, 185, 191; number in Minnesota estimated: *1849*, 254, *1860*, **2**: 64, *1895*, **3**: 226, *1900*, 251, 251n; character, **2**: 213; U. S. Indian system criticized, 207–209, 213–216, 395, 409, **4**: 194n, 201n, 305n, 323, 473; exile demanded, **2**: 255, 256; investigation of Indian affairs requested, 256; plans for civilizing, 256, 257n, **3**: 27–29, *see also* Dawes Act; plans for removal suggested, **2**: 256–258; murders and depredations in spring of *1863*, 282, 288; protective measures against, 282, 287; cause flight of whites, 287; troops in wars against, 339; in Civil War, 421; extension of suffrage to, **3**: 7, 8, **4**: 332; demand for reform of policies relating to, **3**: 25, 27–29; attempts to determine blood status, **4**: 285–288, 291–293, 324n; bring claims into court, 306, 328; ruling of Supreme Court regarding control, 308; attitude toward missionaries, *see* Missionaries; education, *see* Missionaries. *See also* British; Chippewa Indians; French; Fur trade; Indian treaties; individual Indian agents and agencies; individual tribes; Missions; Mixed-bloods; Sibley expeditions of *1862* and *1863*; Sioux Indians; Sioux Outbreak; Sully expeditions of *1863* and *1864*; Traders; Winnebago Indians

Indians of Red Lake Reservation, **4**: 305n

Indians Who Served in the Army, **2**: 421n

Indrehus, Edward, **3**: 551n

Industrial Workers of the World, **3**: 568

Industries, *1860*, **2**: 64n, 65n. *See also* Agriculture; Dairy industry; Economic conditions; Financial conditions; Flour-milling; Labor; Lumber industry; Manufacturing; Trade

Inebriates, hospital for, **4**: 421, 421n

Infantry, number in Civil and Indian wars, **2**: 339. *See also* individual regiments

Inheritance tax, *see* Taxation

Initiative, advocated, **3**: 200, 202, 288, 550n

Inkpaduta, Sioux chief, **1**: 325; heads insurrection, **2**: 223, 224, 231, 401, 402, 404, 406, 429; pursued, 408. *See also* Spirit Lake massacre

Insane asylums, established, **3**: 248, **4**: 408; recommendations relating to, **3**: 288; conditions, **4**: 409

Insurance, legal code relating to, **3**: 226, 287; accident, **4**: 455

Interest laws, revised, **2**: 63

Internal improvements, fund, **3**: 225, 225n. *See also* Roads; Transportation

International Joint Commission, **3**: 382n

INTERNATIONAL JOINT COMMISSION, *Final Report*, **1**: 503n

International Lumber Co., **4**: 309, 310

International Steam Transportation Co., **3**: 355

Interstate commerce commission, *see* U. S. Interstate Commerce Commission

Investigation of Steel Corporation, **4**: 34n

Iowa, organization of territory, **1**: 486; establishment of state government and boundaries, 486–489; grasshopper plague, **3**: 97; represented at conference on grasshopper plague, 103; administration of charitable and penal institutions, 262; agricultural college, **4**: 93

Iowa Indians, **1**: 41

Ireland, Rt. Rev. John, **3**: 348; chaplain Fifth Minnesota, **2**: 97; character and services, 98; sketch, **3**: 175; advocates temperance reforms, 175–178; delivers address, 268; eulogizes Johnson, 286n; in educational controversy, **4**: 177, 180–182; sends delegate to councils of U. S. Chippewa commission, 227; approves park project, 255

IRELAND, JOHN, "Memoir of Rev. Lucian Galtier," **1**: 224n; "Address at the Unveiling of the Statue of Shields," **2**: 7n; *The Church and Modern Society*, **4**: 181n

Irish, number, *1860*, **2**: 64n, *1870*, **3**: 59

Iron Cloud, Sioux chief, **1**: 153

Iron Junction, **4**: 21

Iron mining, **3**: 162; iron lands acquired by speculators in half-breed scrip, **1**: 485; taxation of mining properties, **3**: 199, 288–290, 307–309, 551, **4**: 11, 53–58; early explorations for ore, 1–4; on Vermilion Range, 8–17; effect of mining act of *1872*, 13; methods of acquiring ore lands, 14; first shipment of ore, 16; methods of prospecting, 17; on Mesabi Range, 17–22; leasing of state mineral lands, 18, 58; methods, 22; on Cuyuna Range, 22; marketing of ores, 23–28, 57; price of ore, 24, 31; beneficiation of ores, 25, 41; ore production, 28, 40; combinations of mine owners, 28–41; freight rates on ore, 37, 40; future of ore deposits, 41–43; estimates of tonnage of iron formations, 42; conditions affecting demand for ore, 43; origin of ore formations, 43, 483; loss of Mountain Iron Mine property, 44–48; on lands under public waters, 48–50; growth of mining communities, 50–53; statistics, 50, 51, 54, 59; investigation of pig iron industry, 57n; administration of state ore lands, 145. *See also* Cuyuna Iron Range; Mesabi Iron Range; Mining; Vermilion Iron Range

Iron Nest, Sioux Indian, **2**: 133n

Ironton, **4**: 23

Iroquois Indians, **1**: 2, 4n, 43, 44, 50, 80; campaigns against, 2, 6, 22, 26, 33, 37; check French settlement, 3

Irvine, Col. A. G., **3**: 376n

Irvine, W. N., **2**: 313

Irwin, David, **1**: 234

Isanti County, **3**: 216, 393

Isanti Indians, **1**: 182, 200

Island mill, **3**: 338

Isle Pelée, **1**: 12, 39

Isle Royale, **1**: 4n; suggested as home for outlawed Indians, **2**: 257

Itasca, village, **3**: 36, 37n

Itasca County, **1**: 352n, **4**: 7, 103n

Itasca Lake, source of Mississippi, **1**: 110n, 116; Schoolcraft reaches, 114; named, 114; Nicollet's survey, 124, 125; Glazier on, 127; Brower's survey, 127–129

Itasca State Park, **1**: 128

Iuka, battle, **2**: 95n, 102

Iverson, S. G., **4**: 48n

Iverson, S. G., "Public Lands and School Fund," **4**: 146n

Ives, G. S., **2**: 371

Ives, W. J., **3**: 411n

Izatys, **1**: 23

Jackson, Leroy, "Enmegahbowh," **2**: 380n

Jackson, O. F., **2**: 29

Jackson, village, **2**: 223, 402, 404, 405

Jackson County, Sioux attacks, **2**: 123, 223; number massacred, 392; ravaged by grasshoppers, **3**: 97, 102; disloyalty, 572. *See also* Spirit Lake massacre

Jacobson, J. F., **3**: 282

Jails, **4**: 410, 411n

James, J. A., ed., *Clark Papers*, **1**: 69n

James River, **2**: 193, 260, 277, 278, 295, 404, 419, 429

Jay's treaty, *1794*, **1**: 71, 499

Jefferson, Thomas, **1**: 71, 89, 90, 91, 132n, 499

Jefferson, Thomas, *Works*, **1**: 71n; "Life of Captain Lewis," 89n; *Writings*, 132n

Jenkins, J. E., **4**: 247, 247n

Jenks, Dr. A. E., **4**: 292

Jenks, A. E., *Indian-White Amalgamation*, **4**: 292n

Jennison, Col. S. P., **2**: 77n; commander Tenth Minnesota, 305; wounded at Nashville, 326

Jesuit Relations, **1**: 5n

Jesuits, **1**: 18, 25; missionary activities, 7, 15, 45; writings, 8, 11; interest in science, 45n

Jesus College, **4**: 439

Jesus College, **4**: 440n

Jewett, A. J., and members of family, murdered, **2**: 346–349, 350; panic caused by murders, 349–351

Jewish war relief, **4**: 463

Jogues, Isaac, **1**: 6

Johns Hopkins University, **4**: 68

Johnson, President Andrew, **3**: 4; confirms sentences of Little Six and Medicine Bottle, **2**: 350, 448; impeached, **3**: 6, 326, 406

Johnson, C. F., **3**: 554n

Johnson, C. W., "Narrative of the Sixth Regiment," **2**: 101n; *Another Tale of Two Cities*, **3**: 481n

Johnson, E. B., **4**: 86, 97

Johnson, E. B., *University of Minnesota*, **4**: 60

Johnson, F. W., **2**: 364, 368n

Johnson, F. W., *Glimpse of New Ulm*, **2**: 364n

Johnson, J. A., **3**: 293, **4**: 271; addresses by, read, **2**: 314, 315; elected governor, **3**: 272, 275, 277; accuses railroads of dominating politics, 273n; sketch, 275–277; recommends extension of governor's term, 278; career as governor, 279; reëlected, 279, 282; speaking tours, 280; suggested for presidential nomination, 281, 285, 286n; legislation during administration, 286–288; views on taxation of iron ore property, 288–290, 307, **4**: 55; appoints tax commission, 54; death and burial, **3**: 283; eulogized, 283,

284n, 285, 285n, 286n; erection of statues, 283–285; collection of clippings relating to, 285n; memorial meeting, 285n

JOHNSON, J. W., "History of Fort Snelling," 1: 219n; "Fort Ridgely," 2: 127n; "Fort Ripley," 127n

Johnson, John, see Enmegahbowh, J. J.

Johnson, Magnus, candidate for governor, 3: 320, 551; elected U. S. senator, 320, 552; defeated for reëlection, 321, 552; eulogizes Nelson, 499; sketch, 551, 551n

Johnson, Gen. R. W., 1: 454; sketch, 3: 144; candidate for governor, 144

JOHNSON, R. W., "Fort Snelling," 1: 454n

JOHNSON MEMORIAL COMMISSION, Final Report, 3: 277n

Johnston, Gen. A. S., 2: 85

JOHNSTON, D. S. B., "Minnesota Journalism," 1: 241n

Jolliet, Louis, discovers Mississippi, 1: 14, 19; sketch, 18; exploring expedition, 18–22; report, 21, 22; historical importance, 22

Jones, Capt. John, 2: 130, 132; on Sibley expedition of 1863, 267n; on Sully expedition of 1864, 296; commands detachment sent to Devil's Lake, 300

Jones, R. A., 3: 7n

Jones, Robinson, 2: 415, 416, 417

Jones, Mrs. Robinson, 2: 417

Jones, T. C., 1: 477

Jones, William Ashley, 2: 28n

Jones, William A., commissioner of Indian affairs, 4: 300n, 305n, 318–320

JOUTEL, HENRI, Journal historique, 1: 35n; Journal of the Last Voyage, 35n

Judiciary, see Courts

Judson, garrisoned, 2: 243

Julia, Lake, 1: 110

Juni, Benedict, 2: 125n

Junior Colleges, see Education

Kanabec County, 1: 10

Kandiyohi County, 3: 109; in Sioux Outbreak, 2: 123, 161, 392; bill to remove capital to, 3: 9

Kandiyohi lakes, 2: 283

Kansas, admitted to Union, 2: 10–12, 15; represented at conference on grasshopper plague, 3: 104; adopts prohibition, 300

Kansas Constitution, 2: 15n

Kaposia, 1: 156, 2: 233; battle, 1: 180; missions, see Missions

KAPPLER, C. J., ed., Indian Affairs, 2: 439n

Kaskaskia, 1: 69, 73

Kasota, quarries, 3: 270

Kathio, 1: 23

Kavenaugh, Rev. B. T., 1: 206

Kearful, F. J., 4: 290

KEARNEY, S. W., "Journal," 1: 138n

Keating, W. H., expedition, 1: 107, 108, 455, 457

KEATING, W. H., Narrative, 1: 42n, 107n

Keegan, Owen, assists in arresting Lord Gordon, 3: 373, 374; arrested and tried, 375, 376, 377, 383

Kegwedzissag, Chippewa guide, 1: 124

Keller, Senator Henry, 3: 207, 505

Kelley, O. H., sketch, 3: 36; organizes and promotes Granger movement, 37, 38, 39

KELLEY, O. H., Patrons of Husbandry, 3: 37n

Kellogg, F. B., sketch, 3: 298; elected U. S. senator, 299; defeated for reëlection, 299, 320, 550; ambassador to Great Britain, 299; secretary of state, 299

KELLOGG, L. P., "Memorandum on the Spelling 'Jolliet,'" 1: 18n; Early Narratives of the Northwest, 26n; "Remains of a French Post near Trempealeau," 37n; "Capture of Mackinac," 100n

Kennedy, J. S., and Co., 3: 446, 450, 456, 459, 461, 461n, 466n, 470

Kennedy Mine, 4: 23

Kenwood Parkway, Minneapolis, 4: 428

Keweenaw, 1: 80

KEYES, WILLARD, "Diary," 1: 63n

Kiehle, Rev. D. L., plan for school of agriculture, 4: 94, 96n; advocates free textbooks, 161n

KIEHLE, D. L., Education in Minnesota, 4: 94n; "Education Applied to Agriculture," 95n; "Department of Public Instruction," 152n

KIESTER, J. A., *Faribault County*, **1**: 437n

KILPATRICK, MRS. A. E., "William Holcombe," **1**: 491n

Kimball, De Grove, **2**: 182n

Kindred, C. F., sketch, **3**: 147; political contest with Nelson, 147–149

King, David, **1**: 204, 205

King, W. S., **3**: 327, 300, 396, 397, 485, **4**: 427; denounces Rice, **2**: 71n; sketch, **3**: 90–92

KINGSBURY, D. L., "Sully's Expedition," **2**: 298n

Kingsbury, W. W., **2**: 28n; delegate to Congress, 19; unseated, 19–21

KINGSFORD, WILLIAM, *Canada*, **1**: 6n

Kittson, N. W., fur-trader, **1**: 164n, 293, 352, 454, **2**: 28n, **3**: 451; approves arrest of Lord Gordon, 378; sketch, 452; becomes part owner of St. Paul and Pacific Railroad Co., 453–462; sued for railroad properties, 463–474; death, 469

Kitzman, Paul, **2**: 120, 121

Knatvold, T. V., **3**: 490n

Knife Lake, **1**: 10

Knights of Labor, **3**: 169, **4**: 427, 449

Knights of the Forest, **2**: 256

Knox, H. M., **3**: 121–124

Knox, J. J., **2**: 28n

Koetten, Sister Philomena, **4**: 325

KOOS, L. V., *Junior College*, **4**: 72n

Kraft, John, **3**: 137n

Kreiger, Justina, **2**: 121n, 155

KUHLMANN, C. B., "Development of Flour Milling in Minneapolis," **3**: 70n; "Minneapolis Flour Mills," 389n

KUMM, H. F., *Constitution of Minnesota*, **3**: 521n

La Bathe, François, **2**: 109, 196

La Biche, Lake, *see* Itasca

La Biche River, **1**: 105

Labor, demands, **3**: 169, 170, 550; bureau of labor statistics created, 179, **4**: 449; restriction of child labor, **3**: 170, 201, 226; arbitration of disputes urged, 188, 198, 249; demands incorporated in political platforms, 198, 200, 201; legislation protecting, 205; incorporation of unions recommended, 249; coöperates with Nonpartisan League in elections, 320, 547, 548; growth of unions, **4**: 449, 453. *See also* Bureau of labor; Bureau of labor statistics; Farmer-Labor party; Strikes

Lac Courte Oreille, **1**: 10

Lac la Biche, *see* Itasca

Lac qui Parle, trading post, **1**: 257; Indian murder, **2**: 121; capture of Indians, 193; mission, *see* Missions

La Crescent, designated railroad terminus, **2**: 38, 42

La Croix, E. N., **3**: 69, 71n

Lacy, C. Y., **4**: 87, 88, 90

La Farge, John, **3**: 270

La Follette, Senator R. M., **3**: 315, 566, 567n; platform, 552

Laframboise, Joseph, fur-trader, **1**: 121, 133, 164n, **2**: 117, 405; testifies in Sisseton and Wahpeton claim case, 426, 427

Laframboise, Julia, **2**: 427

Laframboise family, **2**: 252

La Harpe, Bernard de, **1**: 38n

LAHONTAN, L. A., *New Voyages*, **1**: 24n

La Jemeraye, C. D., **1**: 48

Lake, *see* individual names

Lake City, plan to move county seat to, **3**: 21

Lake County, **4**: 3, 7, 15; state lands, 12

Lake of Tears, *see* Pepin, Lake

Lake of the Isles, Minneapolis, parkway, **4**: 428

Lake of the Woods, explorers, **1**: 48, 108; fort, 48

Lake of the Woods County, forest fires, **4**: 391

Lake Superior and Mississippi Railroad Co., **3**: 48, 49, 119n. *See also* Northern Pacific Railroad Co.; St. Paul and Duluth Railroad Co.

Lake Superior Co. Ltd., **4**: 35, 36, 40

Lake Superior Consolidated Iron Mines Co., **4**: 29–32

Lake Superior, Puget's Sound, and Pacific Railroad Co., **1**: 329

Lake Winnibigoshish Indian Reservation, **4**: 193, 195, 196n; established 192; unsuitable for permanent reservation, 201; councils, 212; partly included in forest reserve, 254, 258, 259, 307, 399

Lake Winnibigoshish Indians, habitat, 4: 190n; cede land, 191; acquire reservation, 192; agree to consolidation, 212, 218; census, 227n
Lamar, L. Q. C., 4: 201, 219
Lamb, John, 4: 450
Lame Jim, 2: 441
Lamoreux, S. W., 4: 236n, 237n, 240n
LAMPHERE, G. N., "Wheat Raising in the Red River Valley," 3: 66n
Lampson, Chauncey, 2: 283, 285n
Lampson, Nathan, 2: 283, 286
Land O'Lakes Creameries, 4: 405n
Lands, see Property; Public lands
LANGFORD, N. P., "Louisiana Purchase," 1: 78n
Langum, O. S., 3: 566
La Perrière, sieur de, 1: 45
La Pointe, 1: 175, 4: 215; trading post, 1: 80, 173; Indian agency, 154, 204n, 471, 475; missions, see Missions; treaty, see Indian treaties
LA POTHERIE, BACQUEVILLE DE, L'Amérique Septentrionale, 1: 36n
La Reine, 1: 49
LARPENTEUR, A. L., "Recollections of St. Paul," 1: 180n
Larrabee, C. F., 4: 202
La Salle, sieur de, 1: 31n, 32, 73; sketch, 25; exploring expeditions, 25–27, 28, 33; fur-trader, 26; in command of Fort Frontenac, 26; Indian policy, 32; proclaims French sovereignty, 33, 50; colonizing expedition, 34; death, 35
Lauzon, Jean de, 1: 11
Laverdière, Abbé C. H., 1: 2n
La Vérendrye, chevalier de, 1: 49
La Vérendrye, sieur de, sketch, 1: 47; exploring expedition, 48
Law, practice regulated, 4: 445, 445n
Law school, see University of Minnesota
Lawler, D. W., 3: 196
Lawrence, Abbott, 1: 329
Lawrence, Lorenzo, 2: 391
Laws, code of 1851, 1: 262–264, 265, 381, 3: 228; concerning debts, 1: 380; concerning local government, 2: 63, 3: 161, 224, 226, 287, 516; special, legislative abuse of power regarding, 124, 125, 516, 517, 518n, 520; military code, 161, 226; penal code, 161; probate code, 190; banking code, 226; insurance code, 226, 287; code of 1905, 291; compilations and revisions, 4: 338–341; election code, see elections. See also Banks; Constitution; Corporations; Enabling act; Interest laws; Military laws; Organic act
Laws and Regulations Governing the University of Minnesota, 4: 73n
Laws of Minnesota Relating to the Public School System, 4: 144n
LAWSON, V. E., ed., Kandiyohi County, 2: 123n
Lawton expedition, 3: 232
Lawyers, prominent early, 3: 409
Lea, Luke, 1: 274n, 277–280, 284–288, 296, 467
Leach, Col. G. E., 3: 528n, 534, 535, 538n
LEACH, G. E., War Diary, 3: 528n
League Exchange, 3: 555
Lean Bear, Sioux chief, 2: 123n
Leavenworth, Col. Henry, 1: 62, 231, 232, 437; Indian agent, 135n; locates fort at mouth of Minnesota, 135–138, 143; negotiates Sioux treaty, 144, 437, 446; grant to, 437n
Leavenworth, village, 2: 441
Leavett, S. W., 3: 513n
Le Blanc, see Provençalle
LE CLERCQ, CHRÉTIEN, First Establishment of the Faith, 1: 33n
Lecompton constitution, 2: 10
LE DUC, W. G., ed., Minnesota Year Book, 1: 279n; "The Little Steamboat that Opened the 'Cracker Line,'" 2: 321n
Ledyard, John, 1: 89, 89n
Lee, Col. Francis, 1: 426, 427
LEE, J. T., "Bibliography of Carver's Travels," 1: 54n; "Jonathan Carver: Additional Data," 54n
LEE, L. P., Spirit Lake Massacre, 2: 402n
Lee, Gen. R. E., 2: 308, 315, 316
Leech Lake, 1: 97, 3: 79, 4: 196n, 307; trading post, 1: 68, 69n, 97; explorers, 97, 98, 117, 123; Indian council, 98; mission, see Missions; Pillagers join in insurrection, 2: 375–382; attempts to concentrate Chippewa at, 3: 22–24, 26, 29; lumbering, 30, 208n; Indian uprising, 233, 240, 528, 4: 312–323; dam, 209, 230, 317

Leech Lake Indian Reservation, **1**: 307, **4**: 192, 193, 195, 196n, 201; plans to remove Chippewa to, **3**: 22–24, 26, 27, 29; councils, **4**: 207–212, 215, 228n; Indian agent, 248; partly included in forest reserve, 254, 258–260, 307, 399; uprising, 312–323; annuity payment, 313; Bishop Whipple at, 476

Leech Lake Indians, claim damages, **4**: 210; agree to consolidation, 212, 218; uprising, 312–323

Leech Lake River, **3**: 23

Legislative districts, **1**: 252, 379, 395, **2**: 1, 355

Legislature, provision for territorial, **1**: 247; first state: status questioned, **2**: 5, 6, 13, 21, financial proceedings, 30–33; reapportionment, 63, **3**: 226; political complexion, 49, 85, 189, 246, 491, 553, 553n; meets biennially, 119, 144; quarters in new Capitol, 269; procedure regulated by constitution, **4**: 363; members elected on nonpartisan ballot, 372

LEITH, C. K., *Mesabi District,* **4**: 18n

LEMON, J. J., *Northfield Tragedy,* **3**: 114n

LEONARD, J. A., *Olmsted County,* **4**: 109n

Leonhaeuser, Col. H. A., **3**: 234; handles mutiny, 236, 522, 523, 524; court of inquiry, 236, 524n, 525, 526–528

Leonhart, Rudolph, **2**: 364

Lester, Col. H. C., **2**: 94

Le Sueur, P. C., **1**: 49; sketch, 38; trading and mining operations, 38–42, 118; arbiter between Indians, 81

LE SUEUR, P. C., "Relation de son voyage," **1**: 40n

Le Sueur, **2**: 136, **4**: 109; headquarters Tenth Regiment, **2**: 243; sends reënforcements to New Ulm, 373

Le Sueur County, Indian depredations, **2**: 288

Lettsom, Dr. J. C., **1**: 59

LETTSOM, J. C., "Some Account of Carver," **1**: 54n

Leupp, F. E., commissioner of Indian affairs, **4**: 269, 271, 272, 275, 281

Lewis, J. H., **3**: 254

Lewis, Meriwether, **1**: 89, 90

Lewison, Samuel, **4**: 134

Libby, H. W., **3**: 558n

LIBBY, O. G., "Some Verendrye Enigmas," **1**: 49n; "Fort Abercrombie," **2**: 124n

Liberal Democrats, **3**: 81

Liberal Republicans, **3**: 49, 75, 80, 115

Liberty Bonds, **3**: 560, 562, 563n, 572

Libraries, statistics relating to, *1870,* **3**: 58; suffrage on matters relating to, 227, 307n

Life insurance, *see* Insurance

LICHTNER, W. H., "Judge Flandrau," **2**: 136n

Lignery, sieur de, **3**: 44n

Limping Devil, Sioux chief, **3**: 282n

Lincoln, President Abraham, **2**: 186, 379, **3**: 10, 484, **4**: 81; challenged by Shields to duel, **2**: 9; political campaign of *1860,* 66, 67; action with respect to condemned Sioux, 196n, 197, 202, 209, 249, 336; supports Wilkinson, 340; estimates number killed in Sioux Outbreak, 391

LINCOLN, ABRAHAM, *Works,* **2**: 9n

Lind, John, **3**: 491, 526, **4**: 255; congressman, **3**: 220, 242, 257n, **4**: 401; defeated for governor, *1896,* **3**: 220–222, 221n, 244; sentiments on silver question, 220, 221n; welcomes Thirteenth Minnesota, 232; appeals for return of Thirteenth Minnesota, 233n, 277; sketch, 241; elected governor, *1898,* 241–246, **4**: 123; quartermaster in Twelfth Minnesota, **3**: 243, 245; recommendations to legislature, 246–249, 286, 288; defeated for reëlection, *1900,* 256, 257; appointed senator ad interim, 264; refuses to run for senator, 493, 497; member of commission of public safety, 557, 558n

Lindbergh, C. A., **3**: 547

Linnen, E. B., **4**: 282

Lippmann, Rosenthal, and Co., **3**: 444, 447n

Liquor, sale at Fort Snelling, **1**: 166, 219, 220, **3**: 563; license system, **1**: 256, **3**: 175, 179; restrictions on, **1**: 264, 307, 330; political issue, **3**: 172, 182; temperance agitation, 175–178, 200; commission of public safety regulates, 560, 563, 569; prohibition of sale or gift on election days, 4: 377. See also Indians; Prohibition

Litchfield, E. C., 3: 450, 460

Litchfield, E. D., 3: 450, 461

Litchfield, E. H., 3: 441

Little Canada, population, 1: 352

Little Crow III, Sioux chief, 1: 92, 136, 446

Little Crow IV (Big Thunder), 1: 153, 156, 179, 185, 202, 205, 206, 447n

Little Crow V, Sioux chief, leader in Sioux Outbreak, 1: 92, 201, 202, 285, 286, 2: 152, 157, 158, 178, 187, 191, 194, 287n, 415, 427, 433, 446, 447, 3: 354, 4: 470; directs attack on Sioux agency, 2: 109; captives held in camp, 122, 183, 426, 430; loses opportunity of capturing Fort Ridgely, 127; attack on Fort Ridgely, 129, 130, 132n; at battle of New Ulm, 142n; organizes expedition against Sibley, 158; at battle of Acton, 160; plunders Forest City and Hutchinson, 162, 163; credited with attack near Fort Abercrombie, 168n; Sibley attempts to negotiate with, 171, 174, 176; gives reasons for Sioux Outbreak, 172, 233, 287n; prepares for battle with Sibley, 173; battle of Wood Lake, 178–182; leads expedition in pursuit of Inkpaduta, 224, 412, 413; attitude before outbreak, 232, 233, 236, 239, 4: 474; character and ability, 2: 239n, 286, 287n; accepts command of insurgent Sioux, 240, 399; loss of position, 241, 399; accused of planning Sioux attack in 1863, 266; testimony concerning, given to military commission, 285n; activities in spring of 1863, 287n; defended by half-brother, 287n; Indian names, 287n; alliance with Hole-in-the-Day rumored, 380; at treaty negotiations, 1858, 394–396; complicity in Dustin murders, 443; killed, 283–286

Little Falls, prepares defense against Sioux, 2: 161

Little Fish, Sioux Indian, 2: 428

Little Frenchman, Chippewa chief, 4: 214

Little Paul, Sioux Indian, 2: 433; son, 270; loyalty commemorated, 391

Little Priest, Winnebago chief, 2: 145

Little Rock, occupied by Third Minnesota, 2: 303, 304; battle commemorated, 327n. See also Missions

Little Round Top, 2: 310, 452

Little Sioux River, 2: 401, 402

Little Six (Shakopee), Sioux chief, 1: 136, 156, 197, 2: 24, 122, 239, 240, 4: 470; captured, 2: 293, 443–445; tried and sentenced, 293, 447, 448–450; executed, 293, 450

Lochren, Judge William, delivers address, 2: 314; credits Northrup with relief of Fort Ridgely, 384; cited, 452; candidate for U. S. senator, 3: 86; assists in prosecution of McIlrath, 88; tries suit against Northern Securities Co., 260; connection with Lord Gordon affair, 372, 376, 377; tries Chippewa captives, 4: 320

Lochren, William, "Narrative of the First Regiment," 2: 77n; "The First Minnesota at Gettysburg," 311n

Lochren, McNair, and Gilfillan, 3: 372

Lone Tree Lake, 2: 177n

Long, Maj. S. H., expeditions, 1: 106–109, 134; report, 109

Long, S. H., Voyage in a Six-Oared Skiff, 1: 64n, 134n

Long Prairie, 1: 351, 2: 4

Long Prairie Indian Reservation, 4: 230, 322; territory acquired from Chippewa, 1: 305, 310; removal of Winnebago to, 313–316, 317n; dissatisfaction of Winnebago with, 318, 478; size, 319; exchanged for Blue Earth Reservation, 319

Long Prairie River, 4: 322

Longstreet, Gen. James, 2: 316, 317, 318, 319

Longyear Lake, 4: 49, 50

Lookout Mountain, 2: 319, 320

Loomis, Maj. Gustavus, 1: 192

Loomis, Col. J. J., 3: 362, 364, 365, 366, 367

Loomis, proposed town, **3**: 362
Loras, Bishop Mathias, **1**: 219
Lord, Judge Samuel, **3**: 409
LORIN, HENRY, *Frontenac*, **1**: 19n
Loring, C. M., sketch, **4**: 425; services in development of Minneapolis park system, 426–429, 430, 432–434; encourages civic improvement, 430; work in California, 431; death, 434
LORING, C. M., "Parks and Public Grounds," **4**: 427n
Loring, G. B., **4**: 90
Loring Park, Minneapolis, **4**: 428, 432, 470
Loring Scrapbooks, **4**: 430n
Losey, J. W., **3**: 405n
Louisiana, claimed by French, **1**: 34; under Spanish, 74, 75, 76, 78; Upper Louisiana: set off, 75, immigration to, 76, Minnesota West included, 88; regained by French, 76; purchased by U. S., 77–79
Lovely, Judge J. A., **3**: 405n
Lower Sioux agency, *see* Redwood agency
Lowry, Gen. S. B., **2**: 28n, 34–36
Ludden, J. D., **1**: 390
Lumber industry, **3**: 2, 63; on Chippewa and Black rivers, **1**: 159; pineries opened by treaties, 209, 227, 307, 358; centers of lumber manufacture, 227, 229, 356; on St. Croix, 227, 233, 356; on upper Mississippi, 356; surveys of pine lands, 357; on unsurveyed lands, 357; franchises granted, 379; pine lands acquired through: half-breed scrip, 472, 477, 478, 484, Homestead Act, **2**: 332; value of exports, *1860*, 65n; transportation, 2, 60; at Leech Lake, **3**: 30, 208n; milling at Falls of St. Anthony, 30, 216, 480; statistics: *1870*, 60, *1880*, 141, *1894*, 208n, *1895*, **4**: 395, *1900*, **3**: 252, 253; investigations of timber sale, 88, 206, 229, 273, 500–512; laws regulating sale of timber, 208, 287, 500, 501n, 503, 504, 507, 513–515; in Hubbard County, **4**: 199; on Chippewa lands, 224, 225, 238–253, 267, 272–276, 279, 285n, 289, 295, 307–312; activities at Walker, 465. *See also* Forests; individual lumber companies

Lutherans, **3**: 221n, **4**: 171
Lyman Irwin Lumber Co., **4**: 274, 275n
Lynd, J. W., **2**: 109, 390
Lyon County, ravaged by grasshoppers, **3**: 102; land office, 242

Macalester, Charles, **4**: 441
Macalester College, established, **4**: 441. *See also* Baldwin University
McArthur, Helen, **3**: 79
McArthur, Gen. John, **2**: 325
Macaulay, W. J., **3**: 383
McBAIN, H. L., *Municipal Home Rule*, **3**: 518n
McCleary, J. T., **3**: 221, 268n, **4**: 250
McClellan, Gen. G. B., **2**: 101, 102
McClure, Col. A. K., **3**: 367
McClure, Charles, **1**: 403, 418, **2**: 68n
McCONKEY, H. E. B., *Dakota War Whoop*, **2**: 367n
McConnell, J. M., **4**: 189
MACDONALD, C. F., "Narrative of the Ninth Regiment," **2**: 307n
McDonald, Sir John, **3**: 382
McDowell, Malcolm, **4**: 295, 296n
McElroy, R. H., **2**: 182n
MacFarland's Gap, **2**: 317
McGannon, James, **2**: 283, 286
McGaughey, E. W., **1**: 248
McGaughey, J. P., **4**: 454n
McGee, J. F., **3**: 557, 563n
McGEE, W. J., *The Siouan Indians*, **1**: 79n
McGill, A. R., **4**: 450; sketch, **3**: 171; elected governor, 171–173, 178; on liquor question, 173, 175; legislative activities during term, 173–175, 179; later career, 174, 181; announces enlargement of university, 180; fails of renomination, 182; delivers address, 268; death, 181
McGillis, Hugh, **1**: 97, 100
McGillivray, William, **1**: 24n
McGolrick, Rev. James, **3**: 176
McGregor Western Railroad Co., **3**: 44. *See also* Minnesota Central; Milwaukee and St. Paul
McGUIRE, A. J., "Minnesota Dairy School," **4**: 405n
McIlrath, Charles, **3**: 88–90, 500–503
Mack, C. C., **2**: 346
Mack, Jesse, **2**: 345

McKay, James, 3: 374
McKee, T. H., *National Conventions and Platforms*, 3: 117n
McKenzie, F., 3: 379
McKenzie, J. H., 2: 443, 444, 445
McKenzie, J. H., *Capture of Little Six and Grey Iron*, 2: 293n
McKenzie, Kenneth, 1: 239, 283n
Mackinac (Michilimackinac), 1: 20, 30, 54; trading post: 98, of the British, 53, 67, 88, 132, of American Fur Co., 103, 133, 172, 443; Indian agency, 112n, 141n, 146; mission, *see* Missions
McKinley, President William, elections, 3: 194, 221, 222, 257; war message, 231; reviews Thirteenth Minnesota, 232; pardons Chippewa captives, 4: 320
Mackubin, Senator C. N., 2: 56
McLaren, Col. R. N., 2: 181, 449, 450
McLaughlin, James, 4: 270, 272, 300–304
McLean, Nathaniel, 1: 283, 284, 289, 290, 297, 299, 464
McLeod, Maj. G. A., 2: 267n
McLeod, Martin, fur-trader, 1: 164n, 293, 466, 2: 28n; sketch, 1: 256; legislator, 256, 261, 425, 4: 136, 141; character, 1: 257; at treaty negotiations, 283; interest in college at Glencoe, 4: 81
McLeod County, 1: 257, 4: 81, 83, 84; exodus of settlers during Sioux Outbreak, 2: 161; number massacred, 392; ravaged by grasshoppers, 3: 98, 102. *See also* Agricultural College of Minnesota; Glencoe; Hutchinson
McLeod County Register, quoted, 4: 85
"MacLeod Manuscript," 1: 214n
McMillan, Senator James, 3: 491
McMillan, Judge S. J. R., 3: 174, 175n, 4: 387; elected U. S. senator, 3: 87; reëlected, 87, 116
McMillen, Col. W. L., 2: 326
McNair, W. W., 3: 388
McNulty, Rev. Ambrose, 3: 266n
McNulty, Ambrose, *Diocese of St. Paul*, 1: 47n; "Chapel of St. Paul," 224n
Macomb, Col. J. N., 3: 340, 341, 342
McPhail, Col. Samuel, 2: 28n; relieves Fort Ridgely, 150, 383; commands reënforcements sent to Birch

Coulee, 153, 389; on Sibley expedition of *1863*, 267n, 272, 277; estimates Indian losses at battle of Big Mound, 429
McVey, F. L., 4: 54
Madelia, 3: 294; garrisoned, 2: 170, 243
Madeline Island, 1: 173; mission, *see* Missions: La Pointe. *See also* La Pointe
Madrid, treaty, *1801*, 1: 76n
Madwaganonint, Chippewa chief, 4: 476
Maginnis, Maj. Martin, 2: 314, 315
Mahnomen, 4: 265n
Mahoning Mine, 4: 33, 35
Mails, carried by stage, 2: 64; improved by railroads, 3: 32, 62; federal aid for post roads, 309; failure of route to Montana, 355. *See also* Transportation
Maine Prairie, 2: 161
Mallmann, John, 4: 18
Malmros, Oscar, 2: 149, 176, 390; organizes volunteer scouts, 288; offers bounty for Sioux scalps, 289; reports on first battle of New Ulm, 366
Malvern Hill, battle, 2: 102
Mandan Indians, 1: 111n
Manderfield, Anton, 2: 434
Manila, capture, 3: 232, 238; Thirteenth Minnesota, 232; arrival of Forty-fifth Infantry, 239
Manitoba, 3: 375, 376, 386, 451
Mankahta County, population, *1850*, 1: 352n
Mankato, Sioux chief, 2: 132n
Mankato, 2: 138, 144, 148n, 202, 256n, 260, 346, 347, 404, 441, 3: 60, 294, 4: 67n; designated railway terminus, 2: 42; objective of Sioux, 126; attack rumored, 157; imprisonment of Sioux convicts, 210, 249–251, 252, 254, 255, 262, 265, 336; execution of condemned Sioux, 210, 249, 336, 351n, 437; refuge from Sioux, 224, 3: 409; garrisoned, 2: 243; sends force against Indians, *1864*, 349, 350, 351n; fears Indian attack, 351; sends aid to New Ulm, 362, 373; Granger meeting, 3: 54; quarries, 270; home guard station, 318; election laws applicable to, 4: 347n, 360n

Mankato House, **2**: 205

Mantorville, **3**: 67

Manufacturing, growth in Minneapolis, **3**: 30; statistics: *1870*, 58, *1880*, 141, *1900*, 252, *1920*, 322; law governing, 205. *See also* Flourmilling; Lumber industry

MANYPENNY, G. W., *Our Indian Wards*, **2**: 259n

Marble, Mrs. M. A., **2**: 402, 407

Marble, William, **2**: 402

March, C. H., **3**: 557

MARGRY, PIERRE, *Decouvertes*, **1**: 16n; *Relations et mémoires, inédits*, 27n

Marine, **2**: 375; lumber manufacture, **1**: 227, 356

Marine corps, **3**: 316

Marine insurance, *see* Insurance

Marksman, Peter, **1**: 205

Marne, battle of the, **3**: 532

Marquette, Father Jacques, **1**: 16, 43; discovers Mississippi, 14, 19; exploring expedition, 18–20, 22n; death, 20; narrative by, 21; historical importance, 21

MARQUETTE, JACQUES, "Voyage," **1**: 21n

Marryat, Capt. Frederick, **1**: 119n

MARRYAT, FREDERICK, *Diary in America*, **1**: 119n

Marsh, Capt. J. S., **2**: 127; goes to aid of settlers at Sioux agency, 112; at battle of Redwood Ferry, 113, 147, 152, 392; recalls detachment of Fifth Minnesota to Fort Ridgely, 128; goes to Yellow Medicine to quiet Indians, 230; drowned, 114, 129; monument, 390

MARSHALL, A. B., *First Presbyterian Church of Minneapolis*, **1**: 193n

Marshall, W. R., **1**: 229, 403, **2**: 193, 275n, **3**: 34, 339, 438n, **4**: 6, 152; character, **1**: 375; candidate for territorial delegacy, 376; on Sibley expedition of *1862*, **2**: 177, 181; member of military commission, 192n; conducts uncondemned Sioux to Fort Snelling, 200, 252; on Sibley expedition of *1863*, 267n, 270, 271, 272; pursues Indian marauders, 281; commands Seventh Minnesota, 326, 327, 337; in battle of Nashville, 326, 327; supports Ramsey in politics, 337; elected governor, 343; accompanies McPhail

to Fort Ridgely, 384, 385; credits Grant with command at Birch Coulee, 387; delivers address, 388; captures Indian band, 431; approves fourteenth amendment, **3**: 4; urges extension of suffrage, 8; opposes removal of capital, 9, 10n; reëlected, 10; urges establishment of bureau of statistics, 20; recommends revision of election laws, 21; railroad commissioner, 52; supports Davis, 83; urges use of land grant for payment of state railroad bonds, 423, 424, 425; vetoes bill for redemption of bonds, 425; investigates land frauds, **4**: 14; interest in agricultural college, 84n; prosecutes claim of university, 101n; on Chippewa commission, 210, 211n; school trustee, 435n

MARSHALL, W. R., "Henry M. Rice," **1**: 239n; "Reminiscences of Wisconsin," 493n

Marshall Journal, **2**: 269n

MARTIN, CHARLES, *Selkirk's Work in Canada*, **1**: 213n

Martin, M. L., **1**: 234, 489, 491, 494

Martin County, ravaged by grasshoppers, **3**: 97, 102; district court, 410; sale of liquor restricted, 563; Nonpartisan League activities, 571

Marty, Rt. Rev. Martin, **4**: 226, 227, 229n, 232

Mason, J. H., **3**: 481–483

Mason, Senator J. M., **2**: 13

Mason, J. W., **3**: 366

Materials for the Future History of Minnesota, **1**: 116n

Mather, J. C., **1**: 505–514

Mather, Lieut. W. W., **1**: 118

Mattson, Col. Hans, **2**: 28n, **3**: 1

MATTSON, HANS, *Reminiscences*, **3**: 2n

Maumee River, fort, **1**: 72n

May, Lieut. W. I., **2**: 451n

Mayo, Dr. C. H., sketch, **4**: 111; connection with Mayo Clinic and Mayo Foundation, 111–122; gives address, 125

Mayo, Dr. W. J., sketch, **4**: 111; connection with Mayo Clinic and Mayo Foundation, 111–122; university regent, 114, 134

Mayo, Dr. W. W., sketch, **4**: 109; pioneer physician at Rochester, 110, 111; state senator, 111n

Mayo Clinic, 3: 283, 4: 116n; development and expansion, 112–114, 119–122

Mayo Clinic and Foundation, 4: 109n

Mayo Foundation for Medical Education and Research, 4: 114–119, 128n

Mayo Properties Association, 4: 120

Mazahota, Sioux Indian, 1: 152

Mazakutemani, Paul, 2: 429, 4: 332n

Mdewakanton (lower Sioux) Indians, 1: 182, 353, 446, 2: 207n; activities during Sioux hostilities, 183, 429, 430, 431, 433. *See also* Indian treaties; Santee Indians; Sioux Indians; Sioux reservations

Medary, Samuel, 1: 325, 401, 421, 2: 3, 4, 5, 407, 413; appointed governor, 1: 394; messages, 395, 2: 5, 406; leaves state, 21

Medicine, practice regulated, 3: 156, 157

Medicine Bottle, Sioux Indian, 4: 470; captured, 2: 293, 443–445; tried and sentenced, 293, 445–449, 450; executed, 293, 450

Medicine men, hostility to missionaries, 2: 222

Meeker County, 3: 102; exodus of settlers during Sioux Outbreak, 2: 161; number massacred, 392. *See also* Acton Township; Forest City

Meeker and McLeod Counties, 2: 109n

Meeker dam, proposed, 3: 325, 326

Melrose, railroad station, 3: 444, 447, 459, 460

Memorial Tributes to Windom, 3: 74n

Mendota, 1: 143, 143n, 147n, 244, 294, 427, 438, 3: 162, 268n; Sibley's home, 1: 125, 161, 162, 365, 440; trading post, 161, 164n, 216, 219, 240, 351, 422, 440; settlement, 219, 223, 229; trade center, 230; designated railroad junction, 2: 42; Sioux settlement, 263, 264; treaty, *see* Indian treaties

Menominee Indians, 1: 100n, 320, 321, 4: 192n; proposed reservation, 1: 321, 4: 230, 322; plan for exiling, 2: 2. *See also* Indian treaties; Wolf River Reservation

Mercer, W. A., 4: 248, 249n

Merchant's Hotel, St. Paul, 4: 255

Merriam, G. N., 3: 78, 376, 377, 378, 383

Merriam, J. L., 3: 335

Merriam, W. R., 3: 195, 293, 4: 450; speaker of House, 3: 174; elected governor, 182, 183; sketch, 183, 194; reëlected, 187–189; legislative activities during term, 189; attitude toward Davis, 204; refers to evils of grain inspection, 209; interest in agriculture, 217; attitude in Nelson-Washburn campaign, 495, 497

Merriam Park, 3: 271

MERRICK, G. B., *Recollections,* 1: 225n

Merrill, D. D., contract for school textbooks, 4: 155–160

Merrill, G. A., 3: 153

Merriman, Capt. O. C., 2: 154n, 193; at battle of Birch Coulee, 154n; captures Indian Camp, 193

Merritt, Alfred, 4: 19n

Merritt, Leonidas, 4: 18, 19

Merritt brothers, 4: 18, 19, 20, 28–30, 31

Mesabi Iron Range, 4: 27, 50; beginning of mining operations, 3: 162, 4: 20; explorations for and discovery of ore, 9, 17, 19, 20; described, 19; control of ore properties, 19, 28, 29, 31, 34–40; mining boom, 20; transportation facilities, 20, 29, 37, 38n; nature and extent of ore deposits, 21, 24, 41n; production of ore, 21, 40, 53; mining methods, 22; schools, 52. *See also* Iron mining

Messick, Capt. N. S., 2: 313

Methodist missions, *see* Missions

Meuse-Argonne offensive, 3: 536

Mexico, difficulties with, 3: 529

MEYER, B. H., *Northern Securities Case,* 3: 260n

Miami Indians, 1: 28

Michaux, André, 1: 89

Michelet, Simon, 4: 268–272, 278n, 279n, 280

Michilimackinac, *see* Mackinac

Michigan, territorial boundaries, 1: 102, 231, 486; reduced by creation of Wisconsin Territory, 231, 486; state government organized, 486; adjusts railroad debt, 3: 424; iron-bearing region, 4: 43n; agricultural college, 93; land grant, 135

Middle Creek, **2**: 239n
Middle-of-the-Road Populists, in elections: *1898,* **3**: 241, *1900,* 257. *See also* People's party
Milford, **2**: 115, 134, 361, 362, 363
Military Department of the Northwest, **2**: 170, 187, 189, 266. *See also* Pope, Gen. John
Military District of Minnesota, **2**: 189, 202, 295, 336, 350, 449
Military laws, revision recommended, **2**: 62; revised, **3**: 161, 226
Military Reservation at Fort Snelling, **1**: 515n
Military Reserve at Fort Snelling, **1**: 512n
Military Reserve on the St. Peter's River, **1**: 425n
Militia, provided for by constitutional convention, **1**: 413; reorganization urged by Sibley, **2**: 23, 26; provisions in Code of *1851,* 26; organization in *1852,* 26; revision of laws, 27, 28n, 106; Sibley's reorganization, 27, 28n; ordered to Wright County, 29; called out by president, 77–79. *See also* individual regiments; Sibley expeditions of *1862* and *1863;* Sioux Outbreak; Sully expeditions of *1863* and *1864*
Mill Springs, battle, **2**: 91, 91n, 102
Mille Lacs, **1**: 23, 29, 30; battle, 81
Mille Lacs County, sale of timber, **3**: 504
Mille Lacs Indian Reservation, **4**: 218; plans to remove Indians, **3**: 22–24, 26, 29; established, **4**: 92; ceded, 193; unsuitable for permanent reservation, 201
Mille Lacs Indians, **2**: 243; loyalty commemorated, 382; remain at Mille Lacs, **4**: 194; councils with government commissions, 214, 215, 228n; refuse to consolidate, 214, 218; condition, 214, 228n; complaints, 230. *See also* Chippewa of the Mississippi
Miller, C. B., **2**: 438
Miller, Stephen, **2**: 68n, 314n, 337, 342, 350, **3**: 7, 422; regimental colonel, **2**: 106; in command of Camp Lincoln, 202, 336; orders dispersion of mob at Mankato, 205; in charge of execution of Sioux, 210n, 336; acting commander of District of Minnesota, 278, 336; sketch, 335; recruiting of regiments, 337; elected governor, 337; messages, 338, 340; estimates population, *1865,* 334; urges execution of Little Six and Medicine Bottle, 449; interest in search for minerals, **4**: 3–5
Millier, Hubert, **2**: 109
Milling, *see* Flour-milling
Milwaukee and St. Paul Railway Co., builds in Minnesota, **3**: 2, 61; buys McGregor Western, 44; competition with, 48
Mining, **3**: 252; early reports of and explorations for minerals, **1**: 4, 6n, 102, 305, **3**: 162, **4**: 1, 2, 3; Le Sueur's concession and alleged operations, **1**: 41, 118; value of products in *1920,* **3**: 322. *See also* Copper; Gold; Iron mining; Silver
Mining Directory of Minnesota, **4**: 21n
Minneapolis, **2**: 82, 159n, 383, 385, **3**: 45, 179, 196, 217, 234, 325, 341, 384, 556, 570n, **4**: 79, 85n, 105, 199, 242n, 309, 464, 465; beginnings, **1**: 429, **4**: 79; designated railway station, **2**: 38, 42; population: *1860,* 64n, **3**: 480n, **4**: 425, *1865,* **3**: 480n, *1870,* 480n, **4**: 105, *1875,* **3**: 480n, **4**: 427, *1880,* **3**: 139, 480n, **4**: 105, 123, 427, *1885,* **3**: 480n, **4**: 105, 123, 427, *1890,* **3**: 487; opens telegraph office, **2**: 66; refuge from Indians, 124; lumber milling, **3**: 30, 216, 480; flour milling, 30, 70, 131; grain elevator, 68, 208; rivalry with St. Paul, 91, **4**: 425; aids victims of grasshopper plague, **3**: 99, 100n; mill explosion, 131–136; grading of grain, 161, 210; mayors, 172, 244, 373, 376, **4**: 123; election rally, *1886,* **3**: 173; temperance society, 176; legislation for, 189, 391, 518, 518n; quarrel with St. Paul over census of *1890,* 193, 480–489; welcomes returning soldiers, 232, 537; furnishes companies to Fifteenth Minnesota, 234; political conventions, 241, 549, **4**: 31; takes measures to preserve Falls of St. Anthony, **3**: 334, 342, 343, 345; Lord Gordon in, 362, 363, 364, 365, 366, 371n; in congressional elections of

1898, 392, 393; unites with St. Anthony, 480; Associated Charities, 482; artillery unit, 528; regulation of liquor sales, 563; headquarters Industrial Workers of the World, 568; board of education receives gift of land, **4**: 124; special school district, 142n; commercial club appeals for preservation of forest reserve, 260, 261n; election laws for, 339n, 347n; use of voting machines, 351; permanent registration of voters, 358; primary election system, 366; development of park system, 426–429, 430, 432–434; election of *1890,* 429, 429n

Minneapolis and Cedar Valley Railroad Co., chartered, **2**: 42; property sold to state, 328n; succeeded by Minnesota Central, **3**: 2, 44; foreclosure of mortgage on property, 419n; restoration of property to, 420

Minneapolis Athenæum, **4**: 467

Minneapolis Board of Trade, **3**: 161, 334, **4**: 427

Minneapolis Bureau of Information, **3**: 480, 481, 482, 488

Minneapolis Business Men's Union, **3**: 481, **4**: 466

Minneapolis Club, **4**: 256

Minneapolis, Faribault, and Cedar Valley Railroad Co., **3**: 422n

Minneapolis Gas Light Co., **3**: 229

Minneapolis Institute of Fine Arts, **4**: 463

Minneapolis Mill Co., **3**: 30, 84, 333

Minneapolis Millers' Association, **3**: 148, 389

Minneapolis Philharmonic Association, **4**: 105, 106

Minneapolis Public Library, **4**: 467

Minneapolis, St. Paul, and Sault Ste. Marie Railroad, **3**: 494, 541, **4**: 264, 282

Minneapolis Society of Fine Arts, **4**: 105, 469

Minneapolis Tribune, **3**: 363, 366, 380, **4**: 105, 106, 107; *State Atlas* merged into, **3**: 90; editor, 366; position on Nelson's candidacy for senator, 492

Minneapolis Water Co., **1**: 424

Minneapolis Water Power Co., **3**: 131, 137

Minnehaha Creek, **1**: 232

Minnehaha Falls, **1**: 139, 232, 232n, **4**: 108

Minnehaha Park, **3**: 179

Minnehaha Parkway, **4**: 428

Minnesota, spelling, **1**: 235n, 454; meaning, 455–457; admission to Union, **2**: 9–18, 22, 23; name and boundaries, 355

Minnesota Academy of Sciences, **4**: 467, 484

Minnesota and Northwestern Railroad Co., **1**: 337n, 350, 378, **2**: 37, 343, **3**: 36; incorporation, **1**: 329–332; organization, 336; suit against, 341–343; attempt to annul charter, 343, 344; reënactments and amendments of charter, 345–349

Minnesota and Pacific Railroad Co., **3**: 142n; incorporated, **2**: 42; opposes attempt to secure priority of lien of state bonds, 50; property sold to state, 328n; construction, 330; forfeits rights, 330; foreclosure of mortgage on property, **3**: 419n, 421; restoration of property to, 420, 441; attempts to renew building, 420–422; surrenders franchise, 422, 422n; land grants to, 441; change of name, 441. *See also* St. Paul and Pacific Railroad Co.

Minnesota Central Railroad Co., **3**: 2, 44

Minnesota Commission of Public Safety, created, **3**: 317, 556; powers and duties, 318, 556, 557, 557n, 570, **4**: 364; organization and personnel, **3**: 318, 557, 558n, 559; organizes home guard, 318, 559; appoints woman's committee, 559; penalty for violation of orders, 560; regulates places of amusement and sale of liquor, 560, 563, 569; prohibits unemployment, 561; orders registration of aliens, 561; provides for soldier vote, 562, **4**: 364; encourages sale of Liberty Bonds, **3**: 562; orders farm-crop and stock census, 563; activities relating to forest fires, 564; activities relating to sedition, 565–569, 570; investigates use of foreign languages in schools, **4**: 166

Minnesota Dairyman's Association, **3**: 157, **4**: 407

Minnesota Democrat, **1**: 339, 343, 465, 479, **3**: 38

Minnesota East, **1**: 231; under British, 53, 64; acquired by U. S., 69, 88; merged into Northwest Territory, 70

Minnesota Eastern, *see* Eastern Railway of Minnesota

Minnesota Educational Association, **4**: 187

Minnesota Election Case, **2**: 18n

Minnesota Federation of Women's Clubs, **4**: 254, 256, 258, 259, 261n

Minnesota Gold Mining Co., **4**: 5

Minnesota Historical Society, **1**: 128, 129, 257; collections rescued from fire, **3**: 138; Hubbard's services, 163; Ramsey's services, 267; memorial meetings for Ramsey, 268

Minnesota Hospital and Home for Crippled Children, **4**: 108, 124, 125

Minnesota Hospital College, **3**: 180

Minnesota in the Civil and Indian Wars, **2**: 77n, **3**: 163

Minnesota Iron Co., **4**: 32; incorporated, 11; railroad, 12, 15, 17; acquires lands, 13; operations in Vermilion district, 16; opens mine on Mesabi Range, 18

Minnesota Iron Mine, **3**: 162

Minnesota Iron Mining Co., **3**: 299

Minnesota Land Grant Bill, *see* Railroads

Minnesota Leader, **3**: 546

Minnesota Mounted Rangers, *see* First Regiment Minnesota Mounted Rangers

Minnesota National Forest, *see* Chippewa National Forest

Minnesota National Park and Forestry Association, **4**: 255, 256, 256n

Minnesota Pioneer, cited, **1**: 250, 343, 370, 372, 479, **3**: 350; established, **1**: 251, 361; editors, 251, 260, 343; organ of Democrats, 369

Minnesota Public Library Commission, **4**: 188

Minnesota River, **1**: 135, 144, **2**: 169, 252, 282, 288, 404, **3**: 61, **4**: 193; explorers, **1**: 40, 56, 92, 106, 107; Carver's description, 56n, 106; navigation, 257, 361; trading post, 437; Indian names for, 455; provisions for railroad along, **2**: 38

Minnesota State Agricultural Society, **3**: 184, 217

Minnesota State Bonds, **3**: 419n

Minnesota State Federation of Labor, **3**: 547, 548

Minnesota State Forestry Association, **4**: 258, 393

Minnesota State Grange, **3**: 38, 39, **4**: 96n

Minnesota State Horticultural Society, **4**: 94

Minnesota State Live Stock Sanitary Board, **4**: 419

Minnesota State Railroad Adjustment Bonds, **3**: 139, 439. *See also* Five Million Loan

Minnesota State Railroad Bonds, *see* Five Million Loan

Minnesota State Teachers' Association, **4**: 67n, 75

Minnesota State Training School, **4**: 164, 408

Minnesota State University, **4**: 102n

Minnesota Statesman, **2**: 369, 371

Minnesota Steel Co., **4**: 27

Minnesota tax commission, *see* Tax commission

Minnesota Territorial Agricultural Society, **1**: 361

Minnesota Territory, organized, **1**: 235–247; officers: listed, 252n, salaries, 379. *See also* Organic act

Minnesota Territory Election Case, **2**: 20n

Minnesota Valley, resources, **1**: 109; German communities, **3**: 553

Minnesota Valley Historical Society, **2**: 390

Minnesota West, acquired by U. S. **1**: 79n; part of Upper Louisiana, 88

Minnesotian, **1**: 260, 340, 376, 479, **3**: 427n

Minnetonka, Lake, **4**: 109n

Misquadace, Chippewa chief, **3**: 26

Missabe Mountain Mine, **4**: 31, 59

Missionaries, **1**: 285; influence, 85, 170, 181n, 202, 293, **4**: 198; problems confronting, **1**: 170, 178, 207, **2**: 215, 222; schools and teaching, **1**: 171, 172, 173, 178, 190n, 195, 198, 205, 206, 210; attitude of Indians toward, 174, 207, 208, 210, 211; build first church in Minnesota, 192; competition among, **3**: 59. *See also* individual missionaries; individual religious denominations; Missions

Missionary Ridge, **2**: 316, 317; battle, 91, 319–321, 327n
Missions:
American Board of Commissioners for Foreign Missions, Mackinac, **1**: 172, 173n; La Pointe, 173, 175, 181n; Yellow Lake, Wisconsin, 174; Sandy Lake, 174, 178; Lake Pokegama, 174, 177, 178, 179, 181; Leech Lake, 175–177, 178; Fond du Lac, 178; Red Lake, 182n; Lake Harriet, 190n, 193, 195, 196, 200; Lac qui Parle, 192, 194, 197, 198–201, 202, 203, 211, 212, **2**: 207n; Oak Grove, **1**: 196, 211, 212; Prairieville, 198, 211; Red Wing, 200, 203, 211; Traverse des Sioux, 201, 211; Kaposia, 201, 211; Hazelwood, **2**: 118, 118n, 183, 434; Yellow Medicine (Pajutazee): location, 118, 118n, 250, escape of settlers, 119, 264, Sioux depredations, 434
Episcopal, Gull Lake, **1**: 181, **2**: 206, 380, **3**: 26, **4**: 227, 472; Leech Lake, **1**: 182; Redwood Agency, **2**: 207, 239, 399, **4**: 474; White Earth, 197, 198, 200
Methodist, **1**: 181, 204, 207; Kaposia, 205–207, 452n; Red Rock, 206, 452n
Roman Catholic, **1**: 207; La Pointe, 16, 43; Fort Frontenac, 27; Sault de Ste. Marie, 43; Straits of Mackinac, 43; St. Michael the Archangel, 46, 47n; Chaska (Little Rock), 207; White Earth, **4**: 197, 198, 208, 318, 324
To Chippewa, **1**: 172–178, 181
To Sioux, **1**: 190, 192, 193–212
Mississippi Chippewa, *see* Chippewa of the Mississippi
Mississippi River, **1**: 4, 30, 84, 89, **3**: 337, 338, **4**: 190, 196; early reports and ideas concerning, **1**: 4, 6, 7, 13, 16, 17, 18, 20, 21, 25, 159; alleged discovery by Groseilliers and Radisson, 11, 13; discovery and exploration by Jolliet and Marquette, 14, 18–20; Jolliet's map, 21; explorations, 27–30, 36–38, 39n, 40, 42, 46n, 47n, 55, 90–99; trade route, 73, 77, 164n, 225, 230, **3**: 2, 479; Pike's fort, **1**: 95; search for source, 97, 98, 101, 104, 109, 113n, 114–116, 124, 128, **4**: 1; Long's

survey, **1**: 134; boundary of Wisconsin Territory, 159; regarded as western limit of settlement, 266; railroad route along, **3**: 61; proposed improvement, 325, 326; pineries, 333; reservoirs: dams constructed, **4**: 209, damages to Chippewa property, 200, 210–212, 230, 234, 322, 322n. *See also* Lumber industry; St. Anthony, Falls of; Steamboat transportation
Mississippi Valley, **1**: 33, **4**: 255
Missouri, represented at conference on grasshopper plague, **3**: 103; establishes home rule for cities, 519; admitted to Union, **4**: 190
Missouri River, **2**: 265, 266, 268, 274, 275, 275n, 276, 287n, 294, 295, 429, 440; Jolliet's map, **1**: 21; expedition to explore, 90
Mitchell, Col. A. M., **1**: 252n, 315, 370, 371
Mitchell, W. B., "St. Cloud in the Territorial Period," **2**: 34n; *Stearns County*, 34n
Mitchell, Judge William, **2**: 95n, **3**: 7n, 211, 409, 440
Mix, C. H., **2**: 28n
Mixed-bloods, **1**: 86, 464, 465; concerned in treaty of northwestern tribes, *1830*, 158, 270, 322, 482, *see also* Wabasha Reservation; concerned in Chippewa treaties: *1837*, 160, *1851*, 288, *1854*, 307, 470, issue of scrip in execution of, *see* Scrip, *1855*, 307, *1864*, **4**: 477; concerned in Sioux treaties: *1837*, **1**: 160, *1841*, 274n, 323, 458n, Mendota, *1849*, 274, 323, Traverse des Sioux, *1851*, 282, 302, 303, unratified provisions in treaty of Mendota, *1851*, 284, 291, 324; in Winnebago treaty, *1838*, 309; factors in treaty negotiations, 269, 275, 298, 301, **2**: 215, 216; granted suffrage, **1**: 412, **3**: 7, 8, **4**: 331; captives released, **2**: 183–185; fail to aid in civilization of Indians, 223; foment trouble among Sioux, 234; accompany Indians to camp at Fort Snelling, 252, 253n, 254; scouts on Sibley expedition of *1863*, 267n; inform Sibley of movements of Sioux, 284; in Civil War, 421; number in *1895*, **3**: 226; on White Earth Reservation, **4**: 197; as farm-

ers, 198; land allotments, 268, 269, 271; status, 272; authorized to sell allotments, 277, 278, 280; take advantage of Clapp rider of 1906, 277, 278n, 280; attempts to define, 285–288, 291–293; Beaulieu faction, 290n; reservation, see Wabasha Reservation

Mobile, siege, 2: 305

Moes, Mother Mary Alfred, 4: 110, 110n, 111

Monticello, 2: 29, 376

Montreal, Canada, 1: 8; French trading center, 44; surrendered to British, 51; headquarters of Northwest Co., 67

Montreal-Michilimackinac Co., 1: 132

Monzoomannee, see Mouzoomaunnee

Mooers, Calvin, 2: 443n

MOONEY, J. A., "Catholic Controversy about Education," 4: 182n

Moore, A. W., 2: 29

Moore, G. W., 2: 48

MOORE, J. B., International Arbitrations, 1: 500n

Moore, J. K., 2: 368

Moore, Lieut. J. T., 4: 317

Moorehead, W. K., 4: 246n; sketch, 281; investigates White Earth situation, 281, 283, 284n

MOOREHEAD, W. K., American Indian, 4: 268n

Moorhead, W. G., 3: 443n, 444

Moorhead, 3: 376, 4: 190; railroad terminal, 3: 61, 366; Lord Gordon in, 364

Moose Lake (village), destroyed by fire, 3: 564

Morcom, Elisha, 4: 16

Morgan, Capt. G. H., 3: 524

Morgan, John, 1: 351, 352n

Morgan, Col. Willoughby, 1: 158

Morgan Park, 4: 28

Morgan Park Co., 4: 28

Morrill, A. C., 2: 377, 378, 379

Morrill, J. S., 4: 77, 78, 80, 94

Morrill Act, 4: 61n, 77, 78, 82, 82n, 103

Morris, Judge Page, 4: 250, 251n, 252, 253n, 259, 287n, 288, 289, 293

Morris, school of agriculture, 4: 108

Morris Act, 4: 249, 251, 251n, 252, 253, 259, 399

Morrison, William, 1: 69n, 116n

Morrison County, 1: 116n

Mortgages, 4: 457

Morton, 2: 173n, 386, 389, 390; Sioux settlement, 264

Moscow Expedition, 2: 260, 261n, 439 441

Moss, H. L., "Wisconsin Territory," 1: 234n; "Old Settlers," 237n

Motor corps, 3: 319

MOTT, E. H., Story of Erie, 3: 364n

Mountain Iron Mine, 4: 19, 20, 29, 44–48

Mounted Rangers, see First Regiment Minnesota Mounted Rangers

Mouzoomaunnee, Chippewa Indian, 2: 133n, 382

Mower, W. H., 2: 28n

Mower County, Granger convention, 3: 47; aids victims of grasshopper plague, 99; ravaged by grasshoppers, 103; citizens demand impeachment of Judge Page, 129; district court, 129, 400; school superintendency, 400

MOYER, L. R., ed., Chippewa and Lac qui Parle Counties, 3: 296n

Moynihan, Rt. Rev. H., 4: 193n

Mud Creek, 1: 110

Munch, Capt. Emil, 2: 99, 307

Municipalities, see Cities

Munro, Alexander, 3: 386

Munson, S. A., 4: 9, 10

Murfreesboro, surrender of Third Minnesota, 2: 92–95; battle, 1864, 302n

Murphy, W. J., 4: 128n

Murray, W. P., 1: 383, 2: 6n, 3: 4, 481, 4: 75n, 137

Murray County, 2: 201; number massacred during Sioux Outbreak, 2: 392; ravaged by grasshoppers, 3: 97, 102. See also Shetek, Lake

Musical festival, 4: 106, 107n

MUSSEY, H. R., Combination in the Mining Industry, 4: 30n

Mutual Protection Gold Miners Co. of Minnesota, 4: 4, 5

Myrick, A. J., 2: 109, 233, 399n, 446

Myrick, Nathan, 2: 109, 399n

NASH, C. W., "Hatch's Battalion," 2: 292n

Nashville, battle, 2: 323–327; painting commemorating, 327n

National Defense Act, 3: 316, 529

National Education Association, 4: 180

National Exchange Bank, Minneapolis, **3**: 362, 364, 366
National Farmers' Alliance, **3**: 187, 188. *See also* Farmers' Alliance of Minnesota
National Federation of Women's Clubs, **4**: 462
National Guard, **4**: 317, 361; called out during war with Spain, **3**: 231; provisions for, 314, 529; World War service, 316, 530; Mexican border service, 529, 557n
National Leader, **3**: 553. *See also Nonpartisan Leader*
National Nonpartisan League, *see* Nonpartisan League
National Park and Forestry Association, *see* Minnesota National Park and Forestry Association
National Producers' Alliance, **3**: 556
National Republican League, **4**: 466
National Statuary Hall, **3**: 214, 268n
Native-born, number, in *1895*, **3**: 226. *See also* Population
Natural history survey, **4**: 478, 483
Naturalization, **4**: 333
Naval Reserve, **3**: 316
Neal, H. S., **1**: 475
Nebraska, represented at conference on grasshopper plague, **3**: 103
Nebraska City, **3**: 353, 354, 354n
Negroes, condition after Civil War, **3**: 3; legislation against, 3, 13; suffrage extended to, 7, 8, **4**: 333; federal aid for, **3**: 13; education urged, 13
Neill, Rev. E. D., **1**: 253, 257; cited, 250, 450, 456, 462; regimental chaplain, **2**: 84, 84n, **4**: 184, 438, 439; secretary to president, **2**: 84n, **4**: 439; superintendent of public instruction, **2**: 360, **4**: 152, 183, 184; school land commissioner, 141n; educational work, 434–442; sketch, 434; hospital chaplain, 439; U. S. consul, 439
Neill, E. D., "Groseilliers and Radisson," **1**: 8n; "Discovery along the Great Lakes," 15n; *Minnesota*, 23n; *Writings of Hennepin*, 32n; "Early Wisconsin Exploration," 37n; "History of the Ojibways," 43n; *Last French Post*, 47n; "Fort Snelling," 90n, 141n; *Minnesota Valley*, 107n; "Boutwell," 173n; "Battle of Lake Pokegu-

ma," 180n; "The Brothers Pond," 185n; "Renville," 191n; "Beginning of Organized Society in the Saint Croix Valley," 227n; "Goodhue," 251n; "Reminiscences of the Last Year of Lincoln's Life," **2**: 84n; *Descendants of Henry Neill*, **4**: 435n; *Macalester College*, 435n; *Presbyterian Church in Minnesota*, 436n; *Jesus College*, 440n
Neill Papers, **1**: xi
Nelson, Capt. A. D., **2**: 149n
Nelson, B. F., **3**: 283
Nelson, Knute, **3**: 209, 210, 568, **4**: 75n, 387n, 401n; sketch, **3**: 146; opposes Kindred in congressional election, 146–149; elected to Congress, 149, 195; character and ability, 195, 494; advocates revision of tariff, 195; elected governor, 195, 197; reëlected, 197, 203, 490; legislation during administration, 205; elected U. S. senator, 205, 217, 489–497; reëlected, 205, 205n, 264, 498; senatorial career, 205, 497–499; furthers timber investigations, 206, 504, 506, 507, 507n; aids victims of Hinckley fire, 212; activities in connection with erection of Rice statue, 214; on silver question, 220; urges economy, 226; recommends extension of state census, 226; activities in connection with Indian affairs, **4**: 219, 222, 223, 224n, 249, 251n, 286, 300; promotes park project, 307; university regent, 404; death, 205, 320, 498, 551; eulogies of, 498
Nelson, O. N., ed., *History of the Scandinavians*, **3**: 146n
Nelson, Judge R. R., **1**: 326, 387, **3**: 264n, 464, 488, 489
Nelson Act, **4**: 243, 244, 245, 299, 306, 323n; history, 219, 222–224, 242n; provisions, 220–222, 223, 229, 297, 307n, 326, 399; commission to carry out provisions, 226; copies distributed, 227; amended, *1896*, 237; dissatisfaction with, 249, 250, 313; amended by Morris Act, 251, *see also* Morris Act; results, 328
Nelson-Washburn campaign, *1895*, candidacy of Washburn, **3**: 205, 489; rumors of Nelson's candidacy, 205, 489–492; announcement of Nelson's candidacy, 205, 492; Re-

publican caucus, 205, 493; election of Nelson, 205, 493, 495; attitude of candidates toward outcome, 495–497

Nett Lake Indian Reservation, 4: 192

NEUHAUS, EUGEN, *Walker Art Collections,* 4: 469n

"Neutral Ground," 1: 308, 309, 310, 312

New France, *see* Canada

New Hope, *see* Mendota

New Jersey, land grant, 4: 82n

New Orleans, 1: 52; founded, 40, 73; trade center, 73; retained by French, *1763,* 73, 495; under Spanish, 74, 75; Sixth Minnesota, 2: 305. *See also* Louisiana

"New Orleans and the Minnesota Railroad," 1: 327

New Ulm, 2: 148n, 200, 236, 445, 446, 3: 60, 243; refuge from Sioux, 2: 115, 224; reported in danger of attack, 119; first battle: 121, 133, various accounts, 361–374, monument commemorating, 368; second battle: 132n, 139–144, 432, monument commemorating, 142n, evacuation of town, 144, retreat of Sioux, 145, 156; founding and growth, 133n; preparation for defense, 136, 137–139, 3: 409; objective of Sioux, 2: 137; garrisoned, 169, 281; trial of Sioux participants in battles of, 196n; whites killed, 392; Indians killed, 393n; Twelfth Minnesota mustered out, 3: 233, 245; home of Lind, 242, 497; labor convention, 548; disloyalty, 558, 565

New York, natives of, in Minnesota, 3: 59, 73

New York City, transportation to, 3: 61; activities of Lord Gordon in, 77, 366–370

New York Colonial Documents, 1: 15n

Newson, T. M., 2: 102n, 4: 4, 5

NEWSON, T. M., *Pen Pictures,* 1: 57n

Newspapers, 1: 361; preservation of files, 254, 257; number in *1870,* 3: 58; used by Nonpartisan League, 545. *See also* individual newspapers

Nicholas, E. H., 3: 572, 573, 574

Nichols, E. T., 4: 36

Nichols, Capt. J. A., 4: 19

Nichols-Chisholm Lumber Co., 4: 242n, 274, 275n, 280, 285n, 287n, 289n, 295n

Nicolay, J. G., 2: 186n

Nicolet, Jean, 1: 4, 5, 6n, 320

Nicollet, J. N., sketches, 1: 122, 126; explorations, 123–126; map, 123n, 125; examines Itasca basin, 124, 125; writings, 126, 127n; places named for, 127; at Leech Lake mission, 176

NICOLLET, J. N., *Report,* 1: 123n

Nicollet, 2: 138

Nicollet County, 2: 362; Sioux attacks, 115; number killed during Sioux Outbreak, 392; ravaged by grasshoppers, 3: 101; offices held by McGill, 171; fair association, 276; erects statue of Johnson, 285

Nicollet House, Minneapolis, 4: 80n

Nicollet Island, 3: 333, 335, 336, 337, 340, 347, 4: 427

Nicollet Papers, 1: 127n

Nicols, John, 3: 423, 4: 72n

Nika, Sioux Indian, 1: 155, 157n

Niles, Sanford, 4: 155

NILES, SANFORD, "Common Schools," 4: 139n

Nilsson, Christine, 4: 106

Nininger, 2: 60, 3: 11, 165

Ninth Regiment Minnesota Volunteer Infantry, 2: 205n, 307n; organized, 103, 104, 106; on Sibley expedition of *1862,* 177; garrisons frontier posts, 243, 282; on Sibley expedition of *1863,* 267n; Civil War service, 305–307, 326; casualties, 306; number engaged in Civil and Indian wars, 339

Niobrara River, Santee reservation, 2: 261; agency, 262, 431

Nipigon, Lake, post, 1: 48

Nix, Capt. Jacob, in first battle of New Ulm, 2: 361, 361n, 362, 363, 364, 365, 368, 369; account of battle, 362, 373

NIX, JACOB, *Ausbruch der Sioux-Indianer,* 2: 139n

Noah, J. J., 2: 28n

Noble, J. W., 3: 487, 4: 236

Noble, Mrs. Lydia, 2: 404, 407, 408

Nobles County, 3: 97

Non-partisan, anti-Townley paper, 3: 554n

Nonpartisan, Farmer-Labor paper, 3: 553

Nonpartisan Leader, **3**: 544, 546, 554; becomes *National Leader*, 553

Nonpartisan League, organization in North Dakota, **3**: 319, 542–544; aims, 319, 543; membership and fees, 319, 320, 543, 544, 546, 547, 553, 571; in North Dakota elections, 319, 544, 546n; organized in Minnesota, 320, 546, 571; in Minnesota elections of *1918* and *1920*, 320, 547, 548; publications, 544, 545, 546; uses newspapers to disseminate ideas, 545; expansion, 546; antiwar activities, 553, 558, 566, 571–573; opposition to, 553, 554n; decline, 553; ancillary organizations, 554. *See also* Farmer-Labor party

Nonpartisan League of Minnesota, **3**: 554n

Nonpartisan Publishing Co., **3**: 554, 555

Normal school board, **4**: 444

Normal schools, **3**: 31, 262. *See also* Education

Norman County, **4**: 280n

Norris, J. S., **1**: 230n, **4**: 99n

North, J. W., **1**: 261, 399, 403, 413, 414, **4**: 98

North Central Agricultural Experiment Station, **4**: 258

North Dakota, passes prohibition law, **3**: 300; Nonpartisan League, 319, 541–545, 546n, 555

North Star Grange, **3**: 38

Northern Pacific Railroad Co., **3**: 79, 443n, 455, 458n, 461, **4**: 20; builds in Minnesota, **3**: 61; land agencies, 77, 147, 362, 364, 365, 366, 541; duped by Lord Gordon, 77, 362, 363, 364, 365, 366, 368; attempted merger with Great Northern, 260, 272; organization, 445; controls St. Paul and Pacific and First Division companies, 445, 448, 450, 454; bankrupt, 446, 450

Northern Securities Co., **3**: 260

"Northerner," steamboat, **2**: 259

Northfield, **3**: 180, **4**: 443; bank robbery, **3**: 113; college town, 294

Northrop, Cyrus, **2**: 314n, **3**: 283, **4**: 72, 94

Northrop, Cyrus, *Addresses*, **4**: 93n

Northrup, Capt. Anson, **2**: 383, 384–386

Northwest Co., **1**: 111, 116, 133, 161, 437; posts: on Pigeon River (Grand Portage), 24n, 67, Fort William, 24n, Mackinac, 67, Green Bay, 67, Prairie du Chien, 67, Fond du Lac, 68, 88, 97, Sandy Lake, 68, 68n, 96, Leech Lake, 68, 69n, 97; organized, 66; headquarters, 67; policies, 67; monopolizes fur trade, 68, 131; retention of posts after *1783*, 72, 87, 88, 100; merged into Hudson's Bay Co., 87; liquor traffic, 87; agreement with Southwest Co., 132; controls trade through Americans, 133; surrenders posts in U. S., 133; struggle with Selkirk colony, *see* Selkirk colony. *See also* Fur trade

Northwest Indian Commission, appointed, **4**: 202; duties, 202; negotiates with Chippewa, 203–217; agreements, 217, 218, 220, 222

Northwest Indian Commission Report, **4**: 207n

Northwest Ordinance, **1**: 70, 75, 390, 490, 491, 494, **4**: 72, 135, 330n

Northwest Territory, **1**: 65, 131, 231, 391, **4**: 72, 135

Northwestern Indian expedition, *see* Sully expedition of *1864*

Northwestern Service Bureau, **3**: 545

Norton, D. S., **3**: 409, **4**: 5n; elected senator, **2**: 340–342, **3**: 4; senatorial career, 4–6; censured by legislature, 5; death, 7, 73; eulogies of, 7, 7n

Norwegians, *see* Scandinavians

Nourse, G. A., **2**: 150, 328n

Nyack and Northern Railroad, **3**: 369

Oak Grove mission, *see* Missions

Oak Lake, **3**: 362, 363

Oakes, C. H., **2**: 28n

Oakland Cemetery, St. Paul, **3**: 267

O'Brien, C. D., **3**: 283

O'Brien, H. D., **2**: 313

Occupation tax, **3**: 308, 551, **4**: 55, 56

Ochagach, draws map for La Vérendrye, **1**: 48

O'Connell, Dennis, **3**: 522, 528

O'Connor, R. T., **4**: 314, 315

Officers, salaries and terms, **1**: 379, **2**: 30, 63, **3**: 77, 145, 357, 361; provided for by constitution, **2**:

356. *See also* Government of Minnesota

Official Records, **2**: 76n

Ogden, Lieut. E. A., **1**: 188

Ogema, **4**: 265n, 279, 282

O'Gorman, Rev. Thomas, **3**: 176, **4**: 182n

Ohio, natives of, in Minnesota, **3**: 73; admitted to Union, **4**: 97; land grant, 135

Ohio River, Jolliet's map, **1**: 21

Ohio Valley, French and English claims, **1**: 50

Oil Creek and Allegheny Valley Railroad, **3**: 369

Ojibway Indians, *see* Chippewa Indians

Okoboji, Lake, Indian massacre, *see* Spirit Lake massacre

Old Crossing, **4**: 476

Olesen, Anna D., **3**: 299n

Olin, Lieut. R. C., **2**: 174, 181n, 192n

Oliver, H. W., **4**: 30, 32n

Oliver Iron Mining Co., **3**: 299, 308, **4**: 31–33, 38n, 59

Olmsted, David, **1**: 311n, 315, 316; candidate for territorial delegacy, 371, 376; public printer, 379

Olmsted County, **4**: 109

Olsen, J. W., **4**: 164

Olson, A. J., **4**: 134

Olson, F. B., **3**: 321

One Hundred and Fifty-first Field Artillery, **3**: 317, 531–538. *See also* First Minnesota Field Artillery

One Hundred and Thirty-fifth Infantry, **3**: 316

One Hundred and Thirty-sixth Infantry, **3**: 316

One Hundred and Twenty-fifth Field Artillery, **3**: 317

Ordinance of *1787, see* Northwest Ordinance

Ore Lands, *see* Iron mining; Mesabi Range; Vermilion Range; Cuyuna Range

ORFIELD, M. N., *Federal Land Grants,* **4**: 46n

Organic act, **1**: 243–246, 247, 264, 265, 382, 385, **4**: 331

"Organization of Minnesota Territory," **1**: 237n

Orphanages, **3**: 153

Orr, J. L., **2**: 19

Otakle, *see* Godfrey

Other Day, John, Sioux chief, **1**: 186n, **2**: 118n, **4**: 470; aids whites during Sioux Outbreak, **2**: 117; brother tried, 196, 196n; rewarded for loyalty to whites, 264; monument, 391; aids in rescue of captives, 407; on expeditions in pursuit of Inkpaduta, 408, 409n, 413

Otis, G. L., **2**: 31, **3**: 18

Oto Indians, **1**: 41

Ottawa Indians, **1**: 43, 457

Otter Tail, defense planned by Pope, **2**: 187; land office, **4**: 480

Otter Tail County, **4**: 7; Lord Gordon's proposed colony, **3**: 77, 362, 364; ravaged by grasshoppers, 102, 111; history cited, 366; state lands, 480

Otter Tail Indians, remove to White Earth Reservation, **4**: 197, 198n; represented at council, 270. *See also* Pillager Indians; White Earth Reservation

Otter Tail Lake, **2**: 277, **4**: 197, 322

Ourcq, battle of the, **3**: 534

Overton's Hill, **2**: 325

Owatonna, political conventions, **3**: 33, 48, 49, 116, 117; railroad station, 45. *See also* State Public School

OWEN, D. D., *Geological Survey of Wisconsin, Iowa, and Minnesota,* **1**: 306n

Owen, S. M., **3**: 188, 197, 203, 241

Ozawindib (Yellow Head), Chippewa Indian, **1**: 114, 116, 117n, 125

Page, Judge Sherman, criticism of, **3**: 129, 401–403, 407, 408; impeached, 129, 174, 403–407; previous career, 400; attempts to force resignation, 408; defeated for reëlection, 408; leaves state, 408

Pajutazee mission, *see* Missions

Panics, financial, *1857,* **2**: 39, 43, **4**: 80, 436; *1873,* **3**: 52, 53, 55, 72, 126, 141, 143, 447, 480; *1893,* 198, **4**: 29

Papers Relating to the Red River Settlement, **1**: 215n

Pardee, J. S., **4**: 19n

Paris, treaty, *1763,* **1**: 51, 73; *1898,* **3**: 237

Park Rapids, **4**: 280n, 282

Park Rapids Lumber Co., **4**: 280, 285n, 295n

Parker's Prairie, **3**: 541

PARKMAN, FRANCIS, *Pioneers of France*, **1**: 3n; *Old Régime*, 6n; *La Salle*, 18n, 25n; *Frontenac*, 19n; *Discovery of the Great West*, 25n; *Half-Century of Conflict*, 43n; *Montcalm and Wolfe*, 50n; *Conspiracy of Pontiac*, 53n

Parrant, Pierre, **1**: 219, 220n, 223n

Partridge, G. H., **4**: 134

Pasteur institute, **4**: 419, 421, 421n

PATCHIN, S. A., "Banking in Minnesota," **2**: 58n

Patrons of Husbandry, **4**: 86; growth, **3**: 37–39, 46, 54, 55; oppose railroad abuses, 47; representation in legislature of *1874*, 50; criticize Granger law of *1874*, 54; decline, 55; aid victims of grasshopper plague, 99. *See also* Granger movement

Pattee, W. S., sketch, **3**: 180, **4**: 443; dean of university law school, 444–448; death, 445

PATTEE, W. S., *Essential Nature of Law*, **4**: 447, 448n

Paul, Daniel, **2**: 429

Paul, Edwin, **2**: 451n

Paul Ernest, **2**: 182n

Pauli, Emilie, **2**: 364

Paywashtay, Sioux Indian, **2**: 196n

Peabody, A. P., **2**: 70

Peach Orchard, **2**: 309, 310

Peake, Rev. E. S., **4**: 227, 472

Pearl Lake, **1**: 124

Peat, extent and value, **4**: 479

Peck, L. W., **3**: 133

Peckham, S. F., **3**: 133, 134

Pelican Rapids, **3**: 362, 363, 366

Peller, John, **2**: 311

Pembina, **1**: 108, 109, 129, 217, 230, 288, 414, **2**: 159, 163, 444, **3**: 374, 376; population: *1823*, **1**: 108, *1849*, 352; treaty, *see* Indian treaties; Hatch's Battalion ordered to, **2**: 291, 292; surrender of Sioux Indians, 293; customs office, **3**: 78, 375, 377; grasshopper plague, 102; railroad station, 357, 451; fur-trading station, 452

Pembina County, population, *1850*, **1**: 352n

Pembina Indians, habitat, **4**: 190n; cede land, 191; land held by, 192; remove to White Earth Reservation, 197, 198n; census, 227n; population statistics, 323. *See also* Chippewa Indians; Chippewa reservations; Indian treaties

Penal code, revised, **3**: 161

Penal institutions, examination of accounts, **3**: 121; board of pardons, 224, 226; board of control, 248, 262, 287; abuses in administration, 261; board of visitors, 263; established, **4**: 408; administration, 410–412; conditions, 410. *See also* Correctional institutions; Prison

PENDERGAST, W. W., "History of Hutchinson," **2**: 163n

Pénicaut, Jean, **1**: 41

PÉNICAUT, JEAN, "Relation," **1**: 38, 40n

Pennington, W. S., **1**: 248

Pennsylvania, natives of, in Minnesota, **3**: 73; land grant, **4**: 26, 82n

Pennsylvania Railroad Co., **3**: 367, 420

Pentland, Thomas, **3**: 386

People's party, **3**: 490; supported by Scandinavians, 195; in elections: *1892*, 196, 199, *1894*, 197, 199, 203, 491, *1896*, 220, 222, 223, 223n, *1898*, 241, *1900*, 257; platforms, 196, 199, 220, 296, 298; decline, 553. *See also* Farmers' Alliance of Minnesota

People's Peace Council, **3**: 558, 566

Pepin, Lake, **1**: 28, 37, 46, 56n

Pepin Reservation, *see* Wabasha Reservation

Perkins, Mrs. Alma D., **2**: 443

Perrault, J. B., **1**: 69

PERRAULT, J. B., "Narrative," **1**: 68n

Perrot, Nicolas, **1**: 18n, 36–38, 49

PERROT, NICOLAS, *Mémoire*, **1**: 17n

Perry, Abraham, **1**: 223

Perryville, battle, **2**: 91, 99, 307

Pershing, Gen. J. J., **3**: 529, 530, 535, 537

PERSHING, J. J., *Final Report*, **3**: 531n

Peters, Rev. Samuel, **1**: 61–63

Pettigrew, R. F., **2**: 423, 424

Pettijohn, Jonas, **2**: 120n

Pettit, C. H., **3**: 438n

Pettit-Robinson mill, **3**: 131

Pfaender, William, **2**: 68n

Pfau, Charles, **2**: 363

Pfefferle, Richard, **2**: 133n, **3**: 72n
Phalen's Creek, **1**: 29
PHELPS, ALONZO, *Biographical History*, **3**: 84n
Phelps, W. W., **2**: 18, 51n
Philippine Insurrection, **3**: 238-240, 256
Pickett, Gen. G. E., **2**: 312, 313n
PIERCE, E. D., "French Post near Trempealeau," **1**: 37
Pig iron industry, *see* Iron mining
Pigeon Point, **4**: 42
Pigeon River, explorers, **1**: 23n, 48, 58; trading post, 24n, 67
Pig's Eye, **1**: 220n, 223n, 429
Pike, Lieut. Z. M., sketch, **1**: 90, 100; expedition, 90-101, 190; negotiates treaty with Sioux, *1805*, 92-94, *see also* Indian treaties; trade agreement with Northwest Co., 97; death, 100; centennial celebrations, 100n
PIKE, Z. M., *Expeditions*, **1**: 47n, 91n
Pike's Island, **1**: 92, 144, 437; Faribault claim to, *see* Faribault claim
Pike's Rapids, **1**: 95
Pillager Indians, **1**: 182, 305n, 321, **2**: 277, **3**: 79, **4**: 194; attack by, feared, **2**: 243; disturbance of *1862*, 375-382; reservations, **3**: 22, **4**: 192; habitat, 190n; cede land, 191, 230, 322; claim damages for destruction of property, 210, 230, 322; census, 227n; councils with U. S. Chippewa Commission, 228n; uprising, 312-323; complaints, 322. *See also* Chippewa Indians; Chippewa reservations; Indian treaties; Leech Lake Indian Reservation; Cass Lake Indian Reservation; Otter Tail Indians
Pillsbury, C. A., **3**: 437n
Pillsbury, J. S., **3**: 89, 110, 172, 460, **4**: 159, 429n; combats grasshopper plague, **3**: 100n, 103-105, 108, 109, 115; sketch, 112; elected governor, 112, 113, 115; delivers inaugural address, 113, 121; services evaluated, 113, 115; favors redemption of state railroad bonds, 113, 139, 430, 431, 432, 433, 436, 438, 439n; appoints Edgerton senator, 115; legislation during administration, 119-121, 124, 139; praises of-

fice of public examiner, 123; criticizes special legislation, 124, 517, 518n; recommendations relative to new capitol, 188, 189n; declines nomination for fourth term, 143; lumber interests, 208n; services to university, **4**: 60; university regent, 72n, 96n, 404; donates land to university, 95n; approves textbook legislation, 155; donates land to state, 393; later career and death, **3**: 266; statue, 267, 267n
PILLSBURY, J. S., *Address before the Alumni*, **4**: 84n
Pilot Knob, **3**: 268n
Pinchot, Gifford, **4**: 259
Pine Bluff, **2**: 303
Pine Coulie, battle, **1**: 180
Pine County, forest fires, **3**: 212, **4**: 388
Pine Land Investigating Committee, **3**: 514; created to investigate timber sales, 207, 273, 506; findings, 207, 229n, 508-512. *See also* Lumber industry
Pine Lands and Timber on Red Lake Reservation, **4**: 239n
Pine Point, **4**: 260, 281
Pine River, **4**: 210, 230
Pine timber, amount, **4**: 395, 395n; sale, 399. *See also* Chippewa Indians; Red Lake Indian Reservation; Red Lake Indians; White Earth Indian Reservation
Pinkerton's National Detective Agency, **3**: 559
Pioneer and Democrat, **1**: 388, 396, 421
Pioneer Press, see St. Paul Pioneer Press
Pioneer Press Building, **3**: 485
Pipestone County, liquor sales, **3**: 563
Pipestone quarry, **1**: 119-121
Plummer, Le V. P., **2**: 150n
Plummer Diary, **2**: 150n
Plympton, Maj. Joseph, commandant at Fort Snelling, **1**: 152, 153, 196, 217, 218, 220, 221, 422, 439, 442; competitor for preëmption at Falls of St. Anthony, 452-454
Poehler, Henry, **2**: 28n
Poinsett, J. R., **1**: 126, 160, 439, 440, 441, 443
Point Douglas, **1**: 225
Point Prescott, battle, **1**: 81

Pokegama, Lake, **3**: 23; Indian reservation, **4**: 192, 193; mission, *see* Missions

Pokegama Falls, **4**: 209

Political parties, regulated by law, **4**: 340, 365, 369, 372–374, 380. *See also* individual parties

Politics, *see* Elections; Farmers' Alliance of Minnesota; Government of Minnesota; Granger movement; individual parties; Nonpartisan League; Patrons of Husbandry

POLK, R. L., ed., *County of Brown*, **2**: 133n

Polk County, **3**: 98, **4**: 305

Pollock, R. L., **3**: 285n

Pond, G. H., missionary, **1**: 151, 176, 189, 193, 194, 198, 456, **2**: 227, 249, 250, 253; sketch, **1**: 183; aided by Taliaferro, 184, 186; devises Dakota alphabet, 188, 447; at Lac qui Parle mission, 194, 199; ordained, 197; compiles Dakota dictionary, 198, 203, 449, 450, 451, 452n; aids in translation of Scriptures into Dakota, 200; quoted, 209; death, 197. *See also Grammar and Dictionary of the Dakota Language*

POND, G. H., "Dakota and Chippewa Wars," **1**: 84n

POND, PETER, Journal, **1**: 56n

Pond, S. W., missionary, **1**: 151, 156, 176, 189, 194, 198, **2**: 207n, 249; sketch, **1**: 183; aided by Taliaferro, 184, 186; devises Dakota alphabet, 188, 447; prepares Sioux spelling book, 193; ordained, 194; translates Scriptures into Dakota, 194; at Lake Harriet mission, 195; compiles Dakota grammar, 195, 448, 450; compiles Dakota dictionary, 195, 198, 203, 449, 450, 451, 452n; at Lac qui Parle mission, 197; explanation of Sioux Outbreak, **2**: 213n; estimate of Little Crow, 239n; death, **1**: 198. *See also Grammar and Dictionary of the Dakota Language*

POND, S. W., "The Dakotas in *1834*," **1**: 80n; *Two Volunteer Missionaries*, 151n; "Indian Warfare," 154n; "Pioneer Work among the Dakotas," 184n; Hebrew-Dakota dictionary, 198n

Pond Papers, **1**: 171n

Poorhouses, conditions, **4**: 410

Pope, Gen. John, **2**: 190, 193, 201, 204n, 251, 267, 277, 279, 287n, 341, 345, 440; Civil War service, 86, 100, 187; commands Military Department of the Northwest, 170, 187, 189, 266; sends replacements to Minnesota, 170, 181; plans defense against Sioux, 187; removal recommended, 188; transfers headquarters to Wisconsin, 189; attitude toward punishment of Sioux, 191–193, 197, **4**: 475; orders arrest of Sioux at Indian camps, **2**: 194; countermands order to try Sioux at Fort Snelling, 195; fears mob violence to condemned Sioux, 204; informs Halleck of end of Sioux war, 242; submits plan for removal of Indians from state, 257; plans expedition against Sioux, *1863*, 266; opposed to organization of Hatch's Battalion, 291; plans operations against Sioux, *1864*, 294; declines Chippewa offer of service against Sioux, 380; forwards proceedings of trial commission, 448

POPE, JOHN, *Report of an Exploration of Minnesota*, **1**: 129n

Pope County, **3**: 147n

Population, *1840*, **1**: 351; *1849*, 244, 316, 351; *1850*, 352; *1855*, 359, 380n, 388; *1857*, 359, 389, 418, **2**: 1, 12; *1860*, 64, 344, **3**: 1, 58; *1865*, **2**: 344, **3**: 1; *1870*, 58, 59, 143, **4**: 414; *1875*, **3**: 62, 73; *1880*, 139, 143; *1890*, 192, **4**: 147; *1895*, **3**: 226; *1900*, 251, 251n; *1910*, 558; *1920*, 322; of Minneapolis, St. Anthony, and St. Paul, *1860–90*, **2**: 64, **3**: 480, 487, **4**: 105, 123, 425, 427; foreign, **2**: 64n; growth after Civil War, **3**: 1, 2; of Wabasha County, *1865–67*, 21; of mining communities, **4**: 51; of St. Louis County, 51n; statistics relating to Chippewa, 196, 227n, 285, 293, 297, 323; of Red Lake County, 299

Populists, *see* People's party

Porter, E. D., **3**: 181n, **4**: 89–92, 94

Porter, Gen. Fitz John, **2**: 101

Porter, R. P., **3**: 483, 486, 487

Postal service, *see* Mails

Potawatomi Indians, **1**: 107, 457
Potter, Capt. T. E., **2**: 373
POTTER, T. F., *Autobiography*, **2**: 374n; "Recollections," 374n
Powderly, T. V., **4**: 449
Powell, R. J., **4**: 287n, 289n, 291
Powers, Le Grand, commissioner of labor, **4**: 451–459
Prairie du Chien, **1**: 57, 63n, 231; trading post, 57, 67, 88, 240, 437; population, 92, 92n, 105; British occupation, 100n, 101; Indian agency, 135n; treaties, *see* Indian treaties. *See also* Fort Crawford; Fort Shelby
Prairie Island, **1**: 12, 39
Prentiss, Gen. B. N., **2**: 98
Presbyterian Church, *see* Pond, G. H. and S. W.; Riggs, Rev. S. R.; Williamson, Rev. J. P.; Williamson, Rev. T. S.
Presbyterians, in educational field, **4**: 436, 441
Presbytery of St. Paul, **3**: 427n
Prescott, Philander, **1**: 147n, 186, 425, **2**: 110, 404, 445, 446
PRESCOTT, PHILANDER, "Autobiography and Reminiscences," **1**: 138n
Presidential elections, *see* Elections
Preston, Gen. William, **2**: 318
Preston, C. H., and Co., **4**: 129
Preus, J. A. O., sketch, **3**: 295; elected governor, 295, 320, 549, 551; reëlected, 320, 551; defeated for senatorship, 321, 551, 552; advocates ore tax, 307, **4**: 55
PRICE, H. B., *Farmers' Co-operation*, **4**: 405n
Price, Gen. Sterling, **2**: 307
Primary elections, *see* Elections
Prince, J. S., **2**: 28n, **4**: 5
Princeton, **1**: 504, **2**: 243
Princeton Union, **3**: 273
Prison, **1**: 260; existing location confirmed, **3**: 9; established, **4**: 408; management and policies, 410; codification of laws relating to, 412. *See also* Penal institutions
Probate code, **3**: 190
"Proceedings of Military Commission Held at Fort Abercrombie and Fort Snelling," **2**: 284n
Proceedings of the Board of Commissioners Appointed under the Provisions of an Act Approved February 28, 1866, **2**: 56n

Progressive Republicans, **3**: 539, 547
Prohibition, agitation for, **3**: 179, 196, 200, 300–302; effected by constitutional amendment, 179, 300, 302, 303. *See also* Liquor
Prohibition party, **3**: 486; in elections: *1890*, 189, *1892*, 197, *1894*, 197, 200–202, *1900*, 257; supported by Scandinavians, 195; organization, 301
Property, value: *1870*, **3**: 60, *1900*, 251, 251n, 252, *1922*, 322; aliens' holding of, 188, 199, 202; laws relating to, 224, 263; Torrens title, 263. *See also* Public lands; Taxation
Protestant Episcopal Church, *see* Episcopal Church
Protestants, number in *1900*, **3**: 255n; controversy with Catholics over school matters, **4**: 175–182. *See also* Churches; various denominations
Provençalle, Louis, **1**: 119, 120, 120n, 133, 164n
PROVOST MARSHAL GENERAL, *Final Report*, **3**: 315n
Public charities, *see* Charitable institutions
PUBLIC EDUCATION COMMISSION, *Report*, **4**: 169n
Public examiner, provided for, **3**: 121, 124n; findings, 121–124; duties curtailed, 287
Public health, promotion, **3**: 154–156, **4**: 413–423; work among Chippewa, 325
Public Health in Minnesota, **4**: 420
Public highways, *see* Roads
Public lands, sales offices, **1**: 70, 225, 229, 240, 428; sales, 225, 229, 354, 360, 363, 428; surveys, 225, 229, 354, 357, **4**: 465; set apart for schools, **1**: 244, 393, **4**: 44, 78, 82, 82n, 83, 85, 436, 443; speculation, **1**: 254, 363, 434; Homestead Act, **2**: 331, 333; grants to Minnesota, **3**: 8, 34, 119, 119n, 423; grants to railroads, 32, 32n, 45, 53, 60, 119n, 159, 441, **4**: 12; proposed grant to railroads, **3**: 34–36; extent of surveys in *1870*, 60; opened to homesteaders, 62; investigations of sales of timber, 88, 206, 229, 273, 500–512; disposal of swamp lands, 119, 119n,

4: 12, 84, 85n; royalties yielded by ore lands, **3:** 120n; reservation for settlers demanded, 170, 188, 198, 199, 202; legislation relating to sale of timber, 208, 287, 500, 501n, 503, 504, 507, 513–515; loss of ore lands by state, 223, **4:** 14, 44–48; land offices, **3:** 242, **4:** 45, 46; supervisory bureau recommended, **3:** 288; proposed grant for improvement of Mississippi, 325, 326; exchange of state railroad bonds for: proposed, 423, 424, 425, 431, 433, provided for, 439; legislation relating to acquisition of ore lands, **4:** 13; sale of timber lands, 15; leasing of ore lands, 18, 58; under public waters, 48–50; granted to states for education, 77, 79n, 82n, 97, 135; double university grant, 97–103; value of pine lands, 103; administration of school lands, 137, 139, 140, 141, 143, 145–149, 183; auditor made commissioner, 140, 146; ceded Chippewa lands: appraisal and sale, 235–243, logging of dead and down timber, 244–249, provisions of Morris Act for sale of pine, 249–253; state claims lands on Red Lake Reservation, 300n; refusal of Red Lake Indians to give land for schools, 304; donated to state for forestry purposes, 393, 400, 401; salt spring lands, 480. *See also* Education; Lumber industry; Railroads; Settlement; Scrip; Fort Snelling; Squatters; Town site speculation

Public Library Commission, *see* Minnesota Public Library Commission

Public safety commission, *see* Minnesota Commission of Public Safety

Public schools, *see* Education; State Public School

Public utilities, legislation concerning, **3:** 287

Pugh, G. E., **2:** 13

Purchase of Island, **1:** 144n

Purdie, T. W., **3:** 128

Pure-food laws, **3:** 158

Pusey, Pennock, **3:** 20, 104, 392n

Putnam, G. W., **3:** 411n

Pyle, Howard, **2:** 327n

Pyle, J. G., *Hill,* **3:** 452n

Quackenbos, G. P., *To the Legislators and Teachers,* **4:** 157n

Quaife, M. M., "Carver and the Carver Grant," **1:** 54n; *Chicago and the Old Northwest,* 168n

Quarries, **3:** 269, 270

Quarrying, **4:** 17n. *See also* Building stones

Quebec, **1:** 9, 73; founded, 2; surrendered to British, 14, 51

Quebec Act, **1:** 65, 496

Queen Anne's War, **1:** 44

Quinn, Peter, **2:** 112, 114

Quinn, W. L., **1:** 304; interpreter, **2:** 154; testifies before military commission, 285n; testifies in Sisseton and Wahpeton claim case, 431

Rabbit Lake Indian Reservation, **3:** 23, **4:** 192, 193

Rabbit Lake Indians, **4:** 192, 196n, 213. *See also* Chippewa of the Mississippi; Chippewa reservations; White Earth Indian Reservation; White Oak Point Indian Reservation

Radisson, sieur de, **1:** 79; sketch, 7; narrative, 7–13; and formation of Hudson's Bay Co., 8; alleged discovery of Mississippi, 4n, 11–13

Radisson, sieur de, *Voyages,* **1:** 8n

Railroad and Warehouse commission, **3:** 210, 211

Railroads, **3:** 449; land grants advocated, **1:** 130, 256n, 327, 329, 388; legislation for Illinois, 327, 346; land grant bill of *February 7, 1854,* 332–334; charters granted, 350, 378, **2:** 39, 41–43; "Great Railroad Excursion," **1:** 358; Pacific railroad advocated, 389; land grant bill of *May 6, 1854:* **2:** 37, provisions, **1:** 334, passed, 335, altered, 335–338, repealed, 338, efforts to annul repeal, 340–344, 349; land grant bill of *1857:* **2:** 37–40, transmitted to legislature, 40; combination to eliminate competition, 39; affected by panic, 43, 44; aided by Five Million Loan, 44–47; construction, 49, 52, 53, 330; depreciation of bonds loaned to, 52; suspension of construction, 52, 53; charters to new companies urged by Ramsey, 53; redemption of bonds urged, 62; properties acquired by state, 328;

conditions governing restoration of property, 329; need for, **3**: 2, 32, 44, construction in decade after Civil War, 2, 32, 60, 61; dissatisfaction with, 32–34, 39, 40, 44–49, 54, 159, 160, 170, 188, 196, 198, 201; land grants, 32, 32n, 45, 53, 60, 119n, 159, 411, **4**: 146n; scheme for acquiring lands, *1871*, **3**: 34–36; Granger act of *1871*: passage and provisions, 36, 40–42, 55, disobeyed, 42, 44, 50, 55, declared constitutional, 42; railroad commissioners, 41, 42, 45, 50, 52, 54, 159–161, 179, 208, 209; bond issues limited, 44; Granger act of *1874*: passage and provisions, 51, opinions regarding, 51, 53, operation, 52–55, 56; land sales, 52; affected by panic of *1873*, 52, 53, 55, 72, 141; cost of construction and operation, 53; Granger act of *1875*, 55; declared subject to state control, 57, 113, 142, 159; displace other means of travel, 61; affect settlement, 62, 67; regulation discussed by Congress, 74; resumption of building after *1873*, 141, 143; regulatory act of *1885*, 159–161; regulatory act of *1887*, 179; accused of interference in politics, 202, 273n; taxation, 218, 225, 249; abolition of passes, 248, 287; project for line from Taylor's Falls to western Minnesota, 325; extended to Red River, 355, 357; demand for public ownership, 552; land grant bill of *1870*, **4**: 8; in mining region, 11–13, 15–17, 20, 29, 30, 33, 37, 38n. *See also* Five Million Loan; individual companies

Rainbow Division, *see* Forty-second Division

Rainy River, **4**: 191

Ramsey, Alexander, **1**: 290, 291, 294, 312, 314, 315, 403, 433, **2**: 17, 48, 81, 87, 129, 169, 186n, 191, 197, 257, 342, 361, 375, 377, 378, 390n, 451, **3**: 5, 19, 37, 74, 116, 214, 251, 348, 350, 422, **4**: 435; sketch, **1**: 248; appointment to governorship and assumption of office, 248, 252; character, 249, 275; friendship with Sibley, 249, 276, 276n; messages, 253–255, 266n, 271, 327, 353n, 354,

355, 459, **2**: 43n, 53, 63, 68, 251, 255, 391, **4**: 2, 135, 136, 139, 140; holds Indian councils, **1**: 258, 289; commissioner on territorial seal, 267, 459–462; treaty commissioner, 271–275, 277–280, 284–290, 295–303, 323, 463, 464; interest in railroads, 330, 335, 336, 339, 340, 341; investigation of conduct as treaty commissioner, 464–470; favors repurchase of Fort Snelling, 515n; candidate for governor, *1857*, **2**: 3; attitude toward Five Million Loan, 48; elected governor, 53, 60–63; plan for cancellation of railroad bonds, 53; supports Donnelly for lieutenant governor, 61; recommended for secretary of interior, 67; elected U. S. senator, 68, 106–108, 334; receives letters relating to situation in South, 70, 71, 72; tenders troops for Civil War service, **2**: 76, 79, 88, 89, **4**: 81; directs organization of troops, **2**: 89–91, 92, 96, 103, 105; reëlected, 100; attacks on, 106, 217n; receives appeal for help from Fort Ridgely, 115; organizes Indian campaign of *1862*, 147, 149, 168; sends aid to Meeker County, 158, 159, 161; sends aid to Fort Abercrombie, 167; notifies U. S. government of Sioux war, 186; attempts to organize mounted rangers for Indian war, 190; attitude toward punishment of Sioux, 202, 204, 251, 255; fears attack on Sioux prisoners, 205; informs president of end of Sioux war, 242; authorizes impressment of supplies for Indian war, 244; appeals to secretary of war for reimbursements, 245; urges protection of frontier against Indian attack, 281; political supporters, 335, 337; supports Miller for governor, 336; sends reënforcements to Fort Ripley, 376; negotiates with Chippewa, 378; declines Chippewa offer of service against Sioux, 380; delivers address at dedication of Birch Coulee monument, 388; estimates number killed in Sioux Outbreak, 391; heads faction in Republican party, **3**: 15–17, 18, 81; reëlected U. S. senator, *1869*, 16; services in behalf of arrested Minnesotans, 78, 380; supports Davis for district attorney, 82; in senatorial election of *1875*, 85–87; appointed secretary of war, 87; opposes squandering of school lands, 268; lays corner stone of new Capitol, 269; urges reduction of salaries, 357; purchases properties of defaulting railroads, 418; interest in railroad building, 421, 422; interest in mining development, **4**: 2; services in securing second university land grant, 99–101; school land commissioner, 141n; school trustee, 435; advocates revision of school fund, 438; later career and death, **3**: 267

RAMSEY, ALEXANDER, Diary, **1**: 279n

Ramsey County, **3**: 211, **4**: 88, 108; population, *1850*, **1**: 352n; district court, **3**: 88, 260, 392, 463, 569, **4**: 130–132; aids victims of grasshopper plague, **3**: 99; representation in Republican convention of *1904*, 274, 275

Ramsey County Picket Guard, **2**: 375

Ramsey Investigation Report, **1**: 269n

Ramsey Papers, **1**: xi

Randall, Maj. B. H., **2**: 128n, 131n

RANDALL, J. H., "Railroad Building in Minnesota," **3**: 422n

Randall, J. J., **3**: 52

Rankin, A. W., **4**: 186

RANKIN, A. W., "High Schools," **4**: 77n; "State Aid Imbroglio," 150n

Rapidan Township, Blue Earth County, Indian attack, **2**: 346

Rascher's Atlas of St. Paul, **3**: 485

Raven's Point, **4**: 212

Ravoux, Father Augustin, **1**: 207, **2**: 449, 450; baptizes Sioux convicts, 210, 211n; baptizes converts at Fort Snelling, 254

RAVOUX, AUGUSTIN, *Reminiscences*, **1**: 207n; *Labors among the Sioux*, 207n; *Path to the House of God*, 207, 207n

Raymbault, Charles, **1**: 6

Recall, rejection of constitutional amendment providing, **3**: 307; advocated by labor, 550n

Reconstruction, **3**: 3, 4, 12, 75

Recruiting, for World War, **3**: 316

Red Bird, Sioux Indian, **1**: 155, 156, 157, 158

Red Iron, Sioux chief, **1**: 300, 301, 464, **2**: 120n, 178, 182, 428, 431; at treaty negotiations, *1858*, 394

Red Lake, **1**: 110, 111n, **4**: 297, 298, 307, 309

Red Lake Chippewa Indians, **4**: 220n

Red Lake County, **3**: 563, **4**: 299, 300

Red Lake Indian Forest, **4**: 307–311

Red Lake Indian Reservation, "diminished reservation" defined, **4**: 216, 297–299; bills relating to cession and sale, 219, 219n; population and area, 297; agitation for cession of western portion, 299–304; act of *1904*, providing for cession of part, 304; sales of land under act of *1904*, 305; legality of act of *1904*, contested, 306; partly included in forest reserve, 307–310; lumbering, 308–312; school, 309; Bishop Whipple at, 476. *See also* Red Lake Indian Forest; Red Lake Indians

Red Lake Indian Reservation, **4**: 305n

Red Lake Indian School, **4**: 309

Red Lake Indians, **2**: 376, 378, 381; habitat, **4**: 190n, 192; cession of *1863*, 191; excluded from plans for consolidation of Chippewa, 202, 215, 234, 262; appraisal and sale of lands and timber, 215–219, 220–224, 229n, 231, 235–240, 305; complain of incorrect boundary line, 216, 230; unsuccessful attempts to provide for land allotments, 216, 219n, 301, 302; allotments provided for, 220, 231, 234, 262, 297–299, 305; census, 227n; accept "diminished reservation," 297–299; condition, 307; farming, 307; fund, 308; population statistics, 323; number of full-bloods, 323; attempt to negotiate treaty in *1861*, 476. *See also* Chippewa reservations; Indian treaties; Red Lake Indian Reservation

Red Lake mission, **1**: 182n

Red Lake River, **1**: 109, 111n, **3**: 447, **4**: 194

Red River, **1**: 111n, 129, **2**: 265, 294, 376, 419, **4**: 191, 195; railroad to, planned, **2**: 38; Fort Abercrombie established, 163; steamboat transportation, **3**: 452

Red River carts, **1**: 226
Red River Lumber Co., **4**: 466
Red River settlement, *see* Selkirk colony
Red River trade, **2**: 164, 282
Red River Transportation Co., **3**: 447, 452
Red River Valley, **1**: 108, **4**: 197, 219n; patrolled by Hatch's Battalion, **2**: 293; resources, **1**: 106, 109, 129; trade, 226; transportation to, **3**: 61, 355, 357, 447; grasshopper plague, 102; settlement, 139, 140, **4**: 199, 263, 299
Red Rock mission, **1**: 206, 452n
Red Wing, Sioux chief, **1**: 136, 203, **3**: 350n
Red Wing, **3**: 163, 501n, 572, **4**: 414, 418; state training school, 164, 408; election law applicable to, 347n
Redby, **4**: 310n, 311
Redfield, South Dakota, **2**: 260
Redstone Ferry, **2**: 136, 369
Redwood, **2**: 252, 253
Redwood agency, **1**: 353, **2**: 193, 223, 264, 408, 409, **4**: 474; location, **2**: 109, 111n, 394; attacked by Sioux, 109, 112–114; trouble over non-payment of annuities, 231–237; monument to Lynd, 390; number killed by Sioux, 392; appealed to for protection against Inkpaduta, 402, 404. *See also* Missions; Sioux Outbreak
Redwood County, **3**: 102; number killed during Sioux Outbreak, **2**: 392
Redwood Ferry, battle, **2**: 113, 392; monument commemorating, 390
Redwood River, **2**: 266, 408
Reed, J. A., **3**: 351, 352, 353, 354n, 355, 357
Reeve, Gen. C. McC., **3**: 233
Referendum, on legislation: advocated, **3**: 196, 200, 202, 249, 550n, practiced, 225, 423, 426, 428, 432, 433, 439; on senatorial candidates, 205n; on constitutional amendments, *see* Constitution
Reformatory institutions, *see* Correctional institutions
Registration of electors, *see* Elections
Rehfeld, Fred, **2**: 362
Religion, *see* Churches; Education; Indians; Missionaries; Missions; Protestants; various religious denominations
Renville, Antoine, **2**: 118
Renville, Gabriel, **2**: 172n, 270, 418, 420, 428
RENVILLE, GABRIEL, "Sioux Narrative of the Outbreak in *1862*," **2**: 172n
Renville, Isaac, **2**: 428
Renville, Rev. J. B., **2**: 249, 428
Renville, Joseph, fur-trader, **1**: 100n, 133, 164n, 190, 199, 455; on Long's expedition, 107; promotes Columbia Fur Co., 161, 190; difficulties with Chippewa, 191; at Lac qui Parle mission, 192, 199, 202; aids in translation of Scriptures into Dakota, 200; death, 202
Renville family, **2**: 252
Renville County, Sioux attacks, **2**: 110, 120; number killed during Sioux Outbreak, 392; ravaged by grasshoppers, **3**: 98, 102. *See also* Birch Coulee
Renville Rangers, **2**: 430; reënforce garrison at Fort Ridgely, 129; casualties, 133n; on Sibley expedition of *1862*, 177, 180, 181
"Report as to Amendments and Revision of the Railroad and Warehouse Laws," **3**: 209n
Report of the Pine Land Investigating Committee, **3**: 208n
Report of the Tax Commission, 1901, **3**: 258n
Report of the Special Senate Committee, **3**: 502n
Representatives, state: apportioned, **2**: 1, election, *1857*, 1, 2, *1858*, 59, 62, *1860*, 68, *1862*, 333; U. S.: election, *1857*, 1, 2, 12, 18, *1862*, 333, 334, 336; number: provided by constitution, 12, debated in Congress, 13. *See also* individual representatives
Republicans, organize, **1**: 375, 393; in political campaigns: *1856*, 394, 396, *1857*, **2**: 2–4, *1858*, 59, *1859*, 59, 61, 62, *1860*, 66–68, *1862*, 333, 334, **3**: 11, *1863*, **2**: 108, 336, 337, *1864*, **3**: 11, 25, *1865*, **2**: 340–342, 343, *1866*, **3**: 11, *1867*, 10, *1868*, 10, *1869*, 17, *1870*, 17, *1873*, 49, 82–85, *1874*, 410, *1877*, 115, *1878*, 388, 390, *1879*, 115, *1880*, 118, *1881*, 144, *1882*, 147–149, *1883*, 144, *1884*, 166, *1886*, 171–173, 175, 242, *1888*, 182,

242, *1890*, 187, 189, 486, *1892*, 195, *1894*, 197, 202, 491, 505, *1896*, 219, 221, 244, *1898*, 245, *1900*, 256, 257, *1902*, 257n, *1904*, 272, 275, *1906–12*, 279, 293, *1916*, 299, *1922*, 299, 320, *1923*, 320, 552, *1924*, 321, 552; attitude toward Five Million Loan, **2**: 48; control legislatures: *1859*, 62, *1860*, **4**: 338, *1861*, **2**: 68; attitude toward abolitionists, 69; criticize Sibley expedition of *1863*, 277; denounce Hatch, 290; supported by Miller, 335; supported by Marshall, 337; denounce antinegro legislation, **3**: 3; vote on fourteenth amendment, 4; censure Norton, 4–6; favor negro suffrage, 7; strength, *1860–65*, 10, *1870–76*, 75, *1876–81*, 115; relations with Donnelly, 10, 11, 15, 16, 17, 18; in senatorial elections by legislature: *1869*, 16, *1871*, 73, *1875*, 85, 87, *1881*, 116, *1883*, 149, 150, *1887*, 174, *1889*, 184–186, *1893*, 203, *1895*, 204, 489–497, *1899*, 250, *1901*, 264, *1905*, 265, *1911*, 265; views on tariff, 17; attitude toward railroads, 33, 36, 49; pass Granger law of *1874*, 51; organization of new factions, 81, 83, 84, 400; newspaper organs, 82, 83; decline of power, 118, 189, 319, 320, 548, 550, 551; follow practice of renomination, 182, 184; monetary principles, 194, 218, 219–221; denounced by Prohibitionists, 202; accused of subservience to railroads, 273n; in constitutional convention, 516; in North Dakota elections of *1916*, 544; denounce Nonpartisan League, 554n; national convention, **4**: 30; in state and national elections, *see* Elections. *See also* Constitutional convention; Liberal Republicans; Progressive Republicans; Silver Republicans

Reservation at Fort Snelling, **1**: 222n
Rhode Island, land grant, **4**: 82n
Rice, Edmund, **1**: 336, 349, 513n, **2**: 39, **3**: 348, 421
Rice, H. M., **1**: 250, 311, 426, 471, **2**: 9, 89, 333, 397, 398, **3**: 251, 320, 348, 550, **4**: 100, 208, 437; sketch, **1**: 239; relations with American Fur Co., 240, 367, 371; relations with Sibley, 240, 260, 313–318, 341, 347, 369–372, 376; obtains consent of Sioux to treaty amendments, 293–295, 462, 467; selects site for Winnebago reservation, 310, 478; contract to transport scattered Winnebago to reservation, 313–318; territorial delegate: 324, 408, 431, 481n, favors railroad legislation, 329, 332, 333, 340, secures extension of preëmption rights, 356, reëlected, 373–377, influence, 388, favors statehood, 390, 431, opposes Watab treaty, 481, introduces bill for enabling act, **4**: 98, secures land grant for university, 98n; stimulates development of St. Paul, **1**: 367; aids in establishment of Minnesota Territory, 368; character, 368; party affiliation, 369; favors sale of Fort Snelling Reservation, 404, 405; aspires to senatorship, 411; elected senator, **2**: 6, 8; seated, 17; credited with securing passage of land grant bill of *1857*, 38n; advocates passage of Five Million Loan amendment, 48; attitude on mandamus issued to Sibley, 51; in political campaign of *1860*, 66; opposes Civil War, 70, 71, 73; supports administration during Civil War, 74–76; accused of political machinations, 108, 341; instrumental in securing opening of Red River trade, 164; suggested as successor to Pope, 188, 242; approves execution of condemned Sioux, 203n; explanation of Sioux Outbreak, 212; supports bill for relief of victims of Sioux Outbreak, 247; urges formation of regiment for campaign against Sioux, 290; criticized by Sibley, 291; hospitality, 340; declines Republican senatorial nomination, 341; candidate for governor, 343; member of commission negotiating with Chippewa, *1862*, 378; reports Indian treaties, 396; represents Chippewa at treaty of *1863*, **3**: 22, 23, **4**: 193; votes on Morrill bill, 79n; on U. S. Chippewa Commission, 226, 227, 227n, 229, 233n, 234, 235; death and burial, **3**: 213; statue, 214

Rice commission, *see* U. S. Chippewa Commission

Rice County, **3**: 103, 114; Indian depredations, **2**: 288

Rice Creek, **2**: 239, 239n, 240, 415

Rice Lake (Clearwater County), **4**: 195

Rice Lake Indian Reservation, **3**: 23, 30, **4**: 192, 193

Rice Lake Indians, *see* Rice Lake Indian Reservation; Chippewa Indian Reservation; White Earth Indian Reservation

Rice Report, **4**: 227n

Richardson, Harris, **3**: 207n, 507n, 513n

RICHARDSON, J. D., *Messages and Papers,* **1**: 290n

RICHARDSON, NATHAN, "Morrison County," **1**: 95n

Riggs, Rev. S. R., **1**: 282n, 283n, **2**: 196n, 248, 262, 350, 407, 409n, 412n; sketch, **1**: 200; mission stations, 200, 201, 203, **2**: 118, 207n, 220; character, **1**: 201; publishes Sioux grammar and dictionary, 203, 448, *see also Grammar and Dictionary of the Dakota Language;* learns of Sioux Outbreak, **2**: 118, 119; on Sibley expedition of *1862,* 173, 181, 182n; at trial of Sioux, 198; attitude toward execution of condemned Sioux, 203; preaches memorial sermon on J. R. Brown, 210; explanation of Sioux Outbreak, 212, 231; called to Yellow Medicine agency to quiet Indians, 230; testifies before Sioux claims commission, 247, 250, 434; ministration to Sioux convicts, 249; aids in listing loyal Sioux, 264; on Sibley expedition of *1863,* 277

RIGGS, S. R., *Dakota Grammar,* **1**: 79n; *Tah-koo Wah-kan,* 170n; *Forty Years with the Sioux,* 171n; "Protestant Missions in the Northwest," 173n; *Grammar and Dictionary of the Dakota Language,* 448n; "Memoir of Lynd," **2**: 111n; "Narrative of Paul Mazakootemane," 430n

RILEY, C. V., *Locust Plague,* **3**: 93n

Ripley, Judge Christopher, **3**: 409

Rippe, Henry, **3**: 211

River transportation, **2**: 65. *See also* Mississippi River; Red River

Roads, proposed, **1**: 254, 263; provided for, 265, **2**: 21; federal aid, **1**: 361, **2**: 64, **3**: 309, 311, 312; legislation for improvement, **2**: 63, **3**: 309, 310, 312; county system recommended, 226; constitutional amendment relating to, 309, 310. *See also* Transportation

Roaring Cloud, Sioux Indian, **2**: 408

Robbins, A. B., **3**: 109

Robert, Louis, **2**: 129n, 399n

Roberts, A. F., relations with Lord Gordon, **3**: 370, 372, 377, 378, 379, 382

Robertson, D. A., **3**: 38, **4**: 86; charges against Ramsey, **1**: 465, 469, 469n; commands Twenty-third Regiment of Militia, **2**: 28n; criticizes Five Million Loan, 48; offers regiment for Civil War service, 88; rejection of regiment, 89–91

Robertson, T. A., **2**: 172, 173n; testifies in Sisseton and Wahpeton claim case, 426, 427

ROBERTSON, T. A., Reminiscences, **2**: 173n

Robertson family, **2**: 252

ROBINSON, DOANE, "Verendrye Calendar," **1**: 47n; "Additional Verendrye Material," 49n; *Sioux Indians,* **2**: 168n; "Sioux Indian Courts," 401n

ROBINSON, E. V., *Agriculture in Minnesota,* **1**: 361n, **3**: 21

Rochester, designated railroad junction, **2**: 42, **4**: 109; antimonopoly meeting, **3**: 33; railroad station, 42, 45; temperance society, 176; hospital facilities, **4**: 110–112, 122; academy, 110, 110n; tornado, 110; election law applicable to, 347n, 360. *See also* Mayo Clinic; Mayo Foundation; Mayo Properties Association

Rochester State Hospital, **4**: 408. *See also* Insane asylums

Rock County, **3**: 97

Rockefeller, J. D., **4**: 29, 31

Rockford, **2**: 442

RODDIS, L. H., "The Last Indian Uprising," **3**: 240n

ROGERS, G. D., "Flour Manufacture in Minnesota," **3**: 70n

Rogers, Maj. Robert, **1**: 55, 56

Rolette, Joseph, **1**: 100n, 133; connection with capital removal

scheme, 384, 385; in constitutional convention, 403; legislator, 2: 41
Rolling Stone, 1: 360
Roman Catholic Church, bishops, 4: 110, 213, 226
Roman Catholics, advocate temperance reform, 3: 176; number in 1900, 255n; among foreign element, 4: 171; controversy over school matters, 175–182. See also individual priests and bishops; Missions
Rondo, Joseph, 1: 223
Roos, Charles, 2: 362, 364; criticizes Sibley, 176n; account of battle of New Ulm, 361
Roosevelt, Theodore, 4: 271, 281; Minnesota vote for, 3: 275; desires command of army corps, 315n; third party leader, 539, 540
Root, Elihu, 3: 280, 371
Root, N. G., 2: 345
Root River Valley and Southern Minnesota Railroad Co., 3: 422n; proposed, 1: 38; chartered, 2: 42
Rose, A. P., Yellow Medicine County, 2: 116n; Jackson County, 124n
Rose, E. E., 2: 182n
Rosecrans, Gen. W. S., 2: 96, 316, 319, 323
Ross, Alexander, Red River Settlement, 1: 214n
Ross, Lieut. Tenny, 4: 315
Rosser, J. T., 1: 336, 378
Rossman, L. A., Iron Ore Industry, 4: 52n
Rossville Gap, 2: 318
Round Wind, Sioux Indian, 2: 210, 210n, 211n
Roverud, E. K., 3: 494n
Royalty tax, 3: 288, 4: 51, 55, 56, 57
Royce, C. C., Indian Land Cessions, 1: 79n
Rum River, 1: 29, 30, 138, 139; battle, 157, 158
Russell, C. E., Nonpartisan League, 3: 542n
Russell, Jeremiah, 1: 178
Russell, Judge R. D., 3: 229n
Russell, R. P., 1: 402
Russell, William, 4: 316

Sabin, D. M., elected senator, 3: 149, 150, 497; sketch, 150; fails of renomination, 184, 495; charges of corruption unproved, 185n; sup-

ports Nelson, 495; interest in Nelson Act, 4: 223n
Saby, R. S., "Railroad Legislation in Minnesota," 1: 378n
Sacred Heart, Sioux attack settlers, 2: 120
Sagard-Théodat, Gabriel, Histoire du Canada, 1: 4n
St. Anthony, 1: 260, 2: 4, 82, 3: 112, 374, 4: 64, 108, 439; beginnings, 1: 229; population: 1849, 251, 352, 358, 1860, 2: 64, 3: 480n, 4: 425, 1865, 3: 480n, 1870, 3: 480n; Ramsey's prophecy concerning, 1: 255; obtains university, 261; incorporated, 379; designated railway station, 2: 38, 330; opens telegraph office, 66; liberation of slave, 69, 70n; refuge from Indians, 124; sends reënforcements against Sioux, 385; raises funds for preservation of falls, 3: 334, 345; railway terminal, 421, 441, 442; growth, 480; absorbed by Minneapolis, 480; lumber office, 501n. See also Minneapolis; Twin Cities
St. Anthony Express, 1: 430
St. Anthony, Falls of, 1: 13, 32n, 45n, 63n, 82, 3: 91, 4: 79, 108; discovered and named, 1: 29; explorers, 55, 94, 99, 105, 123, 134; Carver's description, 55; government sawmill erected, 139, 140; land claims, 228, 428, 452–454; land sale, 229; lumber industry, 229, 356; establishment of industries, 3: 30, 131, 333; recession, 30, 333–335, 4: 482; local, state, and federal activities for preservation, 3: 31, 334, 335, 336–346, 4: 209; mill explosion, 3: 131–136. See also Flour-milling; Lumber industry
Saint Anthony Falls Water Power Co., incorporated, 3: 30; controls power at falls, 333; litigation, 335, 346; damage to construction work, 338
St. Benedict's Mission, 4: 318
St. Benedict's Orphan Industrial School, 4: 325
St. Cloud, 2: 292, 376, 379, 3: 60, 504, 4: 190, 387; activities of Mrs. Swisshelm, 2: 33–36; designated railway station, 42; refuge from

Sioux, 124; fortifies against Sioux, 161; sends force against Indians, *1864*, 350; reformatory, **3**: 179, **4**: 412; quarries, **3**: 269; railway station, 325, 441, 443, 444, 447; lumber office, 501n; election law applicable to, **4**: 360n
St. Croix County, **1**: 233, 234, 236, 351, **4**: 330, 331n
St. Croix Falls, **1**: 225; battle, 81
St. Croix River, **1**: 24, 30, 39, 58n, 117, 227, **3**: 212, 325, 333, **4**: 190; lumbering, *see* Lumber industry
St. Croix Valley, geological survey, **4**: 3
St. Ignace, **1**: 20
St. James, **3**: 293, 294
St. John, Mission of, **4**: 474
St. John's Abbey, **4**: 324
St. Joseph, **2**: 161, 292
St. Lawrence River, **1**: 1, 2, 6, 6n, 7, 14, 27
St. Louis, Missouri, **1**: 75, 76, 78, 90, 91; political conventions, **3**: 187, 222, 223n; banking center, 253; adopts home-rule charter, 519
St. Louis County, **3**: 563, 563n, 564, **4**: 3, 7; state lands, 12; pine timber, 18; iron-bearing region, 20; district court, 49; statistics relating to mining and settlement, 51; forest fires, 390; forestry, 394, 401. *See also* Iron mining; Mesabi Iron Range; Vermilion Iron Range
St. Louis River, **1**: 4n, 104, 111n, **3**: 61, **4**: 192; trading posts, **1**: 68, 104
St. Lusson, sieur de, **1**: 17
St. Mark's Church, Minneapolis, **4**: 464
St. Mary's Hospital, Rochester, **4**: 111, 122
St. Mary's River, **1**: 5n, 9
St. Michael the Archangel, Mission of, **1**: 46, 47n
St. Mihiel offensive, **3**: 535
St. Paul, **1**: 229, 287, 428, **2**: 4, 83, 203, 260, 277, 282, 283, 376, 380, 381n, **3**: 31, 37, 86n, 149, 325, 352, 379, 388, 503, 570n, **4**: 5, 86, 105, 110, 203, 314. 321; first settlements on site, **1**: 219, 223; early development, 223–226, 368; named, 224; population: *1845*, 224, *1849*, 250, 352, *1855*, **4**: 436, *1860*, **2**: 64, **3**:

480, *1865–85*, 480, *1890*, 487; land sale, **1**: 225; early trade, 225, 226, 229, 230, 361; made capital, 244, 260, 382, **3**: 8–10, 10n; Ramsey's prophecy concerning, **1**: 255; affected by panic, 364; incorporated, 368, 379; designated railway station, **2**: 38, 42, 330; political meetings and conventions, 59, **3**: 15, 33, 39, 81, 84, 169, 171, 188, 546, 547, 548, 566, 567n, **4**: 449; opens telegraph office, **2**: 65; departure of First Minnesota, 84; refuge from Indians, 124; objective of Sioux, 133; Red River trade, 164; headquarters Military District of Minnesota, 202; relief of refugees, 244; embarkation of exiled Sioux, 259; railroad facilities, **3**: 2, 45, 48, 60, 61, 179, 421, 460; blizzard of *1873*, 71; rivalry with Minneapolis, 91, **4**: 425; growth, *1870–80*, **3**: 139; grain elevators, 161, 196, 208; banquet for Sibley, 162; home of prominent Minnesotans, 163, 174, 181, 182, 183, 196, 234, 294, 298, 405, 414, **4**: 387; Roman Catholic cathedral, **3**: 175; organization of temperance society, 176; Australian ballot adopted, 189; census fraud of *1890*, 193, 480–489; military activities, 231, 233, 236, 528, 537; home guard station, 318; Lord Gordon in, 363; in congressional election of *1878*, 391; early supremacy, 479; attitude in Nelson-Washburn campaign, 495; charter, 520, 520n; headquarters Nonpartisan League, 546; school legislation for, **4**: 136; special school district, 142n; educational convention, 180; memorial of commercial club in behalf of forest reserve, 260, 261n; election laws applicable to, 339n, 347n; permanent registration of voters, 358. *See also* Capital; Capitol; Twin Cities
St. Paul and Duluth Railroad Co., **3**: 467, **4**: 20
St. Paul and Milwaukee Railroad Co., **3**: 38
Saint Paul and Minneapolis Pioneer Press, **3**: 403
St. Paul and Pacific Railroad Co., **3**: 148, 424n; succeeds Minnesota and

Pacific Railroad Co., **2**: 330; extended to Red River Valley, **3**: 61, 355, 447; defaults interest payments, 389, 446; franchise, 422n; First Division Co., formed, 441; leases property to First Division Co., 443, 445; Northern Pacific in control, 445, 454; in receivership, 446; bill to forfeit franchise, 449; Hill and others obtain control, 453–462; merged in St. Paul, Minneapolis, and Manitoba Railway Co., 462. *See also* Minnesota and Pacific Railroad Co.

St. Paul and Sioux City Railroad Co., sued, **3**: 428–430

St. Paul Chamber of Commerce, **3**: 97, 484, 487n

St. Paul Choral Society, **4**: 106

St. Paul Daily Dispatch, **3**: 83

St. Paul Dispatch Building, **3**: 485

St. Paul, Minneapolis, and Manitoba Railway Co., organized, **3**: 462; sued by Farley, 463. *See also* St. Paul and Pacific Railroad Co.

St. Paul Pioneer, **3**: 24, 29, 332, 347, 380

St. Paul Pioneer Press, **2**: 251, **3**: 109, 213, 245, 273, 482, 483, 484, 495

Saint Paul Press, **3**: 7, 14, 24, 82, 83, 87, 325, 326, 380, 425

St. Paul Trust Co., **3**: 469

St. Paul Union Depot, **3**: 485, 488

St. Peter, **2**: 128, 138, 148, 148n, 149n, 205n, 236, 383, 384, 385; scheme to remove capital to, **1**: 381–387, 405, **3**: 9; designated railway station, **2**: 38, 42; objective of Sioux, 126; sends reenforcements to New Ulm, 134, 362, 365, 367, 368, 370, 371, 372, 373; learns of Sioux Outbreak, 135; founding, 143; Indian attack rumored, 157; arrival of Sibley's troops, 168, 176; refuge from Sioux, 224; garrisoned, 243; home of prominent Minnesotans, **3**: 18, 171, 275, 276, 283, 380, 409; celebrates election of Johnson, 278n; statue of Johnson, 285; college town, 293

St. Peter Co., **1**: 381, 382, 383, 386

St. Peter Free Press, **1**: 407

St. Peter Frontier Guards, **2**: 142

St. Peter Herald, **3**: 276

St. Peter State Hospital, **4**: 408. *See also* Insane asylums

Saint Peter Tribune, **3**: 171

St. Peter's, *see* Mendota

St. Peter's River, *see* Minnesota River

St. Vincent, railroad station, **1**: 42, **3**: 443, 444, 445, 447, 455, 458, 459, 460

Sale of Fort Snelling Reservation, **1**: 422n

Salt spring lands, history, **4**: 479–481

Salt Spring Lands in Minnesota, **4**: 481n

San Ildefonso, treaty, *1800*, **1**: 77

Sanborn, Gen. J. B., **2**: 28n, **3**: 84n, 437, 486; eulogizes Rice, **2**: 75; adjutant general, 90, 95; commands Fourth Minnesota, 95; promoted brigadier general, 322; painting of, 322n

SANBORN, J. B., *Congressional Grants in Aid of Railways*, **1**: 328n; " Minnesota in the National Congress," **2**: 75n; " Bishop Whipple as a Mediator," **4**: 475n

Sanborn, W. H., **3**: 411, 413

Sanders, Capt. E. C., **2**: 373, 374

Sandy Lake, **1**: 82, **4**: 296; explorers, **1**: 23, 39n, 96, 99, 104, 105, 111n, 114; trading post, 68, 68n, 96, 104, 151n, 174; battle, 81; mission, *see* Missions; plans to remove Chippewa Indians, **3**: 22–24, 26, 29

Sandy Lake Indian Reservation, **4**: 192, 193, 201

Sandy Lake Indians, **4**: 192, 196n, 213. *See also* Chippewa of the Mississippi; Chippewa reservations; Sandy Lake Indian Reservation; White Earth Indian Reservation; White Oak Point Indian Reservation

Sanford, H. S., **2**: 87

Sanford, Maria L., principal of school of agriculture, **4**: 95; sketch, 459–465

Sanford Niles' Academy, **4**: 111

Sanitation, *see* Public Health

Santee Indians, **2**: 257n, 297, 432; removed to Crow Creek reservation, 259–261, 263, 439; significance of name, 260, 261n; removed to Niobrara reservation, 261, 262, 437;

civilization, 261; agencies, 262, 280, 431, 433; claim for restoration of annuities, 437–439. *See also* Indian treaties; Mdewakanton Indians; Moscow Expedition; Sioux Indians; Sioux Outbreak; Wahpekute Indians

Satterlee, M. P., **2**: 392

SATTERLEE, M. P., *Victims of the Indian Massacre*, **2**: 110n, 392n; *Massacre at the Redwood Indian Agency*, 111n; "Narratives of the Sioux War," 161n

Sauk Center, **2**: 277; fortified against Indians, 161, 243; railroad station, **3**: 459, 460

Sauk Indians, **1**: 457

Sauk River route, **1**: 226

Sault de Ste. Marie, **1**: 103, **4**: 2; explorers, **1**: 4n, 5n, 6, 6n, 9, 23, 36, 58, 103, 114; Indian councils, 17, 36, 103; military post, 43

Sault Ste. Marie, Indian agency, **1**: 112n, 146

Saulteur Indians, **1**: 6. *See also* Indian treaties

Saunders, William, **3**: 37n

Sauntry, William, **3**: 509

Savage's Station, battle, **2**: 101, 102

Scandinavians, number: *1860*, **2**: 64n, *1870*, **3**: 59, *1875*, 73, *1880*, 140; at Belmont, attacked by Sioux, **2**: 123; invited to settle in Minnesota, **3**: 1; support Lind, 221, 246, 246n, 257, 493; support Nelson, 494. *See also* Aliens

Scarlet Plume, Sioux chief, **2**: 122, 270, 427, 428

Scattered Lake, **2**: 285

Schall, T. D., **3**: 321, 552

Schaper, W. A., **3**: 567n

Schell, Richard, **1**: 505

Schilling, Robert, **3**: 196

Schofield, Gen. J. M. **2**: 323, 324

School for the Blind, Faribault, **4**: 408

School for the Deaf, Faribault, **4**: 408

School for the Feeble-Minded, Faribault, **4**: 408, 410

School lands, leased in mining region, **4**: 19; loss by state, 44–48. *See also* Education

School of Christian Literature, **4**: 439

Schoolcraft, H. R., **1**: 115n, 192, 455; on Cass expedition, 102, 104, 105; arbiter between Sioux and Chippewa, 112; expeditions, 112–117, 175; sketch, 112n; Indian agent, 112n, 146; at Lake Itasca, 114, 124

SCHOOLCRAFT, H. R., *Indian Tribes*, **1**: 81n; *Summary Narrative*, 90n; *Narrative Journal*, 102n; *Personal Memoirs*, 112n; *Narrative of an Expedition*, 112n; *Northwestern Indians*, 117n; "History and Physical Geography of Minnesota," 455n

Schoolcraft Island, **1**: 124

Schoolcraft Manuscripts, **1**: 68n

Schoolcraft River, **1**: 114, 124

Schools, *see* Education

Schurz, Carl, **2**: 60

Schuyler, Robert, **1**: 330n

SCHWANDT-SCHMIDT, MARY, "Story of Mary Schwandt," **2**: 116n

Schwartz, H. H., **4**: 246, 247n

Scotch, intermarry with Chippewa, **4**: 294

Scotch Lake, **2**: 288

Scott, Capt. Martin, **1**: 453, 454

Scott, Col. T. A., **3**: 367, 368

Scott, Maj. Gen. Winfield, **1**: 140, 509

Scott County, **3**: 103; salt mining enterprise, **4**: 480

Scotti, François, **4**: 482n

Scrip, Sioux half-breed: issue, **1**: 324, 382, fraudulent operations connected with, 483–486, increase in value, **4**: 4, used for location of lands, 5n; Chippewa half-breed: issue, **1**: 470, fraudulent operations connected with, 471–475, **4**: 395, motives of operators, **1**: 472, investigation of operations, 475, 477, legitimate claims recognized, 476–478; half-breed, iron lands acquired with, **4**: 13n, 14; public land, 78, 79, 79n, 82

Seal of Minnesota Territory, suggested, **1**: 254; description and significance, 267, 461, 462; first seal, 459; designs and mottoes suggested, 460–462; adopted, 461; modified and adopted as state seal, **2**: 26, 359–361; recommendations of Republican constitutional convention, 357; constitutional provision for, 358; legislative bill for, 358

Searle, Judge D. B., **3**: 504

Searles, J. N., **2**: 314

SEARLES, J. N., " First Minnesota," **2**: 86n

Secession, resolution of legislature, **2**: 72

Secombe, D. A., **3**: 347n, 435, 439, **4**: 98

Second Battery of Minnesota Light Artillery, **2**: 99, 307. *See also* Artillery

Second Co. of Minnesota Sharpshooters, **2**: 86, 100

Second Minnesota Infantry, **3**: 316

Second Regiment Minnesota Veteran Volunteer Infantry, **2**: 225; organized, 89–91; frontier service, 91; Civil War service: summarized, 91, at Missionary Ridge, 91, 319, 321, on Sherman's march, 91, 302, defense of Snodgrass Ridge, 318; memorials to, 316, 319n, 321, 327n; casualties, 318, 321; number in Civil and Indian wars, 339

Second Regiment of Cavalry, Minnesota Volunteers, service against Indians, **2**: 296, 299, 346, 350, 351n; organized, 339; number in Indian wars, 339; officers form military commission, 445

Second Regiment of U. S. Sharpshooters, **2**: 99, 100

Second U. S. Volunteer Engineers, **3**: 237

Sedition, during World War, **3**: 553; activities of commission of public safety, 565–569, 570; trials, 571– 574. *See also* Germans; New Ulm; Nonpartisan League

Seeger, William, **3**: 76, 357–362

Seignelay, marquis de, **1**: 23, 36

Selective Service Act, **3**: 315

Selkirk, Earl of, **1**: 214, 215. *See also* Selkirk colony

Selkirk colony, **1**: 108, 129n, 288n; founded, 213; purpose, 213; struggle with Northwest Co., 213; dispersion of settlers, 214, 215, 216, 220

"Selkirk," steamboat, **3**: 452

Semple, Robert, **1**: 214

Senatorial elections, *see* Elections

Senators, state: apportioned, **2**: 1; U. S.: manner of election prescribed, 6, election, *see* Elections

Settlement, after Civil War, **3**: 1, 2; extent in *1870*, 59; extends to prairie lands, 62, 139, 140; affected by railroads, 62, 67. *See also* Population; Public lands

Setzer, H. N., **1**: 390

Seven Years' War, **1**: 51, 74

Seventh Regiment Minnesota Volunteer Infantry, **2**: 192n, 193, 202, 336, 343, **3**: 172; organized, **2**: 103, 104; commanders, 106, 305, 336, 337; on Sibley expedition of *1862*, 154, 174, 177, 178, 181; retained for protection against Sioux, 243; on Sibley expedition of *1863*, 267n, 269, 270, 271, 272, 273; pursues Indian marauders, 281; Civil War service: summarized, 305, 306, in battle of Nashville, 307, 326; number in Civil and Indian wars, 339

Severance, Judge M. J., **2**: 222

Severance tax, **3**: 308, **4**: 55

Sewall, J. S., **3**: 424

Seward, William, **2**: 13, **3**: 13; delivers political address in St. Paul, **2**: 66; supported for presidency by Minnesota Republicans, 67

SEYMOUR, E. S., *Minnesota*, **1**: 251n

Shagoba, Chippewa Indian, **1**: 326

Shakopee, Sioux chief, *see* Little Six

Shakopee, town, **2**: 126, 148

SHAMBAUGH, B. F., *Constitutions of Iowa*, **1**: 488n; ed., *Debates of the Iowa Constitutional Conventions*, 488n

Shandrew, Col. J. C., **3**: 234

SHARP, ABBIE G., *Spirit Lake Massacre*, **2**: 401n

Sharpshooters, **2**: 339. *See also* First Co. of Minnesota Sharpshooters; Second Co. of Minnesota Sharpshooters

SHEA, J. G., *Discovery and Exploration*, **1**: 21n; *Early Voyages*, 35n

Sheehan, Col. T. J., **2**: 383, 388; at Fort Ridgely: reënforces garrison, 128, 230, directs defense of fort, 129, 130n, 431, relieved by Col. McPhail, 384; sent from Birch Coulee for reënforcements, 154; aids in quieting Indians at Yellow Medicine, 229, 230, 231n, 431; testifies in Sisseton and Wahpeton claim case, 431; Indian agent at

White Earth, **4**: 203, 208, 213; at Leech Lake Indian uprising, 315, 317, 317n

Shelby Township, Blue Earth County, Indian attack, **2**: 345

Sheldon, Rev. C. B., **1**: 402

Shepard, D. C., **3**: 424

Shepley, J. C., **2**: 34, 35

Sherburne, Moses, territorial judge, **1**: 378; in constitutional convention, 403, 415, 417, 419, **4**: 99n

Sherburne County, **3**: 36, 103

Sherman, John, **2**: 16, 18, 23

Sherman, Maj. T. W., **2**: 409, 410, 411

Sherman, Gen. W. T., **2**: 319, 320, 322, 323; march to the sea: 322, Minnesota troops participating, 91, 302, 307; on treaty commission, 439

Sherman bill, **3**: 243

Shetek, Lake, **2**: 281, 349; Sioux murders, 123; expedition sent to, 201

Shevlin, T. H., **4**: 238n, 240n; entertains excursion party, 256; interest in sale of Chippewa pine, 274, 275

Shevlin-Carpenter and Co., **4**: 238n

Shiegley, A. P., **2**: 402

Shields, Gen. James, **1**: 483, **3**: 16; elected U. S. senator, **2**: 6, 8; sketch, 7, 8; urges admission of Minnesota, 12; seated, 17; expiration of term, 59

Shifting Wind, Sioux Indian, **2**: 414

Shillock, Daniel, **2**: 369

Shiloh, battle, **2**: 98, 307

Shippee, L. B., "Jane Grey Swisshelm," **2**: 34n

Shipstead, Senator Henrik, elected, **3**: 299, 550; candidate for governor, 320, 549; eulogizes Nelson, 498; sketch, 548, 549n

Shiras, Judge George, Jr., **3**: 473, 489n

Shortridge, W. P., " Life of Sibley," **1**: 163n; " Sibley and the Minnesota Frontier," 163n

Shortt, Adam, ed., *Constitutional History of Canada*, **1**: 51n

Shutter, M. D., ed., *Progressive Men of Minnesota*, **3**: 474n

Sibley, H. H., **1**: 119, 119n, 162, 235, 269n, 301, 423, 424, 440, 441, 442, 443, **2**: 7, 53, 78n, 169, 387, 428, 440, **3**: 348, 350, 409, **4**: 71,

480; friendship with Nicollet, **1**: 125, 126; cited, 158, 274, 291, 304, 323, 459; sketch, 161; employee and partner in American Fur Co., 161, 162, 240, 283n, 371; character, 161, 242, 244, 365; elder of first Minnesota church, 192; at land sale, 225; relations with Rice, 240, 260, 313–318, 341, 347, 369–372, 376; delegate to Congress from rump of Wisconsin Territory, 241–246, 365–367, **4**: 331; friendship with Ramsey, **1**: 249, 276n; territorial delegate, 253, 271, 275, 291, 313, 318, 323, 365–367, 369, 425, 427, **4**: 135; commissioner on territorial seal, **1**: 267, 459–462; assists in execution of treaty, 293, 297, 303; interest in railroads, 329, 341, 343, 372; in territorial legislature, 341, 343, 347, 372, 381; attitude toward Indians, 366; aspires to governorship, 377; in constitutional convention, 400, 403, 404, 412, 416, 419, **4**: 99n, 332n; connection with Ramsey investigation, **1**: 464–468; position on Wisconsin boundary question, 494; elected governor, **2**: 3, 7, 23; messages, 23, 26, 52, 59, 62, 63, **4**: 138, 139, 141; adopts territorial seal as state seal, **2**: 26, 359; calls out militia to suppress Wright County insurrection, 29; vetoes school bills, 33, **4**: 140, 183; protests against appropriation bill of *1858*, **2**: 33; attitude toward Five Million Loan, 48; fails to secure priority of lien for state railroad bonds, 49–51; in political campaign of *1860*, 66; appeals for volunteers, 102n; promotes trial and punishment of Sioux, 145, 191, 192, 193, 194, 195, 285n, **4**: 475; receives colonel's commission and command of Indian expedition, *1862*, **2**: 147; appointed brigadier general of volunteers, 186; appointed brevet major general of volunteers, 186n; commands Military District of Minnesota, 189, 202, 243, 336; attitude toward punishment of convicted Sioux, 204, 210n; fears attacks on Sioux prisoners, 205; arranges frontier defense, 243, 282; receives orders respecting Sioux convicts, 249; submits plan for removal of Sioux, 256; Indian settlement on property, 263; aids in listing loyal Sioux, 264; fears general Indian uprising in *1863*, 266; opposed to organization of Hatch's Battalion, 291; plans operations against Sioux, *1864*, 294, 295; replies to criticism of expedition of *1863*, 350; receives payment of Indian debt, 399n; holds upper bands guilty of hostilities, 434; appoints commission to try Little Six and Medicine Bottle, 445; approves action of commission, 448; eulogizes Norton, **3**: 7n; friendship for J. R. Brown, 76, 349; aids victims of grasshopper plague, 97, 99; defeated for Congress, 118; honored at banquet, 162; urges redemption of state railroad bonds, 163, 426; receives degree from Princeton University, 163; works for conservation of school fund, 268; criticizes multiplication of cities, 516; president of mining company, **4**: 5; university regent, 72n, 104, 106; obtains land grant for university, 98; on Chippewa commission, 210; death, **3**: 163; proposed memorial to, 268n

Sibley, H. H., "Reminiscences," **1**: 90; "Memoir of Nicollet," 122n; "Memoir of Faribault," 144n; "Sketches of Indian Warfare," 157n; "Memoir of Dousman," 163n; "Reminiscences of the Early Days of Minnesota," 183n; "American House Letter," 369n

Sibley County, **3**: 242, **4**: 83n; ravaged by grasshoppers, **3**: 98, 101, 102

Sibley Day Book, **1**: 126n

Sibley Diary, **2**: 267n

Sibley expedition of *1862*, **2**: 105, **3**: 18, 354; organized, **2**: 147–150; inadequacy of troops and supplies, 149, 171, 175; arrival of detachment at Fort Ridgely, 150, 171, 383, 386; detachment buries dead, 150; battle of Birch Coulee: 152–156, 158, 176, 386–391, casualties, 392, 393n; Indian expedition down Minnesota River, 157; attempted negotiations with Little Crow, 171, 174, 176; Sioux chiefs make overtures to Sibley, 172; training of troops at Fort Ridgely, 173; arrival of reënforcements, 174; trials encountered by Sibley, 174–176; reduction of forces, 175; criticism of, 176; march to Yellow Medicine, 177; battle of Wood Lake, 178–182, 265; dispersal of Indians, 182; release of captives, 183–185, 190, 430, 433; appeals to Washington, 186; results of expedition, 186, 265; Pope's plans for defense, 187; Indian war declared ended, 188; expedition to Lake Shetek, 201; cost, 244; plundering by whites, 248, 249n; promise of immunity to friendly Sioux, 265, 427

Sibley expedition of *1863*, **2**: 536, **3**: 18, 354; organized, **2**: 266; concentration of troops and supplies, 266; departure from Camp Pope, 267; march to Big Mound, 267–269; battle of Big Mound, 270–272, 275, 275n, 429, 434; battle of Dead Buffalo Lake, 273; battle of Stony Lake, 273, 274n; nature of battles, 274; number of Indians engaged, 274; arrival at Missouri River, 274; pursuit of Indians, 274–276; casualties of whites, 275, 275n; Indian losses of life and property, 275, 275n, 429; return march, 276–278; capture of Wowinapa, 284; results, 294; criticism of, 350

Sibley Letter Books, **1**: 164n

Sickles, Gen. D. E., **2**: 308, 309

Silver, money: demonetized, **3**: 126, 220, 243, demand for remonetization, 126, 198, 199, 201, 243, remonetization, 126–128, Bland-Allison Act, 127, 243, free coinage, 219, 220, Sherman bill, 243; metal, **4**: 2, 6, 7

Silver Republicans, in elections: *1896*, **3**: 220, *1898*, 241, 245, *1901*, 264. *See also* Republicans

Simcoe, Lake, **4**: 1

Sioux claims commission, *1863*, provided for, **2**: 247; report, 247, 366; takes testimony on Acton murders, 417n

Sioux Indians, **1**: 6, 10, 17, 18, 23, 28, 39, 41, 43, 53, 57n, 68, 100n, 107, 141, 487, **3**: 22, 479, **4**: 190, 193, 231n, 322; habitat, **1**: 29,

79, 80, 81, 84, 88, 150, 182, 353, 437, **4**: 296; Carver among, **1**: 56; name, 79n; culture, 80; land cessions: *1805*, 92–94; *1820*, 144, *1837*, 160, **2**: 216, *1841*, **1**: 266n, *1851*, 281, 287, **2**: 216, 217, 393, 424, **4**: 225, *1858*, **2**: 218, 227, 394–396, **4**: 225, *1867*, **2**: 419, *1873*, 420; councils with, **1**: 92, 99, 144, 257, 258, 278–281, 285–287, 289, 296, 446; Pike among, 92–94, 98; Catlin among, 120; divisions and tribes, 182; language: 188, 447, alphabet devised, 188, 447, spelling book, 193, translations of Scriptures, 194, 200, grammar, 195, dictionaries, 195, 198, 203, 452n, *Grammar and Dictionary of the Dakota Language*, 203, 448–452, Ravoux's *Path to the House of God*, 207, *Dakota Friend*, 209; decline, 208; reservations: lower bands, 211, 284, 286, 291, 353, 354n, 503; upper bands, 281, 291, 353, 354n, 503; outbreak of *1862*, *see* Sioux Outbreak; demands for punishment of, **2**: 190, 202–204, 209; trials by military commission, 191–193, 195–200; arrests at Camp Release and Yellow Medicine, 194, 196n; uncondemned Indians encamp at Fort Snelling, 200, 203, 249, 251, 252–255, 263; danger of mob attacks on convicts, 204; interest of Bishop Whipple, 206–208, **4**: 474; sale of liquor to, **2**: 207, 222, 228, 395, 415; execution of convicts, 209, 210, 249, 254, 336, 351n, 437, **4**: 475; imprisonment of convicts, **2**: 210, 249–252, 254, 255, 262, 265, 285n, 293, 301, 336, 437; claims of traders, 214, 216, 218, 395, 396, 399, 400; plans for civilization, 219–223, 227, 261; size of nation, 225; effects of concentration, 227; demands for exile, 255; plans for removing, 256–258; abrogation of treaties, 258, 300; removal of lower bands to Crow Creek reservation, 258–261, 263, 437, 439; pardon of convicts, 262; settlements at Mendota, Faribault, Morton, 263; loyal Indians rewarded and commemorated, 264, 390; distribution after Indian war of *1862*, 265, 418; frontier attacks,

1863, 281, 282, 288, *see also* Sibley expedition of *1863*, Sully expedition of *1863*; bounties paid for killing of, 289; Hatch's Battalion organized for campaign against, 289–292; battle with Hatch's Battalion, 292; surrender to Hatch, 293; unvanquished by operations of *1863*, 294; protection of frontier against, 299; results of expeditions against, 300; agitation for restoration of annuities, 301, 418, 421–426, 435, 437; attacks and depredations, *1864*, 345, *see also* Sully expedition of *1864*; depredations, *1865*, 346, *see also* Sully expedition of *1865*; alliance with Chippewa unproved, 380; treatment by government criticized by Little Crow, 395; partial restoration of annuities, 422, 435–437, 438; insurrection of *1857*, *see* Spirit Lake massacre; services of J. R. Brown, **3**: 354. *See also* Half-breeds; Indian treaties; Indians; individual chiefs; Mdewakanton Indians; Missions; Redwood agency; Santee Indians; Sibley expeditions of *1862* and *1863*; Sioux claims commission; Sioux Outbreak; Sioux reservations; Sisseton Indians; Sully expeditions of *1863*, *1864*, and *1865*; Wahpekute Indians; Wahpeton Indians; Yankton Indians; Yanktonai Indians; Yellow Medicine agency

Sioux Outbreak, **1**: 92, 320, 325, **3**: 1, 22, 354, 409; causes: Ramsey blamed, **2**: 106, stated by contemporaries, 207, 212, 213n, Indian policy of government, 213–216, **4**: 474, treaty of *1851*, **2**: 216–218, treaty of *1858*, 218, 418, Indians' ignorance of power of U. S., 223–226, 234, failure of government to punish Spirit Lake murderers, 225, 231, 415, effects of concentration, 227, character of reservations, 227, demoralization caused by whiskey, 228, nonpayment of annuities, 228–239, injustice in payments of *1861*, 231, attributed to rebel agents, 234, investigation requested, 256; attacks on lower agency, 109, 112–114; attacks in Renville County, 110; battle of Redwood Ferry, 113; reënforcements requested, 114; arrival of reënforcements, 128; attacks on Milford, West Newton, Courtland, 115; escape of settlers: from upper agency, 116–118, 119, from Hazelwood and Yellow Medicine missions, 118–120; attack on Sacred Heart settlers, 120; murder at Lac qui Parle, 121; attacks in Brown County, 121; escape of J. R. Brown's household, 121; attacks in Kandiyohi, Murray, and Jackson counties, 123; attacks at and near Big Stone Lake, 123, 434; attack on Breckenridge, 124; exodus of settlers to river towns, 124, 161; Indian methods of warfare, 125; arrival of reënforcements at Fort Ridgely, 128; attack on Fort Ridgely: 129–132, results, 132, casualties, 132; first battle of New Ulm, 133; St. Peter warned, 135; preparations for defense of New Ulm, 136, 137–139; second battle of New Ulm: 132n, 139–144, 432, monument commemorating, 142n; evacuation of New Ulm, 144; retreat of Indians, 156; battle of Acton, 158–160, 174; Forest City and Hutchinson plundered, 162, 163; attacks on Fort Abercrombie, 165–168, 428, 430, 431, 434; volunteer militia organized, 168–170, 188; attacks in Blue Earth County, 170; Acton murders, 239, 283, 392, 415–417, 432; relief of victims, 244, see also Sioux claims commission; number killed and wounded: whites, 391–393, Indians, 393, 393n; stories of atrocities, 393. See also Chippewa Indians; Fortifications; Indians; Sibley expeditions of 1862 and 1863; Sioux claims commission; Sioux Indians; Sisseton and Wahpeton claim case; Spirit Lake massacre; Sully expeditions of 1863, 1864, and 1865; Winnebago Indians

Sioux reservations, lower bands, on Minnesota River, 2: 217, 227, 393, 394, 4: 193, 474; on Crow Creek: removal of Indians to, 2: 259, 439, Moscow Expedition to, 260, 261n, 440, agency, 280; on Niobrara River, 261, 262, 431; upper bands, on Minnesota River, 217, 227, 393, 394, 4: 192; Sisseton reservation,

2: 419, 422; on Devil's Lake, 419, 422, 428; in western South Dakota, 439

Sioux-Chippewa warfare, 1: 42, 191, 196, 318; arbiters, 39, 81, 98, 104, 112; campaigns, 81–84, 92, 148–158, 179, 257–259

Sisseton and Wahpeton Bands of Dakota or Sioux Indians, 2: 420n

Sisseton and Wahpeton Bands of Sioux Indians, 2: 423n

Sisseton and Wahpeton Bands of Sioux or Dakota Indians, 2: 423n

Sisseton and Wahpeton claim case, 2: 426–435

Sisseton and Wahpeton Claim Case Record, 2: 11n, 426n

Sisseton and Wahpeton Indians, 2: 423n

Sisseton Indians, 1: 183, 201, 2: 228, 230, 408, 412n; attitude during Sioux hostilities: 119, 122, 123n, 131, 184, 201, 424, investigated by U. S. court of claims, 426–435; casualties at battle of Wood Lake, 182n; Sibley's attempt to negotiate with, 265, 427; defeated by Sibley, 274n; disperse after battle of Wood Lake, 418, 427; agency, 426, 427; partial restoration of annuities, 435–437. See also Indian treaties; Missions; Sibley expedition of 1862; Sioux Indians; Sioux Outbreak; Sioux reservations; Yellow Medicine agency

Sisters of Saint Francis, see Congregation of our Lady of Lourdes

Sixth Minnesota Infantry Association, 2: 388

Sixth Minnesota Infantry Regiment, 2: 192n; organization, 100, 102, 102n; on Sibley expedition of 1862: 148, 149, 150, 177, reënforces detachment at Birch Coulee, 153, 154, 387, at battle of Wood Lake, 178, 181; captures Sioux camp, 193; garrisons frontier posts, 243; on Sibley expedition of 1863: 267n, 273, 274, 275n, at battle of Big Mound, 269, 272; Civil War service, 303, 304; number in Civil and Indian wars, 339; on Moscow Expedition, 440

Sixty-seventh Field Artillery Brigade, 3: 531

Skaro, A. K., 2: 28n
Sketch of Andrews, 4: 386n
Skinner, J. D., 4: 480
Skunk Lake, South Dakota, 2: 413
SLAFTER, E. F., " Champlain," 1: 4n;
" Memoir of Champlain," 15n
Slate deposits, 4: 3
" Slaughterhouse Cases," 3: 46
Slavery, negro, 1: 143n, 204; exten-
sion: political issue, 365, 373–375,
394, 396, 488, 2: 68; deprecated
by legislature, 5; abolished, 342, 3:
3. *See also* Civil War; Negroes
Sleepy Eye, Sioux chief, 1: 279, 200,
2: 123n
Sloane, R. T., 3: 523
Slocum, Isaac, 2: 404, 405, 406n
SMALLEY, E. V., ed., *Republican Par-
ty,* 1: 365n; *Republican Manual,*
3: 76n; *Northern Pacific Railroad,*
446n
Smelting plants, 4: 27
Smith, Judge A. C., 2: 158, 417n
SMITH, A. C., *Meeker County,* 2: 159n
Smith, Gen. A. J., 2: 325, 327n
Smith, C. A., and Co., 3: 207n
Smith, C. B., 2: 258, 399
Smith, Col. C. F., 2: 164
Smith, C. K., 1: 252n, 257
Smith, D. A., sketch, 3: 451, 452n;
friendship with Hill, 452; acquires
part ownership in St. Paul and Pa-
cific Railroad Co., 453–462, 463,
467
Smith, Lieut. E. K., 1: 139n, 218,
221
Smith, E. P., 4: 196
Smith, G. A., 3: 69, 71n
Smith, Gerritt, 1: 334
Smith, Hoke, 4: 236, 237n, 239
Smith, J. D., 2: 314, 3: 507n
Smith, James, Jr., 2: 102n, 3: 411n
Smith, L. A., 3: 557, 558n
Smith, L. D., 2: 28n
Smith, Robert, 1: 508, 3: 30;
leases property at Falls of St. An-
thony, 1: 423, 426, 428
Smith, Rev. S. G., 3: 172
Smith, Capt. T. D., 2: 166
Smith, T. M., 1: 385
SMITH, W. R., *Wisconsin,* 1: 63n
Smith, Warren, 3: 101n
Smith Map, 1: 139n
SMITH-GORDON, LIONEL, " Co-operation
in the New World," 4: 405n

Smith-Hughes Act, 4: 187
Snake Indians, 1: 49
Snana (Mrs. Maggie Brass), 2: 391,
432, 433
Snelling, Mrs. Abigail, 1: 232
Snelling, Col. Josiah, commandant at
Fort Snelling, 138, 145; sketch,
138; punishes Sioux murderers,
148
Snelling, W. J., 1: 232
SNELLING, W. J., " Running the
Gantlet," 1: 147n; *Tales of the
Northwest,* 214n
Snodgrass Ridge, 2: 316, 317, 318
Snyder, F. B., 4: 119n, 133, 134
Snyder, Capt. S. P., 2: 384
Social conditions, *1860–65,* 2: 344.
See also Economic conditions; Edu-
cation; Population
Social Democrats, 3: 257
Socialist-Labor party, 3: 257
Socialists, rise of American school, 3:
539; in elections, 540, 546n; activi-
ties in North Dakota, 542; coöp-
erate with Nonpartisan League,
553, 554n
Soldiers' Home, Minneapolis, 3: 179,
262
" Soo " Railroad, *see* Minneapolis, St.
Paul, and Sault Ste. Marie Rail-
road
Soudan, 4: 16, 22n
Sounding Moccasin, Sioux chief, 1:
282n
South Bend, 2: 138, 205; headquarters of Flandrau, 169; Sioux camp,
200; garrisoned, 243
South St. Paul, 1: 250
South Vermilion River, 4: 5
Southern Minnesota Railroad Co.,
property sold to state, 2: 328n; attempts to obtain public lands, 3:
36; extension, 61; foreclosure of
mortgage on property, 419n; property restored, 420; sued, 429
Southwest Co., 1: 132
Spanish, 1: 16; acquire Louisiana,
52, 74, 495; territorial cessions, 74,
77
Spanish-American War, 3: 163, 256;
declaration of war and call for
troops, 231, 233, 243; Minnesota
troops in, 231–237, 240, 240n; casualties, 233, 236; treaty of peace,
237, 256

Spencer, George, **2**: 111n
Spencer, J. C., **1**: 443
Spencer Brook, **3**: 216
Spenner, John, **2**: 363
Spirit Lake massacre, **1**: 325; depredations and murders, **2**: 223, 400–404; pursuit of murderers, 223, 404–406, 408; rescue of captives, 406–408; responsibility for capture of Inkpaduta's band placed upon Sioux tribes, 223, 410, 412–414; cause of Sioux Outbreak, 225, 231, 415
Spooner, **4**: 391
Spring Wells, treaty, *1815*, **1**: 103n
Springer, W. M., **3**: 394–398
Springfield, Indian massacre, **2**: 223, 402, 404, 405
Squatters, at Fort Snelling: **1**: 216, 217, evicted from military reservation, 218, 220–223, 423, preëmption claims, 254, 424, 425, 426, 427, 429, 430–432; in "Suland," 352, 354–356
Stage transportation, **2**: 64, **3**: 2, 61. *See also* Roads; Transportation
Stambaugh, S. C., **1**: 438, 439, 441, 442, 443
STANCHFIELD, DANIEL, "Pioneer Lumbering on the Upper Mississippi," **1**: 228n
Standing Buffalo, Sioux chief, **2**: 122, 265, 269, 270, 275n, 410n, 434; council with, 230; attitude during Sioux hostilities, 427, 428, 429, 431, 433
Staples, C. F., **3**: 513n
Staples, Franklin, **4**: 418n
Starkey, Capt. James, **1**: 326
State Agricultural Society, **4**: 80, 83, 97
State Atlas, **3**: 90
State prison, *see* Prison
State Public School, Owatonna, **3**: 153, **4**: 412
State Reformatory, St. Cloud, **3**: 170, **4**: 412
Statistics, commissioner of: provided for, **3**: 18, 19, 20; reports, 19, 20, 59, 73, 139
Steamboat transportation, **1**: 225, 257, 359, 361, **3**: 2, 61, 452, 479, **4**: 25. *See also* Transportation
Stearns, Judge O. P., **3**: 73
Stearns County, **3**: 147n, **4**: 7, 324; exodus of settlers during Sioux

Outbreak, **2**: 161; ravaged by grasshoppers, **3**: 102; railroad building, 444; coöperation between parochial and public schools, **4**: 177
Steel Corporation Hearings, **4**: 30n
Steel production, **4**: 23, 24, 27, 39, 43
Steele, Franklin, **1**: 298, 465, 466, **2**: 79; preëmption claim at Falls of St. Anthony, **1**: 228, 423, 428, 452–454, **3**: 30; railroad incorporator, **1**: 329; purchase of Fort Snelling Reservation, 432–434, 504–515; Pike's Island patented to, 446n; aspires to senatorship, **2**: 7, 8; urges ratification of Five Million Loan amendment, 48; loses Nicollet Island, **3**: 335
Steele County, ravaged by grasshoppers, **3**: 103; liquor sales, 563
Steele Papers, **1**: xi
Steenerson, Halvor, **4**: 266, 267n, 276, 286, 304
Steenerson Act, **4**: 273, 278n; provision for allotments to Indians, 266; land allotted, 267–272
Stephen, George, **3**: 469; obtains part control of St. Paul and Pacific Railroad Co., 455–462, 463
Stephens, W. R., **3**: 319
Stevens, E. A., **2**: 82n
STEVENS, H. F., ed., *Bench and Bar of Minnesota*, **1**: 387n
Stevens, J. H., **1**: 428, 432, 453, **2**: 28n, 61; pioneer of Minneapolis and Glencoe, 159n; in Sioux Outbreak, 159n, **4**: 81; sketch, 79, 84; interest in agricultural college at Glencoe, 80, 81n, 84; in Mexican War, 81; statue, 85n
STEVENS, J. H., *Personal Recollections*, **1**: 185n
Stevens, Capt. J. T., **3**: 337, 342
Stevens, Rev. Jedediah, missionary, **1**: 155, 174n, 189; character, 193; establishes Lake Harriet mission, 193; alleged author of "Sioux Spelling Book," 193; resigns from Lake Harriet mission, 195
Stevens, Thaddeus, **3**: 24, 25
STEVENS, W. E., "Organization of the British Fur Trade," **1**: 67n; "Fur Trading Companies in the Northwest," 87n
Stevens County, **3**: 102, 147n, 387
Stevens Papers, **1**: xi

Stevens Seminary, 4: 85
Stewart, Dr. J. H., 2: 28n, 3: 390n
Stewart, Joshua, 2: 404
Stickney, A. B., 3: 33n
STICKNEY, A. B., *Railway Problem*, 3: 33n
STICKNEY, G. P., *Nicholas Perrot*, 1: 36n
Stillwater, 1: 229, 234, 239, 2: 4, 3: 60, 150, 4: 190; post office, 1: 225; lumber manufacturing, 227, 356; convention, 237; population, *1849*, 251, 352, *1860*, 2: 64n; Ramsey's prophecy concerning, 1: 256; prison, 260; incorporation, 379; designated railway terminus, 2: 42; sends force against Chippewa, 375; Australian ballot adopted, 3: 189; lumbering town, 216, 501n; co-operation between parochial and public schools, 4: 176–179; election law applicable to, 347n
Stimpson, D. H., 3: 402, 407
Stock-raising, 3: 92, 157
Stockwell, S. A., 4: 134
Stoddard, Capt. Amos, 1: 78
Stone, G. C., 4: 8, 11, 13, 15
STONE, J. A., *Flouring Mills of Minneapolis*, 3: 136n
Stone River, battle, 2: 307
Stony Brook, 4: 20
Stony Lake, battle, 2: 273, 274n
Strait, H. B., 3: 166, 410
STRAND, A. E., ed., *Swedish-Americans of Minnesota*, 3: 277n
Strikes, forbidden, 3: 561
Striped Wing Feather, Sioux Indian, 2: 133
STRONG, M. M., *Territory of Wisconsin*, 1: 233n
Strong Earth, Chippewa Indian, 1: 149n
Strout, Capt. Richard, 2: 159, 160, 162, 163, 174
Stuart, C. E., 2: 43n
Stuart, Robert, 1: 103, 162, 172, 443
Stuntz, G. R., 4: 11
Sturgis, W. J., 2: 115, 147
STURTEVANT, E. A., ed., *Mill Explosion at Minneapolis*, 3: 133n
Sudley Springs, 2: 85
Suffrage, provisions governing, 2: 3, 356; discussed in Congress, 15; constitutional amendments, 3: 7, 224, 227, 307; on educational questions, 120, 227, 307n, 520; denied

aliens, 224; history, 4: 330, 338. *See also* Woman suffrage
Sugar Point, 4: 260; battle, 312–323
"Suland," desire for acquisition, 1: 254, 266–270; area, 287; acquisition, *see* Indian treaties, *1851*
Sully, Gen. Alfred, 2: 411
Sully expedition of *1863*, fails to join Sibley expedition, 2: 276, 278, 279; battle of White Stone Hill, 279; version of S. J. Brown, 280; casualties, 280n; results, 294
Sully expedition of *1864*, planned, 2: 295; organization, 296; westward marches, 296, 298; battle with Sioux, 297; return march, 299; results, 345; criticized, 350
Sully expedition of *1865*, 2: 346
Sulpicians, 1: 25, 26n
Summit mill, destroyed, 3: 338
Sumner, Maj. Gen. E. V., 1: 129n
Sumner, Gen. S. S., 3: 524
Sundberg, J. E. G., 4: 134
Sunrise, 2: 375
Superior, 4: 16, 20, 25
Superior, Lake, 1: 3, 4, 6n, 39, 3: 26, 162, 4: 42, 190; discovery, 1: 6, 6n; explorers, 7, 9, 16, 18, 23, 58, 104, 111n, 114, 4: 1; French proclamation of sovereignty over, 1: 17; trade, 44; minerals sought for, 4: 1–3; iron region, 42n, 43, 57; triangle ceded by Indians, 191; Chippewa of, *see* Chippewa of Lake Superior. *See also* Iron mining
Superior National Forest, 4: 400
Supreme Court of Minnesota, upholds constitutionality of act regulating railroads, 3: 43; justices, 7n, 88, 272, 289n, 404, 405n, 409, 414, 435, 464; term of clerk, 145; quarters in new Capitol, 269; decision relating to ratification of tax amendment of *1906*, 289n; authorized to revise general laws, 291; decision in suit against Saint Anthony Falls Water Power Co., 346n; delegated to pass on validity of railroad bonds, 434; upholds constitutionality of law applying to Minneapolis, 518n; tries cases involving rights of home-rule cities, 520; tries Nonpartisan League leaders, 571; upholds constitutionality of act authorizing the leasing of ore lands, 4: 19n; decision relating to

ownership of land under public waters, 49; decision relating to power of regents to manage university, 132. *See also* Courts

Supreme Court of Minnesota Territory, **1**: 252n, 264, **3**: 300

Supreme Court of the U. S., tries railroad cases, **3**: 43, 46, 52, 55, 56, 113, 142, 179, 260, 430; passes on constitutionality of income-tax laws, 296, 297; passes on validity of ore tax, 308, **4**: 56; case of Farley *v.* Hill, **3**: 454n, 465, 473; congressional review of decisions advocated, 552; decisions in proceedings against Nonpartisan leaders, 571, 574; decisions relating to Indian affairs, **4**: 288, 289, 300n, 308

Surveys, *see* Public lands

Swamp lands, fund augmented, **4**: 59; administration, 146, 146n. *See also* Public lands

Swan, Lieut. J. H., **2**: 201

Swan Lake, party from, at first battle of New Ulm, **2**: 364, 366, 367, 369, given credit for saving New Ulm, 370, 371, 373

Swan River, **3**: 501n, **4**: 33, 191

Swedes, **4**: 16. *See also* Scandinavians

Sweeny, R. O., **2**: 357

SWEET, MRS. J. E. DEC., "Narrative of Captivity," **2**: 125n

Sweet Corn, Sioux Indian, **2**: 430

Sweetser, Madison, **1**: 299, 304, **2**: 399n; locates at Traverse des Sioux, **1**: 288, 462; alliance with Sioux against traders, 290, 291, 293, 295, 301, 302, 462–464; charges against Ramsey, 465, 468, 469

Swenson, L. S., **3**: 490n

Swift, H. A., state senator, **2**: 75; lieutenant governor, 78n, 335; governor, 335, **3**: 293, 409, 422; sketch, **2**: 335; candidate for U. S. senator, 341; at first battle of New Ulm, 365, 366, 367, 371, 373; account of battle, 371; interest in mining development, **4**: 3

Swisshelm, Mrs. Jane G., sketch, **2**: 34; arouses opposition in St. Cloud, 34–36; criticizes Sibley, 176n; favors expulsion of Sioux, 247n

SWISSHELM, JANE G., *Half a Century*, **2**: 36n

Taché, Rt. Rev. A. A., **3**: 378n

Taft, President W. H., **3**: 282, 285n, 539, 540

Taliaferro, Maj. Lawrence, Indian agent, **1**: 119n, 125, 133, 140, 146, 151, 152, 155, 156, 159, 160, 175n, 191, 205, 210, 216, 220, 322, 437, 439, 446, 447; relations with Schoolcraft, 115n; sketch, 141; reasons for resignation, 142n; relations with Leavenworth, 143; slave owner, 143n; Indian policy, 145, 158; relations with Pond brothers, 184, 186; agricultural establishment, *see* Eatonville

TALIAFERRO, LAWRENCE, "Autobiography," **1**: 91n, 141n

Taliaferro Journal, **1**: xi, 94n, 141n

Taliaferro Letter Books, **1**: xi, 141n

Taliaferro Papers, **1**: xi, 141n

Talon, J. B., **1**: 15, 16, 17, 18, 19, 25

TANNER, G. C., *Diocese of Minnesota*, **1**: 182n

Taopi, Sioux chief, **2**: 183, **4**: 474; makes overtures to Sibley, **2**: 172, 173n, 427, 433; witness in trial of Little Six, 447

Tariff: political issue, *1870*, **3**: 17; demands of Farmers' Alliance, 188; Morrison bill, 195; Mills bill, 195; position of Republicans in *1894*, 198; Democrats approve Wilson tariff, 198; Prohibitionist views, 201; on pig iron, **4**: 57n

Tasagi, Sioux chief, **2**: 401, 401n

Tatemima, Sioux Indian, **2**: 210, 210n, 211n

TAUSSIG, F. W., *Silver Situation*, **3**: 127n

Tawney, J. A., **3**: 491, **4**: 250

Tax commission, Minnesota, **4**: 32, 40n, 54, 56, 57, 59

Taxation, territorial, **1**: 388; revision of laws relating to, **2**: 62, 63; in *1860*, 65; after Civil War, **3**: 1; income from, *1870*, 60; of incomes, 170, 199, 249, 296; demands for reform, 199, 246, 249, 257–259, 286, 543, **4**: 458; of inheritances, **3**: 199, 227, 249, 286; of mining properties, 199, 288–290, 307–309, 551, **4**: 51, 53–58; of railroads and other corporations, **3**: 218, 224, 225, 226, 226n, 249; code, 258; constitutional amendments relating to,

259, 286, 289, 289n; of mortgages, 286; for road and bridge fund, 309; of motor vehicles, 310; exemption of iron ore, **4**: 11; in mining communities, 51–53; for schools, 136, 139, 142–145, 147, 149, 151, 184; for forestry purposes proposed, 397
Taylor, J. W., **2**: 102n, 257, **3**: 377, 379
TAYLOR, J. W., *Railroad System of Minnesota*, **2**: 45n, 51n
Taylor, Oscar, **2**: 28n
Taylor's Falls, **2**: 375, **3**: 325
TEAKLE, THOMAS, *Spirit Lake Massacre*, **2**: 401n
Teigen, F. A., **3**: 573, 574
TEIGEN, F. A., *Nonpartisan League*, **3**: 554n
Teigen, L. O., **4**: 134
Telegraph, **2**: 65
Temperance, *see* Liquor; Prohibition
Tennessee Coal, Iron, and Railroad Co., **4**: 39n
Tenney, Lieut. D. D., **3**: 523
Tenth Regiment of Minnesota Volunteers, **2**: 168, **3**: 42, 373; organized, **2**: 103, 104; at battle of Acton, 159, 160; garrisons frontier, 243, 282; on Sibley expedition of *1863*, 267n, 269, 271, 272, 277; Civil War service: summarized, 305, 306, at battle of Nashville, 307, 326; number in Civil and Indian wars, 339; detachment pursues Inkpaduta, 404
Tenure of Office Act, **3**: 6
Teton Indians, **1**: 182, **2**: 274n, 295, 297, 429. *See also* Sioux Indians
Thatcher, Mrs. Elizabeth, **2**: 404
Theobald, Louis, **2**: 363
Thief River, **4**: 298
Thief River Falls, **4**: 298, 299, 305
Third Battery of Minnesota Light Artillery, on Sibley expedition of *1863*, **2**: 267n; on Sully expedition of *1864*, 296; on frontier duty, 300; mustered out, 300. *See also* Artillery
Third Minnesota Infantry, **3**: 316
Third Regiment of Minnesota Volunteer Infantry, **2**: 190, 192n, 243, 390; chaplaincy, 84n, **4**: 184; organized, **2**: 92; Civil War service: surrenders at Murfreesboro, 92–95, summary, 303, painting at Little Rock, 327n; detachment reënforces Fort Abercrombie, 167; detach-

ments on Sibley expedition of *1862*, 174, 177, 201; detachments at battle of Wood Lake, 178–182; number in Civil and Indian wars, 339
Third U. S. Cavalry, **3**: 235, 523
Third U. S. Infantry, **3**: 239, **4**: 314, 315, 316, 321
Thirteenth Regiment of Infantry, Minnesota Volunteers, in Spanish-American War, **3**: 231–233, 233n, 277
Thomas, Cyrus, **3**: 104
Thomas, Gen. G. H., at battle of Chickamauga, **2**: 316, 317, 318; at Missionary Ridge, 320; at Nashville, 323, 324, 325
Thomas, J. B., **2**: 402
Thomas, Col. Lorenzo, **1**: 509
Thomas, M. T., **2**: 106
Thomas, Theodore, **4**: 105, 106, 107
Thompson, Col. C. W., **2**: 68n; superintendent of Indian affairs, 257n, 258, 440, **3**: 22, 26, 356
Thompson, David, **1**: 111
Thompson, Horace, **3**: 378
Thompson, J. E., **3**: 420
Thompson, Lieut. J. L., **1**: 221, 423
Thompson, James, **1**: 204
THOMPSON, RUTH, "Sioux Treaties at Traverse des Sioux," **1**: 273n
Thompson Brothers, **2**: 244
Thompson Map, **1**: 139n
Thomson, **4**: 10
Thornton, Sir Edward, **3**: 382n
THORPE, F. N., ed., *Constitutions*, **1**: 69n
Three Mile Creek, **3**: 352
THWAITES, R. G., *France in America*, **1**: 1n; *Wisconsin*, 5n; ed., *Jesuit Relations*, 5n; *Story of Wisconsin*, 19n; *Historic Waterways*, 19n; *Father Marquette*, 20n; *How Clark Won the Northwest*, 43n; ed., *Early Western Travels*, 68n; ed., *Original Journals of the Lewis and Clark Expedition*, 89n; "Sketch of Martin," 234n; "Narrative of Martin," 234n; "Boundaries of Wisconsin," 490n
Tighe, Ambrose, **3**: 558n
Tilden, S. J., **3**: 115, 115n
Tilton and Co., **1**: 107, 161, 190
Timber, *see* Lumber industry; Pine Land Investigating Committee
Timber on the Chippewa Reservations, **4**: 239n, 245n

Tinker, A. M., 4: 317
Todd, Col. John, Jr., 1: 70
Todd County, 3: 102, 541, 4: 7
Toka, Sioux Indian, 1: 152, 153
Tomazin, Rev. Ignatius, 4: 197, 324
Tonnage tax, 3: 288–290, 307, 550, 4: 53, 55, 56
Tonti, Henri de, 1: 33, 34, 40
Torrance, Judge Ell, 4: 434n
Torrens title, 3: 263
Tourtellotte, Col. J. E., 2: 28n, 322, 3: 423
Tousley, O. V., 4: 109n
Tower, Charlemagne, 4: 9–16
Tower, Charlemagne, Jr., 4: 11, 15
Tower, town site platted, 4: 12
Town site speculation, 1: 361, 364, 383, 434
Towne, C. A., 3: 264, 491
Townley, A. C., 3: 550, 553; sketch, 541; organizes Nonpartisan League, 542–547; later career, 554–556; examined by commission of public safety, 566; tried, 571, 572, 573, 574
Townships, provisions for government, 2: 62, 63, 64n, 357
Tracy, land office, 1: 242
Trade, in Mississippi Valley, 1: 73, 77; of Red River Valley, 226; commodities: imported, 230, shipped down river, 362, increase during Civil War, 3: 1; number engaged in, 1870, 58; boards of, 161; in early St. Paul, 479. See also Economic conditions; Financial conditions; Flour-milling; Fur trade; Lumber industry; other industries; Transportation
Trade marks, 3: 161
Traders, 2: 257; responsibility for Sioux Outbreak, 172; claims against Indians, 214, 216, 218, 394, 395, 399, 400, 3: 23; opposed to civilization of Indians, 2: 223; at annuity payments, 232; intermarry with Chippewa, 4: 294. See also Coureurs de bois; Fur trade; Indians; individual traders and trading companies
"Traders' papers," 1: 282–284, 289, 295, 295n, 296, 297, 299, 301, 464, 467, 468
Trade-unions, see Labor
Transcript of Record, 4: 288
Transit Railroad Co., chartered, 2: 42; failure to sell lands, 43; foreclosure of mortgage on property, 328n, 3: 419n; property restored to, 420
Transportation, in 1860, 2: 64; inadequate facilities for, 3: 2; of products, 2, 41, 45, 48, 54, 61, 62, 70; cost, 45; number engaged in, 1870, 58; railroads displace other means, 61; motor vehicles: invented, 351–354, unsuccessful projects for use, 354–357; canoe route along international boundary, 387. See also Mississippi River; Railroads; Red River; Red River Valley; Roads; Steamboat transportation
Transportation-Routes to the Seaboard, 3: 75n
Traveling Hail, Sioux chief, elected to Little Crow's position, 2: 399; attitude during Sioux hostilities, 433
Traverse, Lake, 1: 107, 2: 267, 427; trading post, 1: 107, 351; Indian villages, 2: 265
Traverse des Sioux, 1: 294, 2: 366; explorers, 1: 107, 121, 129n; town, 107n; trading post, 120; mission, see Missions; telegraph terminal, 2: 65n; refuge from Sioux, 224; treaty, 1851, see Indian treaties
Treasurer of Minnesota, legislation relating to, 3: 77, 357, 361
Treat, Judge Samuel, 3: 464
Treaties, Indian, see Indian treaties; international, see individual treaties
Trial of Cox, 3: 131n
Trial of Page, 3: 129n
Trust companies, 3: 161, 253, 469, 4: 466
Trusts, suppression of, 3: 198, 199, 201, 538, 540
Tunnel Co., 3: 336, 346
Tupelo, battle, 2: 306
Turner, E. C., ed., Rice County, 2: 109n
Turner, T. A., Fifteenth Minnesota, 3: 234n
Turtle Lake, 1: 111n
Tuttle, W. G., 3: 366
Tweedy, J. H., 1: 239
Twelfth Regiment of Infantry, Minnesota Volunteers, 3: 231, 233, 243, 245
Twenty-fifth Wisconsin Regiment, 2: 170

Twenty-third Regiment of Minnesota Militia, **2**: 88; rejected, 89–91
Twin Cities, growth as metropolitan center, **3**: 253. *See also* Minneapolis; St. Paul
Two Harbors, **4**: 16, 25
Two Stars, Sioux Chief, **2**: 426
Tyler, Charles, **2**: 347
Tyler, Hugh, **1**: 276, 288, 465; character, 292n; assists in execution of treaty, 292, 296, 299, 302–304; charges against, 465, 466, 468

Underwood, J. M., **3**: 186n
Undine Region, **1**: 183, 268, 320, **2**: 400
Union Pacific Railroad Co., **3**: 188, 326, 327
U. S. Board of Indian Commissioners, **4**: 281
U. S. Chippewa Commission, appointed, **4**: 226; work, 227–235, 266, 297–299; duties, 231, 234, 262; changes in personnel, 236n; discontinued, 236n
U. S. circuit court of appeals, **4**: 288
U. S. court of claims, **4**: 328, 329
U. S. district courts, *see* Courts
U. S. Guaranty Co., **3**: 555
U. S. Interstate Commerce Commission, **4**: 75, 211
U. S. representatives, *see* Representatives
U. S. senators, *see* Senators
U. S. Steel Corporation, **4**: 25n, 27, 28, 30, 32, 36–41, 58; investigations, 38–40
U. S. Supreme Court, *see* Supreme Court of the U. S.
U. S. Tariff Commission, **4**: 57n
Universal Portland Cement Co., **4**: 28
University of Iowa, **4**: 64
University of Michigan, **4**: 61n, 64
University of Minnesota, **4**: 439, 443; incorporated, **1**: 261; land grants, 366, 393, **3**: 31, **4**: 73, 97–103; site, **3**: 9, **4**: 108; growth, **3**: 31, **4**: 108; pays debt with land grant, **3**: 31, 424; enlarged, 180; attendance in *1900*, 254; financial supervision of board of control, 262; Pillsbury's services, 266; fund depleted through timber frauds, 506, 515; commandant of cadets, 524; students in artillery unit, 529; investigation of disloyalty, 567; fund increased, **4**: 56, 56n, 59; organization: plan of committee on organization, 60–65, Minnesota plan, 62n, 65–72, 443; department of medicine: provided for, 60, 61, affiliated with Mayo Foundation, 114–119, established, 422; department of law, 60, 61; preparatory work, 60, 61, 71, 73, 84, 436, 440; college of agriculture and mechanic arts: provided for, 60, 61, 63, land grant, 77–79; military tactics, 62, 86, 103; coeducation, 64; enrollment statistics, 68, 73n, 77; powers of president, 68n; board of regents: early policy regarding control, 68n, policy regarding agricultural education, 86, 94, charged with diversion of land grant fund, 93, state board succeeds territorial board, 99n, status affected by court decision, 132, elected by legislature, *1929*, 134; academic department: 72, provided for, 60, 61, 63, administration, 73n, opened, 74, 443; chartered, 73, 436, 443; extricated from debt, 84; college of agriculture: established, 84, beginnings, 85–89, farmers' lecture course, 89–91, farmers' institutes, 91, movement to separate from university, 93, 95n, enrollment, 97, advanced degrees granted, 97, *see also* Agricultural College of Minnesota; buildings erected, 87, 91, 104–106, 108, 125, 436; agricultural experiment station: established, 89, work, 405, 406; school of agriculture, **3**: 180, **4**: 92–97; department of agriculture: plant evaluated, 96, 96n, tardy development, 96, campus, 97, enrollment, *1925*, 97; Coliseum, 103–108; proposal for removal, 109n; Eustis trust, 122–126; contest between regents and commission of administration and finance, 127–133; financial statistics: *1926–27*, 128n, *1927–28*, 130; staff insurance system adopted, 129; presidency, 134, 443; chancellorship, 134, 437, 438; faculty members serve as school inspectors, 185; dairy school, 404, 406; public health work, 421; reorganized: *1860*, 437, *1868*, 60–62, 73, 84, 86, 103; law school, 443–

447; rhetoric department, 460; conducts geological survey, 478–483

UNIVERSITY OF MINNESOTA, BOARD OF RECENTS, Minutes, 4: 61n; *Minutes*, 116n

UNIVERSITY OF MINNESOTA AGRICULTURAL EXPERIMENT STATION, *Agriculture in Minnesota*, 4: 405n

University of Wisconsin, 4: 64

Unveiling of the Statue of Pillsbury, 3: 267n

Upham, H. P., 3: 453, 468n

Upham, Warren, 4: 482

UPHAM, WARREN, "Groseilliers and Radisson," 1: 4n; "Life and Services of Pike," 100n; *Altitudes between Lake Superior and the Rocky Mountains*, 125n; *Minnesota Geographic Names*, 235n; *Minnesota Biographies*, 249n

Upper Red Cedar Lake, *see* Cass Lake

Upper Sioux agency, *see* Yellow Medicine agency

Usher, J. P., 2: 434, 435

Valentine, R. G., 4: 284, 295

VAN BARNEVELD, C. E., *Iron Mining in Minnesota*, 4: 26n

VAN BRUNT, WALTER, *Duluth and St. Louis County*, 4: 6n

VAN CLEVE, CHARLOTTE O., "*Three Score Years and Ten*," 1: 137n; "Reminiscence of Fort Snelling," 149

Van Cleve, Col. H. P., 2: 28n, 91

Vanderburgh, Judge C. E., 3: 409

Vander Horck, John, 2: 28n; commands garrison at Fort Abercrombie, 164, 167, 431; testifies in Sisseton and Wahpeton claim case, 431

Van Etten, Isaac, 1: 466, 2: 33n, 359

VAN HISE, C. R., *Lake Superior Region*, 4: 20n

Van Lear, Thomas, 3: 549n

VAN OSDEL, A. L., "The Sibley Expedition," 2: 272n

Van Sant, S. R., sketch, 3: 256; elected governor, 256, 257; advocates reform of taxation, 257, 258n, 259, 286; disapproves consolidation of railroad companies, 260, 272; urges reform of state institutions, 261, 262; aspires to senatorship, 265; delivers address on Ramsey, 268; occupies offices in new Capitol, 269; aspires to third term, 272

Vaudreuil, marquis de, 1: 44n

Vermilion Iron Range, 4: 50; exploration and discovery of ore, 8–10, 13, 17; transportation facilities, 11, 15, 17; production of ore, 16; mining boom, 17, 20; nature of ore deposits, 21, 24; mining methods, 22n; extent of ore beds, 41n

Vermilion Lake, 3: 162, 4: 16; discovery of iron ore, 3; gold rush, 4–6; geological surveys, 5–8, 9–11. *See also* Vermilion Iron Range; Iron mining

Vermilion Lake Indian Reservation, 4: 192

Vermilion River, 3: 12n, 4: 191

Vermillion Falls Gold Mining Co., 4: 4, 5n

Vernon Center, 2: 346

Verrazano, Giovanni da, 1: 1

Vervais, J. O., 3: 488, 489

Vesle, battle of the, 3: 534

Vicksburg, siege, 2: 303, 307, 322

Victory Memorial Drive, 4: 433, 433n

Vilas, W. F., 3: 146

Villages, incorporation, 2: 21, 3: 161. *See also* Cities

Vincennes, 1: 69, 73

Vincent, G. E., 4: 114

Vineyard, Maj. M. W., 1: 141n

Virginia, 3: 318, 4: 19, 20; population statistics, 51; schools, 52; election law applicable to, 360n

Visiter, St. Cloud newspaper, 2: 34, 35

Vital statistics, 4: 420

Volk, Douglas, 2: 321

Volstead, A. J., 3: 214, 302, 4: 401

Voyageurs, 1: 16, 19, 27, 67, 103, 105, 133, 219, 351

Waanatan, Sioux chief, 2: 427, 428, 431

Wabasha, Sioux chief, 1: 99, 136, 278, 311, 468, 2: 183, 241, 4: 474; at treaty negotiations, *1837*, 1: 285, 286, 297, 298; makes overtures to Sibley, 2: 172, 173n, 433; instructed by missionary, 254; at treaty negotiations, *1858*, 394

Wabasha County, population, **3**: 21; election returns for *1867*, 21; aids victims of grasshopper plague, 99

Wabasha Indian Reservation, established, **1**: 159, 270, 322, 482; surrender proposed, 273, 274, 274n, 284, 291, 323; exchanged for scrip, 324, 482; surveyed and apportioned, 483. *See also* Scrip

Wabashaw County, population, *1850*, **1**: 352n

Wacouta, Sioux chief, **1**: 153, 286, 468, **2**: 241n

Wahnahta County, population, *1850*, **1**: 352n

Wahpekute Indians, **1**: 182, 203, 353; reservation, *see* Sioux Indians; history, **2**: 400. *See also* Indian treaties; Indians; Santee Indians; Sioux Indians; Sioux Outbreak; Sioux reservations

Wahpeton Indians, **1**: 183, 199, 202, 211, **2**: 122, 184, 207n; reservation, *see* Sioux Indians; attitude during Sioux hostilities: 117, 131, 424, investigated by U. S. court of claims, 426–435; casualties at battle of Wood Lake, 182n; disperse after battle of Wood Lake, 418, 427; partial restoration of annuities, 435–437. *See also* Indian treaties; Indians; Sioux Indians; Sioux Outbreak; Sioux reservations

Waite, Senator H. C., **3**: 7n

WAKEFIELD, MRS. SARAH F., *Six Weeks in the Sioux Tepees*, **2**: 125n

Wakeman, Rev. J. W., **2**: 286n

Wakeman, Thomas, *see* Wowinapa

Walker, L. C., Indian agent, abandons agency, **2**: 374, 376; incurs enmity of Indians, 381; commits suicide, 376

Walker, R. J., **1**: 329

Walker, T. B., **3**: 208n, 268n, **4**: 103n; sketch, 465–468; art collector, 468–472

WALKER, T. B., " Early Life and Development of Minnesota," **2**: 376n; *Low Tariffs and Hard Times*, **4**: 466, 466n; "Ancient Glass and Pottery," 467n; *Son of Man*, 467, 628n; *Testimony of the Ages*, 468n

Walker, village, **4**: 255, 314, 315, 317, 321

Walker Art Galleries, **4**: 469–472

WALKER ART GALLERIES, *List of Artists*, **4**: 470n

Walker Foundation, **4**: 471

Walking Spirit, Sioux chief, **2**: 431

WALL, O. G., *Sioux Massacre*, **2**: 114n

Wamdiyokiya, Sioux Indian, **1**: 155n

War of *1812*, **1**: 100, 132, 145, 214. *See also* Ghent, treaty

WARNER, C. E., ed., *Washington County and the St. Croix Valley*, **1**: 227n; *Hennepin County and Minneapolis*, **2**: 165n

Warner, W. P., **4**: 47

Warren, Gen. G. K., **3**: 339, 340

Warren, J. E., suit against Minnesota and Northwestern Railroad Co., **1**: 341–343; removed from office, 343, 349; advocates statehood, 388

Warren, L. M., **1**: 173

Warren, W. W., **1**: 81, 259, **4**: 296

WARREN, W. W., " History of the Ojibways," **1**: 67n

Warrenton, **2**: 85

Waseca, **4**: 108

Washburn, Gen. C. C., milling interests, **3**: 70, 71n, 131, 137; family, 329n

Washburn, Israel, **3**: 329n

Washburn, W. D., **3**: 15, 328n, 380; candidate for congressman, *1864*, 25, 328; candidate for governor, 84; sketch, 84, 494, 496; aspires to senatorship, *1875*, 85; election to Congress, *1878*: 118, 388–390, contested by Donnelly, 118, 165, 390, **4**: 346; reëlected, **3**: 118; congressional career, 118, 204; elected U. S. senator, *1889*, 184; fails of reëlection, *1895*, 205, 222, 489–494; relations with Clough, 222, 244; family, 329n; entertains Lord Gordon, 364. *See also* Nelson-Washburn campaign

Washburn, Rev. W. W., **4**: 61n, 68n

Washburn family, **3**: 329n

Washburn A mill, **3**: 132, 133, 134, 135, 137n

Washburn B mill, **3**: 132, 137

Washburn Home, **3**: 153

Washburne, Elihu, controversy with Donnelly, **3**: 14, 325–332; family, 329n

Washington County, population, *1850*, **1**: 352n

Watab treaty, *see* Indian treaties

Water power, *see* St. Anthony, Falls of

Watertown, **2**: 442

Waterville, **2**: 288

Watonwan County, **2**: 346, 392n; ravaged by grasshoppers, **3**: 97, 101, 102

Watonwan River, **2**: 281, 404

Waubun, **4**: 265n

Waverly, **2**: 442

Wealth, growth after *1860*, **3**: 1; in *1870*, 60; in *1900*, 251, 252; in *1922*, 322

Webb, Gen. A. S., **2**: 313n

Webster, Mrs. R. A., **2**: 416, 417, 417n

Webster, Viranus, **2**: 416, 417

Webster-Ashburton treaty, *1842*, **1**: 502

Weetjen, L. H., **3**: 458n

Weiser, Dr. J. S., **2**: 270, 272, 274, 275n, 430

Weiss, A. C., **3**: 557

Welch, Maj. A. E., **2**: 174, 180

Welch, W. H., **1**: 342, 378

Welles, H. T., **2**: 337, **3**: 334, 345, **4**: 5n

Welles, H. T., *Autobiography*, **2**: 38n

Welsh, in Blue Earth County, attacked by Sioux, **2**: 170

West, Nathaniel, *Sibley*, **1**: 162n

West, W. M., "University of Minnesota," **4**: 72n

West Newton, Sioux attack, **2**: 115

Westfall, W. P., **3**: 362, 364, 366

Weyerhaeuser and Co., **4**: 238n

Wheat, production: *1860–66*, **2**: 345, **3**: 66, *1868*, 3, *1870*, 60, 66, *1877*, 110, 111n, *1880*, 111, 140, *1890*, 193, *1900*, 252, 252n; transportation, 2, 48, 54, 61; introduction of grain elevator, 66–68; graded, 68, 208, 389; culture of spring wheat, 68; damage by grasshopper plague, 97, 100, 101, 105; chief crop before *1870*, 157; price drop, *1893*, **4**: 457. *See also* Agriculture; Flourmilling; Grain

Wheelock, J. A., **1**: 359, **3**: 348; commissioner of statistics, 19; postmaster, 87; evaluates J. R. Brown's career, 348

Wheelock, J. A., *Minnesota: Its Place among the States*, **1**: 360n; *Minnesota: Its Progress and Capabilities*, 360n

Whigs, **1**: 374, 377, 458, 489; attitude toward territorial organization, 244, 245; indorse Mitchell, 370; indorse Wilkin, 373

Whipple, Bishop H. B., **2**: 215, 263, **3**: 29, 98, 99n, 378; elected regimental chaplain, **2**: 84n; sketch, 206, **4**: 472; interest in Indians, **2**: 207–209, **4**: 193, 200–217, 227, 262, 473–478; calls on Lincoln in interests of Sioux, **2**: 208; confirms Sioux converts, 254; selects Sioux to be rewarded for loyalty, 264; testimony relative to Sioux-Chippewa alliance, 380; commends White Earth Chippewa, **4**: 198; criticizes U. S. Indian system, 201n; death, 296

Whipple, H. B., "Civilization of the Ojibways," **1**: 171n; *Lights and Shadows*, **4**: 200n

Whipple Diary, **4**: 472n

Whisky trade, *see* Indians; Liquor

Whitcomb, Capt. G. C., **2**: 159n

White Cloud, Chippewa chief, **4**: 204, 207, 210, 228n, 233, 271

White Dog, Sioux Indian, **2**: 113

White Earth, **3**: 80

White Earth Lake, **3**: 30, **4**: 195

White Earth Indian Reservation, **4**: 480; efforts to concentrate Chippewa on, 192–235, 261, 262, 324; established, 195, 324; conditions on, 196–198, 201, 283; population statistics, 196–198, 262, 293, 323; agriculture, 196, 197, 262; agency established, 196; removals to, 196, 197, 234, 262, 324; allotments, 196, 205–207, 220–222, 231, 234, 235, 262, 265–272, 302; area, 196n, 199n; mission, 197, 198, 200, 208, 318, 324; fair held, 198; appropriation for relief of Indians, 198n; township purchased for Pembina Indians, 198n; greed of whites for land on, 199, 203; agents, 203, 268–272, 278n, 279n, 280, 282n; appraisal and sale of land and pine, 204, 217, 220, 229n, 231–233, 236–243; cutting of dead and down timber, 244n, 247, 249; exploitation of Indians by whites, 261–283, 295; town sites laid out, 264, 265n; railroad, 264; litigation in connection with land sales, 284, 287–295; attempts to define mixed-bloods and full-bloods, 285–288, 291–293; value of lands, *1906*, 293; number of full-bloods, 293, 323; schools, 324; complaints of Indians, 328; Indians bring claims into court, 328, 329. *See also* Chippewa Indians; Chippewa of the Mississippi; Indian treaties

White Fish Lake, **1**: 99, 123

White Fisher, Chippewa Indian, **1**: 151

White Iron Lake Iron Co., **4**: 49

White Lodge, Sioux chief, **2**: 123n, 410n

White Oak Point Indian Reservation, established, **4**: 196n; unsuitable for permanent reserve, 201; conditions, 213; Indians agree to consolidation, 213, 218. *See also* Chippewa of the Mississippi; Rabbit Lake Indians; Sandy Lake Indians

White Stone Hill, battle, **2**: 279

Whiteman, A. J., **4**: 15

Whiting, J. B., **4**: 227, 228, 229n

Whitman, Allen, **3**: 101n, 104

WHITNEY, HELEN, *Maria Sanford*, **4**: 460n

Whitney, Capt. J. C., **3**: 133; on Moscow Expedition, **2**: 440

Whitney, Prof. W. D., **4**: 69

Wilcox, Gen. C. M., **2**: 310, 311

Wild Rice Lumber Co., **4**: 242n, 280, 285n, 295n

Wild Rice River, **3**: 26

Wildes, F. A., **4**: 22n

Wilkie, J. B., **2**: 269

Wilkin, Col. Alexander, **2**: 106, 306

Wilkin, Judge Westcott, **3**: 88

Wilkin County, state lands, **4**: 480

Wilkinson, James, **1**: 78, 90, 91

Wilkinson, Maj. M. C., **4**: 315, 316, 317n

Wilkinson, M. S., **1**: 263, **2**: 66, 209, 267n, 340; sketches, 62, 341; elected U. S. senator, 62; expresses views on situation prior to Civil War, 71; presents resolution and memorial to Congress, 72, 73; reports Sioux Outbreak to president,

186; approves execution of condemned Sioux, 203n; supports bill for relief of victims of Sioux Outbreak, 247; urges formation of regiment for campaign against Sioux, 290; urges payment of Sioux, 398; approves Moscow Expedition, 440; elected to Congress, **3**: 10; aspires to senatorship, 16; votes on Morrill bill, **4**: 79n

WILKINSON, WILLIAM, *Minnesota Forest Fires*, **3**: 213n

"William Crooks," locomotive, **3**: 422n

Williams, J. F., **1**: 364

WILLIAMS, J. F., *Saint Paul*, **1**: 141n; "Henry Hastings Sibley," 162n; "Memoir of J. R. Brown," **3**: 349n

Williams, J. G., **4**: 134

Williamson, Rev. J. P., missionary, **2**: 207n; ministrations to Sioux, 253, 254; accompanies Sioux exiles, 259, 260, 261, 262

WILLIAMSON, J. P., ed., *English-Dakota Dictionary*, **1**: 448n

Williamson, Jane, **2**: 220, 412n

Williamson, Rev. T. S., **1**: 189, 283, 283n, 448, 450, 451, 456, 464, **2**: 118, 119, 233, 253, 393, 409n, 412n; establishes Lac qui Parle mission, **1**: 192, 198; sketch, 198; translates Scriptures into Dakota, 199; at Kaposia, 201; at Yellow Medicine mission, **2**: 118, 220; escapes from Sioux, 120, 250; criticizes Sioux trials, 198n; services to Sioux, 207n; baptizes Sioux convicts, 211n, 250; explanation of Sioux Outbreak, 225, 415; ministrations to Sioux convicts, 249; aids in listing loyal Sioux, 264; sympathy with Indians, 351; on board of visitors for Chippewa, **4**: 193

Willis, Judge, J. W., **3**: 211

WILLSON, BECKLES, *Lord Strathcona*, **3**: 452n

Wilson, Bess M., **4**: 134

Wilson, C. D., **2**: 415

Wilson, E. M., **2**: 28n, 105, 270, **3**: 376; elected to Congress, 16; candidate for governor, 183, 189; counsel in trial of captors of Lord Gordon, 377; introduces bill for university land grant, **4**: 100

WILSON, E. M., "Narrative of the First Regiment of Mounted Rangers," 2: 105n
Wilson, F. M., 2: 315
Wilson, H. B., 2: 181, 4: 72n, 76, 153
Wilson, John, 1: 431
Wilson, Thomas, 2: 48, 3: 436n, 437, 438, 438n; in constitutional convention, 1: 403, 406, 408, 417; candidate for governorship, 3: 187
Wilson, W. L., 3: 328n, 331n
Wilson, President Woodrow, vetoes prohibition act, 3: 303; favors woman suffrage, 305; correspondence with Germany, 312–314; elections, 313, 540; approves war resolution, 314
WINCHELL, A. N., "Minnesota's Northern Boundary," 1: 503n
Winchell, N. H., urges development of ore industry, 4: 9, 18; state geologist, 478–483; other activities, 484; death, 485
WINCHELL, N. H., Aborigines, 1: 23n; Geology of Minnesota, 42n, 3: 162n; "Northern Boundary of Minnesota," 1: 503n; Geological Surveys in Minnesota, 3: 162n; "Iron Ores of Minnesota," 3: 162n
Windom, William, 2: 264, 3: 380, 409; expresses views on situation prior to Civil War, 2: 72; approves execution of condemned Sioux, 203n; urges passage of bill for relief of victims of Sioux Outbreak, 246; reëlected to Congress, 333; candidate for U. S. senator, 341; sketch, 3: 73; elected U. S. senator, 73, 74; supported by King, 91; reëlections, 115, 116; becomes secretary of the treasury, 115, 151; resigns, 116; fails of senatorial reëlection in 1883, 149, 184; votes on Morrill bill, 4: 79n; death, 3: 151
Winnebago, 2: 351n; railroad terminal, 3: 61
Winnebago Indians, 1: 5, 100n, 240, 305n, 308, 457, 2: 119, 3: 22, 479, 4: 192n, 193, 193n, 230, 322; provisions for reservation in Watab

treaty, 1: 318, 319, 479, 482; attitude during Sioux hostilities, 2: 124, 138, 145, 168, 188, 243; agency garrisoned, 243; demand for removal, 255, 256n; agent, 257n; plan for exiling, 258; taken to Crow Creek, 260, 439, 440; attacks by, feared, 287; suspected of depredations, 288. See also Blue Earth Reservation; Indian treaties; Long Prairie Reservation
Winnibigoshish, Lake, 4: 196n, 209, 212, 230, 317
Winnibigoshish Indian Reservation, 1: 307, 3: 22
Winnipeg, 3: 372, 375, 376, 382, 386; railroad station, 42, 45, 451, 459. See also Fort Garry
Winona, 1: 12, 311, 2: 65, 3: 189, 256, designated railroad terminus, 2: 38, 42; vote on Five Million Loan, 48; population, 1860, 64n; presents banner to First Minnesota, 82; refuge from Indians, 124; normal school, 3: 31; railroad station, 61; home guard station, 318; election laws applicable to, 4: 347n, 360n
Winona and Olmsted Counties, 4: 109n
Winona and St. Peter Railroad Co., popular disapproval of, 3: 33; sued, 42; freight rates, 45; extension to Dakota boundary, 61; franchise, 422n
Winona County, aids victims of grasshopper plague, 3: 99
Winona Republican, 3: 83, 490
Winslow, J. M., 2: 328n
Winslow House, 2: 69, 4: 439, 442
WINSOR, JUSTIN, ed., America, 1: 1n; Cartier to Frontenac, 5n; Mississippi Basin, 49n
Winston, Eliza, 2: 69, 70n
Winston, 4: 6
Winter, Mrs. T. G., 3: 559
WIRTH, F. P., "Disposition of Iron Lands," 4: 12n
Wirth, Theodore, 4: 433
Wisconsin, establishment of state government and boundaries, 1: 236, 489–495; natives of, in Minnesota, 3: 59, 73; administration of state

institutions, 262; iron-bearing district, 4: 43n; land grant, 135
Wisconsin Territory, 4: 330, 331; establishment of government and boundaries, 1: 159, 231, 234; furnishes model for Minnesota laws, 4: 338
Wise, J. C., 3: 101n
Wolf, A., 2: 102n
Wolf River Reservation, 1: 321
Woman suffrage, 3: 120, 551, 4: 333–337, 347; advocated, 3: 200, 201, 540; history, 304–306. See also Suffrage
Woman's Christian Temperance Union, 3: 301
Wood, George, 2: 402, 404
Wood, William, 2: 402, 404
Wood Lake, battle, 2: 177n, 178–182, 190, 242, 250, 265, 286, 336, 346, 418, 427, 428, 432, 433, 446, 447; monument commemorating, 182n; trial of Sioux participants, 196n; losses, 392, 393, 393n
WOODBRIDGE, D. E., ed., Duluth and St. Louis County, 4: 24n
Woodbury, Joseph, 4: 313n
Woods, Maj. Samuel, 1: 424, 513n
Wool, Gen. J. E., 1: 221, 442
Working People's Nonpartisan Political League, 3: 320, 548, 550
Workmen's compensation, 4: 455
World War, hastens woman suffrage, 3: 304; American participation: causes, 312–314, war resolution, 314, 530, 556, raising of troops, 315, 530; Minnesota troops, 316, 531; home activities, 317–319, 4: 463, 464; effect on Nonpartisan League, 3: 553; disloyalty and sedition, 565–574; manufacture of material for, 4: 27. See also Aisne-Marne offensive; Germans; Minnesota Commission of Public Safety; One Hundred and Fifty-first Field Artillery
World's Exposition, 4: 92n
World's Fair, 4: 108n
Wowinapa, 2: 286; tells of death of Little Crow, 284; tried by military commission, 285n; founds Y.M.C.A. among Sioux, 285n; sons, 286n
Wright, A. W., 4: 33, 34, 40, 238n

Wright, Rev. Charles, 4: 271, 272
Wright, Ely, 4: 323n
Wright, C. B., 3: 362
WRIGHT, J. A., "Story of Company F," 2: 86n
Wright, J. G., 4: 239n
Wright, Judge J. V., 4: 202, 203
Wright, Sela G., 1: 182n
Wright County, insurrection, 2: 28–30; settlers flee from Sioux, 161, 287; Indian depredations and attacks, 282, 283, 442
Wrightstown, 3: 541
Wyoming, 3: 304

X Y Co., 1: 116

Yale, Senator W. H., 3: 7n
Yankton Indians, 1: 182, 2: 119, 201, 225, 260, 265
Yanktonai Indians, Sioux tribe, 1: 182, 2: 228, 274n, 297, 429, 431; opposition to whites, 11, 265, 277
Yellow Head River, see Schoolcraft River
Yellow Lake mission, see Missions
Yellow Medicine agency, 1: 211, 354, 2: 407, 412, 414; location, 116, 394; escape of settlers, 116–118, 119, 264; Sioux attack, 117, 119; Sioux camp, 192, 440; arrest of Indians, 194; trouble with Indians over annuities, 228–231
Yellow Medicine Church, 2: 286n
Yellow Medicine mission, see Missions
Yellow Medicine River, 2: 156, 177, 178, 179, 207n, 222, 349, 408
Y.M.C.A., 4: 467; founded among Sioux, 2: 285n
Young, G. B., 3: 473
Young, R. M., 1: 466, 468
Young, Gen. S. B. M., 3: 521, 525, 526, 527
Youngdahl, E. S., 4: 134
Younger, James, 3: 114
Younger, Robert, 3: 114
Younger, T. C., 3: 114
Youngquist, G. A., 4: 133, 133n

Zenith Furnace Co., 4: 27, 28
Zenith mill, 3: 131
Zumbra Heights, 4: 108
Zumbrota, 1: 360